Psalms

Westminster Bible Companion

Series Editors

Patrick D. Miller
David L. Bartlett

Psalms

JAMES LIMBURG

WESTMINSTER
JOHN KNOX PRESS
LOUISVILLE · KENTUCKY

Book design by Publishers' WorkGroup
Cover design by Drew Stevens

First edition

Published by Westminster John Knox Press
Louisville, Kentucky

This book is printed on acid-free paper that meets the American National Standards Institute Z39.48 standard. ∞

PRINTED IN THE UNITED STATES OF AMERICA

05 06 07 08 09 — 10 9 8 7 6 5 4

Library of Congress Cataloging-in-Publication Data is on file at the Library of Congress, Washington, D.C.

ISBN 0-664-25557-4

Contents

2. Book II   **140**

Psalm 42–72

Series Foreword

This series of study guides to the Bible is offered to the church and more specifically to the laity. In daily devotions, in church school classes, and in listening to the preached word, individual Christians turn to the Bible for a sustaining word, a challenging word, and a sense of direction. The word that scripture brings may be highly personal as one deals with the demands and surprises, the joys and sorrows, of daily life. It also may have broader dimensions as people wrestle with moral and theological issues that involve us all. In every congregation and denomination, controversies arise that send ministry and laity alike back to the Word of God to find direction for dealing with difficult matters that confront us.

A significant number of lay women and men in the church also find themselves called to the service of teaching. Most of the time they will be teaching the Bible. In many churches, the primary sustained attention to the Bible and the discovery of its riches for our lives have come from the ongoing teaching of the Bible by persons who have not engaged in formal theological education. They have been willing, and often eager, to study the Bible in order to help others drink from its living water.

This volume is part of a series of books, the Westminster Bible Companion, intended to help the laity of the church read the Bible more clearly and intelligently. Whether such reading is for personal direction or for the teaching of others, the reader cannot avoid the difficulties of trying to understand these words from long ago. The scriptures are clear and clearly available to everyone as they call us to faith in the God who is revealed in Jesus Christ and as they offer to every human being the word of salvation. No companion volumes are necessary in order to hear such words truly. Yet every reader of scripture who pauses to ponder and think further about any text has questions that are not immediately answerable simply by reading the text of scripture. Such questions may be about historical and geographical details or about words that are obscure or so loaded with meaning that one cannot tell at a glance what is at stake. They may be about the fundamental meaning of a passage or about what connection a particular text might have to our contemporary world. Or a teacher preparing for a church school class may simply want to know: What should I say about this biblical passage when I have to teach it next Sunday? It is our hope that these volumes, written by teachers and pastors with long experience studying and teaching the Bible in the church, will help members of the church who want and need to study the Bible with their questions.

The New Revised Standard Version of the Bible is the basis for the interpretive comments that each author provides. The NRSV text is presented at the beginning of the discussion so that the reader may have at hand in a single volume both the scripture passage and the exposition of its meaning. In some instances, where inclusion of the entire passage is not necessary for understanding either the text or the interpreter's discussion, the presentation of the NSRV text may be abbreviated.

We hope this series will serve the community of faith, opening the Word of God to all the people, so that they may be sustained and guided by it.

Introduction: The People's Book

My grandfather ran a general store that carried everything necessary for life in a small Iowa town, from groceries and hardware to candy and clothing. On the floor in the middle of the store was a large heat register, surrounded by benches, where farmers sat on Saturday evenings and told stories. We children liked to gather around behind the benches and listen. We heard local gossip or the latest humorous anecdote brought to town by a traveling salesman. After a funeral in town, there might be serious reflections on life and death. The conversation offered advice on everything from repairing tractors to raising children. The sign out in front of the building read "The People's Store."

The Bible's collection of 150 psalms has a way of providing what is necessary for the lives of God's people. In this book, one discovers sad songs for times of sorrow and happy songs celebrating good times. The Psalms offer reflections on the mysteries of death and life, on poverty and prosperity. And the book provides advice on everything from balancing work and rest to finding a marriage partner and raising children. The sign in front of this collection could well be "The People's Book."

HAPPINESS AND TEARS

The scene is a wedding, taking place in Tevye's yard, in a village in Russia. It is night, and the guests are entering, carrying candles. Tevye looks at the bridal couple and asks, "Is this the little girl I carried? Is this the little boy at play?" His wife responds, "I don't remember growing older. When did they?" Then the women of the village sing:

> Sunrise, sunset, sunrise, sunset,
> Swiftly fly the years.
> One season following another,
> Laden with happiness and tears.
> (from *Fiddler on the Roof*, p. 97)

"Happiness and tears" mark the poles of our lives. They also mark the two fundamental notes running through the Psalms: praise that comes from the good times and laments that arise out of times of sadness.

The Old Testament is made up of three fundamental kinds of material. The first are stories that were passed on from one generation to the next, telling what God has done. They range from the stories of creation, through the stories about ancestors such as Abraham and Sarah, through judges such as Gideon and Samson, to kings such as David and Hezekiah (Genesis–2 Kings). The children must have enjoyed listening in on their parents and uncles and aunts telling these stories!

The second are prophetic writings, reporting what God has said (Isaiah–Malachi). Finally come the psalms and wisdom writings, offering the people's response to the acts and the words of God in the form of praise and lament, reflection, and advice on how to live (Psalms, Job, Ecclesiastes, and Proverbs).

The psalms give expression to the people's response to the words and the acts of God. It is important to notice that the great majority of the psalms are addressed to God. This is evident as one pages through them, after the introductory Psalms 1 and 2. They begin "O LORD" (3:1), "O God" (4:1), "O LORD" (5:1), "O LORD" (6:1), and so on.

Lament and praise are the two fundamental themes running through the Psalms, but the basic theme is praise. This is why the name of the book of Psalms in its original Hebrew form is one word: *tehillim*, which means "praises."

TAKE IT TO THE LORD

It is important to notice that a majority of the Psalms arose out of two fundamental situations in the lives of God's people. Coming from those times "laden with tears," the sad times, are prayers for help or *laments* (note, for example, Psalms 3–7, 13, 22, 51, 102, 130, 140–143). The heading for Psalm 102 expresses a typical situation giving rise to a lament: "A prayer of one afflicted, when faint and pleading before the LORD." The story of Hannah, brokenhearted and praying that the Lord would give her a child, provides an example for the setting in which laments were prayed (1 Samuel 1). A whole community may bring its sorrows before the Lord, in community laments such as Psalms 44, 74, 79, 80.

Sadness and sorrow brought before the Lord is lament. The old hymn "What a Friend We Have In Jesus" had it right:

Have we trials and temptations?
Is there trouble anywhere?
We should never be discouraged—
Take it to the Lord in prayer.

Originating in the good times are the psalms of thanksgiving and *praise*. Psalm 30, for example, is an individual's thanks to the Lord for a particular healing and a call to the congregation to join in praise. Psalm 8 is an example of a more general psalm of praise, a hymn, as are Psalms 19, 29, 33, 95–100, 113, 134–136, 146–150, and others.

HYMNBOOK, PRAYER BOOK, INSTRUCTION BOOK

Eventually, individual psalms were gathered into collections of psalms. Some of the psalms were used in the people's worship, for times of community lament (for example, Psalms 44, 80, and 137) or community praise (Psalms 95–100, 146–150). The New Testament book of Acts shows how a psalm could be used in a spontaneous gathering of believers (Acts 4:23–31). The book of Psalms provides hints at processions (Ps. 118:19–29) and rituals (Pss. 66:13–15; 116:12–19). In these ways, the collected psalms began to function as a *hymnbook* (see also Eph. 5:19–20).

The large number of laments functioned in the lives of the people as prayers in times of trouble, for both individuals (e.g., Psalms 3–7, 13, 22) and the community (Psalms 44, 80, 137). The settings for such individual and community prayers continue to be debated: Did individuals pray them at the temple? Were there small support groups that prayed these psalms? Did the people gather regularly to pray the community laments, or in times of national emergency, or both? In any case, the psalms have reached into times of need and have functioned as a *prayer book*.

Recent study of the psalms has emphasized their importance as sources for teaching. This is clear in psalms that speak of *torah*, or "instruction" (translated as "law" in the NRSV), such as Psalm 1: "but their delight is in the instruction of the LORD, and on his instruction they meditate day and night" (v. 2; see also Psalms 19 and 119). The aim of a good many other psalms is also instruction, whether explicitly or implicitly indicated (Psalms 37, 49, 73, 127, 128, and others). Thus these psalms function as an *instruction book*.

BACK INTO THE MIDST OF LIFE

The psalms have a way of not staying locked up in a book. They originated in real-life situations, and they continue to appear in the midst of life. One thinks immediately of the words of Psalm 22 that appear as a prayer from the cross: "My God, my God, why have you forsaken me?" (Matt. 27:46). In another example, words from Psalm 130, in German, appear on a wall at the memorial to the victims of the concentration camp at Dachau, Germany. Further, I recall visiting with an aging widow at a funeral on the Minnesota prairies. She told me that one of her sons could always get the horses to plow the best "because he sang psalms to them in Dutch." The picture of a young Dutch American farmer plowing with horses on the prairies, singing psalm paraphrases that traveled from Israel to the Netherlands to midwestern America, has always stuck with me.

These psalms that originated in the midst of the lives of the people of God have a way of reappearing in the midst of life today. A former student wrote about having learned a Hebrew song based on a psalm in a college Bible class. She taught it to a group of young Christian campers in New York, who sang it as they hiked through the woods. Suddenly a group of Jewish campers rushed over to join them in singing, in Hebrew: "Hineh mah tov oo-mah na-im, shevet achim gam yachad" (How good and how pleasant it is when God's people live together in unity; Psalm 133).

The psalms won't stay locked up in a book. Another example: late in the night after a spring formal at a college, musician Duke Ellington sat at the piano and gave us a private performance of his setting of Psalm 150. And yet another: once I noticed a sailboat carrying across the blue waters of a Minnesota lake the words of a psalm in the name of the boat, lettered across the stern: "Wings of the Morning" (from Psalm 139).

The psalms originated in the midst of life and continue to appear in the midst of life. The commentary herein will provide examples, and the reader can add his or her own!

GOING BY THE BOOK

Psalms can be interpreted in a variety of ways. Each psalm can be read and studied *on its own*; one thinks of the variety of settings where Psalm 23 has been read.

Especially since the research of Hermann Gunkel at the beginning of the twentieth century, individual psalms have been interpreted *with other psalms of the same type.* Laments may be considered together, or hymns, or royal psalms, and the like.

Now, at the beginning of the twenty-first century, the emphasis is on reading each psalm *in its literary context*, whether that be the context of neighboring psalms (see below on Psalms 103–104) or the context of a smaller collection (Psalms 120–134) or the context of the entire book of Psalms, called the Psalter. This is sometimes called the *canonical* method and is illustrated in the work of a number of recent scholars. James Mays, whose commentary illustrates this method, refers to this approach as "going by the book" (*Psalms* in the Interpretation commentary series; see also his *The Lord Reigns*). Erich Zenger of Münster, Germany, has summarized the method simply: "Interpret the psalm, then interpret the Psalter"; the results of his work on the psalms are beginning to appear in German (see *Psalmen 1–50* in Hossfeld and Zenger, *Die Neue Echter Bibel*) and in English translation. J. Clinton McCann's commentary in the *New Interpreter's Bible* provides yet another helpful example of this canonical approach.

The following illustrates the method of "going by the book":

Psalms 1 and 2 furnish an *introduction* to the entire book of Psalms. Neither has a heading; the two psalms appear to have been added to the collection to provide an introduction. The appearance of the expression "Happy are . . ." in 1:1 and 2:11 forms a bracket, linking the two psalms. Psalm 1 suggests that the way to find happiness is to meditate on the psalms. Psalm 2 suggests that the psalms that follow be read as providing clues for a coming messiah. As a double entrance into the book of Psalms, these two suggest that the psalms be *meditated* upon and that they be read with *messiah* in mind. (See the commentary for further observations.)

Psalms 146–150 are a group, each beginning and ending with "Praise the LORD" (in Hebrew, "Hallelujah"). Psalm 145:21 promises that "all flesh" will praise the Lord; Psalm 150 shows how this universal praise works out (v. 6). Considering the book of Psalms as a whole, there is a clear movement from lament (most of the psalms in Book I, Psalms 3–41) to praise.

The Psalter has been edited by persons who wanted to highlight the "praise" theme. There are five subcollections or "books," each concluding on a note of praise: Psalms 1–41, 42–72, 73–106, 107–150, with Psalm 150 as a whole furnishing the concluding praise.

THE POETRY OF THE PSALMS

Noticing some of the poetic forms and devices in the Psalms is helpful in understanding them. The most obvious characteristic of Hebrew poetry is called parallelism. In *synonymous parallelism*, the first half of a line (a) states a thought and the second half (b) balances it with a similar thought. Psalm 114 provides a good example:

> 1 (a) When Israel went out from Egypt,
>   (b) the house of Jacob from a people of strange language . . .
> 4 (a) The mountains skipped like rams,
>   (b) the hills like lambs.

In verse 1, "Israel" and "Egypt" are balanced by "house of Jacob" and "people of strange language"; in verse 4, "mountains" and "rams" are balanced by "hills" and "lambs." (See also Pss. 19:1–2; 24:1–3, etc.)

With *antithetic parallelism*, the second half of a line balances the first half by saying the opposite, as in Psalm 37:

> 22 (a) for those blessed by the LORD shall inherit the land,
>   (b) but those cursed by him shall be cut off.

In this case, "those blessed" is countered by the opposite, "those cursed," and "shall inherit the land" is countered by "shall be cut off." (For further examples of antithetic parallelism, see Pss. 1:6; 20:8; 32:10; Proverbs 10; Eccl. 10:2.)

Repetition is a characteristic of the poetry of the psalms, usually serving to emphasize that which is repeated. A psalm may begin (Ps. 22:1, "My God . . .") or end (Ps. 27:14, "Wait for the LORD . . .") with repetition, for emphasis. Repetition may take the form of a refrain (Pss. 42:5, 11; 43:5), or a thematically central expression may recur, such as the sevenfold "the voice of the LORD" in Psalm 29. Psalm 136 repeats the refrain in each verse.

A number of psalms are *alphabetic acrostics*, the initial letters of each line following the order of the Hebrew alphabet; for examples, see the commentary on Psalms 9–10.

For a discussion of metaphors and similes for God and for people, see my article "Psalms, Book of" in the *Anchor Bible Dictionary*; and for a recent discussion of Hebrew poetry, see the work of Adele Berlin in the *New Interpreter's Bible*, 4:301–15.

1. Book I
PSALMS 1–41

THE WAY TO GO
Psalm 1

1:1 Happy are those
> who do not follow the advice of the wicked,
> or take the path that sinners tread,
> or sit in the seat of scoffers;
2 but their delight is in the law of the LORD,
> and on his law they meditate day and night.
3 They are like trees
> planted by streams of water,
> which yield their fruit in its season,
> and their leaves do not wither.
> In all that they do, they prosper.

4 The wicked are not so,
> but are like chaff that the wind drives away.
5 Therefore the wicked will not stand in the judgment,
> nor sinners in the congregation of the righteous;
6 for the LORD watches over the way of the righteous,
> but the way of the wicked will perish.

The book of Psalms is a book filled with pictures. The Lord may be portrayed as a shepherd (Psalm 23), a king (5, 93), a rock (92), a father (103), or a mother (131). The Lord's people are pictured as sheep (23, 80) or servants (90) or dependent children (131) or vines (128) or arrows (127).

When Jesus taught by using a picture of a waiting father or a rebelling child or a woman searching for a lost coin (Luke 15), this was nothing new. Jesus was doing what psalm writers and prophets and preachers and pedagogues have always done: using pictures to make a point or convey a message.

1

A Poem as Lovely . . .

The first picture in the first psalm is a picture of a tree. Call up that tree on the video screen of your imagination! Make it a sturdy oak or a maple with red and yellow leaves or an apple tree loaded with fruit. Place it alongside a stream with clear, rushing water. Notice the colors: the red of fresh, healthy fruit; the green of the leaves; the white of the foaming water; the blue of the sky and the stream. Look for a moment at that imaginary tree. Think of some words to describe what you see: alive, sturdy, rooted, productive, bending without breaking, beautiful. "I think that I shall never see a poem lovely as a tree," the poet Joyce Kilmer wrote.

"This tree can be a picture of your life," says the first psalm. "Your life can be like that tree: rooted, productive, flexible, truly alive, marked by beauty."

"How can that be?" is the question the reader or hearer of these words asks. "How can my life be vital, productive, rooted, even beautiful—like that tree?"

The Way of Happiness (1:1–3)

The answer is given in the first words of this psalm. The opening describes those persons who are happy (vv. 1–3). First come three negatives: such people don't follow the advice of wicked people; they don't take the paths that sinners take; and they don't associate with cynics and scoffers. Then comes the positive, and here is the point of this psalm in this place: those who are truly happy—whose lives can be represented by that tree—are those people who take delight in the Lord's *teaching*.

The Hebrew text says, "Surely in the *torah* of the LORD is their delight." The Hebrew word *torah* can mean "law," and so it is translated in most modern English Bibles. But it is often better translated as "teaching" or "instruction," and such is the case here. The Jewish Publication Society translation puts it this way: "rather, the teaching of the LORD is his delight, and he studies that teaching day and night."

The psalm says that those people are truly happy who delight in the "teaching of the LORD." It also says that these people "meditate" on that teaching "day and night," that is, at all times. The word translated "meditate" is a form of the Hebrew *hāgāh*. The same word occurs in a passage from Isaiah: "As a lion or a young lion *growls* [a form of *hāgāh*] over its prey . . ." (Isa. 31:4). This time *hāgāh* is translated as "growl." But how could a word mean both "growl" and "meditate"?

Imagine reading this text as it is read in a traditional Jewish synagogue, even today. The entire congregation is standing. Each person has a Bible. Each reads Psalm 1 aloud, but not in unison. Some read quickly, some slowly, some quietly, some loudly. Almost all sway back and forth as they read, getting their bodies involved in the expression of this psalm. Now imagine the sound of all those people reading the psalm on their own. That is what the word *hāgāh* means: to meditate, yes; but to meditate aloud, at times in the company of others.

The Way to Death (1:4–6)

Verses 4–5 describe those who are wicked. Once again, the writer of the psalm provides a picture. The wicked person is like chaff. When it is threshing time, the farmer scoops up the grain, lets it fall to the ground, and lets the wind blow the husks, the scraps, the chaff, away. Quite a different picture from the previous one! Not much is said about this chaff—because there is not much to say. Job 21:18 uses the same "chaff" imagery; note the context in verses 7–18. Psalm 1:5 comments on the ultimate end of the wicked.

Finally, verse 6 wraps up the entire psalm. The first word in this first psalm began with *alef*, the first letter of the Hebrew alphabet. The last word in this psalm begins with *tav*, the last letter of the alphabet. This first psalm offers the "*alef* to *tav*," the "A to Z" of living the life of the godly. The Lord watches over the way of the righteous. The way of the wicked? They will perish.

The "two ways" theme occurs frequently in the Bible; read through Jeremiah 17:5–8 and Matthew 7:24–27 for a couple of examples. But the point the psalm is making is clear. These are not really two options, equally valid. There is only one way to go.

Jesus spoke of himself as "the way, and the truth, and the life" (John 14:4–6). The earliest Christians were called those who "belonged to the Way" (Acts 9:2; 19:9, 23; 22:4; 24:22).

Getting Going

The first word in the first psalm is *happy* (or, in the older translations, *blessed*). "I want to be happy," goes an old song; the book of Psalms opens with an acknowledgment of that universal human wish. Other psalms discuss the same theme. Psalm 41:1, the last in this first "book," suggests that happiness can be found in caring for the poor. Psalm 127:5 speaks of the happiness to be found in family life. Psalms 65:4 and 89:15 hint at happiness connected with participation in worship, while 119:1–3 and 128:1 link happiness with walking in the Lord's ways.

The reader's or hearer's question remains: What would that way of happiness look like? How would I get started on that way? This psalm says, Find that path by considering, meditating on, the psalms that follow. There you will discover the way that leads to happiness. These psalms will teach you the way to go.

THE PLOTTING POLITICIANS
Psalm 2

2:1 **Why do the nations conspire,**
    and the peoples plot in vain?
  2 **The kings of the earth set themselves,**
    and the rulers take counsel together,
    against the LORD and his anointed, saying,
  3 **"Let us burst their bonds asunder,**
    and cast their cords from us."

  4 **He who sits in the heavens laughs;**
    the LORD has them in derision.
  5 **Then he will speak to them in his wrath,**
    and terrify them in his fury, saying,
  6 **"I have set my king on Zion, my holy hill."**

  7 **I will tell of the decree of the LORD:**
    He said to me, "You are my son;
      today I have begotten you.
  8 **Ask of me, and I will make the nations your heritage,**
    and the ends of the earth your possession.
  9 **You shall break them with a rod of iron,**
    and dash them in pieces like a potter's vessel."

 10 **Now therefore, O kings, be wise;**
    be warned, O rulers of the earth.
 11 **Serve the LORD with fear,**
    with trembling 12**kiss his feet,**
    or he will be angry, and you will perish in the way;
      for his wrath is quickly kindled.

   Happy are all who take refuge in him.

The first psalm began on a note of happiness, with the sounds of prayer and meditation and the sight of a tree planted by a stream. Psalm

2 returns to the everyday world of politics and of plots. These two psalms are artfully linked. They are bracketed by a pair of "Happy are . . ." sayings (1:1; 2:12), and both use that rather rare word *hāgāh*. This time the word refers not to pious meditation (Ps. 1:2) but to political plotting (2:1). Neither psalm has a heading, and the pair form an introduction and a kind of "reader's guide" to understanding the psalms that follow.

Politics as Usual?

To understand Psalm 2, one ought to remember that the psalm came out of a time when the form of government was a monarchy. The psalm was designed for an occasion when a new king was being installed. Other nations were subject to the king in Jerusalem, and the kings of these nations were on hand for the event.

Imagine their mood. These minor kings ruled over nations that were satellites of Jerusalem. This meant they had to pay taxes and furnish military troops when needed. They and their people wanted one thing: freedom. Especially at the time of a new king, they were tempted to plot a rebellion and declare independence.

The background for understanding this psalm is not the quiet time of meditation alone or in the synagogue but the noisy sort of conspiring and plotting that goes on in the smoke-filled rooms of a political convention.

The Lord and His Messiah (2:1–12)

Verses 1–3 set the scene. Representatives of these nations are gathered in Jerusalem for the installation of a new king. They are gathering together in the back rooms, planning a rebellion. The writer of the psalm reminds us who they are rebelling against: not only against the king but against the Lord and his king! The Hebrew text has "against the LORD and his *messiah*," here translated "anointed." This is the first occurrence of "messiah" in the book of Psalms.

As if the back rooms were electronically bugged, we can listen in on the exact words of the plotting politicians. "Let us burst their bonds asunder, and cast their cords from us," they say. Transposed into another era, they are saying, "Enough of the monarchy and these high taxes! Let's throw the tea into the harbor!"

With verses 4–6, the scene shifts to the place where the Lord sits on a heavenly throne. The first thing that we hear from the Lord in the book of Psalms is *laughter*! Such is the Lord's reaction to this pitiful plotting. That laughter will turn to fury, and the Lord will inform these would-be rebels that "I have set *my* king on Zion, *my* holy hill." Here are two important themes that run through the psalms that speak of the king: (1) the Lord has chosen Zion as the *place* where the king will rule, and (2) the Lord has chosen the king, the *person* who will rule.

With verses 7–9, the king himself speaks. He makes some extravagant claims, which must be understood against the background of the notion of kingship in ancient Israel. No doubt referring to a statement in the installation ceremony, the Lord has declared the king to be the Lord's son. And the king has been told that he will smash these small-time plotters as easily as one might walk into a pottery shop with an iron rod and break everything to pieces. Then the king will rule over these nations; indeed, his rule will extend over the entire earth. Some remarkable expectations, indeed!

The psalm comes to an end with some words of warning in verses 10–12, addressed to the plotting politicians. They would do well to "serve the LORD," which, in terms of practical politics, means to be loyal to the king. Finally, there is a "Happy are . . ." saying, which links up with the first words of Psalm 1 and concludes this double introduction to the Psalms.

The Royal Psalms: Seedbed for Messianic Hope

These first two psalms introduce the 148 psalms that follow. Psalm 1 suggests that the way to happiness is a delightful path, which involves reflecting on the Lord's teachings. The Lord will watch over such a life and will shape it in the manner of a well-rooted, well-nourished, productive tree.

The second psalm also speaks of happiness, this time in the context of lives that enjoy the Lord's protection in the midst of a world filled with conspiracies and assassinations and power-hungry dictators. In a world where even the best of monarchs was involved in a sex scandal and a murder (2 Samuel 11), the hope for an ideal anointed one, a truly magnificent messiah, never died. Originating with the promises of the prophet Nathan in 2 Samuel 7, those hopes were nourished in the eleven *royal psalms*, so named because they played a part in the life of the king. These royal psalms were used at such occasions as a royal wedding (Psalm 45), a time before a king entered battle (20), or after a king won a victory (21). They were frequently part of the installation ceremony for a new king (Psalms 2, 72, 101, 110). They speak of the king in most hopeful and extravagant language, calling him a *messiah*, an anointed one (Pss. 2:2; 45:7), a son of God (Psalm 2), seated at the Lord's right hand (Psalm 110), who will rule over the nations of the earth (Pss. 2:8–9; 72:8–11, 19). This anointed one will have special concern for the poor and powerless (72:2–4, 12–14), will rule with justice and righteousness (Ps. 72:1), and will bring about *shalom* (Ps. 72:3, translated by the NRSV as "prosperity"; 72:7 translated "peace"). Other royal psalms include 18, 89, 132, and 144.

But as history played itself out, king after king was a disappointment. One need only read the books of 1 and 2 Kings to catch the biblical writer's negative evaluation of each successive monarch: "He did what was evil in the sight of the LORD" (e.g. , 1 Kings 15:25–26, 34).

Finally the monarchies came to an end, first in 722 B.C. , when Israel fell to Assyria, then in 587 B.C. , when Judah fell to the Babylonians. Even though there were no more kings, no more coronations, no more celebrations involving the monarch, the royal psalms were still used. Now they expressed the people's hope for an ideal ruler who would come in the future. In this way the hope for an ideal king, an ideal anointed one, a *messiah*, was born. The royal psalms became the seedbed for messianic hope. The people sang of these hopes in their worship services. Prophets drew on these psalms to describe the messiah who would one day appear (Isaiah 9, 11). And centuries later, when Jesus asked the disciples what people were saying about him, Simon Peter answered in the language of these royal psalms: "You are the Messiah, the Son of the living God" (Matt. 16:16).

One could write a book on the "messiah" theme. In fact, it's been done. The church calls it the New Testament.

NOW I LAY ME DOWN TO SLEEP
Psalm 3

A Psalm of David, when he fled from his son Absalom.

3:1 **O LORD, how many are my foes!**
    Many are rising against me;
 ² **many are saying to me,**
    "There is no help for you in God."   *Selah*

 ³ **But you, O LORD, are a shield around me,**
    my glory, and the one who lifts up my head.
 ⁴ **I cry aloud to the LORD,**
    and he answers me from his holy hill.   *Selah*

 ⁵ **I lie down and sleep;**
    I wake again, for the LORD sustains me.
 ⁶ **I am not afraid of ten thousands of people**
    who have set themselves against me all around.

⁷ **Rise up, O Lᴏʀᴅ!**
   Deliver me, O my God!
   For you strike all my enemies on the cheek;
   you break the teeth of the wicked.

⁸ **Deliverance belongs to the Lᴏʀᴅ;**
   may your blessing be on your people!   *Selah*

The first thing one notices about this psalm after reading Psalms 1 and 2 is that it has a heading. The same is true of almost all the remaining psalms in Book I, Psalms 1–41. These headings are the work of the editors who put the book of Psalms together and can furnish the earliest commentary on the psalm texts.

The heading for Psalm 3 is a good example. The English says, "A Psalm of David . . . ," but the Hebrew can also be translated as "for David" or "to David." Therefore the heading could mean the psalm was written *by* David, indicating authorship. But it could also mean that the psalm was written *for* David or was dedicated *to* David. Seventy-three biblical psalms are so designated.

In thirteen instances, including this one, the heading associates the psalm with an event in David's life: Psalms 3, 7, 18, 34, 51, 52, 54, 56, 57, 59, 60, 63, 142. In this psalm the editor links it to a time when David was running away from his rebelling son Absalom (2 Samuel 13–18). "This is the sort of prayer that David prayed," the editor is saying, "when his life was in extreme danger." The heading suggests that this psalm was constructed for such high-stress situations.

The psalm is made up of elements typical of a *lament*, that is, an individual prayer in a time of trouble (see on Psalm 13). Verses 1–3 are a *complaint*, verses 3–6 an *affirmation of trust*, verse 7 a *call for help* or *request*, and verse 8 again a statement of *trust*.

The word *Selah* at the end of verses 2, 4, and 8 is also the work of the editors who put the book of Psalms together. *Selah* most likely indicates a pause for a musical interlude when the psalm was used in worship. The word should be omitted when reading the psalm aloud.

The Lord Is My Shield (3:1–8)

The psalm begins with a prayer, an urgent complaint about the enemies of the psalmist (vv. 1–2). The writer is in a dire situation and begins simply, "O Lᴏʀᴅ" (also Psalms 6 and 7). Certain contemporaries are advising the psalmist to give up on his or her religion. "God isn't going to help you out!" they are saying.

But the writer will not so easily be talked out of his or her faith and addresses the Lord with words of trust: "But you, O LORD, are a shield around me, my glory, and the one who lifts my head." Following this affirmation are words to others *about* the Lord, who answers the psalmist's prayers, watches over the psalmist in the night, and makes possible a life that is free from fear (vv. 4–6).

With verse 7 comes the urgent request that is at the heart of this psalm. The Hebrew expresses it with one word: "Deliver me!" The psalm concludes with a statement Jonah made after being saved from the big fish, "Deliverance belongs to the LORD!" and then with a wish that the Lord's people may experience the Lord's blessing (v. 8).

Sleeping and Trusting (3:5)

"I lie down and sleep," declares verse 5. Sleep can come as a great blessing. Sleep-robbing worry can be a curse. A friend once described a sleepless night to me: "It was one of those nights when I was lying awake, baby-sitting the world."

At the heart of this psalm is this expression of calm trust, like the child's bedtime prayer "Now I lay me down to sleep. . . ." Enemies are making fun of the psalmist's religious convictions (vv. 1–2). Their threat is serious enough that violence may erupt (v. 7). But no matter; the writer says, "I lie down and sleep."

The rhythm of sleeping and waking runs through these first psalms. Psalm 4:8 expresses the same calm trust: "I will both lie down and sleep in peace; for you alone, O LORD, make me lie down in safety." Psalm 5:3 speaks again of waking, and 6:6 is the expression of one who can't sleep because of illness. "Sweet is the sleep of laborers," says Ecclesiastes 5:12, and Psalm 127:2 speaks of sleep as one of God's great gifts.

The psalm encourages one to sleep, trusting that the Lord can run things on the planet for a few hours, without the person's help.

Deliverance Comes from the Lord (3:2, 7–8)

Central to this psalm is a theme that is central to the Bible: the Lord *delivers*. The Hebrew word that occurs here is *yeshua*, from which comes the name Joshua, the great deliverer in the Old Testament. The Greek version is Jesus, which means "he shall *save* his people from their sins" (Matt. 1:21).

The word occurs three times: the psalmist's enemies are saying, "There is no *help*" [translation of *yeshua*] for you in your God" (v. 2); the one praying asks, "*Deliver* me, O my God" (v. 7); and the person finally observes, "*Deliverance* belongs to the LORD" (v. 8).

God, says this psalm, is a God who delivers. Christians regularly pray, "Lead us not into temptation, but *deliver* us from evil." But this is not the only way in which God relates to God's people. God also gives everyday good gifts, such as sunshine and rain, health and success, family and friends. The giving of these gifts the Bible calls the *blessing* activity of God. Psalm 3:8 nicely ties deliverance and blessing together.

Corners of Heaven, Pits of Hell

Psalm 3 is the first of a series of five prayers from times of trouble. Very quickly the book of Psalms makes clear that "the way of the righteous" (Ps. 1:6) may be a way that goes through valleys of darkness. But these psalms also indicate that the believer will never need to go through those valleys alone: "But you, O LORD, are a shield around me . . . I lie down and sleep; I wake again, for the LORD sustains me" (3:3, 5).

The heading links this psalm with a time when an aging King David was running away from his son Absalom (2 Samuel 13–18). One can hardly imagine a more difficult situation: the king feared for his life because of a rebellious favorite son! After an especially difficult time of dealing with a rebelling teenager, a friend once observed to me, "There are corners of heaven and pits of hell that people without children don't even know about."

This psalm, the heading tells us, has been created for just such times.

THE PEACE OF THE LORD
Psalm 4

To the leader: with stringed instruments.
A Psalm of David.

4:1 **Answer me when I call, O God of my right!**
    You gave me room when I was in distress.
    Be gracious to me, and hear my prayer.

  2 **How long, you people, shall my honor suffer shame?**
    How long will you love vain words, and seek after lies?

                                                       Selah

  3 **But know that the LORD has set apart the faithful for himself;**
    the LORD hears when I call to him.

  4 **When you are disturbed, do not sin;**
    ponder it on your beds, and be silent.   *Selah*

5 **Offer right sacrifices,**
   and put your trust in the LORD.

6 **There are many who say, "O that we might see some good!**
   Let the light of your face shine on us, O LORD!"
7 **You have put gladness in my heart**
   more than when their grain and wine abound.

8 **I will both lie down and sleep in peace;**
   for you alone, O LORD, make me lie down in safety.

Shalom. For the first time in the book of Psalms that word occurs, translated as "peace," in Psalm 4:8. The word may have been used as a greeting in biblical times (Gen. 37:4) and remains the standard greeting in Israel and among Jewish people today. *Shalom* means "Hello, with a little goodbye in it, and goodbye, with a little hello in it," as the song puts it. In the Bible, its fundamental meaning is more than just "peace" in the sense of absence of warfare. *Shalom* means abundant, prosperous crops (Ps. 72:3, translated "prosperity") or that feeling of security as one drifts off to sleep in one's own bed (Ps. 4:8). This psalm concludes with a word about *shalom.*

A Note about the Heading

The heading for this psalm suggests three stages in its history. As a "Psalm of David," it was in some way associated with that king. The note "To the leader: with stringed instruments" was intended for the choir director in the temple, when the psalms functioned as the hymnbook for the Old Testament company of believers. Finally, the psalm became part of a book, the second in a series of five laments, after two introductory psalms. The words of this psalm have demonstrated power. The psalm keeps appearing in new settings. In modern books of worship, for example, it is a part of the service of Compline or "Prayer at the Close of the Day" (for example, see *Lutheran Book of Worship,* p.155).

Elements of the form of the lament are present in this psalm; see the comments on Psalm 13.

From Desperate Prayer to Restful Sleep (4:1–8)

The opening request in this psalm reflects a situation of desperation. The one praying gets right to the point: "When I call, answer me, God of my right!" is the ordering of the Hebrew. After reminding God of God's previous help, the one praying fires off a pair of imperative verbs: "*Be gracious* to me, and *hear* my prayer" (v. 1).

"I can't hang on much longer" is the meaning of the "How long?" of verse 2. The psalmist is speaking about certain persons in the community. They have been slandering him, speaking lies, so that his reputation has been called into question. He is, however, confident that the Lord keeps an ear open to the faithful, of whom he is one (v. 3). *Selah* probably indicates an interlude (see on Psalm 3).

With verses 4 and 5, the psalm offers some instruction for those verbally attacked by others in the community. How should this troubling matter be handled? The psalm says, "Don't do anything rash. Think about it for a while, in silence. Participate in the community worship services. And then leave things in the hands of the Lord."

The psalmist brings the prayers of the community to the Lord's attention by quoting them in verse 6. "Let the light of your face shine on us" means to show favor (Num. 6:25).

The mood changes with verses 7–8. Something has happened to the one who was so desperate. Did the psalmist himself put into practice the advice given in verses 4 and 5? Perhaps the psalmist has withdrawn from the difficult situation, pondered the problem in silence, gone to worship, and finally decided to leave things in God's hands. Once again there is some joy in the psalmist's heart. The one who was desperate can now lie down and sleep in peace, confident that matters can be left in the hands of the Lord.

Trust, Joy, *Shalom*

This psalm indicates that the "way of the righteous" as recommended in Psalm 1:6 is not a way that is free from difficulties. In this case, the one offering the prayer has been slandered by members of the community and has then survived the situation, as the final words of the psalm indicate. The message of this psalm may be summarized by focusing on three important words.

First, verse 5 counsels putting *trust* in the Lord. The best biblical picture is that of the child resting in its mother's arms, contented, after having been nursed (Psalm 131). Verse 8 speaks of lying down "in safety." The Hebrew word is the same as that translated *trust* in verse 5. What should one do when one's life, one's world, is coming unglued? This psalm suggests, Ease off. Reflect. Be silent. Go to worship. And then turn things over to God, so that you can lie down and sleep, trusting in that God.

Second, when one reads verse 7, one might think the psalmist knew the old song "I've got the joy, joy, joy, joy down in my heart." The Hebrew word here is *simchah*, translated as "gladness." Once I attended a

Jewish fall festival called *simchat torah*, which means "joy in the scriptures" or perhaps "joy with the Bible." The synagogue service appeared to begin normally. Then two senior members of the community took the biblical scrolls out of their place in the front of the synagogue, carried them down the aisle, and soon the entire congregation, men and women, old people and children, were involved in a lively snake dance, singing, clapping hands, dancing with the Torah scrolls, passing them on, rejoicing in the fact that the Lord had given them the Bible. The picture in this psalm is of the kind of happiness, singing, and dancing that came at the time of a good harvest. "The Lord," says the psalm writer, "has put that sort of joy down in my heart."

The third word is *shalom*, here translated as "peace" (v. 8). The word can refer to a time when there is no warfare (1 Sam. 7:14; Ps. 72:7) but can also denote a prosperous harvest (Ps. 72:3). Ultimately, *shalom* refers to the peace that will abound when the messiah comes (Isa. 9:7). It is this sort of peace, on which the Lord's face shines (v. 6), that has been wished for gatherings of God's people since the time of Moses:

> The LORD bless you and keep you;
> the LORD make his face to shine upon you, and be gracious to you;
> the LORD lift up his countenance upon you, and give you *shalom*.
> (Num. 6:24–26)

MORNING PRAYER
Psalm 5

**To the leader: for the flutes.
A Psalm of David.**

5:1 **Give ear to my words, O LORD;
    give heed to my sighing.**
2 **Listen to the sound of my cry,
    my King and my God,
    for to you I pray.**
3 **O LORD, in the morning you hear my voice;
    in the morning I plead my case to you, and watch.**

4 **For you are not a God who delights in wickedness;
    evil will not sojourn with you.**
5 **The boastful will not stand before your eyes;
    you hate all evildoers.**
6 **You destroy those who speak lies;
    the LORD abhors the bloodthirsty and deceitful.**

⁷ But I, through the abundance of your steadfast love,
    will enter your house,
  I will bow down toward your holy temple
    in awe of you.
⁸ Lead me, O LORD, in your righteousness
    because of my enemies;
    make your way straight before me.

⁹ For there is no truth in their mouths;
    their hearts are destruction;
  their throats are open graves;
    they flatter with their tongues.
¹⁰ Make them bear their guilt, O God;
    let them fall by their own counsels;
  because of their many transgressions cast them out,
    for they have rebelled against you.

¹¹ But let all who take refuge in you rejoice;
    let them ever sing for joy.
  Spread your protection over them,
    so that those who love your name may exult in you.
¹² For you bless the righteous, O LORD;
    you cover them with favor as with a shield.

After two psalms appropriate for evening prayer (3:5; 4:8), this one addresses the Lord in the morning (5:3). There is a reason for starting out with evening prayers and then moving to the morning, instead of the other way around. The day begins, still for Jewish persons today, when the sun goes down. Synagogues will post the exact time of sundown, so that members will know when the Sabbath begins and when worship services start. Why start the day in the evening? Because the refrain running through Genesis 1 is "and there was evening and there was morning, the first day," and not the other way around.

The freshness of the morning hour seems a good time to pray. "In the morning, while it was still very dark, he got up and went out to a deserted place, and there he prayed," says Mark 1:35 of Jesus. "In the morning my prayer comes before you," says the writer of Psalm 88:13. Psalm 55:17 refers to prayers at evening, morning, and noon. It is reported of faithful Daniel that he went out to pray three times a day (Dan. 6:10–13). Another characteristic of the lives of those who are trying to walk in the "way of the righteous" (Pss. 1:6; 5:8) is the framing of each day, evening and morning, with prayer.

The heading indicates that this psalm is to be associated with David; see the comments on Psalm 3. The note to the music director suggests that the musical setting of this psalm will feature the flutes. The location of the psalm in the book suggests that this morning prayer is placed here to balance the two evening prayers that precede it.

Some Requests for the King (5:1–12)

The psalm begins immediately with a request, using a series of imperative verbs ("Give ear . . . give heed . . . listen . . ."; vv. 1–2). Verse 2 offers the first metaphor or picture for God in the entire book of Psalms: "my King." The same expression, "my King and my God," occurs in Psalms 44:4 and 84:3. If God is "my King," then I am a subject, presumably a loyal one.

Twice the one who is praying speaks of the time of this prayer: "in the morning." The day begins with prayer, with a request to God the King. As the day continues, the one who has prayed keeps waiting and watching.

With verses 4–7, the psalmist reveals something of his theology, his notion of God. What he has to say, however, is addressed *to* God, in the form of prayer. He begins with three negatives: "You don't like wickedness; you won't put up with evil; you won't tolerate braggarts." The address to the Lord continues, "You hate . . . You destroy," but then there is a word *about* the Lord, directed toward those listening to this psalm, providing them with some theological instruction: "the Lord abhors the bloodthirsty and deceitful."

The psalmist has been speaking to God about evildoers and to the congregation about the Lord. Now, with an abrupt "But I," he speaks of himself. These are words of a loyal subject, coming before a loving king. The major point of the psalm finds expression in the request for the Lord's guidance in verse 8. There are those in the community who are making the psalmist's life miserable. He asks that the Lord show the *way* (Ps. 1:6) he should follow in the midst of this difficult situation. (See also Pss. 25:4–5; 27:11; 32:8; 86:11, for this way imagery.)

Verses 9–11 offer a double request, asking the Lord to punish these enemies (vv. 9–10) and to give blessing and happiness to those who take refuge with the Lord (v. 11). What were these "enemies" of the psalmist doing? These verses suggest that their wrongdoing included both wrong speaking, such as lying and flattering, and wrong actions, such as transgressing and rebelling. (See also Rom. 3:10–13, where Paul cites verse 9 of this psalm.) The seriousness of these actions is indicated when the psalm says that these were sins against the King, "against you" (v. 10).

"But let all who take refuge in you rejoice," the psalm continues in verse 11. The language is the same as that at the end of Psalm 2, where happiness was promised to those who "take refuge" in the Lord. After the prayer against the enemies comes this prayer for the Lord's people.

The psalm ends on a note of trust and praise (v. 12).

Who Is God Like?

What is God like? Or better, who is God like? These are questions asked by children, adults, and students and professors in theological schools.

One way in which the Bible answers these questions is to provide pictures, or metaphors, to illustrate something of the reality of God. This psalm introduces a very important biblical picture of God: God is king (v. 2). There are a number of psalms, sometimes called "enthronement psalms," that celebrate the Lord's being king: 47:2, 6, 7, 8; 93:1; 95:3; 96:10; 97:1; 98:6; 99:1. Others, like this one, address God as King (145:1).

What does that picture of the Lord as king mean for us, especially for those of us who have never lived under a king or queen? As we read this psalm, at least two things come to mind. First, a king has power, and God has power. Verses 4–6 refer to a God who will not tolerate evil deeds or evildoers and who is capable of destroying such persons. Second, a king may have compassion and care for those over whom he rules. The central phrase here is "steadfast love," which translates the Hebrew word *hesed*. Because of this steadfast love, an individual can come before the King with a request (vv. 1–3). The privilege of an audience with the king was not automatic (see Esth. 4:11). This heavenly King, whom the Israelites know as the Lord, will pay attention to the prayers and problems of an individual, offering guidance (v. 8), protection (v. 11), and the possibility of a life marked by singing and rejoicing (v. 11).

Kingly power and kingly compassion—these two aspects of the Lord's kingship run through the entire Bible. The Lord, the King, formed the earth and all that is in it (Ps. 95:3–5) and also cares about the earth and its creatures, nourishing life on the planet (Ps. 145:13–16) and eventually sending Jesus to announce the coming of the kingdom of God (Mark 1:14–15).

A TEXT OF TERROR
Psalm 6

> **To the leader: with stringed instruments; according to The Sheminith.**
> **A Psalm of David**

> 6:1 **O LORD, do not rebuke me in your anger,**
>   **or discipline me in your wrath.**
>   2 **Be gracious to me, O LORD, for I am languishing;**
>   **O LORD, heal me, for my bones are shaking with terror.**

³ My soul also is struck with terror,
   while you, O LORD—how long?

⁴ Turn, O LORD, save my life;
   deliver me for the sake of your steadfast love.
⁵ For in death there is no remembrance of you;
   in Sheol who can give you praise?

⁶ I am weary with my moaning;
   every night I flood my bed with tears;
   I drench my couch with my weeping.
⁷ My eyes waste away because of grief;
   they grow weak because of all my foes.

⁸ Depart from me, all you workers of evil,
   for the LORD has heard the sound of my weeping.
⁹ The LORD has heard my supplication;
   the LORD accepts my prayer.
¹⁰ All my enemies shall be ashamed and struck with terror;
   they shall turn back, and in a moment be put to shame.

This psalm is driven by the prayer of one who is terrified before the anger of God (vv. 2–3). Shaking with terror because of bodily illness (v. 2) and experiencing terror deep in the soul (v. 3), the psalmist fires a question heavenward: "O LORD—how long?"

"How long?" is what the psalm says. What the psalmist means is "Lord, this has been enough. Too long have I suffered in body and in spirit. And you, Lord, where are you? I can't hang on much longer. My bones are shaking and there's terror in my soul. So how about it, Lord? How long are you going to let this go on?"

Terror. Such is the thematic word of this psalm: terror because of physical symptoms (v. 2), terror that lives deep in the soul (v. 3), and terror wished upon enemies (v. 10).

The heading associates the psalm with David (see on Psalm 3) and dedicates it to the music director; "Sheminith" probably refers to a melody. The typical elements of a lament are present in this psalm (see on Psalm 13): a *request* or *call for help* in vv. 1–2 and 4–5; a *complaint* in the "I" form (vv. 2, 3a, 6–7), the "they" form (v. 7), and the "you" form (v. 3b); and an *affirmation of trust* (vv. 8b–10).

Lord, I Am Terrified! (6:1–10)

As is the case with Psalms 3, 7, and 8, the psalm begins with "O LORD." Immediately following is a call for help (vv. 1–2). After a pair of negative verbs (v. 1), the cry for help is put into a positive form: "Be gracious . . . heal me."

The one praying has experienced the Lord's anger. In our own age, which has little sense of the "wrath of God," the report of that experience is striking, even terrifying. Three times the psalmist refers to the wrath of God in terms of terror (vv. 2–3, 10). That wrath can move mountains (Job 9:5), consume human beings (Ps. 90:7), and destroy entire nations (Jer. 10:10).

The first complaint appears in verse 2, in the "I" form: "I am languishing . . . my bones are shaking with terror." After describing these outer symptoms, the psalmist speaks of the terror that is within: "My soul also is struck with terror."

This first section concludes with a "you" complaint, directed to God: "while you, O LORD—how long?" The "how long" question is a frequent one in psalms, usually in laments (Pss. 74:10; 80:4; 90:13; 94:3). Whatever the problems of the one praying in Psalm 6, they are described here as having physical (v. 2), psychological (vv. 2–3), and theological dimensions (v. 3).

Verses 4 and 5 once again present a call for help. The psalmist's situation is desperate, a matter of life or death. The only hope is the Lord's steadfast love (v. 4). Verse 5 indicates the direct, childlike relationship of the psalmist to the Lord. "Save me from death," says the one praying, "because if I die, you'll hear no more praises from me!"

The Old Testament thinks of Sheol as the place of the dead, located in the mysterious regions beneath the earth (Num. 16:30–33). It is a dismal place of darkness and gloom (Job 10:20–22), of maggots and worms (Isa. 14:11), where there is no praise of God (v. 5; also Ps. 115:17). God, however, can be present even there (Ps. 139:8).

What is the situation of the one who is praying? Verse 2 points toward physical illness. Verse 3 gives expression to a terror that resides deep in the soul. Verses 6 and 7 fill in the picture. The psalmist is grieving "because of all my foes." The problem includes both personal illness and troubles with others in the community ("my foes," v. 7).

Verse 8 expresses a wish that these "workers of evil" go away. Then, beginning with verse 8b, the mood changes to one of quiet trust. The psalmist has the sense that the Lord has heard the prayer.

A Penitential Psalm

Psalm 6 has been called the *sick* psalm, because of the situation of illness as described in verses 2, 6, and 7. As such, it has been used in times of sickness. It has also been classified as the first of the church's seven "penitential" psalms, along with Psalms 32, 38, 51, 102, 130, 143. These psalms consider human beings in their relationships to God, to others, and to themselves. These dimensions of human existence are interrelated. When the relationship to God is distorted by unconfessed sin, for example, the body may react with illness (Pss. 32:1–4; 38:3–8; 51:8). When relationships to one's colleagues or associates are strained, again, there may be physical symptoms (Ps. 102:3–4, 7, 9).

Certainly, the one praying this psalm is physically ill (6:2, 6, 7). But in considering the psalm as a whole, it is clear that the problem is more than physical. The psalmist believes that God is neglecting him. The one praying lives in terror and asks the Lord, "How long can this go on?" (v. 3).

The relationship to others in the community is also not what it ought to be (vv. 8, 10). Put in other terms, the psalmist's problems with God as expressed in verses 1–3 have physical, psychological, and social dimensions. Wise healers, whether they be pastors, physicians, psychologists, or social workers, have always known that all of these dimensions are important for wellness.

A Day of Penitence

The church has assigned this psalm to an observance of a "Day of Penitence," or sorrow over sins, along with Nehemiah 1:4–11a; 1 John 1:5–2:2; and Luke 15:11–32. One worship handbook suggests that this can be a day remembering the Holocaust. One of the suggested prayers for such a remembrance day:

> Almighty God, in penitence we come before you,
> acknowledging the sin that is within us. We share
> the guilt of all who, bearing the name Christian,
> slay their fellow human beings because of race or
> faith or nation. Whether killing or standing silent
> while others kill, we crucify our Lord anew. Forgive
> us and change us by your love, that your Word of
> hope may be heard clearly throughout the world.
> (*Lutheran Book of Worship: Minister's Desk Edition*, p. 186)

THE HIDING PLACE
Psalm 7

A Shiggaion of David, which he sang to the LORD concerning Cush, a Benjaminite.

7:1 O LORD my God, in you I take refuge;
  save me from all my pursuers, and deliver me,
 2 or like a lion they will tear me apart;
  they will drag me away, with no one to rescue.

 3 O LORD my God, if I have done this,
  if there is wrong in my hands,
 4 if I have repaid my ally with harm
  or plundered my foe without cause,
 5 then let the enemy pursue and overtake me,
  trample my life to the ground,
  and lay my soul in the dust.   *Selah*

 6 Rise up, O LORD, in your anger;
  lift yourself up against the fury of my enemies;
  awake, O my God; you have appointed a judgment.
 7 Let the assembly of the peoples be gathered around you,
  and over it take your seat on high.
 8 The LORD judges the peoples;
  judge me, O LORD, according to my righteousness
  and according to the integrity that is in me.

 9 O let the evil of the wicked come to an end,
  but establish the righteous,
 you who test the minds and hearts,
  O righteous God.
 10 God is my shield,
  who saves the upright in heart.
 11 God is a righteous judge,
  and a God who has indignation every day.

 12 If one does not repent, God will whet his sword;
  he has bent and strung his bow;
 13 he has prepared his deadly weapons,
  making his arrows fiery shafts.
 14 See how they conceive evil,
  and are pregnant with mischief,
  and bring forth lies.
 15 They make a pit, digging it out,
  and fall into the hole that they have made.
 16 Their mischief returns upon their own heads,
  and on their own heads their violence descends.

 17 I will give to the LORD the thanks due to his righteousness,
  and sing praise to the name of the LORD, the Most High.

The lines of those waiting to get into the small house on the Prinsengracht Canal in Amsterdam are long, every day. The total number of visitors has run into the millions. In the top and back of the building, Otto Frank had built a hiding place, with secret passageways and sliding panels. An entire Jewish family and some friends lived there in secret during the years of World War II, hiding during the daytime and moving about only at night. When there was a knock on the door of the family living downstairs or when they had visitors, the Jewish family and friends took refuge in their hiding place. One member of that family made the house famous. Her name was Anne Frank, and the discovery and publication of her diary has inspired books, plays, and movies.

This psalm, like a good many others, speaks of the Lord as a "hiding place," a place to find security and refuge.

The sense of "Shiggaion" in the title is uncertain. The incident between David and Cush is not known from the Bible. The psalm has the marks of an individual lament (see on Psalm 13), with *calls for help* or *requests* (vv. 1–2, 6–9), an *affirmation of trust* (vv. 10–16), *complaint* about enemies (vv. 1b–2, 6, 9), and a *vow to praise* (v. 17).

My God, Help Me! (7:1–5)

The psalm begins with an urgent call for help:

> O Lord my God, in you I take refuge;
> *save me* from my pursuers and *deliver me*.
>
> (v. 1)

One could imagine the family of Otto Frank praying these words as they entered their secret refuge. Apparently, the writers of the psalms often had to seek refuge. The word *refuge* also occurs at the beginning of Psalm 11, "In the Lord I take refuge," as well as Psalm 16, "Protect me, O God, for in you I take refuge," and in Psalm 31, "In you, O Lord, I seek refuge. . . . Be a rock of refuge for me, a strong fortress to save me." There are many other examples where psalms speak of the Lord as a hiding place (e.g. , 37:40; 57:1; 64:10; 71:1; 118:8–9). This prayer presents no long and drawn-out introductory words of praise to the God being addressed. As was the case in Psalms 3 and 6, the first word is *Lord*, and the writer gets to the point immediately: "O Lord my God, in you I take refuge."

The consequences of *not* finding a hiding place are spelled out in the imagery of verse 2, which compares the psalmists' enemies to a ferocious lion. The psalms often portray enemies as wild animals (see Pss. 10:9; 17:12; 22:12–13; 58:3–6; and other passages).

The psalm continues with a section in which the writer asserts innocence of wrongdoing (vv. 3–5). Balancing the beginning of the psalm is
the address "O LORD *my God*" (v. 3). The bond between the one praying
and the one addressed remains real!

"If I have done this . . . ," continues the psalm (v. 3). Of what wrong
was the psalmist being accused? The answer is not clear. Perhaps the
accusation had to do with some inappropriate action during the course of
military duty (v. 4). What is clear is that the psalmist is dead certain he is
innocent of the charges. (For *Selah*, see the comments on Psalm 3.)

My God, Wake Up! (7:6–9)

The bond between the one praying and the God prayed to is affirmed a
third time with another "my God" (v. 6). The writer calls the Lord to
"awake." This is, of course, picture-language and does not mean to imply
that there are times when the Lord fails to pay attention. In fact, Psalm
121 declares, "He watching over Israel, slumbers not nor sleeps," to use
the version from the chorus of Mendelssohn's *Elijah*.

To paraphrase what the psalmist says: "I know that God doesn't sleep,
but it surely seems that the Lord is napping right now!" Certain of his
innocence, the writer calls on the Lord to judge his case. The God of this
psalm is not too small. The Lord is portrayed here as judging the nations
of the earth. Nor is the psalmist's God too big to be concerned with one
individual. The psalmist asks, "Judge me, O LORD," praying that the
Lord bring the evil of the wicked to an end and vindicate his own cause
(vv. 7–8). If verse 8 has something of a self-righteous ring, it should be
observed that the psalmist is speaking about his innocence in this particular instance.

God, My Shield (7:10–17)

The mood of these verses is one of trust and, finally, praise. Two pictures
of God lead off the section. First, God is a shield (v. 10). The shield is a
frequently used picture for God, all the way from the promise to Abram,
"I am your shield" (Gen. 15:1), through a promise to the people, "the
LORD, the shield of your help" (Deut. 33:29), to David's song, "my God,
my rock in whom I take refuge, my shield" (2 Sam. 22:3; also vv. 31, 36).
The imagery continues into the books of Psalms (3:3; 28:7; 33:20) and
Proverbs (2:7; 30:5).

Second, God is a judge (v. 11). The "judge" imagery continues
through the psalms (50:6; 82:1; 94:2) and the entire Bible (e.g. , Judg.
11:27; Job 23:7; Jer. 11:20) into the New Testament (Matt. 25:31–46).

Verses 14–16 offer a variation of the "they" complaint observed in the psalms of lament. The psalm closes with the vow to praise, an element typical of the psalms of lament.

My God, My Refuge

This has not been one of the more popular psalms. It offers, however, some themes for reflection, teaching, and preaching.

There are some interesting pictures of God in the psalm. God is the *hiding place* or *refuge* and also the *saver* and *deliverer* (v. 1). God is the *judge* over the nations (vv. 6–8) and over the individual (v. 8). God is a *swordsman* and an *archer* with specially enhanced weapons (vv. 12–13).

This psalm addresses a God who can call the powerful nations of the world to account, but who will also be a hiding place for individuals who are persecuted and pursued. Such a God is deserving of thanks and praise (v. 17).

HOW DOES IT ALL FIT TOGETHER?
Psalm 8

To the leader: according to The Gittith.
A Psalm of David.

8:1 O LORD, our Sovereign,
   how majestic is your name in all the earth!

   You have set your glory above the heavens.
 2   Out of the mouths of babes and infants
   you have founded a bulwark because of your foes,
       to silence the enemy and the avenger.

 3 When I look at your heavens, the work of your fingers,
       the moon and the stars that you have established;
 4 what are human beings that you are mindful of them,
       mortals that you care for them?

 5 Yet you have made them a little lower than God,
       and crowned them with glory and honor.
 6 You have given them dominion over the works of your hands;
       you have put all things under their feet,
 7 all sheep and oxen,
       and also the beasts of the field,

⁸ **the birds of the air, and the fish of the sea,**
   whatever passes along the paths of the seas.

⁹ **O Lᴏʀᴅ, our Sovereign,**
   how majestic is your name in all the earth!

When the *Apollo 11* spacecraft was sent to the moon in July 1969, each of the heads of the nations of the earth sent along a message, engraved on a silicon disk the size of a fifty-cent piece, which was left on the moon. Pope Paul VI, as political head of the Vatican, sent along the text of Psalm 8. When you next look at the moon, you can know that parked on that silvery ball are the words of the Eighth Psalm! (NASA News Release No. 69–83F).

If there is a psalm for stargazers, this is it. Gazing at the night sky has a way of raising the big questions, such as "Who am I? Who is God? What should I do with the few years I have on this planet?"

With this psalm, the mood of the book of Psalms changes. After the two introductory pieces (Psalms 1 and 2) and a quintet of laments (Psalms 3–7) comes this hymn. Psalm 7 concluded with the writer's resolve to "sing praise to the name of the Lᴏʀᴅ." That resolve to praise is carried out in Psalm 8.

Like most of the psalms in Book I, this one is linked to David (see on Psalm 3). The note to the choir director says that it can be sung to a tune called "The Gittith." (The same melody was also used for Psalms 81 and 84.)

The structure of the psalm is reminiscent of the standard pattern for a hymn (see on Psalm 113). The psalm is framed with statements of *praise* (vv. 1a, 9). In between are *reasons* for praising, considering first the heavens (vv. 1b–3), then human beings and the earth and its creatures (vv. 4–8).

"For purple mountains' majesty" goes the line from "America the Beautiful," and it is just this sense of *majesty* that is expressed in vv. 1a and 9, which frame this psalm (see also Ps. 76:4). The same Hebrew word is used in describing the thundering waves at sea (Ps. 93:4) or a whole forest of cedars in Lebanon (Isa. 10:34).

Considering the Heavens (8:1b–3)

Verses 1b–2 refer to the voices of children praising God; one thinks of the sounds of a children's choir. The praises of these children provide a sturdy wall, protecting the Lord from enemies.

Verse 3 indicates that the psalmist has been out gazing at the night sky. These are "*your* heavens, the work of *your* fingers," the writer concludes.

The intricate work of putting the heavens together was accomplished with the Lord's *fingers*; the less delicate task of assembling sheep and oxen was the work of God's *hands* (vv. 6–7).

Considering Humans and the Universe (8:4)

"What are human beings in the context of such immensity?" is the question raised in verse 4, and also the question that comes to any reflective person in such a setting. Once I heard astronomer Karel Vanderlugt suggest this model: Imagine that the sun, which is a star, is the size of a grapefruit. Then the earth would be the size of a grain of sand, about thirty-five feet away. The moon would be a tiny speck of sand about an inch from the earth. Venus would be twenty-five feet distant, Mars fifty-three feet. On this scale, the next grapefruit-star would be two thousand miles away, about the distance from Minneapolis to Los Angeles. To model our home galaxy, the Milky Way, we would need some 10 billion of those grapefruit-stars, each sixteen hundred miles apart. And our universe is made up of billions of such galaxies, all moving away from one another.

Given such a universe, one can only say of the Creator, "How majestic is your name!"

Considering Humans and the Earth (8:4–8)

How does it all fit together? The psalm's answer is quite clear. At first, we humans appear to be quite insignificant in the context of the vast universe (vv. 3–4). Yet this psalm identifies humans as "a little lower than the angels" (NRSV footnote) and says that earthlings have been created as royalty. We are kings and queens, crowned with glory and honor and called to have "dominion" over the works of the Lord's hands. This dominion is first of all over "all things" (v. 6). But then the realm over which humans are to rule is made more specific. Moving from those nearby to those far off, these creatures include domestic animals (sheep and oxen), animals that roam the fields (the beasts of the field), and creatures of the sky and the sea (the birds, the fish, whatever is in the seas).

Midway between the Apes and the Angels

Such was the title of a lecture I once heard from a biologist, helping us humans to locate ourselves in the scheme of created things. We are lower than the angels but higher than the apes and orangutans. We are not up there with the angels, just under the ranking of gods. But neither are we

merely advanced primates, the last figures on a long chart beginning with
stooped, apelike creatures, gradually standing more erect, until at the end
of the line is a smiling couple in business suits. If this were the case, then
the accomplishments of Bach or Michelangelo or da Vinci would be but
the final chapters in a book of advanced biology.

The Responsibility of Royalty

This psalm helps us determine how humans fit in with the rest of creation. It also indicates what we ought to do. Humans are viewed as royalty, "crowned with glory and honor" and given "dominion" over all that
God has created. Humans are to the earth and its creatures as a king or a
queen is to his or her subjects.

How does the Bible view that royal relationship? Psalm 72, designed
for a king's installation, provides an answer. The king is to be especially
concerned for the poor and needy, the weak and powerless (Ps. 72:4,
12–14). Royalty are responsible for caring for the weakest, the least powerful, over whom they rule. Translated to the concern of Psalm 8, this
means that humans, who are here identified as royalty, are to exercise
care for the earth and its creatures. They are asked to be responsible royalty. The same notion is developed on the first page of the Bible, in Genesis 1:26–28.

In these times of ecological crisis, Psalm 8 is a call for humans to act as
responsible royalty and to care for the fragile blue planet we call our home.

HOPE FOR THE DOWN-AND-OUT
Psalms 9–10

Psalm 9

To the leader: according to Muth-labben.
A Psalm of David.

9:1 **I will give thanks to the LORD with my whole heart;**
     I will tell of all your wonderful deeds.
  2 **I will be glad and exult in you;**
     I will sing praise to your name, O Most High.

  3 **When my enemies turned back,**
     they stumbled and perished before you.
  4 **For you have maintained my just cause;**
     you have sat on the throne giving righteous judgment.

⁵ You have rebuked the nations, you have destroyed the wicked;
    you have blotted out their name forever and ever.
⁶ The enemies have vanished in everlasting ruins;
    their cities you have rooted out;
    the very memory of them has perished.

⁷ But the LORD sits enthroned forever,
    he has established his throne for judgment.
⁸ He judges the world with righteousness;
    he judges the peoples with equity.

⁹ The LORD is a stronghold for the oppressed,
    a stronghold in times of trouble.
¹⁰ And those who know your name put their trust in you,
    for you, O LORD, have not forsaken those who seek you.

¹¹ Sing praises to the LORD, who dwells in Zion.
    Declare his deeds among the peoples.
¹² For he who avenges blood is mindful of them;
    he does not forget the cry of the afflicted.

¹³ Be gracious to me, O LORD.
    See what I suffer from those who hate me;
    you are the one who lifts me up from the gates of death,
¹⁴ so that I may recount all your praises,
    and, in the gates of daughter Zion,
    rejoice in your deliverance.

¹⁵ The nations have sunk in the pit that they made;
    in the net that they hid has their own foot been caught.
¹⁶ The LORD has made himself known, he has executed judgment;
    the wicked are snared in the work of their own hands.
                                        Higgaion. Selah

¹⁷ The wicked shall depart to Sheol,
    all the nations that forget God.

¹⁸ For the needy shall not always be forgotten,
    nor the hope of the poor perish forever.

¹⁹ Rise up, O LORD! Do not let mortals prevail;
    let the nations be judged before you.
²⁰ Put them in fear, O LORD;
    let the nations know that they are only human.   *Selah*

Psalm 10

10:1 Why, O Lᴏʀᴅ, do you stand far off?
    Why do you hide yourself in times of trouble?
  2 In arrogance the wicked persecute the poor—
    let them be caught in the schemes they have devised.

  3 For the wicked boast of the desires of their heart,
    those greedy for gain curse and renounce the Lᴏʀᴅ.
  4 In the pride of their countenance the wicked say, "God will
    not seek it out";
    all their thoughts are, "There is no God."

  5 Their ways prosper at all times;
    your judgments are on high, out of their sight;
    as for their foes, they scoff at them.
  6 They think in their heart, "We shall not be moved;
    throughout all generations we shall not meet adversity."

  7 Their mouths are filled with cursing and deceit and oppression;
    under their tongues are mischief and iniquity.
  8 They sit in ambush in the villages;
    in hiding places they murder the innocent.

    Their eyes stealthily watch for the helpless;
  9   they lurk in secret like a lion in its covert;
    they lurk that they may seize the poor;
    they seize the poor and drag them off in their net.

10 They stoop, they crouch,
    and the helpless fall by their might.
11 They think in their heart, "God has forgotten,
    he has hidden his face, he will never see it."

12 Rise up, O Lᴏʀᴅ; O God, lift up your hand;
    do not forget the oppressed.
13 Why do the wicked renounce God,
    and say in their hearts, "You will not call us to account"?

14 But you do see! Indeed you note trouble and grief,
    that you may take it into your hands;
    the helpless commit themselves to you;
    you have been the helper of the orphan.

15 Break the arm of the wicked and evildoers;
    seek out their wickedness until you find none.

¹⁶ The LORD is king forever and ever;
    the nations shall perish from his land.

¹⁷ O LORD, you will hear the desire of the meek;
    you will strengthen their heart, you will incline your ear
¹⁸ to do justice for the orphan and the oppressed,
    so that those from earth may strike terror no more.

The Bible has a special concern for the widow, the orphan, and the poor. One hears this from the prophets, for instance, when Isaiah calls the political leadership of his day to "rescue the oppressed, defend the orphan, plead for the widow" (Isa. 1:17), or when he accuses the politicians of enacting laws that were biased against the powerless (Isa. 10:1–2). Micah contended that the Lord would rather have justice done than receive massive offerings (Micah 6:6–8), and Amos spoke on behalf of the powerless when he called for justice to roll down like waters (Amos 5:21–24). When the prophets speak about "doing justice," they are speaking about taking up the cause of the powerless in society, that is, the widow, the orphan, and the poor. Psalms 9 and 10 have a good deal to say about the powerless; more specifically, about the poor and the oppressed.

One Psalm Out of Two

There are a number of reasons to believe that Psalms 9 and 10 were originally a single psalm and therefore to consider them together. There is no heading for Psalm 10; this is quite unusual, since, after the introductory Psalms 1 and 2, only Psalm 33 in Book I (Psalms 1–41) lacks a heading. The two psalms appear as one in early Greek and Latin translations. Certain expressions occur only in these two psalms ("times of trouble" in 9:9 and 10:1). Most important is the fact that the two psalms together follow the pattern of an alphabetical acrostic, every other line beginning with a successive letter of the Hebrew alphabet (though a few letters have been disrupted or omitted). A number of psalms exhibit this alphabetical acrostic pattern: 25, 34, 111, 112, 145, and 119.

Because of the restrictions of the alphabetical scheme, the broad outline of Psalms 9–10 is not obvious. The heading is similar to the headings of Psalms 4–6 and 8, with its dedication to the choir director, a (probable) indication of the tune, and the association with David.

The Wonderful Deeds of the Lord (9:1–20)

The piece begins on a positive note (vv. 1–2). The first half of verse 1 speaks *about* the Lord, announcing to others that the psalmist is going to give thanks. This suggests that the psalm was designed to be read or sung in the context of the gathered congregation, where others could hear this recital of the "wonderful deeds" of the Lord. With the second line, the writer switches to "you," addressing the Lord directly. The reference to "your *name*" calls to mind the mention of the Lord's name in the first and last verses of Psalm 8. Psalm 111, another acrostic, begins in the same manner.

Verses 3–6 indicate what some of these "wonderful deeds" have been. This section is framed by references to "enemies" (vv. 3, 6) and apparently refers to military victories that have been achieved through the Lord's help. "God was at work in those victories," the psalmist is saying, "and for that I give thanks!"

With verses 7–10 the focus changes from "wonderful deeds" in the past to the present and the future. The psalm speaks *about* the Lord, giving instruction to those listening. The Lord is going to be enthroned forever and will judge the world fairly. Then comes the central teaching point of the psalm in verse 9:

> The LORD is a stronghold for the oppressed,
> a stronghold in times of trouble.

The word translated "stronghold" has the sense of a place of refuge high in the mountains (the "high citadel" in Deut. 2:36).

After a word expressing trust in the Lord (v. 10), the psalm addresses the congregation. The psalmist had announced that he would tell what the Lord had done for him (v. 1); now the entire congregation is invited to give testimony concerning the deeds of the Lord (v. 11). The major reason for praise is that the Lord doesn't forget the prayers of the down-and-out (v. 12).

From this point, the psalm moves back and forth quickly, from praise to instruction to affirmation of trust and back to praise. These sudden shifts are an accommodation to the acrostic form. The writer had to keep the alphabetical sequence in mind! Verses 13 and 14 present the psalmist's own prayer for deliverance from enemies. He asks that the Lord, who took him from the "gates of death," bring him safely to the "gates of Zion," that is, to Jerusalem.

Verses 15 and 16 look back at what happened to those nations who had been plotting evil: they have fallen into their own trap! (The same idea occurs in Psalm 7:15–16.) Verses 17–18 offer a hopeful view of the future, when the wicked will be off the scene, and the poor and needy will be restored to normal sorts of lives. Finally, the Lord is asked to do something dramatic (vv. 19–20) so that these wicked ones will know who they are ("only human") and who the Lord is (the one who "executes judgment").

Why, O Lord? (10:1–18)

The opening "Why . . . ?" introduces an urgent call for help and reminds one of a similar desperate cry at the beginning of Psalm 22 ("My God, my God, *why*. . . ?). The congregation had earlier affirmed the Lord's help "in times of trouble" (9:9). Now there are such "times of trouble," and, says the psalmist to the Lord, "You are nowhere to be found! Why are you hiding?"

Psalm 10:2 summarizes the psalm's complaint and expresses a call for help regarding the wicked. "In arrogance the wicked persecute the poor," declares the psalmist; "let them be caught in the schemes they have devised."

Verses 3–11 present a detailed description of the actions of the wicked, in the form of a complaint in "they" form (see comments on Psalm 13). Their words and their thoughts are quoted three times in this section. They believe that God will not discover their greed; in fact, they say that God does not exist! "God will not seek it out. . . . There is no God" (v. 4). Yet they are certain that nothing bad will happen to them: "We shall not be moved; throughout all generations we shall not meet adversity" (v. 6). And they reaffirm their conviction that God will never see what they have done to the poor, the helpless, the oppressed: "God has forgotten, he has hidden his face, he will never see it" (v. 11).

"Why do good things happen to bad people?" the psalmist asks (v. 5). The same question is asked in Psalm 73:3–12. The description in Psalm 10 continues. These persons are guilty of mischief and iniquity and even murder. Their crimes are especially reprehensible because they are against the innocent and helpless (vv. 8, 10, 14) and the poor, the meek, and the oppressed (vv. 2, 9, 12, 17, 18).

Verses 12–15 articulate a call for help on the part of the psalmist, beginning with "Rise up, O LORD" and ending with "Break the arm of the wicked and evildoers." The piece concludes with praise to the Lord as king and an expression of trust that the Lord will hear the prayers of the meek and will take up the cause of the orphan and the oppressed (vv. 16–18).

Hope for the Down-and-Out

We have already observed that the demands of following the alphabetical pattern may account for some difficulties in following the line of thought in this psalm. Perhaps the psalm was broken into two parts because there are two themes: praise and thanksgiving dominate Psalm 9, whereas Psalm 10 is preoccupied with complaints about the wicked (vv. 2–11).

Because this psalm has such a rich variety of words describing the poor and oppressed, and because concern for these groups comes up throughout the book of Psalms, it seems good to note some of these descriptions: "the oppressed" (9:9; 10:12, 18), "those who know your name" (9:10), "those who seek you" (9:10), "the afflicted" (9:12), "the poor" (9:18; 10:2, 9), "the meek" (10:17), "the needy" (9:18), "the innocent" (10:8), "the helpless" (10:8, 10, 14), "the orphan" (10:14).

Most of these terms designate those persons in society who have no power. Some are suffering a lack of someone or something: the orphan has no parents; the helpless has no one who cares; the needy and poor have no money. Others are victims of life's tragedies and inequities: the oppressed, the afflicted, the innocent.

The point of the psalm is that there is hope for these persons. The Lord is their stronghold in times of trouble (9:9). Jesus would one day name these persons "blessed" (Matt. 5:1–12). The hymn "This Is My Father's World" expresses what the psalmist says in 10:16–18: "though the wrong seems oft so strong, God is the ruler yet."

IN GOD I TRUST
Psalm 11

To the leader. Of David.

11:1 In the Lord I take refuge; how can you say to me,
    "Flee like a bird to the mountains;
  2 for look, the wicked bend the bow,
    they have fitted their arrow to the string,
    to shoot in the dark at the upright in heart.
  3 If the foundations are destroyed,
    what can the righteous do?"

  4 The Lord is in his holy temple;
    the Lord's throne is in heaven.
    His eyes behold, his gaze examines humankind.
  5 The Lord tests the righteous and the wicked,
    and his soul hates the lover of violence.
  6 On the wicked he will rain coals of fire and sulfur;
    a scorching wind shall be the portion of their cup.

7 **For the** LORD **is righteous;**
   he loves righteous deeds;
      the upright shall behold his face.

The motto found on every American coin or item of paper money is "In God We Trust." Shifted into the singular form, that motto well catches the theme of this psalm: "In God I trust."

One of the standard elements in the psalms of lament is an *affirmation of trust* (see on Psalm 13). These brief expressions of trust may be observed in the lament psalms 3:3–6; 4:8; 6:8b–9; 13:5; 22:4–5, 9–10; and others.

With Psalm 11, that element of trust is expanded so that it dominates the entire psalm. This is the first of a number of psalms often called "Psalms of Trust" because that theme dominates (Psalms 11, 16, 23, 27, 62, 63, 131).

Psalm 2, part of the double introduction to the book of Psalms, concluded with an expression of trust: "Happy are all who take refuge in him." Psalm 11 picks up that thematic word, beginning with the affirmation of trust that sets the tone for the psalm: "In the LORD I take refuge." The same "take refuge" theme occurs in Psalms 5:11; 7:1; 31:1; and 71:1.

The structure of this psalm is quite clear. After the heading, dedicating the psalm to the choir director and associating it with David (see on Ps. 4:1), the psalm falls into two major sections. Verses 1–3 focus on the individual, stating the theme "In the LORD I take refuge." Verses 4–7 focus on the Lord, promising that the upright will come into the Lord's presence.

The psalm is somewhat unusual in that it does not speak *to* the Lord (contrast Pss. 10:1 and 12:1) but rather tells *about* the Lord. It certainly has an *instructional* aim, addressed as it is to a gathered congregation.

Flee like a Bird! (11:1–3)

The psalm indicates that the writer was experiencing some sort of harassment. Certain persons were making the psalmist's life miserable, persons identified as a "lover of violence" or simply "the wicked" (vv. 5–6). In the face of this difficult situation, there were some among the psalmist's associates who were willing to offer advice. "Get out of town for a while" was their counsel; "take off for the mountains." For persons living in Jerusalem, surrounded by mountains, this advice would be quite in order.

The imagery here is dramatic. The psalmist is pictured as a bird and those pursuing the psalmist as hunters, hiding in the darkness, bows fitted with arrows, ready to cut short the flight of that winged creature.

The writer, however, has declared the intention to ride out the storm, whatever it may be. The psalmist's refuge will be in trusting in the Lord. The writer will stay with the people in this difficult time, helping to keep the foundations of their community in good repair.

Behind the Scenes (11:4–7)

The first words of this second part of the psalm take the focus away from the enemies and the psalmist and portray a scene in heaven. One hears the calm announcement "The LORD is in his holy temple." The prophet Habakkuk's version of this saying has quite appropriately been used at the beginning of worship services:

> But the LORD is in his holy temple;
>   let all the earth keep silence before him!
>   (Hab. 2:20)

The scene here is no naive declaration that "God's in his heaven, and all's right with the world." For certain, God is in heaven, but all is far from right with the world as the situation is described here. The world is filled with violence and wickedness, as the writer, who has to seek refuge, knows all too well. The conclusion of this psalm instructs all who have experienced the shaking of the foundations of their lives that though the Lord is enthroned in heaven, the Lord is not unaware of what is happening on the earth. The Lord will act to punish the wicked and deliver the Lord's own people. The upright, that is, those who trust in the Lord, will in fact experience that which has been so often declared at the end of a service of worship. They will "behold his face," that is, experience the Lord's presence, and the Lord will give them peace (Num. 6:24–26).

STICKS AND STONES
Psalm 12

To the leader: according to The Sheminith.
A Psalm of David.

12:1 **Help, O LORD, for there is no longer anyone who is godly;**
        the faithful have disappeared from humankind.
    2 **They utter lies to each other;**
        with flattering lips and a double heart they speak.

³ May the LORD cut off all flattering lips,
   the tongue that makes great boasts,
⁴ those who say, "With our tongues we will prevail;
   our lips are our own—who is our master?"

⁵ "Because the poor are despoiled, because the needy groan,
   I will now rise up," says the LORD;
   "I will place them in the safety for which they long."
⁶ The promises of the LORD are promises that are pure,
   silver refined in a furnace on the ground,
   purified seven times.

⁷ You, O LORD, will protect us;
   you will guard us from this generation forever.
⁸ On every side the wicked prowl,
   as vileness is exalted among humankind.

This is a psalm that has to do with words.

It begins with the desperate words of one crying out in prayer, "Help, O LORD!" It continues by referring to the misuse of words by the wicked: lies, flattery, boasting, speaking from a "double heart," which means speaking half-truths (vv. 2–4).

There is only a hint concerning the words of the poor and needy. The psalm speaks of their "groaning."

One does hear the words of the Lord. In verse 5, the Lord promises to give the needy help or safety (the Hebrew means both); this promise links the second half of Psalm 12 with the opening in verse 1. The psalm winds down with a statement about the reliability of the words of the Lord, the "promises . . . promises" (v. 6), and concludes as it began, with words addressed *to* the Lord (vv. 7–8). The heading is similar to that of Psalm 6.

Help, O Lord! (12:1–4)

The psalm begins with a *cry for help*, an element typical of psalms of lament (see on Psalm 13). The psalmist gives a reason for this desperate cry for help: he believes that he is alone, without any like-minded believers to be found (v. 1).

With verses 2–4, the psalmist's judgment on the persons surrounding him in his community (and on humankind) is quite pessimistic. These persons give no evidence of godliness or faithfulness. One of the elements in a psalm of lament is a *complaint* (see on Psalm 13); the psalmist's complaint here has to do with the *words* of his contemporaries. These persons are liars. They speak not the truth but rather flattery (translated "smooth things," the opposite of the truth, in Isa. 30:10). They are not persons of wholehearted integrity but say one thing here and another there; they are "double-hearted." In other words, they are half-hearted about their religion.

After this "they" complaint, the psalmist expresses a wish, asking that the Lord put an end to the lying and flattery. The language is clear and it is shocking: the psalmist would like the Lord to cut out the tongues of these liars!

Promises, Promises (12:5–8)

The mood of the psalm changes dramatically with verse 5. The speaker is no longer the suffering psalmist but the Lord. When the psalm was used in a service in the temple, these words would likely have been spoken by a priest. "I have seen what is happening to the poor and have heard the sounds of their suffering," says the Lord. "Now I will answer their call for help [yāša', v. 1] and bring them to a place of safety [a form of yāša', v. 5]."

Such is the Lord's promise. And what of these promises? Verse 6 offers a word of *instruction* about them. The promises of the Lord are pure. They are as pure as silver that has been refined by fire seven times. (See Isa. 1:25 for the same vocabulary.)

After words *from* the Lord in verse 5 and words *about* the Lord in verse 6, verses 7–8 are once again words addressed to the Lord. Verse 7 is an *affirmation of trust*, again typical of laments (see on Psalm 13). The Hebrew word here translated "protect" occurs six times in Psalm 121, translated as "keep." That psalm may be read as a commentary on this statement.

The psalm concludes with a reminder of the realities of the writer's situation. The wicked are described as "walking back and forth" (the literal Hebrew), like an animal prowling about (v. 8). The psalm ends as it began, with a reference to the general worthlessness of humankind (vv. 1, 8).

Sticks and Stones

"Sticks and stones may break my bones, but words can never hurt me" were the lines we learned as children. But as we grow older, we discover that this saying is not true. Words can hurt us terribly. What we thought was honest praise turns out to be self-serving flattery. The boastful promises didn't come true! And one we thought we could count on lied about us in our absence.

The letter of James provides some memorable instruction about words, observing that while most wild creatures can be tamed, "no one can tame the tongue" (James 3:1–12).

But the instructional point of this psalm is expressed in verse 6. Here is a word about the promises of the Lord. These promises, whether read in scripture or heard in proclamation, are said to be both pure and sure.

ASKING THE HARD QUESTIONS
Psalm 13

To the leader. A Psalm of David.

13:1 **How long, O LORD? Will you forget me forever?**
How long will you hide your face from me?
2 **How long must I bear pain in my soul,**
and have sorrow in my heart all day long?
How long shall my enemy be exalted over me?

3 **Consider and answer me, O LORD my God!**
Give light to my eyes, or I will sleep the sleep of death,
4 **and my enemy will say, "I have prevailed";**
my foes will rejoice because I am shaken.

5 **But I trusted in your steadfast love;**
my heart shall rejoice in your salvation.
6 **I will sing to the LORD,**
because he has dealt bountifully with me.

Elie Wiesel once told of a young Jew who was struggling with life's hard questions: Why was there so much evil in the world? Why didn't the Lord do something about it? He went to various rabbis for help, but the answer was always the same: "Go and study!"

So the young man did. He studied the Bible. He immersed himself in the Talmud. But those questions were not answered, and they would not go away. Then he learned that a great rabbi was going to speak in a distant city, and the young man went there to hear him. He sat in the audience, listening. He knew it could not be so, but it seemed the rabbi was looking only at him. He knew it could not be so, but it seemed the rabbi was speaking directly to him. He joined in the singing and the prayers of fellow believers.

When he returned to his home, he was asked about the visit. "My questions have remained questions," he said, "but somehow, now I can go on."

This psalm begins with a quartet of questions, each introduced by "How long . . . ?" The writer is saying, "Lord, there's been enough of this pain and trouble. I can't hold out any more."

The heading informs the worship leader that this is once again a psalm associated with David. Psalm 13 provides an excellent example of a *psalm of lament* and may be taken as a model for understanding the many psalms of lament. The psalmist is in a desperate situation. Out of this time of trouble comes a lament, a prayer for help. This psalm is made up of the four basic elements found in psalms of lament: a *complaint*, in three forms (vv. 1–2); a *call for help* (vv. 3–4); an *affirmation of trust* (v. 5); and a *vow to praise* (v. 6).

How Long, O Lord? (13:1–2)

In the opening complaint section of the psalm, the question "How long?" occurs four times. These questions express three aspects of the psalmist's complaint: "How long, O LORD? Will *you* forget me forever? How long will *you* hide your face from me?" The subject of the verbs in these first complaints is "you," referring to God. The psalmist believes that God has forgotten him or that God is hiding (which would be worse because it would be an intentional act on God's part). In any case, the psalmist believes that the Lord has let him down. The psalmist does not speak to others *about* the Lord's behavior ("I think the Lord has forgotten about me!"). Rather, the complaint is directly to the Lord: "Will *you* forget me forever?" Since "you" referring to God is the subject of the sentence here, we can name this the "you" complaint or the *theological* complaint.

In the next statement, in verse 2, the subject of the verb is "I": "How long must *I* bear pain in my soul, and have sorrow in my heart all day long?" This "I" complaint expresses the *psychological* dimension of the suffering being experienced. The pain is deep, involving both the heart and the soul.

Finally, the psalmist points to the *sociological* dimension of his troubled situation, asking, "How long shall *my enemy* be exalted over me?"

In sum, every aspect of the writer's existence is strained, hurting, coming apart. Other persons, enemies, are making life miserable. In his own heart the psalmist is experiencing pain and sorrow. And most emphatically, as the first doubled "How long?" indicates, it appears that the Lord has forgotten him.

Claus Westermann has pointed out that these words, "How long?" are found in Babylonian and in Egyptian psalms. He observes that this cry is therefore "not specifically biblical, nor specifically Israelite, but is very, very human" (*Der Psalter*, p. 48, my translation).

Answer Me, O Lord My God (13:3–4)

The elements in the call for help in these verses match up with those of the complaint. Since the Lord seems to have forgotten the psalmist, the prayer is "Consider and answer me, O LORD my God!" Because the one praying is pained in the depths of his heart and soul, the prayer is "Give light to my eyes, or I will sleep the sleep of death." Since enemies have been making life miserable, the prayer is that they will not be victorious.

Trust and a Promise to Praise (13:5–6)

Despite the difficulties of the situation, the psalmist still affirms trust in God, expressing that trust in some of the traditional language of the faith. The object of trust is the Lord's steadfast love, or *hesed*. This *hesed* is an utterly dependable sort of love that exists between persons in a covenant relationship, such as marriage (Hos. 2:19) or friendship, like that between David and Jonathan (1 Sam. 20:14–17), or the relationship between the Lord and the Lord's people (Hos. 6:6). This sort of "covenant love" is especially celebrated in Psalm 136, where the second half of each verse refers to it.

The Hebrew word *salvation* also occurs in Psalm 12:1 (translated "Help") and 12:5 (translated "safety"); see also the comments on Psalm 3:2, 7, 8.

Finally, with verse 6 the one praying believes that the Lord will be able to get the psalmist out of this troubling situation, and that one day the writer will again praise and sing to the Lord.

Those Hard Questions

One contemporary hymnbook prints a selection of biblical psalms in the front part of the book. Twenty-eight psalms are eliminated, including twenty-one laments, or prayers from times of trouble. A realistic view of our lives on this earth will not suppress these psalms from times of trouble and keep only the "happy" psalms. The song from *Fiddler on the Roof* cited in the "Introduction" has it right:

> Sunrise, sunset, sunrise, sunset,
> Swiftly fly the years.
> One season following another,
> Laden with happiness and tears.

Our lives are made up of both happiness and tears, and the Psalter includes psalms both of praise and of lament. It may well be that the greatest contribution the psalms can make to our own lives will be to help us through those times of tragedy and tears.

WHERE IS GOD?
Psalm 14

To the leader. Of David.

14:1 **Fools say in their hearts, "There is no God."**
     They are corrupt, they do abominable deeds;
     there is no one who does good.

2 **The LORD looks down from heaven on humankind**
  to see if there are any who are wise,
  who seek after God.

3 **They have all gone astray, they are all alike perverse;**
  there is no one who does good,
  no, not one.

4 **Have they no knowledge, all the evildoers**
  who eat up my people as they eat bread,
  and do not call upon the LORD?

5 **There they shall be in great terror,**
  for God is with the company of the righteous.
6 **You would confound the plans of the poor,**
  but the LORD is their refuge.

7 **O that deliverance for Israel would come from Zion!**
  When the LORD restores the fortunes of his people,
  Jacob will rejoice; Israel will be glad.

The question is a burning one and is still raised in our own time. Psalm 12 made the promise that the Lord would respond to the groans of the poor and needy by rising up to help. These were "the promises of the Lord" that people assumed they could count on. But Psalm 13 raised another sort of problem. There was a person bearing pain and sorrow whose life was made miserable by those who had turned against him or her. This person was counting on those promises of the Lord—and yet nothing was happening. In Psalm 14, too, the person's prayer is "How long, O Lord?" The underlying question is "Where is God?" Again, the psalm is associated with David and dedicated to the worship leader (see Psalm 11).

The Absence of God (14:1)

Like Psalm 13, this psalm is concerned with the absence of God. The writer hears persons saying, "There is no God," and designates such people as "fools" (Hebrew, *nābāl*). What is the sense of that word? It may be translated "impious" and can be used to refer to people who scoff at the Lord: "remember how the *impious* scoff at you all day long" (Ps. 74:22; also v. 18). The *nābāl* is also a person who is out of control, who does not know how to control appetites or actions after eating heartily (Prov. 30:21–23) or the words spoken to others (Ps. 39:8). Nabal was a rich man who provides an illustration of what a fool is by living up to his name (1 Samuel 25; note v. 25). He doesn't have the common sense to accept a genuine offer of peace. He scoffs at God and scorns others. Such is a fool.

This psalm fills in one more dimension on the portrait of a fool. The fool does not believe in God. "There is no God," the fool says and acts in ways that fit in with that attitude. The fool's premise of practical atheism results in a life marked by perverse actions. When there is no God, says the psalmist, there is no good (v. 1).

The Absence of Good (14:2–4)

Verses 2–4 look at the human situation from God's perspective. The Lord is in heaven and looks down at humans to see if there are indeed any who are smart enough to be looking for God. There are not. In fact, all humans have gotten off the right path. In its Arabic cognate, the word translated "perverse" is used for milk that has turned sour. These people, who should be walking in the way of the righteous (Psalm 1), have soured on religion and their lives are derailed. The statement made in verse 1 is reaffirmed and repeated in verse 3: "there is no one who does good, no, not one." The fools' wrong attitude toward God has resulted in wrong actions toward their fellow humans. In Jeremiah's day, the situation had become so bad in the city of Jerusalem that the Lord advised the prophet to look for even one person concerned with truth and justice (Jer. 5:1).

Other prophets spoke the same way, saying that the people's sins against one another had cut off their relationship to the Lord (Isa. 59:1–8). Hosea said that lack of religious education ("knowledge of God") had resulted in people sinning against one another, with implications even for the natural environment (Hos. 4:1–3).

The psalmist traces both the sociological and theological problems of society to a lack of religious education. These persons "have no knowledge," they chew up "my people" as they chew up bread, and they don't pray (14:4). Others also used this "chew up" imagery: Psalm 27:2; Proverbs 30:14; Micah 3:1–3.

God with Them (14:5–7)

With verses 5–6, the psalmist affirms trust in what the Lord will do. God is *with* the righteous, and these evildoers shall be terrorized. (For "God is with," see the comments on Psalm 23.) The "refuge" theme is also sounded in Psalms 2:12; 11:1; 46:1; 61:3.

The psalm concludes with a confident wish that God deliver the people (v. 7).

What about Atheism?

The Bible does not deal with the question of theoretical atheism, that is, whether or not God exists. The existence of God is an assumption for the biblical writers. The biblical writers do, however, pick up the question of what we might call a practical atheism. This may be a sense that God is not paying attention to me (Psalm 13) or even that God has abandoned me (Psalm 22).

The question behind Psalm 14 is "Where is God now?" In the day of the psalmist, there were those who put it clearly and said, "There is no God!" And in our own time we continue to hear not only of individual atheists but of societies of those who make a point of declaring their lack of belief in God.

This psalm deals with the question "Where is God?" in two ways. First, it locates God in heaven, from which place God "looks down" on humankind. And where is heaven? The language of the Bible simply asserts that the place where God dwells is "up," that is, beyond the earth (v. 2). Jesus told his followers to pray to "our Father in heaven," without explaining things further. That may be about as well as we can do with this question, though some have found other imagery, such as "ground of our being," to be more effective.

But Psalm 14 has another response to the question "Where is God?" "God is with the company of the righteous," it states (v. 5), adding that the Lord is the refuge of the poor. These two themes run through the Bible. On the one hand, God is high and lifted up, "high above all nations, and his glory above the heavens," as Psalm 113:4 puts it. But God also "looks far down" and is with the poor, the needy, and the infertile woman who is praying that she might have a child (Ps. 113:9). "When you see her happily playing with her children," Psalm 113 is saying, "then you see what it means that God is 'with the company of the righteous,'" as Psalm 14 puts it.

The Bible offers an updated version of this psalm in Psalm 53. The apostle Paul quotes from Psalm 114 in Romans 3:10–12.

HOW DO I GET IN?
Psalm 15

A Psalm of David.

15:1 **O LORD, who may abide in your tent?**
        Who may dwell on your holy hill?

   2 **Those who walk blamelessly, and do what is right,**
        and speak the truth from their heart;
   3 **who do not slander with their tongue,**
        and do no evil to their friends,
        nor take up a reproach against their neighbors;
   4 **in whose eyes the wicked are despised,**
        but who honor those who fear the LORD;
      who stand by their oath even to their hurt;
   5 **who do not lend money at interest,**
        and do not take a bribe against the innocent.

      Those who do these things shall never be moved.

Our question was, "How do we get into this place?"

We were seeking entrance to a synagogue in the downtown area of a large German city. We had the address, but in the mass of large buildings there was nothing that looked like a synagogue. Then we noticed it. Alongside a door was a small black plaque with the words "Israelite Community" in Hebrew and in German. Alongside the plaque was a button. I pressed the button. A buzzer sounded and the door clicked. We walked into a corridor and saw a young man sitting in a glassed-in booth. "Shalom," he said. "Shalom" was our response. Then he asked some questions: "What do you wish? Where are you from? May I see your passport?" Then another buzzer, another door, and we walked into the place of worship.

A modern-day "entrance liturgy" of sorts, I thought. "Shalom." Then questions and answers. Then the opening of the door and admittance.

Who May Enter? (15:1)

It appears that Psalm 15 was originally used in the Jerusalem temple as something of an entrance liturgy. This time the one seeking entrance asked the first question: "O LORD, who may abide in your tent? Who may dwell on your holy hill?"

Then a priest or temple official answered, "Those who walk blamelessly, and do what is right. . . ." After this ritual, the worshiper entered the temple area.

"A Psalm of David" associates the psalm in some way with that king (see on Psalm 3). The psalm consists of a pair of questions (v. 1) and then a series of answers to the questions (vv. 2–5). After a series of psalms that focus on the theme of the poor and needy (Psalms 9–14), this one sounds a different note. It deals with the question "What sort of people are found in this company known as the people of God?" Psalm 24 has the same sort of entrance liturgy (vv. 3–6) and furnishes a closing bracket for the group running from Psalm 15 through 24.

In the earliest setting for this entrance liturgy, we could imagine a worshiper approaching the temple area. At the gate or the doorway was a temple official. There were no buzzers or glassed-in booths, but there was a procedure. The worshiper asked,

> O LORD, who may abide in your tent?
> Who may dwell on your holy hill?
> (v. 1)

The reference to the "holy hill" referred to Mount Zion, where the temple was located. "Tent" was something of an old-fashioned name for the temple, recalling the days when the people of Israel worshipped in a tent in the wilderness (2 Sam. 7:6; also Pss. 27:5–6; 61:4; 78:60).

Who May Enter? (15:2–5)

The temple official then provided some answers to the worshiper's questions. The first is brief and general, using participles in the Hebrew to suggest continuing action rather than a single act:

> Those walking blamelessly,
> and doing what is right,
> and speaking truth from their heart.
> (v. 2; my translation)

The "walking" word takes us right back to the first psalm: "Happy are those who do not walk in the way of the wicked" (Ps. 1:1; my translation). This "walking" refers to the conduct of one's entire life. "Doing what is right" speaks of one's everyday actions.

After these references to actions, the psalm refers to words, calling for words that are truthful and sincere, in contrast to the sort of lying, flattering, and deceiving described in Psalm 12:2.

After the general statement in verse 2, verses 3–5 provide more specific instruction. The person about to worship ought to reflect on his or her neighbors and friends. Verse 3 refers to those "who do not slander with their tongue." The Hebrew verb translated "slander" is from the word for "foot." The sense here seems to refer to someone who goes about on foot, from place to place, spreading gossip. Sandwiched between two statements about words is some advice about acts toward one's friends.

Further instruction regarding the lifestyle of those who worship the Lord is then given (vv. 4–5). Once again, a general statement comes first: these people about to participate in worship ought to distinguish between the wicked and those who believe in the Lord, despising the one and honoring the other (v. 4). After this general statement are comments that have to do with specific words (oaths) and specific acts, in this case actions involving money (interest, bribes). Those persons who belong to the congregation of God's people ought to stick by promises sealed with oaths (see also Num. 30:2–16). They ought not to oppress the poor by charging exorbitant interest rates (see Ezek. 18:8, 13; also Lev. 25:37). Nor should they accept bribes to testify against the innocent in court procedures. That there are so many biblical warnings against bribery indicates that it must have been a serious and ongoing problem (see Exod. 23:8; Deut. 10:17; 16:19; 27:25; Prov. 17:23; Ezek. 22:12).

The concluding line declares that those persons living in this way "shall never be moved." They will never totter, never be shaken, never be knocked over by adversity (Ps. 10:6; see also Pss. 16:8; 30:6; 62:2, 6).

Religion Outside the Temple

This psalm is concerned with some basics in the life of faith: believing, speaking, and doing. The one asking the opening question is a believer who has come to worship the Lord in the temple. But to believe in the Lord does not have to do only with what happens in the temple. The remainder of the psalm is concerned to describe the lifestyle of the believer outside the temple. Such persons will act in ways that are blameless and right. They will not do evil to their friends, nor will they oppress the poor through wrong handling of their money. They will speak the truth, stand by their promises, and avoid running about as gossips. Their lives will not easily be shaken. They will be as deeply rooted as trees planted by streams of water (Psalm 1) or as solid as houses built on rock (Matt. 7:24–27).

SHOW ME THE WAY TO GO
Psalm 16

A Miktam of David.

16:1 Protect me, O God, for in you I take refuge.
   2 I say to the LORD, "You are my Lord;
     I have no good apart from you."

   3 As for the holy ones in the land, they are the noble,
     in whom is all my delight.

   4 Those who choose another god multiply their sorrows;
     their drink offerings of blood I will not pour out
     or take their names upon my lips.

   5 The LORD is my chosen portion and my cup;
     you hold my lot.
   6 The boundary lines have fallen for me in pleasant places;
     I have a goodly heritage.

   7 I bless the LORD who gives me counsel;
     in the night also my heart instructs me.
   8 I keep the LORD always before me;
     because he is at my right hand, I shall not be moved.

   9 Therefore my heart is glad, and my soul rejoices;
     my body also rests secure.
   10 For you do not give me up to Sheol,
     or let your faithful one see the Pit.

   11 You show me the path of life.
     In your presence there is fullness of joy;
     in your right hand are pleasures forevermore.

Once again, this psalm pictures life as a path along which one walks. The first psalm speaks of two ways, the way of the righteous and the way of the wicked. Psalm 15:2 issues an encouragement to "walk blamelessly." Now, this psalm speaks of a "path of life" that God reveals and where joy can be found, because as one walks that path, the Lord goes along (v. 11).

Psalm 16 is once again associated with David. (See the comments on Psalm 3.) The meaning of "Miktam" is not clear; another set of these Davidic "Miktams" occurs in Psalms 56–60.

The Lord Is My Protector (16:1–6)

The psalm begins with a call for help, an element typical of laments (see on Psalm 13). This is a prayer for protection, using the "refuge" imagery at the close of Psalm 2: "Happy are all who take refuge in him." After this brief prayer, the psalmist speaks of his or her relationship to the Lord (vv. 1b–2).

Verses 3 and 4 speak of the delight of living with other believers, the "holy ones in the land" and then expresses disgust with those who worship other gods.

Using some fresh imagery, verses 5 and 6 describe God and the life of the believer. The image of the cup calls to mind the picture of the Lord's hospitality in Psalm 23:5, "my cup overflows." The main picture here, however, is that of dividing up an inheritance of land. "I have been given a good place to live and to work," the psalmist is saying.

The Lord Is My Guide Along Life's Way (16:7–11)

Verses 7 and 8 speak of the way in which the Lord advises and guides the one praying. The Lord gives counsel and instruction and even gives instruction in the night (v. 7). During the day, the Lord is at the psalmist's right hand, prepared to rescue him or her should the writer fall. Another psalm put it this way: "though we stumble, we shall not fall headlong, for the LORD holds us by the hand" (Ps. 37:24).

A sense of happiness, joy, and security arises from the knowledge that the Lord is "at my right hand, I shall not be moved." The notion of joy and security is developed further in verses 9–10 with the additional statement that the psalmist knows the Lord will never abandon him or her in Sheol, the place of the dead (see on Psalm 6).

The psalm comes to a conclusion with an affirmation of trust, the psalmist declaring that the Lord has shown the writer the path his or her life should take. It speaks of the pleasure and joy that are present along the way when that way is accompanied by the Lord (v. 11).

The Lord is responsible for protecting the one who prays from times of trouble (vv. 1–2). The Lord is also the one who can be counted on to go with the believer along life's way (v. 11).

A Psalm of Trust

This psalm is usually grouped with the "individual psalms of trust" (Psalms 11, 16, 23, 27, 62, 63, 131) because of the ringing confessions of confidence in the Lord in verses 1b–2 and 5–11. God continues to be a mighty fortress where the writer can find safety and security and thus live a good life (vv. 1b–2). Twice reference is made to the Lord's *closeness*, in the language of the Lord's being at the psalmist's right hand, which gives both stability (v. 8) and joy (v. 11) to life.

Given such a life—provided with safety and security (vv. 1, 8–9), a good place to live and work (vv. 5–6), an opportunity for religious instruction (v. 7); not dreading death but enjoying a day-by-day walking with the Lord (vv. 10–11)—who would not be happy (vv. 9–11)?

The Psalm in Two Sermons

In two instances, preaching reported in the New Testament quotes from this psalm. The first is Peter's sermon to the crowd gathered in Jerusalem to celebrate the Jewish festival of Pentecost. It is nine o'clock in the morning and something strange is going on. There is a sound like a wind, then something like flames appears, and the followers of Jesus begin speaking in the languages of those gathered.

Peter speaks of the fulfilling of prophecy (Acts 2:14–21), then of the life and death of Jesus (2:22–23), and finally of God's raising Jesus from the dead (2:24–35). After announcing, "But God raised him up," the apostle cites Psalm 16:8–11 as a witness to the resurrection of Jesus (Acts 2:25–28; also v. 31). When those first believers in Jesus Christ looked at the Psalms in the light of what had been happening among them, Psalm 16 was one of those passages they found fulfilled in the resurrection of Jesus.

The other link between Psalm 16 and New Testament preaching is found in connection with an important sermon of Paul. As reported in Acts 13, the apostle is a guest speaker in the synagogue of Antioch. After the texts from the Pentateuch and the Prophets have been read, Paul addresses the gathering. He begins with recalling the Lord's mighty acts in Israel's history, from the ancestors through David (Acts 13:17–22). After speaking briefly of that king, Paul skips a millennium to report that "what God promised to our ancestors he has fulfilled for us, their children, by raising Jesus" (v. 32). Then Paul cites texts from Psalm 2, from Isaiah 55, and from Psalm 16:10: "Therefore he has also said in another psalm, 'You will not let your Holy One experience corruption'" (Acts 13:35).

These early believers were convinced that the promises found in the Old Testament were being fulfilled in the life, death, and resurrection of Jesus. And when they had experienced the resurrection, they thought of Psalm 16.

The Way

Finally, we have observed that this psalm speaks of the Lord showing the way to go along the path of life. The earliest believers used that same imagery, referring to the new Christian movement as "the Way" (Acts 9:2; 19:9, 23; 22:4; 24:22). And of course, that designation was not original to them. When Thomas asked, "How can we know the way?" Jesus answered, "I am the way, and the truth, and the life" (John 14:6).

THE APPLE OF YOUR EYE
Psalm 17

A Prayer of David.

17:1 Hear a just cause, O LORD; attend to my cry;
　　　give ear to my prayer from lips free of deceit.
　2 From you let my vindication come;
　　　let your eyes see the right.

　3 If you try my heart, if you visit me by night,
　　　if you test me, you will find no wickedness in me;
　　　my mouth does not transgress.
　4 As for what others do, by the word of your lips
　　　I have avoided the ways of the violent.
　5 My steps have held fast to your paths;
　　　my feet have not slipped.

　6 I call upon you, for you will answer me, O God;
　　　incline your ear to me, hear my words.
　7 Wondrously show your steadfast love,
　　　O savior of those who seek refuge
　　　from their adversaries at your right hand.

　8 Guard me as the apple of the eye;
　　　hide me in the shadow of your wings,
　9 from the wicked who despoil me,
　　　my deadly enemies who surround me.
　10 They close their hearts to pity;
　　　with their mouths they speak arrogantly.
　11 They track me down; now they surround me;
　　　they set their eyes to cast me to the ground.
　12 They are like a lion eager to tear,
　　　like a young lion lurking in ambush.

　13 Rise up, O LORD, confront them, overthrow them!
　　　By your sword deliver my life from the wicked,
　14 from mortals—by your hand, O LORD—
　　　from mortals whose portion in life is in this world.

May their bellies be filled with what you have stored up for them;
  may their children have more than enough;
  may they leave something over to their little ones.
¹⁵ As for me, I shall behold your face in righteousness;
  when I awake I shall be satisfied, beholding your likeness.

For the first time in the book of Psalms, the heading refers to a psalm as a "prayer" (Hebrew, *tephillāh*). This description of the psalm is taken from the text itself: the psalm begins with "give ear to my *prayer*." Psalms 86, 90, 102, and 142 are also designated "prayers" in their headings, and Psalm 72:20 looks back at previous psalms and concludes, "The *prayers* of David son of Jesse are ended." The heading indicates that this prayer is to be associated with David. (See comments on Psalm 3.)

The psalm includes typical elements of the lament (see on Psalm 13). Especially dominant are *calls for help*, indicating something of the desperation of the one praying (vv. 1–2, 6–9, 13–14). Other lament elements are a threefold *"they" complaint* about the enemy (vv. 10–12) and an *affirmation of trust* (v. 15). What makes this psalm different from the standard lament is an *assertion of innocence* in verses 3–5. This would seem to indicate that the one praying has been falsely accused.

Both beginning and ending suggest that the psalm was intended to be prayed at the end of the day, before drifting off to sleep (vv. 3, 15).

A Desperate Call for Help (17:1–15)

The psalm begins with an intense triple request for a hearing with the Lord and for justice to be done (vv. 1–2; see also Ps. 5:1–2 for a triple request). A person who is innocent has come to the place of worship to appeal to God for help in regard to a legal difficulty. Deuteronomy 17:8–11 and 1 Kings 8:31–32 hint at such procedures.

With verses 3–5, the psalmist claims to be innocent of any charges that might be brought against him or her. Does "visit me by night" mean that the Lord is "cross-examining" the psalmist during sleep? The parallel expressions "try my heart . . . test me" suggest that this is the sense. (See also Ps. 139:1, 23–24, which may reflect such an examination.)

The picture of life as a journey, as in Psalm 16:11, recurs in verse 5 with the assertion that the psalmist has been keeping on track and has not "slipped" away (the same verb was translated "moved" in 16:8). This theme of life as a walk or a journey is found in other psalms (Pss. 1; 23:3) and also in Proverbs (4:11, 26; 5:21).

In verses 6–9 the psalmist calls again for God's help. Verse 6 asks for a hearing with the Lord. Verse 7 uses familiar vocabulary to request help from the Lord, referring to "your steadfast love" and indicating something of the reason for this prayer: it is necessary to seek refuge from enemies. "Guard me" and "hide me" are also typical vocabulary of psalms calling for help. The two images in verse 8, however, are fresh and striking. "The apple of the eye" refers to the pupil, the most precious part of the eye, which is the most precious part of the body (see also Deut. 32:10; Prov. 7:2; Zech. 2:8). "The shadow of your wings" portrays the Lord as a mother bird, protecting her young by covering them with her wings (see also Deut. 32:11–12).

Verses 10–12 develop the "enemies" theme introduced in verse 9 into a "they" complaint typical of laments (see on Psalm 13). These persons are first described literally, as arrogant, without pity, surrounding and attacking the psalmist (17:9–11). These vicious, violent people are then described figuratively, compared to lions lurking, eager to pounce on their prey (v. 12; see also Ps. 10:8–9).

The third call for help in the psalm is the sharpest (17:13–14). The one praying asks that the Lord overthrow these enemies and at the same time rescue the psalmist. The English word *mortal* (which appears twice in v. 14) is derived from the Latin *mors*, "death"; the Hebrew word used is also derived from the word for death and again carries with it a reminder of the limits of human life. One might expect a curse on these enemies at this point; instead, the psalmist prays that they be blessed (v. 14b).

Apples and Eagles

"Guard me as the apple of your eye, hide me in the shadow of your wings" (v. 8, Jewish Publication Society translation) is the central request of this psalm. The writer uses two especially effective pictures here. First, the Hebrew translated "apple of your eye" has the literal sense "little person of your eye," referring to the pupil; when one is very close, one can see a "little person" in the pupil. The expression means something precious; we might say, "Their little daughter is the apple of her father's eye."

The second picture portrays God as a bird under whose wings the psalmist, like a chick under the wings of a mother hen, seeks protection (see also Pss. 63:7; 91:4). Both images are also combined in Deuteronomy 32, where it is said the Lord watches over the Lord's people "as the apple of his eye" (Deut. 32:10) and also that the Lord cares for them as an eagle cares for its young (Deut. 32:10–12).

Here are two arresting pictures for the relationship between God and people. God's people are as precious to the Lord as the pupil of one's eye is to a person! And God cares for God's people as a mother bird cares for her young.

The Mother Hen

The same imagery is transformed into a different key in the New Testament when Jesus speaks of Jerusalem:

> Jerusalem, Jerusalem . . . How often have I desired to gather your children together as a hen gathers her brood under her wings, and you were not willing! (Matt. 23:37)

The Lord as eye protector, as bird, as hen—these are fresh pictures illustrating God's care for God's own. Trust in that caring God is expressed in literal language in the prayer at the end of the psalm: "when I awake I shall be satisfied, beholding your likeness."

WITH MY GOD I CAN LEAP OVER A WALL
Psalm 18

To the leader. A Psalm of David the servant of the Lord, who addressed the words of this song to the Lord on the day when the Lord delivered him from the hand of all his enemies, and from the hand of Saul. He said:

18:1 **I love you, O Lord, my strength.**

2 **The Lord is my rock, my fortress, and my deliverer,**
    my God, my rock in whom I take refuge,
    my shield, and the horn of my salvation, my stronghold.
3 **I call upon the Lord, who is worthy to be praised,**
    so I shall be saved from my enemies.

4 **The cords of death encompassed me;**
    the torrents of perdition assailed me;
5 **the cords of Sheol entangled me;**
    the snares of death confronted me.

6 **In my distress I called upon the Lord;**
    to my God I cried for help.
  From his temple he heard my voice,
    and my cry to him reached his ears.

⁷ Then the earth reeled and rocked;
    the foundations also of the mountains trembled
    and quaked, because he was angry.
⁸ Smoke went up from his nostrils,
    and devouring fire from his mouth;
    glowing coals flamed forth from him.
⁹ He bowed the heavens, and came down;
    thick darkness was under his feet.
¹⁰ He rode on a cherub, and flew;
    he came swiftly upon the wings of the wind.
¹¹ He made darkness his covering around him,
    his canopy thick clouds dark with water.
¹² Out of the brightness before him
    there broke through his clouds
    hailstones and coals of fire.
¹³ The LORD also thundered in the heavens,
    and the Most High uttered his voice.
¹⁴ And he sent out his arrows, and scattered them;
    he flashed forth lightnings, and routed them.
¹⁵ Then the channels of the sea were seen,
    and the foundations of the world were laid bare
  at your rebuke, O LORD,
    at the blast of the breath of your nostrils.

¹⁶ He reached down from on high, he took me;
    he drew me out of mighty waters.
¹⁷ He delivered me from my strong enemy,
    and from those who hated me;
    for they were too mighty for me.
¹⁸ They confronted me in the day of my calamity;
    but the LORD was my support.
¹⁹ He brought me out into a broad place;
    he delivered me, because he delighted in me.

²⁰ The LORD rewarded me according to my righteousness;
    according to the cleanness of my hands he recompensed me.
²¹ For I have kept the ways of the LORD,
    and have not wickedly departed from my God.
²² For all his ordinances were before me,
    and his statutes I did not put away from me.
²³ I was blameless before him,
    and I kept myself from guilt.
²⁴ Therefore the LORD has recompensed me according to my
  righteousness,
    according to the cleanness of my hands in his sight.

²⁵ With the loyal you show yourself loyal;
    with the blameless you show yourself blameless;
²⁶ with the pure you show yourself pure;
    and with the crooked you show yourself perverse.
²⁷ For you deliver a humble people,
    but the haughty eyes you bring down.
²⁸ It is you who light my lamp;
    the LORD, my God, lights up my darkness.
²⁹ By you I can crush a troop,
    and by my God I can leap over a wall.
³⁰ This God—his way is perfect;
    the promise of the LORD proves true;
    he is a shield for all who take refuge in him.

³¹ For who is God except the LORD?
    And who is a rock besides our God?—
³² the God who girded me with strength,
    and made my way safe.
³³ He made my feet like the feet of a deer,
    and set me secure on the heights.
³⁴ He trains my hands for war,
    so that my arms can bend a bow of bronze.
³⁵ You have given me the shield of your salvation,
    and your right hand has supported me;
    your help has made me great.
³⁶ You gave me a wide place for my steps under me,
    and my feet did not slip.
³⁷ I pursued my enemies and overtook them;
    and did not turn back until they were consumed.
³⁸ I struck them down, so that they were not able to rise;
    they fell under my feet.
³⁹ For you girded me with strength for the battle;
    you made my assailants sink under me.
⁴⁰ You made my enemies turn their backs to me,
    and those who hated me I destroyed.
⁴¹ They cried for help, but there was no one to save them;
    they cried to the LORD, but he did not answer them.
⁴² I beat them fine, like dust before the wind;
    I cast them out like the mire of the streets.

⁴³ You delivered me from strife with the peoples;
    you made me head of the nations;
    people whom I had not known served me.
⁴⁴ As soon as they heard of me they obeyed me;
    foreigners came cringing to me.

⁴⁵ **Foreigners lost heart,**
  and came trembling out of their strongholds.
⁴⁶ **The LORD lives! Blessed be my rock,**
  and exalted be the God of my salvation,
⁴⁷ **the God who gave me vengeance**
  and subdued peoples under me;
⁴⁸ **who delivered me from my enemies;**
  indeed, you exalted me above my adversaries;
  you delivered me from the violent.

⁴⁹ **For this I will extol you, O LORD, among the nations,**
  and sing praises to your name.
⁵⁰ **Great triumphs he gives to his king,**
  and shows steadfast love to his anointed,
  to David and his descendants forever.

There are a number of unique features about this psalm. It is the third longest of the psalms, ranking after Psalms 78 and 119. The heading is the longest of all the psalm headings. This psalm has a duplicate in 2 Samuel 22.

Another notable characteristic of this psalm is its imagery, including the great variety of pictures for God (seven in vv. 1–2 alone) and for human beings (lamp carrier, deer, archer, superhero, warrior). This is a *royal psalm*, that is, a psalm that played a role in the life of the king. The king is the one who is speaking in the psalm (vv. 49–50; see the comments on royal psalms in connection with Psalm 2).

The Earliest Commentary (The Heading)

The heading associates the psalm with David's deliverance "from the hand of all his enemies, and from the hand of Saul." The editors who placed the same psalm near the end of the second book of Samuel (chap. 22) are suggesting that the psalm expresses David's thanks to God after a lifetime of deliverances, some of which are recorded in the books of Samuel. That setting of the psalm suggests that it be viewed as words of thanks from the old king to the God who had been faithful to him for a lifetime, since his deliverance from the hand of Goliath.

The biblical report on David's career begins and ends with stories of encounters with Philistine supermen (1 Samuel 17; 2 Sam. 21:18–22). The heading thus suggests that Psalm 18 would be appropriate for such a time of looking back and giving thanks.

But the purpose of the psalm is not only to give thanks for great victories in the past. It also points forward and carries assurance that the Lord will continue to prosper the Davidic kings of the future (vv. 49–50).

After the introduction (vv. 1–3) is a story of distress and deliverance, in the manner of a psalm of thanksgiving (vv. 4–30; see on Psalm 30). The second major section is a song of a king giving thanks for a victory and anticipating continued success (vv. 31–50).

This God—His Way Is Perfect (18:1–30)

The psalm begins in verses 1–3 with a triple address to the Lord. Following the declaration "I love you, O LORD, my strength" is a confession with a listing of descriptive names for God: "my rock, my fortress, my deliverer, my God, my rock in whom I take refuge, my shield, the horn of my salvation, my stronghold." Finally comes the confident assertion "I call upon the LORD . . . so I shall be saved from my enemies."

Verses 4–19 tell a story of distress and deliverance. As in psalms of thanksgiving (see comments on Psalm 30), there is a brief summary of what the psalmist has experienced (vv. 4–6), followed by a more detailed telling of the entire story (vv. 7–19). The Lord was in his temple, heard the psalmist's cry, and came to the rescue, accompanied by earthquake and darkness, wind and hail, thunder and lightning, and storms at sea (vv. 6b–15). The psalmist is pictured as drowning, fighting for breath in mighty waves, but then brought out to a safe, wide-open place (vv. 16–19).

Do verses 20–24 have something of a self-righteous ring to our ears? This is the flowery language of royalty, the king describing his own administration in glowing terms! The "clean hands" imagery at the beginning and end is explained in the literal language of verses 21–23.

Verses 25–30 consist of praise accompanied by instruction. The king speaks of what the Lord has done for his people (v. 27). Then, with striking imagery and exaggeration, the king tells what the Lord means for his own life: "Lord, you light my lamp, you give me the strength to take on an entire army, with you I can leap over a wall!" (vv. 28–29 paraphrased). The tone of verse 30 is instructional, telling about the ways and the promises and the works of the Lord. The "refuge" language of verse 30 recalls that theme at the end of Psalm 2.

You Delivered Me; for This I Praise You (18:31–50)

Verses 31–50 present the song of one giving thanks to the Lord for achieving a victory. The final verse identifies the victor as King David. The king tells of the God who has given him strength; who has made his feet, hands, and arms strong for warfare; and who has supported him in battles (vv. 32–36). With verses 37–42 the king gives his account of a victory, giving credit to the Lord for help (vv. 39–40). Verses 43–45 report the king's international successes. Verses 46–50 present the king as praising the Lord.

A Royal Psalm

Like the other royal psalms, this one continued to be used during the time of the monarchy and was canonized long after David and the Davidic monarchy were off the scene. (See the comments on royal psalms in connection with the discussion of Psalm 2.) Psalm 2 spoke of the king as the Lord's anointed, as son of God, and as one ruling over the nations of the earth. Psalm 18 promises that the Lord will give great victories to the king and show steadfast love to his anointed, his messiah, and to the descendants of the messiah, forever (v. 50). This psalm, too, was part of that seedbed that contributed to the full-blown flowering of messianic hope.

A Jagged Integrity

We have already alluded to the rich imagery in this psalm, which could serve to enliven proclamation and instruction. After the abstract notion that God is "my strength" (v. 1), there follows a series of concrete images, each of which could be developed in preaching or teaching. Each is used with the pronoun *my*, signaling the close relationship between the psalmist and the Lord. The Lord is "my rock" (Hebrew, *selaʿ*), that is, my place of security and solidarity (see Pss. 31:3; 42:9; 71:3). Jesus used this "built on a rock" imagery at the conclusion of the Sermon on the Mount (Matt. 7:24–27). The Lord is "my fortress" (Pss. 31:2–3; 71:3; 91:2; 144:2). The Lord is "my deliverer," or better, "my shelter, place of escape" (see Ps. 55:8). The Lord is "my rock in whom I take refuge," this time using the word *ṣūr,* for rock, as in verses 31 and 46 (also Ps. 19:14). Finally, the Lord is described as "my shield" (Ps. 3:3), "the horn [a symbol of power] of my salvation" (Jer. 48:25), and "my stronghold" (Ps. 9:9).

In addition to these concrete pictures for God at the opening, the psalmist uses others during the course of the psalm: the Lord is a storm God who can set the earth quaking with a blast of breath from his nostrils (18:12–15). God is a lamplighter, helping God's people to make their way through life's dark places (v. 28). God is a trainer who prepares the feet, hands, and arms of persons for warfare (vv. 33–34). God is an equipper in the spiritual armory, furnishing people with weaponry, such as the "shield of your salvation" (v. 35). Finally, God is a promise keeper who continues to show caring love to the descendants of David (v. 50).

There is also fresh imagery describing people: the one who prays for help is a drowning person (v. 16), or one who carries a lamp through the darkness (v. 28), or something of a superman, who can crush an army and leap over the walls of a city (v. 29). This person has feet like a deer (v. 33), the hands of a warrior carrying a shield (vv. 34–35), and arms like an archer (v. 34). Enemies have been beaten like fine dust (v. 42) and have been left like refuse in the streets (v. 42).

I once heard Edward R. Murrow's news reporting characterized as having a "jagged integrity." The fresh and sometimes jagged imagery of this psalm can be an encouragement to strive for equally creative language when seeking to communicate the biblical message in our own time.

A TALE OF TWO BOOKS
Psalm 19

To the leader. A Psalm of David.

19:1 **The heavens are telling the glory of God;**
    and the firmament proclaims his handiwork.
  ² **Day to day pours forth speech,**
    and night to night declares knowledge.
  ³ **There is no speech, nor are there words;**
    their voice is not heard;
  ⁴ **yet their voice goes out through all the earth,**
    and their words to the end of the world.

  In the heavens he has set a tent for the sun,
  ⁵ **which comes out like a bridegroom from his wedding canopy,**
    and like a strong man runs its course with joy.
  ⁶ **Its rising is from the end of the heavens,**
    and its circuit to the end of them;
    and nothing is hid from its heat.

  ⁷ **The law of the LORD is perfect,**
    reviving the soul;
  the decrees of the LORD are sure,
    making wise the simple;
  ⁸ **the precepts of the LORD are right,**
    rejoicing the heart;
  the commandment of the LORD is clear,
    enlightening the eyes;

⁹ the fear of the LORD is pure,
    enduring forever;
the ordinances of the LORD are true
    and righteous altogether.
¹⁰ More to be desired are they than gold,
    even much fine gold;
sweeter also than honey,
    and drippings of the honeycomb.

¹¹ Moreover by them is your servant warned;
    in keeping them there is great reward.
¹² But who can detect their errors?
    Clear me from hidden faults.
¹³ Keep back your servant also from the insolent;
    do not let them have dominion over me.
Then I shall be blameless,
    and innocent of great transgression.

¹⁴ Let the words of my mouth and the meditation of my heart
    be acceptable to you,
    O LORD, my rock and my redeemer.

Many a sermon, Bible study, or class period has begun with the prayer that concludes this psalm:

> Let the words of my mouth and the meditation of my heart
>   be acceptable to you,
>   O LORD, my rock and my redeemer.

This prayer is appropriate at the beginning of a teaching or preaching situation. But the scope of the psalm of which it is a part is broader than a classroom or a church. The vision of this psalm includes the whole earth (v. 4) throughout all time (v. 9). Psalms 19, 20, and 21 have identical headings. (See the comments on the heading of Psalm 4.)

What the Heavens Tell (19:1–6)

The first segment of this psalm is framed with references to "the heavens" (vv. 1, 6). Parallel to "heavens" in verse 1 is a reference to "the firmament" or "dome" (NRSV footnote), indicating that "heavens" and "dome" are here used with the same meaning. The biblical view of the world imagined a huge, transparent Plexiglas-like dome that was mounted over the flat earth, like an inverted soup bowl. Below the earth was water, as was obvious when one dug a well. Above the dome was water, as could be observed from the blue of the sky and from rainfall, when openings in the dome allowed water to pass through. At the time of the great flood, the fountains of the deep beneath the earth burst with water, and the windows of the dome were opened, the water then inundating the entire earth (Gen. 7:11; see also Ps. 148:4). The blue sky, the heavenly dome above us, somehow testifies to the magnificence of God, says this psalm.

Psalm 8 speaks dramatically about the moon and the stars and the heavens at night. The writer of Psalm 19 is reflecting on the daytime sky and thus offers some thoughts about the sun. God has put the sun in its place. It emerges each day with the freshness and newness of a bridegroom on the first day of married life. Joyfully it runs its daily course, like a perpetually jubilant celestial jogger. Each day it moves from one edge of the dome to the other—and nothing can be hidden from it.

What the Scriptures Teach (19:7–10)

With verse 7, the psalm modulates into another key. The focus is no longer on the world (v. 4) but on words. The spotlight is no longer on God's handiwork in space but on human beings and speech. For the first time, the psalm uses the personal name Yahweh (NRSV, "LORD") for God. The writer is concerned about the *torah* (NRSV, "law"). As was the case with Psalm 1, the word here is better translated "instruction" than "law": "the instruction of the LORD is perfect, reviving the soul."

The psalm fires off a series of six statements indicating how God communicates with God's people. The *torah* of the Lord refers to religious instruction. The *decrees* of the Lord refer to specific directives on how one should live. When one attends to the *precepts* of the Lord, one's life goes along better and one is happy. When the *commandments* are kept, they help one "see" better. The *fear of the Lord* is the biblical expression meaning respect for and reliance on the Lord; the expression occurs frequently in Proverbs (see, e.g. , Prov. 1:7; 9:10). The *ordinances* of the Lord refer to legal decisions. The psalmist goes off on a side trip to praise these decisions, comparing them to gold and to honey (vv. 9–10).

A Prayer for Telling and Teaching (19:11–14)

The psalm comes to a conclusion with words addressed, for the first time, to God (vv. 11–14). Here is a recognition that seeking to follow the instruction of the Lord will result in a better life (v. 11). The psalmist also admits that leading such a scripture-directed life is not easy, and thus the psalm requests forgiveness and guidance (vv. 12–13).

Psalm 1 recommends meditation on the instruction of the Lord, day and night (Ps. 1:2). This psalmist asks for the Lord's help in continued reflection on the Lord's teaching (Ps. 19:14). Verses 1–6 speak of God the Creator, focusing on God's work in nature. The last phrase of this psalm is "my redeemer," thus pointing to the work of God the Saver, or Savior, pointing toward the work of God in history.

It has often been said that two books tell of God and of what God has done. The book of nature speaks of God's work in creating the world and all that is in it; verses 1–6 of this psalm speak of that book. Then the book of *torah*, of instruction, tells more about the godly life (vv. 7–13) and about God's saving work (v. 14).

The themes are three: *creation* (how the world began), *redemption* (what God has done to save humans), and *sanctification* (living a godly life). This psalm deals especially with the first and last of these themes. The next two psalms will have more to say about the middle one.

V IS FOR VICTORY
Psalm 20

To the leader. A Psalm of David.

20:1 **The LORD answer you in the day of trouble!**
    The name of the God of Jacob protect you!
  2 **May he send you help from the sanctuary,**
    and give you support from Zion.
  3 **May he remember all your offerings,**
    and regard with favor your burnt sacrifices. *Selah*

  4 **May he grant you your heart's desire,**
    and fulfill all your plans.
  5 **May we shout for joy over your victory,**
    and in the name of our God set up our banners.
  May the LORD fulfill all your petitions.

  6 **Now I know that the LORD will help his anointed;**
    he will answer him from his holy heaven
    with mighty victories by his right hand.
  7 **Some take pride in chariots, and some in horses,**
    but our pride is in the name of the LORD our God.
  8 **They will collapse and fall**
    but we shall rise and stand upright.

  9 **Give victory to the king, O LORD;**
    answer us when we call.

For those who grew up during the days of World War II, it was the word that focused the hopes and dreams of all: *victory!* We helped tend and harvest the "victory gardens" that our parents planted. We learned that the first four notes of Beethoven's Fifth Symphony sounded out the letter V in Morse code (dit-dit-dit-dah). We were inspired by the sturdy figure of Winston Churchill, cigar in one hand, fingers formed in a V formation with the other, symbolizing the toughness and hope of England and the free world.

If there is a thematic word in this psalm, it is that word *victory.* The Hebrew is *yeshua,* which can be translated "salvation" or "help" or "victory." The psalm says, "May we shout for joy over your *victory*" (v. 5); "Now I know that the LORD will *help* [Hebrew, 'give *victory* to'] his anointed . . . with mighty *victories* by his right hand" (v. 6); "Give *victory* to the king, O LORD" (v. 9).

This is the second in a series of three psalms with the same heading, "To the leader. A Psalm of David." (See the comments on Psalm 4.)

Just Before the Battle

This psalm was written for use in connection with an event in the life of the king (see also Psalms 2, 18) and may therefore be called a *royal psalm* (see the comments on Psalm 2). The occasion for Psalm 2 was a coronation; that for Psalm 18 was a time of giving thanks after military triumph. Psalm 20 was composed as a prayer for the king before he went into battle.

Second Chronicles 20 reports a service of worship before King Jehoshaphat led Judah's army into battle and may give an idea of the sort of situation in which this psalm was used. The point of the psalm is compactly expressed by the prayer in verse 9: "Give victory to the king, O LORD; answer us when we call."

Some Take Pride in Chariots (20:1–9)

The psalm begins with a series of eleven verbs, expressing the wishes of those praying: "The LORD answer . . . protect . . . send . . . give . . . remember . . . regard . . . grant . . . fulfill. . . . May we shout for joy . . . set up. . . . May the LORD fulfill all your petitions" (vv. 1–5).

With verses 6–8, the writer expresses trust in the Lord, saying, "the LORD will protect his anointed." "The LORD will protect his *messiah*," says the Hebrew text, a reminder that these royal psalms provided the seedbed out of which messianic hope developed. (See the discussion with Psalm 2.) The Lord will help the king in a very concrete way, by giving the king and his armies victories on the battlefield. "Some people," says the writer, "take pride in huge military parades, displaying their most sophisticated and recent weaponry. But our pride is in the name of the Lord our God." Deuteronomy 17:16 also sounds a warning against putting too much trust in military armament. Isaiah 31:1 expresses a prophetic warning about trusting in weaponry rather than in the Lord. "With the Lord on our side," Psalm 20 continues, "the enemy will collapse, and we will stand tall!"

We can imagine a chaplain on the king's staff concluding with the words "Give victory to the king, O LORD," and then sending the troops off to battle with a blessing in their ears and with hope in their hearts (v. 9).

Joshua (Jesus) Means Victory

After the collapse of the monarchy, when there were no more kings in Israel or Judah, it would have seemed that there was no further need for these royal psalms. They could have been stored in some military museum, along with antique spears, swords, and chariots, all to recall the glories of days gone by.

But when the prayers and songs and miscellaneous pieces that were to make up the book of Psalms were collected, these royal psalms were included. These psalms spoke of an anointed one—in Hebrew, a *messiah* (v. 6)—who would lead God's people to victories (vv. 5, 6, 9). The armies of the Assyrians, the Babylonians, the Persians, the Greeks, could march down the halls of history, horses prancing, pulling ever more sophisticated weaponry. But our people? Our hope, our trust, our pride is in the name of the Lord our God, says the psalmist.

The thematic word *yeshua* that runs through this psalm may be translated as "victory" but also as "salvation." It appears in the name Joshua, who led his people in many victories, from the battle of Jericho on. And in Greek the name is Jesus, whose mission was to give his people victory over their sins (Matt. 1:21).

According to the New Testament, this Jesus came to give victory not only to his own people but also to the peoples of the world (John 3:16; Acts 4:5–12; 13:16–41; 17:22–31).

BLESS YOU!
Psalm 21

To the leader. A Psalm of David.

21:1 **In your strength the king rejoices, O LORD,**
    and in your help how greatly he exults!

² You have given him his heart's desire,
    and have not withheld the request of his lips.   *Selah*
³ For you meet him with rich blessings;
    you set a crown of fine gold on his head.
⁴ He asked you for life; you gave it to him—
    length of days forever and ever.
⁵ His glory is great through your help;
    splendor and majesty you bestow on him.
⁶ You bestow on him blessings forever;
    you make him glad with the joy of your presence.
⁷ For the king trusts in the LORD,
    and through the steadfast love of the Most High he shall
    not be moved.

⁸ Your hand will find out all your enemies;
    your right hand will find out those who hate you.
⁹ You will make them like a fiery furnace
    when you appear.
The LORD will swallow them up in his wrath,
    and fire will consume them.
¹⁰ You will destroy their offspring from the earth,
    and their children from among humankind.
¹¹ If they plan evil against you,
    if they devise mischief, they will not succeed.
¹² For you will put them to flight;
    you will aim at their faces with your bows.

¹³ Be exalted, O LORD, in your strength!
    We will sing and praise your power.

If you are on the bus or are in the subway and someone sneezes, you are likely to hear one of a couple of responses. In Germany, someone will say, "Gesundheit!" that is, "Health!" In the United States or Canada you might hear "Gesundheit" or even a "Bless you!" The sense of the latter expression is also "Good health!" although it is actually a shortened form of "God bless you!"

God Saves and God Blesses

God "blesses." The Bible speaks of two fundamental ways in which the Lord acts among people, and God's activity of blessing is one of them. While Psalm 20 is concerned with the *saving* action of God, Psalm 21 centers on the Lord's activity of *blessing*. Psalm 20 speaks much about *victory* (vv. 5, 6, 9) and about the Lord *helping* (v. 6) the anointed king; "victory" and "help" are translations of the same Hebrew word *yeshua*, which means salvation or deliverance or victory. Both Psalms 20 and 21 were designed to function in the life of the king and may thus be designated *royal psalms* (see on Psalm 2). In the case of Psalm 20, reference is to victory over the king's enemies. The pattern runs through the Bible: the people are in trouble; they pray to the Lord; the Lord delivers them from trouble; and life goes back to normal again. For a good example of this pattern, read the first chapters of Judges.

There are two especially significant demonstrations of God's saving action in the Bible. The first is the deliverance from Egypt at the Sea of Reeds, or Red Sea, as reported in Exodus 14–15 and recalled throughout the Old Testament. The second is the deliverance from the power of sin, death, and the devil that was achieved in the events of the cross and resurrection and is reported in the New Testament.

The biblical God is a God who delivered Israel from Egypt and who sent his Son to deliver all who believe in him from the power of sin and death.

But the Bible portrays another major way in which God acts. This is not a single, dramatic, never-to-be repeated act, like the exodus or the crucifixion and resurrection. God also works through an ongoing, quiet, steady action that the Bible calls *blessing*. God's action of blessing is a major theme of Psalm 21 (vv. 3, 6).

The King Trusts in the Lord (21:1–7)

For the heading, see the comments on Psalm 4.

Verses 1 and 2 set the mood for the psalm: the king is rejoicing because the Lord has answered his prayer and given him help! Psalm 20 ends with a prayer that the Lord will *give victory* to the *king*; Psalm 21 begins by linking up with these words, saying that the *king* has received *help* (the same Hebrew word as *victory* in Ps. 20:9). In other words, Psalm 20 is a prayer for victory and Psalm 21 announces that the prayer has been answered. (For the word *Selah*, see the comments on Ps. 3:2.)

Verses 3–6 speak of the "blessings" the Lord has given to the king. The king wears a crown, symbolizing the power and authority that are his. The king has prayed for a long life (note the prayer for the king in Ps. 72:5), and, says the psalm, the Lord has given it to him. Verse 5 indicates again how the "help, give victory" theme links with the "blessing" theme: the Lord has given the king help (the *yeshua* word again) and therefore the king has a certain presence, a splendor. Verse 6 summarizes the happy state of the king by speaking of the Lord's blessings and also of the joy the king has in his life and work (note *joy, rejoice* in vv. 6 and 1). The repetition of the *blessing* word links up with the same word in verse 3, at the beginning of the segment in verses 3–6.

A statement that is central to this psalm occurs in verse 7: "For [Hebrew *kî*] the king trusts in the LORD." This declaration is literally at the center of the psalm, since in the Hebrew text there are forty-eight words before it (not counting the heading or the *Selah*) and forty-eight words after it. The same centering technique occurs with the words "for [Hebrew *kî*) you are with me" in Psalm 23. Central to the sense of this psalm is the assertion of the king's loyalty to the Lord.

We'll Sing and Praise (21:8–13)

The tone of the psalm changes with verses 8–13. Instead of the calm and reassuring language of blessing, we hear the militaristic and realistic language of God acting to save from the attacks of enemies. With the Lord's help, the enemies will be destroyed, and they will not succeed in any battles against the Lord's people.

As is the case with Psalm 20, the end of Psalm 21 reaches back to the beginning. "Be exalted, *O LORD, in your strength*," says the writer, picking up the language from verse 1. "We will sing and praise your power."

The Good Times

With these references to the king, Psalms 20 and 21 may seem quite remote from our own time, especially for persons who do not live under the rule of royalty. Nonetheless, Psalm 21 has something important to say.

It is quite easy to praise and thank God after a dramatic act of deliverance, whether it be when an individual regains health or survives a car crash or when a nation achieves independence or enjoys a reunification. But this psalm reminds us that there is another shape of God's action. It calls attention to the everyday gifts that God has given and gives: meaningful tasks, life itself, success in one's work, family and friends, years laden with happiness. These steady, ongoing good things and good times that the Lord gives are what the Bible means by God's blessings. In reflecting on these, one can understand the central statement of this psalm about trusting in the steadfast love of the Lord (v. 7) and can also join in the chorus of those singing and praising the Lord's power (v. 13).

"AND NOT SO HOT ON WHY!"
Psalm 22

To the leader: according to The Deer of the Dawn.
A Psalm of David.

22:1 My God, my God, why have you forsaken me?
    Why are you so far from helping me, from the words
    of my groaning?
² O my God, I cry by day, but you do not answer;
    and by night, but find no rest.

³ Yet you are holy,
    enthroned on the praises of Israel.
⁴ In you our ancestors trusted;
    they trusted, and you delivered them.
⁵ To you they cried, and were saved;
    in you they trusted, and were not put to shame.

⁶ But I am a worm, and not human;
    scorned by others, and despised by the people.
⁷ All who see me mock at me;
    they make mouths at me, they shake their heads;
⁸ "Commit your cause to the Lord; let him deliver—
    let him rescue the one in whom he delights!"

⁹ Yet it was you who took me from the womb;
    you kept me safe on my mother's breast.
¹⁰ On you I was cast from my birth,
    and since my mother bore me you have been my God.
¹¹ Do not be far from me,
    for trouble is near
    and there is no one to help.

¹² Many bulls encircle me,
    strong bulls of Bashan surround me;
¹³ they open wide their mouths at me,
    like a ravening and roaring lion.

¹⁴ I am poured out like water,
    and all my bones are out of joint;
my heart is like wax;
    it is melted within my breast;
¹⁵ my mouth is dried up like a potsherd,
    and my tongue sticks to my jaws;
    you lay me in the dust of death.

¹⁶ For dogs are all around me;
    a company of evildoers encircles me.
My hands and feet have shriveled;
¹⁷ I can count all my bones.
They stare and gloat over me;

¹⁸ they divide my clothes among themselves,
   and for my clothing they cast lots.

¹⁹ But you, O Lᴏʀᴅ, do not be far away!
   O my help, come quickly to my aid!
²⁰ Deliver my soul from the sword,
   my life from the power of the dog!
²¹   Save me from the mouth of the lion!

   From the horns of the wild oxen you have rescued me.
²² I will tell of your name to my brothers and sisters;
   in the midst of the congregation I will praise you:
²³ You who fear the Lᴏʀᴅ, praise him!
   All you offspring of Jacob, glorify him;
   stand in awe of him, all you offspring of Israel!
²⁴ For he did not despise or abhor
   the affliction of the afflicted;
   he did not hide his face from me,
   but heard when I cried to him.

²⁵ From you comes my praise in the great congregation;
   my vows I will pay before those who fear him.
²⁶ The poor shall eat and be satisfied;
   those who seek him shall praise the Lᴏʀᴅ.
   May your hearts live forever!

²⁷ All the ends of the earth shall remember
   and turn to the Lᴏʀᴅ;
   and all the families of the nations
   shall worship before him.
²⁸ For dominion belongs to the Lᴏʀᴅ,
   and he rules over the nations.

²⁹ To him, indeed, shall all who sleep in the earth bow down;
   before him shall bow all who go down to the dust,
   and I shall live for him.
³⁰ Posterity will serve him;
   future generations will be told about the Lord,
³¹ and proclaim his deliverance to a people yet unborn,
   saying that he has done it.

   The scene is from the rock opera *Jesus Christ Superstar*. Jesus is alone
in the garden of Gethsemane, praying, struggling with the realities of
what he knows lies ahead of him. Jesus speaks to God:

Can you show me now that I would not be killed in vain?
Show me just a little of your omnipresent brain!
Show me there's a reason for your wanting me to die!
You're far too keen on where and how,
   and not so hot on why.

"My God, my God, why . . . ?" The question at the beginning of Psalm 22 is especially important because Jesus asked it from the cross. Christians across the world hear it year after year in its Hebrew form, when the story of the death of Jesus is read on Good Friday: "And about three o'clock Jesus cried with a loud voice, 'Eli, Eli lema sabachthani?' that is, 'My God, my God, why have you forsaken me?'" (Matt. 27:46).

The heading for this psalm is the same as that of the previous three psalms, with the addition "according to The Deer of the Dawn," which apparently refers to a melody to which the psalm was once sung.

The structure of the psalm is clear, since it is made up of the typical elements of an individual lament, as noted in the comments on Psalm 13: *complaint* (in "I," "you," and "they" forms), *affirmation of trust, call for help,* and *vow to praise.*

My God, Why? (22:1–21a)

Verses 1–2 present the opening complaint. The doubled "My God," "Eli, Eli," is unique in the Bible and indicates the intensity of the prayer. The prayer in this case is a complaint, addressed to God directly as "you": "*you* have forsaken me, *you* are far from helping me, *you* do not answer." The one praying thinks in terms of the basics of human existence: God is "so far" away in *space;* the psalmist cries for help day and night, through all *time.*

With verses 3–5 the psalmist shifts to a typical element of the lament, an affirmation of trust. (Notice the tripling of "trust" in vv. 4 and 5.) After a word of praise (v. 3), the psalmist recalls stories of how his ancestors trusted in God and how they were never disappointed. "I remember," a modern-day believer might say, "my grandparents telling how they lost their farm during the depression of the 1930s. They didn't know whether they would survive. But they didn't quit going to church and they didn't give up on God. They kept on hoping and praying. And the Lord helped them get through it." In this psalm, the one who feels forsaken by God finds it helpful to remember the stories of what God did for his ancestors.

The complaint returns in verses 6–8: "And I? I'm a worm, not a human being!" (For the worm metaphor, see Job 25:6.) Since it is difficult to get lower than a worm, this puts the one praying at considerable distance from God, who is "holy, enthroned on the praises of Israel" (v. 3). This "worm anthropology" is in considerable contrast to the view of humans as royalty, as in Psalm 8:5–8. Combined with the "I" complaint is a "they" complaint, referring to the behavior of contemporaries, who are making fun of the psalmist's religious convictions (vv. 7–8).

The trust theme emerges again in verses 9–10. Once more the psalmist looks back, this time at what God has done for him in his own life. Referring to his birth with four differing descriptions, he recalls, "You have been my God [*Eli*]." Here is the same *Eli* ("my God") that introduced the psalm, but this time in a more positive context.

Verse 11 is the psalm's first cry for help, stated clearly and supported by a pair of reasons. The psalmist has said, "You are far from helping me" (v. 1). Now, using the same words, the psalmist begs, "Do not be far from me." Why does the one praying need help? Trouble is near. And the one who is crying out is alone.

Verses 12–18 clarify the nature of the trouble. Certain members of the community are making life miserable (vv. 12–13). The one praying is hurting, aching, both outwardly ("my bones") and inwardly ("my heart"). There is no doubt in the psalmist's mind about the cause of these problems: "It's *you*, Lord, who have put me here!" (v. 15c).

The complaints continue with vivid pictures. These enemies are like a pack of wild dogs circling for an attack (see 1 Kings 22:38). To paraphrase the words of the sufferer: "Because of my sickness, I'm thin enough to count my bones. And these people in my community? I am lying here, terribly ill, and they think I can't hear. What are they doing? They are dividing up my possessions. I can hear them saying, 'I'm about his size and could use a new sport coat; you can have the leather jacket!'" (vv. 17–18).

The extended and intensified cry for help in verses 19–21 once again picks up the "far away" phrase from verses 1 and 11 and for the first time uses the more personal name for God, Yahweh (NRSV, "LORD"): "But you, O LORD, do not be *far away*!" This is a desperate cry for help, made in both literal and figurative language: "Save me from the sword, those dogs, that lion!" (see vv. 13, 16).

A Modulation into a New Key (22:21b–31)

With verse 21b the psalm modulates from a mournful minor into a bright, major key. The psalmist reports being rescued and resolves to do two things: he will tell the congregation about his rescue, and he will praise God, because God heard him when he cried for help (vv. 21b–24)! The psalmist has recalled the saving work of God in the past (vv. 3–5,

9–10), has experienced it in the present (v. 21b), and anticipates that stories about God's mighty acts will be told to generations to come in the future (vv. 30–31).

For Future Generations

What does this psalm mean for those "future generations" that it speaks about (v. 30)? What does it mean for those who read it in our time?

First of all, this is a lament and obviously speaks quite immediately to one who feels forsaken, forgotten by God. The psalm makes it clear that at such times the one who is hurting needs community. Here is a reminder of the importance of the community of the past that first nurtured faith (vv. 4–5), a pointer to the present community that gives faith expression in the form of lament and praise (vv. 22, 25), and an anticipation of the future community where stories of faith will continue to be told (vv. 30–31). The one despairing ought not despair alone. This psalm can be a means of bringing that despair before God. As I noted earlier, the old hymn "What a Friend We Have In Jesus" had it right:

> Have we trials and temptations?
> Is there trouble anywhere?
> We should never be discouraged —
> Take it to the Lord in prayer.

Second, we notice that the "why" questions are not answered. In discussing Psalm 13, I related Elie Wiesel's account of a young student going to a synagogue to hear a particularly powerful rabbinic teacher. When the young man returned he reported, "My questions remained questions. But somehow I could go on." There are questions that we shall never have answered. Many of them begin with "Why?" like the questions in this psalm. The psalm suggests that the place to bring these questions is before God, in the company of the gathering of believers. The questions may well remain questions. But we may discover that, somehow, we shall be able to go on with life.

Finally, we remember the reports that Jesus prayed this psalm on the cross (Matt. 27:46; Mark 15:34). If Jesus believed himself forsaken, far from God, it should not be surprising that ordinary believers feel that way at times! In that most difficult time of his life, Jesus reached for Psalm 22. This suggests we could do no better.

But more than that, this psalm sketched out the pattern of Jesus' own life. He felt forsaken, lying in the dust of death, but was then rescued. According to both the Old and the New Testament, the story of these events ought to be told to the ends of the earth (Acts 1:8; see also Ps. 22:27) and even to people not yet born (see Ps. 22:31).

THE POWER OF A PREPOSITION
Psalm 23

A Psalm of David.

23:1 **The LORD is my shepherd, I shall not want.**
  2   **He makes me lie down in green pastures;**
      he leads me beside still waters;
  3   **he restores my soul.**
      He leads me in right paths
          for his name's sake.

  4 **Even though I walk through the darkest valley,**
      I fear no evil;
      for you are with me
          your rod and your staff—
          they comfort me.

  5 **You prepare a table before me**
          in the presence of my enemies;
      you anoint my head with oil;
          my cup overflows.
  6 **Surely goodness and mercy shall follow me**
          all the days of my life,
      and I shall dwell in the house of the LORD
          my whole life long.

It was the hour for morning Bible study, at a camp in the mountains of southern California. "Tell me," my co-leader said to the group, "what is your favorite preposition?"

My favorite preposition? Come now. I had to admit, I'd not thought much about prepositions as such, and certainly not about any favorites. I was about to lead the group in a study of Psalm 23 and had that text on my mind. I heard someone say, "In," and then there was some discussion about "in Christ." Then suddenly I understood what my partner was up to. At the middle of this psalm is a preposition, a prepositional phrase, and as we shall see, it provides the key for opening up the meaning of the psalm.

For "A Psalm of David," see the comments on Psalm 3. The psalm divides into two sections, each with a picture of the God-people relationship. In the first, the Lord is Shepherd, the psalmist a sheep (vv. 1–4). In the second part of the psalm, the Lord is Host and the psalmist a guest (vv. 5–6). There is a progression in the psalm. It begins with a picture of one who is guided by the Lord on a journey (vv. 1–3), hints at the dangers along the way (v. 4), pauses at a table for mealtime (v. 5), and ends with the expressed hope of living in this "house of the LORD" forever (v. 6).

The Shepherd and the Sheep (23:1–4)

The shepherd/sheep imagery in the first part of the psalm provides a picture of the Lord's care for an individual. "I shall not want" is a general statement, developed in the sentences that follow. The psalm opens on a note of peace and calm, portraying the green pastures, the blue waters, the safe paths along which the shepherd leads his sheep. With verse 4, however, the tranquil mood is shattered. The psalmist refers to going through dangerous places and reports, surprisingly, that even then, "I fear no evil." The reason for this absence of fear follows immediately, as the psalmist switches from talking *about* the Lord, the Shepherd, to speaking *to* the Lord: "for you are with me." The "rod" refers to the short wooden club that the shepherd would use for protection against animal or human enemies. The "staff" was longer and could be used to help sheep struggling up a difficult path or through whatever darkness and wilderness they must pass (see Jer. 2:6).

The Host and the Guest (23:5–6)

The second half of the psalm shifts to another picture. Now the Lord is a host, carefully preparing a marvelous meal. Though there are enemies in the vicinity, the guest enjoys the host's hospitality and protection. The host Lot once extended hospitality to some strangers, saying to those who would harm them, "Do nothing to these men, for they have come under the shelter of my roof" (Gen. 19:8). Judges 19:23 speaks of a host's responsibility toward a guest, and Sirach 32:1–2 provides a picture of the sort of hospitality a good host provides:

> If they make you master of the feast, do not exalt yourself;
>> be among them as one of their number.
> Take care of them first and then sit down;
>> when you have fulfilled all your duties, take your place,
> so that you may be merry along with them
>> and receive a wreath for your excellent leadership.

The Psalms often speak of enemies in pursuit of the psalmist: "let the enemy pursue and overtake me" (Ps 7:5; also 71:11, e.g.). In this psalm, however, it is goodness and mercy that will chase after the psalmist, for a lifetime and even beyond (the NRSV "my whole life long" can also be translated "forever").

The Lord Be with You (23:4)

Now for a few comments based on the original Hebrew text. At the center of this psalm is the statement "for you are with me." The number of words leading up to the expression in the Old Testament (Hebrew Bible) is twenty-six, not counting "A Psalm of David," which was the work of later editors. If one counts back from the end of the psalm toward this expression, the number of words is also twenty-six. The words "for you are with me" appear precisely in the middle of the psalm. Was the writer of the psalm using this centering technique to emphasize these words, which are at the heart of what the psalm has to say? (The number twenty-six is itself of interest because the numerical value of the Hebrew letters in the word YHWH [Yahweh, the name for God] is $10 + 5 + 6 + 5 = 26$.)

In any case, the notion that the Lord is "with" someone occurs frequently at crucial points in the Bible. For example, the Lord appeared to Isaac in the night and said, "Do not be afraid, for I am *with* you" (Gen 26:24). Genesis 39 tells how the Lord was *with* Joseph in Egypt (vv. 2, 3, 21, 23). When a frightened Gideon was threshing wheat, hiding in the pit dug for the wine press, an angel appeared to him and said (not without some irony), "The LORD is *with* you, you mighty warrior." Whereupon Gideon responded, with understandable skepticism, "But sir, if the LORD is *with us*, why then has all this happened to us?" (Judg. 6:12–13).

When Jeremiah was fearful about taking up the task of a prophet, the Lord said, "Do not be afraid of them, for I am *with you*" (Jer. 1:8; also 15:20). And when Paul was fearful about continuing his missionary work, the Lord said to him in a dream, "Do not be afraid, but speak and do not be silent; for I am *with* you, and no one will lay a hand on you to harm you" (Acts 18:9–10).

Finally, one can recall the power of that preposition in the name given to Jesus: "and they shall name him 'Emmanuel,' which means 'God is *with* us'" (Matt. 1:23; see also the words to Mary in Luke 1:28).

In reading these texts, one discovers that the Lord's being *with* someone means that the Lord will prosper and protect that person. The greeting often heard in a church service "The Lord be with you" and the response "And with you, too" have a long history and are meant to wish the hearers prosperity and the Lord's protection.

Finally, Christians can hardly hear this psalm without thinking of the One who announced, "I am the good shepherd," and who laid down his life for the sheep (John 10:11–18).

WHO'S THERE?
Psalm 24

Of David. A Psalm.

24:1 **The earth is the LORD's and all that is in it,**
  the world, and those who live in it;
 2 **for he has founded it on the seas,**
  and established it on the rivers.

 3 **Who shall ascend the hill of the LORD?**
  And who shall stand in his holy place?
 4 **Those who have clean hands and pure hearts,**
  who do not lift up their souls to what is false,
  and do not swear deceitfully.
 5 **They will receive blessing from the LORD,**
  and vindication from the God of their salvation.
 6 **Such is the company of those who seek him,**
  who seek the face of the God of Jacob.   *Selah*

 7 **Lift up your heads, O gates!**
  and be lifted up, O ancient doors!
  that the King of glory may come in.
 8 **Who is the King of glory?**
  The LORD, strong and mighty,
  the LORD, mighty in battle.
 9 **Lift up your heads, O gates!**
  and be lifted up, O ancient doors!
  that the King of glory may come in.
 10 **Who is this King of glory?**
  The LORD of hosts,
  he is the King of glory.   *Selah*

Some psalms cannot be read without hearing music. This is one of them. The composition is "Lift Up Your Heads" from Handel's *Messiah*. After a brief orchestral introduction, the soprano and alto voices give the orders:

> Lift up your heads, O ye gates!
>   And be ye lift up, ye everlasting doors,
>   and the King of glory shall come in.

Then the tenors and basses ask the question "Who is this King of glory?" repeat it several times, and the women's voices provide the answer "The Lord strong and mighty, the Lord strong and mighty, the Lord strong and mighty in battle."

This is surely an example of a psalm composed for a ceremony of some sort at the temple. Was this an "entrance liturgy" for those entering the temple area, like Psalm 15? Was it used in connection with a procession reenacting David's bringing the ark into Jerusalem (2 Samuel 6)? The nature of the ceremony is not clear. But the hymn, the entrance liturgy, the call to open the gates, all indicate that something festive was going on. Handel's instincts in setting a portion of this psalm to celebratory music were on target.

For an explanation of "Of David. A Psalm," see the comments on Psalm 3. The psalm consists of a short introductory hymn about the ownership of the earth (vv. 1–2), a question-and-answer liturgy (vv. 3–6), and the script for a ceremony for entering the temple area (vv. 7–10).

Whose Is It? (24:1–2)

The psalm opens with a bold claim: the planet, all that is on it, including all who live on it, belongs to the Lord, the God of Israel! Psalm 50 makes a similar claim; God is speaking:

> For every wild animal of the forest is mine,
>   the cattle on a thousand hills.
> I know all the birds of the air,
>   and all that moves in the field is mine. . . .
>   the world and all that is in it is mine.
>   (Ps. 50:10–12)

Verse 2 in Psalm 24 indicates the reason for making this claim: the earth is the Lord's because the Lord made it. Behind this assertion is the biblical view of the universe: below the earth is a vast sea (Gen. 1:6; 7:11; Exod. 20:4; Deut. 33:13).

One could pause to reflect on verse 1 in our own context. The earth, all living things on it, does not belong to Baal or to Buddha or to big business or to any god. Nor do the earth and its creatures belong to Americans or to Europeans or even to a representative group assembled from the United Nations. Quite simply, the earth and all that is in it belong to the Lord. We humans are here as guests, invited to enjoy and care for the earth and its creatures in a manner that is ecologically responsible (Psalms 8, 104).

Who Gets In? (24:3–6)

Verses 3–6 present a liturgy for entrance into the temple area, in the manner of Psalm 15. We imagine a potential worshiper asking a pair of questions of a priest at the temple gate: "Who shall go up to the hill of the Lord? And who shall stand in the place of the Lord's holiness?"

The priest or some other temple official would then give the answer, in the words of verses 4–6. As with Psalm 15, the first response is general, involving both outer actions ("Those who have clean hands") and inner thoughts ("and pure hearts"). Then more specific entrance requirements are set forth: those who wish to worship at this place ought not pray to false gods (perhaps even gods who claimed the earth was theirs; recall v. 1) and ought not lie under oath (Lev. 19:12; Zech. 8:17).

Persons who meet these entrance requirements and who come seeking the Lord (v. 6) will receive both blessing and salvation (v. 5).

Who's There? (24:7–10)

Finally, verses 7–10 are the script for a ceremony celebrating the entrance of royalty. The command is given: "Open the gates to the temple area! The King of glory wants to enter!" The logical question is "Who is there? Who is the King of glory?" The answer is given: "The LORD strong and mighty, the LORD mighty in battle."

Then the command is given again: "Lift up your heads, O gates!" The "Who's there?" question is repeated, and the final answer is given: "The LORD of hosts, he is the King of glory." "LORD of hosts" means the Lord, with all the angelic beings surrounding the throne (Ps. 89:6–8; see also 1 Kings 22:19–23), perhaps represented by a procession with the ark of the covenant. "King of glory" occurs five times, indicating the importance of the picture for God: our Lord is royalty, a king!

Whose Is the Earth?

This psalm, with its hints of ancient liturgy and ceremonial acts and exchanges, has a certain fascination, rather like a curious antique. But few parts of scripture are more relevant or significant for our situation today than its opening two verses.

In this time of environmental crisis, Psalm 24 provides a reminder that the earth does not belong to humans. It is not ours to do with as we please. The earth, all that is in it and on it, belongs to the Lord, who made it. While we are here, we are invited to enjoy the earth and its creatures (Psalm 104). The Bible even identifies us as royalty, kings and queens, called to exercise responsible care for this beautiful and fragile planet we call our home (Gen. 1:26–28; Psalm 8).

And what about the music? That chorus from *Messiah* won't be stilled as we hear these words about the "King of glory" at the conclusion of the psalm. Handel's interpretation of the text can provide a clue for our own interpretation. The One who entered Jerusalem in the procession on Palm Sunday was, according to the Christian way of looking at things, the King of glory (Matt. 21:1–11).

LEARNING AND LIVING
Psalm 25

Of David.

25:1 **To you, O LORD, I lift up my soul.**
   2 **O my God, in you I trust;**
      do not let me be put to shame;
      do not let my enemies exult over me.
   3 **Do not let those who wait for you be put to shame;**
      let them be ashamed who are wantonly treacherous.

   4 **Make me to know your ways, O LORD;**
      teach me your paths.
   5 **Lead me in your truth, and teach me,**
      for you are the God of my salvation;
      for you I wait all day long.

   6 **Be mindful of your mercy, O LORD, and of your steadfast love,**
      for they have been from of old.
   7 **Do not remember the sins of my youth or my transgressions;**
      according to your steadfast love remember me,
      for your goodness' sake, O LORD!

   8 **Good and upright is the LORD;**
      therefore he instructs sinners in the way.
   9 **He leads the humble in what is right,**
      and teaches the humble his way.
  10 **All the paths of the LORD are steadfast love and faithfulness,**
      for those who keep his covenant and his decrees.

¹¹ **For your name's sake, O L**ORD**,**
       pardon my guilt, for it is great.
¹² **Who are they that fear the L**ORD**?**
       He will teach them the way that they should choose.

¹³ **They will abide in prosperity,**
       and their children shall possess the land.
¹⁴ **The friendship of the L**ORD **is for those who fear him,**
       and he makes his covenant known to them.
¹⁵ **My eyes are ever toward the L**ORD**,**
       for he will pluck my feet out of the net.

¹⁶ **Turn to me and be gracious to me,**
       for I am lonely and afflicted.
¹⁷ **Relieve the troubles of my heart,**
       and bring me out of my distress.
¹⁸ **Consider my affliction and my trouble,**
       and forgive all my sins.

¹⁹ **Consider how many are my foes,**
       and with what violent hatred they hate me.
²⁰ **O guard my life, and deliver me;**
       do not let me be put to shame, for I take refuge in you.
²¹ **May integrity and uprightness preserve me,**
       for I wait for you.

²² **Redeem Israel, O God,**
       out of all its troubles.

This psalm has something of the scent of the classroom about it. As an aid to memorization, it is an alphabetical acrostic, each line except the last running through the ABC's of the Hebrew alphabet (see the comments on Psalms 9–10). It uses the teacher's device of a rhetorical question (v. 12). The psalm expresses an eagerness for instruction. "Make me to know," the writer asks the Lord (v. 4), "teach me" (vv. 4, 5), "lead me in your truth" (v. 5). The psalmist thinks of the Lord as a teacher, instructing sinners (v. 8), leading and teaching the humble (v. 9), and teaching those who fear the Lord how they ought to live (v. 12).

Framing the instructional core of the psalm (vv. 4–15) are segments suggesting that the context for this instruction was not peaceful and tranquil. The psalmist has experienced hatred, is being threatened by enemies, and fears for life itself (vv. 1–3, 19–20). The writer is lonely and hurting, troubled, needing protection, forgiveness, and refuge (vv. 11, 16–20).

In such a dire situation, the psalmist prays for immediate help and sanctuary (v. 20) but also for instruction about the ways of the Lord (v. 4) and the path that life ought to take (v. 12).

This is the first of a set of four psalms that are identified simply "Of David." (See the comments on Psalm 3.) While the shape of the psalm is determined by the alphabetical pattern, one can sense in it the elements of an individual (vv. 1–2, 16–21) or community (v. 22) lament (see Psalm 13).

The ABC's of Theological Instruction (25:1–22)

The psalm begins with an *affirmation of trust* in the Lord God (vv. 1–2a). Following this are a series of *requests* for protection and security for those who are loyal to the Lord (vv. 2b–3).

Then the psalm shifts into that which provides its distinctive stamp, a series of requests for and reflections on *instruction* (vv. 4–15). "Teach me," the psalmist asks, "make me to know your ways. . . . Lead me in your truth" (vv. 4–5). (For a discussion of "way," "ways," see the comments on Psalms 1 and 16.) The requests continue in verses 6–7, with the psalmist asking the Lord to remember past demonstrations of motherly love ("mercy"; see on Psalm 103:8) and covenant love ("steadfast love"; see on Psalm 136), and to forget the "sins and transgressions" of the psalmist's youth.

This psalm uses the three most important biblical words for sin. The first is *ḥāṭā'*, translated "sins, sinners" in verses 7, 8, and 18. The sense is to miss the target, as in the case of the seven hundred left-handed sling-shot marksmen from the tribe of Benjamin who could fire at a hair and not *miss* (*ḥāṭā'*; Judg. 20:16). Behind the word *transgressions* (v. 7) is the Hebrew *pāša'*, which means "to rebel," like the rebelling of a teenager against parents (Isa. 1:2) or of one treaty partner against another (2 Kings 1:1; 3:5, 7). The third word, *guilt* (v. 11), is from the Hebrew verb *'awōn*, which has the sense of being twisted out of shape (Isa. 24:1) or bent over, bowed down (Ps. 38:6; Isa. 21:3). Here, then, are three dramatic pictures of life that is not right with God: a life that is not headed in the right direction, off target; a life of rebelling; a life twisted out of shape.

Verses 8–10 offer some thoughts about theological education. This time God is not the object of the educational efforts (*theology* may be defined as what can be said about God) but rather the subject. God is not "that which is being taught about" but the teacher. Those being instructed are identified as "sinners" (again from *ḥāṭā'*; v. 8). Once again, this instruction involves not only the head but the feet; not only talking but also walking "in the way" (vv. 8, 9) and in the "paths" of the Lord (v. 10).

How was this theological instruction actually carried out? One thinks of the priests, as the Lord's representatives, who had responsibility for the temple's educational program (Hos. 4:6; Jer. 18:18).

Verse 11 is again a request. After speaking about the Lord teaching sinners, the psalmist expresses the central request of the psalm: "pardon my guilt, for it is great."

While verses 8–10 speak of the Teacher, verses 12–15 focus on the students being instructed. It is assumed that they "fear the LORD" (v. 12), since such fear is the beginning of wisdom (Prov. 1:7). Once again, this instruction has a practical aim, directing students in "the way" (see on v. 4), or how they should live. The results will be prosperity, including landownership, and a life lived in close context with the Lord as friend. The psalmist ends this educational section with a declaration of his own *trust* in the Lord (v. 15).

The remainder of the psalm is dominated by *requests* and *complaints*, of the sort found in psalms of lament (vv. 16–22). The complaints provide a clue to the psalmist's situation: lonely and afflicted (vv. 16, 18), troubled (vv. 17, 18), burdened by sin within (v. 18; the miss-the-target word, as in v. 7) and enmity and hatred from without (v. 19). One also hears the *affirmation of trust* typical of lament psalms in vv. 20 ("for I take refuge in you") and 21 ("for I wait for you"). The final request, asking that the Lord save all of Israel, is outside the acrostic pattern and sounds as if it was added to the psalm as it was adapted for use in congregational life.

Thoughts on Religious Education

The psalmist's notion of religious education here is of interest. First, such education has to do with God; that is, it has a strong *theological* dimension. This teaching comes from the Lord: "*your* ways . . . *your* paths . . . *your* truth" (vv. 4–5). In fact, the Lord will be the teacher (v. 12). Second, this instruction has a strong *relational* dimension, assuming that those being instructed are believers in God. "You are the God of my salvation" (v. 5), says the psalmist, and those who will be taught are those who fear the Lord (vv. 12, 14). Third, this instruction has both *cognitive* ("your truth"; v. 5) and *practical*, down-to-earth dimensions, as is apparent from the talk about "paths" and "ways" (vv. 4–5, 8–9, 12).

Here is a program of religious instruction, in other words, that involves talking but also walking. This is about words but also about action. One thinks of Jesus' program of discipleship, which involved cognitive learning (the word *disciple* is from *mathētēs*, "learner," in Greek) but also concrete living, summarized in the characteristic invitation "Follow me."

Is it not true that all religious education ought to have these theological, relational, cognitive, and practical dimensions?

"Not Many of You Should Become Teachers" (James 3:1)

Learning is something to pray about. The psalm asks the Lord to "teach me . . . lead me . . . teach me" (vv. 4–5). It is quite within the biblical tradition to begin a class studying the Bible with prayer: "O Lord, teach me your paths. Lead me in your truth."

Finally, it is apparent from reflection on this psalm that Jews and Christians are a people with a long tradition of teaching and learning. Paul spoke of the gift of teaching (Rom. 12:6–8), and James, surprisingly, suggested that not everyone ought to teach (James 3)!

MY CONSCIENCE IS CLEAR
Psalm 26

Of David.

26:1 Vindicate me, O LORD,
　　　for I have walked in my integrity,
　　　and I have trusted in the LORD without wavering.
　2 Prove me, O LORD, and try me;
　　　test my heart and mind.
　3 For your steadfast love is before my eyes,
　　　and I walk in faithfulness to you.

　4 I do not sit with the worthless,
　　　nor do I consort with hypocrites;
　5 I hate the company of evildoers,
　　　and will not sit with the wicked.

　6 I wash my hands in innocence,
　　　and go around your altar, O LORD,
　7 singing aloud a song of thanksgiving,
　　　and telling all your wondrous deeds.

　8 O LORD, I love the house in which you dwell,
　　　and the place where your glory abides.
　9 Do not sweep me away with sinners,
　　　nor my life with the bloodthirsty,
　10 those in whose hands are evil devices,
　　　and whose right hands are full of bribes.

　11 But as for me, I walk in my integrity;
　　　redeem me, and be gracious to me.
　12 My foot stands on level ground;
　　　in the great congregation I will bless the LORD.

Paul's life was on the line. The old apostle had been in mortal danger many times before. Once, in a letter, he recalled some of those events:

Three times I was beaten with rods. Once I received a stoning. Three times I was shipwrecked; for a night and a day I was adrift at sea . . . in toil and hardship, through many a sleepless night, hungry and thirsty, often without food, cold and naked. (2 Cor. 11:25–27)

But this time it was clearly a matter of life or death. It was in Jerusalem, after the last of his missionary journeys; the story is told in Acts 21–23. Someone had spotted him in the crowd. They recognized him as Paul, who had been going about the Mediterranean world teaching and preaching in a way that was a threat to the present Jerusalem religious establishment. They jumped him, were about to lynch him, when the Roman police came. "Let me speak to them," Paul asked.

So he spoke to the mob briefly about his call, his work among the Gentiles, and that did it. The crowd was "shouting, throwing off their cloaks, and tossing dust in the air" (Acts 22:23). The Romans, who were then ruling and keeping order in the world, discovered that Paul was a Roman citizen and saved him from being killed by the unruly bunch. The next day, he was invited to make a speech before the Jewish council.

Again, his life was on the line. The council was quiet. Paul looked at them intently and said, "Brothers, up to this day I have lived my life with a clear conscience before God" (Acts 23:1).

Paul had been falsely accused. His life was in danger. Such also was the situation of the one who wrote Psalm 26.

The "Of David" heading again associates the psalm with that king (see on Psalm 3). The psalm consists of elements typical of the individual lament (see on Psalm 13). It begins with an urgent *request*, this time a desperate call for help including an assertion and demonstration of innocence (vv. 1–7). Verse 8 affirms *trust* in the Lord, and verses 9–10 present another desperate request, coupled with a *complaint* in the "they" form. The "I walk in my integrity" of verse 11 links with verse 1, and the psalm concludes with more requests for deliverance and finally with a *vow to praise* the Lord.

A Life of Integrity (26:1–12)

As Paul claimed a "clear conscience before God," so the writer of the psalm speaks with realism, but without pride, of his own integrity. Three times he describes his life as a "walk," a walk faithful to and trusting in the Lord (vv. 1, 3, 11).

With verses 4–7 the psalmist indicates this "clear conscience," first with a negative and then with a positive picture. He or she has not been involved with circles of phonies, criminals, or mobsters (vv. 4–5).

Verse 6 refers to some sort of hand-washing ceremony, indicating cleansing from sin, that took place in the temple. As in Psalm 24:4, "clean hands" symbolizes integrity. Hand washing can also symbolize innocence, as in Deuteronomy 21:1–9, when the elders indicate that they have had nothing to do with a murder. The Roman governor did the same thing when he wanted to disassociate himself from the evil that he knew was about to happen to Jesus (Matt. 27:24–26).

The procession around the altar appears to have been a time for singing thanksgiving hymns and telling things that the Lord had done for members of the community (see Ps. 22:22–31). In worship, these people seem to have shared not only their mutual woes but also their mutual joys. The two groups are in sharp contrast here: the gang sitting and plotting (vv. 4–5) and the group singing and processing in the temple (vv. 6–7).

The section in verses 8–10 begins with the psalmist declaring her affection for happenings in the temple, the "house in which you dwell." Psalms 23:6 and 27:4 express the same sentiments:

> One thing I asked of the LORD,
>   that will I seek after:
> to live in the house of the LORD
>   all the days of my life,
> to behold the beauty of the LORD,
>   and to inquire in his temple.
>   (Ps. 27:4; also Ps. 84:1, 3)

Verses 9 and 10 in Psalm 26 are a reminder that this psalm came out of a life-or-death situation. The psalm is a cry for help!

Verse 11 picks up the "walk in integrity" theme with which the psalm began and once again asks for the Lord's help and compassion. The psalm involves the entire person. After referring to the heart and mind (v. 2), the eyes (v. 3), and the hands (vv. 6, 10), the psalmist speaks of her or his foot, not about to slip or stumble (Ps. 73:2) but enabling a walk in integrity and faithfulness (26:1, 3, 11) and now firmly planted, providing a foundation for praise (v. 12).

On the Solid Rock I Stand

Some have been uncomfortable with the seemingly self-righteous "What a good boy am I" tone of the declaration of innocence in verses 4–7 of this psalm. The psalm itself, however, provides clues to the context out of which this declaration came. Here was one desperate for vindication (v. 1), fearing that life itself might be swept away (vv. 9–10). When Paul, who can hardly be accused of self-righteousness, stood before the Jerusalem council in a life-or-death situation, he could say, "Up to this day I have lived my life with a clear conscience before God" (Acts 23:1).

In the life-or-death situation assumed by this psalm, it is not surprising to hear a similar declaration. Here is a prayer from one deathly afraid and desperately seeking deliverance (vv. 9–10, 11b). This psalmist had experienced the Lord's love and actions (vv. 3, 7) and knew what it was to live in the Lord's presence (v. 8). On the basis of this past history, the psalmist could declare that her feet were still on solid ground and that one day she would again be singing those songs of praise (v. 12).

WHY PRAY WHEN YOU CAN WORRY?
Psalm 27

Of David.

27:1 **The LORD is my light and my salvation;**
  whom shall I fear?
The LORD is the stronghold of my life;
  of whom shall I be afraid?

2 **When evildoers assail me**
  to devour my flesh—
my adversaries and foes—
  they shall stumble and fall.

3 **Though an army encamp against me,**
  my heart shall not fear;
though war rise up against me,
  yet I will be confident.

4 **One thing I asked of the LORD,**
  that will I seek after:
to live in the house of the LORD
  all the days of my life,
to behold the beauty of the LORD,
  and to inquire in his temple.

5 **For he will hide me in his shelter**
  in the day of trouble;
he will conceal me under the cover of his tent;
  he will set me high on a rock.

6 **Now my head is lifted up**
  above my enemies all around me,
and I will offer in his tent
  sacrifices with shouts of joy;
I will sing and make melody to the LORD.

⁷ Hear, O Lord, when I cry aloud,
    be gracious to me and answer me!
⁸ "Come," my heart says, "seek his face!"
    Your face, Lord, do I seek.
⁹   Do not hide your face from me.

    Do not turn your servant away in anger,
        you who have been my help.
    Do not cast me off, do not forsake me,
        O God of my salvation!
¹⁰ If my father and mother forsake me,
        the Lord will take me up.

¹¹ Teach me your way, O Lord,
        and lead me on a level path
        because of my enemies.
¹² Do not give me up to the will of my adversaries,
        for false witnesses have risen against me,
        and they are breathing out violence.

¹³ I believe that I shall see the goodness of the Lord
        in the land of the living.
¹⁴ Wait for the Lord;
        be strong, and let your heart take courage;
        wait for the Lord!

We noticed the sign as we were driving through downtown Denver. It was high up on an old building, in faded yellow letters against a red brick background. On that wall someone had painted the words "Why Pray When You Can Worry?" I remember the conversation in the car. Who put that up there? Why put it there? What does it mean? We finally concluded that it meant just the opposite of what it said. It meant "Why worry—when you can pray?" Another building just down the street in Denver, it appeared, had been working with the same theme. On each coin turned out at the Denver mint are the words "In God We Trust."

These themes are the themes of this psalm: anxiety, prayer, and trust.

For the "Of David" heading, see the comments on Psalm 3. The psalm has three major sections: words addressed to the congregation about the Lord, declaring trust (vv. 1–6, 10); words addressed to the Lord, asking for help (vv. 7–9, 11–12); words addressed to the congregation about the Lord (vv. 13, 14). Since the dominant theme of the psalm is trust in the

Lord (vv. 1–6, 10, 13–14), it may be classified with other psalms of trust (Psalms 11, 16, 23, 62, 63, 131).

Safe in the Shelter of the Lord (27:1–6)

This first section is aimed at the gathered people, telling them about the Lord. The Bible often associates the Lord with light. God is called the "light of Israel" in Isaiah 10:17. Isaiah 60:1–3 proclaims, "Arise, shine; for your light has come," and Isaiah 9:2 promises, "The people who walked in darkness have seen a great light." Micah declares, "When I sit in darkness, the LORD will be a light to me" (Micah 7:8). The New Testament says of Jesus, "The true light, which enlightens everyone, was coming into the world" (John 1:9), and Jesus says, "I am the light of the world" (John 9:5).

The meaning behind "salvation" is rescue or deliverance, while "stronghold" identifies a place of safety and security. This psalm is rich in pictures used for God: "my light," "my salvation," "my stronghold" (v. 1); master (implied by "servant" in v. 9); teacher and leader (v. 11).

Finding himself in the midst of enemies, the psalmist uses military imagery to describe that situation. Attacked by adversaries and foes, the psalmist imagines a situation where a whole army is camped against him! Nonetheless, "as for me, I am trusting," says the Hebrew, quite literally (v. 3).

Verse 4 speaks of enjoying the *beauty* of the Lord in the temple. Psalm 133:1 uses the same Hebrew word to describe how *pleasant* it is to be together with other believers. The psalmist uses three pictures to describe the feeling of security he has in the temple. First, it is the Lord's "shelter." The Hebrew word is *sukkah*, which referred to the portable shelter used by the Hebrews when they wandered in the wilderness after the exodus. Jewish people continue to construct portable shelters in connection with the celebration of Sukkot in the fall. In this way they remember the events in the wilderness when the Israelites lived in such temporary quarters (Lev. 23:42–43).

Second, the psalmist says being in the temple is like being in the Lord's tent, where the Lord provides a hiding place. Third, being in the temple is like being set on a high rock, far above any danger.

Hear Me, Teach Me, Lead Me (27:7–14)

After these words in verses 1–6 *about* trusting in the Lord, the psalm shifts into words addressed *to* the Lord: "Hear, O LORD!" The psalmist speaks of the Lord's "face" (that is, "presence") as in Psalm 24:6. The quadruple repetition of the cry for help emphasizes the urgency of the prayer: "Do not hide your face. . . . Do not turn your servant away. . . . Do not cast me off, do not forsake me" (vv. 7–9). The sense of the desperate plea is "Don't abandon me!"

With verse 10, words are addressed to the congregation: "Even if my parents abandon me, I know the Lord won't!"

The "Teach me . . . lead me" of verse 11 is reminiscent of the requests in Psalm 25:4 and 5. Psalm 26:12 speaks of level ground; Psalm 27, using the same word, asks for guidance "on a level path" (v. 11). Verses 11c and 12 are a reminder that these affirmations of trust and prayers arise out of a situation where enemies are nearby.

Finally, the psalm switches back to addressing the gathered community, with a confession of trust in the Lord for a good future (v. 13). The encouragement to be strong, to take courage, and to wait (twice!) returns to military language, as was used at the beginning of the psalm (vv. 1–3). The word of encouragement sounds much like the Lord's words to Joshua as he was about to step into the leadership shoes of Moses: "Be strong and courageous . . . be strong and very courageous. . . . Be strong and courageous . . . for the LORD your God is with you" (Josh. 1:6–9).

Why Worry When You Can Pray?

This psalm is reminiscent of that other psalm of trust, Psalm 23. Both originate in a situation where the writer is in the midst of enemies (23:5; 27:2, 6, 11–12). Both begin by affirming trust in the Lord, speaking *about* the Lord: "The LORD is my shepherd, I shall not want"; "The LORD is my light and my salvation; whom shall I fear?" Psalm 23's confident assertion "and I shall dwell in the house of the LORD my whole life long" is echoed in Psalm 27's hope "to live in the house of the LORD all the days of my life."

These psalms of trust are designed for tough times, "when other helpers fail, and comforts flee"—times when friends disappoint. The psalmists knew what it was to live "in the presence of enemies" (23:5) or among adversaries and foes and slanderers (27:2, 6, 11–12). In such situations, they affirmed the goodness of the Lord as shepherd and host, light and salvation. They looked forward to ongoing life in the presence of the Lord (23:6; 27:4), and they resolved to keep on singing (27:6).

In tough times, these psalmists asked the Lord for instruction and guidance and advised their fellow believers to be courageous and to wait, yes, to wait. In any case, they made it clear that God is the one to trust and that praying is far better than worrying.

LORD, GIVE THEM A LIFT
Psalm 28

Of David.

28:1 **To you, O LORD, I call;**
      my rock, do not refuse to hear me,
   for if you are silent to me,
      I shall be like those who go down to the Pit.
 ² **Hear the voice of my supplication,**
     as I cry to you for help,
   as I lift up my hands
     toward your most holy sanctuary.

 ³ **Do not drag me away with the wicked,**
     with those who are workers of evil,
   who speak peace with their neighbors,
     while mischief is in their hearts.
 ⁴ **Repay them according to their work,**
     and according to the evil of their deeds;
   repay them according to the work of their hands;
     render them their due reward.
 ⁵ **Because they do not regard the works of the LORD,**
     or the work of his hands,
   he will break them down and build them up no more.

 ⁶ **Blessed be the LORD,**
     for he has heard the sound of my pleadings.
 ⁷ **The LORD is my strength and my shield;**
     in him my heart trusts;
   so I am helped, and my heart exults,
     and with my song I give thanks to him.

 ⁸ **The LORD is the strength of his people;**
     he is the saving refuge of his anointed.
 ⁹ **O save your people, and bless your heritage;**
     be their shepherd, and carry them forever.

At first glance, this psalm appears to be a typical lament, that is, a prayer from a time of trouble. An individual is in distress, calls for the Lord's attention, then asks that God save him or her from the wicked and punish them for their evil deeds (vv. 1–5). Then the psalmist speaks to the congregation, telling them that the Lord has heard the writer's prayers, declaring trust and praising the Lord (vv. 6–7).

Such a scheme, combining the elements of request, complaint, affirmation of faith, and vow to praise, is typical for the psalms of lament (see on Psalm 13). But with Psalm 28 comes something different. The psalm concludes with a declaration about the Lord and a prayer for the Lord's people (vv. 8–9). The imagery of the last verse is familiar from the Bible and also from a thousand altar paintings, church bulletins, and Sunday school books: "be their shepherd, and carry them forever" (vv. 8–9). (For "Of David," see the comments on Psalm 3.)

Lord, Be Their Shepherd (28:1–9)

At the beginning of the psalm, the Lord is addressed as "my rock." That image, which conveys safety and stability, is a frequent one in the Psalms (see Pss. 18:2, 46; 19:14; 62:2, 6; 92:15; 144:1).

But what if the Lord refuses to hear or is silent? Such a silence would not be golden but fatal, says the psalmist, and would send the writer straight to the "Pit," the place of the dead.

Verse 2 puts a request in a positive form: "Hear the voice of my supplication!" Here is an interesting detail about posture and prayer. Contemporary Christians learn from childhood to "fold your hands and pray." This psalm says rather, "Lift up your hands and pray!" Other psalms (63:4; 134:2; 141:2) and biblical texts speak the same way (Neh. 8:6; Lam. 2:19; 3:41; 1 Tim. 2:8). Since there are a variety of settings and postures for prayer given in the Bible, one might conclude that a number of different postures are acceptable to the Lord.

Verses 3–4 present the central request in this psalm, combined with a reason for the request (v. 5). The one praying asks to be preserved from the fate that awaits certain persons in the psalmist's environment. These people are identified in three ways: the wicked, workers of evil, and those who speak peace (Hebrew, *shalom*) with their lips while mischief is in their hearts. The psalmist has three suggestions for dealing with them, all of which amount to the same thing: punish them by treating them the way they have been treating others! Verse 5 provides a theological reason for punishing them: like the drunken carousers described in Isaiah 5:11–12, these people know a lot about partying "but . . . do not regard the deeds of the LORD, or see the work of his hands."

With verse 6, the mood of the psalm changes. Somehow, help has come, and the writer praises the Lord with a "Blessed be the LORD." The reason for the change in mood is clear: the psalmist had prayed, "Hear the *voice of my supplication*" (v. 2), and now declares, "for he has heard *the voice of my supplication*" (NRSV, "sound of my pleadings," but the Hebrew phrases in vv. 2 and 6 are identical). The psalmist's prayers have been answered, and now is the time for praise. The psalm was written down after the distress and deliverance had been experienced, so that others could hear this story.

Verse 7 is an *affirmation of trust*, speaking *about* the Lord to the congregation. If verse 2 suggests that the one praying is in the temple area, this reference to singing would seem to point in the same direction. One could imagine verses 6–7 as the written text for the choir anthem sung one day in the temple!

The psalm could end at that point and could be explained as a prayer for help (lament) followed by a brief song of thanksgiving. Two verses remain, however, which may be the comments of earlier users of the psalm who wished to supplement it further. Verse 8 is again an affirmation of trust, recalling that the Lord is the strong defender of his people and a refuge for the anointed one, or king. With verse 9, the one who has experienced persecution from the people but deliverance from the Lord now prays for the people in the congregation, asking that the Lord save them, bless them, shepherd them, and carry them.

Lord, Give Them a Lift

Particularly interesting in this psalm is what happens after the song has been sung (v. 7) and the confession declaring the Lord's goodness to both king and people has been made (v. 8). The psalmist prays that the Lord *save* this people, rescue them from danger and evil, and also *bless* them, give them ongoing care and ordinary gifts that make life possible and pleasant. (For the *saving* and *blessing* actions of God, see the comments on Psalm 3.)

In a final line notable for its simplicity and sensitivity, the psalmist asks that the Lord act as a good shepherd not only for individuals (Psalm 23) but for the entire people (also Pss. 74:1; 80:1; Isa. 40:11; Ezek. 34:13ff.).

One particular aspect of the work of the shepherd comes into focus here. When a sheep has gotten off the right path and is injured in some dark valley, a good shepherd lifts that sheep to his shoulders and carries it. The prayer of this psalm is especially wide-hearted, asking that the Lord carry not just one hurting sheep but the whole flock, and not just until some suitable place for rest and healing is found but forever.

From one who experienced so much grief at the hands of these people, this prayer asking the Lord to give them a lift is quite remarkable.

THE ROLLING THUNDER
Psalm 29

A Psalm of David.

29:1 Ascribe to the LORD, O heavenly beings,
    ascribe to the LORD glory and strength.
  2 Ascribe to the LORD the glory of his name;
    worship the LORD in holy splendor.

  3 The voice of the LORD is over the waters;
    the God of glory thunders,
    the LORD, over mighty waters.
  4 The voice of the LORD is powerful;
    the voice of the LORD is full of majesty.

  5 The voice of the LORD breaks the cedars;
    the LORD breaks the cedars of Lebanon.
  6 He makes Lebanon skip like a calf,
    and Sirion like a young wild ox.

  7 The voice of the LORD flashes forth flames of fire.
  8 The voice of the LORD shakes the wilderness;
    the LORD shakes the wilderness of Kadesh.
  9 The voice of the LORD causes the oaks to whirl,
    and strips the forest bare;
    and in his temple all say, "Glory!"

 10 The LORD sits enthroned over the flood;
    the LORD sits enthroned as king forever.
 11 May the LORD give strength to his people!
    May the LORD bless his people with peace!

Imagine standing on the shore of a great lake, watching a storm develop. At first there is an eerie calm. The western sky darkens and then turns black. The storm begins to move closer, with jagged flashes of lightning and cracking thunder. Clouds race across the sky. The wind comes, at first gently, then more and more powerfully. White-capped waves pound on the shore. There is a flash of lightning, a clap of thunder, and a branch on a great pine breaks and crashes to the ground. Then, like a huge gray curtain, the rain moves across the water. As you watch the storm from the safety of a lakeside cabin, some words come to your mind:

> O Lord my God, when I in awesome wonder
> Consider all the worlds thy hands have made,

I see the stars, I hear the rolling thunder,
Thy power throughout the universe displayed;
Then sings my soul, my Savior God to thee;
How great thou art! How great thou art!
(*The United Methodist Hymnal*, 77)*

It was this sort of experience of a storm, probably moving in across the sea from the west, that motivated the writing of this psalm. (For the "Psalm of David" heading, see the comments on Psalm 3.)

Give Glory to the Lord (29:1–2)

The psalm displays the structure typical of a hymn (see on Psalm 113). It begins with an *imperative* section, calling on all "heavenly beings" to give "glory" to God (vv. 1–2). The call to praise is sounded three times, each call progressively longer. The "heavenly beings" called to praise are those supernatural creatures (we might call them angels) who surround the Lord's throne. The Bible assumes the presence of these heavenly creatures. Psalm 82:1 calls them "gods":

> God has taken his place in the divine council;
>   in the midst of the gods he holds judgment.

In Psalm 148:1–2 they are named "angels":

> Praise the LORD!
> Praise the LORD from the heavens;
>   praise him in the heights!
> Praise him, all his angels!

Isaiah 6:1–2 speaks of the heavenly beings as "seraphs": "I saw the Lord sitting on a throne, high and lofty. . . . Seraphs were in attendance above him.

"Glory" (Hebrew, *kābôd*) is an important word in this psalm, occurring in verses 1 and 2 as well as verse 9. The fundamental sense of the word is "heaviness, abundance." A cloud, for example, may be described as *kābôd* with rain, meaning that it is thick or heavy with rain (Exod. 19:16); or one may speak of "heavy hail" (Exod. 9:24). The word may also denote a kind of superluxury or splendor, like the splendor of the great banquet given by King Ahasuerus (Esth. 1:4, "splendor"; read 1:5–9 and 5:11). When used of the Lord, *kābôd* denotes splendor, majesty, magnificence. How are these heavenly beings to "ascribe glory" to the Lord? Since they are capable of singing (Isa. 6:3), it appears that they join both supernatural and natural creatures in being called on to sing or shout the word *glory* (*kābôd*). What is called for in verses 1–2 is executed in verse 9, as all in the temple sing out, "Glory!"

The Storm (29:3–11)

After the introductory call to praise, the psalm continues in the manner of a hymn, giving *reasons* for praise (vv. 3–9). The description of the weather system enables one to imagine the storm developing in the west and moving in across the Mediterranean.

The thunder that one hears? For the psalmist, this is the voice of the Lord, powerful and majestic (vv. 3–4). As the psalm goes on, there is more thunder and then a sharp crack, followed by the snapping of branches and finally a mighty thud as a cedar hits the ground (v. 5). Lightning bolts flash and more damage is done to the forests (v. 9).

God in Nature

While the Bible often speaks of God's revelation through mighty acts in history (Deuteronomy 26; Psalms 105, 106), this psalm speaks almost exclusively about the mighty acts of God in nature. The mood is somewhat eerie, with no human beings on the scene until one hears the chorus of "Glory!" in verse 9. The psalm concludes with a wish that this powerful God who works through earthquake, storm, and fire will attend to God's people, giving them strength and providing for them peace (v. 11).

SHALL WE DANCE?
Psalm 30

A Psalm. A Song at the dedication of the temple. Of David.

30:1 **I will extol you, O LORD, for you have drawn me up,**
    and did not let my foes rejoice over me.
  2 **O LORD my God, I cried to you for help,**
    and you have healed me.
  3 **O LORD, you brought up my soul from Sheol,**
    restored me to life from among those gone down to the Pit.

  4 **Sing praises to the LORD, O you his faithful ones,**
    and give thanks to his holy name.
  5 **For his anger is but for a moment;**
    his favor is for a lifetime.
  Weeping may linger for the night,
    but joy comes with the morning.

6 As for me, I said in my prosperity,
   "I shall never be moved."
7 By your favor, O LORD,
   you had established me as a strong mountain;
   you hid your face;
   I was dismayed.

8 To you, O LORD, I cried,
   and to the LORD I made supplication:
9 "What profit is there in my death,
   if I go down to the Pit?
   Will the dust praise you?
   Will it tell of your faithfulness?
10 Hear, O LORD, and be gracious to me!
   O LORD, be my helper!"

11 You have turned my mourning into dancing;
   you have taken off my sackcloth
   and clothed me with joy,
12 so that my soul may praise you and not be silent.
   O LORD my God, I will give thanks to you forever.

The old gospel song declares, "I've got the joy, joy, joy, joy, down in my heart." A good song, but not quite the sort of thing you find in the Bible. When the Bible speaks of joy, that joy is not just "down in my heart" but also in my feet, my legs, my whole body. In other words, the typical expression of joy in the Bible is dancing.

When the Israelites had crossed the Sea of Reeds and escaped from Egypt, Miriam and her friends took out their tambourines and got everybody dancing (Exod. 15:20). When Jerusalem fell to the Babylonians, the young men packed up their instruments and, because of the sadness, called off the dances (Lam. 5:14–15). When the exiles return to Jerusalem, said the prophet, there will be singing and dancing (Jer. 31:12–13). The book of Psalms concludes with a call to strike up the band and dance (Psalm 150).

We've all delighted in watching small children dance their way through an outdoor band concert. Some may recall a whole nation jitter-bugging for joy at the end of World War II, or Germans from east and west singing and dancing when the Berlin Wall came down in 1989. And when "my fair lady" found her true love, remember that she sang, "I could have danced all night!"

Dancing is a human expression of joy. And this psalm is about the Lord turning mourning into dancing.

A Psalm for Hanukkah (The Heading)

The heading provided for Psalm 30 indicates something about how it was used through Israel's history. The psalm originated as an expression of praise and thanksgiving from one who had experienced sickness and then healing (v. 2). When it became part of a collection of psalms, it no doubt continued to be used by individuals expressing their joy in being healed. But sometime after 164 B.C. , when the Jerusalem temple was rededicated after it had been desecrated by the Greek armies, this psalm became associated with the celebration of that event. The heading says, literally, "A Song at the dedication [*hanukkah*] of the temple." In the New Testament the feast is called "Dedication" (John 10:22). A psalm originally written with an individual in mind was used to celebrate an event involving the whole community. (For the reference to David, see the comments on Psalm 3.)

I Cried, You Healed (30:1–5)

The psalm may be categorized as an *individual song of thanksgiving* and, as such, is made of elements characteristic of such psalms. A *summary of the crisis* in verses 1–3 gives a short version of what the writer has experienced. The verb *draw up* is used for drawing water from a well (Exod. 2:16); the idea is that of being rescued from a situation from which one could not escape. Verse 2 provides a summary: "I cried . . . you healed." The writer's situation was so severe that he felt himself to have been among the dead in Sheol (see the comments on Ps. 6:5).

With verses 4–5, the psalm offers a *testimony to the congregation*. The psalmist has experienced rescue and now wants to tell about it. He calls on the congregation to sing and gives them a reason for singing. Experience has taught that the Lord's anger may last for a moment, and weeping may last for a night, but joy will return in the morning, and the Lord's favor endures for a lifetime.

The Inside Story (30:6–12)

Verses 6–10 present a *description of the crisis* and a *request*, telling the same story at greater length, this time with attention to the inner feelings of the storyteller. Once the psalmist had been happy and successful and thought that life would always be that way (v. 6). Writing these things down after the crisis, the psalmist realizes that the prosperity he had been taking for granted was due to the Lord's favor. When the Lord turned away, his life went into a tailspin (v. 7).

The psalmist continues to tell the story for the benefit of the listening congregation (vv. 4–5). In the midst of those desperate times, the psalmist cried out to the Lord for help. The psalm quotes a part of one such prayer, showing the psalm writer bargaining with God: "How will it help you, Lord, if I die?" he asks. "In fact," he argues, "it will be harmful, because there will be fewer voices praising you!" The same argument was used in Psalm 6:5 and also occurs in Sirach 17:27–28:

> Who will sing praises to the Most High in Hades . . . ?
> From the dead . . . thanksgiving has ceased;
>   those who are alive and well sing the Lord's praises.

Verse 10 of Psalm 30 has a trio of big requests: "Hear . . . be gracious . . . LORD, be my helper!"

Verses 11 and 12 report the *deliverance* experienced in poetic language (v. 11) and express a *vow to praise* (v. 12). In verse 5, the writer has addressed the congregation, telling of the return of the Lord's favor. Using figurative language, the psalmist now addresses the Lord. Mourning has been transformed into dancing! And instead of going about dressed in the black garments suited to sadness, the psalmist is "clothed in joy" and promises to live a life of thanksgiving to God.

Post-Easter People

The church has assigned this psalm to the third Sunday after Easter, linking it with John 21. This psalm is suited for seasons when the Lord has turned times of mourning into times of dancing.

The lectionary also ties this psalm to two especially joyful times in the ministry of Jesus: the stories of Jesus restoring life to a widow's only child (Luke 7:11–17; Sunday between June 5 and 11 C) and to the little daughter of Jairus (Mark 5:21–43; Sunday between June 26 and July 2 B).

There is a unique post-Easter joy that describes the lives of those who were lost but have been found (Luke 15:6, 9, 24). There was an everyday kind of joy enjoyed by God's people in Jerusalem (Luke 24:52) and beyond (Phil. 4:4–7), even including those facing trials (James 1:2–4). Perhaps the old gospel song was right after all. There is a joy that runs deep through the New Testament like a steady *cantus firmus*, a fundamental joy, maybe best described as "down in my heart."

MY TIMES ARE IN YOUR HAND
Psalm 31

To the leader. A Psalm of David.

31:1 In you, O LORD, I seek refuge;
          do not let me ever be put to shame;
          in your righteousness deliver me.
    2 Incline your ear to me;
          rescue me speedily.
       Be a rock of refuge for me,
          a strong fortress to save me.

    3 You are indeed my rock and my fortress;
          for your name's sake lead me and guide me,
    4 take me out of the net that is hidden for me,
          for you are my refuge.
    5 Into your hand I commit my spirit;
          you have redeemed me, O LORD, faithful God.

    6 You hate those who pay regard to worthless idols,
          but I trust in the LORD.
    7 I will exult and rejoice in your steadfast love,
          because you have seen my affliction;
          you have taken heed of my adversities,
    8 and have not delivered me into the hand of the enemy;
          you have set my feet in a broad place.

    9 Be gracious to me, O LORD, for I am in distress;
          my eye wastes away from grief,
          my soul and body also.
   10 For my life is spent with sorrow,
          and my years with sighing;
       my strength fails because of my misery,
          and my bones waste away.

   11 I am the scorn of all my adversaries,
          a horror to my neighbors,
       an object of dread to my acquaintances;
          those who see me in the street flee from me.
   12 I have passed out of mind like one who is dead;
          I have become like a broken vessel.
   13 For I hear the whispering of many—
          terror all around!—
       as they scheme together against me,
          as they plot to take my life.

¹⁴ But I trust in you, O LORD;
    I say, "You are my God."
¹⁵ My times are in your hand;
    deliver me from the hand of my enemies and persecutors.
¹⁶ Let your face shine upon your servant;
    save me in your steadfast love.
¹⁷ Do not let me be put to shame, O LORD,
    for I call on you;
  let the wicked be put to shame;
    let them go dumbfounded to Sheol.
¹⁸ Let the lying lips be stilled
    that speak insolently against the righteous
    with pride and contempt.

¹⁹ O how abundant is your goodness
    that you have laid up for those who fear you,
  and accomplished for those who take refuge in you,
    in the sight of everyone!
²⁰ In the shelter of your presence you hide them
    from human plots;
  you hold them safe under your shelter
    from contentious tongues.

²¹ Blessed be the LORD,
    for he has wondrously shown his steadfast love to me
    when I was beset as a city under siege.
²² I had said in my alarm,
    "I am driven far from your sight."
  But you heard my supplications
    when I cried out to you for help.

²³ Love the LORD, all you his saints.
    The LORD preserves the faithful,
    but abundantly repays the one who acts haughtily.
²⁴ Be strong, and let your heart take courage,
    all you who wait for the LORD.

The last words that Jesus spoke before dying, according to Luke's account, were from this psalm:

> Then Jesus, crying with a loud voice, said, "Father, into your hands I commend my spirit." Having said this, he breathed his last. (Luke 23:46; see Ps. 31:5)

Stephen also spoke dying words from this psalm: "While they were stoning Stephen, he prayed, 'Lord Jesus, receive my spirit'" (Acts 7:59; see Ps. 31:5).

The words of Psalm 31:5 served as a last prayer for Jesus and for Stephen. In the context of the psalm, however, they are part of a prayer of one whom the Lord has rescued and who is asking for the Lord's hand to continue to provide direction through life.

The "hand" theme occurs elsewhere in the psalm. The psalmist rejoices because the Lord did not give the writer over "into the hand of the enemy" (v. 8). Looking toward further encounters with those who are hostile, the psalmist says, "I trust in you, O LORD. . . . My times are in your hand" (vv. 14–15) and asks that the Lord provide deliverance "from the hand of my enemies." This attitude of trust is an important theme in the psalm, which contains many of the typical elements of the lament (see Psalm 13). (For the heading, see the comments on Psalm 4.)

Into Your Hand (31:1–8)

Verses 1–8 are a mixture of standard elements of the lament. The statement in Psalm 2:12 promises happiness to those who "take refuge" in the Lord; this psalm begins by declaring that the one praying is seeking just that. The imperatives in this *request* section of the psalm pile up in these opening verses: "do not let . . . deliver . . . Incline . . . rescue . . . Be a rock of refuge . . . a fortress" (vv. 1–3).

After these urgent requests, using a variety of pictures to describe a God who protects (rock of refuge, strong fortress, rock, fortress, refuge) and leads (lead me, guide me) and rescues (take me out of the net), the writer expresses *trust* in the Lord. In the language of the psalm, "Into your hand I commit my spirit," that is, "my life" (v. 5).

The *affirmation of trust* theme continues in verses 6–8. Verse 6 declares, "I hate [Hebrew; see NRSV footnote] those who pay regard to worthless idols, but I trust in the LORD." The psalmist *vows to praise* the Lord (v. 7) because the Lord saw his affliction, took into account his troubles, and established him in a safe and secure (NRSV, "broad") place (v. 8). The psalmist had put his life in the hand of the One who proved to be a rock of ages, a mighty fortress, a trustworthy guide, and that One had proved to be faithful.

In Your Hand (31:9–18)

Verses 9–13 describe the acute situation of the one praying. After a brief cry for help, the reasons for this request are spelled out in a series of intensive *"I" complaints*. This is a pain that involves the entire person: *my eyes* are tired out from crying, *my soul* and body are aching, *my bones* are wasting away. This is no small-time problem but one that has been affecting *my* years, and *my* entire life (v. 10).

With verses 11–13, complaints about others ("they" complaints) are added to the list. Says the psalmist in verse 11: Neighbors and acquaintances who should befriend me, avoid me or run away! In an especially poignant statement, the psalmist says that everyone has forgotten him— he might as well be dead! And, in fact, he has heard rumors that some are plotting his murder.

Then the mood changes as the psalmist shifts out of the complaint mode. He addresses the Lord directly, saying, "But I trust in you, O LORD!" He lets his weight down, saying to the Lord, "My times are in your hand" (v. 15). Then the requests for help begin once again: deliver me, let your face shine (that is, show me your favor; see 27:9 and 30:7), save me, don't put me to shame but let the wicked be put to shame (vv. 14–18)! Here is a clue as to what the "enemies and persecutors" were doing: verse 18 indicates that their wrongdoing grew out of pride and contempt and expressed itself in lying and insolent speech.

You Hold Them Safe (31:19–24)

The psalm winds up on a series of positive notes of *praise, trust,* and *encouragement.* The promise of Psalm 2 proves to be true: if you *take refuge* (Pss. 2:12; 31:19) in the Lord, you will be happy, because the Lord will hide you from plotting enemies and will take you as guest in the Lord's "shelter" (Hebrew, *sukkah*), the small hut still used by Jews today to celebrate the exodus wilderness experience (see on Ps. 27:5). The psalmist praises God because just when he thought God was not around, the Lord heard and helped. The final words encourage all who are hearing or praying this psalm to love the Lord, to be strong, and to wait courageously for the Lord.

My Times Are in Your Hand

Psalm 31 appears in the lectionary for the Sunday between May 29 and June 4 (A), along with the parable of the house built on a rock, from Matthew 7:21–29. "Be a rock of refuge for me" is one of the themes of the psalm. The figure of the Lord as "rock" is a frequent one in the psalms (Pss. 18:2, 31, 46; 19:14; 28:1) as well as in Christian hymnody, for instance, "Built on a Rock the Church Shall Stand" and "Rock of Ages."

Verses 23 and 24 shift the psalm into an instructional mode. These are words addressed no longer to God but to the congregation. Hearers are advised to love the Lord, to be strong, to take courage.

Since Psalm 31:5a is one of the traditional "seven last words" spoken from the cross, it is worth asking, Why did Jesus pick just these words? Did he pray this psalm, or at least a good part of it, on the cross? Such could have been the case, since quotations from a document were often a way to signal the use of the entire document. The entire psalm would have served well as a prayer from the cross.

HAPPINESS IS . . .
Psalm 32

Of David. A Maskil.

32:1 **Happy are those whose transgression is forgiven,**
          whose sin is covered.
   2 **Happy are those to whom the LORD imputes no iniquity,**
          and in whose spirit there is no deceit.

   3 **While I kept silence, my body wasted away**
          through my groaning all day long.
   4 **For day and night your hand was heavy upon me;**
          my strength was dried up as by the heat of summer.
                                                              Selah

   5 **Then I acknowledged my sin to you,**
          and I did not hide my iniquity;
       I said, "I will confess my transgressions to the LORD,"
          and you forgave the guilt of my sin.   *Selah*

   6 **Therefore let all who are faithful**
          offer prayer to you;
       at a time of distress, the rush of mighty waters
          shall not reach them.
   7 **You are a hiding place for me;**
          you preserve me from trouble;
          you surround me with glad cries of deliverance.   *Selah*

   8 **I will instruct you and teach you the way you should go;**
          I will counsel you with my eye upon you.
   9 **Do not be like a horse or a mule, without understanding,**
          whose temper must be curbed with bit and bridle,
          else it will not stay near you.

¹⁰ **Many are the torments of the wicked,**
   but steadfast love surrounds those who trust in the LORD.
¹¹ **Be glad in the LORD and rejoice, O righteous,**
   and shout for joy, all you upright in heart.

"Happiness is a warm puppy" was the caption of the *Peanuts* cartoon, which then set off a whole series of "Happiness is . . ." cards and sayings. The biblical equivalent is the statement beginning "Happy are those . . ." or, in the older translations, "Blessed are those. . . ." These "happy are those" sayings occur in a number of psalms (1:1–3; 41:1–3; 112:1; 119:1–2; 127:5; 128:1), indicating that in biblical times, as well as now, "the pursuit of happiness" was one of the goals in life. In the case of Psalm 32, being happy involves being freed from the guilt that comes from having sinned.

The heading associates the psalm with David (see on Psalm 4) and then identifies it as a "Maskil," which appears to mean an "instructional piece" (see also Psalms 42, 44, 45, 52–55, 74, 78, 88, 89, 142). The same Hebrew word occurs in verbal form in verse 8: "I will *instruct* you and teach you the way you should go." This psalm will provide instruction about "the way you should go."

Happiness Is . . . (32:1–2)

Verses 1–2 gather four major Old Testament words for sin. Each word provides a picture with an insight into the biblical notion. Verse 1 speaks of *transgression* (from the Hebrew, *pāšaʿ*). The same word may be used for the rebellion of one treaty partner against another (2 Kings 1:1) or the rebellion of children against parents (Isa. 1:2). According to this word, happiness is a life no longer being lived in rebellion against God.

The second word, *sin*, comes from the Hebrew *ḥāṭāʾ*, which has the fundamental sense of missing a target. The word occurs in Judges 20:16, which tells of the seven hundred left-handed marksmen from the tribe of Benjamin who could "sling a stone at a hair, and not *miss*." Happiness, according to this picture, is having one's life head in the right direction, on course, no longer wrongly aimed off target.

The third word is *iniquity*, the Hebrew *ʿawōn* (v. 2; also v. 5, translated "guilt"). The sense of this word is to be bent over, twisted, or crooked. Isaiah 24:1 speaks of the Lord *twisting* the surface of the earth; in Psalm 38:6 a sick person says, "I am utterly *bowed down* and prostrate; all day long I go around mourning." According to this word, happiness is being straightened out, no longer twisted and bent out of shape.

Finally, behind *deceit* is the Hebrew *remīyāh*, which has the sense of treachery or not being reliable, like a weapon that backfires or cannot be depended on to function (Hos. 7:16, a "defective bow"). This word defines happiness as living in a manner that is honest and forthright.

In sum, according to this psalm, the person is happy who is not rebelling against God, whose life is on track, straightened out, and marked by honesty. (For *Selah*, see the comments on Psalm 3.)

Confession Is . . . (32:3–5)

The psalm continues with a description of the terrible physical toll that bottled-up sin can take (vv. 3–4). The sense is "When I kept all that to myself, my bones ached. Your hand was heavy upon me, Lord, and I had no vigor!"

Then, continues verse 5, the psalmist took it all to the Lord in prayer: "I acknowledged my sin to you, and I did not hide my iniquity." The next lines are used in the church's liturgies for confession and forgiveness: "I said, 'I will confess my transgressions to the LORD,' and you forgave the guilt of my sin."

The Way to Live (32:6–11)

The important word in verse 6 is *therefore*. The sense is "Therefore, because the Lord forgives sins, and such forgiveness results in true happiness, consider the following!" The first word of advice for believers is simple: pray (v. 6)! The psalmist had experienced the benefits of taking personal troubles to the Lord in prayer (vv. 3–5) and now commends such a practice to others.

Verse 7 identifies the Lord as a "hiding place." When Jonathan knew that his father, King Saul, was out to kill his friend David, he told David to "stay in a *secret place* [the Hebrew is the same as that translated 'hiding place'] and hide yourself" (1 Sam. 19:2). The Lord, says verse 7, is such a "secret place," a place of security and safety for those who seek him (see also Ps. 119:114).

With verse 8, the psalm shifts into a teaching mode, the Lord providing the instruction. Life is pictured as a "way," a journey, as in Psalms 1, 16, 25, 37, and 119. Here again is the promise that this instruction will be "with my eye upon you." The Lord promises to watch over the one being instructed.

The first word of instruction is negative: Don't function at the level of a horse or mule that doesn't even know enough to stay close to its master! The biblical writers often use animals as examples (see Prov. 26:3; Isa. 1:2–3; Jer. 8:6–7; Matt. 6:26).

The instruction continues in verses 10 and 11. The sense of verse 10 is "Trust in the Lord, and you'll be surrounded by the Lord's amazing grace!" Concluding with the happiness theme that introduced it, the psalm closes with a picture of one who is shouting for joy. Such is the one who trusts in the Lord.

Happiness and Repentance

This has been one of the more popular psalms in the Christian tradition. It has been named one of the "penitential psalms," to be used in connection with repentance and forgiveness of sin (also Psalms 6, 38, 51, 102, 130, 143). The lectionary has understood the psalm in this way, tying it to the story of the repentant prodigal son (4 Lent C). The psalm is also linked with the story of the forgiven woman in Luke 7:36–50 and with David and Bathsheba (both for Sunday between June 12 and 18 C). Paul referred to verses 1–2 of Psalm 32 in Romans 4:7–8.

This is a psalm of extremes. It begins and ends on a note of happiness and joy. At its center is a word about sin and about forgiveness, that gift from the Lord that makes a guilt-free, joy-filled life possible (v. 5).

THE EYE OF THE LORD
Psalm 33

33:1 Rejoice in the LORD, O you righteous.
  Praise befits the upright.
  2 Praise the LORD with the lyre;
  make melody to him with the harp of ten strings.
  3 Sing to him a new song;
  play skillfully on the strings, with loud shouts.

  4 For the word of the LORD is upright,
  and all his work is done in faithfulness.
  5 He loves righteousness and justice;
  the earth is full of the steadfast love of the LORD.

  6 By the word of the LORD the heavens were made,
  and all their host by the breath of his mouth.
  7 He gathered the waters of the sea as in a bottle;
  he put the deeps in storehouses.

  8 Let all the earth fear the LORD;
  let all the inhabitants of the world stand in awe of him.
  9 For he spoke, and it came to be;
  he commanded, and it stood firm.

  10 The LORD brings the counsel of the nations to nothing;
  he frustrates the plans of the peoples.
  11 The counsel of the LORD stands forever,

the thoughts of his heart to all generations.
¹² Happy is the nation whose God is the LORD,
    the people whom he has chosen as his heritage.

¹³ The LORD looks down from heaven;
    he sees all humankind.
¹⁴ From where he sits enthroned he watches
    all the inhabitants of the earth—
¹⁵ he who fashions the hearts of them all,
    and observes all their deeds.
¹⁶ A king is not saved by his great army;
    a warrior is not delivered by his great strength.
¹⁷ The war horse is a vain hope for victory,
    and by its great might it cannot save.

¹⁸ Truly the eye of the LORD is on those who fear him,
    on those who hope in his steadfast love,
¹⁹ to deliver their soul from death,
    and to keep them alive in famine.

²⁰ Our soul waits for the LORD;
    he is our help and shield.
²¹ Our heart is glad in him,
    because we trust in his holy name.
²² Let your steadfast love, O LORD, be upon us,
    even as we hope in you.

It was in a Greek Orthodox church that I noticed it. Front and center, near the ceiling of the church, was a painting of a single human eye. The eye was huge, with a brown iris and a black pupil. Our guide was explaining that it was to represent the eye of the Lord. "Wherever you are in this church," she said, "the eye of God is always looking at you."

"Truly the eye of the LORD is on those who fear him," says verse 18 of this psalm; and only in this psalm does this "eye of the Lord" expression appear in the Bible. (Ps. 34:15 speaks of "the eyes of the Lord.") Knowing that the Lord is watching can be comforting, as in the gospel song "His eye is on the sparrow, and I know he watches me." But awareness of being watched can also be unsettling. The apocryphal book of Sirach tells of a person about to become involved in an illicit sexual relationship. But that person

> does not realize that the eyes of the Lord
> are ten thousand times brighter than the sun;
> they look upon every aspect of human behavior
> and see into hidden corners.
>   (Sir. 23:19)

This psalm is an excellent example of a *hymn* (see on Psalm 113). A series of opening imperatives make up a *call to praise* (vv. 1–3). Following this are carefully constructed *reasons for praise* (vv. 4–19), including God's greatness (vv. 4–12) and God's goodness (vv. 13–19). The concluding *statement of trust* (vv. 20–21) and a *request* (v. 22) round off the psalm. The psalm consists of twenty-two verses, the number of letters in the Hebrew alphabet; is this to indicate completeness?

Psalm 30 gave thanks and praise to God for a specific healing. Like Psalm 8, Psalm 33 is a hymn, not related to a specific healing or deliverance but giving praise for what God does continually.

The Same Old Songs? (33:1–3)

Middle-aged song leaders in church contexts know that they can always get a good response from a middle-aged audience with the old favorites such as "How Great Thou Art" and "Amazing Grace." This psalm, however, suggests that singing a few new songs once in a while would be appropriate. This introductory call to praise offers several suggestions for worship. (1) Worship ought to be joyful (v. 1)! (2) Worship may include the use of musical instruments, mentioned here for the first time in the Psalter. (3) Worship of the Creator ought to be characterized by creativity! This psalm encourages contemporary composers and poets to write something fresh, in the language of our own day. (4) Worship ought to call up the best from musicians, who should play "skillfully." (5) Worship should be enthusiastic and may even have the volume turned up ("loud," v. 3). Worship committees in congregations would do well to reflect on this psalm with these suggestions.

Why Praise? The Lord Is Great (33:4–12)

Praising the Lord is a reasonable thing to do, the psalms argue, and Psalm 33 makes that argument quite precisely. The first word in verses 4 and 9 is "for," bracketing these verses as a unit. This section speaks of the Lord's word (v. 6) and then of the great prophetic themes of righteousness and justice (Isa. 1:10–17; 5:1–7; Amos 5:24; Micah 6:6–8) and steadfast love (Hos. 2:19; illustrated in 3:1–5 and 11:1–9). Because the Lord promotes righteousness, justice, and steadfast love and allows them to prosper (Ps. 33:5), the Lord ought to be praised! Once the Lord spoke the word and called into being all that is (Genesis 1); this, too, is a reason for praise (33:6).

Verses 10–12 are a reminder that the Lord not only has created the heavens and the earth but continues to influence the course of history, working on both the international and national levels (vv. 10, 12). Again, this is reason to praise the Lord! Psalm 32 had a good deal to say about personal happiness (vv. 1–2, 11); the same "happy" theme occurs in Psalm 33:12, but the scope broadens to include an entire people: "Happy is the nation whose God is the LORD."

Why Praise? The Lord Watches (33:13–19)

This section of the psalm has much to say about the Lord's seeing. The Lord *looks down* from heaven and *sees* all humankind (v. 13). That huge eye in the Greek Orthodox church is a reminder of the biblical assertion that the Lord sees all. The Lord *watches* everyone on earth and *observes* all their deeds (vv. 14–15). Recall the statement in the book of Sirach that "the eyes of the Lord are ten thousand times brighter than the sun" (Sir. 23:19).

What does it mean that the "eye of the Lord" is upon someone? Verse 18 declares that this watchful eye is "on those who fear" God and "on those who hope in [God's] steadfast love." And with what result? This watchful eye will result in the Lord's rescuing the Lord's people from death and also in keeping them alive in famine (v. 19). Like a loving parent "keeping an eye on" a child that is playing, the Lord who is watching will protect and care for the Lord's people.

Psalm 34 provides a good commentary on this section about the "eye of the Lord," now speaking of the eyes, the ears, and the face of the Lord (34:15–18). Daniel once spoke of the "eyes of God" in prayer: "Incline your ear, O my God, and hear. Open your eyes and look at our desolation" (Dan. 9:18; see also the prayers in 1 Kings 8:52 and Neh. 1:6).

Hesed and Hope (33:20–22)

The hymn concludes with a look toward the future and with an abstract ("help") and a concrete ("shield") reference to the Lord. The "joyful" theme of verse 1 is picked up with "glad" in verse 21, and the hymn ends by recalling the steadfast love, or *hesed*, of God once again (see vv. 5, 18), as the basis for hope in the future.

This psalm, which issues a call to creativity and competence in worship, itself offers praise to the Lord as the creator and the caregiver of the Lord's people.

WHY NOT TRY IT OUT?
Psalm 34

**Of David, when he feigned madness before Abimelech,
so that he drove him out, and he went away.**

34:1 I will bless the Lord at all times;
    his praise shall continually be in my mouth.
2 My soul makes its boast in the Lord;
    let the humble hear and be glad.
3 O magnify the Lord with me,
    and let us exalt his name together.

4 I sought the Lord, and he answered me,
    and delivered me from all my fears.
5 Look to him, and be radiant;
    so your faces shall never be ashamed.
6 This poor soul cried, and was heard by the Lord,
    and was saved from every trouble.
7 The angel of the Lord encamps
    around those who fear him, and delivers them.
8 O taste and see that the Lord is good;
    happy are those who take refuge in him.
9 O fear the Lord, you his holy ones,
    for those who fear him have no want.
10 The young lions suffer want and hunger,
    but those who seek the Lord lack no good thing.

11 Come, O children, listen to me;
    I will teach you the fear of the Lord.
12 Which of you desires life,
    and covets many days to enjoy good?
13 Keep your tongue from evil,
    and your lips from speaking deceit.
14 Depart from evil, and do good;
    seek peace, and pursue it.

15 The eyes of the Lord are on the righteous,
    and his ears are open to their cry.
16 The face of the Lord is against evildoers,
    to cut off the remembrance of them from the earth.
17 When the righteous cry for help, the Lord hears,
    and rescues them from all their troubles.
18 The Lord is near to the brokenhearted,
    and saves the crushed in spirit.

19 Many are the afflictions of the righteous,
    but the Lord rescues them from them all.
20 He keeps all their bones;
    not one of them will be broken.
21 Evil brings death to the wicked,
    and those who hate the righteous will be condemned.

²² **The LORD redeems the life of his servants;**
   none of those who take refuge in him will be condemned.

"Try it out!" suggests Psalm 34. "Experiment! Look at it! Listen to it! Test it! Taste it! See what this religion of the Bible is all about." This is the sense of the most well known verse in this psalm: "O taste and see that the LORD is good" (v. 8). The psalmist was speaking on the basis of a positive experience with the faith and wanted others to have that sort of experience as well.

Two things are puzzling about this psalm. First, the incident to which the heading refers is not known from the Bible or from any other source. Second, while this is an alphabetical psalm (see the comments on Psalms 9–10), the line beginning with the sixth letter of the Hebrew alphabet, *waw*, is missing; apparently it was somehow lost. It should appear after verse 5 in the NRSV.

Verses 1–3 offer a *call to worship*. Verses 4–6 present a *song of thanksgiving* (see on Psalm 30), with words of testimony and instruction following in verses 7–10. With verses 11–22 the emphasis is on *instruction*, with a question and answer (vv. 11–14) followed by some theological observations (vv. 15–22).

The heading, supplied when the psalms were being collected, associates the psalm with a time when David "feigned madness before Abimelech." First Samuel 21:12–15 reports David feigning madness before King Achish of Gath. It is possible that the person providing the headings confused the two kings; or perhaps we no longer understand the allusion.

Good News for the Poor (34:1–3)

While the word *bless* usually refers to something that the Lord does for people, it is used here with a human subject and with the sense "praise," as is evident from the balancing word *praise* (see Ps. 26:12 for this sense of *bless*). The second half of verse 2 indicates that the psalm intends to offer good news for the poor or humble. The psalmist is among this group (v. 6), also identified as the "righteous" (vv. 15, 17, 19, 21).

Try It and See! (34:4–10)

In the manner of a song of thanksgiving (see Psalm 30), the writer offers a short summary of personal experience with the Lord. This story of answered prayers is twice told. The verbs indicate the action: "I sought . . . he answered . . . and delivered." Verse 6 repeats the sequence: "This poor soul cried . . . was heard . . . and was saved." The psalmist has been delivered and has been saved. This becomes the basis for what is said in the remainder of the psalm. In between these two declarations, the writer gives the listeners some advice: Look to the Lord, and be happy (v. 5)! Verse 7 assures the hearers of the Lord's protection.

With verse 8 the psalm shifts into the imperative mood, and the psalmist gives instruction to those listening. The three verbs *taste, see, fear* are a recommendation that those hearing try out the life lived in relationship to the Lord. This is a life marked by happiness and security (v. 8) as well as freedom from want (v. 10). The reference to those who "seek the LORD" closes the section by linking it to the similar expression in verse 4.

Some Theological Instruction (34:11–22)

Verses 11–14 present some instruction that is of basic importance for those who "fear the LORD." The notion of fearing the Lord occurs in verses 7, 9, and 11 and is of central importance for the psalm. It is at the heart of the teacher's curriculum, indicating that "fear of the LORD" is something that can be taught (v. 11). To fear the Lord means to enjoy the Lord's protection (v. 7) and provision (v. 9). The book of Proverbs indicates that it is the starting point for becoming an educated person (Prov. 1:7).

The material in verses 11–14 is in the form of a teacher giving private instruction. The tone is not cool and theoretical. With this teaching, Hans-Joachim Kraus notes in his commentary on *Psalms 1–59*, "there is a burning fire that wants to be applied to the hearers" (p. 387). The question is, "Which of you would like to live for a long time, enjoying the good things of life?" (v. 12). The answer is obvious: "I would!" Then some instruction is given, first negative, advising the avoidance of evil and untruthful speaking (v. 13), and then positive: do good and "pursue *shalom*," which means to work actively for peaceful relationships in the community (v. 14).

The section from verses 15–22 consists of unrelenting instruction about the Lord, or (to use our language) theological instruction. Notice that the Lord is the subject of every sentence except for verse 21.

The references to the Lord's "eyes, ears, face" indicate that the Lord is viewed as a *person* (vv. 15–16). As in Psalm 33, the Lord's eyes are on the people, that is, on "the righteous" (vv. 15, 17), whom the Lord "rescues . . . from all their troubles."

But apparently, not all are instantly rescued. The psalm refers to those who are "brokenhearted" and "crushed in spirit" and recognizes that God's people, too, experience suffering (vv. 18–19). The psalm promises that the Lord is close to those whose hearts have been broken by some tragedy and will save those who are crushed in spirit (v. 18).

On reading verses 11–14, one could get the impression that the psalmist is proposing a simplistic approach to the complexities of human existence: watch your words, stay away from evil, work for peace, and you'll have a long life and be happy! But the psalm is more realistic. It recognizes there are those whose hearts have been broken and whose spirits have been crushed. It is aware that the righteous suffer, too (vv. 18–19).

The reference to evil in verse 21 links up with the comment about evil at the beginning of this section, in verse 13. Evil is tied to death, quite the opposite of the life that these young students desire (v. 12). Finally, a later hand (the verse stands outside the acrostic pattern) has added the promise in verse 22.

TO LIVE QUIETLY IN THE LAND
Psalm 35

Of David.

35:1 Contend, O LORD, with those who contend with me;
    fight against those who fight against me!
2 Take hold of shield and buckler,
    and rise up to help me!
3 Draw the spear and javelin
    against my pursuers;
  say to my soul,
    "I am your salvation."

4 Let them be put to shame and dishonor
    who seek after my life.
  Let them be turned back and confounded
    who devise evil against me.
5 Let them be like chaff before the wind,
    with the angel of the LORD driving them on.
6 Let their way be dark and slippery,
    with the angel of the LORD pursuing them.

7 For without cause they hid their net for me;
    without cause they dug a pit for my life.
8 Let ruin come on them unawares.
  And let the net that they hid ensnare them;
    let them fall in it—to their ruin.

9 Then my soul shall rejoice in the LORD,
    exulting in his deliverance.
10 All my bones shall say,
    "O LORD, who is like you?

You deliver the weak
   from those too strong for them,
   the weak and needy from those who despoil them."

11 Malicious witnesses rise up;
   they ask me about things I do not know.
12 They repay me evil for good;
   my soul is forlorn.
13 But as for me, when they were sick,
   I wore sackcloth;
   I afflicted myself with fasting.
   I prayed with head bowed on my bosom,
     14 as though I grieved for a friend or a brother;
   I went about as one who laments for a mother,
   bowed down and in mourning.

15 But at my stumbling they gathered in glee,
   they gathered together against me;
   ruffians whom I did not know
   tore at me without ceasing;
16 they impiously mocked more and more,
   gnashing at me with their teeth.

17 How long, O LORD, will you look on?
   Rescue me from their ravages,
   my life from the lions!
18 Then I will thank you in the great congregation;
   in the mighty throng I will praise you.

19 Do not let my treacherous enemies rejoice over me,
   or those who hate me without cause wink the eye.
20 For they do not speak peace,
   but they conceive deceitful words
   against those who are quiet in the land.
21 They open wide their mouths against me;
   they say, "Aha, Aha,
   our eyes have seen it."

22 You have seen, O LORD; do not be silent!
   O Lord, do not be far from me!
23 Wake up! Bestir yourself for my defense,
   for my cause, my God and my Lord!
24 Vindicate me, O LORD, my God,
   according to your righteousness,
   and do not let them rejoice over me.

²⁵ **Do not let them say to themselves,**
   "Aha, we have our heart's desire."
Do not let them say, "We have swallowed you up."

²⁶ **Let all those who rejoice at my calamity**
   be put to shame and confusion;
let those who exalt themselves against me
   be clothed with shame and dishonor.

²⁷ **Let those who desire my vindication**
   shout for joy and be glad,
   and say evermore,
"Great is the LORD,
   who delights in the welfare of his servant."
²⁸ **Then my tongue shall tell of your righteousness**
   and of your praise all day long.

The chorus from Felix Mendelssohn's *Elijah* asserts that the Lord is ever watchful, ever awake: "He watching over Israel, slumbers not nor sleeps" (Ps. 121:4). But apparently there were times when it seemed to the psalmists that the Lord *was* sleeping. Psalms 7:6; 44:23; and 59:4, as well as Psalm 35, assume that the Lord has not been alert and must be encouraged to wake up!

This psalm consists of the typical elements of the individual lament (see on Psalm 13), though these elements are not held in balance. Most developed is the *request*, occurring in verses 1–6, 8, 17b, 19, and 22–27, totaling fourteen and a half verses. The extent of this element reflects the desperation of the psalmist's situation.

Next in length is the *complaint*, almost exclusively in "they" form, in verses 7, 11–12a, 15–16, 20–21, with a half verse each of "I" complaint (v. 12b) and "you" complaint (v. 17a), for a total of seven and a half verses. If we count the "protest of innocence" in verses 13–14 as a form of "I" complaint, then the total number of complaint verses reaches nine and a half. Again, the desperate nature of the psalmist's situation is evident from the fact that twenty-four of the twenty-eight verses give expression to *request* or *complaint*.

Strategically placed at the close of each unit of the psalm are *vows of praise*, in verses 9–10, 18, and 28.

Save Me, Lord! (35:1–10)

The first part of this psalm is completely dominated by desperate cries for help, directed to the Lord (vv. 1–6, 8). The opening imagery is military, asking the Lord to take up the battle against the psalmist's enemies and to announce, "I am your salvation." What could have been the situation of the psalmist? Verses 4 and 7 indicate that the problem was not a matter of minor interpersonal differences. No, the psalmist's life was at stake!

The psalmist asks the Lord to deal with these persons and has some suggestions as to what might be done. They could be shamed and dishonored. They certainly ought to be turned back. Picking up language from Psalm 1:4, the psalmist says that he would like to see them blown away like so much chaff before the wind (v. 5). And here are two unusual references to the "angel of the LORD," the psalmist praying that the Lord assign an angel to chase after these enemies (vv. 5–6).

The complaint in verse 7 adds another element to the psalmist's dilemma: twice he emphasizes that these wrongs were done to him "without cause." And then the psalmist prays that the Lord might bring into action what F.-L. Hossfeld in *Die Psalmen* calls the "boomerang effect," causing them to get tangled up in their own evils (v. 8; see also Ps. 9:15).

The desperate tone of this first section of the psalm is brought to a close with the vow to praise in verses 9–10, the psalmist expressing certainty that the Lord will deliver the "weak," "the weak and needy," of whom the psalmist is a part.

How Long, O Lord? (35:11–18)

Dominating this portion of the psalm are further complaints about the writer's enemies. Behind verses 11–12 appears to be some sort of court procedure, where the psalmist is being unfairly manipulated through a diabolical scheme of questioning (v. 11) and where those whom he once helped are now bent on harming him (v. 12).

Verses 13–16 contrast the psalmist's behavior with that of those he had previously helped. When they were ill, he had gone through the appropriate procedures of mourning, including intense (as if for a friend, sibling, or parent) prayer and fasting. But now, in his own time of difficulty (we don't know exactly what the "stumbling" was), these persons have turned against him, mocking him, tearing at him, and all the while enjoying it!

The heart of this psalm is found in verse 17. Here is a desperate and impatient cry for help. Implied with "How long?" are "It's about time!" and "I can't hang on much longer!" The psalmist is not so desperate as to be out of control, however. After this urgent plea for assistance, the psalm writer promises, once again, to thank and to praise (v. 18).

Wake Up, Lord! (35:19–28)

The cries for help continue. Once again, the psalmist reminds God that his suffering is "without cause" (v. 19; see also v. 7, twice). Another charge against these enemies is that they do not speak the words that lead to *shalom* (peace) in the community. Their words have turned against those who wish to live peacefully and, in a phrase unique in the Bible, against those who are "quiet in the land" (v. 20).

Verses 22–27 are another gathering of a half dozen cries for help, balancing a similar series at the beginning of the psalm. The official theology of the day asserted that the Lord would speak, would be near, would defend the Lord's people, but certainly would not be asleep. But now it seems to the psalmist as if the Lord is silent, far away, and sound asleep. And so the Lord must be awakened!

The psalm finishes up with some further requests to save the one praying and to shame the enemies (vv. 24–26). Apparently, the psalmist knows of a support group that wants his deliverance, and he reminds the Lord how good it would be to hear their praises upon the restoration of *shalom* (welfare) to the psalmist (v. 27). If and when this deliverance happens, there will be continuous praises ascending to heaven (vv. 27–28).

Can we find ourselves in this psalm? When might it touch our own lives? Not often, one would hope. But there are times of desperation, when one's own prayer will be "How long, O Lord, will you look on?" or simply "Rescue me!" or "Don't be far from me!" or even "Wake up, Lord!"

In such situations, it is helpful to know that other of God's people have been there, too, and that despite the desperation of their situation, they could look forward to rejoicing, giving thanks in the congregation, praising the Lord, and once again living quietly in the land.

HUMANS AND ANIMALS ALIKE
Psalm 36

To the leader. Of David, the servant of the LORD.

36:1 **Transgression speaks to the wicked**
    deep in their hearts;
  there is no fear of God
    before their eyes.
2 **For they flatter themselves in their own eyes**
    that their iniquity cannot be found out and hated.
3 **The words of their mouths are mischief and deceit;**
    they have ceased to act wisely and do good.

⁴ They plot mischief while on their beds;
   they are set on a way that is not good;
   they do not reject evil.

⁵ Your steadfast love, O LORD, extends to the heavens,
   your faithfulness to the clouds.
⁶ Your righteousness is like the mighty mountains,
   your judgments are like the great deep;
   you save humans and animals alike, O LORD.

⁷ How precious is your steadfast love, O God!
   All people may take refuge in the shadow of your wings.
⁸ They feast on the abundance of your house,
   and you give them drink from the river of your delights.
⁹ For with you is the fountain of life;
   in your light we see light.

¹⁰ O continue your steadfast love to those who know you,
   and your salvation to the upright of heart!
¹¹ Do not let the foot of the arrogant tread on me,
   or the hand of the wicked drive me away.
¹² There the evildoers lie prostrate;
   they are thrust down, unable to rise.

I used to see the signs in the shop windows and on the doors each day as I walked down the streets of Munich, Germany, toward the university where I was writing these lines. With a picture of a small dog in the corner, the black letters on the white background read, *Wir müssen draussen bleiben!* "We have to stay outside!" The signs would not be necessary were it not for the fact that many citizens of Munich like to take their dogs downtown and have them go along for coffee in a restaurant or a cruise through the grocery store. "It is not good that the man should be alone," said Genesis 2, and so the Lord God created animals, presumably including dogs, for companionship. The Bible has much to say about God and human beings but also about God and the earth and its creatures.

The psalm divides into three sections. Verses 1–4 are a *"they" complaint* (see on Psalm 13). Verses 5–9 offer a hymn of *praise*. The psalm concludes with the *requests* in verses 10–12. The heading dedicates the psalm to the music director and associates it with David (see the comments on Psalm 4).

Portrait of the Wicked (36:1–4)

The psalm begins by looking deeply into the hearts of certain wicked persons, where one discovers no fear of God, only evil thoughts. These thoughts express themselves first in dishonest and mischievous words and then in actions that are neither wise nor good. Like those greedy persons whom Micah describes as lying in bed, cooking up plots to rob and oppress (Micah 2:1–5), these wicked ones do not have enough hours in the day to plan their evil actions and so make their plans when they should be sleeping. When the daytime comes, their evil thoughts erupt into actions.

The portrait of these persons is painted in exceptionally negative tones, with descriptions like "transgression . . . wicked . . . no fear of God . . . flatter . . . iniquity . . . mischief . . . deceit . . . ceased to act wisely and do good . . . plot mischief . . . set on a way that is not good . . . do not reject evil."

Your Amazing Grace (36:5–9)

In sharp contrast to the cesspool of sin portrayed in the opening of the psalm is the hymn of praise. Our eyes are directed away from the cesspool and toward the celestial realm. No longer is the language about the wicked; but it is now directed to the Lord, in direct, personal "you" form.

The first segment of the hymn is bracketed by "O LORD" (vv. 5–6). The psalmist achieves an expansive sort of praise by naming the extremes. The range of the Lord's love is like the distance from the mountaintops to the deep. Another set of extremes describes the breadth of the Lord's saving work, which includes humans *and animals too.*

With verse 7 the imagery continues. The Lord is like a bird under whose wings the Lord's people may take shelter. Or the Lord is a host, providing abundantly for those who are house guests (v. 8; see also Ps. 23:5–6). Two further images are reminiscent of the imagery of John's Gospel: with the Lord is to be found the source of life and also light (v. 9; see John 1).

As one reads through this hymn section, an array of pictures appears: the heavens and the clouds, the mountains and the deep, humans and animals, a mothering bird, a banquet at home, a fountain, and a great light. And one hears sounds: the thunder of the heavens, the beating of wings, the laughter of a party, the flowing of a river, the bubbling of a fountain. So it is when the Psalms speak of God; a lively display of sights and sounds plays out before one's eyes and ears.

To Be Continued (36:10–12)

The preceding two stanzas began with references to the Lord's steadfast love (vv. 5, 7). Now, as the psalm comes to a close, the psalmist asks the Lord to continue giving that amazing grace to the Lord's people and to send salvation. While verse 10 is something of a general request, verse 11 is quite specific: "Lord, don't let the hands and feet of the arrogant wicked harm me or drive me away!" The psalm ends with a picture of the wicked, defeated, lying down and unable to get up.

Humans and Animals Alike (36:6)

This psalm appears in the lectionary for 2 Epiphany C, where it contributes to the "light" theme of the season, and also for Monday in Holy Week ABC, where verse 9 is again the point of contact with the other texts for the day.

The psalm also has something to say about relationships among God, humans, and the other creatures living on our planet. Most significant is the statement "you save humans and animals alike, O LORD" (v. 6). This could mean that the next time we see a bumper sticker saying, "Jesus Saves," we ought to think that according to Psalm 36, the Lord is interested in saving the nonhuman creatures of the earth as well as humans!

Psalm 8 indicates that the human calling to have "dominion" over the earth includes responsibility toward "all sheep and oxen . . . the beasts of the field, the birds of the air, and the fish of the sea." Psalm 104 also addresses this theme. (See the comments on those psalms.) The fact that humans and animals are ranked together here as twin objects of the Lord's saving activity could remind us that as royalty who exercise dominion (Genesis 1; Psalm 8), we humans have a responsibility for care of the earth and its creatures.

Another detail in this psalm sets us thinking about nonhuman creatures. God is pictured as a bird, sheltering persons under a wing, like a mother bird shelters her young ones (v. 7). The same bird imagery occurs in Psalms 17:8; 36:7; 57:1; 61:4; 63:7; 91:4. Jesus used it, too: "Jerusalem, Jerusalem . . . How often have I desired to gather your children together as a hen gathers her brood under her wings" (Matt. 23:37; Luke 13:34). Reflecting on this imagery encourages imaginative teaching about God and reminds us that we may have too much disdained and neglected these fellow creatures of the sixth day (Gen. 1:24–31), whom we should best think of as our distant cousins.

WHAT I'VE LEARNED ALONG THE WAY
Psalm 37

Of David.

37:1 **Do not fret because of the wicked;**
  do not be envious of wrongdoers,

2 for they will soon fade like the grass,
  and wither like the green herb.

3 Trust in the LORD, and do good;
  so you will live in the land, and enjoy security.
4 Take delight in the LORD,
  and he will give you the desires of your heart.

5 Commit your way to the LORD;
  trust in him, and he will act.
6 He will make your vindication shine like the light,
  and the justice of your cause like the noonday.

7 Be still before the LORD, and wait patiently for him;
  do not fret over those who prosper in their way,
  over those who carry out evil devices.

8 Refrain from anger, and forsake wrath.
  Do not fret—it leads only to evil.
9 For the wicked shall be cut off,
  but those who wait for the LORD shall inherit the land.

10 Yet a little while, and the wicked will be no more;
  though you look diligently for their place, they will not be there.
11 But the meek shall inherit the land,
  and delight themselves in abundant prosperity.

12 The wicked plot against the righteous,
  and gnash their teeth at them;
13 but the LORD laughs at the wicked,
  for he sees that their day is coming.

14 The wicked draw the sword and bend their bows
  to bring down the poor and needy,
  to kill those who walk uprightly;
15 their sword shall enter their own heart,
  and their bows shall be broken.

16 Better is a little that the righteous person has
  than the abundance of many wicked.
17 For the arms of the wicked shall be broken,
  but the LORD upholds the righteous.

18 The LORD knows the days of the blameless,
  and their heritage will abide forever;

¹⁹ they are not put to shame in evil times,
    in the days of famine they have abundance.

²⁰ But the wicked perish,
    and the enemies of the LORD are like the glory of the pastures;
    they vanish—like smoke they vanish away.

²¹ The wicked borrow, and do not pay back,
    but the righteous are generous and keep giving;
²² for those blessed by the LORD shall inherit the land,
    but those cursed by him shall be cut off.

²³ Our steps are made firm by the LORD,
    when he delights in our way;
²⁴ though we stumble, we shall not fall headlong,
    for the LORD holds us by the hand.

²⁵ I have been young, and now am old,
    yet I have not seen the righteous forsaken
    or their children begging bread.
²⁶ They are ever giving liberally and lending,
    and their children become a blessing.

²⁷ Depart from evil, and do good;
    so you shall abide forever.
²⁸ For the LORD loves justice;
    he will not forsake his faithful ones.

    The righteous shall be kept safe forever,
    but the children of the wicked shall be cut off.
²⁹ The righteous shall inherit the land,
    and live in it forever.

³⁰ The mouths of the righteous utter wisdom,
    and their tongues speak justice.
³¹ The law of their God is in their hearts;
    their steps do not slip.

³² The wicked watch for the righteous,
    and seek to kill them.
³³ The LORD will not abandon them to their power,
    or let them be condemned when they are brought to trial.

³⁴ Wait for the LORD, and keep to his way,
    and he will exalt you to inherit the land;
    you will look on the destruction of the wicked.

35 I have seen the wicked oppressing,
   and towering like a cedar of Lebanon.
36 Again I passed by, and they were no more;
   though I sought them, they could not be found.

37 Mark the blameless, and behold the upright,
   for there is posterity for the peaceable.
38 But transgressors shall be altogether destroyed;
   the posterity of the wicked shall be cut off.

39 The salvation of the righteous is from the LORD;
   he is their refuge in the time of trouble.
40 The LORD helps them and rescues them;
   he rescues them from the wicked, and saves them,
   because they take refuge in him.

This is one of two psalms where the author is identified as a senior citizen:

> I have been young, and now am old,
>   yet I have not seen the righteous forsaken
>   or their children begging bread.
>   (v. 25; see also 71:9, 17–18)

Verse 25 indicates that this psalm intends to offer a collection of observations about life, designed to help those who are not as far along the way on life's journey as the psalmist.

The collection is organized in a "user-friendly" manner, if one remembers that the "user" would have been expected to memorize this material. As an aid to memorization, the psalm is an acrostic (see the list with Psalms 9–10), this time with the first word in every other line beginning with a letter of a Hebrew alphabet in sequence.

Though the content of the psalm is somewhat restricted by its alphabetical scheme, one can detect a thematic arrangement. Verses 1–9 are a series of *imperative sayings*, beginning and ending with concern about "the wicked" and advising hearers not to fret about them (vv. 1, 7, 8). Verses 10–26 offer *observations*, mainly about "the wicked" (vv. 10, 12–17, 20–21), and conclude with an autobiographical comment in verses 25–26. Verse 27 picks up with two general imperatives and continues with observations about both "the righteous" (vv. 28–30, 32, 39) and "the wicked" (vv. 28, 32, 35, 40).

Don't Worry! (37:1–9)

Verses 1 and 2 strike a major theme of the psalm: Don't worry about the wicked! They aren't going to be around for long. They will fade and wither like the grass; the same imagery is used in Psalm 90:5–6.

The second important theme is sounded in verse 3: the blessing of living safely in the land. Notice the importance of the theme "inherit the land" in verses 9, 11, 22, 29, 34. When one recalls the central role the land has played in the life of Israel since ancient times, one can understand the passionate debates over the land between Israelis and Arabs in our own time.

The third significant theme is that of "your way" as an image for one's life (vv. 5, 7, 23, 34). The imagery was introduced in the picture of two "ways" in Psalm 1:6 and is developed in Psalms 16, 25, 32, and 119. Verse 5 is an encouragement from an older, experienced believer to live a life trusting in the Lord. Verse 7 speaks again of the prosperity of the wicked "in their way." Verses 23 and 24 speak of the Lord's support "in our way," which is like the support of a parent delighting in a child's first steps and holding that child by the hand (see also Hosea 11). Finally, verse 34 encourages those hearing this psalm to have patience, despite the difficulties with the wicked, and to keep to the Lord's way.

Considered as a whole, this first segment has some practical advice from an older person (v. 25) to the younger generation. Don't worry about the prosperity of the wicked; they'll soon be off the scene (vv. 1–2, 7, 9)! Trust in the Lord and enjoy your days (vv. 3–5). Don't let yourself get angry, but wait for what the Lord has in store (vv. 8–9). Verses 23–24 are again a voice of experience, testifying that the Lord "holds us by the hand."

Don't Worry about the Wicked! (37:10–26)

Now the "wicked" theme that framed verses 1–9 dominates, as the psalm gives a number of reasons for not worrying about them. (1) They are not going to be around much longer (v. 10). (2) The wicked have the Lord against them, even laughing at them, and their success is short-lived (vv. 12–13; see Ps. 59:8). (3) Their evil actions against the poor and needy will backfire, turning against them (vv. 14–15; Matt. 26:52). (4) The wicked will eventually come to ruin (vv. 17, 20). The "better than" saying in verses 16–17 has parallels in form and content in Proverbs 15:16–17; 16:8; and Tobit 12:8, "A little with righteousness is better than wealth with wrongdoing." (5) The wicked are going to die, as surely as the grass in the pastures dies and as surely as smoke fades away (v. 20; also Matt. 6:30).

On the positive side is the assertion that the righteous will eventually inherit the land. The theme was introduced in verse 9 and is sounded again in verses 11 and 22, where the blessing that promised land to Abraham (Genesis 12) is recalled. Finally, in verse 25 the teacher adds a personal endorsement to what has been said: "I've lived a long life, and have discovered that the Lord doesn't forsake the righteous!"

Stay on Track! (37:27–40)

After the initial imperatives "Depart from evil, and do good" (v. 27), this section of the psalm focuses on the righteous. They shall be kept safe and shall inherit the land. Wisdom is on their lips and the teaching (*torah*) of the Lord is in their hearts (vv. 28–31).

Verse 34 offers a compact summary of this psalm's teaching. The two imperatives advise patient waiting and staying on the right path. Two results are promised: "You will inherit the land, and the wicked will be destroyed."

Verses 35–38 continue to play on the theme of the destruction of the wicked and the prosperity of those who are upright and "peaceable" (literally, "people of *shalom*"). Verses 39–40 make clear that salvation and rescue are from the Lord.

This psalm offers good advice for a younger generation from an older believer. But what happens when it appears that the righteous *have been* forsaken and when their children *are* begging for bread? In our own time, what can one say about the millions of innocent sufferers in the world, from the Holocaust to wars in Vietnam and Bosnia or anywhere else? This question of innocent suffering is partially addressed by Psalm 73 and the book of Job. The final answer, however, is known to God alone.

In the meantime, the advice of the psalm is worth hearing. Do not fret. Trust and take delight in the Lord. Keep to the Lord's way, and wait. And recall the one who said, "I am the way, and the truth, and the life" (John 14:6).

ALL MY LONGING
Psalm 38

A Psalm of David, for the memorial offering.

38:1 **O LORD, do not rebuke me in your anger,**
    or discipline me in your wrath.
  2 **For your arrows have sunk into me,**
    and your hand has come down on me.

³ There is no soundness in my flesh
    because of your indignation;
there is no health in my bones
    because of my sin.
⁴ For my iniquities have gone over my head;
    they weigh like a burden too heavy for me.

⁵ My wounds grow foul and fester
    because of my foolishness;
⁶ I am utterly bowed down and prostrate;
    all day long I go around mourning.
⁷ For my loins are filled with burning,
    and there is no soundness in my flesh.
⁸ I am utterly spent and crushed;
    I groan because of the tumult of my heart.

⁹ O Lord, all my longing is known to you;
    my sighing is not hidden from you.
¹⁰ My heart throbs, my strength fails me;
    as for the light of my eyes—it also has gone from me.
¹¹ My friends and companions stand aloof from my affliction,
    and my neighbors stand far off.

¹² Those who seek my life lay their snares;
    those who seek to hurt me speak of ruin,
    and meditate treachery all day long.

¹³ But I am like the deaf, I do not hear;
    like the mute, who cannot speak.
¹⁴ Truly, I am like one who does not hear,
    and in whose mouth is no retort.

¹⁵ But it is for you, O LORD, that I wait;
    it is you, O Lord my God, who will answer.
¹⁶ For I pray, "Only do not let them rejoice over me,
    those who boast against me when my foot slips."

¹⁷ For I am ready to fall,
    and my pain is ever with me.
¹⁸ I confess my iniquity;
    I am sorry for my sin.
¹⁹ Those who are my foes without cause are mighty,
    and many are those who hate me wrongfully.
²⁰ Those who render me evil for good
    are my adversaries because I follow after good.

²¹ **Do not forsake me, O LORD;**
     O my God, do not be far from me;
²² **make haste to help me,**
     O Lord, my salvation.

This is a prayer from a person who is hurting, hurting badly. It is similar to Psalm 6 in this regard. To give expression to this hurting, the psalm uses the typical elements of the individual lament (see on Psalm 13). Identifying these typical elements indicates something of the creative way in which these psalmists worked, using traditional forms but rearranging and adjusting them to fit a particular situation.

The psalm is framed by *requests* for help. These are the first and last things that the one praying has to say to God (vv. 1, 21–22). The *complaints* begin with vigorous *"you" complaints* addressed to the Lord in verses 2 and 3a ("your arrows . . . your hand . . . your indignation") and continue with *"I" complaints* in verses 3b–10. The complaints keep on with *"they" complaints* in verses 11–12 and then move back to an "I" complaint in verses 13–14. Verses 15–16 offer an *affirmation of trust.* Verse 17 is an "I" complaint, while verse 18 is a *confession of sin.* Verses 19–20 present final "they" complaints.

As one considers this analysis of the psalm, two things are clear. (1) The cries for help in verses 1 and 21–22 are cries from one who is in a desperate situation. This is a psalm that has a note of urgency about it. (2) The psalm is a lament, dominated by the element of complaint (seventeen out of twenty-two verses). The trust element is sounded in verses 15–16; the typical vow to praise is absent.

The heading associates the psalm with David (see comments on Psalm 4) and links it (along with Psalm 70) to "the memorial offering," the precise meaning of which is not certain.

My Misery (38:1–8)

The psalmist cannot be accused of bottling up feelings and emotions. Nor is the writer reticent about placing the blame for personal illness. Right off the bat the psalmist names the Lord as the one who is responsible, using two pictures to make the point: the Lord has shot arrows into the writer, and the Lord has struck the writer with his hand (v. 2).

Verses 3 and 5 go beyond a description of the psalmist's ills to indicate what the writer believes is the cause of these ills. Speaking to the Lord, the psalmist links hurting to "your rage" (Jewish Publication Society translation; NRSV, "indignation"; v. 3) and "my sin" and "my foolishness." The psalmist is quite certain in the diagnosis that (1) I have sinned and been foolish, and (2) therefore you are angry and are punishing me. Such a direct correlation between wrongdoing and punishment is found in wisdom literature, where illness may be understood as God's way of disciplining for some specific sin. Just as parents discipline a child because of some wrongdoing ("Those who spare the rod hate their children, but those who love them are diligent to discipline them"—Prov. 13:24; see also 19:18), so it is that "the Lord disciplines those whom he loves, and chastises every child whom he accepts" (Heb. 12:6, citing Prov. 3:11–12, Greek).

The picture behind the Hebrew word translated "iniquities" in verse 4 is that of being bent over or twisted out of shape; the same Hebrew word is translated "bowed down" in verse 6 (see on Psalm 32). Verses 6–8 portray the one praying as a desperate person who is physically ill, exhausted, crushed, and hurting badly.

My Longing and My Sighing (38:9–14)

This section begins with an affirmation of trust. Despite the desperate situation, the psalmist remains certain that the Lord knows of these struggles (v. 9).

Then the complaints start up again, first in "I" form: "my strength fails . . . the light of my eyes . . . has gone" (v. 10). The complaints continue in "they" form: enemies design murder plots (v. 12); friends and neighbors do not wish to get involved (v. 11). Then proceeds a series of complaints in the form of similes, in "I" form: "I am like the deaf . . . like the mute . . . like one who does not hear, and in whose mouth is no retort" (vv. 13–14).

My Waiting (38:15–22)

Another affirmation of trust introduces the last section of the psalm (v. 15). Each of a series of four sentences is introduced with the Hebrew word *kî* used to indicate emphasis (vv. 15–18). Verse 15 uses three different names for God: "LORD" or "Yahweh," the personal name for God in the Old Testament; "O Lord," with the sense "Master"; and "my God," translating *'elohim*, the general Hebrew word for God. The last two *kî* sentences focus on the psalmist's pain (v. 17) and then confess wrongdoing and sinfulness, apparently assuming that there is a link between the psalmist's suffering and a sin that has been committed.

The psalm ends as it began, with a series of requests, finally addressing the Lord as "my salvation."

The Penitential Psalms

The church has traditionally counted Psalm 38 as one of those psalms especially appropriate for expressing sorrow because of sin (penitence) and then for the confessing of sin (see the comments on Psalm 6). Despite its long history of use in the church, Psalm 38 is not listed in the Revised Common Lectionary and therefore is not often heard in public reading in our own time.

Why do bad things happen to good people? That question is easy to ask but most difficult to answer. The writer of this psalm believes that bad things have happened (1) because of the Lord's anger (vv. 2, 3a) and (2) because of the psalmist's own sin and foolishness (vv. 3b, 5). Therefore the writer confesses his or her sins (v. 18).

Suffering may come as a result of wrongdoing. But there is another sort of suffering that comes to the innocent. This is the suffering experienced by the writer of Psalm 73 and in the book of Job. And in an especially profound view of suffering, the prophet claims that through the suffering of one, God takes away the punishment that belongs to many (Isaiah 52–53).

A friend or counselor dealing with one who is suffering will want to avoid giving easy answers to some of these most puzzling of life's questions. This psalm suggests that we can trust in a God who knows all our longing and our sighing, even when we don't have the answers, nor even the strength or clarity of mind to say to that loving God, "Do not forsake me . . . make haste to help me."

A PSALM FOR SOJOURNERS
Psalm 39

To the leader: to Jeduthun. A Psalm of David.

39:1 I said, "I will guard my ways
    that I may not sin with my tongue;
  I will keep a muzzle on my mouth
    as long as the wicked are in my presence."
  2 I was silent and still;
    I held my peace to no avail;
  my distress grew worse,
  3 my heart became hot within me.
  While I mused, the fire burned;
    then I spoke with my tongue:

4 "LORD, let me know my end,
　　and what is the measure of my days;
　　let me know how fleeting my life is.
5 You have made my days a few handbreadths,
　　and my lifetime is as nothing in your sight.
　Surely everyone stands as a mere breath.   *Selah*
6 　Surely everyone goes about like a shadow.
　Surely for nothing they are in turmoil;
　　they heap up, and do not know who will gather.

7 "And now, O Lord, what do I wait for?
　　My hope is in you.
8 Deliver me from all my transgressions.
　　Do not make me the scorn of the fool.
9 I am silent; I do not open my mouth,
　　for it is you who have done it.
10 Remove your stroke from me;
　　I am worn down by the blows of your hand.
11 "You chastise mortals
　　in punishment for sin,
　consuming like a moth what is dear to them;
　　surely everyone is a mere breath.   *Selah*

12 "Hear my prayer, O LORD,
　　and give ear to my cry;
　　do not hold your peace at my tears.
　For I am your passing guest,
　　an alien, like all my forebears.
13 Turn your gaze away from me, that I may smile again,
　　before I depart and am no more."

Sojourner—the word has an old-fashioned, biblical ring. It comes from the Latin *sub* + *diurnus*, through the French *sous* + *jour*, literally "for a day." My dictionary defines the word as one who lives in a place temporarily, as on a visit.

Abraham described himself as "a stranger and a sojourner" when he was living temporarily in Hittite territory (Gen. 23:4, RSV). Moses said of the years he spent living in Midian, "I have been a sojourner in a foreign land" (Exod. 2:22, RSV).

Sojourner can have another sense in the Bible. It can be used for the totality of a person's existence, picturing a whole lifetime as a journey or sojourn. The aged Jacob said to the ruler of Egypt, "The years of my earthly sojourn are one hundred thirty" (Gen. 47:9). The writer of

Hebrews says of Abraham and Sarah that they "sojourned in the land of promise, as in a foreign land, living in tents" (Heb. 11:9, RSV).

It is with this second sense that the word is used in Psalm 39. The writer understands his existence as that of "someone who lives in a place temporarily, as on a visit." The psalmist speaks to God: "For I am your passing guest, a sojourner, like all my ancestors" (v. 12, RSV adapted)

The heading associates the psalm with David and dedicates it to the choir director (see on Psalm 4). Jeduthun was a musician on King David's staff (2 Chron. 5:12); Psalm 62 is also linked with him. The psalm falls into two major sections, with three subdivisions in the second section. Verses 1–3 are an introduction, telling why the writer could no longer keep silent. Verses 4–13 are a prayer in three parts, each new section introduced by "LORD" or "O Lord" (vv. 4–6, 7–11, 12–13).

A Time to Speak (39:1–3)

"Silence is golden," goes the old saying, and the book of Proverbs would agree: "When words are many, transgression is not lacking, but the prudent are restrained in speech," says Proverbs 10:19 (see also 11:12–13; 13:3; 17:27).

The psalmist was quite aware of this advice about too many words and too much babbling. In fact, the writer of this psalm indicates that for a long time, he said nothing about his difficult situation, apparently caused by friction with persons close by. But finally it was too much. "My distress grew worse, my heart became hot within me," he says. The biblical wisdom tradition also says that there is a time to speak (Eccl. 3:7). "And now," the psalmist has finally concluded, "this is such a time!" There was something like a fire within his bones (as in Jer. 20:9) that could no longer be held back. What could be of such burning significance?

A Puff of Smoke (39:4–6)

Something has suddenly made the psalmist aware of the shortness of life. What it was he does not indicate. Other biblical voices also lament the brevity of human life (Job 14:1–2; Ps. 90:9–12; 109:23; 144:3–4; James 4:14). The writer of this psalm asks the Lord to give it to him straight: "Let me know how fleeting my life is!" (Ps. 39:4).

The psalmist offers the results of his considerable reflection on the subject (vv. 1–3; these were no "off-the-cuff" remarks) in a series of three sentences, each beginning with an emphatic "Surely!"

1. "Surely everyone stands as a *mere breath*" (in Hebrew, *hebel*; v. 5). In Ecclesiastes, *hebel* occurs thirty-seven times, usually translated "vanity."

The word means something that is temporary and without substance, like a vapor or a breath (Prov. 21:6; Isa. 57:13). "Blow a puff of smoke into the air and consider it. Our lives are like that," says this psalm. (For *Selah*, see on Psalm 3.)

2. "Surely everyone goes about like a shadow," says verse 6.

3. "Surely for nothing they are in turmoil" (v. 6). What of all our feverish activity, our gathering of goods and goodies? "You can't take it with you" is the old saying. Ecclesiastes had said, "You will leave all you have gathered to someone else!" (Eccl. 2:18–22; 6:2; see also Ps. 49:10; Sir. 11:18–19 and 14:15). Again, it is really all as lasting as a puff of smoke ("for nothing" translates *hebel* in v. 6).

My Hope Is in You (39:7–11)

"And now" signals that something very important is coming. Of first importance is an answer to a question the writer asks himself. This is not a statement *about* the Lord ("My hope is in the Lord") but rather a personal confession of faith, speaking *to* the Lord: "My hope is in you." Following are three requests, addressed to the Lord: (1) "Deliver me from my rebellions against you!" (2) "Don't make me an object of ridicule!" (3) "Take away the blows of your hand!" (vv. 8, 10, paraphrased). These requests reveal the psalmist's situation. He is worn down, an object of scorn, and ill. He sees his illness as coming from the Lord. He understands his suffering as the Lord's punishment (v. 11). And yet, through all this, he says that his only possible hope is with the Lord! Then he takes another look at himself and repeats the Ecclesiastes sort of refrain: "surely everyone is a mere breath" (v. 11; *hebel*).

A Sojourner, like My Ancestors (39:12–13)

The final section of the prayer again begins with an address to the Lord: "Hear my prayer, O Lord!" The one praying is hurting; he refers to tears (v. 12). Here is an illuminating insight into the situation of this person before God: "I am your passing guest, a sojourner, like all my ancestors" (v. 12, RSV adapted).

Like old Jacob, the psalmist understands his life as a journey, a sojourn (Gen. 47:9). Like those ancestors in the faith, the psalmist knows that existence on this earth is "for a time," ever on the way toward that "city that has foundations" (Heb. 11:8–10). He knows what the rich farmer had forgotten: that his earthly sojourn had a beginning and would also have an end (Luke 12:13–21).

Finally, the psalmist can take no more of this suffering, perceived as the Lord's discipline, and asks that the Lord now leave him alone! Then he will smile again, knowing that in the Lord there is hope (v. 13).

GOOD NEWS BULLETIN
Psalm 40

To the leader. Of David. A Psalm.

40:1 I waited patiently for the LORD;
    he inclined to me and heard my cry.
  ² He drew me up from the desolate pit,
    out of the miry bog,
  and set my feet upon a rock,
    making my steps secure.
  ³ He put a new song in my mouth,
    a song of praise to our God.
  Many will see and fear,
    and put their trust in the LORD.

  ⁴ Happy are those who make
    the LORD their trust,
  who do not turn to the proud,
    to those who go astray after false gods.
  ⁵ You have multiplied, O LORD my God,
    your wondrous deeds and your thoughts toward us;
    none can compare with you.
  Were I to proclaim and tell of them,
    they would be more than can be counted.

  ⁶ Sacrifice and offering you do not desire,
    but you have given me an open ear.
  Burnt offering and sin offering
    you have not required.
  ⁷ Then I said, "Here I am;
    in the scroll of the book it is written of me.
  ⁸ I delight to do your will, O my God;
    your law is within my heart."

  ⁹ I have told the glad news of deliverance
    in the great congregation;
  see, I have not restrained my lips,
    as you know, O LORD.
  ¹⁰ I have not hidden your saving help within my heart,
    I have spoken of your faithfulness and your salvation;

I have not concealed your steadfast love and your faithfulness
   from the great congregation.

11 Do not, O LORD, withhold
   your mercy from me;
let your steadfast love and your faithfulness
   keep me safe forever.
12 For evils have encompassed me
   without number;
my iniquities have overtaken me,
   until I cannot see;
they are more than the hairs of my head,
   and my heart fails me.

13 Be pleased, O LORD, to deliver me;
   O LORD, make haste to help me.
14 Let all those be put to shame and confusion
   who seek to snatch away my life;
let those be turned back and brought to dishonor
   who desire my hurt.
15 Let those be appalled because of their shame
   who say to me, "Aha, Aha!"

16 But may all who seek you
   rejoice and be glad in you;
may those who love your salvation
   say continually, "Great is the LORD!"
17 As for me, I am poor and needy,
   but the Lord takes thought for me.
You are my help and my deliverer;
   do not delay, O my God.

The words heard on the radio or seen on a television screen always catch one's attention: "We interrupt this program to bring you an important message!" Then follows a news bulletin, reporting an event of special significance.

There is something of that atmosphere of a news report about this psalm. The psalmist hints at a dramatic rescue (v. 2), refers to a scroll where the event is recorded (v. 7), and indicates that the story of this rescue has been told in the presence of the gathered congregation (v. 9). And now, it appears, the writer is in need of rescue once again (vv. 12, 17).

The heading indicates that the piece is dedicated to the worship leader and identifies it as a psalm linked to the David tradition (see on Psalm 3).

The psalm falls into three sections: (1) verses 1–4 tell a story of a rescue and then conclude with a "happy are those" saying; (2) verses 5–10 speak of a joyful life, guided by the Lord's instruction (NRSV, "law") or *torah* and witnessing to the congregation; (3) verses 11–17 are a cry to be rescued from troubles.

Verses 13–17 are almost identical with Psalm 70. This indicates something about the composition of the psalms. Much like modern-day writers, composers, or preachers, the psalmists often quoted from existing materials. In this case, we cannot tell whether the writer of Psalm 40 was quoting the material in Psalm 70 or the other way around. In either case, we are given an insight into the workshops where these psalms were put together. If a song or a written piece fits in with what the writer wants to say, then why not use it!

A Song and a Saying (40:1–4)

The psalmist wants to tell other members of the community (v. 9) a story about how the Lord's help finally came, after a long period of waiting. Though we are not told exactly what the trouble was, the picture of being pulled out of a slimy swamp and set on a solid rock suggests a dramatic rescue of some sort. Perhaps the psalmist had been ill and experienced an unexpected recovery, in a manner similar to the events behind Psalm 30.

The natural response to such a rescue, from one who believes in God, is to say or to sing "Praise the Lord!" This psalmist gives credit to God not only for the rescue but also for the inspiration that resulted in the "new song" he is now singing.

Some clues here suggest how both biblical psalms and biblical wisdom literature came into being. A person is in a difficult situation and prays for help. The help comes, and that person tells the story to the congregation by means of a song. Then, on further reflection, that individual formulates a saying that summarizes what he learned and that is designed to teach the congregation. The saying in verse 4 fits into the pattern of the "happy are those" sayings and recommends banking on the Lord, rather than on other people or other gods.

What Is True Religion? (40:5–10)

This segment begins with words of praise, directed to the Lord as "You" (v. 5). Religion that is acceptable to the Lord, according to verse 6, does not consist only in the making of offerings and sacrifices. This notion is stated elsewhere in both psalms (51:16–17) and prophetic sayings (Hos. 6:6; Amos 5:21–24). This psalm says that true religion involves *doing*

God's will as expressed in God's *torah*, or instruction, written in the believer's heart (v. 8).

Verses 9–10 give expression to another dimension of true religion in the biblical sense. The psalmist has not kept his experience of being delivered to himself but has "told the glad news" to the congregation. He experienced the Lord's saving help, the Lord's steadfast love, the Lord's faithfulness, and he has made it a point to tell others in the believing community about these things.

Do It Again, Lord! (40:11–17)

With this section of the psalm, the mood changes completely. Now there is no more talk of happiness, delight, and glad news. Now the psalm speaks of evils, iniquities, murderous plots, symptoms of heart failure. Here is a prayer from someone who is in deep trouble. The prayer begins and ends with urgent cries to the Lord for immediate help (vv. 11, 17). The psalmist has told others about the faithfulness and love and mercy of the Lord; now, once again, he is in need of those things himself (v. 11).

Verse 12 describes the difficulty of the situation. The psalmist asks for help—immediate help—and then brings a double request before the Lord: "Let my enemies be shamed, and let all who are on your side rejoice!" (vv. 13–16). The psalm ends with "I am weak, but you are strong!" and then with a final plea for quick action on God's part (v. 17).

I Love to Tell the Story

"I love to tell the story" is the first line of an old favorite hymn, and it fits well with what is said in this psalm. Despite the desperate situation of the writer as expressed in the last part of the psalm, the mood of this piece is one of trust and happiness: "Happy are those who make the LORD their trust" (v. 4). The life of believers is not a lusterless, boring existence, hedged in by "do nots," but is rather a life marked by joy and delight (v. 8). And a part of that life involves telling the entire congregation what God has done (vv. 9–10).

I have been part of worship services where persons have spoken or written out prayer requests for God's help in connection with problems in their lives. I don't recall a service, however, where individuals have spoken or written out stories of healings or good things they have experienced in answer to prayer. Rather than "Let me tell you what the Lord has done," the motto of Christians at worship is often "I've got a secret!"

With the stories and the Story that Christians have to tell, maybe the course of a programmed worship service could be interrupted from time to time for an important message, a special report, a "good news" bulletin.

THE WAY TO HAPPINESS
Psalm 41

To the leader.
A Psalm of David.

41:1 Happy are those who consider the poor;
         the LORD delivers them in the day of trouble.
2 The LORD protects them and keeps them alive;
         they are called happy in the land.
         You do not give them up to the will of their enemies.
3 The LORD sustains them on their sickbed;
         in their illness you heal all their infirmities.

4 As for me, I said, "O LORD, be gracious to me;
         heal me, for I have sinned against you."
5 My enemies wonder in malice
         when I will die, and my name perish.
6 And when they come to see me, they utter empty words,
         while their hearts gather mischief;
         when they go out, they tell it abroad.
7 All who hate me whisper together about me;
         they imagine the worst for me.

8 They think that a deadly thing has fastened on me,
         that I will not rise again from where I lie.
9 Even my bosom friend in whom I trusted,
         who ate of my bread, has lifted the heel against me.
10 But you, O LORD, be gracious to me,
         and raise me up, that I may repay them.

11 By this I know that you are pleased with me;
         because my enemy has not triumphed over me.
12 But you have upheld me because of my integrity,
         and set me in your presence forever.

13 Blessed be the LORD, the God of Israel,
         from everlasting to everlasting.
                                    Amen and Amen.

This psalm closes Book I of the book of Psalms (Psalms 1–41) and gives evidence of that closing function. The opening words, "Happy are those . . . ," reach back to link up with the beginning of Book I, in Psalm 1:1. Psalm 1 described happiness in terms of the delight that comes from studying the scriptures; Psalm 41 speaks of the happiness that results from helping the poor. Considering these two psalms as "bookends" for Book I can be a reminder that biblical religion includes both immersion in the scriptures and involvement in the problems of the poor.

The central part of the psalm is a *prayer*, addressed to the Lord and exhibiting elements typical of the lament (vv. 4–10; see Psalm 13). The *requests* in verses 4 and 10, "LORD, be gracious," frame a *"they" complaint* in verses 5–9. Verses 11 and 12 affirm the psalmist's *trust* in the Lord's ongoing help, while verse 13 functions to wrap up Book I on a note of praise.

The heading dedicates the psalm to the director of worship and concludes the long series of psalms associated with David (see on Psalm 3).

The Way to Happiness (41:1–3)

The psalms that open and close Book I both begin by speaking of happiness. Psalm 1 depicts a person who is truly happy as one who is absorbed in reading, "chewing on" the teachings of the Lord as presented in the psalms (see the comments on Psalm 1). Psalm 41 also speaks of happiness, but now the kind of happiness that comes from giving help to those who are poor.

To "consider" the poor (v. 1) means to reflect on, think about, be attentive to their situation; the same Hebrew word occurs in Proverbs 16:20 ("are attentive"), in Psalm 64:9 ("ponder"), and in Psalm 101:2 and Nehemiah 8:13 ("study"). Concern for the widow, the orphan, and the poor is a mark of biblical ethics from the beginning of the Old Testament and continuing through the New. The idea here is that concern for the powerless is a characteristic of the lifestyle of the people of God.

God Answers Prayer (41:4–12)

Having stated that the Lord helps the Lord's people (vv. 1–3), the writer provides an example of that help with a flashback, telling a story of suffering and deliverance.

The story begins with the teller admitting having sinned and reporting his prayer: "O LORD, be gracious to me; heal me" (v. 4; see also v. 10). Verses 5–9 are an extended "they" complaint, describing the behavior of certain "enemies" of the psalmist. They are "miserable comforters," like those who made a pastoral call on Job (v. 6; see Job 16:2). Far from keeping the discussions confidential, they broadcast the psalmist's problems throughout the community. Even an old, trusted friend turned against the psalmist (v. 9). The writer of the Fourth Gospel understood Judas's actions to be a similar kind of betrayal (John 13:18).

Verses 11 and 12 indicate that the time of being persecuted is past, and life is back on track. That was then, and for the psalmist, now is now. The original psalm closes on a positive note, with words of trust: "you have upheld me . . . and set me in your presence forever" (v. 12).

Verse 13 has been inserted by the editor of the book of Psalms as a word of praise to close Book I. Similar words of praise conclude the other books: Psalms 72:18–20; 89:52; 106:48; and the whole of 150, which closes the entire Psalter.

Will the Poor Have You with Them?

It was Jesus who once said, "The poor you will always have with you" (Matt. 26:11, NIV). This psalm raises the question "Will the poor have you (God's people) with them?" Concern for the widow, the orphan, and the poor is a theme running through the Bible; see Exodus 22:21–24; Leviticus 19:33–34; Deuteronomy 14:28–29; 24:19–22; Isaiah 1:10–17, 21–26; 5:1–7; 10:1–4; Amos 2:6–8; 4:1–3; 5:10–12; 8:4–8; Micah 2:1–5; 6:6–8; Matthew 25:31–46; James 1:26–2:7; and many others.

A story is told about the Hasidic rabbi Levi Yitzhak of Berditchev, Poland. Rabbi Yitzhak was one of the great religious figures of his time and was often sought out for miracles, healings, and the like. One thing was unusual about him: in solidarity with the poor, he dressed like a beggar, going from house to house, person to person, raising funds for widows, orphans, and poor persons.

One day he wished to travel to Pinsk in Poland and so got on the train and took a seat. Two wealthy gentlemen stepped into the same train car. When they could find no seats together and saw this person they thought was a beggar sitting alone, they told him to move to the back of the train. He did.

When they got to the station, the gentlemen noticed a huge crowd, obviously waiting for someone important. Then, to their surprise, they saw that when the man they thought was a beggar stepped out of the train, the crowds shouted and carried him on their shoulders.

"Who is that person?" they asked someone in the crowd. "Are you the only one in Poland that doesn't know?" was the reply. "That's Levi Yitzhak, the greatest rabbi of our time!"

The men felt terrible. They shoved their way through the crowd. They came up to the rabbi. "Rabbi, we apologize for insulting you," they said, "but how could we have known who you were? We thought you were just a poor beggar!"

"Don't worry," said the rabbi. "Don't apologize to me. You didn't insult me. You insulted a poor beggar. So the next time you see a poor beggar, go and apologize to him."

Biblical religion has a long tradition of concern for the poor. Jesus once commended caring for the hungry and thirsty, saying, "Just as you did it to one of the least of these who are members of my family, you did it to me" (Matt. 25:40).

According to Psalm 41, the way to happiness for God's people involves considering not only the Bible (Psalm 1) or even the ravens (Luke 12:24) but also considering and caring for the poor.

2. Book II
PSALMS 42–72

WHY MUST I BE SO SAD?
Psalms 42–43

Psalm 42

To the leader. A Maskil of the Korahites.

42:1 As a deer longs for flowing streams,
    so my soul longs for you, O God.
  ² My soul thirsts for God,
    for the living God.
  When shall I come and behold
    the face of God?
  ³ My tears have been my food
    day and night,
  while people say to me continually,
    "Where is your God?"

  ⁴ These things I remember,
    as I pour out my soul:
  how I went with the throng,
    and led them in procession to the house of God,
  with glad shouts and songs of thanksgiving,
    a multitude keeping festival.
  ⁵ Why are you cast down, O my soul,
    and why are you disquieted within me?
  Hope in God; for I shall again praise him,
    my help⁶ and my God.

  My soul is cast down within me;
    therefore I remember you
  from the land of Jordan and of Hermon,
    from Mount Mizar.
  ⁷ Deep calls to deep
    at the thunder of your cataracts;

all your waves and your billows
    have gone over me.
8 By day the LORD commands his steadfast love,
    and at night his song is with me,
    a prayer to the God of my life.

9 I say to God, my rock,
    "Why have you forgotten me?
Why must I walk about mournfully
    because the enemy oppresses me?"
10 As with a deadly wound in my body,
    my adversaries taunt me,
while they say to me continually,
    "Where is your God?"

11 Why are you cast down, O my soul,
    and why are you disquieted within me?
Hope in God; for I shall again praise him,
    my help and my God.

Psalm 43

43:1 Vindicate me, O God, and defend my cause
    against an ungodly people;
from those who are deceitful and unjust
    deliver me!
2 For you are the God in whom I take refuge;
    why have you cast me off?
Why must I walk about mournfully
    because of the oppression of the enemy?

3 O send out your light and your truth;
    let them lead me;
let them bring me to your holy hill
    and to your dwelling.
4 Then I will go to the altar of God,
    to God my exceeding joy;
and I will praise you with the harp,
    O God, my God.

5 Why are you cast down, O my soul,
    and why are you disquieted within me?
Hope in God; for I shall again praise him,
    my help and my God.

Why must I be so sad? This double psalm raises that question three times (42:5, 11; 43:5). The psalm provides clues for answering that recurring question. The writer longs for the presence of God and for the old, familiar experiences of worshiping with the people of God (42:1–5). The psalmist is far away from home, feeling forgotten by God and being harassed by the people around him (42:6–11). The psalm writer asks God to rescue him and to bring him to the place of worship (43:1–5).

Why must I be so sad? The psalmist's problem could be diagnosed as *homesickness*, a deep longing to be back in familiar places with the family of God and, in fact, to be back with God. What do Psalms 42 and 43 have to say to such sadness, to such longing?

Some Preliminaries

A few preliminary observations are in order. First, it is clear that Psalms 42 and 43 were originally one psalm and, in the process of being passed on, were separated. There is a common refrain in 42:5 and 11 and 43:5. While almost all the psalms of Book II have headings (Psalm 71 is an exception), Psalm 43 has none. Psalm 42 has some elements of the lament (see on Psalm 13): *complaint* in the "I," "you," "they" forms and *affirmation of trust*. Psalm 43 supplies the other elements, with a *request* (v. 1) and a *vow to praise* (v. 4). Taken together, these two psalms make up a typical lament. Finally, a footnote in the Hebrew Bible indicates that many Hebrew manuscripts join these two as one psalm.

Second, the location of Psalms 42–43 in the book of Psalms is of interest. The psalm stands at the beginning of Book II, indicating that the editors thought it was of special importance.

This psalm is also the first of the "Korahite" psalms, a collection associated with professional musicians (2 Chron. 20:19) and including Psalms 42–49, 84–85, and 87–88. Again, this initial position may be an indication of the psalm's special significance. (For a brief discussion of "Maskil," see the comments on Psalm 32.)

Finally, this is the first of the "elohistic psalms," a collection of psalms running from Psalm 42 through Psalm 83 and preferring the more general name *'elohim* or "God" to Yahweh (NRSV, "LORD"), the specific name of the God of Israel. As an example, notice the way in which Psalm 14 has been changed in the elohistic psalter: in Psalm 14, "LORD" (Yahweh) occurs in verses 2, 4, and 7; in Psalm 53 in the elohistic psalter, each of these has been replaced by *'elohim*, translated "God" (Ps. 53:2, 4, 6; compare also Ps. 40:13–17 with the elohistic Psalm 70).

The psalm divides into three sections, each concluding with a refrain: (1) 42:1–5; (2) 42:6–11; (3) 43:1–5.

When Will I See You Again, God? (42:1–5)

Why must I be so sad? The problem animating this prayer is a theological one: the psalmist feels abandoned by God. Such is the sense of the questions raised in verses 5 and 11 and in 43:5. The aching for some sort of connection with God is compared to the sort of thirst a deer has after a strenuous run, when it longs for cool, refreshing water. Even mealtime has not brought relief, only more weeping. And the associates with whom the psalmist is living keep asking the same question the psalmist is asking: "Where is your God?" (v. 3).

With verse 4 the psalmist turns to the past ("These things I remember"), seeking to find help for enduring the present and facing the future. He is lonesome not only for God but also for the people of God, as he recalls those times of festivals and worship, with processions, music, even shouting for joy.

The refrain in verse 5 begins with an "I" complaint. The psalmist is bent over like one going about in mourning (the Hebrew word behind "cast down" is translated "bowed down" in Ps. 35:14). There is a roaring going on inside him, like the roaring of the waves of the sea (Jer. 5:22), that will not be calmed. Nonetheless, he expresses trust and hope in God.

Why Have You Forgotten Me, God? (42:6–11)

Verse 6 makes an important point. Again, the psalmist refers to his soul as "cast down within me." We might put it, "I feel so sad!" And in this situation, the psalmist again says, "I remember"; but this time what he remembers is not the congregation (v. 4). Addressing God, he says, "I remember you."

Part of his problem seems to be geographical. He is located in the north, near Mount Hermon, a long way from the temple in Jerusalem. But even in this situation, he can pray. The direct address to God continues with verse 7, where the psalmist declares, "You have almost drowned me, God!" His troubles have been like mighty waves rolling over him, and he is convinced that these waves have been sent by God. Verse 8 is an interesting description of this psalm: "a prayer to the God of my life."

The two "why" questions raised in verse 9 express all three dimensions of the psalmist's troubles. The questions are raised against the background of trust: "God, my rock" is the way the prayer begins. But now the writer believes that God, who has been the rock on which he relied, is no longer reliable. He puts the question to God directly: "Why have *you* forgotten me?" (See also the discussion of Ps. 22:1.) His life has become miserable; once again there is a "why" question, this time in the form of an "I" complaint: "Why must I walk about mournfully?" In a final "they" complaint, the psalmist repeats the charge made in verse 3: people around him are taunting him with "Where is your God?"

Lead Me! (43:1–5)

At the heart of these combined psalms are the requests expressed in 43:1 and 3: "Take up my cause, Lord! Deliver me! Lead me back to your temple!" The request is supported in verse 2 by another affirmation of trust, "For you are the God in whom I take refuge" (compare "God, my rock" in 42:9), and then the "why" questions of 42:9 are repeated.

The psalm closes with a repetition of the questions in the refrain "Why do I feel so sad?" and then a restatement of the call to hope and the vow to praise. Though the relationship has been strained, God remains "*my* God."

The Big Questions

Why do I feel so sad? That question is stated three times in the psalm. The sadness, we discovered, has three aspects. The psalmist feels alienated from God, cut off from fellow believers, and harassed by those around him. As a result of all of this, he feels bent down, churning inside, about to go under. The psalmist formulates his desperate situation in terms of questions. The psalmist wonders, "When will I be back in touch with God again?" (42:2). People ask him, "Where is your God?" (42:3, 10). He asks God, "Why have you forgotten me? Why must I be so sad?" (42:9; 43:2b).

The psalm does not pick up these questions one at a time and provide answers. The questions remain questions. We also notice that the one in such desperate straits looks to the past, remembering the good times when the community was at worship (42:4), remembering God, even from far away in a distant land (42:6). Remembering what God has done in the past somehow seems to help with the difficulties of the present (see also Psalm 22).

After an honest diagnosis of the situation in the present (the "why" questions in the three refrains) and an intense recall of how things had been with God in the past, the psalmist is able to go on living. In fact, the psalmist ends on a note of hope, with the expectation that one day there will be joy again, and he will again take his place in the temple orchestra, playing music in praise of God (43:4).

WHY US, LORD?
Psalm 44

To the leader. Of the Korahites. A Maskil.

44:1 We have heard with our ears, O God,
  our ancestors have told us,
 what deeds you performed in their days,
  in the days of old:
 ² you with your own hand drove out the nations,
  but them you planted;
 you afflicted the peoples,
  but them you set free;
 ³ for not by their own sword did they win the land,
  nor did their own arm give them victory;
 but your right hand, and your arm,
  and the light of your countenance,
  for you delighted in them.

 ⁴ You are my King and my God;
  you command victories for Jacob.
 ⁵ Through you we push down our foes;
  through your name we tread down our assailants.
 ⁶ For not in my bow do I trust,
  nor can my sword save me.
 ⁷ But you have saved us from our foes,
  and have put to confusion those who hate us.
 ⁸ In God we have boasted continually,
  and we will give thanks to your name forever.   *Selah*

 ⁹ Yet you have rejected us and abased us,
  and have not gone out with our armies.
 ¹⁰ You made us turn back from the foe,
  and our enemies have gotten spoil.
 ¹¹ You have made us like sheep for slaughter,
  and have scattered us among the nations.
 ¹² You have sold your people for a trifle,
  demanding no high price for them.

 ¹³ You have made us the taunt of our neighbors,
  the derision and scorn of those around us.
 ¹⁴ You have made us a byword among the nations,
  a laughingstock among the peoples.
 ¹⁵ All day long my disgrace is before me,
  and shame has covered my face

¹⁶ at the words of the taunters and revilers,
   at the sight of the enemy and the avenger.

¹⁷ All this has come upon us,
   yet we have not forgotten you,
   or been false to your covenant.
¹⁸ Our heart has not turned back,
   nor have our steps departed from your way,
¹⁹ yet you have broken us in the haunt of jackals,
   and covered us with deep darkness.

²⁰ If we had forgotten the name of our God,
   or spread out our hands to a strange god,
²¹ would not God discover this?
   For he knows the secrets of the heart.
²² Because of you we are being killed all day long,
   and accounted as sheep for the slaughter.

²³ Rouse yourself! Why do you sleep, O Lord?
   Awake, do not cast us off forever!
²⁴ Why do you hide your face?
   Why do you forget our affliction and oppression?
²⁵ For we sink down to the dust;
   our bodies cling to the ground.
²⁶ Rise up, come to our help.
   Redeem us for the sake of your steadfast love.

The Jewish writer Abraham Heschel dedicates his study of the prophets "To the martyrs of 1939–1945" and quotes from Psalm 44:

> All this has come upon us,
> Though we have not forgotten Thee,
> Or been false to Thy covenant.
> Our heart has not turned back,
> Nor have our steps departed from Thy way . . .
> . . . for Thy sake we are slain . . .
> Why dost Thou hide Thy face? (vv. 17–24)
> (*The Prophets*)

The feelings of Jews who had experienced the Nazi Holocaust were best expressed by this psalm, Heschel believed.

The psalm is dedicated to the worship leader. For comments on Korahites, see my discussion on Psalms 42–43; for Maskil, see the discussion on Psalm 32.

The psalm falls into three sections: (1) verses 1–8 are introductory, recalling the mighty things God had done in the *past* (vv. 1–3), affirming trust in this God for the *present* (vv. 4–7), and promising to praise God in the *future* (v. 8); (2) the heart of the psalm is the long complaint about the *present* situation in verses 9–22; (3) the conclusion in verses 23–26 looks toward the *future*, addressing the Lord with a series of requests for help and with more complaints.

This is the first of eleven psalms that express prayers of the people from various situations of distress. These are the *community laments* and include Psalms 44, 60, 74, 79, 80, 83, 85, 90, 94, 123, and 137.

The Past: You Have Done Much for Us, Lord! (44:1–8)

An individual speaking for the assembled congregation addresses God in prayer, reminding the Lord (and the congregation) that their parents and grandparents had told them many stories about how God had helped them in the past (vv. 1–3). The psalmist puts in a good word for the people: "Remember," he says to the Lord, "how you delighted in them!" (v. 3).

The psalm identifies God as king, commander, saver from enemies, and the object of the community's boasting. It assures the Lord, "We will give thanks to your name forever." (For *Selah*, see the comments on Psalm 3.)

The Present: The Bad Shepherd (44:9–22)

That was then, says the psalm, but this is now! This section dealing with the present begins with a series of unusually sharp barbs aimed directly at "you, God." In the past, God had given the people victories (vv. 2–3); now there are only defeats (vv. 9–10). In the past, the Lord had been known as the "good shepherd" for these people (Pss. 23; 74; 79:13; 80; 95:7; 100:3); now the Lord is like a bad shepherd, scattering the people among the nations like so many sheep, selling them off for less than they are worth (vv. 11–12). Verses 13–16 report the scorn and taunting experienced from neighbors; again, the fault is placed clearly with "you," referring to the Lord (vv. 13–14).

Behind verses 17–22 lies one question: Why? These people knew that breaking the agreement or covenant with God would bring trouble; a quick reading of the book of Judges makes that clear. But the psalmist claims they have not done that, saying, "We have not forgotten you, Lord, we have not been unfaithful!" Lest this sound like boasting, we have been reminded that these people have a long history with God (vv. 1–3) and have been faithful in giving thanks (vv. 1–8).

The Future: Why Won't You Help Us, Lord? (44:23–26)

The last section of the psalm is framed with a series of desperate cries addressed to the Lord: "Rouse yourself! Wake up! Don't cast us off! Rise up! Come to our help! Save us!" These are prayers from a people who don't know what to do or where to turn. These "why" questions are fired at the Lord: "Why do you sleep? Why do you hide? Why do you forget?"

The last word of the psalm, only one word in Hebrew, gives a ray of hope in all this darkness. "Redeem us for the sake of *your steadfast love.*"

Why, Lord?

The Jewish writer Elie Wiesel tells the story of a caretaker of a synagogue in a town in Eastern Europe in World War II. It was the caretaker's custom to prepare the synagogue for worship each morning, then to step to the front and address the Lord in a strong and confident voice: "I have come to inform you, Master of the Universe, that we are here!" After that introduction, the service would begin.

Then came the first massacre of the Jews, followed by others. Somehow the caretaker escaped. He would continue each morning to run to the synagogue, pound his fist on the lectern, and announce, "You see Lord, we are still here."

The morning after the last massacre, he did what he always did, sweeping, cleaning, preparing the synagogue for worship. This time he, the last living Jew in the town, was the only one who came for worship. Alone in the deserted synagogue, he stood in the front, stretched out his hands in prayer, and whispered, "Master of the Universe, you see? I am still here!"

He stopped before continuing in his sad, quiet voice, addressing the Lord: "But you, where are you?" (as heard; see Wiesel's *One Generation After*, pp. 90–91, for a printed version).

Where are you, Lord? Why did you allow this to happen, Lord? These are the hard questions that the psalms ask and that believers continue to ask. Some have said, Why must a whole people suffer? The biblical books from Deuteronomy through 2 Kings give one answer. After recounting example after example of the people's rebellion against God, 2 Kings 17 reports the destruction of the capital city of Israel and the deportation of the people. "This occurred," says the biblical writer, "because the people of Israel had sinned against the LORD" (v. 7).

But this time, says Psalm 44, the people have not sinned but have remained faithful. So why should these innocent persons suffer? The psalm does not answer the "why" question. Psalm 73 wrestles with it at an individual level, as does the book of Job. The best the psalmist can do is affirm continued trust and hope in the Lord's "steadfast love" (v. 26).

That hope and trust are taken up into a longer melody in a brighter key by the apostle Paul, who cites verse 22 of this psalm and declares that nothing, no matter what the world throws at us, "will be able to separate us from the love of God in Christ Jesus our Lord" (Rom. 8:38–39; see vv. 18–39).

HERE COMES THE BRIDE
Psalm 45

To the leader: according to Lilies.
Of the Korahites. A Maskil. A love song.

45:1 My heart overflows with a goodly theme;
    I address my verses to the king;
    my tongue is like the pen of a ready scribe.

  2 You are the most handsome of men;
    grace is poured upon your lips;
    therefore God has blessed you forever.
  3 Gird your sword on your thigh, O mighty one,
    in your glory and majesty.

  4 In your majesty ride on victoriously
    for the cause of truth and to defend the right;
    let your right hand teach you dread deeds.
  5 Your arrows are sharp
    in the heart of the king's enemies;
    the peoples fall under you.

  6 Your throne, O God, endures forever and ever.
    Your royal scepter is a scepter of equity;
  7   you love righteousness and hate wickedness.
  Therefore God, your God, has anointed you
    with the oil of gladness beyond your companions;
  8   your robes are all fragrant with myrrh and aloes and cassia.
  From ivory palaces stringed instruments make you glad;
  9   daughters of kings are among your ladies of honor;
    at your right hand stands the queen in gold of Ophir.

  10 Hear, O daughter, consider and incline your ear;
    forget your people and your father's house,

¹¹   and the king will desire your beauty.
      Since he is your lord, bow to him;
¹²   the people of Tyre will seek your favor with gifts,
      the richest of the people ¹³with all kinds of wealth.

      The princess is decked in her chamber with gold-woven robes;
¹⁴   in many-colored robes she is led to the king;
      behind her the virgins, her companions, follow.
¹⁵ With joy and gladness they are led along
      as they enter the palace of the king.

¹⁶ In the place of ancestors you, O king, shall have sons;
      you will make them princes in all the earth.
¹⁷ I will cause your name to be celebrated in all generations;
      therefore the peoples will praise you forever and ever.

Certain selections have become part of the traditional music used at weddings. There was a time when brides marched in to Richard Wagner's "Wedding March," popularly identified as "Here Comes the Bride." More recently, a trumpet and organ will bring in the bride with "Trumpet Voluntary" by Jeremiah Clarke or "Trumpet Tune" by Henry Purcell.

Weddings in Old Testament times also had their musical traditions. When a king married, one of the traditional songs accompanying the marriage was Psalm 45. Certain psalms were composed for events in the life of the king, designed to be used at an installation (Psalms 2, 72), before going into battle (Psalm 20), or after having won a victory (Psalm 21; see the discussion of these "royal psalms" with Psalm 2 above). To understand Psalm 45, we should consider it first of all in its connection with the wedding of a king.

The heading indicates that the psalm is dedicated to the director of music and that it was to be sung to a melody called "Lilies." Psalms 69 and 80 used the same melody. (For "Korahites" and "Maskil," see my comments on Psalms 42–43 and 32.)

After the introduction, in which the writer declares that his heart is bubbling over (v. 1), the poet addresses words to the royal bridegroom (vv. 2–9) and then to the bride (vv. 10–13a). A short description of the wedding procession follows (vv. 13b–15), and the piece concludes with some final words to the king (vv. 16–17).

Here Is the King! (45:2–9)

The writer of this psalm (not forgetting who was paying his salary!) begins by describing the king as handsome, a gifted speaker, and blessed by God (v. 2). He continues by describing his king as a great military leader who has achieved international success (vv. 3–4). The address "O God" in verse 6 has puzzled commentators: How could anyone, even a great king, be addressed as "God"? The answer appears to lie in the fact that these royal psalms (see the comments on Psalm 2) speak of the king in the most extravagant terms, much as poems and songs in neighboring countries did. Psalm 2:7 identifies the king as the Lord's son, and Isaiah 9:6 calls the future king "Mighty God." The extravagant language continues: the king is described as ruling forever, ruling with equity and righteousness. The king is, in fact, described as "messiah"; the Hebrew word behind *anointed* (v. 7) is from the same root as *messiah*.

The whole scene here is described in terms of beautiful sights (the handsome king, v. 2), smells (the perfumed robes, v. 7), and sounds (the string orchestra, v. 8). Present at the wedding are princesses from other lands, including the one who will become the wife of the king (v. 9).

Here Comes the Bride! (45:10–15)

With verse 10, the singer of this wedding song turns to address the bride, dressed in gold and standing to the right of the king (v. 9). In rather strong language, she is advised to forget her own people and her own family and to show loyalty to her new husband (vv. 10–11). Representatives from other nations are on hand for the wedding, bringing gifts—but also seeking the favor of the new monarch (vv. 12–13).

Verses 13b–15 provide a glimpse of the wedding procession. Again, the future queen is described as wearing gold. Following her are her friends, chosen as bridesmaids. The whole ceremony is marked by an atmosphere of celebration.

Children for the Future (45:16–17)

The biblical writers often remind their readers and hearers of what God has done for them in the past: "We have heard with our ears, O God, our ancestors have told us, what deeds you performed in their days" (Ps. 44:1–3). Here the focus is not on the parents and grandparents but on the children, and the concern is not with the past but with the future. "Your ancestors will disappear, but in their place you shall have sons," promises this psalm, "and these sons will occupy positions of leadership in nations throughout the world" (v. 16).

In another look at the future, the psalm promises that the name of this anointed one will be celebrated throughout earthly space ("in all the earth") and time ("forever and ever").

In These Last Days . . .

The writer of Hebrews in the New Testament began the letter by saying, "Long ago God spoke to our ancestors in many and various ways by the prophets, but in these last days he has spoken to us by a Son." As this writer reflected on the story of Jesus as the writer had heard it, a number of passages from the Hebrew Bible came to mind. After citing Psalm 2:7; 2 Samuel 7:14; Deuteronomy 32:43; and Psalm 104:4, the writer of Hebrews quotes Psalm 45:6–7, understanding these words as finding their fulfillment in the person of Jesus Christ, God's Son (Heb. 1:8–9).

The psalm had spoken about a king especially blessed, victorious, ruling forever, promoting equity and righteousness, and identified as anointed (literal Hebrew, "messiahed") by God. This king's name would be celebrated and praised by people from all over the world, forever and ever (Ps. 45:16–17).

As history worked itself out, the king for whom this wedding song was originally written did not measure up to the extravagant picture sketched by this and the other royal psalms. (See the discussion on Psalm 2.) Nor did the kings who followed. But when Jesus of Nazareth appeared on the scene, the writer to the Hebrews saw this psalm as yet another pointer to Jesus as the Son of God, the Messiah.

A MIGHTY FORTRESS
Psalm 46

To the leader. Of the Korahites.
According to Alamoth. A Song.

46:1 **God is our refuge and strength,**
    a very present help in trouble.
  2 **Therefore we will not fear, though the earth should change,**
    though the mountains shake in the heart of the sea;
  3 **though its waters roar and foam,**
    though the mountains tremble with its tumult.   *Selah*

  4 **There is a river whose streams make glad the city of God,**
    the holy habitation of the Most High.
  5 **God is in the midst of the city; it shall not be moved;**
    God will help it when the morning dawns.
  6 **The nations are in an uproar, the kingdoms totter;**
    he utters his voice, the earth melts.

⁷ **The LORD of hosts is with us;**
 the God of Jacob is our refuge. *Selah*

⁸ **Come, behold the works of the LORD;**
 see what desolations he has brought on the earth.
⁹ **He makes wars cease to the end of the earth;**
 he breaks the bow, and shatters the spear;
 he burns the shields with fire.
¹⁰ **"Be still, and know that I am God!**
 I am exalted among the nations,
 I am exalted in the earth."
¹¹ **The LORD of hosts is with us;**
 the God of Jacob is our refuge. *Selah*

"A mighty fortress is our God." So begins one of the most well known Christian hymns, written by Martin Luther and based on this psalm. The opening words appear in huge letters on the top of the tower of the Castle Church in Wittenberg, Germany, where Luther lived and taught: EIN FESTE BURG IST UNSER GOTT.

I gained a new insight into the sense of these words after a visit to the Wartburg Castle near Eisenach, where Luther lived in hiding for ten months in 1521 and 1522. "A half-hour," says the sign just out of Eisenach, as one begins hiking up the hill. After weaving back and forth through woods and rocks, one arrives finally at the Wartburg. *Ein' feste Burg*, that is, a mighty fortress, and so it is indeed: situated high on a hill, majestic, sturdy, solid, a place to live in security and safety, a place to get a new perspective on things. Such is the Wartburg—and our God is something like this, said Luther in his hymn.

The heading identifies this as another Korahite psalm, dedicated to the leader. (See the comments on Psalm 42.) "Alamoth" in Hebrew means "young women"; does the word here refer to a melody or to a song for women's voices? The matter is not clear.

The psalm divides into three sections, each concluded with *Selah*, indicating a pause: God and the threats of nature (vv. 1–3); God and the threats of the nations (vv. 4–7); God and the threat of war (vv. 8–11). The last two sections end with refrains in verses 7 and 11; a similar refrain may have once concluded the first section, after verse 3. The psalm, which celebrates the city of Jerusalem, can be considered a "song of Zion" along with Psalms 48 and 76, which also focus on that city. (See the comments with Psalm 87.) The dominant theme is trust in God, expressed in verses 1, 7, and 11. A similar *affirmation of trust* is one of the typical elements in the psalms of lament. (See the comments on Psalm 13.)

God and Nature (46:1–3)

Verse 1 states the theme of the psalm, affirming trust in God as "our refuge and strength." The same word *refuge* occurs in Psalm 104:18, referring to a place high in the mountains where rock badgers (NRSV, "coneys") may find safety. In Isaiah 25:4 the word denotes a "*shelter* from the rainstorm," and in Isaiah 4:6, a "*refuge* and a shelter from the storm and rain." If "refuge" refers to God as a place where one may find safety and security, "help" has a more active sense, identifying God as one who takes action to assist those in trouble. Such is the theme for this psalm.

Verses 2 and 3 then spell out some implications of that theme. We need not fear the worst that nature can throw at us, whether it be the earth quaking, mountains shaking, or floods.

God and the Nations (46:4–7)

Verses 4 and 5 identify the place where the protected people live. Watered by a river, it is the "city of God, the holy habitation of the Most High," that is, Jerusalem. The temple was located in Jerusalem. This was God's house, and God was there "in the midst of the city."

The reference to God's help "when the morning dawns" reminds the Bible reader of the dramatic rescue of the city that took place in the days of Isaiah, around 701 B.C. As reported in 2 Kings 19, the Assyrian emperor Sennacherib came up to Jerusalem with his armies to capture the city. But during the night, something terrible happened in the camp. In the morning, 185,000 Assyrian soldiers were lying dead. It was "the angel of the LORD" that struck them down, says 2 Kings 19:35. Is this psalm referring to this long-remembered, dramatic deliverance?

Verse 6 goes on to speak of a battle involving a number of nations. Kingdoms are falling; the heavens are thundering; the earth is melting. Is this some cosmic battle at the end of the world? Even if such were to come, continues the psalm, we would not need to fear, because

> the LORD of hosts is with us;
> the God of Jacob is our refuge.

God is our refuge and strength. The Lord is with us. And the God of Jacob, our ancestor, is our *refuge* (a different Hebrew word from that translated "refuge" in v. 1). This word refers to a high place, where inhabitants of a city find security (Deut. 2:36; Isa. 26:5, "lofty").

God and the Stillness (46:8–11)

After the roaring of the sea and the warring of the nations, the psalm portrays a time of quiet. The wars have come to an end. Programs of disarmament have been carried out, and the battlefields have been cleared. A voice says, "Be still, and know that I am God!" The nations have quit their battling; the earth its quaking. There is only this "Be still!" The psalm concludes with the congregation joining in the refrain a final time:

> The LORD of hosts is with us;
>   the God of Jacob is our refuge.

Peace, Be Still!

The working of God can be accompanied by the sounds of the storm and the roaring of waters and the whirling and crashing of great oak trees (Psalm 29). The Creator God may be acting through the roaring wind, through lightning and thunder (Psalm 104).

It is also possible that God works through less spectacular means. It may be that the Lord is not in the windstorm, the earthquake, or the fire. God may work through the "sound of sheer silence" (1 Kings 19:12).

Once a group of fishermen feared for their lives, out in a boat on the storming Galilean Sea. Then one whom they called Teacher stood up and said to the wind and the sea, "Peace! Be still!" The wind quit, and there was a dead calm. The fishermen asked one another, "Who then is this, that even the wind and the sea obey him?" (Mark 4:35–41).

One could be reminded of the words at the end of this psalm—"Be still, and know that I am God!"—or those words at the beginning, about God as a place of refuge and a very present help in trouble.

GOD IS THE RULER YET
Psalm 47

To the leader. Of the Korahites. A Psalm.

47:1 **Clap your hands, all you peoples;**
        shout to God with loud songs of joy.
   2 **For the LORD, the Most High, is awesome,**
        a great king over all the earth.
   3 **He subdued peoples under us,**
        and nations under our feet.

⁴ He chose our heritage for us,
    the pride of Jacob whom he loves.   *Selah*

⁵ God has gone up with a shout,
    the LORD with the sound of a trumpet.
⁶ Sing praises to God, sing praises;
    sing praises to our King, sing praises.
⁷ For God is the king of all the earth;
    sing praises with a psalm.

⁸ God is king over the nations;
    God sits on his holy throne.
⁹ The princes of the peoples gather
    as the people of the God of Abraham.
  For the shields of the earth belong to God;
    he is highly exalted.

Psalm 46 offers pictures of God as refuge in times of natural disaster (vv. 1–3), as rescuer in times of national difficulty (vv. 4–7), and as peacemaker in times of war (vv. 8–9). It concludes with a voice from the throne of God saying, "Be still, and know that I am God! I am exalted among the nations, I am exalted in the earth." Then the participating congregation is asked to join in the final refrain (v. 11).

Psalm 47 begins where Psalm 46 left off: God is in heaven, ruling as king over all the earth (vv. 2, 7) from God's throne (v. 8).

Enthronement Psalms

Eleven psalms are associated with events in the life of the king on the throne in Jerusalem, such as a king's wedding or the installation of a new king. These are the *royal psalms* and are discussed in connection with Psalm 2. The king about whom these psalms speak is the ruling monarch in Jerusalem.

Psalm 47 is the first of seven psalms that speak of the Lord being acclaimed king at some sort of festival. These are the *enthronement psalms* and include Psalms 47, 93, 95, 96, 97, 98, 99. Like the royal psalms, these enthronement psalms have to do with a king. In the royal psalms, the king is the king, but in the enthronement psalms, the Lord is King.

Psalm 47 names the Lord as king in verses 2, 6, and 7. Some of the enthronement psalms include the cry "The LORD is king!" (Pss. 93:1; 96:10; 97:1; 99:1), or they may refer to the Lord as "a great King above all gods" (Ps. 95:3) or "the King, the LORD" (Ps. 98:6).

Two Typical Hymns

Psalm 47 falls into two sections, each built on the typical pattern of the *hymn*, beginning with a *call to praise* in the imperative mood, followed by *reasons for praise* (see Psalm 113). The first section (vv. 1–4) consists of the imperatives in verse 1 ("Clap . . . shout") followed by reasons, introduced by "For," in verses 2–4. Verse 5 describes what is happening in the worship service and is followed by another series of imperatives in verse 6 ("sing" four times), followed by reasons, again introduced by "For," in verses 7 and 9b.

For "To the leader," see the comments on Psalm 4; "the Korahites" are discussed in connection with Psalm 42. "A Psalm" in the heading translates the Hebrew, *mizmor*. Since the related verb *zamar* occurs five times in verses 6 and 7 and is translated as "sing," the connection between the heading and the psalm would be more clear by translating "A Song."

International Applause (47:1–5)

Psalm 46 concluded with the picture of the Lord God having settled the storming seas and having saved the city of Jerusalem from her enemies and now calling for stillness, for recognition as the God of all the earth and all nations. Psalm 47 begins with an invitation to the peoples of the earth to applaud these actions and to shout, loudly!

Why applaud? There are plenty of reasons. The writer picks up the image of the time that conveys the greatest personal power: the Lord, the Most High, is *King*, not only over Israel or Judah or even Assyria or Babylon but over the entire earth.

Verse 3 offers a picture of a king with his foot on the neck of the enemy, a familiar victor's gesture in the ancient world (Josh. 10:24; Ps. 110:1). Verse 4 provides a further reason for praise: the Lord has given this people the land where they live. *Selah* marks a pause; see my comments on Psalm 3.

Verse 5 has to do with the performance of the psalm in the service of congregational worship. It may refer to a procession that was part of a celebration with the ancient portable altar (see Psalms 24, 132), accompanied by trumpet playing, but the matter is not certain.

Sing, Sing, Sing! (47:6–9)

What must this celebration have sounded like? Reading the words of the psalm provides only a pale approximation of what must have been happening. The text suggests the sounds of clapping and shouting, trumpet playing, and enthusiastic singing (vv. 1, 5–7).

All this was directed to God, named "our King," "king of all the earth," "king over the nations," and described as "highly exalted."

Taken together, Psalms 46–48 indicate that while the people of the Psalms knew how to complain and bring their troubles to the Lord (Psalms 42–43, 44), they also knew how to celebrate. They knew that no matter what, God was still God, and God was with them (Psalm 46). In a time and place where kings ruled the nations of the earth, they knew that the God who had revealed himself to their ancestor Abraham was king over the nations, over the entire earth. All of this was reason enough to sing, shout, and trumpet God's praises.

When Jesus announced that "the kingdom of God is at hand" (Mark 1:15, NRSV footnote), he spoke against the background of what these psalms said about God: "God is the king of all the earth" (Ps. 47:7).

In the face of evil and troubles of all kinds, that fundamental biblical assertion can be, and has been, forgotten. The writer of "This Is My Father's World" had it right: "though the wrong seems oft so strong, God is the Ruler yet!" (*Lutheran Book of Worship*, no. 554).

THIS IS THE CITY
Psalm 48

A Song. A Psalm of the Korahites.

48:1 Great is the LORD and greatly to be praised
    in the city of our God.
His holy mountain, 2beautiful in elevation,
    is the joy of all the earth,
Mount Zion, in the far north,
    the city of the great King.
3 Within its citadels God
    has shown himself a sure defense.

4 Then the kings assembled,
    they came on together.
5 As soon as they saw it, they were astounded;
    they were in panic, they took to flight;
6 trembling took hold of them there,
    pains as of a woman in labor,
7 as when an east wind shatters
    the ships of Tarshish.

⁸ As we have heard, so have we seen
   in the city of the Lord of hosts,
in the city of our God,
   which God establishes forever.   *Selah*

⁹ We ponder your steadfast love, O God,
   in the midst of your temple.
¹⁰ Your name, O God, like your praise,
   reaches to the ends of the earth.
Your right hand is filled with victory.
¹¹   Let Mount Zion be glad,
let the towns of Judah rejoice
   because of your judgments.

¹² Walk about Zion, go all around it,
   count its towers,
¹³ consider well its ramparts;
   go through its citadels,
that you may tell the next generation
¹⁴   that this is God,
our God forever and ever.
   He will be our guide forever.

We walked into the small bookshop in Tel Aviv. Among the volumes on display was a compact one titled *Israel Atlas*. The shopkeeper saw us looking at it. "I wrote that myself!" he announced with obvious pride. "How did you happen to do that?" we asked him. "Let me tell you the story," he said.

"I grew up in a village in Eastern Europe, where there was a very small Jewish community. One day I went into the post office to mail a letter to an uncle who lived in Jerusalem. The man behind the window handed the letter back to me.

"'You can't mail this,' he said.

"'Why not?' I asked.

"'It's addressed to Jerusalem!' was his reply.

"'So? There's the address. There's the stamp,' I said.

"'But there *is* no Jerusalem!' he declared, 'Jerusalem doesn't really exist. Jerusalem is only in the Bible.'

"And so," continued the shopkeeper, "I resolved that if I ever got to Israel, I would write an atlas, listing the height of every mountain, the depth of every lake, the name of every river, the population of every village and town and city. And I would tell the whole world about Jerusalem, so that everyone would know that it's not just in the Bible, but it really does exist!"

I bought the book, and with it got a reminder that the Bible tells of real people and real events and real places.

This is the third in a series of psalms that center on a real place, the city of Jerusalem. Psalm 46 declared that God was present there. Psalm 47 celebrated that presence with singing, shouting, and clapping. Now Psalm 48 takes us by the hand, points toward those honey-colored stone buildings, and says, "Jerusalem. There really is such a place. This is the city."

The heading indicates that this is a song, probably accompanied by instruments, associated with the Korahites. (See the comments on Psalm 42.) Since its theme is Jerusalem, this is one of those psalms called a "song of Zion"; see my comments on Psalm 87.

Verses 1–3 state that the Lord is to be praised in the city and then tell why; verses 4–8 tell a story and then speak again of the city; verses 9–11 offer some reflections about God; and verses 12–14 offer an invitation to a tour of the city.

What's So Great about Jerusalem? (48:1–3)

The first words of the psalm make clear that it is not the city that is being praised here, though it is praiseworthy. We could imagine a real estate brochure:

> Choose Jerusalem!
> "Ideal elevation. Lovely mountain location. Stunning sunsets.
> Fine array of interesting shops. A happy place,
> where you'll meet people from all over the world."

But this song of praise is being sung for another reason. Jerusalem is "the city of our God" (vv. 1, 8). It is "the city of the great King" (v. 1), "the city of the LORD of hosts" (v. 8), the city that God dramatically defends (see 2 Kings 18–19).

God Saves the City (48:4–8)

This section describes a situation in which Jerusalem is surrounded by enemy troops. They move in for the attack and then suddenly withdraw in panic. Is this a memory of the last-minute rescue from the Assyrians in the days of Isaiah (2 Kings 18–19)? Or does this refer to a future deliverance from some as yet unknown foe, maybe in the last days? In any case, the pictures describing the deliverance are arresting: the enemy armies are writhing, shaking, hurting, like a woman giving birth. The soldiers are shattered like the majestic sailing ships of Spain might be shattered by a wind (Tarshish; see Ezek. 27:25–36).

"We've heard of these things and have seen them," says verse 8, coming to a climax with the assertion that God has established this city—forever! (*Selah* marks a pause; see on Psalm 3.)

A Few Theological Reflections (48:9–11)

Now, for the first time in this psalm, there are words of response from the congregation. What do they think of Jerusalem? What of this story of miraculous deliverance?

Worship, it would appear, is not only a time to clap hands, sing, and shout (Ps. 47:1) but also a time to sit quietly and reflect, to ponder (v. 9). The people begin by reflecting on God's unshakable love, unlimited influence, and innumerable victories (vv. 9–10). Then they conclude that with such a God, the people living on Mount Zion, that is, in Jerusalem, ought to live happily (v. 11).

A Guided Tour (48:12–14)

The psalm begins by speaking of Jerusalem as a city of beauty and joy, and it ends in the same way. "Walk around Jerusalem!" it says. "Here it is. This is the city." Is this an invitation to join in some sort of liturgical procession around the city? Or is the writer inviting hearers to join an imaginary tour? Either way, the psalm ends as it began, with an appreciation of the magnificence of Jerusalem.

And the author has an eye on the children. They should be told not only about the city but about the God of the city. They should be told that this is "our God," who will be a guide not just for a city tour but for the journey of a lifetime (v. 14).

Jerusalem, Jerusalem

For the first-time visitor, the sign on the highway suggests that the city really does exist:

```
+----------------------------+
|                            |
|         Jerusalem          |
|        22 kilometers       |
|                            |
+----------------------------+
```

For one who has grown up hearing stories and singing songs about Jerusalem, seeing the city for the first time evokes a sense of wonder. It may be that to see Jerusalem is to fall in love with it. What city has known more prophets, poets, and dreamers? What city has heard more tales? What city is the subject of more stories and songs?

It could well be that to live in Jerusalem is to fall in love with it. Perhaps that explains the sadness in those words of Jesus, addressed to the city as he sat looking over it:

> O Jerusalem, Jerusalem . . . How often would I have gathered your children together as a hen gathers her brood under her wings, and you would not! (Matt. 23:37, RSV)

PUTTING THINGS IN PERSPECTIVE
Psalm 49

To the leader. Of the Korahites. A Psalm.

49:1 **Hear this, all you peoples;**
    give ear, all inhabitants of the world,
  2 **both low and high,**
    rich and poor together.
  3 **My mouth shall speak wisdom;**
    the meditation of my heart shall be understanding.
  4 **I will incline my ear to a proverb;**
    I will solve my riddle to the music of the harp.

  5 **Why should I fear in times of trouble,**
    when the iniquity of my persecutors surrounds me,
  6 **those who trust in their wealth**
    and boast of the abundance of their riches?
  7 **Truly, no ransom avails for one's life,**
    there is no price one can give to God for it.
  8 **For the ransom of life is costly,**
    and can never suffice,
  9 **that one should live on forever**
    and never see the grave.

  10 **When we look at the wise, they die;**
    fool and dolt perish together
    and leave their wealth to others.
  11 **Their graves are their homes forever,**
    their dwelling places to all generations,
    though they named lands their own.

¹² Mortals cannot abide in their pomp;
    they are like the animals that perish.

¹³ Such is the fate of the foolhardy,
    the end of those who are pleased with their lot.   *Selah*
¹⁴ Like sheep they are appointed for Sheol;
    Death shall be their shepherd;
  straight to the grave they descend,
    and their form shall waste away;
  Sheol shall be their home.
¹⁵ But God will ransom my soul from the power of Sheol,
    for he will receive me.   *Selah*

¹⁶ Do not be afraid when some become rich,
    when the wealth of their houses increases.
¹⁷ For when they die they will carry nothing away;
    their wealth will not go down after them.
¹⁸ Though in their lifetime they count themselves happy
    —for you are praised when you do well for yourself—
¹⁹ they will go to the company of their ancestors,
    who will never again see the light.
²⁰ Mortals cannot abide in their pomp;
    they are like the animals that perish.

After psalms dealing with broader issues such as war and peace (Psalm 46), God's rule over the earth (Psalm 47), and God's care for the city (Psalm 48), this one focuses on concerns of the individual. After psalms reporting mountains shaking, trumpets playing, ships being wrecked at sea, the mood of this psalm is calm, quiet, and reflective. It invites us to sit back and think about how we are leading our lives. It is an invitation to reflection on wealth and poverty, life and death.

For "To the leader," see the comments on Psalm 4; "the Korahites" are discussed with Psalm 42. "A Psalm" is considered with Psalm 47.

The psalm consists of an introduction identifying the targeted audience and the source of the teaching (vv. 1–4), some thoughts about fearing certain wealthy persons (vv. 5–15), and an exhortation not to be afraid (vv. 16–20).

Your Attention Please! (49:1–4)

The "hear" and "give ear" language at the opening of the psalm could be the way a teacher begins a class session; Psalm 78 begins in a similar way. Unless this is an imagined audience, one might think of the speaker addressing persons gathered in Jerusalem for a festival, such as that described in Acts 2:1–11. The speaker calls attention to the international variety of the audience but also to the variation in economic and social status. His words are addressed to "low and high, rich and poor together."

Verses 3 and 4 explain the origin of the speaker's message. There is much here in the description that we can no longer understand. Was this instruction delivered to the accompaniment of music (v. 4)? Does the "proverb" refer to the saying in verses 12 and 20, which is then the "text" for this speech? The "riddle" appears to be "Why does God allow the wicked to prosper?"

Some things in this introduction are clear: (1) the origin of the material comes from outside the prophet himself (the proverb, v. 4); (2) the message is of sufficient importance to deserve an international hearing; and (3) while the teacher is sensitive to the problems of poor people and explicitly names them, the message is aimed at *both* the poor and the rich (v. 2).

They Can't Take It with Them (49:5–15)

The problem that gave rise to these thoughts is identified at the beginning of each of the two main parts of the psalm: certain wealthy persons are making the lives of others in the community miserable, so that they live in fear (vv. 5, 16). The teacher follows the ancient advice given to all educators: *repetitio mater studiorum*, "repetition is the mother of learning," or in other words, the way to teach is to repeat the same thing over and over again.

In this first major section the same argument is made three times: these wealthy persons who put their trust in their magnificent houses and impressive bank accounts are going to be gravely disappointed because (1) they are not going to live forever (v. 9, summarizing vv. 5–9); (2) whether they are wise or foolish, one day they will die and leave their wealth to others (v. 10, summarizing vv. 10–12); (3) like so many sheep, these wealthy oppressors are marching toward Sheol, the place of the dead, and the shepherd they are following is Death itself (vv. 13–14 in vv. 13–15).

The three arguments are summarized in the refrain of verse 12, to be repeated in verse 20: "Mortals cannot abide in their pomp; they are like the animals that perish." Then the writer ties up the section from verses 5–15 with a second "I" statement (the first is in v. 5) that is the high point of the psalm: "But God will ransom my soul from the power of Sheol, for he will receive me" (v. 15; for Sheol, see on Psalm 6). Here is one of those rare places in the psalms with a hint that beyond death, the believer will be with God. Another psalm comes close to saying the same thing: "Nevertheless I am continually with you . . . and afterward you will receive me with honor" (Ps. 73:23–24).

So Don't Be Afraid! (49:16–20)

If verse 15 makes the main point about God for this psalm, verse 16 states its application. The problem had to do with certain arrogant persons who, heady with their success, were making life miserable for others with less impressive financial resources. The first response to the problem began, "Why should I fear?" (v. 5) The second is more direct: "Do not be afraid!" The writer argues: these people may be wealthy, persecuting others in the community now, but they too will die, and they won't take their wealth with them (v. 17)! And these rich (and the poor, too; v. 2) ought to remember what the refrain says: we humans are not gods but are like the animals that also die. The Hebrew word translated "mortals" in verses 12 and 20 is *'ādām*, as used in Genesis 1:26 and 2:7, 8, 15–16, 18–21, where the link between humans and the earth is accented (the Hebrew for "earth" is *'adāmāh*, Gen. 2:7).

Putting Things in Perspective

"If I were a rich man . . . ," sings Tevye the milkman in *Fiddler on the Roof*, fantasizing about the happiness of a wealthy life. But does wealth necessarily bring happiness? In an often inaccurately quoted sentence, Paul wrote, "For the *love of* money is a root of all kinds of evil" (1 Tim. 6:10).

The Bible has much to say about finances. One could start with the story of the wealthy but bored person described in Ecclesiastes 2:1–23. The New Testament gives the account about the rich man whose possessions owned him (Mark 10:17–22), and Jesus told stories about a foolish farmer who was more than right with the bank but not right with God (Luke 12:13–21) and about a wealthy citizen who never noticed the poverty in his own town, on his own doorstep, until it was too late (Luke 16:19–31).

For more, one could read through from Proverbs 10 to the end of that book, marking those sayings that have to do with riches and poverty, and discuss them with someone else. Note, for example, Proverbs 10:15; 11:28; 14:21; 15:16; 16:16; 21:13; 22:1–2; 28:6, 11; 30:8; 31:9, 20. Then recall what Jesus said about the limitations of money in the bank (Matt. 6:19–21)!

THE TROUBLE WITH RELIGION
Psalm 50

A Psalm of Asaph.

50:1 The mighty one, God the LORD,
    speaks and summons the earth
    from the rising of the sun to its setting.
2 Out of Zion, the perfection of beauty,
    God shines forth.

3 Our God comes and does not keep silence,
    before him is a devouring fire,
    and a mighty tempest all around him.
4 He calls to the heavens above
    and to the earth, that he may judge his people:
5 "Gather to me my faithful ones,
    who made a covenant with me by sacrifice!"
6 The heavens declare his righteousness,
    for God himself is judge.   *Selah*

7 "Hear, O my people, and I will speak,
    O Israel, I will testify against you.
    I am God, your God.
8 Not for your sacrifices do I rebuke you;
    your burnt offerings are continually before me.
9 I will not accept a bull from your house,
    or goats from your folds.
10 For every wild animal of the forest is mine,
    the cattle on a thousand hills.
11 I know all the birds of the air,
    and all that moves in the field is mine.

12 "If I were hungry, I would not tell you,
    for the world and all that is in it is mine.
13 Do I eat the flesh of bulls,
    or drink the blood of goats?
14 Offer to God a sacrifice of thanksgiving,
    and pay your vows to the Most High.
15 Call on me in the day of trouble;
    I will deliver you, and you shall glorify me."

16 But to the wicked God says:
    "What right have you to recite my statutes,
    or take my covenant on your lips?

¹⁷ **For you hate discipline,**
   and you cast my words behind you.
¹⁸ **You make friends with a thief when you see one,**
   and you keep company with adulterers.

¹⁹ **"You give your mouth free rein for evil,**
   and your tongue frames deceit.
²⁰ **You sit and speak against your kin;**
   you slander your own mother's child.
²¹ **These things you have done and I have been silent;**
   you thought that I was one just like yourself.
But now I rebuke you, and lay the charge before you.

²² **"Mark this, then, you who forget God,**
   or I will tear you apart, and there will be no one to deliver.
²³ **Those who bring thanksgiving as their sacrifice honor me;**
   to those who go the right way
   I will show the salvation of God."

I recall a college campus where an annual religious emphasis week was being celebrated. Prominently displayed over the door of the gymnasium where the sessions were being held was a huge banner that stated the theme "Religion and Life."

After a couple days into the week, an unauthorized change was made in the banner. Instead of "Religion and Life," the middle word was crossed out and "in" was substituted. Apparently someone thought that religion and life ought not be separated but that religion ought to be integrated into all of life. I think the writer of this psalm would have considered the change an improvement.

This psalm falls into four parts. The introduction describes the appearance of God on earth for a time of judgment (vv. 1–6; for *Selah*, see Psalm 3). Verses 7–15 are words from God critical of the people's relationship to God. Verses 16–21 are again words from God (spoken by a priest) and are critical of the people's relationship to their neighbors. Verses 22 and 23 shift into the imperative mood and offer a summary of the entire psalm. After a series of Korah psalms (Psalms 42–49), Psalm 50 is identified as a psalm of Asaph (see on Psalm 73). Its theme of sacrifices links it to Psalm 51:19.

Here Comes the Judge (50:1–6)

We should imagine this psalm as part of a religious ceremony, where one speaker introduces the ceremony (vv. 1–4, 6) and another, presumably a priest, speaks the words from God (vv. 5, 7–15, 16b–23). The psalm begins by setting a vast scene: the Lord God is summoning all people, from east to west (the horizontal dimension), and calling the heavens above and the earth below (the vertical) to witness an act of judgment.

The arrival of the judge in any courtroom is always a moment of drama, and the account here is no exception. The coming of the Judge into this court is described in cosmic terms, accompanied by a consuming fire and a tempestuous windstorm. Out of the storm comes the voice of God: "Gather to me my faithful ones!"

The scene is set. There is order in the court. Now, what does the Judge have to say?

The Cattle on a Thousand Hills (50:7–15)

God speaks, announcing a case against the people, Israel. Something is wrong with what is happening at the place of worship. Sacrifices are being offered, apparently in a proper and timely manner (vv. 8–13), but something is wrong. That something has to do with what happens outside the place of worship. These people had hung a banner over their place of worship that said, "Religion and Life." In other words, they were keeping their religion and their everyday living in two separate compartments.

Other biblical voices are critical of this sort of split. The prophet Amos announced the Lord's fury against a people who were conducting extravagant worship ceremonies (religion) but who showed no concern for the poor and the orphan in their midst (life), neglecting any sort of social justice (Amos 5:21–24). Isaiah announced that the Lord was fed up with a people who were busy bustling about with the business of liturgies and sacrifices (religion) but who neglected the powerless (Isa. 1:10–17) and who put into effect legislation biased against widows and poor people (Isa. 10:1–4; life). Isaiah went so far, in fact, as to call the Jerusalem of his day not holy but a whore (Isa. 1:21–26)! Speaking in the name of God, Hosea said, "I desire steadfast love [*in* life] and not sacrifice [religion]" (Hos. 6:6). Jeremiah had sharp words of criticism for those who made the temple a fetish and whose religion never got out of the worship place and into daily living (Jer. 7:1–15).

Psalm 50 sets forth no call to put away the priesthood. It does not demand shutting down all sacrifices or doing away with liturgies (v. 8), even though the Lord does not need the blood and meat being offered (v. 13). Indeed, says God, "every wild animal of the forest is mine, the cattle on a thousand hills. I know all the birds of the air, and all that moves in the field is mine . . . the world and all that is in it is mine" (vv. 10–12).

Then what does God want? The psalm says it clearly: God wants God's people to give thanks; to keep promises made to God. And finally, just as a parent finds joy when a child asks for help, so God would like to have God's children call for help in times of trouble. They would discover that God would help them out, and they would praise God (vv. 14–15)!

Talking and Walking (50:16–23)

In this second part of the scene in court, the charge against the people is that their religion is only lip deep, a matter of words but not works. They know how to recite the creeds but do not take God's words seriously (vv. 16–17). They are strong on words but weak on works (vv. 16–18). The charges continue with the speaker addressing the people: The commandment says, "You shall not steal," but you make friendships with thieves. The commandment says, "You shall not commitment adultery," but you hang around with adulterers. The commandment says, "You shall not bear false witness," but you slander even your own brother and sister!

The speech concludes on a grim note, accusing the hearers of forgetting God and advising them to get their lives in order or face the wrath of a God who will tear them apart as a lion tears up a lamb (see Hos. 5:14 and Amos 3:4, 8, 12).

Finally, verse 23 sums up the two parts of the speech. What God wants is not the making of sacrifices but giving thanks! What God wants is a people whose religion involves not only lips but also legs, that is, who "go the right way."

Somehow these words have a familiar ring. Didn't Jesus speak about being *doers* of the word (Matt. 7:24–27)? And didn't James say not that faith without *words* is dead but that faith without *works* is dead (James 2:14–26)?

Psalm 50 remains a call not only to talk the talk of religion but to walk the walk as well.

WHAT CAN YOU DO WITH A BROKEN HEART?
Psalm 51

> To the leader. A Psalm of David, when the prophet Nathan
> came to him, after he had gone in to Bathsheba.

> 51:1 **Have mercy on me, O God,**
> **according to your steadfast love;**

according to your abundant mercy
    blot out my transgressions.
2 Wash me thoroughly from my iniquity,
    and cleanse me from my sin.

3 For I know my transgressions,
    and my sin is ever before me.
4 Against you, you alone, have I sinned,
    and done what is evil in your sight,
so that you are justified in your sentence
    and blameless when you pass judgment.
5 Indeed, I was born guilty,
    a sinner when my mother conceived me.

6 You desire truth in the inward being;
    therefore teach me wisdom in my secret heart.
7 Purge me with hyssop, and I shall be clean;
    wash me, and I shall be whiter than snow.
8 Let me hear joy and gladness;
    let the bones that you have crushed rejoice.
9 Hide your face from my sins,
    and blot out all my iniquities.

10 Create in me a clean heart, O God,
    and put a new and right spirit within me.
11 Do not cast me away from your presence,
    and do not take your holy spirit from me.
12 Restore to me the joy of your salvation,
    and sustain in me a willing spirit.

13 Then I will teach transgressors your ways,
    and sinners will return to you.
14 Deliver me from bloodshed, O God,
    O God of my salvation,
    and my tongue will sing aloud of your deliverance.

15 O Lord, open my lips,
    and my mouth will declare your praise.
16 For you have no delight in sacrifice;
    if I were to give a burnt offering, you would not be pleased.
17 The sacrifice acceptable to God is a broken spirit;
    a broken and contrite heart, O God, you will not despise.

18 Do good to Zion in your good pleasure;
    rebuild the walls of Jerusalem,

¹⁹ **then you will delight in right sacrifices,**
   in burnt offerings and whole burnt offerings;
   then bulls will be offered on your altar.

The heading points to the story in 2 Samuel 11–12 as a way of getting into this psalm.

It was springtime, and for King David, the autumn of his life. No longer did spring mean new military ventures, going out with the army to make new conquests. This year, the king was staying home (2 Sam. 11:1).

Late one afternoon, after his usual nap, David was strolling about on the roof of the royal palace. He noticed a woman bathing on the outdoor patio of the house next door. She was beautiful. An inquiry indicated that she was Bathsheba, and her husband was away with the army. Since David was the king and could have whatever (or whomever) he wanted, he sent for the woman and they spent the remainder of the day together, making love. A pleasant afternoon diversion for the aging monarch!

Some time later David received a letter with a short message: "Your Majesty: I'm pregnant. What do I do now? Bathsheba." The king went into action, arranging for her husband Uriah to have a brief furlough. He met the man. "How goes the war?" he asked. "We who are back here at home appreciate what you men are doing! Take a few days off. Go home to your wife." The king had a choice bottle of wine delivered to the couple and hoped that this surprise furlough would explain the pregnancy.

But Uriah, good soldier that he was, would not go home while his comrades were roughing it in the field, and instead he camped out. David invited him for a meal, got him drunk, and still Uriah would not go home.

So the king arranged to have Uriah killed in battle. And then David did what must have seemed to many an act of kindness: he took the poor, pregnant widow as his own wife.

The tawdry affair might have ended there. But one day the prophet Nathan came to see the king. He told David about a rich man who had many sheep and who had stolen the one precious lamb belonging to a poor man. "Who is this fellow?" said the king. "Tell me! He deserves to die!"

Nathan looked the king in the eye. "You are the man!" he said. David got the point. He saw that he had sinned. David and Bathsheba's baby was born, and after just a week, the child died. And David was broken-hearted. In this situation, suggests the psalm heading, David prayed the prayer now known as Psalm 51.

The psalm consists of elements typical of the lament (see Psalm 13), with those elements modified to fit the situation. Verses 1–5 are a request for forgiveness (vv. 1–2) coupled with a confession of sin (vv. 3–5). Verses 6–12 offer another request for forgiveness. Once forgiven, the psalmist vows to praise God (vv. 13–17); verses 18–19 present some comments designed to adapt the psalm to a later situation.

My Sin, My Own Grievous Sin (51:1–5)

The psalm begins with an urgent cry for help: "Have mercy on me, O God!" The one crying out gives two reasons why God might be expected to help: because of God's *steadfast love* and God's *mercy*. The Hebrew word translated "steadfast love" is *hesed*, with the sense "undeserved love." A good illustration is the prophet Hosea, who found that even though his wife, Gomer, had been unfaithful, he still loved her (Chapter 3; 3:1 uses a different Hebrew word for love but with the same sense). Such is the kind of undeserved love that the Lord has for the Lord's people (Hosea 2; note "steadfast love" in v. 19). Hosea 2:19 also speaks of the Lord's *mercy*, translating the Hebrew *rehem*, related to the word for "womb." It describes the sort of love a mother has for her own child (see also Ps. 103:4, 13). The Lord's love also is like a parent's love for a rebelling teenager (Hos. 11:1–9).

Verses 2–5 of Psalm 51 offer a short course on the Old Testament notions of sin and forgiveness. Here are three words for sin and three words for forgiveness, each associated with a picture. The picture behind "transgressions" (vv. 1, 3, 13) is rebellion, as when children rebel against parents (Isa. 1:2). The literal sense of the Hebrew word translated "iniquity" (vv. 2, 9; translated "guilty" in v. 5) is to be bent over or bent out of shape; in Psalm 38:6 that word is translated "bowed down." The literal meaning of the Hebrew *ḥāṭā'*, translated "sin" (vv. 2, 3, 4, 9; "sinner" in vv. 5 and 13) is to "miss the target," as in the report in Judges 20:16 about the seven hundred left-handed sling-shooters from the tribe of Benjamin who could "sling a stone at a hair, and not *miss* [*ḥāṭā'*]."

Balancing these words for sin are three words for forgiveness. The word translated "blot out" in verse 1 can mean to wipe away, as one wipes away tears (Isa. 25:8) or wipes off a dish (2 Kings 21:13). To "wash" away iniquity (vv. 2, 7) means to scrub, as one scrubs dirty clothes (Exod. 19:10, 14). The word translated "cleanse" (vv. 2, 7; "be clean") can be used for washing clothes in a river, to make them ritually clean (Lev. 13:6, 34, 58).

The psalm makes clear that the one praying is burdened by a great sense of having sinned against God. David understood what he had done in that way (2 Sam. 12:13). Now the one who prays this psalm wants to experience God's forgiveness.

Heart Transplant (51:6–12)

The one who prays this psalm wants and needs help. Those needs can be seen by observing the imperative verbs in this section. "Teach me," says the psalmist, hoping to learn something through this experience. Following are more requests for the Lord to help with the problem of the sin: "Purge me . . . wash me . . . blot out all my iniquities."

A number of requests also have to do with getting a fresh start, getting life going again. Central is the request "Create in me a clean heart, O God" (v. 10). *Create* is a word known from the first chapter of Genesis. The Hebrew dictionaries make the point that in the Bible the subject of this verb is always God—and the result is always something entirely new. "Heart" and "spirit" here both refer to the controlling center of the whole person.

After being forgiven, the one praying hopes to be happy again and to be right with God once more (vv. 8, 11–12).

How Can I Keep from Singing? (51:13–19)

Having experienced forgiveness, the psalmist vows to do three things: teach, sing, and praise the Lord (vv. 13–15). One can understand that having experienced forgiveness, the one forgiven will want to tell—or more precisely, to sing—the story of what God has done (v. 14). That one will praise God and asks that God help him in praising (v. 15). The psalmist's devotion will not express itself in offering sacrifices but in offering himself to God.

Along with the vow to sing and to praise, here is a promise to engage in teaching (v. 13). The response to experiencing forgiveness is portrayed as a life conscious of the Lord's presence, a life marked by joy and gladness, singing and praising, and passing on the faith to others —even those outside the family of believers—through teaching.

The concluding comments in verses 18 and 19 assume the destruction of Jerusalem and balance the harsh words about sacrifices and offerings in verse 16 with hope that the whole sacrificial system will one day again be in operation.

A Psalm for Ash Wednesday

The Christian church has considered this one of the *penitential psalms* (see the discussion with Psalm 6) and has used it in connection with worship

on Ash Wednesday, the first day of the Lenten season. Whether for a
season of the year or a season in one's life when one is especially aware
of having done wrong, this is the psalm to call on when dealing with sin
and for help in formulating a prayer for forgiveness.

A GREEN OLIVE TREE
Psalm 52

> To the leader. A Maskil of David, when Doeg the Edomite came to Saul
> and said to him, "David has come to the house of Ahimelech."

> 52:1 Why do you boast, O mighty one,
>   of mischief done against the godly?
>   All day long ²you are plotting destruction.
>   Your tongue is like a sharp razor,
>   you worker of treachery.
>   ³ You love evil more than good,
>   and lying more than speaking the truth.   Selah
>   ⁴ You love all words that devour,
>   O deceitful tongue.
>
>   ⁵ But God will break you down forever;
>   he will snatch and tear you from your tent;
>   he will uproot you from the land of the living.   Selah
>   ⁶ The righteous will see, and fear,
>   and will laugh at the evildoer, saying,
>   ⁷ "See the one who would not take
>   refuge in God,
>   but trusted in abundant riches,
>   and sought refuge in wealth!"
>
>   ⁸ But I am like a green olive tree
>   in the house of God.
>   I trust in the steadfast love of God
>   forever and ever.
>   ⁹ I will thank you forever,
>   because of what you have done.
>   In the presence of the faithful
>   I will proclaim your name, for it is good.

The psalms use a variety of pictures when speaking of God and of
human beings. The writer of this psalm says, "I am like a green olive tree
in the house of God" (v. 8).

Tree imagery occurs elsewhere in the psalms. The first picture for the believer in the book of Psalms is that of a tree, planted by a stream, firmly rooted and productive (Ps. 1:3). Psalm 92 calls to mind palm trees and cedars:

> The righteous flourish like the palm tree,
>   and grow like a cedar in Lebanon.
> They are planted in the house of the LORD . . .
> In old age they still produce fruit;
>   they are always green and full of sap.
>
> (Ps. 92:12–14)

To understand Psalm 52, one might begin by asking, In what ways does an olive tree or a palm tree or a mighty cedar help us understand our existence as believers in God?

The psalm contains the elements of an individual lament (see on Psalm 13). It begins with a strong *"you" complaint* addressed to an enemy of the godly (vv. 1–4), combined with an announcement of future punishment (vv. 5–7). It concludes with an *affirmation of trust* in God (v. 8) and a *vow to praise* (v. 9).

The heading furnishes a good example of how the first commentaries on the psalms grew. After "To the leader" and the identification as a "Maskil of David" (see on Psalms 4 and 32), an early interpreter locates the psalm in the life of King David, referring to the events described in 1 Samuel 21–22 (see especially 21:7–9 and 22:9–10, 18–19). The commentator saw Psalm 52:1–7 as David's words aimed at the foreigner, Doeg the Edomite, after Doeg had told Saul about David's contact with Ahimelech.

Who Do They Trust? (52:1–7)

When the Old Testament prophets delivered a message of God's judgment against an individual or against a nation, they began with an accusation in the past or present tense and continued with an announcement of punishment in the future tense (see, for example, the sayings in Amos 1:3–2:16). The beginning of Psalm 52 follows this prophetic pattern, with words of accusation (vv. 1–4) followed by an announcement of future punishment (vv. 5–7).

The one being accused is addressed, with bitter sarcasm, as "mighty one." The general accusation against this person, apparently someone in the community, is that of planning and doing evil (NRSV, "mischief") against God's people and then boasting of those deeds. Verse 2 indicates that this evildoing involves words that slash and cut other persons like a sharp razor. Verses 3 and 4 suggest that the cutter and slasher enjoys this activity, loving evil (linking up with the same Hebrew word in v. 1) more than good and preferring lying to speaking the truth.

Verse 5 now speaks of the future, announcing what God will do to this one whose lies are making life so miserable for the godly. "You have been plotting evil *for a whole day?* God will shut down your activities *forever!*" says the psalmist (vv. 1, 5, NRSV paraphrase). The wrongdoing is viewed as serious enough to warrant the death penalty.

With verse 7 the one who is being accused comes into sharper focus. This individual has lied and cheated God's people (vv. 1–4). Now we hear something about the person's religion. The theme song of this person's life is not "A mighty fortress is our God" but rather "A mighty fortress is my gold—and my silver and my high-yield stocks and bonds."

"Who do these people trust?" this psalm asks in regard to those who are making life so miserable for God's people. The answer that the psalm gives is that these people do not trust in God. Rather, they buoy themselves up in times of trouble by reviewing, with pleasure, their investment portfolios (v. 7). Their trust is in their wealth.

Who Do I Trust? (52:8–9)

After looking at one of "them," that is, one of those trying to undermine faith in God, the psalmist makes a two-part confession of faith (v. 8). To be "like a green olive tree in the house of God" means to be living in the presence of God, to be deeply and sturdily rooted in God, to be dependent on God for nourishment and continued life, and to produce olives, that is, to be productive. What is said with a picture in the first half of the verse is stated in nonpicture language in the second half. Others may trust in riches or power or other gods, "but as for me," says the psalmist, "I trust in the steadfast love [*hesed*] of God." (For *hesed*, see the comments on Psalm 136.)

Finally, the psalmist speaks to God with direct "you" address. For the first time, the psalm shifts into a prayer. The psalmist is confident of being delivered from these verbal attacks and, after this deliverance, promises to give thanks to God forever because of God's mighty acts (v. 9).

Who Do You Trust?

The central theme in this psalm is expressed in the verb *trust*, which occurs in verses 7 and 8. The first occurrence refers to one who refuses to trust in God, choosing rather to trust in wealth, stocks, and securities. The person who builds a life on these foundations looks somewhat familiar. Jesus encountered a wealthy young politician who couldn't quite bring himself to let go of his "many possessions" and let God take over his life (Matt. 19:16–30; Mark 10:17–31; Luke 18:18–30). Jesus also told about a wealthy farmer who was good at buying and selling but who had forgotten about his soul. God addressed that person as "You fool!"; a contemporary German Bible translates, "Du Dummkopf!" (Luke 12:13–21).

The second occurrence of the verb *trust* occurs in the confession of faith in verse 8: "I trust in the steadfast love of God forever and ever." Thanks to what God has done (v. 9), the life of the one who so trusts in God can be compared to "a green olive tree in the house of God"; or to a tree planted by streams of water (Ps. 1:3); or perhaps even to a cedar tree— green, full of sap, and still producing fruit, even in old age (Ps. 92:12–15).

WHERE IS GOD?
Psalm 53

To the leader: according to Mahalath.
A Maskil of David

53:1 **Fools say in their hearts, "There is no God."**
　　　 They are corrupt, they commit abominable acts;
　　　 there is no one who does good.
　² **God looks down from heaven on humankind**
　　　 to see if there are any who are wise,
　　　 who seek after God.

　³ **They have all fallen away, they are all alike perverse;**
　　　 there is no one who does good,
　　　 no, not one.

　⁴ **Have they no knowledge, those evildoers,**
　　　 who eat up my people as they eat bread,
　　　 and do not call upon God?

　⁵ **There they shall be in great terror,**
　　　 in terror such as has not been.
　　 For God will scatter the bones of the ungodly;
　　　 they will be put to shame, for God has rejected them.

　⁶ **O that deliverance for Israel would come from Zion!**
　　　 When God restores the fortunes of his people,
　　　 Jacob will rejoice; Israel will be glad.

Psalm 53 offers a shorter and slightly different version of Psalm 14; see the discussion of that psalm for comments. The following differences may be noted:

1. The headings are different. Psalm 53 adds "according to Mahalath," apparently referring to a melody (see also Psalm 88) and "A Maskil" (see the comments on Psalm 32).

2. The names for God are different. Psalm 53 is a part of the *elohistic psalter* (see on Psalm 42) and provides a good example of the way in which *'elohim* is substituted for "LORD" in this collection. Psalm 14 has "LORD" (The Hebrew name is Yahweh) in vv. 2, 4, and 7; in each case, Psalm 53 has substituted the name God (Hebrew, *'elohim*).

3. Verse 5 of each psalm is different after the first line, and verse 6 of Psalm 14 is not found in Psalm 53. Verses 1–4 and 6 of Psalm 53 are almost the same as verses 1–4 and 7 of Psalm 14.

A comparison of Psalm 14 and Psalm 53 suggests that this was once a popular psalm existing in two slightly different versions in two separate psalm collections. When the book of Psalms was put together, the editors decided to keep both versions. For a modern analogy, one could think of the slightly different versions of popular hymns such as "Beautiful Savior" or "Silent Night" that may be found in various modern hymnbooks.

IN THE NAME OF GOD
Psalm 54

> To the leader: with stringed instruments. A Maskil of David,
> when the Ziphites went and told Saul, "David is in hiding among us."

54:1 Save me, O God, by your name,
    and vindicate me by your might.
² Hear my prayer, O God;
    give ear to the words of my mouth.

³ For the insolent have risen against me,
    the ruthless seek my life;
    they do not set God before them.   *Selah*

⁴ But surely, God is my helper;
    the Lord is the upholder of my life.
⁵ He will repay my enemies for their evil.
    In your faithfulness, put an end to them.

⁶ With a freewill offering I will sacrifice to you;
    I will give thanks to your name, O LORD, for it is good.
⁷ For he has delivered me from every trouble,
    and my eye has looked in triumph on my enemies.

Names have power because they have a way of making present the person named. When Peter said to a lame man in Jerusalem, "In the name of Jesus Christ of Nazareth, stand up and walk" (Acts 3:6), the man stood up and walked because the power of Jesus became present. If someone calls out, "Police officer! Stop, in the name of the law!" that order will likely be obeyed because the power of a government is made present in that command.

This psalm begins by calling on the name of God (v. 1) and concludes by giving thanks to God's name (v. 6). In each case, calling on the name means calling on the person, here the person of God.

After a word of dedication to the choir director and an indication about musical accompaniment (see also Psalm 4) and the "Maskil" designation (see the comment on Psalm 32), the heading links this psalm to an incident described in 1 Samuel 23:19–29. Ziph was a town about five miles southeast of Hebron. Certain persons from that place told Saul that "David is hiding among us" (1 Sam. 23:19; see also 26:1). This report set off a search operation by Saul and his soldiers (1 Sam. 23:19–29). The heading suggests that in this situation, where David was running for his life, David prayed the prayer found in Psalm 54.

The psalm is built of the typical elements of the individual lament (see on Psalm 13): a *request* for help (vv. 1–2), a *"they" complaint* (v. 3), an *affirmation of trust* (vv. 4–5a), another *request* (v. 5b), and a *vow to praise* (vv. 6–7).

Your Mighty Name (54:1–3)

The opening sentence is a desperate cry for help. In the Hebrew word order, the first word of this prayer is *God*: "God, by your name, save me!" The earliest commentator on the psalm, the one who produced the heading, suggested that the psalm came from a time when David was running for his life. The implication is "This can also be your prayer, if there is a time when your own life is in danger."

The sense of *save* and *vindicate* is "to rescue," as one might be rescued from drowning. The expression "by your name" means something like "by your powerful presence" or "by your might," as the balancing line indicates.

In the Hebrew word order, the first word of verse 2 is also *God*: "God, hear my prayer." This sentence seems oddly out of place. One might expect the psalm to *begin* with this call for God to "hear my prayer," as is the case with Psalm 55 that follows: "Give ear to my prayer, O God." But the situation behind Psalm 54 is too desperate for a formal beginning. Psalm 54 gets right to the Person, then right to the point: "God, save me."

With verse 3, the one praying hints at the situation being faced. Certain persons are out to kill him. The psalm heading directs us to 1 Samuel 23 as a clue for understanding this psalm. The expression "seek my life" is also used in 1 Samuel 23:15 to describe Saul's purpose in pursuing David: "Saul had come out to seek his life." Who were these pursuers? The psalm does not identify them, but it does describe how they act. These are people who have no regard for God at all. (*Selah* marks a pause in the sequence of the psalm; see on Psalm 3.)

Your Good Name (54:4–7)

With verse 4 the mood of the psalm changes. Though we do hear yet one more *request* in verse 5b ("put an end to them"), the second half of the psalm consists mainly of words of *trust* and a promise of *praise*. The psalmist calls God "my helper" (see Ps. 121:1–2) and "the upholder of my life." The psalmist is certain that God will settle up with the enemies and offers a suggestion about what form that settlement should take (v. 5).

Verses 6–7 look forward to a time after the anticipated deliverance, when the psalmist will express thanks to God by making an offering at the place of worship (see Ps. 50:14). After addressing the Lord, telling what "I" will do (v. 6), the psalmist hints that he will tell those gathered for worship what the Lord has done (v. 7).

The psalm began by referring to God's name as the expression of God's mighty saving presence. Instead of the usual "O give thanks to the LORD, for he is good" (Pss. 106:1; 136:1; and many others), it ends by referring to the Lord's *name* as an expression of God's goodness ("for it is good," v. 6).

Hallowed Be Your Name

One of the Ten Commandments says, "You shall not make wrongful use of the *name* of the LORD your God, for the LORD will not acquit anyone who misuses his *name*" (Exod. 20:7). Jesus suggested that a proper way to pray is to begin "Our Father in heaven, hallowed be your *name*" (Matt. 6:9). Since one of the commandments deals with God's name, and since the most well known of Christian prayers begins by speaking of God's name, the matter is obviously an important one.

As this psalm indicates, God's name is one of the ways in which God is represented on earth. It follows that God's name is to be held in regard and respected (the commandment), because such regard and respect are the proper attitude toward the God whom the name represents. The commandment in Exodus 20 speaks a negative word, warning against using God's name casually or in cursing. The prayer in Matthew 6 speaks a positive word, indicating how God's people can access God through prayer. A prayer ought to begin with a reminder of God's loving closeness ("Our Father") and then, suggests Jesus, continue with a reminder of God's powerful otherness ("hallowed be your name").

Both dimensions of the "name" are present in Psalm 54, which speaks of God's might (v. 1) and of God's goodness (v. 6).

WHEN FRIENDS FAIL
Psalm 55

**To the leader: with stringed instruments.
A Maskil of David.**

55:1 **Give ear to my prayer, O God;**
 do not hide yourself from my supplication.
 ² **Attend to me, and answer me;**
 I am troubled in my complaint.
 I am distraught ³**by the noise of the enemy,**
 because of the clamor of the wicked.
 For they bring trouble upon me,
 and in anger they cherish enmity against me.

 ⁴ **My heart is in anguish within me,**
 the terrors of death have fallen upon me.
 ⁵ **Fear and trembling come upon me,**
 and horror overwhelms me.
 ⁶ **And I say, "O that I had wings like a dove!**
 I would fly away and be at rest;
 ⁷ **truly, I would flee far away;**
 I would lodge in the wilderness;   *Selah*
 ⁸ **I would hurry to find a shelter for myself**
 from the raging wind and tempest."

 ⁹ **Confuse, O Lord, confound their speech;**
 for I see violence and strife in the city.
 ¹⁰ **Day and night they go around it**
 on its walls,
 and iniquity and trouble are within it;
 ¹¹ **ruin is in its midst;**
 oppression and fraud
 do not depart from its marketplace.

¹² It is not enemies who taunt me—
    I could bear that;
  it is not adversaries who deal insolently with me—
    I could hide from them.
¹³ But it is you, my equal,
    my companion, my familiar friend,
¹⁴ with whom I kept pleasant company;
    we walked in the house of God with the throng.
¹⁵ Let death come upon them;
    let them go down alive to Sheol;
  for evil is in their homes and in their hearts.

¹⁶ But I call upon God,
    and the Lord will save me.
¹⁷ Evening and morning and at noon
    I utter my complaint and moan,
    and he will hear my voice.
¹⁸ He will redeem me unharmed
    from the battle that I wage,
    for many are arrayed against me.
¹⁹ God, who is enthroned from of old,   *Selah*
    will hear, and will humble them—
  because they do not change,
    and do not fear God.

²⁰ My companion laid hands on a friend
    and violated a covenant with me
²¹ with speech smoother than butter,
    but with a heart set on war;
  with words that were softer than oil,
    but in fact were drawn swords.

²² Cast your burden on the Lord,
    and he will sustain you;
  he will never permit
    the righteous to be moved.

²³ But you, O God, will cast them down
    into the lowest pit;
  the bloodthirsty and treacherous
    shall not live out half their days.
  But I will trust in you.

There was a knock on the door of my office at the college. It was one of my favorite students. He had stopped by a few days earlier to tell me that he and the young woman he had been dating had broken up. I knew both of them well and was saddened to hear the news. In the course of our conversation I had suggested that he sit down with the book of Psalms and a red pencil and mark any passages that seemed to address his situation.

He sat down in my office and took out a Bible. "Listen to this," he said. "This is amazing. It's about her and me!" Then he showed me a section underlined in red, from Psalm 55:12–14:

> It is not enemies who taunt me—I could bear that. . . .
> But it is you [he had circled the "you"], my equal,
>   my companion, my familiar friend,
> with whom I kept pleasant company;
>   we walked in the house of God with the throng.

We talked about this and a few other psalm texts. Then it was time for class. Whenever I read this psalm, I recall that conversation and the pain that student was experiencing. Somehow, this psalm helped him get through it.

Once again, this is an individual lament. The familiar elements are evident (see Psalm 13), with the exception of a vow to praise: *request* (vv. 1–2a, 9a, 15), *complaint* (vv. 2b–8, 9b–11, 12–14, 20–21), and *affirmation of trust* (vv. 16–19, 22–23). The heading dedicates the piece to the choir director, suggests string accompaniment, and identifies the psalm as a Maskil or "instructional piece" to be associated with David (see comments on Psalm 32).

I'd Like to Get Out of Town (55:1–11)

In contrast to the more desperate and immediate call for help at the opening of Psalm 54, Psalm 55 begins by calling for the Lord's attention (vv. 1–2a). The writer says, "I am troubled in my complaint," and then begins to spell out the disturbing situation. Certain persons have been making the psalmist's life miserable (vv. 2b–3). Switching to "I" statements, the psalmist speaks of personal anguish (vv. 4–5) and envisions two ways of dealing with his painful situation. He imagines taking off like a bird and escaping to the desert (vv. 6–7); or he would be satisfied hiding out in a shelter somewhere, to get away from the storm he is experiencing in his life (v. 8; for *Selah*, also in v. 19, see on Psalm 3).

Verses 9b–11 describe the negative effects these persons are having on the community. The words pile up: *violence, strife, iniquity, trouble, ruin, oppression, fraud.* Clearly, things are in bad shape! The psalmist asks the Lord to put an end to all of this (v. 9a).

You, of All People! (55:12–14)

Among those people lining up against the psalmist is one person who is causing exceptional pain. The writer builds to a climax:

> It is not my enemies—I could bear that.
>   It is not my adversaries—I could hide from them.
> But it is you, my friend!
>
> (vv. 12–13, paraphrased)

Following are words describing the former good relationship that existed between these two. The psalmist describes the other: a person who is like me, my companion, my close friend. Both were believers and had enjoyed times of worship together with the congregation (vv. 13–14).

I Will Trust in You, Lord (55:15–23)

The remainder of the psalm jumps back and forth among affirmations of trust, complaints, and a request for help. The writer doesn't think much of these enemies: "evil is in their homes and in their hearts!" Therefore, he asks the Lord to let them die (v. 15).

Verses 16–19 express trust in God, despite these outward circumstances. As is the case with Muslims today, for the Hebrews there were three times daily for prayer. The psalmist knows what to do with complaints: as "What a Friend We Have in Jesus" puts it, "Take it to the Lord in prayer" (v. 17). Throughout this section is a confidence that the Lord will rescue (v. 16) and the Lord will hear this prayer (vv. 17, 19).

The betrayal of friendship is recalled once again in verses 20–21. The "friend's" words appeared to be smooth and soft as butter but were in fact as sharp and injurious as swords used in warfare.

The psalm ends on a positive note, with an encouragement to others to let the Lord handle troubles (v. 22). The writer of 1 Peter read this psalm and picked up some advice from verse 22 to pass on to his readers: "Cast all your anxiety on him, because he cares for you" (1 Peter 5:7). The psalm concludes with an affirmation of trust, which will be picked up three times in the next psalm (56:3, 4, and 11).

In Praise of Friendship

This psalm tells of a friendship that failed. "You always hurt the one you love," goes an old saying. The failure of the writer's friend to remain loyal hurt badly, precisely because the relationship of friendship had been so deep and genuine.

This report about the failure of a friendship can be balanced by the positive things the Bible has to say about friendship, especially in the book of Proverbs and in the apocryphal book of Sirach. A true friend is one who can be counted on, in good times and bad (Prov. 17:17). Friends can be more loyal than one's own relatives (Prov. 18:24)! Friends at hand are better than relatives at a distance (27:10). The book of Sirach says,

> Do not abandon old friends,
>   for new ones cannot equal them.
> A new friend is like new wine;
>   when it has aged you can drink it with pleasure.
> (9:10)

(See also Sirach 6:5–17 and the advice in 14:13: "Do good to friends before you die, and reach out and give to them as much as you can.")

GOD CARES WHEN YOU CRY
Psalm 56

To the leader: according to The Dove on Far-off Terebinths.
Of David. A Miktam, when the Philistines seized him in Gath.

56:1 **Be gracious to me, O God, for people trample on me;**
       all day long foes oppress me;
   2 **my enemies trample on me all day long,**
       for many fight against me.
   O Most High, 3**when I am afraid,**
       I put my trust in you.
   4 **In God, whose word I praise,**
       in God I trust; I am not afraid;
       what can flesh do to me?

   5 **All day long they seek to injure my cause;**
       all their thoughts are against me for evil.
   6 **They stir up strife, they lurk,**
       they watch my steps.
   As they hoped to have my life,
   7   **so repay them for their crime;**
       in wrath cast down the peoples, O God!

   8 **You have kept count of my tossings;**
       put my tears in your bottle.
   Are they not in your record?
   9 **Then my enemies will retreat**

> in the day when I call.
> This I know, that God is for me.
> 10 In God, whose word I praise,
>   in the LORD, whose word I praise,
> 11 in God I trust; I am not afraid.
>   What can a mere mortal do to me?
>
> 12 My vows to you I must perform, O God;
>   I will render thank offerings to you.
> 13 For you have delivered my soul from death,
>   and my feet from falling,
>   so that I may walk before God
>   in the light of life.

"Don't cry!" the five-year-old might be told after walking out of a frightening kindergarten classroom or falling down with a tricycle.

But "Don't cry!" is not always the best advice.

"Let the tears come!" the confused parent might be advised after telling a pastor or counselor about the most recent escapade of a problematic teenager.

There are times when crying is the right thing to do. According to Ecclesiastes, there is "a time to weep" (Eccl. 3:4). Those exiles living in Babylon sat down by the river there and wept when they thought about their homeland (Ps. 137:1). And who can forget the picture of Jesus weeping over his beloved city (Luke 19:41)? Or Jesus weeping at the death of his friend Lazarus (John 11:35)?

"Cast your burden on the LORD, and he will sustain you" is the advice given in Psalm 55:22. "Cast all your anxiety on him, because he cares for you" is how the writer of 1 Peter understood that text (1 Peter 5:7). This psalm also has a word about burdens and about anxiety. The psalmist says to God, "You have kept count of my tossings; put my tears in your bottle" (Ps. 56:8). According to this psalm, God cares about you when you cry.

After the dedication to the choir director (see on Psalm 4), the heading suggests a melody that is no longer known: "The Dove on Far-off Terebinths." (For David, see on Psalm 3; for Miktam, see the note on Psalm 16.) The editors suggest that the psalm would fit a situation such as David faced when he was captured in Gath (1 Sam. 21:10–15).

The psalm consists of the typical elements of a lament (see on Psalm 13): *request* and *"they" complaint* (vv. 1–2); *affirmation of trust* in God (vv. 3–4); *"they" complaint* and *request* (vv. 5–7); *affirmation of trust* (vv. 8–11); and *vow to praise* (vv. 12–13).

Trampled On, but Trusting (56:1–7)

Most of this psalm is a prayer, the words addressing God directly. The psalmist begins by asking for God's mercy because certain persons are walking all over him; the exact nature of the difficulties is not indicated (vv. 1–2).

After this complaint comes a statement of trust directed to the Lord: "O Most High, when I am afraid, I put my trust in you." Then the psalmist addresses the gathered congregation, testifying to faith in God:

> In God, whose word I praise,
>> in God I trust, I am not afraid;
>> what can flesh do to me?
>>> (v. 4)

Three different Hebrew words are used to refer to humans in this psalm. The first, translated "people," is *'enōš* (v. 1); the second, occurring here and translated "flesh," is *bāśar* (v. 4); the third, "mere mortal," is *'ādām* (v. 11). All three words emphasize the contrast between humans and God. Apparently the writer is varying vocabulary to avoid sounding monotonous.

The complaint against these people making the psalmist's life miserable continues in verses 5–6. The sense of the word translated "lurk" is to prowl about in secret, like a lion on the lookout for prey (Ps. 10:9).

A Bottle Full of Tears (56:8–13)

God is the "Most High" (v. 2) who is mighty enough to deal with entire nations (v. 7). But verse 8 indicates that God is also nearby, caring enough to deal with an individual. In fact, God treasures the tears of those whom God loves and has kept careful records about things that have happened to each of them (see also Ps. 139:16).

With the last line of verse 9, the writer of the psalmist turns from addressing God to speaking to the congregation. His testimony is short and rock solid:

> This I know, that God is for me. (v. 9)

Then he repeats the confession of faith already made in verse 4, this time adding a statement about "the LORD" and using one of the words for humans, *'ādām* (as in the story in Genesis), here translated "mere mortal."

The psalm concludes as the psalmist once again speaks directly to God (vv. 12–13ab). Verse 12 promises a proper offering for the deliverance described in the first part of verse 13. The last lines of the psalm again speak *about* God, describing life as a walk in the sight of God (see Ps. 116:9), in fact, a walk in the light (see Pss. 27:1; 43:3).

If God Is for Me . . .

There are three points at which this psalm makes contact with the lives of contemporary believers. First, the theme of trust is sounded three times in the psalm (vv. 3, 4, and 11). Two of these statements are close to the motto that stands on coins and currency of the United States of America: "In God We Trust" (vv. 4, 11). The difference is that the national motto speaks with the plural "we" while the psalm is the voice of an individual, "I." In any case, this is a teaching point that the author of the psalm wants to make with the congregation. In the middle of sentences addressing God as "you" in prayer, the author has some important instructional words *about* God, in verses 4, 9b–11, and 13c. These words tell others what the psalmist has learned about God: God cares, and we can trust God with our lives.

Second, the confession in verse 9 sounds very much like that confession of faith made by the apostle Paul: "If God is for us, who is against us?" This statement sets off one of the greatest of the Bible's affirmations of trust in God (Rom. 8:31–38).

Finally, the psalm is reminiscent of the story of Jesus healing a blind man, told in John 9. The writer says, "This I know, that God is for me" (Ps. 56:9). The man who was healed testified, "One thing I do know, that though I was blind, now I see" (John 9:25). The psalm ends with a resolve to "walk before God in the light of life." The Fourth Gospel identifies Jesus as the light of the world (9:5), and the writer of 1 John calls on those who believe in Jesus to walk in the light (1 John 1:5–2:11).

LIE DOWN WITH THE LIONS AND STILL GET SOME SLEEP!
Psalm 57

To the leader: Do Not Destroy.
Of David. A Miktam, when he fled from Saul, in the cave.

57:1 **Be merciful to me, O God, be merciful to me,**
   for in you my soul takes refuge;
 in the shadow of your wings I will take refuge,
   until the destroying storms pass by.

² I cry to God Most High,
   to God who fulfills his purpose for me.
³ He will send from heaven and save me,
   he will put to shame those who trample on me.   *Selah*
   God will send forth his steadfast love and his faithfulness.

⁴ I lie down among lions
   that greedily devour human prey;
   their teeth are spears and arrows,
   their tongues sharp swords.

⁵ Be exalted, O God, above the heavens.
   Let your glory be over all the earth.

⁶ They set a net for my steps;
   my soul was bowed down.
   They dug a pit in my path,
   but they have fallen into it themselves.   *Selah*
⁷ My heart is steadfast, O God,
   my heart is steadfast.
   I will sing and make melody.
   ⁸ Awake, my soul!
   Awake, O harp and lyre!
   I will awake the dawn.
⁹ I will give thanks to you, O Lord, among the peoples;
   I will sing praises to you among the nations.
¹⁰ For your steadfast love is as high as the heavens;
   your faithfulness extends to the clouds.

¹¹ Be exalted, O God, above the heavens.
   Let your glory be over all the earth.

Swim with the Sharks without Being Eaten Alive is the title of entrepreneur Harvey Mackay's book about surviving in the competitive world of high finance. Had the author of this psalm written a book, he might have titled it *Lie Down with the Lions and Still Get Some Sleep!* (see v. 4). The imagery is different, but the idea is the same: since life can be such a stressful, dangerous business, one must learn how to survive!

The heading includes a dedication to the choir director (see on Psalm 4), a reference to David (see on Psalm 3) and to a melody no longer known ("Do Not Destroy"), and finally a term no longer understood (Miktam; see on Psalm 16). The editor suggests that this psalm would fit the situation when David was running for his life from Saul (1 Samuel 22–24), thus a time of swimming with sharks or lying down with lions.

As is the case with all the psalms from 54–59, this is an individual lament with the elements of that psalm type: a *request* in the imperative mood (v. 1a,), *affirmations of trust* (vv. 1b–3, 7, 10), *complaints* in the "I" and "they" forms (vv. 4, 6), *words of praise* (vv. 5, 11), and *vows to praise* (vv. 8–9).

These writers often quoted from popular songs or from each other: verses 7–11 of this psalm are almost identical to Psalm 108:1–5.

In the Shadow of Your Wings (57:1–5)

As is the case with the neighboring psalms of lament, this one comes out of a difficult, even life-threatening situation. To speak of the psalmist's life as stressful would be too mild a description. The psalmist speaks rather of trying to exist while living in the midst of a pack of lions (v. 4); the story of Daniel comes to mind (Daniel 6).

The writer does not provide the literal details of the situation being faced. The psalm begins with a desperate, doubled call for mercy, addressed to God as "you." The one who is praying pictures God as a mother hen, protecting her little chicks from a thunderstorm (v. 1).

After speaking to God, the psalmist addresses those in the assembled congregation. His God is not "too small"! The God in whom he expresses confidence is the "Most High," residing in heaven, and from there will send his steadfast love (*hesed*) and faithful help. The psalmist is sure that God will deal with those who are walking all over him (v. 3; the same word, *trample*, appears in Ps. 56:2). (*Selah* indicates a break; see the comments on Psalm 3.)

With this sort of confidence in God's love and protection, the psalmist will be able to survive in the midst of the sharks, the lions, the dangers threatening him (v. 4). He can lie down and sleep, entrusting his life to a God who presides over the heavens and the earth (v. 5). He has learned to let God be God and to give himself over to God's care (v. 1).

Let God Be God! (57:6–11)

What were these people doing to make the psalmist's life so miserable? The psalm gives only pictures. They have been trampling on him, as certain persons trampled on the poor in the days of Amos (Amos 2:7; 8:4). They have set a net trap, as a hunter sets a trap for a bird (Prov. 1:17). They have dug a pit, just as hunters dig a pit and cover it with branches to catch a lion (Ezek. 19:4, 8). But now these enemies have fallen into their own trap (v. 6; see also Prov. 26:27)! After verse 6 is a *Selah*, indicating a break (see on Psalm 3).

The mood of the psalm's conclusion in verses 7–11 is upbeat. The writer is probably quoting a popular song (see also Ps. 108:1–5). In the Hebrew text, each line gets longer, so that the text looks like the side of a pyramid (see Klaus Seybold, *Die Psalmen*, 229). Beginning with a focus on the individual, with "my heart" and "I" in verse 7, the psalm continues with a resolve to sing and a request for orchestral accompaniment (v. 8). The song that began in the heart of an individual continues to expand, calling on others present, then other peoples, then the nations of the world to praise this God whose steadfast love and faithfulness (v. 3) are as high as the heavens and the clouds above them (v. 10)! We could imagine all joining in on the refrain once again (v. 11; see also v. 5), in praise of the God who created the heavens and the earth (v. 11; see Gen. 1:1).

Letting God Be God

So what sort of survival techniques does this psalm suggest for living in a world where one feels trampled on, surrounded by lions—or by sharks?

Certainly, the psalmist is experiencing troubles and stresses enough in the rough-and-tumble of everyday life. The writer speaks of storms (v. 1), of being trampled on (v. 3), of being pursued by those setting traps (v. 6), and of being surrounded by greedy lions with sharp teeth—and sharp tongues (v. 4)! Here is no dreamy poet or disengaged professor, living in some ivory tower away from the troubles of the world!

What does the psalmist suggest for survival in such an environment? We are well advised to pay close attention to the repeated sections, the refrain, in verses 5 and 11. We discover that the one in trouble does nothing but follow the advice "Let go and let God!" The psalmist is concerned that God be properly regarded and praised (vv. 5, 11) and is then content to live in God's protection, praying to the Lord (vv. 1, 2) and living in the confidence of God's care.

We do not discover much focus on the psalmist's own troubles. One has to look carefully to discover what they are. The focus of this psalm is rather on God: the loving and protecting mother hen (v. 1); the Most High in heaven, who is concerned with problems of an individual on earth (vv. 2–3); the One whose splendor can be seen the world over (vv. 5, 11).

Remembering what this God is like, it would be difficult to keep from singing, from cranking up the orchestra, from praising God in all ways and in all places. If praises can come from the belly of a big fish (Jonah 2) or from a furnace of fire (The Prayer of Azariah in the Apocrypha), why not from a sea full of sharks?

PROBABLY NOT FOR OPENING DEVOTIONS
Psalm 58

To the leader: Do Not Destroy.
Of David. A Miktam.

58:1 Do you indeed decree what is right, you gods?
    Do you judge people fairly?
² No, in your hearts you devise wrongs;
    your hands deal out violence on earth.

³ The wicked go astray from the womb;
    they err from their birth, speaking lies.
⁴ They have venom like the venom of a serpent,
    like the deaf adder that stops its ear,
⁵ so that it does not hear the voice of charmers
    or of the cunning enchanter.

⁶ O God, break the teeth in their mouths;
    tear out the fangs of the young lions, O LORD!
⁷ Let them vanish like water that runs away;
    like grass let them be trodden down and wither.
⁸ Let them be like the snail that dissolves into slime;
    like the untimely birth that never sees the sun.
⁹ Sooner than your pots can feel the heat of thorns,
    whether green or ablaze, may he sweep them away!

¹⁰ The righteous will rejoice when they see vengeance done;
    they will bathe their feet in the blood of the wicked.
¹¹ People will say, "Surely there is a reward for the righteous;
    surely there is a God who judges on earth."

How are psalms most often used in our time? An individual may read through a psalm a day, as part of a program of Bible reading. A psalm may be read as part of a Sunday worship service, linked to the other biblical texts for the day. Small groups of Christians may gather in convents or monasteries or deaconess houses, opening and closing the day with a psalm as part of matins and vespers services.

This psalm, however, does not appear in the listing of texts for Sunday morning. It is, of course, read by those who take the psalms as they come, one at a time. One suspects, however, that it is seldom selected as a text for opening or closing a gathering of believers.

Some psalms are that way. Nevertheless, Psalm 58 is of interest and one can learn from it.

The heading gives a clue as to why the psalm is found in this location. It is the second of a series of three psalms, each dedicated "To the leader," associated with David, to be sung to the tune "Do Not Destroy" (a tune no longer known) and classified as a "Miktam" (a term no longer understood; see my comments on Psalm 57). The editors obviously were grouping psalms according to similarities, and here they placed together three using the same tune.

There are a good number of difficulties in understanding this psalm. First off, who is being addressed in verse 1? The NRSV translates the Hebrew as "gods" but has a footnote indicating that the translation could also be "mighty lords," that is, human rulers. If the translation is "gods," then God is calling to judgment certain heavenly beings who rule the earth, as in Psalm 82. "You rulers" (NIV, GNB) seems the more likely translation, because verse 3 then describes the wickedness of these persons.

In either case, with verses 1–2 certain gods or leaders are accused of wrong judgment and provoking too much violence. Verses 3–5 are a "they" complaint (see on Psalm 13) against certain wicked persons. Verses 6–9 are a prayer, asking God to punish these wicked. Finally, verses 10 and 11 anticipate a time after the wicked have experienced punishment.

The Problem of Violence (58:1–5)

The psalm begins by identifying a problem that continues to be at the top of the agenda for concerned citizens of our own day: violence. Violence is planned in the heart, then carried out in the towns and cities (v. 2).

Though the precise nature of the violence is not described, something is said about those who carry it out. These persons have tended toward wickedness since birth (v. 3). With verse 4, the writer of the psalm begins a series of descriptions that indicate considerable imagination and great poetic gifts. These wicked ones spew venom, like poisonous serpents. They are as fierce as snakes that cannot be stopped, even by an expert snake charmer! The prophet Jeremiah also speaks of these fearsome creatures (Jer. 8:17; note also Eccl. 10:11, for a comment on snake charmers).

Snails into the Slime (58:6–9)

Verses 6–9 are most imaginative in their imagery but quite frightening in the realities they portray. The psalmist is asking that God deal with these wicked ones. The pictures are chilling. The psalmist asks God to break their teeth and tear out their fangs. God should let them vanish like water that runs away, or let them be trampled down like grass, so that they dry up and wither away. God should let them become like tiny snails that make their way along the beach and then dissolve into the slime, or like an embryo or fetus that never comes to life. "May they disappear," says the psalm, "just as quickly as a pot of soup heats up over a blazing fire!"

The violent imagery continues, as the righteous are pictured rejoicing at a victory over these wicked ones, washing their feet in their blood (v. 10). One thinks of similar gruesome imagery in Psalm 68:23 or Isaiah 63:1 ("garments stained crimson") or the description of judgment in Revelation 14:20: "And the wine press was trodden outside the city, and blood flowed from the wine press, as high as a horse's bridle, for a distance of about two hundred miles."

But Surely There Is a God (58:11)

This is certainly not one of the first psalms that one would choose for opening a meeting of the church council or even for private devotional reading. For those who have for a lifetime heard those words from the Sermon on the Mount "Love your enemies and pray for those who persecute you" (Matt. 5:44) or from the cross "Father, forgive them; for they do not know what they are doing" (Luke 23:34), this prayer that God might "break the teeth in their mouths" will not do; not for those who call themselves Christians.

The prayer in verses 6–9 is not appropriate, but it is understandable. These are words from the depth of some human pain, perhaps directed at murderers of the innocent and of children. These words are not to be appropriated, but they can be understood as giving expression to a very human response from some very desperate situation.

And in such a situation of extreme hurt and justifiable anger, the final words of this psalm can point the way to healing and to comfort: "surely there is a God who judges on earth" (v. 11).

PROWLERS IN THE NIGHT
Psalm 59

To the leader: Do Not Destroy. Of David.
A Miktam, when Saul ordered his house to be watched in order to kill him.

59:1 Deliver me from my enemies, O my God;
protect me from those who rise up against me.
² Deliver me from those who work evil;
from the bloodthirsty save me.

³ Even now they lie in wait for my life;
the mighty stir up strife against me.

For no transgression or sin of mine, O LORD,
4   for no fault of mine, they run and make ready.

Rouse yourself, come to my help and see!
5   You, LORD God of hosts, are God of Israel.
Awake to punish all the nations;
    spare none of those who treacherously plot evil.   *Selah*

6 Each evening they come back,
    howling like dogs
    and prowling about the city.
7 There they are, bellowing with their mouths,
    with sharp words on their lips—
    for "Who," they think, "will hear us?"

8 But you laugh at them, O LORD;
    you hold all the nations in derision.
9 O my strength, I will watch for you;
    for you, O God, are my fortress.
10 My God in his steadfast love will meet me;
    my God will let me look in triumph on my enemies.

11 Do not kill them, or my people may forget;
    make them totter by your power, and bring them down,
    O Lord, our shield.
12 For the sin of their mouths, the words of their lips,
    let them be trapped in their pride.
For the cursing and lies that they utter,
13   consume them in wrath;
    consume them until they are no more.
Then it will be known to the ends of the earth
    that God rules over Jacob.   *Selah*

14 Each evening they come back,
    howling like dogs
    and prowling about the city.
15 They roam about for food,
    and growl if they do not get their fill.

16 But I will sing of your might;
    I will sing aloud of your steadfast love in the morning.
For you have been a fortress for me
    and a refuge in the day of my distress.
17 O my strength, I will sing praises to you,
    for you, O God, are my fortress,
    the God who shows me steadfast love.

It is nighttime and they are back, prowling about the city like a pack of dogs. They think that no one sees them. "Who will hear us?" they say. Each evening, the same thing. They are back in the city, plotting, prowling about, howling, growling when they do not get what they want.

So the psalmist describes those persons who have become enemies, workers of evil in the city where he lives (vv. 6–7, 14–15).

The elements in the heading are familiar from the preceding two psalms and are discussed with Psalm 57. The editors have linked this psalm to events described in 1 Samuel 19. Saul sought to put an end to David's musical career with his spear (1 Sam. 19:8–10) and then sent some of his own people to "guard" David in his own home overnight. David's wife warned him of the danger and planted a dummy in his bed, while David escaped during the night and the would-be assassins found the dummy (vv. 11–17). The editors imagine the psalm fitting into such a heated and dangerous situation.

Psalm 59 is made up of the typical elements of the individual lament (see on Psalm 13): *requests* for help (vv. 1–2, 4b–5, 11–13), *"they" complaint* (vv. 3–4a, 6–7, 14–15), *affirmation of trust* (vv. 8–10), and a concluding *vow to praise* (vv. 16–17). The *Selah*s mark points of pause (see the comments on Psalm 3).

Howling and Prowling (59:1–7)

The editorial suggestion in the title sets the right tone for this psalm. It was night. David feared for his life. His wife lied to Saul's messengers about his whereabouts, and he escaped. This psalm did not arise from quiet meditation alongside the still waters of a stream running through green pastures. This is more the prayer of a fugitive, a desperate cry of someone on the run, trying to escape those who, like wild dogs, are howling, growling, out to kill him.

The verbs asking God for help multiply in verses 1–2: "Deliver me . . . protect me. . . . Deliver me . . . save me." The descriptions of those pursuing the psalmist escalate. They are "enemies . . . those who rise up against me . . . those who work evil . . . people of blood" (the literal Hebrew; NRSV, "bloodthirsty").

The atmosphere of verse 3 is equally intense: "Look! They lie in wait for my life!" (my translation). The psalmist declares innocence, using all three of the classic Old Testament words for sin: *peša'* (= rebellion, like children rebelling against parents; see Isa. 1:2), *ḥāṭā'* (= missing the target, literally, see Judg. 20:16), *'āwōn* (= being distorted, bent over; Psalm 38:6). The mood is one of action, with these enemies rushing about, getting themselves ready for the next round of fighting (v. 4a).

Though the Lord does not sleep (Ps. 121:3–4), in the urgency of the moment the one praying thinks it will help to ask God to "wake up" (see also Pss. 7:6; 44:23) and punish those who are engaged in evil plots (v. 5b).

The psalmist compares these enemies to stray dogs, prowling through the garbage of the city at night, rummaging about and growling (vv. 6–7; 14–15; for the dogs, see also 1 Kings 14:11; Jer. 15:3). With words sharp as swords (v. 7; see Pss. 55:21; 57:4; 64:3), they carve out what they believe are totally secret schemes that will be harmful to the community of believers.

A Mighty Fortress (59:8–17)

The refrain catches the theme of this final section of the psalm: "for you, O God, are my fortress" (vv. 9, 17; see also v. 16). The affirmation of trust in verses 8–10 brings to expression two aspects of the reality of the biblical God: (1) God's strength and might, superior over all the nations (v. 8), and a secure place of refuge for the psalmist (v. 9), and (2) God's steadfast love that reaches down into the life of the besieged believer (v. 10). The "strength/fortress" theme and the "steadfast love" theme are again picked up in the vow to praise in vv. 16–17, the psalm ending on the words *steadfast love*.

The wishes expressed in verses 11–13 sound unnecessarily harsh and are reminiscent of similar wishes for the enemy expressed in Psalm 58:6–9. As we have seen in connection with that passage, Jesus advised another sort of attitude toward enemies. The very human and hateful attitude expressed by the writer here ("consume them") is not to be taken as exemplary for Christian readers. It may be explained by the acute life-or-death situation of the one praying and by the end the psalmist has in view: "Defeat them, Lord, so that the whole world will recognize that you are the true God" (v. 13, emphasized with a break signaled by *Selah*).

God Who Meets Me

The writer of this psalm has an exalted view of God. God is addressed as Lord God of hosts (v. 5), that is, commander of the heavenly armies that may be seen in the stars at night (Isa. 40:25–26). God is the God of Israel and Jacob but also God of the nations, who controls all the nations and who will be known to the ends of the earth (vv. 5, 8, 13). The psalmist will gladly sing of the might of such a God (v. 16).

This psalm also sees this exalted God as concerned about an individual. The psalmist can say to God, "Deliver *me*, protect *me*, save *me*"

(vv. 1–2). The psalmist can speak to God in one-on-one terms, asking this mighty God to take time out and "come to *my* help" (v. 4) and living in the certainty that the Lord will be "*my* strength" and "*my* fortress"(vv. 9, 16, 17).

The central notion expressing the relationship between God and humans is steadfast love, or *hesed* (vv. 10, 16, 17; see the discussion on *hesed* in connection with Psalm 136). One sentence expresses what is at the heart of this psalm, and at the heart of the entire Bible: "My God in his steadfast love will meet me" (v. 10). The prospect of such a meeting is nothing but good news.

GOD, FIX THE CRACKS!
Psalm 60

To the leader: according to the Lily of the Covenant.
A Miktam of David; for instruction; when he struggled with
 Aram-naharaim and with Aram-zobah, and when Joab on his
 return killed twelve thousand Edomites in the Valley of Salt.

60:1 O God, you have rejected us, broken our defenses;
       you have been angry; now restore us!
   2 You have caused the land to quake; you have torn it open;
       repair the cracks in it, for it is tottering.
   3 You have made your people suffer hard things;
       you have given us wine to drink that made us reel.

   4 You have set up a banner for those who fear you,
       to rally to it out of bowshot.   *Selah*
   5 Give victory with your right hand, and answer us,
       so that those whom you love may be rescued.

   6 God has promised in his sanctuary:
       "With exultation I will divide up Shechem,
       and portion out the Vale of Succoth.
   7 Gilead is mine, and Manasseh is mine;
       Ephraim is my helmet;
       Judah is my scepter.
   8 Moab is my washbasin;
       on Edom I hurl my shoe;
       over Philistia I shout in triumph."

   9 Who will bring me to the fortified city?
       Who will lead me to Edom?

¹⁰ **Have you not rejected us, O God?**
  You do not go out, O God, with our armies.
¹¹ **O grant us help against the foe,**
  for human help is worthless.
¹² **With God we shall do valiantly;**
  it is he who will tread down our foes.

Here is the prayer of a people who have experienced war and have lost. Because they live by the motto "In God we trust," they understand their present tragic situation in the light of God. When their armies win a victory, they are quick to give the credit to God and to sing praises (Psalm 21; see also Exodus 15). When they have lost a battle or a war, they are also quick to associate this experience with God. Such is the case in the situation that gave rise to this psalm. These are a people who have been defeated in warfare and have another battle before them. Their once-proud kingdom has been badly damaged. The nation's structure is cracked, tottering and badly in need of repair (v. 2).

The heading is the longest of any in the book of Psalms. (For Miktam, see my comments on Psalm 16; for the dedication to the choir leader, an indication of the unknown melody, and the association with David, see the comments on Psalms 3 and 4.) In this instance, the editors furnish a specific context for the psalm, associating it with the time when King David was developing a reputation as a great fighter. The books of Samuel indicate that David fought with two Aramaean states (2 Sam. 8:3–8) and, through Joab, brought Edom under control (2 Sam. 8:13–14). Psalm 60 is placed in this context of David's military struggles.

The psalm is a *lament of the community* (see Psalm 44 and the listing there) and is made up of the elements characteristic of the lament (see on Psalm 13), as well as a word from God: *"you" complaint* with *requests* for help (vv. 1–3, 5, 9–11), *affirmation of trust* (vv. 4, 12) and a word from God (vv. 6–8).

Restore, Repair, and Rally Us (60:1–5)

It has been suggested that the central message of biblical faith is a word from God saying, "You are accepted. Now accept the fact that you are accepted." The writer of this psalm imagines God's attitude as quite the opposite. The psalms speaks not of acceptance but of rejection: "O God, you have rejected us," it begins. And it concludes with a question: "Have you not rejected us, O God?" (v. 10).

The implications of God's alleged switch from an attitude of accepting to one of rejecting are pictured in two areas. First, as the people suffer, so does the land, which has been quaking and is torn up, cracked, and ready to collapse because of God's anger toward the people (v. 2). What is probably meant is the kind of beating that the land and the natural environment take in warfare. The second evidence of God's rejection is the political instability of the nation, described as staggering about like a drunken person. The blame for these natural and national difficulties is laid squarely on God: "You have made your people suffer" (v. 3).

There is a sign of hope, however. Just as an army in the field would set up a banner to mark a place for troops to rally in battle (Isa. 5:26, "signal"), so the Lord has set up a banner to indicate a place where the people can gather in safety and rally for a new beginning (v. 4). (*Selah* marks a break in the movement of the psalm; see on Psalm 3.)

The request in verse 5 asks for the Lord's help in rescuing the people, here named "those whom you love."

My Washbasin, the Dead Sea! (60:6–8)

At the heart of this psalm is a message from God's heavenly quarters. This message has little to do with heaven but much to do with down-to-earth political realities. Speaking through a priest or prophet in some sort of sanctuary service, God promises a redividing of territory.

In the future, says God, the area around the city of Shechem and in the Vale of Succoth to the east of the Jordan, under Assyrian control after 722 B.C., will once again be divided among God's people (v. 6). The northern territories of Manasseh and Ephraim and Gilead and Judah will belong to God's people once again (v. 7).

But God's power extends beyond the narrow confines of what were once the states of Israel and Judah. Moab's sea, the Dead Sea, will be the Lord's washbasin, and Edom will be the Lord's shoebox! A cry of victory will resound over the feared cities of Philistia (v. 8).

For a people rejected and broken, suffering and stumbling (vv. 1, 3), these must have been encouraging words indeed! God said, "Don't fear, my people! I rule over all the nations of the earth and also have my eye on you!"

With the Help of God (60:9–12)

With verses 6–8, the psalm has presented words from God, restating the power of God over the nations. Now a representative of the army speaks, trying to integrate faith in God with the task of leading his nation's armies into battle.

"Who's going to help us now, to defeat Edom?" this person asks (v. 9).

And then addressing God, that person, perhaps a priest or maybe the king himself, says, in effect, "You've not been giving us victories lately, God. Have you *rejected* us—the very people you once chose as your own? I know, God, that Edom is nothing more than a shoebox to you. So now will you help us in the battle against these Philistines? We know that as humans, we can't do it alone!" (vv. 1, 10–11).

The psalm concludes with a prayer of the sort a leader might pray before going into battle (v. 11; compare Psalm 20) and then an assurance that sounds as if it is aimed to encourage troops who have the jitters before being sent off on a mission: "With God we shall do valiantly" (v. 12).

God, Fix the Cracks!

The fact that this prayer comes from a time of national disaster is a reminder that biblical faith is concerned not only with individuals but also with communities. After many psalms dealing with individual problems, this one focuses on the problems of the whole people of God (vv. 3, 10–12). It also witnesses to God's regard for the people of the world, people whom God knows (vv. 6–8) and even loves (John 3:16).

ROCK MUSIC
Psalm 61

To the leader: with stringed instruments. Of David.

61:1 **Hear my cry, O God;**
      listen to my prayer.
  2 **From the end of the earth I call to you,**
      when my heart is faint.

   Lead me to the rock
      that is higher than I;
  3 **for you are my refuge,**
      a strong tower against the enemy.

  4 **Let me abide in your tent forever,**
      find refuge under the shelter of your wings.   *Selah*
  5 **For you, O God, have heard my vows;**
      you have given me the heritage of those who fear your name.

  6 **Prolong the life of the king;**
      may his years endure to all generations!
  7 **May he be enthroned forever before God;**
      appoint steadfast love and faithfulness to watch over him!

⁸ **So I will always sing praises to your name,**
as I pay my vows day after day.

One of the old favorites in the musical tradition of the church is "Rock of Ages," which uses the image of a rock to refer to the crucified Christ:

> Rock of ages, cleft for me,
> let me hide myself in thee.

Or there are the lines from "My Hope Is Built on Nothing Less":

> On Christ the solid rock I stand,
> all other ground is sinking sand.

These hymn writers use "rock" imagery to refer to Christ. The writers of the psalms use rock imagery to refer to God.

"Rock" psalms are often paired together. Psalm 18 begins, "The LORD is my rock . . . my rock in whom I take refuge"; it continues, "And who is a rock besides our God?" (v. 31); and it comes to a conclusion with "The LORD lives! Blessed be my rock" (v. 46). Psalm 19 concludes, "O LORD, my rock and my redeemer." Psalm 27 confesses trust in the Lord with the words "he will set me high on a rock" (v. 5), while Psalm 28 says to the Lord, "My rock, do not refuse to hear me" (v. 1). Psalm 94 names God "the rock of my refuge" (v. 22), and Psalm 95 praises "the rock of our salvation" (v. 1).

"Lead me to the rock that is higher than I," says Psalm 61, and the next psalm refers to God as "my rock and my salvation, my fortress" (Ps. 62:2, 6) and also "my mighty rock, my refuge" (v. 7).

The heading indicates to the worship leader that this psalm should be accompanied by stringed instruments and associates it with David (see on Psalm 3), as is true for the collection of psalms running from Psalms 51–65. The psalm identifies itself as a prayer (v. 1) and includes the typical elements of a lament (see on Psalm 13): *request* (vv. 1, 2c ["Lead me . . . ,"] 4, 6–7), *"I" complaint* (v. 2ab), *affirmation of trust* (vv. 3, 5), and a *vow to praise* (v. 8).

Lead Me to the Rock (61:1–4)

The psalm begins with a desperate call for the Lord to hear the prayer for help that follows. The one praying is not in the temple but is far away geographically ("the end of the earth" means far away; see Deut. 28:49) and not in good shape physically (see the heading for Psalm 102 as well as Pss. 142:3 and 143:4 for the same "faint" vocabulary).

The one praying is sinking, as one sinks in water, and asks God to put him in a place of safety, described with three images: "the rock that is higher than I" (v. 2), a "strong tower" (v. 3), and a "refuge" (v. 4). As is clear from the use of the same vocabulary in the next psalm, the rock and the refuge is God (Ps. 62:7).

With verse 4 the one praying expresses a wish to live in God's temple forever ("your tent"; Pss. 15:1; 27:5), under the protection of the wings of the cherubim, the winged creatures supporting the Lord's throne in the temple (Ps. 17:8; 57:1). (*Selah* marks a break in the psalm; see on Psalm 3.)

Politics and Piety (61:5–8)

In the second half of the Psalm 61, a prayer for the king (vv. 6–7) is framed by statements about vows and God's name (vv. 5, 8). The psalm does not indicate which king is being prayed for. In any case, it appears that politics and piety are quite naturally bound together. The language is typical of the extravagant and exaggerated language of the royal psalms: the prayer is that the king will rule forever. Then the psalm asks that God provide the king with those qualities so essential to good rule: steadfast love and faithfulness.

With the framing statements in verses 5 and 8, the one praying acknowledges the heritage God has given and promises to sing praises to "your name" and to keep vows (see v. 5). Does "paying my vows" refer to the vows mentioned in verse 4, to remain attached to the temple for a lifetime?

God and Government

This psalm succeeds in bringing together prayer and praise, God and government. As it begins, it sounds the typical themes of the laments. The one praying is in a desperate state (v. 2) and asks God to rescue and to provide refuge. Apparently that rescue was experienced, and now that prayers have been answered, it is time to praise God (v. 8).

Having had prayers answered, the psalmist does not stop the act of praying but expands the prayer to a circle wider than his own concerns. The psalmist prays for the one who has political responsibility over his life, the king. Here is no absolute separation between the responsibilities of those in the temple and those in the state house. The prayer of verse 7 catches it just right, asking that the king have a long rule, marked by steadfast love, faithfulness, and walking rightly before God.

This psalm begins (the heading) and ends (v. 8) by referring to music. It appears that some things in human life are best done with the help of music. Included in this category, according to this psalm, is bringing praise to "the rock that is higher than I."

BUILT ON A ROCK
Psalm 62

To the leader: according to Jeduthun.
A Psalm of David.

62:1 **For God alone my soul waits in silence;**
        from him comes my salvation.
   2 **He alone is my rock and my salvation,**
        my fortress; I shall never be shaken.

   3 **How long will you assail a person,**
        will you batter your victim, all of you,
        as you would a leaning wall, a tottering fence?
   4 **Their only plan is to bring down a person of prominence.**
        They take pleasure in falsehood;
     they bless with their mouths,
        but inwardly they curse.   *Selah*

   5 **For God alone my soul waits in silence,**
        for my hope is from him.
   6 **He alone is my rock and my salvation,**
        my fortress; I shall not be shaken.
   7 **On God rests my deliverance and my honor;**
        my mighty rock, my refuge is in God.

   8 **Trust in him at all times, O people;**
        pour out your heart before him;
        God is a refuge for us.   *Selah*

   9 **Those of low estate are but a breath,**
        those of high estate are a delusion;
     in the balances they go up;
        they are together lighter than a breath.
  10 **Put no confidence in extortion,**
        and set no vain hopes on robbery;
        if riches increase, do not set your heart on them.

  11 **Once God has spoken;**
        twice have I heard this:
        that power belongs to God,

12   **and steadfast love belongs to you, O Lord.**
      For you repay to all
          according to their work.

The song known as Psalm 61 asked God, "Lead me to the rock that is higher than I." Psalm 62 also refers to God as "my rock," even "my mighty rock" (vv. 2, 6, 7).

Yet another old favorite hymn, "Built on a Rock," also picks up "rock" imagery from the New Testament, suggesting that when everything else in the world is falling apart, the church will continue to stand because it is built on the rock of Christ:

> Built on a rock, the church shall stand
> even when steeples are falling.

The picture of God as rock is central to Psalm 62, since it occurs in the refrain in verses 2, 6 and also in verse 7.

The heading dedicates the psalm to the music director and associates it with David (see on Psalm 3). Jeduthun may refer to a tune of the day, though the matter is not certain.

This is a psalm with a refrain (vv. 1–2, 5–6) and with a few differences in the repetition of that refrain (the second lines of vv. 1 and 5). Since a refrain carries that which is especially important in a text, we shall pay careful attention to it.

The psalm is made up of elements of the lament (see on Psalm 13), but with some variations. Verses 1–2 and 5–7 are *affirmations of trust*, speaking *about* God. Since the element of trust is sounded in the refrain and is of central importance, this psalm is often classified as a *psalm of trust* (see the list with the comments on Psalm 11). Verses 3–4 are *complaints*, first *to* the enemy in "you" form and then *about* the enemy in "they" form; the complaints conclude with a *Selah*, indicating a break (see on Psalm 3). The section in verses 8–10 is framed by imperative verbs, offering instruction ("Trust . . . pour out . . . put . . . set"). Verse 9 makes an observation about humanity as a whole. The psalm winds down with the writer reporting a message twice received from God (v. 11) and concludes by addressing God for the first time, with words of *trust* (v. 12).

Solid as a Rock (62:1–7)

Verses 3 and 4 hint at the trouble that gave rise to this psalm. First, the writer speaks directly to the troublemakers, asking them how long they are going to keep up the "battering" that has been going on. The psalmist pictures himself as a wall about to fall over and these individuals as a wrecking crew, hammering, banging, ramming it until it topples.

What could they have been doing? A hint is given: through their lies, they are trying to ruin one of the prominent members of the community (v. 4).

The affirmations of trust in verses 1–2 and 5–7 should be read in this context of suffering under the attack of such reputation wreckers. Verses 1 and 5 speak of the psalmist ("my soul" is "I") riding out the struggle in silence, relying on God. For the sake of encouragement for self and testimony to others, these confessions of faith are repeated. The psalmist is able to look away from the immediate batterings and remember that the big things that hold life together, such as salvation (v. 1) and hope (v. 5), come from God. And even though asking every day, "How long?" (v. 3), the psalmist can wait it out.

We could imagine the refrain in verses 2 and 6 sung to some majestic melody. Three words are used to refer to God. God is pictured as "rock" dozens of times in the Bible (see the discussion of Psalm 61 for references). The idea behind the Hebrew word translated "fortress" is that of being high and thus protected from attackers (Deut. 2:36 refers to these high "citadels," as does Ps. 48:3). This word is often used for God (Pss. 18:2; 46:7, 11; translated "refuge") and was the inspiration for the hymn "A Mighty Fortress" (Ps. 59:9, 16, 17). The idea behind the word translated as "salvation," as used in verses 1 and 2, 6 and 7 (translated "deliverance"), is that of being rescued, as in being rescued from drowning. God is all of these: the solid *rock* that one can depend on for support, the *fortress* where one finds safety and refuge, the *rescuer* who comes out to save the drowning person.

Build on the Rock (62:8–12)

The mood of the psalm changes from complaint and confession of faith to *instruction*: "Trust in [the Lord] at all times," says the writer, "pour out your heart before him" (v. 8). The reason for doing this? "God is a refuge for us." The writer's own experiences (vv. 3–4) give this advice a ring of authenticity. A second time (see also v. 7) God is described as "refuge"; the word can be used for a shelter from the rain (Isa. 25:4; see also Ps. 61:4, translated "refuge").

Verse 9 refers to those people who have been causing problems for the psalmist; the Hebrew translated "low estate" and "high estate" has the sense of "human beings." These enemies of the writer are weighed in the balances and found to be as significant as a puff of smoke or a breath of air. The Hebrew behind *breath* is the word translated "vanity" in Ecclesiastes, meaning nothingness, worthlessness, emptiness. Verse 10 warns against thinking that money will buy happiness and security; the story Jesus told in Luke 12:13–21 makes the same point, as do the words in 1 Timothy 6:10 and 17.

Finally, verse 11 claims that the writer is delivering what was heard from God, and verse 12 ends the piece by speaking to God for the first time.

The most famous sermon that Jesus preached is remembered as ending with a story about two home builders and with some advice to those engaged in building lives. Those who hear the words of Jesus and put them into action are compared to a wise person who builds a house on a rock. That rock provides a sturdy foundation that withstands storm and flood. Those hearing the words of Jesus and not acting on them are compared to the person who builds on sand and whose life totally collapses under the storms of life (Matt. 7:24–27).

Jesus did not harp on the foolishness of those who build on the sand, nor did the psalmist harangue about the mistake of building a life on riches (62:10). Both the sermon and the psalm simply point to the Rock as the best place to found a life.

WITHIN A WEARY LAND
Psalm 63

A Psalm of David, when he was in the Wilderness of Judah.

63:1 **O God, you are my God, I seek you,**
   my soul thirsts for you;
   my flesh faints for you,
      as in a dry and weary land where there is no water.
2 **So I have looked upon you in the sanctuary,**
   beholding your power and glory.
3 **Because your steadfast love is better than life,**
   my lips will praise you.
4 **So I will bless you as long as I live;**
   I will lift up my hands and call on your name.

5 **My soul is satisfied as with a rich feast,**
   and my mouth praises you with joyful lips
6 **when I think of you on my bed,**
   and meditate on you in the watches of the night;
7 **for you have been my help,**
   and in the shadow of your wings I sing for joy.

⁸ My soul clings to you;
    your right hand upholds me.

⁹ But those who seek to destroy my life
    shall go down into the depths of the earth;
¹⁰ they shall be given over to the power of the sword,
    they shall be prey for jackals.
¹¹ But the king shall rejoice in God;
    all who swear by him shall exult,
    for the mouths of liars will be stopped.

One of the classic hymns of the church, "Beneath the Cross of Jesus," uses imagery that reminds one of this psalm:

Beneath the cross of Jesus I long to take my stand;
The shadow of a mighty rock within a weary land.
A home within the wilderness, a rest upon the way,
    From the burning of the noontide heat and the burdens of the day.
                                    (*Lutheran Book of Worship*, 107)

The psalmist expresses something of these same feelings in saying to God, "My soul thirsts for you; my flesh faints for you, as in a dry and weary land where there is no water" (v. 1).

A human being, battered by conflict with contemporaries, can thirst for God just as intensely as parched and weary land can long for water. This is the situation setting off the story that unfolds in this psalm.

The heading associates the psalm with David, but in a most general way, "when he was in the Wilderness of Judah." We assume this was a time before David became king, when he was running from his former friend Saul, in a "dry and weary land" both literally and figuratively (see 1 Sam. 23:14–15; for David, see on Psalm 3).

Though the psalm arises from a time when the writer's life is in danger (v. 9), it fits the "lament" category only approximately (see on Psalm 13). Verse 1 is an *"I" complaint*, expressing the loneliness of the writer. With verses 2–4 one senses an *affirmation of trust* as well as a *vow to praise* God for a lifetime. The theme of *trust* dominates verses 5–8. Verses 9–11 envision better times, when enemies will be destroyed, liars will be stilled, and God's people and their king will rejoice.

Body and Soul (63:1–4)

"My days have grown so lonely," begins the old love song, continuing, "'cause I have lost my one and only . . . I'm yours, body and soul." "Body and soul" means the whole person, so the sense of that last line is "I'm totally yours!"

Psalm 63 speaks the same way. The psalmist is lonely, looking for God, and feels the pain of God's absence in "soul and flesh," in his entire person (v. 1). The imagery that comes to the psalmist's mind can best be understood by farmers or ranchers, whose existence is closely tied to the productivity of the land. When lack of rainfall means loss of a year's work, when the sun beats down week after week without a cloud in sight, when the sky is black with clouds of topsoil being blown away, then one can understand what the psalmist means by comparing the dryness in his own existence to drought in normally fertile farm country. "My God," says the writer, "I'm as totally dried up as our farms were during last summer's drought" (v. 1 paraphrase).

But just as weary farmers do not close down their churches during summers when there are no crops, so the psalmist continues to structure worship into the pattern of life. In the sanctuary, in the place of worship, one can find a break from the "burning of the noontide heat and the burdens of the day." Lifting one's eyes from immediate troubles, one can once again be reminded not only of God's power and glory but also of God's steadfast love. This is the sort of unmotivated love (*agape*) of which the New Testament speaks; this is the John 3:16 sort of love that keeps on loving, no matter what. Living in the certainty of that love, even in the midst of a time of personal dryness, it is still possible to praise God with one's lips and even with one's hands (v. 4, referring to the practice of lifting hands during prayer; see also Pss. 28:2; 141:2).

It Helps to Remember (63:5–8)

The psalm speaks of a period of spiritual dryness and weariness (v. 1). The question when reading it might well be "What shall I do, God, when I am experiencing such a stretch of weariness and dryness?"

In response, notice what the psalmist does. First, rather than cut himself off from the community and live in loneliness, the psalmist goes where the worshipers are and joins in praising God (vv. 2–5). Second, he does some remembering. While lying in bed at night, rather than tossing and turning with worry over those nagging problems, this person looks back at a lifetime, putting the day's problems in the perspective of months or years. Then the writer can say to God, "You have been my help!" (v. 7). Does "the shadow of your wings" refer to the wings of the cherubim in the temple, or is this a picture of God as a nurturing eagle (Ps. 91:4) or a mother hen (Matt. 23:37)? Whatever the case, the sense of security will enable this person to sing "Praise God from whom all blessings flow" once again, and mean it.

The sense of verse 8 is that of the children's prayer "Now I lay me down to sleep." When a child, or a parent, continues, "I pray the Lord my soul to keep," the one praying knows that this is asking that God care for one's whole life. The sense is the same here; the expression balancing "my soul" is simply "me."

From Weariness to Rejoicing (63:9–11)

The psalm began with a person speaking from a time of life marked by thirst, fainting, dryness, and weariness. It ends with the sounds of rejoicing and exulting in God. The psalmist speaks of "my life" (v. 9); the Hebrew is "my *nephesh*," the same word translated as "soul" in verses 1, 5, and 8. The point, once again, is that when the Bible speaks of "soul," or when a child prays "my soul to take," what is meant is the entire person.

Envisioned here is a time when God and government will be rightly ordered (v. 11a) and when the psalmist's enemies will be no more. These negative sentiments regarding enemies indicate something about the genuine human feelings of the psalmist; they are not meant to serve as examples for our own attitude toward enemies. Jesus had other things to say about that issue (Matt. 5:43–48).

The hymn "Beneath the Cross of Jesus" has a way of linking the imagery in these last three psalms, when it speaks of the cross as "the shadow of a mighty rock" (Pss. 61:2; 62:2, 6–7) "within a weary land" (Ps. 63:1).

READY, AIM, FIRE!
Psalm 64

To the leader. A Psalm of David.

64:1 **Hear my voice, O God, in my complaint;**
      preserve my life from the dread enemy.
   2 **Hide me from the secret plots of the wicked,**
      from the scheming of evildoers,
   3 **who whet their tongues like swords,**
      who aim bitter words like arrows,
   4 **shooting from ambush at the blameless;**
      they shoot suddenly and without fear.
   5 **They hold fast to their evil purpose;**
      they talk of laying snares secretly,
  thinking, "Who can see us?

⁶ **Who can search out our crimes?**
   We have thought out a cunningly conceived plot."
   For the human heart and mind are deep.

⁷ **But God will shoot his arrow at them;**
   they will be wounded suddenly.
⁸ **Because of their tongue he will bring them to ruin;**
   all who see them will shake with horror.
⁹ **Then everyone will fear;**
   they will tell what God has brought about,
   and ponder what he has done.

¹⁰ **Let the righteous rejoice in the LORD**
   and take refuge in him.
   Let all the upright in heart glory.

Maybe at some point in your childhood you chanted that old rhyme, in self-defense on a schoolyard: "Sticks and stones may break my bones, but words can never hurt me." This saying, however, is just not true. Words can hurt deeply; words like "We're downsizing, and the company won't really be needing you anymore from now on!" or "I'm sorry, but I just don't love you anymore."

This is not a particularly happy psalm. It is about schemes and plots, about swords and arrows, about life and death, and about words.

The psalm is made up of some of the typical elements of the lament (see on Psalm 13). It begins with a *request* that God hear and help the one praying (vv. 1–2) and moves quickly to a *"they" complaint* about the psalmist's enemies (vv. 3–6). The psalmist expresses *trust* that God will help (vv. 7–9) and concludes with a *call to praise* and rejoicing (v. 10). (For mention of the leader and of David, see on Psalm 4.)

Ready, Draw, Aim, Fire! (64:1–6)

"Save my life," the psalmist asks God in the first verse of this psalm. The situation here is one of life or death. The one praying is being pursued and is the object of hostile plots. Words are involved, words developing schemes and plots to wipe out the life of the one praying this prayer (vv. 2–3).

Two images are used. First, these evildoers are preparing and polishing up their tongues just as one prepares a sword for battle. Second, their words are compared to arrows. A good deal of preparation goes into the shooting of an arrow. One must learn how to tie and attach the bowstring, how properly to string the bow. And then there is target practice. The instructor calls out the commands: "Ready, draw, aim, fire!" and the arrows are off on their way to their targets. There is something sinister about the delivery of the words of these evildoers (vv. 3–4). They are not spoken face to face, like Nathan's "You are the man!" to David (2 Sam. 12:7). There is something behind-the-back about these words, something secret. The picture is of a sniper lying in the bushes, waiting, the bowstring taut. The victim comes down the path, and the arrow is on its way (v. 4).

Verses 5–6 describe in plain language what is going on. These enemies are devising an elaborate plan to ruin their victim. Since they deal in words, perhaps it will involve innuendo, generating suspicion, planting rumors. They think that their plotting is being done in 100 percent secrecy; they don't know that God sees and hears them (see Ps. 139:11–12).

The section concludes with a sentence about the depths of the human heart and mind—depths that in this case seem more like the dank recesses of a polluted cesspool than the deep mysteries of a vast ocean (v. 6).

On Target (64:7–10)

The Bible has a good number of pictures for God. One thinks immediately of God as king (Isaiah 6) or as loving parent (Hosea 11) or as good shepherd (Psalm 23). The picture in this psalm is the same as that used in Psalm 38:2: God as archer! "These scoundrels," announces the psalm, "will be paid back in kind." They have shot their cutting, wounding words like arrows; now they will be wounded by God's arrows. Why will it be necessary for God to punish them in this way? The case is clear. They caused all this trouble through the scheming they accomplished with their sharp tongues; now, because of their tongues, they will be ruined (vv. 7–8).

After the ruin of these schemers, continues the psalm, others will fear and worship God, will tell stories about what God has done, and will reflect on God's mighty acts. God's people will be safe and will rejoice (vv. 9–10).

I Wonder As I Ponder

This psalm can touch our modern lives at a number of points. Psychologists could help us understand the words of verse 6, "For the human heart and mind are deep." The book of Proverbs and the letter of James have much to say about words and the power of the tongue.

With verse 9, the writer is imagining a situation when the life-and-death dangers are past and things are back to a normal rhythm. Then three things will happen. First, everyone will fear God. The sense of fear is not "to be afraid of" but rather "to have respect and regard for." All will give proper recognition to the God of Israel. Second, God's people will tell the story of what God has done. This is how the faith is passed on. Finally, persons will "ponder what [God] has done." Theology means talk about God. The word here translated "ponder" occurs in Nehemiah 8:13, translated as "study": "On the second day the heads of ancestral houses of all the people, with the priests and the Levites, came together to the scribe Ezra in order to *study* the words of the law."

After experiencing God's acts of deliverance, God's people study the records of those acts, think about those acts in relation to God, and tell the story to others. This is where theology gets started.

The word *ponder* occurs in another well-known biblical context. Here again is an example of doing theology. This time it was a woman, caring for a newborn baby, amazed at what certain shepherds had reported about encountering some angels. She heard their stories, looked at her child lying in a manger, and "treasured all these words and pondered them in her heart" (Luke 2:19). What things did she conclude? We wonder.

THE BLUE PLANET
Psalm 65

To the leader. A Psalm of David. A Song.

65:1 **Praise is due to you,**
> **O God, in Zion;**
> **and to you shall vows be performed,**
> 2   **O you who answer prayer!**
> **To you all flesh shall come.**
> 3 **When deeds of iniquity overwhelm us,**
> **you forgive our transgressions.**
> 4 **Happy are those whom you choose and bring near**
> **to live in your courts.**
> **We shall be satisfied with the goodness of your house,**
> **your holy temple.**

> 5 **By awesome deeds you answer us with deliverance,**
> **O God of our salvation;**
> **you are the hope of all the ends of the earth**
> **and of the farthest seas.**
> 6 **By your strength you established the mountains;**
> **you are girded with might.**

⁷ You silence the roaring of the seas,
    the roaring of their waves,
    the tumult of the peoples.
⁸ Those who live at earth's farthest bounds are awed by your signs;
    you make the gateways of the morning and the evening shout
        for joy.

⁹ You visit the earth and water it,
    you greatly enrich it;
  the river of God is full of water;
    you provide the people with grain,
    for so you have prepared it.
¹⁰ You water its furrows abundantly,
    settling its ridges,
  softening it with showers,
    and blessing its growth.
¹¹ You crown the year with your bounty;
    your wagon tracks overflow with richness.
¹² The pastures of the wilderness overflow,
    the hills gird themselves with joy,
¹³ the meadows clothe themselves with flocks,
    the valleys deck themselves with grain,
    they shout and sing together for joy.

"Space travel," said science fiction writer Ray Bradbury, "has made children of us all." He was referring to the sense of childlike wonder that results whenever one sees photographs from space, especially photographs of our own spaceship Earth. *Blue Planet* is the name of an Imax film production that views the earth from a camera mounted on a satellite orbiting in space. What is amazing in this film is that the planet we call our home, seen from so far away, looks like a beautiful round jewel, blue because it consists of roughly 80 percent water.

View the earth from outer space. Consider the planet as a whole. Such is the perspective of those spectacular photographs, and it is also the perspective of this psalm.

The heading dedicates the psalm to the music director and associates it with David (see the comments on Psalm 4). This is the first of a quartet of psalms designated as a "Song" (Psalms 65–68); the precise nature of such songs remains unknown.

This a *hymn* with a *call to praise* (v. 1), introducing *reasons* for praise (vv. 2–13; see on Psalm 113). The movement of the psalm goes thus: Praise God (v. 1) who answers prayer (vv. 1–5), who has made the earth and seas (vv. 6–8), who continues to water the earth (vv. 9–13).

The best preparation for understanding this psalm would be to walk along the shores of the ocean when the wind is blowing in from the sea and the waves are crashing on the shore (v. 7), or to get up early and hike up a mountain path to watch the sunrise and then, at the end of the day, to see it set (vv. 6, 8). It would help to understand this psalm if one could look at sheep safely grazing in a green pasture (vv. 12–13) or watch a gentle rain falling on amber waves of grain (v. 9). Such are the images that animate this hymn.

Through a Wide-Angle Lens (65:1–5)

This is a psalm of broad perspectives. It speaks not only of Israel or the church praising God but of "all flesh" on this blue planet coming to worship (v. 2). It praises God not only as "our hope" but as "the hope of the ends of the earth and of the farthest seas" (v. 5).

Within this broad perspective of all those who live on the planet Earth, the psalm zooms in on specific persons, to praise God for specific acts of care. First, God answers individual prayers. When a child asks, "I pray the Lord my soul to keep," before drifting off to sleep, God hears that prayer (vv. 2, 5). Second, God straightens out what we have bent and distorted (the literal meaning of the Hebrew behind "iniquity") and forgives us when we act like rebelling teenagers (the literal sense behind "transgressions"; v. 3). Third, God answers our prayers for help when we are in a bind, by acts of deliverance or salvation (from the Hebrew *yāša‘*, the word from which *Jesus*, that is, "saver," comes; v. 5).

At the close of this first section, the camera lens moves from "zoom" back to "wide angle," speaking of God as the hope of "the ends of the earth" and "the farthest seas" (v. 5).

The Seas and the Earth (65:6–13)

Verse 5 speaks of the earth and the seas, and now those themes are developed. The focus is on the creation of the mountains (v. 6) and then on God's control of the seas (v. 7). Twice God's action of calming and silencing the roaring seas is mentioned as evidence of God's power. The New Testament reader thinks of the story of Jesus stilling the storm at sea and thus doing the same things that God does (Mark 4:35–41). Verses 5b–7 speak of God's control over the earth's space, including mountains and seas. Verse 8a again speaks of space, but the subject of verse 8b is time, God setting the limits for morning and evening. This short summary of creation in verses 6–8 concludes on an upbeat note, describing each day as beginning and ending with joy.

The Hills Are Alive (65:9–13)

This psalm is matched only by Psalm 104 in delighting in the gift of water. The first line of verse 9 sets the theme for the entire section, saying to God, "You visit the earth and water it." "The river of God" is a picture for the place where God has stored waters for this blue planet. Verse 10 speaks of the way in which the farmer skillfully channels water to places where it is needed. Verse 10b is a good illustration of what the Bible means by "blessings": everyday gifts that are given to all people, such as rain. Verse 11 apparently refers to wagon wheels making ditches where water will flow.

Finally, verses 12 and 13 describe the result of all this watering of the earth. The center of concern is the land, now experiencing the good that comes with an abundance of water. The pastures have plenty of water for the grazing cattle, and the hills are clothed in grass and flowers, lending a note of beauty and joy to the whole area (v. 12). The green meadows are dressed with white flocks of sheep and the valleys with amber waves of grain. Replacing the roaring of the sea and of the crowds (v. 7) are more pleasant and joyful sounds heard from the pastures and hills, the meadows and valleys. The hills are alive, one could say, with the sounds of music.

The Care of the Earth

The emphasis in this psalm is on what God has done and continues to do: in answering prayers (vv. 1–5), in the work of creation (vv. 6–8), and in caring for the earth and providing the earth's inhabitants with food (vv. 9–13).

Today, however, the picture of our rivers and lakes, meadows and pastures, hills and valleys, is no longer as lush and beautiful as that portrayed in the last section of this psalm. The forests are disappearing; the grasslands are no longer green; the rivers and lakes are no longer blue; the sounds of the music of millions of species in the rainforests are being stilled. Is the blue planet on the way to becoming the brown planet?

This psalm, with its description of a beautiful and harmonious earth, could well be balanced by a hearing of Psalm 8, which issues a call for the care of this earth.

THE MIGHTY ACTS OF GOD
Psalm 66

To the leader. A Song. A Psalm.

66:1 Make a joyful noise to God, all the earth;
  ² sing the glory of his name;
   give to him glorious praise.
 ³ Say to God, "How awesome are your deeds!
  Because of your great power, your enemies cringe before you.
 ⁴ All the earth worships you;
  they sing praises to you,
  sing praises to your name."   *Selah*

 ⁵ Come and see what God has done:
  he is awesome in his deeds among mortals.
 ⁶ He turned the sea into dry land;
  they passed through the river on foot.
 There we rejoiced in him,
  ⁷ who rules by his might forever,
  whose eyes keep watch on the nations—
  let the rebellious not exalt themselves.   *Selah*

 ⁸ Bless our God, O peoples,
  let the sound of his praise be heard,
 ⁹ who has kept us among the living,
  and has not let our feet slip.
 ¹⁰ For you, O God, have tested us;
  you have tried us as silver is tried.
 ¹¹ You brought us into the net;
  you laid burdens on our backs;
 ¹² you let people ride over our heads;
  we went through fire and through water;
  yet you have brought us out to a spacious place.

 ¹³ I will come into your house with burnt offerings;
  I will pay you my vows,
 ¹⁴ those that my lips uttered
  and my mouth promised when I was in trouble.
 ¹⁵ I will offer to you burnt offerings of fatlings,
  with the smoke of the sacrifice of rams;
  I will make an offering of bulls and goats.   *Selah*

 ¹⁶ Come and hear, all you who fear God,
  and I will tell what he has done for me.
 ¹⁷ I cried aloud to him,
  and he was extolled with my tongue.
 ¹⁸ If I had cherished iniquity in my heart,
  the Lord would not have listened.
 ¹⁹ But truly God has listened;
  he has given heed to the words of my prayer.

²⁰ **Blessed be God,**
    because he has not rejected my prayer
    or removed his steadfast love from me.

This is a psalm that stretches the imagination.

It begins with a focus on the "blue planet" (see Psalm 65), calling on the people of "all the earth" (vv. 1, 4) to worship and praise God because of what God has done (vv. 1–4). It continues with something of the story of what God has done for one people on that planet (vv. 5–12). The psalm concludes by narrowing the focus to one individual who is promising to fulfill some vows (vv. 13–15) and who is telling the story of what God has done for him (vv. 16–20).

Calling Planet Earth (66:1–4)

Psalm 65 ended with a picture of planet Earth with its blue seas, amber grain fields, green pastures, and forests (Ps. 65:9–13). Psalm 66 links up with the "earth" theme (Pss. 65:9; 66:1, 4) but now focuses on the people of the planet. Psalm 65 concluded by describing the rejoicing of the hills and the singing of the meadows and valleys (vv. 12–13). Psalm 66 begins with a call to all human beings living on the earth to praise God.

The people of the planet are called to praise because of God's "awesome deeds" (v. 3). The question arises: What were those mighty deeds of God? (*Selah* indicates a break; see on Psalm 3.)

What God Has Done for the People (66:5–12)

The psalm writer is eager to tell about "what God has done" (v. 5). The focus moves immediately to the exodus from Egypt. Since the congregation knows the story well, it is not necessary to retell it in detail. The psalmist recalls the crossing of the Sea of Reeds, or Red Sea (Exodus 14–15); "the river" refers to crossing the Jordan (Josh. 3:14–17).

The story began by speaking of the Israelites as "they" (v. 6). As it continues, the storyteller switches to "we," as if he and the gathered congregation had themselves been present. In this way, a story of events that happened long ago and far away becomes a story in which the listeners are involved, *our story*.

The farmer's creed in Deuteronomy 26:5–10 offers a parallel example of how the switch from "they" (long ago) to "we" and "I" (the present) is made. The creed begins with he/they language (v. 5). When the one confessing speaks of the Egyptian experience, the creed switches to "we" and "us," indicating that the speaker identifies with these experiences as if he had been present (vv. 6–9). Finally, when the worshiper presents the offering, the language is "I," thus identifying the speaker's daily work with the whole story of what God did for this people (v. 10).

The statement in Psalm 66:7 "whose eye keeps watch on the nations" is a reminder that the God being praised is the God not only of Israel but of the other nations of the world as well. The same point may be noted in the address "O peoples" (v. 8).

The meaning of all the allusions in verses 9–12 is not certain. Most likely, reference is being made to God watching over Israel after the exodus (v. 6) for forty years in the wilderness, in the midst of various difficulties. Finally, however, the psalmist recalls, "You have brought us out to a spacious place" (v. 12).

What God Has Done for Me (66:13–20)

One of the standard elements in a prayer from a time of trouble, or lament, is a *vow to praise* (see Pss. 7:17; 13:6; 18:49–50). The laments make a vow to praise God; here that vow is being fulfilled. The fulfillment is substantial, even amazing: the psalmist will bring a variety of offerings, ranging from rams and goats to bulls (vv. 13, 15). All of this was to say "thank you" to God for answering prayers.

In the first segment of this psalm, the focus was on the awesome deeds of God on behalf of the entire earth (vv. 1–4). In the second segment, the psalmist called attention to what God had done for God's people (vv. 5–12). Now, in this final part of the psalm, the focus is on "me":

> Come and hear, all you who fear God,
> and I will tell what he has done *for me*.
> (v. 16)

This is the typical pattern of a psalm of thanksgiving, recalling that prayers were made (v. 17) and that God heard those prayers and answered them (vv. 18–19). The psalm ends on a note of thanks to God for listening to the prayer of an individual and for not taking away God's steadfast love.

Tell Me a Story

When the Bible speaks of God, it most often does so by telling what God has done. In other words, when the Bible speaks of God, it tells a story.

The Bible as a whole follows the pattern of a story, beginning in the Old Testament with creation and continuing through the call to the ancestors, the exodus from Egypt, the giving of the commandments, the wilderness wandering, the conquest of the land, the monarchy, and finally the exile. The New Testament picks up on the story, telling of Jesus as the fulfillment of Old Testament promises and spelling out the meaning of his death and resurrection.

When a parent or grandparent or professor or teacher is telling a story from the Bible, that person is doing what has always been at the heart of the biblical faith: passing on the story of what God has done. When a child asks, "Tell me a story," the one who responds is keeping alive the sort of thing called for in this psalm: "Come and hear, all you who fear God, and I will tell what he has done for me" (v. 16).

MULTIPURPOSE THANKSGIVING
Psalm 67

To the leader: with stringed instruments.
A Psalm. A Song.

67:1 **May God be gracious to us and bless us**
       and make his face to shine upon us,   *Selah*
   2 **that your way may be known upon earth,**
      your saving power among all nations.
   3 **Let the peoples praise you, O God;**
      let all the peoples praise you.

   4 **Let the nations be glad and sing for joy,**
      for you judge the peoples with equity
      and guide the nations upon earth.   *Selah*
   5 **Let the peoples praise you, O God;**
      let all the peoples praise you.

   6 **The earth has yielded its increase;**
      God, our God, has blessed us.
   7 **May God continue to bless us;**
      let all the ends of the earth revere him.

Even if there are no other religious observances in a home, that which often remains is a prayer at mealtime. A child might say, "Lord we thank you for this food, in Jesus' name. Amen." Or the whole family might pray together, "Come, Lord Jesus, be our guest, and let these gifts to us be blessed."

Mealtime is prayer time. Why? As one of my teachers used to say, "It is appropriate to give thanks to God over a plate of food because it took a whole universe to produce it" (Gerhard Frost).

Even if there are no other religious observances in a community, one that often is still observed in the United States is the national holiday of Thanksgiving. Schoolchildren hear stories about pilgrims and draw pictures of turkeys. If there is ever a time for joint worship services in a town or community, it will likely be on this day.

Despite the fact that we are no longer a nation of farmers or of those who work the land directly, it seems right that at the time of the fall harvest we give thanks, and give thanks together.

This psalm is designed for such thanksgiving occasions.

The heading indicates its dedication to the music director and suggests that as a "song," it be sung with instrumental accompaniment. Verses 3 and 5 are identical and no doubt functioned as a refrain. (For the *Selahs* after verses 1 and 4, see on Psalm 3.)

Benediction, Blessing, and Saving (67:1–3)

A *benediction* is a word wishing someone well. In a religious context, it is a word pronounced as part of a worship service, wishing that God's gifts be given to someone.

Benedictions have a way of being passed on from one generation to the next. The "Aaronic benediction" is described in the Bible as given by God to Moses, who passed it on to his brother Aaron, who passed it on to his sons, who passed it on to the people of Israel. It was used in Old Testament times at the end of a service of worship (Lev. 9:22–23) and continues to be used that way in both Judaism and Christianity today:

> The LORD bless you and keep you;
> the LORD make his face to shine upon you, and be gracious to you;
> the LORD lift up his countenance upon you, and give you peace.
> (Num. 6:24–26)

Psalm 67 begins with a similar benediction, asking that the Lord give love and blessing to those gathered, and also that the Lord "make his face to shine" upon them (v. 1). The imagery here describes the Lord in human terms. When the Lord is angry, the Lord turns away, paying no attention to the people (see also Pss. 13:1; 27:9; 30:7). When the Lord shows favor, the Lord turns toward the people, with a beaming face (see also Pss. 4:6; 31:16; 80:3, 7, 19).

What is meant by "blessing"? Verses 6 and 7 indicate that this means causing the earth to produce crops. Thus the blessing activity of God in this context means the giving of sunshine and rain, good weather, so that the crops grow and the harvest will be good. When the earth yields such a harvest, it is an occasion to praise God, from whom such blessings flow (vv. 3, 5).

The psalm also refers to the "saving power" of God, which is another type of God's action (v. 2). This is the sort of rescuing action that Israel experienced in coming out of Egypt (Exodus 14–15) or that an individual might experience in being delivered from danger or healed from an illness (Psalm 30).

Blessing and Mission (67:4–7)

This is a psalm that was used in worship in Jerusalem, and it begins with a request that God bless "us" (v. 1). What is the purpose of this blessing? One answer is obvious in verses 6 and 7: God's blessing us and giving us a good harvest enable us to live and enjoy the life God has given to us.

But as we look more closely at this psalm, it appears there is another purpose for God's blessing. The psalm asks that the people be blessed "that your way may be known upon earth, your saving power among all nations" (v. 2). The people Israel are blessed so that the other nations of the world may know about the God of Israel. The people of Israel are blessed—to be a blessing to other nations (Gen. 12:1–3). These nations will then join in praising God!

The refrain in verses 3 and 5 makes the same point. One might expect that Israel would be called to praise God. But the focus of the psalm is wider. "Let the peoples praise you, O God," it begins. And then, as if to second that suggestion, the next line repeats the idea and expands it: "let all the peoples praise you."

Verse 4 is not concerned only for gladness and joy in Israel but asks that God allow all the nations to celebrate. The reason? Again, the psalm makes a wide-hearted claim. God, it says, judges not only Israel, punishing the evil and rewarding the faithful, but all the nations! And not only has God guided Israel out of Egypt through the wilderness to the promised land, but God works in the history of other nations as well!

This is indeed an appropriate psalm for thanksgiving, because it praises God for what God has done both in nature and in the lives of God's people. But a careful reading indicates that the psalm has another purpose. It is designed to praise God but also to encourage making the story of God's saving power known "among all nations."

This is a psalm with broad horizons, calling not only on Israel to praise God but on the peoples of the earth. It speaks of God's working not only with a single people but with "the nations upon earth" (v. 4). In its concluding wish that "all the ends of the earth revere him," it links up with the words of Jesus in Matthew 28:18–20 and Acts 1:8.

This psalm is a call to thanksgiving, but that is not its only purpose. This is a multipurpose psalm. It is also a call to mission.

THE LORD WHO DAILY BEARS US UP
Psalm 68

To the leader. Of David. A Psalm. A Song.

68:1 **Let God rise up, let his enemies be scattered;**
      let those who hate him flee before him.
  2 **As smoke is driven away, so drive them away;**
      as wax melts before the fire,
      let the wicked perish before God.
  3 **But let the righteous be joyful;**
      let them exult before God;
      let them be jubilant with joy.

  4 **Sing to God, sing praises to his name;**
      lift up a song to him who rides upon the clouds—
    his name is the LORD—
      be exultant before him.

  5 **Father of orphans and protector of widows**
      is God in his holy habitation.
  6 **God gives the desolate a home to live in;**
      he leads out the prisoners to prosperity,
      but the rebellious live in a parched land.

  7 **O God, when you went out before your people,**
      when you marched through the wilderness,   *Selah*
  8 **the earth quaked, the heavens poured down rain**
      at the presence of God, the God of Sinai,
      at the presence of God, the God of Israel.
  9 **Rain in abundance, O God, you showered abroad;**
      you restored your heritage when it languished;
  10 **your flock found a dwelling in it;**
      in your goodness, O God, you provided for the needy.

  11 **The Lord gives the command;**
      great is the company of those who bore the tidings:
  12   **"The kings of the armies, they flee, they flee!"**
    The women at home divide the spoil,
  13   **though they stay among the sheepfolds—**

the wings of a dove covered with silver,
    its pinions with green gold.
¹⁴ When the Almighty scattered kings there,
    snow fell on Zalmon.

¹⁵ O mighty mountain, mountain of Bashan;
    O many-peaked mountain, mountain of Bashan!
¹⁶ Why do you look with envy, O many-peaked mountain,
    at the mount that God desired for his abode,
    where the LORD will reside forever?

¹⁷ With mighty chariotry, twice ten thousand,
    thousands upon thousands,
    the Lord came from Sinai into the holy place.
¹⁸ You ascended the high mount,
    leading captives in your train
    and receiving gifts from people,
    even from those who rebel against the LORD God's abiding there.
¹⁹ Blessed be the Lord,
    who daily bears us up;
    God is our salvation.   *Selah*
²⁰ Our God is a God of salvation,
    and to GOD, the Lord, belongs escape from death.

²¹ But God will shatter the heads of his enemies,
    the hairy crown of those who walk in their guilty ways.
²² The Lord said,
    "I will bring them back from Bashan,
    I will bring them back from the depths of the sea,
²³ so that you may bathe your feet in blood,
    so that the tongues of your dogs may have their share from
    the foe."

²⁴ Your solemn processions are seen, O God,
    the processions of my God, my King, into the sanctuary—
²⁵ the singers in front, the musicians last,
    between them girls playing tambourines:
²⁶ "Bless God in the great congregation,
    the LORD, O you who are of Israel's fountain!"
²⁷ There is Benjamin, the least of them, in the lead,
    the princes of Judah in a body,
    the princes of Zebulun, the princes of Naphtali.

²⁸ Summon your might, O God;
    show your strength, O God, as you have done for us before.

²⁹ Because of your temple at Jerusalem
    kings bear gifts to you.
³⁰ Rebuke the wild animals that live among the reeds,
    the herd of bulls with the calves of the peoples.
  Trample under foot those who lust after tribute;
    scatter the peoples who delight in war.
³¹ Let bronze be brought from Egypt;
    let Ethiopia hasten to stretch out its hands to God.

³² Sing to God, O kingdoms of the earth;
    sing praises to the Lord,   *Selah*
³³ O rider in the heavens, the ancient heavens;
    listen, he sends out his voice, his mighty voice.
³⁴ Ascribe power to God,
    whose majesty is over Israel;
    and whose power is in the skies.
³⁵ Awesome is God in his sanctuary,
    the God of Israel;
    he gives power and strength to his people.

    Blessed be God!

The book of Psalms provides some of the Bible's most crystal-clear texts: one thinks of Psalm 23, Psalm 104, or Psalm 130. Psalm 68, however, is not part of that group. In fact, almost every commentator remarks on how hard it is to understand. After calling this "the most difficult of all the Psalms," one American scholar suggested that it is not a psalm at all but a catalog of psalm titles! In fact, a German scholar published a study of this psalm in 1851, bringing together some four hundred differing interpretations of the psalm!

It is possible, however, to read through the psalm and understand parts of it, even to be bolstered in one's faith by it. One could start by reflecting on verse 19, which speaks of the Lord's day-by-day involvement in the lives of believers:

> Blessed be the Lord,
>   who daily bears us up;
>   God is our salvation.

The heading is made up of familiar elements, identifying the piece as a psalm and a song (see on Psalm 65), associating it with David, and dedicating it to the worship leader (see on Psalms 3 and 4). It is best not to suggest an outline for this psalm, since none is easily to be seen. But the movement of the psalm can be traced, section by section.

The Face of God (68:1–3)

Psalm 67 expresses the wish that God's face "shine upon us" (v. 1). Psalm 68 links up with that imagery, expressing the wish that those who hate God "flee from his face" (Hebrew; NRSV, "before him"). The psalm wishes that the wicked perish and the righteous be joyful "before the face of God" (the literal Hebrew; NRSV, "before God," v. 3). The picture in verse 3 is of God's people celebrating in the presence of a God who is looking on, smiling.

Rider in the Heavens, Rescuer of the Homeless (68:4–6)

This section is a reminder that at one point in their history, these psalms were sung. It follows the pattern of a hymn, first calling on those present to sing praises, then giving reasons for singing praise (see Psalm 113). In this case, praise of God makes sense for two reasons: (1) God is mighty, using the clouds as a chariot (Ps. 104:3); (2) God is also merciful, concerned about individuals needing help, such as orphans and widows, the homeless, and those in prison.

Drum Major for the People, Provider for the Needy (68:7–10)

The psalm is still giving reasons for praising God. The imagery shifts from God as cloud rider to God as drum major, leading the people of Israel as they march out of Egypt, through the wilderness. *Selah* suggests a pause to reflect on that scene. (For *Selah*, see on Psalm 3.)

God was uniquely present at Mount Sinai, where the earth quaked and the heavens poured out rain. Judges 5:4–5 describes God in the same language. With verse 10, God is pictured as a shepherd, leading the people into the well-watered pastures of the promised land and caring especially for the weak and needy.

Commander of Armies, Sender of Snow (68:11–14)

The psalm continues to speak of God with a variety of pictures. Here the Lord gives a command, the armies are victorious, and the enemies run away. The women, who have been staying home caring for the flocks, have the joy of dividing up that which was captured. As in verses 7–9, historical and natural events are linked: the armies won a victory, and in what must have been a rare occurrence, it snowed on Mount Zalmon!

God of Sinai, God of Our Salvation (68:15–23)

With a good deal of poetic imagination, the psalmist now addresses a mountain of Bashan, the area east of the Sea of Galilee, assuming that this mountain is jealous of Zion, which God has chosen as God's place to reside. The Lord's move from residence at Mount Sinai to Mount Zion is described (vv. 17–18). After all this language about mountains and majesty, the section ends with a word of praise for the Lord "who daily bears us up," who cares for the Lord's people individually, who rescues and saves them from death (vv. 19–20), and who defeats their enemies (vv. 21–23).

Do It Again, God! (68:24–31)

Verses 24–27 describe a procession into the temple for a worship service. The point of this section appears to be made in verse 28, which asks God to help Israel achieve a victory as God has done before. The enemy appears to be Egypt, "the wild animals that live among the reeds" (v. 30).

Power Move (68:32–35)

The key word in the last section is *power*. God is described as riding through the heavens, sending out his *powerful* ("mighty," NRSV; Hebrew, *'ōz*) voice. Verse 34 speaks twice of God's *power* (*'ōz*) in the skies. Then, after all this language about the whole earth praising God (v. 32) and God's power in the skies, the psalm declares that God does not hoard that power but passes it on to strengthen God's people (v. 35). For all this God is praised with a "Blessed be God!"

God of Power, God of the People

Despite the difficulties with details in the interpretation of this psalm, the psalm as a whole makes a clear and important contribution to our understanding of God and of God's people.

The God of whom this psalm speaks is a *God of power*. This is a God who rides on the clouds and whose power is not limited to earth but is "in the skies" (v. 34). This is a God who acts with power in history, driving away enemy armies (vv. 1, 11–14, 21–23, 30–31). And this God acts in nature, through earthquake and thunder and rain (vv. 8–10, 33).

This God, however, is not power hungry but gives *power to the people of God* (v. 35). God watches over orphans, protects widows, and is concerned for the homeless and for prisoners (vv. 5–6). Should not God's people use their God-given power to do the same? The psalm suggests another reason to bless and praise God: the Lord not only acts in mighty and dramatic ways but "daily bears us up . . . [and] is our salvation" (v. 19).

DO NOT HIDE YOUR FACE, LORD
Psalm 69

To the leader: according to Lilies. Of David.

69:1 Save me, O God,
     for the waters have come up to my neck.
  ² I sink in deep mire,
     where there is no foothold;
  I have come into deep waters,
     and the flood sweeps over me.
  ³ I am weary with my crying;
     my throat is parched.
  My eyes grow dim
     with waiting for my God.

  ⁴ More in number than the hairs of my head
     are those who hate me without cause;
  many are those who would destroy me,
     my enemies who accuse me falsely.
  What I did not steal
     must I now restore?
  ⁵ O God, you know my folly;
     the wrongs I have done are not hidden from you.

  ⁶ Do not let those who hope in you be put to shame because of me,
     O Lord GOD of hosts;
  do not let those who seek you be dishonored because of me,
     O God of Israel.
  ⁷ It is for your sake that I have borne reproach,
     that shame has covered my face.
  ⁸ I have become a stranger to my kindred,
     an alien to my mother's children.

  ⁹ It is zeal for your house that has consumed me;
     the insults of those who insult you have fallen on me.
  ¹⁰ When I humbled my soul with fasting,
     they insulted me for doing so.
  ¹¹ When I made sackcloth my clothing,
     I became a byword to them.
  ¹² I am the subject of gossip for those who sit in the gate,
     and the drunkards make songs about me.

  ¹³ But as for me, my prayer is to you, O LORD.
     At an acceptable time, O God,
     in the abundance of your steadfast love, answer me.

With your faithful help ¹⁴rescue me
    from sinking in the mire;
  let me be delivered from my enemies
    and from the deep waters.
¹⁵ Do not let the flood sweep over me,
    or the deep swallow me up,
    or the Pit close its mouth over me.

¹⁶ Answer me, O LORD, for your steadfast love is good;
    according to your abundant mercy, turn to me.
¹⁷ Do not hide your face from your servant,
    for I am in distress—make haste to answer me.
¹⁸ Draw near to me, redeem me,
    set me free because of my enemies.

¹⁹ You know the insults I receive,
    and my shame and dishonor;
    my foes are all known to you.
²⁰ Insults have broken my heart,
    so that I am in despair.
  I looked for pity, but there was none;
    and for comforters, but I found none.
²¹ They gave me poison for food,
    and for my thirst they gave me vinegar to drink.

²² Let their table be a trap for them,
    a snare for their allies.
²³ Let their eyes be darkened so that they cannot see,
    and make their loins tremble continually.
²⁴ Pour out your indignation upon them,
    and let your burning anger overtake them.
²⁵ May their camp be a desolation;
    let no one live in their tents.
²⁶ For they persecute those whom you have struck down,
    and those whom you have wounded, they attack still more.
²⁷ Add guilt to their guilt;
    may they have no acquittal from you.
²⁸ Let them be blotted out of the book of the living;
    let them not be enrolled among the righteous.
²⁹ But I am lowly and in pain;
    let your salvation, O God, protect me.

³⁰ I will praise the name of God with a song;
    I will magnify him with thanksgiving.
³¹ This will please the LORD more than an ox
    or a bull with horns and hoofs.

32 **Let the oppressed see it and be glad;**
      you who seek God, let your hearts revive.
33 **For the LORD hears the needy,**
      and does not despise his own that are in bonds.

34 **Let heaven and earth praise him,**
      the seas and everything that moves in them.
35 **For God will save Zion**
      and rebuild the cities of Judah;
   and his servants shall live there and possess it;
36   **the children of his servants shall inherit it,**
      and those who love his name shall live in it.

According to the New Testament, when those who lived at the time of Jesus observed what Jesus said and did, they often made connections with this psalm.

At the beginning of his work, when Jesus chased the money changers out of the temple, his disciples remembered words from Psalm 69:9: "Zeal for your house will consume me" (John 2:17). When Jesus spoke of the hatred his followers would experience, he referred to Psalm 69:4: "They hated me without a cause" (John 15:25). When Jesus was very near death, he said, "I am thirsty," and was offered soured wine; John understands this as fulfillment of Psalm 69:21 (John 19:28–29; see also Matt. 27:34; Mark 15:36; Luke 23:36). Finally, Acts 1:20 gives an account of the death of Judas that is understood as the fulfillment of Psalm 69:25.

Paul made reference to Psalm 69:23 and 24 in Romans 11:9, 10 and to Psalm 69:9b in Romans 15:3. Thus the earliest Christians understood events running from the beginning of Jesus' ministry, to the cross and beyond, as somehow related to this psalm.

The psalm is dedicated to the music director and associated with David (see on Psalm 3). The note, "according to Lilies," is apparently reference to a melody (see also Psalm 45).

Elements of the *individual lament* are evident (see on Psalm 13). Especially frequent are the desperate *cries for help* or *requests*: verses 1, 6, 13–18, 22–28, 29. There are also a good number of *complaints* (vv. 2–4, 7–8, 9, 10–12, 19–21), an *affirmation of trust* (v. 5), and a *vow to praise* (vv. 30–36).

Save Me, God (69:1–6)

The one praying this psalm is desperate, even near death. "Save me, O God!" the psalm begins, and then the situation of the psalmist is described in a mixture of figurative and literal language: the psalmist is about to drown, sinking in a pit of quicksand, worn out from crying to the Lord, and so tired that he or she can no longer see straight (vv. 1–3).

Verse 4 provides a clue to the situation. Apparently the one praying has been falsely accused of stealing: "What I did not steal, must I now restore?" The psalmist says to God, "You know me," and trusts that God knows of his or her innocence in this case (v. 5; also v. 19). Verse 6 sounds an important note: the one praying is concerned for the others in the community.

Set Me Free, Lord! (69:7–18)

Verses 7–8 present an "I" complaint that adds information about the situation of the one praying. My suffering is "for your sake," says the psalmist to God. The writer has become alienated from his or her family, including even siblings (v. 8). A second time the psalmist claims to be taking on the insults that are aimed at God. Is this person among the group rebuilding the temple, after the first one was destroyed? Is the psalmist's enthusiasm for building a new place of worship drawing the fire of neighbors (v. 9)?

Verses 10–12 express a series of complaints about others in the community. These persons have made fun of the writer's observances of fasting and repentance. Those who sit "in the gate," the equivalent of the modern downtown cafe, gossip about the psalmist and even make fun of this person with songs!

Verses 13–18 offer a series of cries for help that indicate once again the desperation of the psalmist. "Answer me, rescue me, let me be delivered! Don't let me drown or be swallowed up by the Pit of death" (vv. 13–15).

But God seems to be unresponsive, silent. And so the psalmist says a second time, "Answer me," and continues with more cries for help: "Turn to me. . . . Do not hide your face." Then the writer petitions a third time, "Make haste to answer me. . . . Draw near to me . . . redeem me, set me free" (vv. 16–18).

The request for help, or better, cry for help, is a standard element in the psalms of lament (see on Psalm 13). This psalm is dominated by such cries.

O God, Protect Me! (69:19–36)

With verse 19, the psalmist once again acknowledges that God knows all (also v. 5). Verses 20 and 21 continue with complaints about those who are making the psalmist's life miserable. Verse 22 introduces a series of curses on these enemies, climaxing with the request that they "be blotted out of the book of the living" (v. 28). This section, too, contains a cry for help: "let your salvation, O God, protect me" (v. 29).

Did the psalmist at this point receive a word of assurance that God would indeed help? In any case, the mood changes with verse 30, and the psalm ends with a vow to praise God, which assumes that the desired deliverance has come (vv. 30–36). The psalmist has learned that the Lord hears those who are in trouble (v. 33) and calls on the entire universe— heaven, earth, the seas—to praise God. Verse 35 assumes that Jerusalem is in ruins and looks forward to the rebuilding of the city.

Your Servant, Lord

This is the third in a sequence of psalms that speak of the face of God. Psalm 67 begins with the blessing "May God . . . make his face to shine upon us." Psalm 68 speaks of the wicked fleeing and perishing and the righteous rejoicing "before the face of God" (v. 3, Hebrew). And now this desperate cry begs God, "Do not hide your face from your servant" (v. 17). In the course of this psalm the servant is described in a way that shows this person to be one who is eager and excited about God's house—but who has also suffered, and suffered even though innocent.

We have noted that the New Testament cites this psalm in at least four different contexts: at the cleansing of the temple, in the prayer Jesus prayed for his disciples in the upper room, on the cross, and after the death of Judas. Jesus, it appears, knew this psalm well and found in it clues for his own life and work; the New Testament, at any rate, describes things this way.

Certainly, the royal psalms help us to answer the question "Who is Jesus?" (see the comments on Psalm 2). It is evident that with its portrayal of God's suffering servant, Psalm 69 has something to say to that question, too.

MAKE IT QUICK, LORD!
Psalm 70

To the leader. Of David, for the memorial offering.

70:1 **Be pleased, O God, to deliver me.**
    O LORD, make haste to help me!
  ² **Let those be put to shame and confusion**
    who seek my life.
  Let those be turned back and brought to dishonor
    who desire to hurt me.

³ **Let those who say, "Aha, Aha!"**
turn back because of their shame.

⁴ **Let all who seek you**
rejoice and be glad in you.
Let those who love your salvation
say evermore, "God is great!"
⁵ **But I am poor and needy;**
hasten to me, O God!
You are my help and my deliverer;
O LORD, do not delay!

This is a desperate prayer from a person who needs help and needs it right now. The one praying says, "O LORD, make haste to help me! . . . hasten to me, O God! . . . O LORD, do not delay!" (vv. 1, 5). What is the situation that occasions this prayer? We are told that certain persons are out to hurt the one praying; in fact, they are out to kill the psalmist (v. 2). This is a desperate prayer from within a situation that could lead to life or to death.

It has been suggested that prayers such as this one were available in written form in the temple. When in distress, one could come to the temple and choose a prayer that fit one's situation.

For the heading, see the comments on Psalms 3 and 4. Psalm 38 is also linked to the "memorial offering"; the nature of such an occasion is not known.

Something of a Mystery

Of special interest is the fact that this psalm is almost identical with Psalm 40:13–17; see the comments in connection with that psalm. In some Hebrew manuscripts, Psalms 70 and 71 are linked together, suggesting they be considered as one psalm. The fact that Psalm 71 has no title might also point in this direction (see Psalms 9–10). To add more to this mystery, the Leningrad Manuscript, the Hebrew manuscript on which most Hebrew Bibles are based, does not have a number before Psalm 71! Upon examining a photocopy of the manuscript, however, one sees that Psalm 70 is numbered 70, and 72 is numbered 72. Why is there no number for Psalm 71? Such are the puzzles that intrigue Old Testament textual specialists.

A Prayer for People in a Hurry?

The psalm is a prayer for help, addressed to God, and contains most of the typical elements of an *individual lament* (see on Psalm 13). The *request* or *cry for help* dominates and is found in verses 1–3 ("deliver me, help me, let my enemies be turned back": paraphrase) and in part of verse 5 ("hasten to me, O God! . . . O LORD, do not delay!"). Verse 5 also contains a brief *"I" complaint* ("I am poor and needy") and an *affirmation of trust* ("You are my help and my deliverer"). Verse 4 has something of the sense of a *vow to praise*.

The Hebrew word translated "hasten" (v. 1) is unusual, occurring elsewhere in prayers in the Psalms only in 22:19, *"come quickly* to my aid"; 38:22, *"make haste* to help me" (another link, in addition to the heading, between Psalms 70 and 38); 71:12, *"make haste* to help me"; 141:1, *"come quickly* to me"; and in the parallel in Psalm 40. "Do not delay" of verse 5 is also unusual vocabulary, occurring in a prayer only in this passage and the parallel in Psalm 40.

Was this a prayer already written out, available in the temple, for someone to use when in a life-or-death situation? Was it short, so that it could be used in a hurry? It gives that impression with its triple "make haste . . . hasten . . . do not delay."

Verses 2–3 ask God to help the one praying by harming those who are persecuting him or her. These persons are saying, "Aha, Aha!" or, in the literal Hebrew, *"He-ach, He-ach,"* which perhaps sounds a bit more sour. This is a mocking word used to indicate joy over the misfortune of innocent people (Ps. 35:21), including the enemies who made fun of the Jews (Ezek. 25:3; 26:2; 36:2).

Jesus advised followers to "pray *for* those who persecute you" rather than to ask God to punish them (Matt. 5:44). This is a prayer, however, from someone running for his or her life. And the prayer is not that these enemies be killed but that they be shamed, confused, and dishonored.

After this prayer against enemies, in verse 4 the psalmist offers a prayer for "those who love your salvation." In contrast to the mocking "Aha, Aha!" of the enemies of God and of the psalmist, these persons are saying, "God is great!"

Verse 5 weaves together in a few lines the typical elements of a lament: an *"I" complaint*, two *requests*, and an *affirmation of trust*. The psalmist identifies with the "poor and needy" who suffer because of the wicked (Ps. 37:14) but whom God has promised to help (note Ps. 35:10).

Pray on the Way

Since this psalm is duplicated in Psalm 40:13–17, one could simply say, "See Psalm 40 and the comments there." But some differences between the two psalms suggest we reflect on this one on its own.

First, with only five verses, Psalm 70 is the shortest psalm thus far in the book of Psalms (Ps. 117 has two verses). The psalm, however, makes sense on its own, without the larger context given to it in Psalm 40. When we recall that the Lord's Prayer is also some five verses, we can be reminded that with prayers, even public prayers, longer is not necessarily better. *Prayers can be short.*

Second, there is a boldness, a directness, an impatience about this prayer that can be instructive. The language of hastening and hustling stands out and is quite rare in the book of Psalms. The person praying this psalm is hurting badly, wants help from God right now, and says so. *Prayers can be honest.*

Finally, the one praying has his or her theology straight. "God is great!" is the confession of God seekers and God lovers (v. 4). The one praying also has his or her anthropology correct: "I am poor and needy." What ties it all together and makes it all good news is the announcement that this great God of the seekers and the lovers is also "my help and my deliverer."

Given all this, the psalm ends, "Do it quickly, Lord!" *Prayers can be urgent.*

"GOD SAVES THE HARDEST PART 'TIL LAST"
Psalm 71

> 71:1 **In you, O LORD, I take refuge;**
> **let me never be put to shame.**
> 2 **In your righteousness deliver me and rescue me;**
> **incline your ear to me and save me.**
> 3 **Be to me a rock of refuge,**
> **a strong fortress, to save me,**
> **for you are my rock and my fortress.**
>
> 4 **Rescue me, O my God, from the hand of the wicked,**
> **from the grasp of the unjust and cruel.**
> 5 **For you, O Lord, are my hope,**
> **my trust, O LORD, from my youth.**
> 6 **Upon you I have leaned from my birth;**
> **it was you who took me from my mother's womb.**
> **My praise is continually of you.**
>
> 7 **I have been like a portent to many,**
> **but you are my strong refuge.**
> 8 **My mouth is filled with your praise,**
> **and with your glory all day long.**

⁹ Do not cast me off in the time of old age;
    do not forsake me when my strength is spent.
¹⁰ For my enemies speak concerning me,
    and those who watch for my life consult together.
¹¹ They say, "Pursue and seize that person
    whom God has forsaken,
    for there is no one to deliver."

¹² O God, do not be far from me;
    O my God, make haste to help me!
¹³ Let my accusers be put to shame and consumed;
    let those who seek to hurt me
    be covered with scorn and disgrace.
¹⁴ But I will hope continually,
    and will praise you yet more and more.
¹⁵ My mouth will tell of your righteous acts,
    of your deeds of salvation all day long,
    though their number is past my knowledge.
¹⁶ I will come praising the mighty deeds of the Lord GOD,
    I will praise your righteousness, yours alone.

¹⁷ O God, from my youth you have taught me,
    and I still proclaim your wondrous deeds.
¹⁸ So even to old age and gray hairs,
    O God, do not forsake me,
  until I proclaim your might
    to all the generations to come.
  Your power ¹⁹and your righteousness, O God,
    reach the high heavens.

  You who have done great things,
    O God, who is like you?
²⁰ You who have made me see many troubles and calamities
    will revive me again;
  from the depths of the earth
    you will bring me up again.
²¹ You will increase my honor,
    and comfort me once again.

²² I will also praise you with the harp
    for your faithfulness, O my God;
  I will sing praises to you with the lyre,
    O Holy One of Israel.
²³ My lips will shout for joy
    when I sing praises to you;
    my soul also, which you have rescued.

²⁴ **All day long my tongue will talk of your righteous help,**
   for those who tried to do me harm
      have been put to shame, and disgraced.

My old teacher and friend sat across from me in my office. Now he was
a visitation pastor, with special responsibility for calling on older members of the congregation. He told me of a few encounters, quoted a couple of conversations. Then he paused and observed, "You know, with all
this calling on senior citizens I've learned that God saves . . ." My mind
raced ahead to complete the sentence: "the best part until last." I should
have known better than to expect a cliché from him. He said, "I've
learned that God saves the hardest part 'til last."

When I visit a nursing home or have a conversation with a lonely older
person, I think of what my teacher said; nothing about golden years or
sunset homes or this being what we've all been waiting for. I think of
what my friend said, and of this psalm.

This is the first psalm since Psalm 33 without a heading. Was it to be
linked with Psalm 70? (See the comments on that psalm.) "Make haste to
help me" of Psalm 71:12 repeats Psalm 70:1b; perhaps for this reason the
psalms stand next to each other.

The psalm contains the typical elements of an *individual lament* (see on
Psalm 13), though these elements are scattered about. Especially dominant are *requests for help* (vv. 1–4, 9, 12–13, 18, in eight verses) and *affirmations of trust* (vv. 3b, 5–7, 14, 17, 20–21, also in eight verses). Verses
10–11 give voice to a *"they" complaint*, and the psalm expresses a good deal
of *praise* (vv. 14–16, 19, 22–24). Considering these segments, one can
understand why many have named it a *psalm of trust.*

The psalm falls into three parts, each ending on a note of praise: verses 1–8, 9–16, 17–24.

From My Youth (71:1–8)

The psalm begins with language typical of an individual in distress; Psalm
31:1–3a reads almost the same. Cries for help dominate the first four
verses: "deliver me . . . rescue me . . . save me . . . Rescue me." God is
described with a number of pictures—"rock of refuge," "strong fortress,"
"my rock," "my fortress"—and then without imagery: "my God"
(71:1–4).

Especially interesting is the first "life review" section in verses 5 and 6.
The one praying is no recent convert to the faith. This person speaks of
the Lord, who has been "my hope, my trust . . . from my youth." When
this psalmist is needing rescue from the wicked and cruel, he looks back

at his own life and concludes that the Lord has been good to him so far, and he can still praise God (v. 6c)! The "strong refuge" picks up from the beginning of the psalm, and the section ends on a note of praise.

In the Time of Old Age (71:9–16)

After reviewing a lifetime of living with the Lord, the psalmist is back to the present. Here is an important insight into the worries of a person facing old age. Even though this psalmist has been a lifelong believer, some worries remain as the writer faces the future, even worries that the Lord might leave him! "Do not cast me off in the time of *old age*" is the psalmist's prayer (v. 9), and later "So even to *old age* and gray hairs, O God, do not forsake me" (v. 18). The repetition of "old age" indicates that this is the central focus of this psalm. *Forsake* is the same word as used in the cry of Psalm 22: "My God, my God, why have you forsaken me?" And this is exactly what others in the community are saying about the psalmist in Psalm 71: "that person whom God has forsaken" (v. 11).

The cry "O my God, make haste to help me!" (v. 12) links this psalm with Psalm 70:1 and adds a note of urgency. After a brief prayer against the enemies in verse 13, the psalmist vows to praise God by telling the congregation stories about the good things God has done (vv. 15–16). This second section, too, ends on a note of praise.

From My Youth, Even to Old Age (71:17–24)

Verses 17 and 18 pick up the "from my youth" and "to old age" themes of the previous sections, tie them together, and offer some further reflections. As the psalmist looks to the future, he resolves to continue doing what he has always done: telling about the "wondrous deeds" of God, as he has experienced them for a lifetime.

Verses 19–20 begin with words of praise and continue with an expression of confidence that God will once again revive and comfort this longtime believer. Apparently the writer is a musician, who promises to praise the "Holy One of Israel" not only with words (v. 22) but also with harp and lyre (v. 22).

Not for Sissies

"Old Age Isn't for Sissies" is the slogan I noticed on a senior citizen's sweatshirt. Psalm 71 also expresses a realistic view of the later years of a lifetime. Here is a recognition that there may still be conflict with others in the community (vv. 4, 10–11, 13). There may also be anxiety about one's relationship to God (vv. 9, 18). That a longtime believer could express such worries might alarm us, until we remember that Jesus expressed the same concerns, with this same language, in praying "My God, my God, why have you forsaken me?" (Mark 15:34).

The book of Sirach says, "Jealousy and anger shorten life, and anxiety brings on premature old age" (30:24). What strikes one about this psalm is the lack of bitterness or anger expressed and the positive notes that keep reappearing (71:1–3, 5–8, 14–24).

What can we do to approach the "hardest part" as God would have us do? The psalm provides yet another clue when it speaks of "a lifetime of praise" (vv. 14, 22–24) that includes telling of God's "deeds of salvation" (v. 15), of "the mighty deeds of the Lord GOD" (v. 16), of "your wondrous deeds" (v. 17) and "your might" (v. 18). It all sounds like taking seriously the words of the old hymn "I Love to Tell the Story."

Feelings of anxiety and lack of trust, the psalm indicates, are to be expected even in the lives of God's senior citizens. Singing praise and telling stories are a part of such lives, too.

PORTRAIT OF A KING
Psalm 72

Of Solomon.

72:1 **Give the king your justice, O God,**
       and your righteousness to a king's son.
   2 **May he judge your people with righteousness,**
       and your poor with justice.
   3 **May the mountains yield prosperity for the people,**
       and the hills, in righteousness.
   4 **May he defend the cause of the poor of the people,**
       give deliverance to the needy,
       and crush the oppressor.

   5 **May he live while the sun endures,**
       and as long as the moon, throughout all generations.
   6 **May he be like rain that falls on the mown grass,**
       like showers that water the earth.
   7 **In his days may righteousness flourish**
       and peace abound, until the moon is no more.

   8 **May he have dominion from sea to sea,**
       and from the River to the ends of the earth.

⁹ May his foes bow down before him,
    and his enemies lick the dust.
¹⁰ May the kings of Tarshish and of the isles
    render him tribute,
  may the kings of Sheba and Seba
    bring gifts.
¹¹ May all kings fall down before him,
    all nations give him service.

¹² For he delivers the needy when they call,
    the poor and those who have no helper.
¹³ He has pity on the weak and the needy,
    and saves the lives of the needy.
¹⁴ From oppression and violence he redeems their life;
    and precious is their blood in his sight.

¹⁵ Long may he live!
    May gold of Sheba be given to him.
  May prayer be made for him continually,
    and blessings invoked for him all day long.
¹⁶ May there be abundance of grain in the land;
    may it wave on the tops of the mountains;
    may its fruit be like Lebanon;
  and may people blossom in the cities
    like the grass of the field.
¹⁷ May his name endure forever,
    his fame continue as long as the sun.
  May all nations be blessed in him;
    may they pronounce him happy.

¹⁸ Blessed be the LORD, the God of Israel,
    who alone does wondrous things.
¹⁹ Blessed be his glorious name forever;
    may his glory fill the whole earth.
        Amen and Amen.

²⁰ The prayers of David son of Jesse are ended.

This psalm shows what a king in Israel looks like—or, more precisely, what a king in Israel ought to look like. The psalm does not offer a photograph of any specific king, not even David or Solomon, but rather a portrait of the ideal king. The entire piece is a prayer, concluding with a doubled "Amen." It belongs to the group of *royal psalms* that played a role in connection with events in the life of a king in Israel or

Judah (see on Psalm 2). This royal psalm was most likely used at a time of the installation of a new king.

The heading, "Of Solomon," identifies the psalm with King David's son. Psalm 127 also is designated "Of Solomon," no doubt because it refers to house building, and it was Solomon who built the "house," or temple, in Jerusalem. After so many psalms linked to David, why should the one that concludes Book II be associated with Solomon? Perhaps after all the attention given to David, the editors wish to point ahead to a new king and a new era.

The psalm falls into five parts (vv. 1–4, 5–7, 8–11, 12–14, 15–17), with a doxology and a concluding comment to bring Book II to a close (vv. 18–20). The editors have placed these royal psalms at strategic locations throughout the book of Psalms. Thus Psalm 2 forms part of the introduction to the entire book of Psalms, Psalm 72 concludes Book II, and Psalm 89 concludes Book III.

Prosperity and Peace (72:1–7)

The psalm is addressed to God as a prayer. It appears to have been used as part of the coronation ceremony of a new king. Since kingship was something new in Israel, beginning with Saul and then continuing with David and Solomon, those ruling in Jerusalem borrowed ideas and no doubt also ceremonies and rituals from neighbors in the ancient Near East who had long experience with monarchy.

The prayer wishes the best for the new king, and in fact, the description of the best often outruns reality. First off, the psalm prays that the king may rule with justice and righteousness (vv. 1–2). Right at the start, the prayer has an eye on the poor; prophets such as Isaiah and Amos and Micah have much to say about "doing justice" as taking up the cause of the widow, the orphan, and the poor (Isa. 1:10–17, 21–26; 10:1–4; Amos 5:21–24; Micah 6:6–8).

Verse 3 is a prayer that "prosperity" may be enjoyed. The Hebrew word translated "prosperity" is *shalom*. Since the language here is about hills and mountains yielding *shalom* (= prosperity), it is clear that the sense of the word is more than "absence of war." Here the word clearly has to do with nature, designating a bountiful harvest.

Verse 4 again focuses on the social responsibility of the new ruler. As king, he is to be especially concerned for the weakest, the least prosperous, the most needy, in the country over which he rules. Fairness in the courts, a special concern for the poor, keeping the land free from oppression—these are things a king can do something about. The good crops will have to be left to the Lord!

"Long live the king," says verse 5, now extending that wish to compare with the lifetime of the sun and the moon. After these words regarding the quantity of life, verses 6 and 7 speak of quality, praying that the king's rule be beneficial for the people, like a nourishing rain on a newly mown field. The wish for righteousness in public life is expressed again, as is the desire for *shalom*, this time translated as "peace," indicating that the word means both prosperity in nature (v. 3) and peace among people (v. 7).

From Sea to Shining Sea (72:8–17)

The extravagant good wishes for the new administration continue. "The River" (v. 8) refers to the Euphrates in the east. Tarshish is an apparent reference to Spain in the west; Sheba and Seba are in southern Arabia. May the king rule, in other words, over the known world! Verse 11 summarizes the scope of the king's dominion with a picture of all kings of the earth falling down before the king in Jerusalem.

After these grandiose dreams of worldwide rule, verses 12–14 bring things down to earth. The focus is again on the powerless, the poor and the weak and the needy. The quality of the king's rule will be judged by the quality of life of the poorest citizens.

These themes are repeated and expanded in verses 15–17. Here are prayers for spiritual support from the people (v. 15), for the growth of crops and the "blossoming" of life in new cities (v. 16), for fame, and for good things to happen to all nations because of this king, recalling the promises of Genesis 12:3, 18:18, and the like.

Pointing toward a Messiah

This psalm adds to the features of the ideal king, as described in the royal psalms. Here is a prayer that the king will live forever, will rule the world, will bring about peace and prosperity, and will be especially concerned about the widow, the orphan, and the poor. When these hopes are thrown in with those of other royal psalms that name the future king "anointed one" or "messiah" (Psalms 2, 45), "son" of God (Psalm 2), and that describe the king as seated at God's right hand (Psalm 110), the portrait of a king that emerges is a dazzling one, indeed.

As the history of Israel, then that of Judah, continued to spiral downward until the last of Judah's kings was executed in 587 B.C. , these descriptions were less and less associated with actual ruling monarchs and more and more projected into the future. In this way, the royal psalms became the seedbed out of which grew messianic hope (see the comments on Psalm 2).

These psalms were read and sung, sorted out and edited, and these hopes survived. When the prophet from Nazareth put the question to his followers "Who do you say that I am?" these royal psalms provided the clue to answering that question: "You are the *Messiah*, the Son of the living God" (Matt. 16:16).

3. Book III
PSALMS 73–89

WHEN GOOD THINGS HAPPEN TO BAD PEOPLE
Psalm 73

A Psalm of Asaph.

73:1 Truly God is good to the upright,
  to those who are pure in heart.
  ² But as for me, my feet had almost stumbled;
  my steps had nearly slipped.
  ³ For I was envious of the arrogant;
  I saw the prosperity of the wicked.

  ⁴ For they have no pain;
  their bodies are sound and sleek.
  ⁵ They are not in trouble as others are;
  they are not plagued like other people.
  ⁶ Therefore pride is their necklace;
  violence covers them like a garment.
  ⁷ Their eyes swell out with fatness;
  their hearts overflow with follies.
  ⁸ They scoff and speak with malice;
  loftily they threaten oppression.
  ⁹ They set their mouths against heaven,
  and their tongues range over the earth.

  ¹⁰ Therefore the people turn and praise them,
  and find no fault in them.
  ¹¹ And they say, "How can God know?
  Is there knowledge in the Most High?"
  ¹² Such are the wicked;
  always at ease, they increase in riches.
  ¹³ All in vain I have kept my heart clean
  and washed my hands in innocence.

14 For all day long I have been plagued,
   and am punished every morning.

15 If I had said, "I will talk on in this way,"
   I would have been untrue to the circle of your children.
16 But when I thought how to understand this,
   it seemed to me a wearisome task,
17 until I went into the sanctuary of God;
   then I perceived their end.
18 Truly you set them in slippery places;
   you make them fall to ruin.
19 How they are destroyed in a moment,
   swept away utterly by terrors!
20 They are like a dream when one awakes;
   on awaking you despise their phantoms.

21 When my soul was embittered,
   when I was pricked in heart,
22 I was stupid and ignorant;
   I was like a brute beast toward you.
23 Nevertheless I am continually with you;
   you hold my right hand.
24 You guide me with your counsel,
   and afterward you will receive me with honor.
25 Whom have I in heaven but you?
   And there is nothing on earth that I desire other than you.
26 My flesh and my heart may fail,
   but God is the strength of my heart and my portion forever.

27 Indeed, those who are far from you will perish;
   you put an end to those who are false to you.
28 But for me it is good to be near God;
   I have made the Lord GOD my refuge,
   to tell of all your works.

When Bad Things Happen to Good People is the title of a book by Rabbi Harold Kushner that appeared in the 1980s. This psalm is concerned with a related issue: when good things happen to bad people. To put it another way, this psalm is about the question "Why do the wicked prosper?" (v. 3).

Psalm 73 is the first psalm in Book III (Psalms 73–89) and also the first in a series of eleven psalms of Asaph, both locations probably a recognition of significance. Asaph is mentioned elsewhere as a singer and cymbal player and chief among David's musicians (1 Chron. 15:17–19; 16:5; see Ezra 3:10).

Since the psalm offers reflections on one of life's great problems, it may be called a *wisdom psalm*. Its concerns are close to those of the book of Job, which asks, "Why do good people suffer?" The question this psalm addresses is "Why do bad people prosper?"

The psalm begins with a confession of faith (v. 1), continues with the psalmist telling "how I almost lost my faith" (vv. 2–16), and concludes with a description of the way back to faith (vv. 17–28). An important structural marker is the Hebrew word *'ak*, translated "Surely" by the NIV, in verses 1, 13, and 18; the NRSV translates as "Truly . . . All . . . Truly."

How I Almost Lost My Faith (73:1–16)

Psalm 73 is framed by two great statements of faith. "Truly God is good to Israel, to those who are pure in heart," it begins (Hebrew; see NIV, NRSV footnote). The psalm ends, "But for me it is good to be near God" (v. 28). In between these two ringing confessions is a story of one who nearly gave up on God.

If there is a thematic word in this psalm, it might be *heart*, which occurs in verses 1, 7, 13, 21, and 26 (twice). The psalm is concerned with the deepest, hidden recesses of human existence, identified as the human heart.

With verses 2–16, the psalmist tells of his own experience. Teachers whose teachings are found in the Bible, like all teachers, use personal illustrations this way; see Psalm 37:25; Proverbs 24:30–34; Sirach 51:13–30. (Like all good teachers, however, they do not use them too often!)

Verse 3 puts the problem into sharp focus: literally, "I saw the *shalom* [peace, prosperity] of the wicked." In other words: Why do the wicked prosper? The same question is asked in Job 21 and Jeremiah 12:1–5. Beginning with verse 4 and continuing through verse 12, the psalm speaks of "they," that is, the wicked. Conventional wisdom said that good people prosper and bad people suffer; Job's friends express this view in Job 4:7–11 and 20:4–29. But the psalmist observes that while he suffers (vv. 14, 26), all sorts of good things are happening to the wicked! They are healthy (v. 4) and seem to lead trouble-free lives (v. 5). They speak evil of their neighbors, mock God in heaven, and yet everyone praises them (vv. 8–10). While they are not atheists who deny God's existence, they deny that God knows what is going on (vv. 10–11; see Eccl. 11:5; Isa. 29:15; Zeph. 1:12). Verse 12 summarizes: this is the way these wicked people are, at ease, getting richer all the time!

The *'ak* of verse 13, "*Surely* in vain . . ." ("All in vain," NRSV), marks the low point of the psalmist's experience. Hand washing signifies innocence; see Psalm 26:6 and Matthew 27:24. But all attempts at clean living have not paid off (vv. 13–14).

Verses 15–16 indicate the writer's concern for the children of the community. He had kept his doubts about the faith to himself, because of the children in the congregation. James Mays writes, "In this restraint he teaches all who teach the faithful that personal doubts, however anguished and authentic, must not be turned quickly into lessons for the community" (*Psalms*, p. 242). Joel 1:3 speaks of the importance of passing on to the children the stories of what God has done, as does Deuteronomy 6:20–25.

The Way Back to Faith (73:17–28)

With verse 17, the mood of the psalm changes. The psalmist, plagued with trouble over the wicked and doubts concerning God, nevertheless went to a service of worship, as was his custom. There, he says, he "perceived their end." From that perspective he could get a view of the lives of the wicked as a whole, and he realized that their prosperity would not last forever (v. 19).

With verse 18, instead of speaking *about* God, the psalmist begins speaking *to* God. Now comes the third *'ak*, "Truly" ("Surely," NIV), calling attention to what follows. "I see what you have done, God," says the psalmist, who then describes the lives of these wicked but prosperous people with two pictures. They are like houses built on slippery foundations that will soon fall to ruin. They will wake up and discover that they have been living in a dream world (vv. 18–20). With verses 21–22 the writer looks back and confesses to the Lord that he has been behaving like an animal, not a reasonable human being.

Some have called this psalm "the great *nevertheless*," indicating the importance of the confession of faith in verse 23. The psalmist says, "No matter what, Lord, I know that I am always with you, and that you are holding me!" Verse 24 is one of those rare passages in the Old Testament that points to hope for life after death with God in heaven, and verse 25 develops the notion.

The psalm ends with a resolve to tell of all God's works. In this story of faith almost lost and then regained, thanks to God's "holding my right hand," this telling is precisely what the psalmist has just been doing.

Good Things, Bad People

This is a psalm that is refreshing in its honesty. As in the later book of Ecclesiastes, here is a biblical writer admitting to a less-than-heroic faith that almost disappeared (vv. 2, 13–15). It was Fyodor Dostoyevsky who wrote somewhere, "My hosannas have arisen from a great furnace of doubt." The writer of this psalm, who went so far as to think that religion was "all in vain," might well have said the same thing.

Psalm 73 also points to the importance of the present community of believers. As long as this person kept these doubts to himself, he was more and more wearied with trying to understand the prosperity of the wicked. Then, as he joined the community of worshipers, somehow he saw how these people's lives would end up. He would never have made it alone with his doubts. The community of believers, which brought him into the presence of God, helped him find a way through.

The psalm is also aware of the future community of believers. The writer did not share his doubts because of the negative influence this might have had on the children (v. 15). At some point, believers move from asking, "What will my parents think?" to "What will my children (or the next generation) think?"

Finally, what of the question about the prospering of the wicked? Claus Westermann has written,

> For the pious, the hardest thing was their having to recognize that God did not invariably reward the pious and punish the godless. And what particularly troubled them was God's blessing the wicked and allowing them to prosper. . . . Some took refuge in asking or praying God to annihilate the wicked. . . . Others, like the author of Job or Psalm 73, realized that this doctrine did not correspond to reality, and from this arose a completely different, and a wholly new, attitude: one must hold fast to God and continue to trust Him even when one no longer understands what He is doing. (*The Living Psalms*, p. 145)

THE NIGHT OF BROKEN GLASS
Psalm 74

A Maskil of Asaph.

74:1 O God, why do you cast us off forever?
   Why does your anger smoke against the sheep of your pasture?
 ² **Remember your congregation, which you acquired long ago,**
   which you redeemed to be the tribe of your heritage.
   Remember Mount Zion, where you came to dwell.
 ³ **Direct your steps to the perpetual ruins;**
   the enemy has destroyed everything in the sanctuary.

 ⁴ **Your foes have roared within your holy place;**

they set up their emblems there.
5 At the upper entrance they hacked
    the wooden trellis with axes.
6 And then, with hatchets and hammers,
    they smashed all its carved work.
7 They set your sanctuary on fire;
    they desecrated the dwelling place of your name,
    bringing it to the ground.
8 They said to themselves, "We will utterly subdue them";
    they burned all the meeting places of God in the land.

9 We do not see our emblems;
    there is no longer any prophet,
    and there is no one among us who knows how long.
10 How long, O God, is the foe to scoff?
    Is the enemy to revile your name forever?
11 Why do you hold back your hand;
    why do you keep your hand in your bosom?

12 Yet God my King is from of old,
    working salvation in the earth.
13 You divided the sea by your might;
    you broke the heads of the dragons in the waters.
14 You crushed the heads of Leviathan;
    you gave him as food for the creatures of the wilderness.
15 You cut openings for springs and torrents;
    you dried up ever-flowing streams.
16 Yours is the day, yours also the night;
    you established the luminaries and the sun.
17 You have fixed all the bounds of the earth;
    you made summer and winter.

18 Remember this, O LORD, how the enemy scoffs,
    and an impious people reviles your name.
19 Do not deliver the soul of your dove to the wild animals;
    do not forget the life of your poor forever.

20 Have regard for your covenant,
    for the dark places of the land are full of the haunts of violence.
21 Do not let the downtrodden be put to shame;
    let the poor and needy praise your name.
22 Rise up, O God, plead your cause;
    remember how the impious scoff at you all day long.
23 Do not forget the clamor of your foes,
    the uproar of your adversaries that goes up continually.

It is a vacant lot now, green with grass, on a busy street in Munich, Germany. Adjacent to it is the bustling Karstadt department store. Across the street is a restaurant where artists used to gather. On the corner of that lot is a stone monument, and carved in the stone are some Hebrew words, from Psalm 74. The words can be translated

> They set your sanctuary on fire . . . they burned all the meeting places of God in the land. . . . Remember this, O LORD, how the enemy scoffs. (vv. 7, 8, 18)

One can stand in that vacant lot today in the sunshine and look at the monument, hear the traffic, watch the children playing on the grass. Once a beautiful synagogue stood in this place, the third largest synagogue in Germany, dedicated on September 16, 1887. But in June 1938 the order was given to take it down; guidebooks will tell you that a certain rising political figure named Adolf Hitler enjoyed lunching in the restaurant across the street and didn't like the looks of that synagogue, so he had it destroyed. A few months later, the order was given to burn down all the synagogues in Germany. That burning, that destruction, took place on the night of November 9/10, 1938. "The night of broken glass," *Kristallnacht*, it is called.

One can stand by the monument in Munich and read the Hebrew words from Psalm 74, remember stories of the Holocaust, and be moved to weep. Who could read Psalm 74 again without thinking of that setting of these words in stone, and of the stories behind these words?

The heading identifies this as a Maskil; see the discussion with Psalm 32. The Asaph psalms are discussed briefly in connection with Psalm 73.

The psalm is one of eleven *community laments* (see Psalm 44) and exhibits the classic elements of the lament (see on Psalm 13): *address* and *"you" complaint* (v. 1), *request* or *cry for help* (vv. 2–3a), *complaint* (vv. 3b–8, 10), *"we" complaint* (v. 9), *"you" complaint* (v. 11), *affirmation of trust* (vv. 12–17), *request/cry for help* (vv. 18–23).

The psalm assumes that the temple had been destroyed a long time ago (v. 3), and it describes the destruction and the burning of that structure (vv. 4–8). It should therefore be dated after the 587 B.C. destruction of the temple (2 Kings 25). The reference to the absence of prophets could refer to a variety of periods.

Why, O God? (74:1–11)

This section of the psalm begins and ends with a Hebrew word known to all who have attended a Good Friday service: *lāmāh*, as in "Eli, Eli *lama* sabachthani" (Matt. 27:46; *lama* in NIV). The word means "Why?" In Psalm 22, the "why" is spoken by an individual; here it is spoken by the community.

The pain behind the question is the same, whether raised by an individual or by the community. The person, the people, can make no sense out of the events that have been happening. They have the sense of being cast off, *forever*. And the Lord's anger is *smoking* against them. Is the writer thinking of the flames and the smoke that arose on that night when the places of worship were burned (vv. 7, 8)?

The community of believers thinks God has forgotten them (vv. 2–3). And God and these people have been together for a long time! They ask God to take a look at where the temple used to stand and see that now there is only a vacant lot, with a few children playing in the sunshine (v. 3).

With verses 4–11 the psalmist describes the events of that terrible *Kristallnacht* when all was destroyed. One can hear the roaring, the hacking, the hatcheting and hammering, the smashing as the armies took out their anti-Judah sentiments on the wood and stone of the temple (vv. 4–6). One can see the flames and smell the smoke and hear the scoffing cries, "We will utterly subdue them!" (v. 8).

The people's prayer in this situation circles around two questions. The first is "How long, O God, is the foe to scoff?" (v. 10) The implication is "Lord, we can't hold on much longer!" The second is "Why do you hold back your hand, Lord? Why don't you do something?" (v. 11 paraphrase) The implication is "Lord, we just don't understand. We know you could help us, but you don't. Why?"

Yours Is the Day, Yours Also the Night (74:12–17)

After these anguished complaints and agonizing questions comes a hymn, affirming trust in this God whose ways cannot be understood. God is named King, even "my King," and is described as doing works of salvation. This hymn remembers the crossing of the Sea of Reeds (the Red Sea) and the Lord's leading the people and providing water in the wilderness. Says the hymn writer, "Day and night, the boundaries between land and water, summer and winter—you control these all, Lord!"

Remember This, O Lord (74:18–23)

"Remember this, O Lord, how the enemy scoffs, and an impious people reviles your name." These words take us back to that monument in Munich, where these words are engraved and where the synagogue once stood. And they recall any similar, senseless acts of needless destruction of holy places. Verses 22 and 23 are once again a reminder of what the enemy has done, a call for God not to forget and to act to save God's people once again.

But You, Where Are You?

The psalm asks the question "Lord, where are you?" I know of no more powerful expression of that cry than this story from the Holocaust after many nights of broken glass, as told by Elie Wiesel:

> This is the story of a ghetto that stopped living, and of a beadle who lost his mind.
>
> It was the beadle's custom to rush to the synagogue each morning, to ascend the bimah and shout first with pride, and then with anger, "I have come to inform you, Master of the Universe, that we are here."
>
> Then came the first massacre, followed by many others. The beadle somehow always emerged unscathed. As soon as he could, he would run to the synagogue, and pounding his fist on the lectern, would shout at the top of his voice: "You see Lord, we are still here."
>
> After the last massacre, he found himself all alone in the deserted synagogue. The last living Jew, he climbed the bimah one last time, stared at the Ark and whispered with infinite gentleness: "You see? I am still here."
>
> He stopped briefly before continuing in his sad, almost toneless voice: "But You, where are You?" (*One Generation After*, pp. 90–91)

PEOPLE ARE TALKING
Psalm 75

To the leader: Do Not Destroy. A Psalm of Asaph. A Song.

75:1 **We give thanks to you, O God;**
    we give thanks; your name is near.
  People tell of your wondrous deeds.

  2 **At the set time that I appoint**
    I will judge with equity.
  3 **When the earth totters, with all its inhabitants,**
    it is I who keep its pillars steady.   ***Selah***
  4 **I say to the boastful, "Do not boast,"**
    and to the wicked, "Do not lift up your horn;
  5 **do not lift up your horn on high,**
    or speak with insolent neck."

⁶ **For not from the east or from the west**
   and not from the wilderness comes lifting up;
⁷ **but it is God who executes judgment,**
   putting down one and lifting up another.
⁸ **For in the hand of the LORD there is a cup**
   with foaming wine, well mixed;
  he will pour a draught from it,
   and all the wicked of the earth
   shall drain it down to the dregs.
⁹ **But I will rejoice forever;**
   I will sing praises to the God of Jacob.

¹⁰ **All the horns of the wicked I will cut off,**
   but the horns of the righteous shall be exalted.

God Who Acts is the title of an influential study of the Old Testament written by G. Ernest Wright in the 1950s. The thesis of the book is that when the Bible speaks of God, it tells what God has done. For example, when an Israelite farmer confessed his faith in God, he told the story of what God had done for his ancestors and for him, beginning with Abraham: "A wandering Aramean was my ancestor." He continued through the events of the exodus and the conquest of the land: "The LORD brought us out of Egypt . . . and he brought us into this place and gave us this land" (Deut. 26:5–10).

In another example, at a Pentecost celebration in Jerusalem, when the earliest apostles were telling about the life, death, and resurrection of Jesus the Messiah, the listeners were amazed, saying, "We hear them telling in our own tongues *the mighty works of God*" (Acts 2:11, RSV).

Psalm 75 begins,

> We give thanks to you, O God;
>   we give thanks; your name is near.
> People tell of your wondrous deeds.
> (v. 1)

To speak *to* God is to give thanks; to speak *about* God is to tell what wondrous things God has done. The psalmist says, "O God, people are talking about the marvelous things you have done!" (v. 1, paraphrase).

The heading dedicates the piece to the director of music and indicates that it is to be used with a tune called "Do Not Destroy" (also Psalms 57, 58, 59). The Asaph psalms are discussed with Psalm 73; "A Song" indicates a musical piece used in worship.

The psalm begins with the community giving thanks to God (v. 1). With verses 2–5, God speaks through a priest to announce an act of judgment; verses 6–8 describe such a judgment act. With verse 9 the psalmist vows to praise God forever, and verse 10 is a final word from God.

The Mighty Acts of God (75:1)

The mood of this psalm stands in sharp contrast to that of the previous one. Psalm 74:1 asked, "O God, why do you cast us off forever? Why does your anger smoke?" Psalm 75 begins with a doubled "We give thanks" (v. 1). Psalm 74 asked God, "Why don't you do something?" Psalm 75 begins by describing people who are celebrating the wondrous deeds God has done. Psalm 74 accuses God of not helping the people (vv. 10–11). Psalm 75 concludes, "I will rejoice forever; I will sing praises to the God of Jacob" (v. 9).

What were the "wondrous deeds" that were being reported? And where did this telling take place? One may imagine recitals telling about God's mighty deeds taking place in some sort of worship gathering, where the people recalled what God had done for them as a community (see Deuteronomy 26; Josh. 24:1–13; Pss. 105:1–6; 106:2; 107:22, 31). Individuals may have told of their experiences of rescue or healing (Pss. 22:22, 31; 30). It seems certain that Old Testament people "loved to tell the story" of what God had done; exactly how and where this was done remains a matter of uncertainty.

The Shaking of the Foundations (75:2–8)

If there is little certainty about just how and where the community told stories about God's wondrous deeds, there is likewise little certainty about the way in which this part of the psalm was used in worship. With verses 2–5, God is the speaker; presumably a worship leader in the temple spoke these words. The judgment act will sort out the "wicked" from the "righteous" (v. 10) and will do so with fairness (v. 2). Involved is God the Creator, who steadies the earth and its peoples when the foundations shake (v. 3; for *Selah*, see on Psalm 3).

The book of Daniel reports visions of rams with powerful horns, which were both means of protection and weapons for attack (Dan. 8:3, 6, 7, 20). Reference to the "horn" of the wicked or righteous refers to their power and strength. The boastful raise themselves up like rams, with mighty horns, poised for an attack (vv. 4–5).

A Cup with Foaming Wine (75:6–10)

The imagery of the cup with a poisonous drink occurs frequently in the Prophets. Jeremiah speaks of the cup containing the wine of God's wrath (Jer. 25:15–29); Ezekiel tells of "a cup of horror and desolation" (Ezek. 23:32–35); Isaiah refers to the cup of the Lord's wrath (Isa. 51:17, 22).

There will be no refreshing, pleasant-tasting drink in this cup, given to the wicked of the earth. This wine is "foaming" and "well mixed," and the wicked must drink it all. They will be put down and cut off (vv. 7, 10).

The coming of the Lord for judgment, however, will be good news for God's people. The writer says, "I will rejoice forever; I will sing praises to the God of Jacob" (v. 9). Finally, in words that remind one of the ending of Psalm 1, the Lord promises to cut the power of the wicked and prosper the way of the righteous.

The Question

Psalm 74 ended with a plea for God to take up the cause of the poor and the needy (Ps. 74:20–23). Psalm 75 begins and ends with thanks and praise for God the Judge (vv. 1, 9). The Judge is powerful (v. 3), attentive to individuals (vv. 4–5), and will punish those wicked who deserve punishment (v. 8).

These assurances are enough to set off thanks and praise in this psalm (vv. 1, 9). The question, however, remains: When is "the set time that I appoint," when God will straighten things out (v. 2)? Surely, God will punish the wicked. But when?

GLORIOUS THINGS OF YOU ARE SPOKEN
Psalm 76

To the leader: with stringed instruments. A Psalm of Asaph. A Song.

76:1 **In Judah God is known,**
     his name is great in Israel.
  2 **His abode has been established in Salem,**
     his dwelling place in Zion.
  3 **There he broke the flashing arrows,**
     the shield, the sword, and the weapons of war.   *Selah*

  4 **Glorious are you, more majestic**
     than the everlasting mountains.

⁵ The stouthearted were stripped of their spoil;
     they sank into sleep;
   none of the troops
     was able to lift a hand.
⁶ At your rebuke, O God of Jacob,
     both rider and horse lay stunned.

⁷ But you indeed are awesome!
     Who can stand before you
     when once your anger is roused?
⁸ From the heavens you uttered judgment;
     the earth feared and was still
⁹ when God rose up to establish judgment,
     to save all the oppressed of the earth.   *Selah*

¹⁰ Human wrath serves only to praise you,
     when you bind the last bit of your wrath around you.
¹¹ Make vows to the LORD your God, and perform them;
     let all who are around him bring gifts
     to the one who is awesome,
¹² who cuts off the spirit of princes,
     who inspires fear in the kings of the earth.

"We give thanks to you, O God," said Psalm 75:1. "People tell of your wondrous deeds." This giving thanks to God apparently involved telling about the things God had done for the people or for an individual. Psalm 76 now presents some examples of the sort of "telling of wondrous deeds" to which Psalm 75 referred.

The heading has a note to the music director that this psalm is to be accompanied with stringed instruments; it is therefore called a "Song." The Asaph psalms run from 73 to 83 (see the comments with Psalm 73): Psalm 76 celebrates the dwelling of God on Mount Zion and is therefore called a *song of Zion* (see the comments with Psalm 87).

The psalm begins with a recalling of one of God's "wondrous deeds" (vv. 1–3), continues with a two-part hymn of praise (vv. 4–6, 7–10), and concludes with a word of advice to the congregation (vv. 11–12).

A "Wondrous Deed" of God (76:1–3)

"Known in Judah is God" is the order of these opening words in Hebrew. The first word in the Hebrew text is *nōdāʿ*, "known," worth noting because the writer uses words beginning with *n* in Hebrew at strategic points in the psalm (see also vv. 4, 7, 11, 12; Hebrew, 5, 8, 12, 13). Salem, which means "peace" (like *shalom*), is an old name for Jerusalem, or Jeru-salem, occurring elsewhere in the Bible only in connection with King Melchizedek of Salem in Genesis 14:18. Zion was the mountain in Jerusalem where the temple was located.

These first verses recall a great victory that was achieved by God. What victory might this have been? The Bible reader thinks immediately of the deliverance of Jerusalem from the Assyrians in 701 B.C. , as reported in 2 Kings 19:35–37. This association is at least as old as the Greek translation of the Hebrew Bible (third century B.C.), which includes in the heading for this psalm "Concerning the Assyrian."

This language about the destruction of weapons reminds one of Psalm 46:8–9. There the reference is clearly to the future, when the Lord of hosts will again achieve a victory and smash the weapons of warfare. The *Selah*, here and at verse 9, frames a quotation of words addressed to "you," the God of Jacob. (For *Selah*, see the comments on Psalm 3.)

Glorious Things of You Are Spoken (76:4–6, 7–9)

After language telling *about* one of God's "wondrous deeds," the psalm shifts into a hymn, speaking *to* God as "you" (vv. 4, 6, 7, 8). The second *n* word in Hebrew, *nā'ōr*, "glorious," introduces the section: "Glorious are you. . . ." Verses 5 and 6 remember a great victory achieved by the Lord. Recalling the Greek heading, one thinks again of the deliverance of Jerusalem from the Assyrians in 701 B.C. as the background for understanding verses 4–6.

With verse 7, the third *n* word in Hebrew appears: "But you indeed are awesome [*nōrā'*]." Here is a description of the appearance of God (a theophany) that appears to outrun any historical events and refers to a future time when God will appear "to save all the oppressed of the earth." Another Asaph psalm asks God not to forget the poor (74:19–21); this one indicates that God has not forgotten (v. 9). Verse 10 is a comment, stating that all the power and wrath that humans exhibit serve only to praise God, as was the case with the defeat of the Assyrians in 701 B.C.

Make Your Vows! (76:11–12)

After this hymn of praise to God, the psalm has a word for worshipers. Using a fourth *n* word, the writer says, "Make vows [*niderū*] to the Lord," encouraging the congregation to continue that praise by making vows and bringing gifts to the one who inspires *nōrā'*, "fear," the fifth and final *n* word, in princes and kings.

One cannot read through this psalm in its Hebrew original without being struck by these *n* words: *nōdā'* ("known," v. 1), *nā'ōr* ("glorious," v. 4), *nōrā'* ("awesome," v. 7), *niderū* ("make vows," v. 11), *nōrā'* ("fear," v. 12).

The theme of the psalm can be traced by following these words, thus telling the story of God's "wondrous deeds" (75:1). God made the divine self *known* in that great act of deliverance in Jerusalem (76:1–3). Ever since that time, *glorious* things have been spoken of you, God (vv. 4–6). God, you are *awesome* and will yet act to save the oppressed (vv. 7–9). And so, congregation, now *make vows* to this one who still evokes *fear* in the hearts of political leaders, as God once evoked fear in acting against the Assyrians at Salem, Mount Zion.

THE UNSEEN FOOTPRINTS
Psalm 77

To the leader: according to Jeduthun. Of Asaph. A Psalm.

77:1 I cry aloud to God,
    aloud to God, that he may hear me.
  2 In the day of my trouble I seek the Lord;
    in the night my hand is stretched out without wearying;
    my soul refuses to be comforted.
  3 I think of God, and I moan;
    I meditate, and my spirit faints.   *Selah*

  4 You keep my eyelids from closing;
    I am so troubled that I cannot speak.
  5 I consider the days of old,
    and remember the years of long ago.
  6 I commune with my heart in the night;
    I meditate and search my spirit:
  7 "Will the Lord spurn forever,
    and never again be favorable?
  8 Has his steadfast love ceased forever?
    Are his promises at an end for all time?
  9 Has God forgotten to be gracious?
    Has he in anger shut up his compassion?"   *Selah*
  10 And I say, "It is my grief
    that the right hand of the Most High has changed."

  11 I will call to mind the deeds of the LORD;
    I will remember your wonders of old.
  12 I will meditate on all your work,
    and muse on your mighty deeds.

¹³ **Your way, O God, is holy.**
    What god is so great as our God?
¹⁴ **You are the God who works wonders;**
    you have displayed your might among the peoples.
¹⁵ **With your strong arm you redeemed your people,**
    the descendants of Jacob and Joseph.   *Selah*

¹⁶ **When the waters saw you, O God,**
    when the waters saw you, they were afraid;
    the very deep trembled.
¹⁷ **The clouds poured out water;**
    the skies thundered;
    your arrows flashed on every side.
¹⁸ **The crash of your thunder was in the whirlwind;**
    your lightnings lit up the world;
    the earth trembled and shook.
¹⁹ **Your way was through the sea,**
    your path, through the mighty waters;
    yet your footprints were unseen.
²⁰ **You led your people like a flock**
    by the hand of Moses and Aaron.

This psalm raises a number of questions; since they involve God, they may be called theological questions:

> Will the Lord . . . never again be favorable?
> Has his steadfast love ceased forever?
>   Are his promises at an end for all time?
> Has God forgotten to be gracious?
> Has he in anger shut up his compassion?
>   (vv. 7–9)

The psalm does not answer these questions. Instead, it tells a story.

The heading dedicates the psalm to the choir director, identifying it as another psalm of Asaph (see on Psalm 73). Jeduthun and his family were on David's musical staff (1 Chron. 16:41–42; 25:1, 3, 6; 2 Chron. 5:11–12).

Psalm 76 offered examples of the "wondrous deeds" of the Lord mentioned in Psalm 75:1; this psalm provides some more. It is also worth noting that three times this psalm refers to meditating (vv. 3, 6, 12). (For *Selah*, see on Psalm 3.)

Those Haunted Nights (77:1–3)

The story told in this psalm begins in the nighttime.

"The nights are the worst times," a woman said to me as she was telling of the loneliness after the death of her husband. The writer of this psalm, it seems, would agree.

During the daytime, the psalmist has been trying without success to make contact with God (vv. 1–2a). And in the night? The description is longer because the pain is more intense. Hands are stretched out in prayer, like a person drowning, reaching out for help (vv. 2bc–3; see Ps. 143:6).

But there is no comfort. There is only that remembering, that moaning, almost fainting. And the nights are the worst times.

Questions in the Night (77:4–10)

The story continues, again at nighttime. Now the psalmist speaks *to* God, declaring that neither sleep nor speech is possible (v. 4). What can be done? Abruptly, the focus shifts to the past. The one praying remembers the good times in those "years of long ago" and muses on the difficulties of the present time (v. 6).

In the nighttime hours, worries can worsen; anxieties can escalate; questions can multiply. These are the questions about God, about which the psalmist thinks and meditates (v. 6).

The Mighty Acts of God (77:11–20)

To this point the writer has told of sleepless nights and of haunting questions about God. All of this has provided fuel for trying to figure things out, for meditating.

With verse 11 the mood changes. No longer does the psalmist brood over the problems and the puzzles of the present. The writer's attention turns to the mighty acts of God in the past:

> I will call to mind the deeds of the LORD;
> I will remember your wonders of old.
> (v. 11)

In the depths of these lonely nights, the psalmist looks back: "I will meditate on all your work, and muse on your mighty deeds." The product of this meditating and musing is that the writer speaks *to* God—"Your way, O God, is holy" (v. 13a)—and also, for the benefit of others, *about* God—"What god is so great as our God?" The sense of "holy" is separate, apart, totally different from the ways and works of anyone on earth.

Verses 14 and 15 recall God's delivering of the people in the events of the exodus (Exodus 19–20). When God appeared at that time, it was an act of deliverance of the Israelites from the power of the Egyptians. Nature was involved as well, however. The language in Psalm 77 is poetic, personalizing powers of nature: the waters (of the Sea of Reeds) saw God, were afraid, and trembled. A mighty storm rose, with lightning, thunder, and high winds. God leading Israel out of Egypt is pictured as a shepherd leading a flock (v. 20). The path went right through the sea. God was the leader, but no footprints could be seen (v. 19).

Footprints on the Sea

The psalm tells a story of a person deeply troubled, meditating deep into the night, haunted by theological questions (vv. 7–9), experiencing the absence of God. The psalm reports that remembering the Lord's works in the past aided in the struggle of trying to understand God's apparent lack of action in the present.

The imagery in verse 19 is worthy of reflection, musing, meditation. "Your way was through the sea, your path, through the mighty waters; yet your footprints were unseen." The psalm has just recalled the story of how the people of Israel came out of Egypt. The Bible makes God the subject of the verbs: "You are the God who works wonders; . . . you redeemed your people" (vv. 14–15). This act of deliverance was accompanied and enabled by acts of God in nature, in the form of thunder and lightning and wind and rain (vv. 16–18). In the midst of this telling of the story of the exodus is the statement "yet your footprints were unseen" (v. 19). God was there, but God's presence was hidden.

In the story of Bel and the Dragon in the Apocrypha, the mystery of the disappearing offering was solved when clever Daniel sprinkled ashes on the floor of the temple and the footprints of the priests and their families could be detected (Bel and the Dragon, vv. 14–20). That sort of evidence would convince any court in any land!

Was the Lord involved in the escape at the Sea of Reeds? Was the Lord involved in what happened to the Egyptians and in the thunder and lightning and storming that accompanied these events? This time there were no footprints to prove that God did it. The questions raised in Psalm 77:7–9 remain questions. There are no footprints. There is only the story of what God has done, told in this psalm and retold from generation to generation a million times since. Even for people who have to live with questions, the story may be enough to invite a confession of faith: "What god is so great as our God?" (v. 13).

DO LOOK BACK
Psalm 78

A Maskil of Asaph.

78:1 Give ear, O my people, to my teaching;
        incline your ears to the words of my mouth.
    2 I will open my mouth in a parable;
        I will utter dark sayings from of old,
    3 things that we have heard and known,
        that our ancestors have told us.
    4 We will not hide them from their children;
        we will tell to the coming generation
      the glorious deeds of the LORD, and his might,
        and the wonders that he has done.

    5 He established a decree in Jacob,
        and appointed a law in Israel,
      which he commanded our ancestors
        to teach to their children;
    6 that the next generation might know them,
        the children yet unborn,
      and rise up and tell them to their children,
        7 so that they should set their hope in God,
      and not forget the works of God,
        but keep his commandments;
    8 and that they should not be like their ancestors,
        a stubborn and rebellious generation,
      a generation whose heart was not steadfast,
        whose spirit was not faithful to God.

    9 The Ephraimites, armed with the bow,
        turned back on the day of battle.
    10 They did not keep God's covenant,
        but refused to walk according to his law.
    11 They forgot what he had done,
        and the miracles that he had shown them.
    12 In the sight of their ancestors he worked marvels
        in the land of Egypt, in the fields of Zoan.
    13 He divided the sea and let them pass through it,
        and made the waters stand like a heap.
    14 In the daytime he led them with a cloud,
        and all night long with a fiery light.
    15 He split rocks open in the wilderness,
        and gave them drink abundantly as from the deep.

¹⁶ He made streams come out of the rock,
    and caused waters to flow down like rivers.

¹⁷ Yet they sinned still more against him,
    rebelling against the Most High in the desert.
¹⁸ They tested God in their heart
    by demanding the food they craved.
¹⁹ They spoke against God, saying,
    "Can God spread a table in the wilderness?
²⁰ Even though he struck the rock so that water gushed out
    and torrents overflowed,
   can he also give bread,
    or provide meat for his people?"

²¹ Therefore, when the LORD heard, he was full of rage;
    a fire was kindled against Jacob,
    his anger mounted against Israel,
²² because they had no faith in God,
    and did not trust his saving power.
²³ Yet he commanded the skies above,
    and opened the doors of heaven;
²⁴ he rained down on them manna to eat,
    and gave them the grain of heaven.
²⁵ Mortals ate of the bread of angels;
    he sent them food in abundance.
²⁶ He caused the east wind to blow in the heavens,
    and by his power he led out the south wind;
²⁷ he rained flesh upon them like dust,
    winged birds like the sand of the seas;
²⁸ he let them fall within their camp,
    all around their dwellings.
²⁹ And they ate and were well filled,
    for he gave them what they craved.
³⁰ But before they had satisfied their craving,
    while the food was still in their mouths,
³¹ the anger of God rose against them
    and he killed the strongest of them,
    and laid low the flower of Israel.

³² In spite of all this they still sinned;
    they did not believe in his wonders.
³³ So he made their days vanish like a breath,
    and their years in terror.
³⁴ When he killed them, they sought for him;
    they repented and sought God earnestly.

35 They remembered that God was their rock,
   the Most High God their redeemer.
36 But they flattered him with their mouths;
   they lied to him with their tongues.
37 Their heart was not steadfast toward him;
   they were not true to his covenant.
38 Yet he, being compassionate,
   forgave their iniquity,
   and did not destroy them;
 often he restrained his anger,
   and did not stir up all his wrath.
39 He remembered that they were but flesh,
   a wind that passes and does not come again.
40 How often they rebelled against him in the wilderness
   and grieved him in the desert!
41 They tested God again and again,
   and provoked the Holy One of Israel.
42 They did not keep in mind his power,
   or the day when he redeemed them from the foe;
43 when he displayed his signs in Egypt,
   and his miracles in the fields of Zoan.
44 He turned their rivers to blood,
   so that they could not drink of their streams.
45 He sent among them swarms of flies, which devoured them,
   and frogs, which destroyed them.
46 He gave their crops to the caterpillar,
   and the fruit of their labor to the locust.
47 He destroyed their vines with hail,
   and their sycamores with frost.
48 He gave over their cattle to the hail,
   and their flocks to thunderbolts.
49 He let loose on them his fierce anger,
   wrath, indignation, and distress,
   a company of destroying angels.
50 He made a path for his anger;
   he did not spare them from death,
   but gave their lives over to the plague.
51 He struck all the firstborn in Egypt,
   the first issue of their strength in the tents of Ham.
52 Then he led out his people like sheep,
   and guided them in the wilderness like a flock.
53 He led them in safety, so that they were not afraid;
   but the sea overwhelmed their enemies.
54 And he brought them to his holy hill,
   to the mountain that his right hand had won.

55 He drove out nations before them;
    he apportioned them for a possession
    and settled the tribes of Israel in their tents.

56 Yet they tested the Most High God,
    and rebelled against him.
    They did not observe his decrees,
57 but turned away and were faithless like their ancestors;
    they twisted like a treacherous bow.
58 For they provoked him to anger with their high places;
    they moved him to jealousy with their idols.
59 When God heard, he was full of wrath,
    and he utterly rejected Israel.
60 He abandoned his dwelling at Shiloh,
    the tent where he dwelt among mortals,
61 and delivered his power to captivity,
    his glory to the hand of the foe.
62 He gave his people to the sword,
    and vented his wrath on his heritage.
63 Fire devoured their young men,
    and their girls had no marriage song.
64 Their priests fell by the sword,
    and their widows made no lamentation.
65 Then the Lord awoke as from sleep,
    like a warrior shouting because of wine.
66 He put his adversaries to rout;
    he put them to everlasting disgrace.

67 He rejected the tent of Joseph,
    he did not choose the tribe of Ephraim;
68 but he chose the tribe of Judah,
    Mount Zion, which he loves.
69 He built his sanctuary like the high heavens,
    like the earth, which he has founded forever.
70 He chose his servant David,
    and took him from the sheepfolds;
71 from tending the nursing ewes he brought him
    to be the shepherd of his people Jacob,
    of Israel, his inheritance.
72 With upright heart he tended them,
    and guided them with skillful hand.

The usual advice is to look toward the future. Common wisdom says, "Let bygones be bygones," "That's water over the dam," "Get a fresh start," or "Don't look back."

We recall what happened when Lot's wife looked back at Sodom, contrary to the Lord's instructions (Gen. 19:15–26). Even Jesus advised against putting one's hand to the plow and looking back (Luke 9:62). And professional "futurists" write books or appear on television to help us prepare for the days and years ahead.

In the context of all this concern for the future, Psalm 78 seems oddly preoccupied with the past. It speaks of "dark sayings from of old," of "things . . . our ancestors have told us," of "wonders that [the Lord] *has done*" (Ps. 78:4).

Contrary to common wisdom, this psalm advises, "Do look back!" But why? The answer comes in the form of a story.

The heading identifies this as a "Maskil of Asaph," that is, an instructional piece associated with the family of Asaph (see on Psalm 32). This psalm is second only to Psalm 119 in length. The Hebrew text has a marginal note alongside verse 36, indicating that it is the middle verse of the book of Psalms. Psalm 78 also is one of a quintet of psalms that recite God's mighty deeds with God's people; the others are 105, 106, 135, and 136.

The aim of this psalm is to teach (v. 1). It may be divided into four major segments: *teaching for the children* (vv. 1–4); *they forgot what God had done* (vv. 5–11); *lessons from the past* (vv. 12–66); *a fresh start* (vv. 67–72).

Teaching for the Children (78:1–4)

The opening words indicate that this is going to be a teaching psalm. The subject matter will be "the glorious deeds of the LORD, and his might, and the wonders that he has done" (v. 4). This is not new material but a curriculum that has been passed down from the ancestors. Now it needs to be taught to the present generation, so that it can be passed on to the next. "So pay attention," says the teacher, "to the instruction I am about to give." This educational project is for the sake of the children (v. 4).

They Forgot What God Had Done (78:5–11)

Verses 5–8 describe a hope for the future and lament a failure from the past. The future hope lies in theological education, that is, in learning the story of what God has done. This teaching has an intellectual component, learning the "works of God," as well as an action component, learning to live in a manner directed by God's commandments (v. 7).

Along with this optimistic look at the future is a pessimistic review of the past (vv. 8–11). Those people "forgot what [God] had done" and "refused to walk according to [God's] law" (vv. 10–11). Teaching means not only pointing the way to live in the present and the future but also remembering the past.

Lessons from the Past (78:12–66)

Now the teacher does just that, telling stories from the past and, every so often, pointing out their significance for the present. First is the story at the center of Israel's faith, the exodus and the wandering in the wilderness (vv. 12–53).

Imagine the teacher writing on a blackboard, in bold capital letters: LESSON ONE: EXODUS AND WILDERNESS (VV. 12–22). Verse 11 announces the theme for the stories that follow: *they forgot what God had done*. Verses 12–16 tell what God has done; the subject of every verb is God! God worked marvels in Egypt, divided the sea, led the people with cloud and fire, gave them water in the desert. And the people's reaction? They rebelled, sinned, and doubted that God would be able to feed them in the wilderness.

So the Lord was angry with them, "because they had no faith in God, and did not trust his saving power" (v. 22). The point of Lesson One is *believe and trust in God's saving power*.

LESSON TWO: WILDERNESS (VV. 23–42): This section also begins with a reminder of what God has done, this time when the people were wandering through the wilderness. God sent manna to eat; God provided quails for meat (vv. 23–29; see Exodus 16). With verse 32 the teacher recalls the reaction of the people, as in verses 10–11: the people neither lived nor believed as they ought (vv. 32, 37). God forgave them, but they kept transgressing, like rebellious children (vv. 40–41). Verse 42 summarizes, suggests the application, and points ahead to the next sections. To summarize Lesson Two: *don't forget the powerful God who rescued you from Egypt!*

LESSON THREE: EXODUS, WILDERNESS, CONQUEST (VV. 43–55). This section returns to the theme of the exodus. Verse 42 had pointed ahead to the exodus. Once again, God is the actor, engineering the plagues and finally leading the people out of bondage and guiding them through the wilderness, like a shepherd leading a flock of sheep (vv. 42–53).

Brief mention is made of the continuation of the story through the time of the conquest, when God "drove out nations before them" and the Israelites were "settled in their tents" (v. 55). This lesson repeats and expands on the point made in Lesson Two: *don't forget the powerful God who led you out of Egypt, led you through the wilderness, and settled you in this land.*

LESSON FOUR: THE DESTRUCTION OF SHILOH (vv. 56–66): Verses
56–57 offer a final judgment on the people's actions. They tested God,
rebelled, and were faithless (vv. 56–57; see vv. 10–11). God's reaction was
anger, and God rejected Israel, going so far as to abandon the place of
worship at Shiloh (vv. 58–61; see Jer. 7:12–14) and to give the people into
the hands of enemies (vv. 62–64).

But then, once again, the Lord acted to help the people. The picture
of God in verses 65–66 is a dramatic one: God goes into action with the
fury of a warrior roused from a drunken sleep! The reference is apparently to the victories over the Philistines during the time of Saul and
David.

The point of the lesson this time is stated at the beginning of the section: *do not rebel against God or God's commandments; you may provoke God
to anger (vv. 56–57).*

A Fresh Start (78:67–72)

In this final section, two themes emerge that are developed in the *royal
psalms* (see on Psalm 2): (1) God has chosen Mount Zion as the place for
God's temple (v. 68); (2) God has chosen King David to be the leader of
God's people (v. 70).

The hope for the future now appears to lie with Judah, the tribe God
chose; with Mount Zion, the place God loves; and with David, the king
God chose to be God's servant.

The Wonders of God's Love

To summarize the teaching of this instructional psalm:

1. Among the people of God, teaching has always been considered
   important (vv. 1–8). This means there must be teachers who have
   researched and *reflected* on both the wondrous deeds of God and the
   rebellious acts of humans.
2. These teachers *report* on those acts and deeds by telling stories of
   what God has done and how people have responded. Here the
   teacher reports on God's marvelous acts (vv. 12–16) but also on the
   people's ungrateful response (vv. 10–11, 17–20, etc.).
3. Reporting on the acts of God and the reactions of the people makes
   obvious the *relevance* of those past events for the present and for the
   next generations. Teachers are to tell the children about the wonderful things God has done "so that they should set their hope in
   God" (v. 7).

4. This teaching calls for a *response* from the hearers, not in the form
of rebellion (vv. 10–11, 17, 56–57) but in lives marked by faithfulness, obedience, and hope (vv. 7–8).

WE, YOUR PEOPLE
Psalm 79

A Psalm of Asaph.

79:1 O God, the nations have come into your inheritance;
  they have defiled your holy temple;
  they have laid Jerusalem in ruins.
 2 They have given the bodies of your servants
  to the birds of the air for food,
  the flesh of your faithful to the wild animals of the earth.
 3 They have poured out their blood like water
  all around Jerusalem,
  and there was no one to bury them.
 4 We have become a taunt to our neighbors,
  mocked and derided by those around us.

 5 How long, O LORD? Will you be angry forever?
  Will your jealous wrath burn like fire?
 6 Pour out your anger on the nations
  that do not know you,
 and on the kingdoms
  that do not call on your name.
 7 For they have devoured Jacob
  and laid waste his habitation.

 8 Do not remember against us the iniquities of our ancestors;
  let your compassion come speedily to meet us,
  for we are brought very low.
 9 Help us, O God of our salvation,
  for the glory of your name;
 deliver us, and forgive our sins,
  for your name's sake.
 10 Why should the nations say,
  "Where is their God?"
 Let the avenging of the outpoured blood of your servants
  be known among the nations before our eyes.

 11 Let the groans of the prisoners come before you;
  according to your great power preserve those doomed to die.

12 **Return sevenfold into the bosom of our neighbors**
   the taunts with which they taunted you, O Lord!
13 **Then we your people, the flock of your pasture,**
   will give thanks to you forever;
   from generation to generation we will recount your praise.

Psalm 78 speaks a good deal about the past, including Israel's wrongdoing in the past. Psalm 78 names the ancestors "a stubborn and rebellious generation . . . whose spirit was not faithful to God" (v. 8) and says of them, "They did not keep God's covenant" (v. 10); "Yet they sinned still more against him, rebelling against the Most High in the desert" (v. 17); "They did not believe in his wonders" (v. 32).

Psalm 79 also looks at the people's past but this time asks God specifically not to hold the sins of the past against the present generation (v. 8). It reminds God who is praying; using the imagery of Psalm 78:52, it speaks of "we your people, the flock of your pasture" (v. 13).

As a psalm of Asaph, this is part of that grouping that includes Psalms 50 and 73–83 (see on Psalm 73). Verse 1 assumes the destruction of Jerusalem by the Babylonians, and thus the psalm is to be dated after 587 B.C. It is one of a number of *community laments* in Book III (Psalms 74, 79, 80, 83, 85) and exhibits the typical elements of the community lament (see on Psalm 44): *complaint* (vv. 1–5, 8c), *request* (vv. 6–8ab, 9–12), *affirmation of trust* (v. 13a), and *vow to praise* (v. 13b–c). The extensive length of the complaint is striking, indicative of the hurting felt in the nation after the events of 587.

How Long, O Lord? (79:1–5)

This psalm gets to the point immediately. It is as if the one praying is standing in the ruins of the city of Jerusalem, pointing at what was once the beautiful temple. "O God, take a look at this!" the writer is saying.

Despite the destruction, those praying continue to consider themselves God's people. Lying there are the bodies of "your servants." The birds are pecking away at the flesh of "your faithful" (v. 2).

Behind the "how long" question in verse 5 is the feeling "We can't hold out much longer!" The subjects of the verbs here are "you" and "your wrath." This is a clear example of a theological complaint, aimed at the Lord. It comes as the climax of this series of complaints, first in the "they" form (vv. 1–3), then in "we" form (v. 4), and finally, as if the Lord has the ultimate responsibility, in "you" form (v. 5).

Help Us! (79:6–12)

This psalm has lots of things to ask of God. First is a request that God punish those nations that have wasted the temple and the holy city (vv. 6–7). Verse 8 should be understood in the light of Psalm 78. In that psalm, rebellions and iniquities of the past are considered as the reason for suffering in the present (Ps. 78:21–22, 30–31, 56–64). God is punishing the people for their past sins. Now the prayer is "let your compassion come," and the prayer is given a reason in the form of a "we" complaint: "for we are brought very low" (v. 8). The cries for help come to focus in verse 9: "Help us . . . deliver us . . . forgive our sins."

The cries for help continue, again asking the Lord to punish those guilty of the destruction of Jerusalem and to save the lives of those who have been taken prisoner (vv. 10–11). The section ends as it began, with a cry to the Lord for revenge (v. 12).

We Will Tell the Story! (79:13)

The psalmist ends by reminding the Lord who is praying, in a literal statement, "We, your people," and then with a picture used in psalms immediately before and after this one, "the flock of your pasture" (see Pss. 77:20; 78:52; 80:1). Once that deliverance has been experienced, there will be no stopping the telling of the story, throughout all generations.

The psalm is a quite remarkable confession of faith from a people who have experienced the destruction of their city and the loss of their place of worship. Through all, they remember who they are ("your servants," "your faithful," "your people"). The sights of dead bodies and the sounds of the taunts of neighbors with which the psalm began (vv. 2–4) are finally replaced by a picture of a flock led by a loving shepherd and by the sound of hymns of praise, passed on from one generation to the next.

LORD, LET YOUR FACE SHINE!
Psalm 80

To the leader: on Lilies, a Covenant. Of Asaph. A Psalm.

80:1 **Give ear, O Shepherd of Israel,**
      you who lead Joseph like a flock!
    You who are enthroned upon the cherubim, shine forth
  2   **before Ephraim and Benjamin and Manasseh.**

Stir up your might,
　　and come to save us!

3 Restore us, O God;
　　let your face shine, that we may be saved.

4 O LORD God of hosts,
　　how long will you be angry with your people's prayers?
5 You have fed them with the bread of tears,
　　and given them tears to drink in full measure.
6 You make us the scorn of our neighbors;
　　our enemies laugh among themselves.

7 Restore us, O God of hosts;
　　let your face shine, that we may be saved.

8 You brought a vine out of Egypt;
　　you drove out the nations and planted it.
9 You cleared the ground for it;
　　it took deep root and filled the land.
10 The mountains were covered with its shade,
　　the mighty cedars with its branches;
11 it sent out its branches to the sea,
　　and its shoots to the River.
12 Why then have you broken down its walls,
　　so that all who pass along the way pluck its fruit?
13 The boar from the forest ravages it,
　　and all that move in the field feed on it.

14 Turn again, O God of hosts;
　　look down from heaven, and see;
　have regard for this vine,
15　　the stock that your right hand planted.
16 They have burned it with fire, they have cut it down;
　　may they perish at the rebuke of your countenance.
17 But let your hand be upon the one at your right hand,
　　the one whom you made strong for yourself.
18 Then we will never turn back from you;
　　give us life, and we will call on your name.
19 Restore us, O LORD God of hosts;
　　let your face shine, that we may be saved.

Both Jewish and Christian worship services include, and often conclude with, these words from Aaron:

The LORD bless you and keep you;
the LORD make his face to shine upon you, and be gracious to you.

(Num. 6:24–25)

Three times in Psalm 80 the praying people ask God, "Let your face shine, that we may be saved" (vv. 3, 7, 19). To "let your face shine" means to be present with someone with good results (Pss. 4:6; 31:16). This refrain is at the heart of Psalm 80, and at the heart of the refrain is the cry "come to save us!"

This psalm is dedicated to the worship leader, to be sung to a tune no longer known, "Lilies, a Covenant" (see also Psalm 45). The piece is a part of the Asaph collection (see on Psalm 73) and, as a "Psalm," is to be sung with instrumental accompaniment.

This is a *lament of the community* ("come to save *us*," v. 2) and contains the same elements as the lament of the individual (see on Psalm 13). The *address* appears in verses 1–2a; *requests* in verses 2b–3, 7, 14–15, 16b–17, and 19; *complaints* in verses 4–6, 12–13, and 16a; an *affirmation of trust* in verses 8–11; and a *vow to praise* in verse 18. A request with an expanding address to God appears in the refrain "Restore us," verses 3, 7, and 19.

The time of this lament's origin is not clear, though mention of the tribes of Joseph's sons Ephraim and Manasseh puts a special emphasis on the Northern Kingdom, which existed from the death of Solomon (922 B.C.) to the fall of Samaria (722 B.C.).

Save Us, O God! (80:1–3)

Psalm 80 begins with "Give ear!" God is not a "saving machine"— *Rettungsautomat*—as Claus Westermann (*Der Psalter*, p. 31) put it, but a person; one must get God's attention! This is a prayer of the people (v. 4), coming from a situation where they are desperately in need of help. The word *save* (vv. 2, 3, 7, 19) is central to the psalm. The Shepherd/sheep imagery appears frequently in the Asaph psalms (see 74:1; 77:20; 78:52–53; 79:13; also 23:1; 28:9; 119:176).

God appears as "enthroned upon the cherubim" (v. 1). Cherubim were winged creatures that decorated thrones in Israel's world. Psalm 99:1 says, "The LORD is king. . . . He sits enthroned upon the cherubim," and this way of speaking was found in Israel from premonarchical times (1 Sam. 4:4; 2 Sam. 6:2). Alongside the picture of God as shepherd is a picture of God as king.

The cry for help is clear in verse 2b and also in the refrain in verse 3. The psalm begins with the people identifying themselves as sheep needing shepherding and as subjects needing their King.

Save Us, O God of Hosts! (80:4–7)

This "people's prayer" (v. 4) now moves into a "you" complaint against God (see on Psalm 13). The Lord is portrayed as the chief of a great army, "LORD God of hosts" (see again 1 Sam. 4:4; also 2 Kings 3:14; Isa. 6:3). The "how long" question implies "Lord help us quickly. We can't hold on much longer!" The same question occurs in the lament Psalms 13:1; 74:10; 94:3.

The sharp complaints against God continue: "Lord, you've been angry too long; we have had only tears as food and drink; our neighbors are laughing at us!" (vv. 5–6 paraphrase).

This time the refrain in verse 7 is expanded to match partially the "LORD God of hosts" in verse 4.

Save Us, O Lord God of Hosts! (80:8–19)

Verses 8–11 affirm trust in the Lord by recalling God's saving acts in the past. The sense is "We remember how you saved us in the past, Lord, and now we trust that you will do it again!" The psalmist reminds God of their previous relationship. The picture is that of a farmer, taking a vine out of Egypt (the exodus), clearing the ground (driving out the nations), planting it, and watching it prosper (the growth of the kingdom under David). Balancing the "how long" question (v. 4), the psalmist asks, "Why?" (v. 12). Why would a farmer exert such effort in planting and nurturing a vineyard only to break down its walls and let it be destroyed (vv. 12–14; see also Isa. 5:1–7)?

The final section of the psalm requests the Lord's help (vv. 14–15), then expresses a complaint and a curse on the enemies who have mistreated Israel (v. 16). Is this a reference to the Assyrians' capture of Samaria in 722 B.C.? Those who translated the Old Testament into Greek in the third century B.C. read it this way, inserting "concerning the Assyrian" into the psalm heading. The psalmist hopes that the enemy will perish and that the king ("at your right hand," v. 17) will prosper. Verse 18 vows to obey and praise God when deliverance has come. The refrain in verse 19 is again a desperate call for help.

Learning to Live with Mystery

Certain questions are asked of God in this psalm, but they are not answered. The people have been faithful in worship, asking for God's help, but God has not responded. The question is "How much longer, Lord?" (v. 4).

The city walls have been broken down, leaving a heap of ruins and rubble. Such scenes have not been uncommon in our times. The city Münster in Germany was bombed on a sunny Sunday afternoon in October 1943. Hundreds of houses and buildings were destroyed, including churches. Hundreds of innocent citizens were killed, including children. The question remains, even today: Why, Lord? In many such cases, the questions will always remain questions. But somehow, despite these unanswered questions, God's people have survived. They have had to learn to live with mystery. Somehow, they have been enabled to go on, remembering mighty acts of God in the past (vv. 8–11), hoping for God's acts in the future (vv. 3, 7, 19), and praying to a God whose ways they do not understand (vv. 4, 12).

They have been enabled once again to call on the name of God and to thank God for the gift of a new kind of life (v. 18), given through one identified as the "good shepherd" (John 10:11) and even as "the way, and the truth, and the life" (John 14:6).

HONEY FROM THE ROCK
Psalm 81

To the leader: according to The Gittith. Of Asaph.

81:1 **Sing aloud to God our strength;**
    shout for joy to the God of Jacob.
 2 **Raise a song, sound the tambourine,**
    the sweet lyre with the harp.
 3 **Blow the trumpet at the new moon,**
    at the full moon, on our festal day.
 4 **For it is a statute for Israel,**
    an ordinance of the God of Jacob.
 5 **He made it a decree in Joseph,**
    when he went out over the land of Egypt.

   I hear a voice I had not known:
 6 **"I relieved your shoulder of the burden;**
    your hands were freed from the basket.
 7 **In distress you called, and I rescued you;**
    I answered you in the secret place of thunder;
    I tested you at the waters of Meribah.   *Selah*
 8 **Hear, O my people, while I admonish you;**
    O Israel, if you would but listen to me!
 9 **There shall be no strange god among you;**
    you shall not bow down to a foreign god.

¹⁰ I am the LORD your God,
  who brought you up out of the land of Egypt.
  Open your mouth wide and I will fill it.

¹¹ "But my people did not listen to my voice;
  Israel would not submit to me.
¹² So I gave them over to their stubborn hearts,
  to follow their own counsels.
¹³ O that my people would listen to me,
  that Israel would walk in my ways!
¹⁴ Then I would quickly subdue their enemies,
  and turn my hand against their foes.
¹⁵ Those who hate the LORD would cringe before him,
  and their doom would last forever.
¹⁶ I would feed you with the finest of the wheat,
  and with honey from the rock I would satisfy you."

In reading through this psalm, one is reminded that these psalms were not originally written to be read, silently, from a book. Like Psalms 50 and 95, this one was intended to be used as part of a festival. What would such a festival have been like? What would one have heard and seen? The psalm calls for singing, even shouting, to the accompaniment of percussion (tambourine), stringed (lyre, harp), and wind instruments ("Blow the trumpet," v. 3). It appears that worship in biblical Israel was not a matter of sitting straight, hands folded, praying silently. According to Psalm 150, it even included dancing!

The heading dedicates Psalm 81 to the worship leader and identifies the melody to which it should be sung as "according to The Gittith" (see also Psalm 8). It is one of the Asaph songs (Psalms 50, 73–83; see on Psalm 73).

There are three major sections: a *call to celebrate* (vv. 1–5a); a word from God *to* Israel, "I rescued you" (vv. 5b–10); and a word from God *about* Israel, "O that my people would listen to me, and walk in my ways!" (vv. 11–16).

Sing and Shout! (81:1–5a)

Psalm 81 gives few clues to the nature of the festival where it was used. It apparently extended from the time of "new moon" to "full moon," that is, for a two-week period (v. 3). It is called "our festal day" (v. 3). While certainty is not possible, the fall Festival of Booths (Sukkot), which begins with trumpet blasts and lasts for two weeks, would seem the most likely candidate (Lev. 23:33–36, 39–43; Deut. 16:13–16).

God Speaks to Israel (81:5b–10)

The speaker claims to hear "a voice I had not known," that is, a voice from God. Prophets claim this same sort of inspiration (for example, Isa. 5:9), as do other psalmists (Ps. 85:8). The words that follow are now given special authority, since they are identified as originating with God.

Verses 6–7 pick up the theme announced in verse 5, the exodus from Egypt. (The story is told in Exodus 1–20.) "The basket" refers to containers used for carrying construction materials when the Israelites were forced to work on Egyptian building projects; Jeremiah uses the same word in reporting visions of baskets of figs (Jer. 24:2). The thunder recalls the events reported in Exodus 19:16 and following; the events at Meribah are reported in Exodus 17. (*Selah* indicates a pause; see on Psalm 3.) The point of these references is to recall what God had done for these people in the past, especially focusing on the events around the time of the deliverance from Egypt.

After this remembrance, following the pattern of the Decalogue itself, is a restatement of the commandment "You shall have no other gods before me" (Exod. 20:3) and of the first words in Exodus 20, recalling the deliverance from Egypt (Ps. 81:8–10). The sense of "Open your mouth" in verse 10c is not clear; should it be placed at the end of the psalm, after verse 16?

God Speaks about Israel (81:11–16)

The tone of "my people" in verse 8 was one of admonishment; now there is a sadness in the doubled expression (vv. 11, 13), recalling the sadness of a parent dealing with a rebelling child, as in Isaiah 1:3, "my people do not understand."

Since these people have chosen not to be obedient, God has given up on them and let them make their own way. One is reminded of the words of Paul: when people who should have known better did not honor or thank God, God "gave them up" to wallow in the consequences of their own wickedness (Rom. 1:24–32).

Now in Psalm 81, if the people at this festival would only listen to God and walk in God's ways, God would deliver them from their enemies, just as God delivered in the days of the judges! (See Judges 2–3 and the entire book.) If the people would only listen to God's words and walk in God's ways, God would give them the finest gifts the land can yield, such as choice wheat and honey from the beehives in the craggy desert rocks (compare Deut. 32:13–14).

Listen!

Twice in this psalm there is reference to listening to the voice of God. The first is a call to *remember* how God delivered God's people and to have none other than God as one's ultimate concern (vv. 8–10). The second is the expression of God's wish that, despite a history of not listening (v. 11), these people now gathered for worship would listen and then *walk* in God's ways (vv. 13–14).

All of this is not far from the way in which Jesus answered a theologian's question about the most important commandment: "You shall love the Lord your God with all your heart, and with all your soul, and with all your mind, and with all your strength" (remembering) and "You shall love your neighbor as yourself" (walking; Mark 12:28–34).

THE SHAKING OF THE FOUNDATIONS
Psalm 82

A Psalm of Asaph.

82:1 **God has taken his place in the divine council;**
  in the midst of the gods he holds judgment:
 2 **"How long will you judge unjustly**
  and show partiality to the wicked?   *Selah*
 3 **Give justice to the weak and the orphan;**
  maintain the right of the lowly and the destitute.
 4 **Rescue the weak and the needy;**
  deliver them from the hand of the wicked."

 5 **They have neither knowledge nor understanding,**
  they walk around in darkness;
  all the foundations of the earth are shaken.

 6 **I say, "You are gods,**
  children of the Most High, all of you;
 7 **nevertheless, you shall die like mortals,**
  and fall like any prince."

 8 **Rise up, O God, judge the earth;**
  for all the nations belong to you!

The world of the psalms is not the world of the twenty-first century. These songs and poems were written in places and times far removed from our own. Often, the key to understanding a psalm consists in asking what it meant in its own time, before asking what it means for our own. Such is the case with this "Psalm of Asaph" (see on Psalm 73). "Gittith" refers to an unknown melody (see Psalm 8).

The Setting: A Council of the Gods (82:1)

The opening sentence of this psalm immediately raises questions for the modern reader. What is going on here? Where is this council being held? Who are these gods?

This psalm picks up on the notion of the "council of the gods" or "divine council," known from ancient texts outside the Bible as well as from the Bible itself. One of the best examples of this notion is found in Isaiah 6. The prophet indicates that he had a vision of the Lord on a throne ("I saw the Lord . . . ," Isa. 6:1) and then goes on to describe what he saw and heard in this vision. He saw the Lord, sitting on a throne, with heavenly beings surrounding and waiting on God (Isa. 6:2). These creatures were singing; the thresholds of the temple were shaking; the place was filled with the smoke of incense. Then one of the creatures took a burning coal from the temple altar, touched Isaiah's mouth, pronounced his sins forgiven, and asked for volunteers for a mission (vv. 6–8). For Isaiah, this was the call to his life's work as a prophet.

Another biblical example is provided in 1 Kings 22:19–23. This time the prophet Micaiah describes a similar vision of the Lord sitting on a throne, again with heavenly beings, "standing beside him to the right and to the left of him." The Lord asks for volunteers for a mission, and once again, one of the heavenly beings volunteers.

The story of Job begins with a report of discussions going on among the "heavenly beings" before the Lord (Job 1:6–12; 2:1–6). Finally, Isaiah 3:13–15 reports another look into the heavenly courtroom, where the Lord is standing up to file a legal complaint (see also Jer. 23:18–22).

Psalm 82 is yet another of these vision reports, telling of a court procedure involving God and divine creatures or gods, about to be held in this divine assembly.

The Story: Gods on Trial (82:1–8)

The psalm invites us to stretch our imagination. A court procedure is going on in heaven, and we are invited to listen in on the proceedings (v. 1).

With verse 2 the first voice heard is that of God, the judge in this courtroom. There are no long speeches for the prosecution (God) or for the defense (the gods) here. The Judge comes right to the point, saying to these heavenly beings, in effect, "How long will you gods keep making decisions that are not just? How long will you keep showing partiality to wicked persons?" The complaint is clear: these gods are making decisions that favor wicked persons. And God the Judge has had enough of such behavior. (For *Selah*, see on Psalm 3.)

According to verses 3 and 4, the Judge switches from complaint to advice. These gods are told to watch carefully over the rights of certain groups of people, "the weak and the orphan . . . the lowly and the destitute . . . and the needy." These are society's powerless. The weak have no strength; the orphans have no parents; the needy and destitute have no money or goods. Therefore these persons have no power. And now the plight of the powerless has come to the attention of God's own supreme court!

In the midst of these words spoken by God the Judge, verse 5 comes as an aside. It is as if the Judge is deliberating and we are waiting for the verdict. In the meantime, the camera leaves the courtroom to focus on a commentator who gives us an editorial opinion: these gods are stupid, they can't see where they are going, and the implications of their actions are such that the structures of society threaten to collapse! Indeed, the foundations of the earth are shaking!

Verses 6 and 7 return to the trial. The Judge speaks: "I say, 'You are gods, children of the Most High, all of you!" We might expect a verdict here, with God saying, "The court finds the defendants guilty/not guilty." But there is no verdict. The Judge immediately pronounces the sentences to those on trial: "You are gods . . . but you shall die like any human being, and come to an end like any ordinary prince!"

The psalm ends in verse 8 with a prayer from the congregation, asking God to go into action, to punish the wicked and to deliver the powerless from the injustices they have had to suffer.

The Significance: When the Foundations Shake

What could the description of this heavenly court scene mean for God's people today? The words of verse 5 are saying that something has happened of such consequence that the foundations of community life have been shaken.

What has happened? It has to do with the way in which certain persons are treated, specifically, the powerless. These are the widows, the orphans, the poor—the list could be extended to include the aged, the stranger, whatever group is "weak, needy, destitute." When such persons are cheated, abused, or neglected, these actions are of such consequence that the fundamental structures of human existence are threatened!

The message is reinforced in the New Testament. Jesus spoke about the eternal consequences of neglecting those who are hungry or naked or hurting (Matt. 25:31–46). James went so far as to define true religion in terms of treatment of the orphan, widow, and poor (James 1:26–2:26).

The focus of Psalm 82 is on the child without parents, the woman without a husband, the woman or man with no financial means. When the powerless are cheated or abused, the foundations of a society are dangerously shaken.

WHEN GOD IS SILENT
Psalm 83

A Song. A Psalm of Asaph.

83:1 **O God, do not keep silence;**
  do not hold your peace or be still, O God!
  2 **Even now your enemies are in tumult;**
  those who hate you have raised their heads.
  3 **They lay crafty plans against your people;**
  they consult together against those you protect.
  4 **They say, "Come, let us wipe them out as a nation;**
  let the name of Israel be remembered no more."
  5 **They conspire with one accord;**
  against you they make a covenant—
  6 **the tents of Edom and the Ishmaelites,**
  Moab and the Hagrites,
  7 **Gebal and Ammon and Amalek,**
  Philistia with the inhabitants of Tyre;
  8 **Assyria also has joined them;**
  they are the strong arm of the children of Lot.   *Selah*

  9 **Do to them as you did to Midian,**
  as to Sisera and Jabin at the Wadi Kishon,
  10 **who were destroyed at En-dor,**
  who became dung for the ground.
  11 **Make their nobles like Oreb and Zeeb,**
  all their princes like Zebah and Zalmunna,
  12 **who said, "Let us take the pastures of God**
  for our own possession."

  13 **O my God, make them like whirling dust,**
  like chaff before the wind.
  14 **As fire consumes the forest,**
  as the flame sets the mountains ablaze,

¹⁵ so pursue them with your tempest
  and terrify them with your hurricane.
¹⁶ Fill their faces with shame,
  so that they may seek your name, O LORD.
¹⁷ Let them be put to shame and dismayed forever;
  let them perish in disgrace.
¹⁸ Let them know that you alone,
  whose name is the LORD,
  are the Most High over all the earth.

Certain psalms seem to be a problem for contemporary Christians and, like problem children, are judged best kept out of sight. When the Roman Catholic *Liturgy of the Hours* was published in 1971, three such problem psalms were omitted: Psalms 58, 83, and 109. The pope explained, "Some few of the psalms and verses which are somewhat harsh in tone have been omitted, especially because of the difficulties that were foreseen from their use in vernacular celebration" (Holladay, *Psalms*, p. 304). In other words, once these psalms were out of Latin and into the language of the people, they were found offensive!

The pope is not alone in this sentiment. Commentaries are often uneasy with this psalm. One has said of Psalm 83, "This psalm is an unedifying and tedious catalogue of bloody violence. . . . These factors are largely responsible for the consensus that regards this psalm as one of the least religious of all the poems in the Psalter" (*Interpreter's Bible*, 4:450–51). As with problem children, however, trying to understand these problem psalms is better than rejecting them.

Psalm 83 is a prayer from the people of God in a time of trouble. Considered in the context of other *community laments*, such as Psalms 44, 74, 79, 80, 85, and 89, Psalm 83 has some unique features. The standard lament form includes an *address* to God; *complaints* in the "we," "you," and "they" forms; an *affirmation of trust*; a *request* for help; and a *vow to praise* (see, for example, the discussions of Psalm 44).

Psalm 83 begins with a brief address ("O God") and a request for God's help (v. 1). Following is a lengthy complaint in the "they" form (vv. 2–8). Verses 9–12 request help and affirm trust in God by recalling some of God's acts of deliverance (compare Pss. 44:1–3, 7; 80:8–11). The remainder of the psalm consists of intense, even desperate requests or cries for help (vv. 13–18). The "they" complaints and requests dominate, indicating the degree of hurting and the intensity of the cries for help.

This is the last in the series of Asaph psalms running from Psalms 73–83 (see the comments on Psalm 73). This is also the last psalm in the "elohistic psalter," which prefers '*elohim* (NRSV, "God") as the name for God to Yahweh (NRSV, "LORD"; see comments on Psalm 42).

Do Something, God! (88:1–8)

The psalm begins with a desperate cry for help: "O God, do not keep silence; do not hold your peace or be still." Verses 2–8 spell out the reasons for the desperation with an extensive "they" complaint about the enemies of Israel: *they* "hate . . . have raised their heads . . . lay crafty plans . . . consult . . . say . . . conspire . . . make a covenant . . . are the strong arm." The psalm even quotes the words of these enemies to indicate that they are making clever and careful plans for a war of total annihilation. They say, "Come, let us wipe them out as a nation; let the name of Israel be remembered no more" (v. 4; vv. 3–5).

Who are these enemies? Ten nations are named, first nine small ones and then, as a climax, Assyria (vv. 6–8). Ten is a biblical number for totality (the commandments, the plagues), and the intent is to say that this will be total war against God's people, including participation even by mighty Assyria.

Do As You Did Before, Lord! (88:9–18)

The effect of verses 9–12 is to give encouragement to the people of the present by looking back at what God has done for them in the past. The psalm recalls events from the time of the judges: Gideon defeated the Midianites and their leaders Oreb and Zeeb, Zebah and Zalmunna (Judges 6–8). Deborah and Barak defeated the armies of Sisera and Jabin (Judges 4–5). Once again, the words of the enemies are quoted (v. 12). The sense is "You defeated our enemies and saved us before, God. Now do it again!"

With verses 13–15 the focus is on the future, moving from historical recollections to poetic imagining. The bond with God is close, as the psalmist prays, "O *my* God!" The images are stunning. God is described in terms of natural catastrophes: God is a mighty wind, and the enemies are dust or chaff; God is a fire, and the enemies are a mountain forest; God is a storm or a hurricane (vv. 13–15).

Verses 16–18 are crucial for understanding this psalm because they indicate the ultimate aim of all this anticipated disaster. The psalmist's hope is that, after being shamed and disgraced, these nations will become seekers of the true God and worshipers of the Most High.

And here, in verses 16 and 18, after great restraint in using the name LORD (Yahweh) in Psalms 73–82 (the elohistic psalter; see on Psalm 42), the name appears in a prayer twice.

When God Is Silent

Is there a word for twenty-first-century Christian believers in Psalm 83? First, the psalm arises in a *desperate situation*, when the survival of God's people is at stake (v. 4). For believers in such a situation, a *desperate prayer* is called for. The one praying has heard the stories of God's deliverances in the past; it certainly does not seem unreasonable to ask for a similar rescue in the present (vv. 9–12). Then the language becomes more imaginative and the prayer more vindictive, as the psalmist speaks in terms of blazing fires and terrifying hurricanes (vv. 13–15, 17). Even in the midst of this language of desperation, however, hope is expressed that these enemies will turn to the Lord (vv. 16, 18).

Those who remember Jesus' advice "Love your enemies and pray for those who persecute you" (Matt. 5:44) will be uneasy with this language about death, dung, and whirling dust. They will not be able to pray for the dismay and disgrace of their enemies. But even the strongest of believers may understand the sense that God is absent, or at best inactive, that informs this psalm. At such a time, the only prayer possible may be "O God, do not keep silence; do not hold your peace or be still."

EVEN THE SPARROW
Psalm 84

> To the leader: according to The Gittith. Of the Korahites. A Psalm.

> 84:1 How lovely is your dwelling place,
>   O LORD of hosts!
>   2 My soul longs, indeed it faints
>   for the courts of the LORD;
>   my heart and my flesh sing for joy
>   to the living God.
>
>   3 Even the sparrow finds a home,
>   and the swallow a nest for herself,
>   where she may lay her young,
>   at your altars, O LORD of hosts,
>   my King and my God.
>   4 Happy are those who live in your house,
>   ever singing your praise.   *Selah*
>
>   5 Happy are those whose strength is in you,
>   in whose heart are the highways to Zion.

⁶ As they go through the valley of Baca
   they make it a place of springs;
   the early rain also covers it with pools.
⁷ They go from strength to strength;
   the God of gods will be seen in Zion.

⁸ O Lᴏʀᴅ God of hosts, hear my prayer;
   give ear, O God of Jacob!   *Selah*
⁹ Behold our shield, O God;
   look on the face of your anointed.

¹⁰ For a day in your courts is better
   than a thousand elsewhere.
   I would rather be a doorkeeper in the house of my God
   than live in the tents of wickedness.
¹¹ For the Lᴏʀᴅ God is a sun and shield;
   he bestows favor and honor.
   No good thing does the Lᴏʀᴅ withhold
   from those who walk uprightly.
¹² O Lᴏʀᴅ of hosts,
   happy is everyone who trusts in you.

"His eye is on the sparrow," goes the old gospel song, "and I know he watches me." That song was based on the saying of Jesus "Are not two sparrows sold for a penny? Yet not one of them will fall to the ground apart from your Father" (Matt. 10:29). The words about the sparrow in this psalm also have caught the imagination of many a songwriter: consider Samuel Liddle's "Yea, the sparrow hath found her a house, where she may lay her young" or Johannes Brahms's setting in the *German Requiem*, "How Lovely Is Thy Dwelling Place."

After a psalm about plots to wipe out entire nations and about crushing enemies so that they are like dung or dust, this psalm about the joys of worshiping in the temple comes as a pleasant change. Here the sights and sounds are beautiful and calming: the loveliness of the temple, the grace of a swallow building a nest, the melodies of praises being sung in the house of God.

The heading dedicates the psalm to the music director and suggests a melody, "The Gittith" (see also Psalms 8, 81). The Korahite psalms and the designation "Psalm" are discussed in connection with Psalms 42–43.

Since the psalm centers on the temple on Mount Zion, this is often designated a *song of Zion* (see the comments with Psalm 87). The psalm falls into three segments, each addressing God in a variation of "O Lᴏʀᴅ of Hosts," and each containing a statement about happiness: verses 1–4, 5–9, 10–12.

The Sights and the Sounds (84:1–4)

The writer of Psalm 84 lives somewhere away from Jerusalem. Something has caused this person to remember good days there, to recall the beauty of "your dwelling place," that is, the temple built by Solomon, and to long to be there once again (vv. 1–2).

The psalmist remembers a detail: while visiting the temple, the writer noticed the sparrows and swallows living in the high corners of the structure. Apparently, they were allowed to live and even build nests there, nurturing their young, undisturbed by overly fussy temple custodians.

After reflecting on the visual beauty of the structure, the writer recalls fondly the beautiful sounds of praises sung in the temple (v. 4). (For *Selah*, see on Psalm 3.)

On the Road Again (84:5–9)

The focus is now on the joys of the journey to Jerusalem, along the "highways to Zion" (v. 5). "The valley of Baca" was apparently a desolate place on the way; the psalmist imagines those making the journey being accompanied by refreshing rains as they pass through it. They are sustained on the journey by the conviction that when they get to Mount Zion, they will meet the God of gods (vv. 6–7).

Verse 8 offers a second prayer (after v. 1) addressed to the Lord of hosts, this time "O LORD God of hosts" (v. 8). To think of the temple is to think of Jerusalem, and to think of Jerusalem is to think of the royal residence there. On the way to the capital city, these travelers pray for the well-being of their king, here named "our shield" and "your *anointed* [Hebrew, 'messiah']."

True Happiness (84:10–12)

The writer is reaching for ways to describe the joy that comes with being present in the temple. Only one day in this place where God is present would be preferred to a thousand days anywhere else! And the humblest position on the temple's custodial staff would be preferred to reveling in the midst of the parties of the wicked!

Why is the writer so eager to live and work in this place of gathering and worship? The answer is clear: The Lord God is present there, as giver and sustainer of life (a sun) and also as protector from danger (a shield;

said of the king in v. 9). Verse 7 speaks of those who "walk" (the literal Hebrew; NRSV, "go") along the way to visit the temple on Mount Zion; verse 11 promises that the Lord will spare no blessing, no favor or honor, for those who walk that way, and the ways of their lives, in integrity.

Finally, verse 12 sums this picture up by addressing God a third time as "LORD of hosts" (vv. 1, 8) and offering a final "happy" statement. The person is truly happy, says the psalm to the Lord, "who trusts in you."

Star Wars, Swallows, and Sparrows

After a long series of psalms where the personal name Yahweh is scarcely mentioned (the elohistic psalter, Psalms 42–83), this psalm comes as a striking contrast, with Yahweh (NRSV, "LORD") mentioned seven times and God referred to in some way in each verse except verse 6.

Statements about God in this psalm fall into two major categories. Some emphasize God's might and power as "LORD of Hosts" or "LORD God of hosts," found in each of the three segments of the psalm (vv. 1, 8, 12). The literal translation would be "Lord God of armies." The Hebrew word translated "hosts" may refer to earthly armies (Gen. 21:22; 2 Sam. 3:23) or to celestial armies, the heavenly creatures surrounding God (Isa. 6:3, "LORD of hosts"). In Isaiah 40, God is portrayed as a commander and the stars as armies at God's command: "Lift up your eyes on high and see: Who created these? He who brings out their host and numbers them" (Isa. 40:26). The stars are portrayed as God's armies, ready to fight at God's command.

Such is the majesty and might of God, says Psalm 84. But it also indicates that this God is related to individuals, "*my* King and *my* God" (v. 3); that an individual can address God in prayer (v. 8); that God is sustainer and protector (v. 11) and the giver of good things to God's people (v. 11).

Beyond all that, we ought not forget that this mighty God has an eye on certain full-time residents of the temple. The only ones who have a permanent home there appear to be the sparrows and swallows and their families (v. 3). Can we not imagine these "creatures of our God and King" adding their voices to the sounds of choirs singing praises there (v. 4)?

YOUR LAND, OUR LAND
Psalm 85

To the leader. Of the Korahites. A Psalm.

85:1 LORD, you were favorable to your land;
   you restored the fortunes of Jacob.

² You forgave the iniquity of your people;
    you pardoned all their sin.   *Selah*
³ You withdrew all your wrath;
    you turned from your hot anger.

⁴ Restore us again, O God of our salvation,
    and put away your indignation toward us.
⁵ Will you be angry with us forever?
    Will you prolong your anger to all generations?
⁶ Will you not revive us again,
    so that your people may rejoice in you?
⁷ Show us your steadfast love, O LORD,
    and grant us your salvation.

⁸ Let me hear what God the LORD will speak,
    for he will speak peace to his people,
    to his faithful, to those who turn to him in their hearts.
⁹ Surely his salvation is at hand for those who fear him,
    that his glory may dwell in our land.

¹⁰ Steadfast love and faithfulness will meet;
    righteousness and peace will kiss each other.
¹¹ Faithfulness will spring up from the ground,
    and righteousness will look down from the sky.
¹² The LORD will give what is good,
    and our land will yield its increase.
¹³ Righteousness will go before him,
    and will make a path for his steps.

This psalm begins and ends by speaking of the land. It recalls the good things the Lord did for land and people (v. 1) and anticipates that one day the Lord will again bring about a time of peace when the land can produce a good harvest (vv. 10–12). But in the meantime, when the psalm is written, things are not going well, and the people are experiencing God's anger.

The psalm is dedicated to the music director. (For Korahites, see Psalm 42; for "A Psalm," see Psalm 98.) It is a prayer of the community in a time of trouble, or *community lament* (in Book III, also Psalms 74, 79, 80, 83, and 89; see the listing with Psalm 44). It consists of an *affirmation of trust*, recalling what God has done (vv. 1–3); an extended *call for help* or *request* (vv. 4–7); and then a *promise of salvation* (vv. 8–13). The *complaint* may be inferred from verses 4b and 5, which speak of "your indignation . . . your anger." The people believe that the Lord has been angry with them for too long.

The psalm divides into three sections. Verses 1–3 address the Lord, speaking of what the Lord did for Israel in the past, in "you-they" form. Verses 4–7 continue to address God, but now the focus is on the present, and the sentences speak of "you" and "us." With verses 8–13, after an introduction (v. 8), a prophet or priest speaks in the name of the Lord, bringing good news.

Lord, We Remember Your Past Favors (85:1–3)

After the brief address, "LORD," those praying remember what the Lord did for them in the past. Such remembering is a typical theme of these community laments (Pss. 44:1–8; 77:11–20; 80:8–11) and is a way for the people to affirm their trust in God. They look back at how the Lord blessed their land and forgave their iniquity and sin. Once there was a time of bountiful harvests when the people knew they were pardoned from sins and when the Lord was generous in forgiving. But those times, says this psalm, are past. (For *Selah*, see on Psalm 3.)

God, Restore Us Now (85:4–7)

Verses 4–7 offer an urgent request, framed by the key word *salvation*. The focus shifts from the loving acts of God *then* (vv. 1–3) to the mysterious inaction of the Lord *now*. The psalmist fires some questions directly at the Lord, in "you" form:

> Are you going to be angry with us forever, Lord?
> Is your anger going to extend to our children?
> Won't you bring us back to life as a people
> so that we can once again experience times of
> celebration and rejoicing?
>
> (vv. 5–6, paraphrased)

The writer does not indicate what happened to set off God's wrath but speaks only of indignation, then anger. We hear of no specific covenant breaking or doing wrong; perhaps the matter is left unspecified so that the psalm can have a wider application.

The psalm leads the people to pray for the Lord's *steadfast love* and, linking up with verse 4, for God's *salvation*.

The Lord Will Give What Is Good (85:8–13)

In the final section, the psalm cites words spoken by a priest or a prophet. This section sounds the great Old Testament words for God's saving activity. The saying is introduced with a promise of *shalom*, "peace" (v. 8). Verse 9 announces that *salvation* is near at hand for the faithful.

The great words of promise continue to pile up, painting the picture of a time coming that will be marked by *steadfast love, faithfulness, righteousness*, and *peace*. The writer's imagination is taking off: righteousness and peace are personified, so closely linked that they kiss each other. From the ground below, faithfulness will spring up like a tree. From the sky above, righteousness will come down like rain.

In these good times of peace with neighbors, the Lord will once again be favorable to the land (v. 12; recall v. 1). It will yield fine crops, and like a farmer striding through fields heavy with the harvest, the Lord will walk among the people (v. 13).

Good Gifts, Good Land, Good News

Psalm 85 is a good reminder that when the Old Testament speaks of salvation (vv. 4, 7, 9), it is not ordinarily referring to life beyond death but to a life in this world, lived in freedom and *shalom* (vv. 8, 10), basking in the Lord's steadfast love (vv. 7, 10) and forgiveness (vv. 2–3), and enjoying the good gifts of the Lord, including a good harvest. All of this is not yet the good news about everlasting life that the gospel announces, but it is a good start in that direction.

TEACH ME TO WALK!
Psalm 86

A Prayer of David.

86:1 **Incline your ear, O LORD, and answer me,**
   for I am poor and needy.
2 **Preserve my life, for I am devoted to you;**
   save your servant who trusts in you.
You are my God; 3**be gracious to me, O Lord,**
   for to you do I cry all day long.
4 **Gladden the soul of your servant,**
   for to you, O Lord, I lift up my soul.
5 **For you, O Lord, are good and forgiving,**
   abounding in steadfast love to all who call on you.
6 **Give ear, O LORD, to my prayer;**
   listen to my cry of supplication.
7 **In the day of my trouble I call on you,**
   for you will answer me.

⁸ There is none like you among the gods, O Lord,
   nor are there any works like yours.
⁹ All the nations you have made shall come
   and bow down before you, O Lord,
   and shall glorify your name.
¹⁰ For you are great and do wondrous things;
   you alone are God.
¹¹ Teach me your way, O LORD,
   that I may walk in your truth;
   give me an undivided heart to revere your name.
¹² I give thanks to you, O Lord my God, with my whole heart,
   and I will glorify your name forever.
¹³ For great is your steadfast love toward me;
   you have delivered my soul from the depths of Sheol.

¹⁴ O God, the insolent rise up against me;
   a band of ruffians seeks my life,
   and they do not set you before them.
¹⁵ But you, O Lord, are a God merciful and gracious,
   slow to anger and abounding in steadfast love and faithfulness.
¹⁶ Turn to me and be gracious to me;
   give your strength to your servant;
   save the child of your serving girl.
¹⁷ Show me a sign of your favor,
   so that those who hate me may see it and be put to shame,
   because you, LORD, have helped me and comforted me.

The Bible speaks a good deal about *walking*. The sense of the word can mean going along by foot, as Abraham and his son Isaac "walked on together" on the way to the mountain in Moriah (Gen. 22:6, 8). The word can also have a wider meaning, which refers to the conduct of one's entire life: "what does the LORD require of you but to do justice, and to love kindness, and to *walk* humbly with your God?" (Micah 6:8).

The word *walk* is used in Psalm 86 with that broader sense, referring to all that one does:

> Teach me your way, O LORD,
>   that I may walk in your truth;
>   give me an undivided heart to revere your name.
>   (v. 11)

The psalm includes a trio of doxologies praising God, functioning as refrains that conclude three major sections: verses 5, 10, and 15. It is made up of elements typical of the *individual lament* (see on Psalm 13). There are *requests* addressed to the Lord, in the imperative mood (vv. 1a,

2, 3, 4, 6, 11, 16–17a); *complaints* in the "I" form (v. 1b) and "they" form (v. 14); *affirmations of trust* (vv. 2, 4b, 7, 13, 15, 17b); and words of *praise* (vv. 5, 8–10, 12). Like Psalm 86, Psalms 17 and 142 are also identified as "A Prayer of David"; for David, see the comments on Psalm 3.

Help Me, Lord! (86:1–5)

The psalm begins by calling for the Lord's attention with the opening "Incline your ear" (see also v. 6). The same request appears in Psalms 17:6; 88:2; and 102:2.

The relationship between the one praying and God is pictured as that between a servant ("your servant" in vv. 2, 4, 16) and a master ("Lord" in vv. 3, 4, 5, 8, 9, 12, 15; note that this is not "LORD," which translates the name Yahweh in vv. 1, 6, 11, and 17).

The one praying also makes self-identifications according to economic status ("poor and needy," v. 1) and religious belief ("devoted" and trusting in the Lord, v. 2). Another expression of the relationship between the one praying and the God addressed is the simple statement "You are my God" in verse 2.

The first segment of the psalm comes to a close in verse 5 with the one praying voicing a traditional confessional statement about the Lord, who is good and forgiving, abounding in steadfast love, or *hesed* (see v. 15; also Exod. 34:6; Ps. 103:8).

Listen to Me, O Lord (86:6–10)

With verse 6, the one praying makes a new beginning. A second time the psalmist seeks to get the Lord's attention by asking the Lord to give a hearing, again referring to the Lord's "ear" (v. 6; see also v. 1). After the request to "answer me" the first time around (v. 1), the psalmist now expresses confidently to the Lord, "you will answer me" (v. 7).

Then the writer launches into a hymn of praise, framed with declarations of the Lord's uniqueness (vv. 8, 10). This short section is theologically packed, assuming that God is unique, that God's works in creation are unique, that God has created all the nations, and that they will all worship this God. The second doxology winds it up by declaring, "You alone are God" (v. 10).

Teach Me, Lord (86:11–15)

At the heart of this psalm is the request for theological instruction in verse 11. (See the comments in "A Note for Teachers," below.)

The vow to praise as found in verses 12 and 13 is a typical element of the individual lament. The writer is anticipating deliverance from present difficulties. For now, however, there are those who are making life miserable (v. 14). Having made that complaint, the psalmist as servant focuses again on the Lord as master and recites a traditional creedlike formulation of what God is like (see on v. 5, above).

Help Me, Lord (86:16–17)

The psalm ends as it began. Having confessed that "you . . . are a God merciful and gracious" (v. 15), the psalmist asks God to demonstrate that grace, that unmerited love. The psalmist prays, "Be gracious to me" (v. 16), thus linking up with the same prayer at the beginning, "Be gracious to me, O Lord" (v. 3). The imagery of the psalmist as servant, even child of a servant, continues (v. 16). The writer concludes by asking for a sign of the Lord's help, not just for the writer's sake but so that others, too, may learn who really is God!

A Note for Teachers

The statements in verse 11 are worthy of reflection as a model for religious instruction anywhere, anytime. This sort of instruction is not only knowledge about God but also teaching about the way in which one ought to *walk*, or conduct the whole of one's life. The psalmist prays that this conduct will match up with God's truth. This instruction thus includes (1) knowledge about the way in which the Lord would have one live; (2) knowledge that is taught in such a way that it leads one to living in that manner (in other words, the learner will not only "talk the talk" but also "walk the walk" of the faithful life); and (3) knowledge that is taught in such a way that the learner will have the right attitude of undivided loyalty and reverence toward God.

In sum, this statement envisions teaching that has a cognitive component ("Teach . . . your way"), that has certain ethical implications ("Teach . . . that I may walk"), and that results in a right relationship to God ("to revere your name").

YOUR HOMETOWN
Psalm 87

Of the Korahites. A Psalm. A Song.

87:1 **On the holy mount stands the city he founded;**
² **the L**ORD** loves the gates of Zion**
more than all the dwellings of Jacob.
³ **Glorious things are spoken of you,**
O city of God.   *Selah*

⁴ **Among those who know me I mention Rahab and Babylon;**
Philistia too, and Tyre, with Ethiopia—
"This one was born there," they say.
⁵ **And of Zion it shall be said,**
"This one and that one were born in it";
for the Most High himself will establish it.
⁶ **The L**ORD** records, as he registers the peoples,**
"This one was born there."   *Selah*

⁷ **Singers and dancers alike say,**
"All my springs are in you."

Whenever I teach a class for the first time, I begin by asking partici-
pants to tell something about their hometowns. When someone comes
from Greensboro, North Carolina, or Washington, D.C. , or Rochester
or St. Paul, Minnesota, a teacher already knows something about that
student. It is always good to discover someone who has a sense of pride
in the place that he or she identifies as "my hometown."

Psalm 87 is concerned with, almost preoccupied with, a particular
hometown. Three times the psalm indicates that it will be said about certain persons, "This one was born in Jerusalem!" The statement is made
with pride. What was so special about Jerusalem?

Songs of Zion

A number of psalms celebrate the glories of the city of Jerusalem. The
city existed before the Israelites invaded and captured it at the time of
King David, a thousand years before the birth of Christ (see 2 Samuel 5).
Since it is partially built on Mount Zion, the name Zion is at times used
to indicate the entire city (Ps. 87:2, 5, for example). The collection of
these psalms called *songs of Zion* takes its name from Psalm 137:3, where
the Babylonian captors ask the Jews living there in exile to "sing us one
of the songs of Zion!"

Those psalms usually designated "songs of Zion" include 46, 48, 76,
84, 87, 122, and 132. Each tells something particular about Zion, or
Jerusalem. Psalm 46 identifies the "city of God" (v. 4) as the place where
the Lord is "with us" as a help in times of trouble (vv. 1, 7, 11). Psalm 48

celebrates the beauty of this "city of our God" (vv. 1, 8) and the security to be found there (especially vv. 3, 12–14). Psalm 76 identifies Salem (Jerusalem) as the place on earth where God lives (vv. 1–2). Psalms 84 and 122 indicate the joy in the heart of a person about to travel to Jerusalem. Psalm 122 prays eloquently for *shalom* in the city. Psalm 132 tells of the Lord's choosing the city as the place where the Davidic king should live (vv. 13–18). Psalm 87 testifies to the Lord's love for the city and the people's pride in it as their hometown.

"Glorious Things of Thee Are Spoken" (87:1–3)

Psalm 87 belongs to the Korahite collection (see on Psalm 42). It divides into two segments, the first celebrating the glories of the city (vv. 1–3) and the second indicating the joy of those who can claim birth there (vv. 4–7).

The psalm portrays Jerusalem's proud heritage: it has been founded by the Lord on Mount Zion and favored by the Lord over any of the cities to be found in Israel (vv. 1–2). Such a place can only be praised, says the psalm. The hymn by John Newton catches the spirit:

> Glorious things of thee are spoken,
> Zion, city of our God!

Augustine took the name for his great work *The City of God* from verse 3 of this psalm. (*Selah* indicates a pause; see on Psalm 3.)

Born in Jerusalem! (87:4–7)

With verse 4 the Lord speaks, identifying the lands where Israelites have been scattered. Rahab is a name for Egypt (Isa. 30:7). The others are areas where Jews scattered to live after the exile in 587 B.C. But even though they live far from the city and the land, their attachment remains, and of them it will be said proudly, "This one was born there," that is, in Jerusalem. The sense is that one could not have a more distinguished birthplace!

The psalm continues along the same lines in verse 5. Now the speakers are the citizens of nations surrounding Jerusalem. Persons with origins in Jerusalem may have settled in other lands, but at times of festivals and on other occasions, they are identified once again proudly with their hometown, saying, "This one and that one were born in [Jerusalem]."

The scene in verse 6 is of the Lord keeping a record book, writing in it the names of the peoples of the world; see also Psalm 69:28 and Isaiah 4:3.

At the proper places, the Lord is writing, "This one was born in Jerusalem." These are the people who can list Jerusalem as their hometown.

Are the "singers and dancers" those taking part in some sort of procession in Jerusalem, perhaps recalling David's procession with the ark, reported in 2 Samuel 6? The question remains open.

Glorious Things Are Spoken of You

One can think of no city that has captured the imagination of people as has Jerusalem. Jews pray, "Next year in Jerusalem," or sing of *Y'rushalayim Shel Zahav* (Jerusalem the golden). Christians sing hymns and songs about "Jerusalem, My Happy Home" or "The Holy City."

The writers of the New Testament were also caught up in the notion of Jerusalem, seeing Christians as part of a great procession moving toward "the city that has foundations" (Heb. 11:10) and declaring to Christians that "our citizenship is in heaven" (Phil. 3:20). The New Testament closes with the vision of the new Jerusalem, where God will wipe away every tear and "Death will be no more" (Rev. 21:4).

According to the New Testament, Christians can count themselves as citizens of "the holy city, the new Jerusalem" (Rev. 21:2), and can rightly look forward to citizenship there. It would be contrary to the spirit of both the Psalms and the New Testament, however, to be so enthralled with the heavenly Jerusalem as to forget the Jerusalem that exists on earth today: the Jerusalem appearing in newspapers and seen on television, with its synagogues, churches, and mosques and also with its shootings, bombings, and stone throwings.

Jesus cared so much for this earthly Jerusalem that he looked at it one day and wept (Luke 19:41; cf. 13:33–34; and Matt. 23:37–39). It may be that such caring is what is called for from followers of Jesus today.

A CRY FROM THE DARKNESS
Psalm 88

A Song. A Psalm of the Korahites. To the leader: according to
Mahalath Leannoth. A Maskil of Heman the Ezrahite.

88:1 O LORD, God of my salvation,
            when, at night, I cry out in your presence,
       2 let my prayer come before you;
            incline your ear to my cry.

³ For my soul is full of troubles,
    and my life draws near to Sheol.
⁴ I am counted among those who go down to the Pit;
    I am like those who have no help,
⁵ like those forsaken among the dead,
    like the slain that lie in the grave,
  like those whom you remember no more,
    for they are cut off from your hand.
⁶ You have put me in the depths of the Pit,
    in the regions dark and deep.
⁷ Your wrath lies heavy upon me,
    and you overwhelm me with all your waves.   *Selah*

⁸ You have caused my companions to shun me;
    you have made me a thing of horror to them.
  I am shut in so that I cannot escape;
⁹   my eye grows dim through sorrow.
  Every day I call on you, O LORD;
    I spread out my hands to you.
¹⁰ Do you work wonders for the dead?
    Do the shades rise up to praise you?   *Selah*
¹¹ Is your steadfast love declared in the grave,
    or your faithfulness in Abaddon?
¹² Are your wonders known in the darkness,
    or your saving help in the land of forgetfulness?

¹³ But I, O LORD, cry out to you;
    in the morning my prayer comes before you.
¹⁴ O LORD, why do you cast me off?
    Why do you hide your face from me?
¹⁵ Wretched and close to death from my youth up,
    I suffer your terrors; I am desperate.
¹⁶ Your wrath has swept over me;
    your dread assaults destroy me.
¹⁷ They surround me like a flood all day long;
    from all sides they close in on me.
¹⁸ You have caused friend and neighbor to shun me;
    my companions are in darkness.

Psalm 88 is a cry for help, from deep in the darkness. It begins in the night (v. 1). The middle part tells of "the regions dark and deep" and asks whether God's saving help can reach into the land of darkness (vv. 6, 12). At the end is loneliness, silence, in the darkness (v. 18).

The contrast with the previous psalm is dramatic. Psalm 87 is about seeing sunlight and enjoying dancing and singing. Psalm 88 is obsessed with the night and the darkness (vv. 1, 6, 12). This psalm reeks with the stench of death, of Sheol (where there is no singing; v. 10) and the Pit and the grave. At the end of the psalm is the loneliness and the silence of the darkness (v. 18). No psalm is as desperate or as hopeless as this one.

The Korahites are discussed with Psalm 42. The piece is dedicated to the music director; "Mahalath Leannoth" may designate a melody (see also Psalm 53). For "Maskil," see the comments on Psalm 32. Heman appears as a wise man in 1 Kings 4:31 and as a singer in 1 Chronicles 6:33 and elsewhere. (For *Selah* in vv. 7 and 10, see on Psalm 3.)

This is an *individual lament* (see on Psalm 13), with special emphasis on the *complaint* sections. *"I" complaints* are found in verses 3–5, 8c–9a, and 15, for a total of five verses. *"You" complaints* occur in verses 6–8ab, 10–12, 14 (question form), 16, and 18, totaling nine verses. With verse 17 as the only *"they" complaint*, the psalm has fifteen out of eighteen verses as complaints. Verse 2 is the only *request*, while verses 1, 9b, and 13 offer *affirmations of trust*, marking the points of division of the psalm.

Lord, It's Dark (88:1–9a)

The psalm begins on a positive, trusting note, with the one praying addressing the Lord as "God of my salvation." From this it would appear that rescue is still possible. After the initial address, the psalmist asks the Lord to hear the prayer. In an unusual detail, the time of the prayer is given: at night (vv. 1–2).

The recital of troubles begins with a series of personal "I" complaints in verses 3–5. The situation is one of life or death. The language has about it the stench of the grave. The writer is described as (1) near Sheol, the place of the dead; (2) already on the list of those who are dead, in the Pit; (3) among those from whom there is no help; (4) like a corpse, abandoned among the dead; (5) like those who have been killed and are lying in a grave; (6) like those persons now off the stage of life, totally forgotten by God and cut off from God's helping hand.

With verses 6–8a, the psalm switches to complaints addressed directly to God, in the "you" form. "You are responsible, Lord," says the psalmist, "for my being in the grave, the place of death, in this place of darkness." A second time (also v. 1) the psalm speaks of the darkness, and now it adds the image of drowning (vv. 6–7). A new dimension of the writer's situation occurs here: the psalmist's friends avoid him or her because of the writer's illness.

A final statement describing the psalmist's loneliness and personal affliction concludes this section (vv. 8c–9a).

A Miracle in the Darkness? (88:9b–12)

To this point, the psalmist has not given up but continues with daily prayers; spreading out the hands is one of the typical biblical postures for prayer (Ps. 143:6; Isa. 1:15).

The one praying is trying to convince the Lord to let him or her live. The answer to each of the questions in verses 10–12 is no. The argument is that if the psalmist dies, the Lord will not be able to perform any miraculous healing! The assumption here is that those in Sheol are out of range of the Lord's help. If the writer dies, one less voice will be in the choir, praising God. The psalmist, who loves to tell the story of God's love, will not be able to tell it in the grave (Pss. 6:5; 30:9; 115:17).

A second time (v.10) the psalmist reminds the Lord that there will be no miracles happening and no salvation going on where he or she is headed. All who are there are forgotten and are in the darkness (v. 12; cf. vv. 1, 6).

Alone in the Darkness (88:13–18)

Once more the psalmist prays in the morning hour. Now the prayer is not for deliverance but simply for understanding. For one who believes in God, there ought to be some sense, some reasonableness in life. But the Lord, who used to let God's face shine upon the psalmist (Num. 6:25), is now in hiding. The question is expressed in only one word, the same word Jesus used from the cross: "Why?" (Matt. 27:46, quoting Ps. 22:1)

The psalm comes to a conclusion with complaints in all three dimensions, involving self (the psychological, "I," v. 15), God (the theological, "you," v. 16), and others (the sociological, "they," v. 17). The psalm began with a lonely prayer in the night, and it ends with the psalmist abandoned, alone in the darkness (v. 18).

Even the Darkness

No other psalm paints such a somber picture of the psalmist's situation. In no other psalm is the darkness as dark as it is here. There are, however, a few notes of hope that will not be suppressed. The one praying addresses the Lord as "God of my salvation" (v. 1), not giving up on God as the one who saves. The one praying has kept on praying, every day (v. 9), in the morning (v. 13) and during the night (v. 1). Despite the darkness, despite the unanswered "why" question, somehow the psalmist can go on, praying.

This is a psalm that reaches into the deepest darkness. Perhaps it can be fully understood only by those who have known that darkness. This is, however, not the last word on death and darkness, from the Old Testament or the Christian faith. "Even the darkness is not dark to you," said the writer in Psalm 139:12. After taking a man out of darkness, Jesus said, "I am the light of the world" (John 9:5; see also 1 John 1:5–10). Finally, 1 Peter speaks of some quite remarkable good news, made possible by the God who "called you out of darkness into his marvelous light" (1 Peter 1:25; 2:9).

LORD, WHERE IS YOUR LOVE?
Psalm 89

A Maskil of Ethan the Ezrahite.

89:1 I will sing of your steadfast love, O LORD, forever;
    with my mouth I will proclaim your faithfulness to all generations.
  2 I declare that your steadfast love is established forever;
    your faithfulness is as firm as the heavens.
  3 You said, "I have made a covenant with my chosen one,
    I have sworn to my servant David:
  4 'I will establish your descendants forever,
    and build your throne for all generations.'"   *Selah*

  5 Let the heavens praise your wonders, O LORD,
    your faithfulness in the assembly of the holy ones.
  6 For who in the skies can be compared to the LORD?
    Who among the heavenly beings is like the LORD,
  7 a God feared in the council of the holy ones,
    great and awesome above all that are around him?
  8 O LORD God of hosts,
    who is as mighty as you, O LORD?
    Your faithfulness surrounds you.
  9 You rule the raging of the sea;
    when its waves rise, you still them.
  10 You crushed Rahab like a carcass;
    you scattered your enemies with your mighty arm.
  11 The heavens are yours, the earth also is yours;
    the world and all that is in it—you have founded them.
  12 The north and the south—you created them;
    Tabor and Hermon joyously praise your name.
  13 You have a mighty arm;
    strong is your hand, high your right hand.

¹⁴ Righteousness and justice are the foundation of your throne;
   steadfast love and faithfulness go before you.
¹⁵ Happy are the people who know the festal shout,
   who walk, O LORD, in the light of your countenance;
¹⁶ they exult in your name all day long,
   and extol your righteousness.
¹⁷ For you are the glory of their strength;
   by your favor our horn is exalted.
¹⁸ For our shield belongs to the LORD,
   our king to the Holy One of Israel.

¹⁹ Then you spoke in a vision to your faithful one, and said:
   "I have set the crown on one who is mighty,
   I have exalted one chosen from the people.
²⁰ I have found my servant David;
   with my holy oil I have anointed him;
²¹ my hand shall always remain with him;
   my arm also shall strengthen him.
²² The enemy shall not outwit him,
   the wicked shall not humble him.
²³ I will crush his foes before him
   and strike down those who hate him.
²⁴ My faithfulness and steadfast love shall be with him;
   and in my name his horn shall be exalted.
²⁵ I will set his hand on the sea
   and his right hand on the rivers.
²⁶ He shall cry to me, 'You are my Father,
   my God, and the Rock of my salvation!'
²⁷ I will make him the firstborn,
   the highest of the kings of the earth.
²⁸ Forever I will keep my steadfast love for him,
   and my covenant with him will stand firm.
²⁹ I will establish his line forever,
   and his throne as long as the heavens endure.
³⁰ If his children forsake my law
   and do not walk according to my ordinances,
³¹ if they violate my statutes
   and do not keep my commandments,
³² then I will punish their transgression with the rod
   and their iniquity with scourges;
³³ but I will not remove from him my steadfast love,
   or be false to my faithfulness.
³⁴ I will not violate my covenant,
   or alter the word that went forth from my lips.
³⁵ Once and for all I have sworn by my holiness;

    I will not lie to David.
36 His line shall continue forever,
    and his throne endure before me like the sun.
37 It shall be established forever like the moon,
    an enduring witness in the skies."   *Selah*

38 But now you have spurned and rejected him;
    you are full of wrath against your anointed.
39 You have renounced the covenant with your servant;
    you have defiled his crown in the dust.
40 You have broken through all his walls;
    you have laid his strongholds in ruins.
41 All who pass by plunder him;
    he has become the scorn of his neighbors.
42 You have exalted the right hand of his foes;
    you have made all his enemies rejoice.
43 Moreover, you have turned back the edge of his sword,
    and you have not supported him in battle.
44 You have removed the scepter from his hand,
    and hurled his throne to the ground.
45 You have cut short the days of his youth;
    you have covered him with shame.   *Selah*

46 How long, O Lᴏʀᴅ? Will you hide yourself forever?
    How long will your wrath burn like fire?
47 Remember how short my time is—
    for what vanity you have created all mortals!
48 Who can live and never see death?
    Who can escape the power of Sheol?   *Selah*

49 Lord, where is your steadfast love of old,
    which by your faithfulness you swore to David?
50 Remember, O Lord, how your servant is taunted;
    how I bear in my bosom the insults of the peoples,
51 with which your enemies taunt, O Lᴏʀᴅ,
    with which they taunted the footsteps of your anointed.

52 Blessed be the Lᴏʀᴅ forever.
    Amen and Amen.

Psalm 89 is a meandering, sprawling psalm that raises a good number of questions about its interpretation. A few basic observations can help to keep on course as one tries to navigate through it.

First, this is a very long psalm, containing a variety of materials that range from exuberant praise (vv. 1–18) to near-despairing lament (vv. 38–51).

Second, this is a *royal psalm*, designed for use in connection with some event in the life of the king. (See the discussion of these psalms in connection with Psalm 2.) It begins with a hymn praising the Lord's steadfast love (*hesed*) and faithfulness and power and restating the promises made to David and David's descendants (vv. 1–18). It continues with a celebration of the Lord's covenant with David, which promises, "His line shall continue forever" (vv. 19–37). It ends by asking how certain present disasters the community is experiencing could have happened, in view of this steadfast love and these promises to David (vv. 38–51).

Third, at the time of the final editing of the book of Psalms, this royal psalm was placed at the end of Book III. A royal psalm concludes the short introduction to the Psalter (Psalm 2), and Book II also closes with a royal psalm (Psalm 72). It would appear that the final editors of the book of Psalms exercised care in the selection of psalms placed at the seams of the five books. An important question for interpreting the psalm will be, Why is this psalm placed at the end of Book III and just before the beginning of Book IV? The concluding "Blessed be the LORD forever. Amen and Amen" (v. 52) is the result of the final editing of the collection.

For Maskil, see the discussion about Psalm 32. Ethan the Ezrahite is noted for his wisdom in 1 Kings 4:31 and is also identified as a musician (1 Chron. 15:17, 19).

I Will Sing of Your Love, Lord (89:1–18)

The psalm begins on a positive, upbeat note. The psalmist resolves to sing and praise the Lord's faithfulness and steadfast love. The writer thinks in terms of long periods of time; the Lord's steadfast love will last forever. At the end of the introductory section in verses 1–4, the writer reminds the Lord of the promises at the time the covenant was made with David (2 Sam. 7:5–17), which included the promise that the Davidic line of kings would be established forever (v. 4). *Selah* marks the end of this first section (see the comments with Psalm 3).

The focus in verses 5–8 is on the heavens, called on to praise the Lord (v. 5). "Who among the heavenly beings is like the LORD?" the writer asks, and the implied answer is "No one!"

With verses 9–10 the psalm focuses on the sea, declaring that the Lord rules it. Rahab was a mythological monster, defeated by the Lord, later used as a name for Egypt (see Ps. 87:4). The psalm turns to the Lord's rule over the earth in verses 11–18. That rule is marked by righteousness and justice, steadfast love (*hesed*) and faithfulness (v. 14). Verses 15 and 16 refer to a ceremony celebrating the Lord's kingship. The present king of the land is called "our shield" and is linked to the "Holy One of Israel."

"I Will Not Lie to David" (89:19–37)

This entire section is presented as a speech of the Lord, setting forth the terms for the covenant with King David and David's descendants on the throne. Here is a picture of the ideal of kingship, as articulated in 2 Samuel 7 and also in the royal psalms. The king is *anointed*; one could also read this as "made messiah," since the Hebrew word translated "anointed" is *mashach*, or "messiah" (v. 20). The Lord promises to support the anointed and give him victory over enemies (vv. 21–23). He will be the son of God, who addresses God as Father (v. 26), and God will give him *hesed*, or steadfast love (v. 28). David's line will be established forever (v. 29).

The psalmist now relates this to the future. If future kings do not keep the commandments, that is, the covenant, then those kings will be punished, but the Lord will not take away the Lord's *steadfast love* (vv. 28–35). The Davidic line will continue, as long as the sun and moon endure. (*Selah* again marks a pause; see on Psalm 3.)

Such are these magnificent promises concerning the king.

Lord, Where Is Your Love? (89:38–52)

After the bright and cheerful hymn of praise, and after these optimistic words of promise, the tone changes. The psalm has just cited the promise that the Lord will always be with the Lord's anointed one (vv. 20–21) and with the Davidic line (vv. 35–37). "But now, Lord," says the writer of the psalm quite abruptly, "you have spurned and rejected him; you are full of wrath against your anointed" (v. 38).

Here are the traditional elements of the lament (see on Psalm 13). The *complaint* is directed against the Lord, with a sequence of repeated "you's" addressing God (vv. 38–46). The king and people have experienced a great defeat. This time, the Lord has not given victory to the king but has hurled him to the ground and, in fact, allowed him to die (vv. 44–45). Now the psalmist begins asking those hard questions: How long will you hide and keep on being angry, Lord? (v. 46). Where is the love (*hesed*) that we used to be able to count on? And what about your promises to David? (v. 49).

This is a lament, but not all the usual elements of the lament are represented (see on Psalm 13). The complaint in the "you" form dominates (vv. 38–46, 48–49) over the "I" complaint (v. 50) and "they" complaint

(v. 51). There is only a glimmer of *affirmation of trust*; verse 46 hopes that the Lord might still act, and verse 49 allows for the possibility that the Lord's *hesed* may still exist. The *request* to remember is very brief (vv. 47, 50). Verse 52 sounds a note of *praise*, though it likely was inserted here by the editors to conclude Book III on a note of praise (see the conclusions of the other books).

This psalm began with words of praise to the Lord and words of promise to the Davidic king (vv. 1–4). In the middle were extravagant words of promise to the Lord's anointed, King David and his line (vv. 19–37). Psalm 89 ends with a report that the Lord is angry with the anointed king and the king has been defeated. The last sounds heard are the insults and taunts of the Lord's enemies, aimed at the Lord's anointed (vv. 50–51).

Where Is Your Love?

What started out as an exuberant hymn, resolving to proclaim the Lord's faithfulness forever, now ends with a burning question: "Lord, where is your steadfast love of old?" The prayer of the psalmist is bold, if not impertinent. It asks, "Lord, where is the love you used to be famous for? What about those promises to David?"

The words that follow, in verses 50–51, speak of a servant suffering insults and taunts. The hymn that began with praise ends as an exhausted cry for help: "Remember, O Lord . . . how I bear . . . the insults of the peoples."

How could an editor follow such a hopeless cry with a word of praise to the Lord (v. 52)? Did that editor know the figure of the servant who would suffer for others, as portrayed in Isaiah 52–53? Or did that editor somehow sense that in the providence of God, a "Hallelujah" chorus could follow a portrayal of a servant who was taunted and insulted, even despised and rejected, and acquainted with grief (Isa. 53:3)?

Book IV, which follows on this psalm, will make clear that despite all, the Lord is still King (Psalms 93, 95–99).

4. Book IV
PSALMS 90–106

IT'S ABOUT TIME
Psalm 90

A Prayer of Moses, the man of God.

90:1 Lord, you have been our dwelling place
    in all generations.
  2 Before the mountains were brought forth,
    or ever you had formed the earth and the world,
    from everlasting to everlasting you are God.

  3 You turn us back to dust,
    and say, "Turn back, you mortals."
  4 For a thousand years in your sight
    are like yesterday when it is past,
    or like a watch in the night.

  5 You sweep them away; they are like a dream,
    like grass that is renewed in the morning;
  6 in the morning it flourishes and is renewed;
    in the evening it fades and withers.

  7 For we are consumed by your anger;
    by your wrath we are overwhelmed.
  8 You have set our iniquities before you,
    our secret sins in the light of your countenance.

  9 For all our days pass away under your wrath;
    our years come to an end like a sigh.
  10 The days of our life are seventy years,
    or perhaps eighty, if we are strong;
    even then their span is only toil and trouble;
    they are soon gone, and we fly away.

11 Who considers the power of your anger?
  Your wrath is as great as the fear that is due you.
12 So teach us to count our days
  that we may gain a wise heart.

13 Turn, O LORD! How long?
  Have compassion on your servants!
14 Satisfy us in the morning with your steadfast love,
  so that we may rejoice and be glad all our days.
15 Make us glad as many days as you have afflicted us,
  and as many years as we have seen evil.
16 Let your work be manifest to your servants,
  and your glorious power to their children.
17 Let the favor of the Lord our God be upon us,
  and prosper for us the work of our hands—
  O prosper the work of our hands!

It was a conversation among old friends, at a time of reunion. As happens on such occasions, the topic turned to the quick passage of time. "Think of life as a football game," suggested one. "If our life expectancy is, say, eighty years, then at age sixty the whistle has just blown for the fourth quarter." Someone calculated the number of books one could still read in this fourth-quarter existence. Another spoke of travels to Europe; yet another of ages of grandchildren.

As we drove home, it occurred to me that we were looking at life from the perspective of Psalm 90, which speaks of an average life span of seventy or eighty years. The psalm has some counsel for those who reflect on such issues.

Introducing Book IV

Psalm 90 introduces Book IV of the Psalter, which consists of seventeen psalms (as does Book III). Does it intend to answer the question raised in Psalm 89:49, "Lord, where is your steadfast love of old?" A few observations about Book IV are in order: (1) in this Book are six of the seven psalms that speak of the Lord's kingship, the *enthronement psalms* (Psalms 93, 95–99); (2) Psalms 103 and 104 are both framed with "Bless the LORD, O my soul"; (3) Psalms 105 and 106 are both recitals of God's acts in history, with similar beginnings and endings; (4) the first "Hallelujah" ("Praise the LORD") in the Psalter occurs at the end of Psalm 104, while Psalm 106 is framed with "Hallelujah"; (5) the heading for Psalm 90, which opens the book, is the only one that associates a psalm with "Moses, the man of God."

Psalm 90 divides into three sections: Who is God? (vv. 1–2); Who are we? (vv. 3–11); How should we live? (vv. 12–17).

Who Is God? (90:1–2)

Today's English Version of the Bible catches the sense of the first line of this prayer by translating "Lord, you have always been our home." There are a good many pictures for God in the Psalms: Father, Mother, Shepherd, King. Here God is pictured as *home*. The hymn writer Isaac Watts caught the sense in his paraphrase of this psalm, "O God, Our Help in Ages Past":

> O God, our help in ages past,
> Our hope for years to come,
> Our shelter from the stormy blast,
> And our eternal home.

The psalm and the hymn emphasize God as *home*. In his poem "The Death of the Hired Man," Robert Frost wrote, "Home is the place where, when you have to go there, They have to take you in." God, says this psalm, is like that.

Who is God? "Our eternal home," said the hymn writer. "Right on," say the first verses of Psalm 90.

Who Are We? (90:3–11)

Now the psalm turns to reflect on human beings. Who are we?

To begin, the question is answered with three pictures (vv. 3–6). We are *dust* and shall eventually return to dust, as Genesis 3:19 indicates and as we are reminded each time we stand by a graveside (see also Ps. 104:29; Eccl. 12:7). Our lives are like a *dream*, dramatically present in the nighttime and then quickly disappearing with the morning light. Again, Isaac Watts got it right:

> Time, like an ever-rolling stream,
> Soon bears us all away;
> We fly forgotten, as a dream
> Dies at the opening day.

Finally, we are like *grass*, fresh and green in the morning but soon dried up and gone. The prophet Isaiah used the same imagery: "The grass withers, the flower fades; but the word of our God will stand forever" (Isa. 40:7; see also 1 Peter 1:24–25).

Verses 7–11 are framed by references to God's anger. The conscious-ness of time continues to dominate: *"our days* pass away," *"our years* come to an end." And "our life" consists of seventy, maybe eighty years. The psalm is not very positive about those years, describing them as "only toil and trouble" (v. 10).

Lament over the shortness of life is a theme found elsewhere in the Psalms: "LORD . . . let me know how fleeting my life is" (Ps. 39:4–6); "Mortals cannot abide in their pomp; they are like the animals that per-ish" (Ps. 49:12, 20). Other biblical texts, too, ponder mortality: "For the fate of humans and the fate of animals is the same; as one dies, so dies the other" (Eccl. 3:19–21); "A mortal, born of woman, few of days and full of trouble, comes up like a flower and withers" (Job 14:1); "When human beings have finished, they are just beginning" (Sirach 18:7–14); "Do good to friends before you die" (Sirach 14:13–14).

Who are we? These three pictures make the matter quite clear: we are transients, here on a visit, persons whose lives are not long. Soon our years will come to an end, and we shall be gone.

How Should We Live? (90:12–17)

With verse 12, we are at the heart of Psalm 90. These are the words that should be underlined, highlighted, or marked in red. "The Latin transla-tion had it all wrong here," said Martin Luther, who translated, some-what freely: "Teach us to reflect on the fact that we must die, so that we become wise" (E. Mülhaupt, ed., *D. Martin Luthers Psalmen-Auslegung* 2:537; my translation from German). In any case, this petition is at the heart of the prayer. From reflecting on death, one can learn how to live. The writer of Ecclesiastes suggested,

> It is better to go to the house of mourning
>   than to go to the house of feasting;
> for this is the end of everyone,
>   and the living will lay it to heart.
>   (Eccl. 7:2)

The writer expresses a number of requests as Psalm 90 ends, speaking on behalf of "your servants" (vv. 13, 16). The final words, doubled for emphasis, are a prayer especially appropriate at the beginning of a task. Verse 10 spoke of the "toil and trouble" of one's years; the final words in the psalm have something more positive to say about work. The expres-sion "the Lord our God" reaches back to the same words at the begin-ning of the psalm that spoke about the almighty and eternal God. The prayer is that this Lord God will reach into our daily lives and bless our work: "O prosper the work of our hands!"

The Work of Our Hands

Adjacent to the "Hospital on the Hill" in Nazareth, Israel, is a small chapel. One steps in and, after a few moments, notices the unusual altar. It is a carpenter's bench, complete with vise—a reminder that Joseph and Jesus who once lived in this town were handworkers, carpenters. "O prosper the work of our hands!"

This story was told in Israel: When Golda Meir, then prime minister, made a visit to the Vatican in Rome, she was quite nervous about the occasion. She said to the pope, "It seems quite unbelievable to me that a carpenter's daughter from Milwaukee is here meeting the pope!" The pontiff's reply was, "Let me remind you, Mrs. Meir, that we hold the profession of carpentry in high regard around here."

Two prayers end this psalm. The first has to do with our attitude toward each day we are given: "Lord, teach us to make each day count, to reflect on the fact that we must die, and so become wise" (v. 12, paraphrase). The second has to do with each day's work: "Lord, prosper the work of our hands" (v. 17). Both prayers are important for those who know who God is, who they are, and what time it is.

ALL THOSE ANGELS
Psalm 91

> 91:1 You who live in the shelter of the Most High,
>   who abide in the shadow of the Almighty,
>   2 will say to the Lord, "My refuge and my fortress;
>   my God, in whom I trust."
>   3 For he will deliver you from the snare of the fowler
>   and from the deadly pestilence;
>   4 he will cover you with his pinions,
>   and under his wings you will find refuge;
>   his faithfulness is a shield and buckler.
>   5 You will not fear the terror of the night,
>   or the arrow that flies by day,
>   6 or the pestilence that stalks in darkness,
>   or the destruction that wastes at noonday.
>
>   7 A thousand may fall at your side,
>   ten thousand at your right hand,

but it will not come near you.
⁸ You will only look with your eyes
    and see the punishment of the wicked.

⁹ Because you have made the Lᴏʀᴅ your refuge,
    the Most High your dwelling place,
¹⁰ no evil shall befall you,
    no scourge come near your tent.

¹¹ For he will command his angels concerning you
    to guard you in all your ways.
¹² On their hands they will bear you up,
    so that you will not dash your foot against a stone.
¹³ You will tread on the lion and the adder,
    the young lion and the serpent you will trample under foot.

¹⁴ Those who love me, I will deliver;
    I will protect those who know my name.
¹⁵ When they call to me, I will answer them;
    I will be with them in trouble,
    I will rescue them and honor them.
¹⁶ With long life I will satisfy them,
    and show them my salvation.

"Even the devil can quote scripture" goes the old saying. According to the Gospels of Matthew and Luke, such is the case with Psalm 91.

Jesus had been fasting in the wilderness for forty days, says chapter 4 of Matthew's Gospel, and was famished. At that time the devil came to him and said, "If you are the Son of God, command these stones to become loaves of bread." Jesus refused, quoting the Old Testament book of Deuteronomy: "It is written, 'One does not live by bread alone, but by every word that comes from the mouth of God'" (Matt. 4:4; citing Deut. 8:3).

The devil took Jesus to the roof of the temple, suggesting that he prove his identity by throwing himself down. Then the devil cited this psalm:

> "He will command his angels concerning you,"
>   and "On their hands they will bear you up,
>   so that you will not dash your foot against a stone."
>   (Matt. 4:6; citing Ps. 91:11–12)

The debate continued as Jesus again quoted Deuteronomy: "Do not put the Lord your God to the test" (Matt. 4:7; citing Deut. 6:16). All of this can be a good reminder that enemies of the faith can twist the Bible to suit their own purposes.

Psalm 91 divides into three sections. Verses 1–2 are addressed to a person who has found security with the Lord; verses 3–13 continue to address this one; and in verses 14–16, the Lord speaks. Who is speaking in each of these cases? Since the psalm has the ring of instruction, the speaker in verses 1–13 may be a priest or a teacher. With verses 14–16, a priest or prophet speaks in the name of the Lord.

In God You Can Trust (91:1–2)

Was the person first addressed here one who had found sanctuary in the Jerusalem temple and who was living there? That is possible. Or does "You who live in the shelter of the Most High" refer to all persons who have found security and safety in a relationship to the Lord? In any case, countless believers have read this psalm in the second manner, considering themselves to be living "in the shadow of the Almighty," that is, enjoying the protection of the Lord.

The words that follow are addressed to such believers.

At Home with the Lord (91:3–13)

One of the pictures of God in this portion of the psalm is the same as that in Psalm 90:1: the Most High is "your dwelling place" (Ps. 91:9). Once again, a psalm says that God is a *home* for those who believe. This section then describes what life at home with the Lord is like.

Life with the Lord, says this psalm, is a life that is remarkably protected from evil, a life that is secure and free from anxiety. A "fowler" was a person who trapped birds (Ps. 124:7); when you feel as if you are caught in a trap, when you cannot get out and get on with your life, the Lord will set you free (v. 3)!

Once freed, says Psalm 91, you will be taken under the Lord's wing and given refuge (v. 4). Here the "wing" imagery switches the picture to the Lord as a bird, perhaps an eagle (Deut. 32:11–12; Pss. 17:8; 36:7; 57:1; 63:7); one is reminded of the Lord pictured as a mother hen (Matt. 23:37; Luke 13:34). "Taken under the Lord's wing, you will fear the terrors neither of the night nor of the daytime!" (vv. 5–6, paraphrase).

Assurance of the Lord's miraculous protection continues in verses 7 and 8. These verses must be read with the promises in verses 9–13 about angels. You will be protected, says the psalmist, and need not fear, for two reasons: (1) the Lord is your home; (2) the Lord has all those angels that are watching over you, guarding you, so that neither inanimate objects (such as stones) nor animate creatures (such as lions) will hurt you (vv. 9–13).

A Promise from the Lord (91:14–16)

The previous section offered instruction *about* the Lord. Now the Lord speaks. When the psalm was used in the temple, we can imagine a priest speaking these words.

The promises pile up, with the Lord saying, "I promise those who love me that I will deliver and protect, I will answer them and be with them in times of trouble, I will rescue and honor them, I will give them long life and show them salvation" (paraphrase).

Promises, Promises

The psalm begins by addressing one who lives "in the shadow of the Almighty," who considers the Lord as a refuge and a mighty fortress (vv. 1–2). It continues with the voice of a priest or prophet declaring the Lord's protection to such a person, for whom God is "home" (vv. 3–13; see v. 9). It concludes with words from a speaker representing God, promising deliverance, protection, and long life (vv. 14–16).

But what about these promises when a life is cut short by death? Or when people pray and there is no answer? Or when there is a terrible accident, and all those angels seem to have failed?

Questions like these may never be answered; after all, as far as *we* know, Jesus received no answer to his "Why have you forsaken me?" question from the cross.

Even Christians will have to live for a while with unanswered questions. But for those for whom the Lord has been a "dwelling place" and "home" for generations (Psalms 90, 91), there is nevertheless hope. There is a promise of a dwelling place in the parental home in the future (John 14:1–7), and a promise that God will be "home" in this place and will wipe away every tear, and death will be no more (Rev. 21:1–4).

ALWAYS GREEN AND FULL OF SAP
Psalm 92

A Psalm. A Song for the Sabbath Day.

92:1 **It is good to give thanks to the LORD,**
 to sing praises to your name, O Most High;

² to declare your steadfast love in the morning,
   and your faithfulness by night,
³ to the music of the lute and the harp,
   to the melody of the lyre.
⁴ For you, O LORD, have made me glad by your work;
   at the works of your hands I sing for joy.

⁵ How great are your works, O LORD!
   Your thoughts are very deep!
⁶ The dullard cannot know,
   the stupid cannot understand this:
⁷ though the wicked sprout like grass
   and all evildoers flourish,
   they are doomed to destruction forever,
⁸   but you, O LORD, are on high forever.
⁹ For your enemies, O LORD,
   for your enemies shall perish;
   all evildoers shall be scattered.

¹⁰ But you have exalted my horn like that of the wild ox;
   you have poured over me fresh oil.
¹¹ My eyes have seen the downfall of my enemies;
   my ears have heard the doom of my evil assailants.

¹² The righteous flourish like the palm tree,
   and grow like a cedar in Lebanon.
¹³ They are planted in the house of the LORD;
   they flourish in the courts of our God.
¹⁴ In old age they still produce fruit;
   they are always green and full of sap,
¹⁵ showing that the LORD is upright;
   he is my rock, and there is no unrighteousness in him.

The book of Psalms begins with a picture of a tree, planted by a stream, beautiful and productive. This was to illustrate the happiness of those who reflect on the teachings of the Lord. In Psalm 92 the picture of a tree occurs again. It is the righteous who flourish like a palm tree or a cedar. Even in old age they are full of freshness and energy, green and full of sap. Who are these persons? And how did they get to be that way?

"A Psalm" in the heading suggests that this piece was sung with instrumental accompaniment (see v. 3). The designation "A Song for the Sabbath Day" occurs only here in the Psalter. The psalm is somehow linked to the celebration of the Sabbath; the exact nature of that connection is not evident.

The writer has experienced deliverance from certain personal enemies (vv. 10–11) and therefore is giving thanks. The psalm begins with praise and thanksgiving for a specific act of deliverance (vv. 1–4), continues with general praise of Yahweh (vv. 5–9), recalls the specific deliverance (vv. 10–11), and concludes with reflections on the happy state of the righteous (vv. 12–15).

I Sing for Joy (92:1–4)

Certainly it would be interesting to hear the way in which psalms like this were performed with music. The *content* of the musical offering was thanks and praise for the steadfast love and the faithfulness of the Lord. The *times* for these offerings were morning and evening services of worship (see Psalm 134 for the latter). The *form* was vocal music accompanied by instruments, such as the lute, the harp, and the lyre. The *reasons* for the thanks and praise were the actions of the Lord, presumably deliverance from personal troubles as described in verses 10 and 11.

How Great Are Your Works! (92:5–11)

After singing about "the works of your hands" (v. 4), the piece continues by linking up with the "works" theme and developing it. The "works and thoughts" theme occurs also in Psalm 40:5; "How weighty to me are your thoughts, O God!" declares Psalm 139:17.

Verses 6–9 offer some reflections on persons who, as we might say, "just don't get it." Verse 6 refers to a "dullard"; the Hebrew word means "cattle," and the sense appears to be a "brutish person." The same word occurs in Psalms 49:10 (NRSV, "dolt") and 73:22 (NRSV, "stupid") and in Proverbs 12:1 and 30:2 (NRSV, "stupid"). There is something that these people without insight do not understand, and that is described in verses 7–9 of this psalm. Evildoers (the word frames section verses 7–9) may immediately prosper, but then they quickly perish. Evildoers are like grass that grows up quickly and then soon dies and dries up and blows away. (The same picture occurs in Psalm 90:5–6.)

Verse 11 says in literal language that the enemies of the psalmist have been destroyed; verse 10 says the same thing using figurative speech. The "horn" is a symbol for power, and to "exalt my horn" means to grant power (see Psalm 89:17; and note Luke 1:69, NRSV footnote). Anointing with oil has a positive meaning (Ps. 133:2); the nature of the ritual act here is not known.

Still Productive (92:12–15)

In verse 7 the wicked are compared to grass that grows quickly and dies. In verse 12 there is a comparison for the righteous. They are like the stately palm tree or the mighty cedar, both of which have a life expectancy of hundreds of years. Though evildoers "flourish" briefly (v. 7), the righteous will "flourish" like the palm and cedar and will indeed "flourish" in their activities in the house of God (v. 13; see also the picture in Psalm 52:8).

The tree imagery continues into the last verses, describing the righteous in their old age. Even as senior citizens, they continue to be productive. They are fresh (the same Hebrew word is used of the oil in v. 10) and full of vitality. They are like that tree portrayed in Psalm 1:3, prospering and productive. The psalm closes with a word praising the Lord, "my rock" (see also Psalm 19:14).

WILL THE CENTER HOLD?
Psalm 93

> 93:1 The LORD is king, he is robed in majesty;
>   the LORD is robed, he is girded with strength.
> He has established the world; it shall never be moved;
> 2   your throne is established from of old;
>   you are from everlasting.
>
> 3 The floods have lifted up, O LORD,
>   the floods have lifted up their voice;
>   the floods lift up their roaring.
> 4 More majestic than the thunders of mighty waters,
>   more majestic than the waves of the sea,
>   majestic on high is the LORD!
>
> 5 Your decrees are very sure;
>   holiness befits your house,
>   O LORD, forevermore.

For those living in the United States, the world of royalty is a foreign world. Our nation was founded by those who wanted to get away from kings and queens and the excesses and abuses that have so often accompanied monarchy.

For the first two centuries of its existence, the nation Israel had no king but was a loosely knit tribal federation. The monarchy eventually came, even though it was not unanimously applauded. The kings of

Israel and Judah move across the pages of the Bible—Saul, David, Solomon, Jeroboam and Rehoboam, and the rest—until Zedekiah, the last ruler, is blinded and dragged off to live in Babylon in exile (2 Kings 25).

The Lord Is King

Psalm 93 is one of seven psalms in the Bible that were used at a festival declaring God to be King: Psalms 47, 93, and 95–99. These *enthronement psalms*, as they are called, are not to be confused with *royal psalms*, which are associated with events in the life of the king in Jerusalem. In the enthronement psalms, God is the king; in the royal psalms, the king is the king.

The first picture for God that appears in the Psalms is that of the Lord as king: "My King and my God" (Ps. 5:2). That picture recurs in these enthronement psalms, often called "kingship psalms," and runs through the book of Psalms: Psalms 10:16; 29:10; 44:4; 48:2; 68:24; 74:12; 84:3; 145:1; 149:2.

To understand these texts portraying the Lord as king, it is helpful to begin by understanding something about kings and monarchies. For the biblical world, the books of Samuel and Kings are useful. To get a contemporary slant on monarchy, watch a television or movie version of a coronation of a king or queen in England.

Psalm 93

This short psalm begins with a cry that is found in a number of these enthronement psalms: "The Lord is king!" (see also Pss. 96:10; 97:1; 99:1). It seems that this cry was a part of a ceremony installing a new king or celebrating the anniversary of that coronation. Though there have been many speculations about the nature of that ceremony, the precise nature of the event is not known (v. 1).

What is known from this psalm is that over which the king rules, which is identified as the entire world, or *tebel* (v. 1c). The same Hebrew word for "world" occurs in Psalms 96:10, 13; 97:4; and 98:9 and may therefore be considered part of the typical vocabulary for these enthronement psalms.

The King, "the Lord," is described as clothed in majesty and strength and ruling from an everlasting throne (vv. 1–2). With verse 2, the psalm switches from language speaking *about* the Lord to words speaking *to* the Lord directly. Now the psalm looks back, recalling the long history of the Lord's rule over the world.

What are "the floods" referred to in verses 3–4? Is there some connection with primeval waters at the time of creation? Is this a reference to Canaanite traditions known and preserved by those outside Israel? The matter is not certain. What is certain, however, is that this short section praises "the LORD," Yahweh, as more powerful than any of these floods or thunderings or waves. *Majestic* is the same word used of the Lord at the beginning and ending of Psalm 8: "how majestic is your name in all the earth!" Whatever the origins of the ideas here, the intent is clear: to praise the Lord, mentioned at the beginning and the ending.

Verse 5 returns to speech addressing the Lord directly (as in vv. 2–3). To a people who were concerned about the shaking of the foundations of both their world and their government (vv. 1–2), these words assuring the reliability of the Lord's works and the authenticity and permanence of the Lord's temple come as good news.

The Shift of the Millennia

Whatever the occasion for this psalm, it is clear that it addresses those who are concerned about the stability of the world and their government as they experience it. In the midst of our own anxieties about these issues at the shift of the millennia, these words about stability, solidarity, permanence, power (even more powerful than the roaring sea), and majesty come as good news.

An old spiritual sang of One who's "got the whole world in his hands." The New Testament starts off with the good news that the rule of the King described in these psalms became present in a dramatic new way with the coming of Jesus (Mark 1:14).

SOLID AS A ROCK
Psalm 94

> 94:1 O LORD, you God of vengeance,
>   you God of vengeance, shine forth!
> ² Rise up, O judge of the earth;
>   give to the proud what they deserve!
> ³ O LORD, how long shall the wicked,
>   how long shall the wicked exult?
>
> ⁴ They pour out their arrogant words;
>   all the evildoers boast.
> ⁵ They crush your people, O LORD,
>   and afflict your heritage.

⁶ They kill the widow and the stranger,
   they murder the orphan,
⁷ and they say, "The LORD does not see;
   the God of Jacob does not perceive."

⁸ Understand, O dullest of the people;
   fools, when will you be wise?
⁹ He who planted the ear, does he not hear?
   He who formed the eye, does he not see?
¹⁰ He who disciplines the nations,
   he who teaches knowledge to humankind,
   does he not chastise?
¹¹ The LORD knows our thoughts,
   that they are but an empty breath.

¹² Happy are those whom you discipline, O LORD,
   and whom you teach out of your law,
¹³ giving them respite from days of trouble,
   until a pit is dug for the wicked.
¹⁴ For the LORD will not forsake his people;
   he will not abandon his heritage;
¹⁵ for justice will return to the righteous,
   and all the upright in heart will follow it.

¹⁶ Who rises up for me against the wicked?
   Who stands up for me against evildoers?
¹⁷ If the LORD had not been my help,
   my soul would soon have lived in the land of silence.
¹⁸ When I thought, "My foot is slipping,"
   your steadfast love, O LORD, held me up.
¹⁹ When the cares of my heart are many,
   your consolations cheer my soul.
²⁰ Can wicked rulers be allied with you,
   those who contrive mischief by statute?
²¹ They band together against the life of the righteous,
   and condemn the innocent to death.
²² But the LORD has become my stronghold,
   and my God the rock of my refuge.
²³ He will repay them for their iniquity
   and wipe them out for their wickedness;
   the LORD our God will wipe them out.

The picture in the magazine is an attention getter: a photograph of a huge, familiar rock, the Rock of Gibraltar. It is an advertisement for an insurance company. That rock is a symbol for stability, safety, and security.

The biblical writers pick up the same imagery, using "rock" as a picture for God. Psalm 19 referred to the Lord as "my rock and my redeemer" (v. 14). The prayer in Psalm 61:2 petitions, "Lead me to the rock that is higher than I," while Psalm 62:2 and 6 assert, "He alone is my rock and my salvation."

The picture of God as rock appears in a number of psalms in this part of the collection. "He is my rock," declares Psalm 92:15. Psalm 95:1 refers to the Lord as "the rock of our salvation," and 94:22 speaks of "my God the rock of my refuge." "My God," this image is saying, "is as secure, as stable, as steady as the Rock of Gibraltar."

Psalm 94 begins with a *cry* to the Lord *for help* and a series of *"they"* *complaints* (vv. 1–7). Verses 8–15 offer *instruction*, countering the assertion in verse 7 "The LORD does not see" (vv. 9, 11, 14). Verses 16–23 affirm *trust* in the Lord's steadfast love (vv. 16–19, 22–23) and offer a *"they"* *complaint* (vv. 20–21).

Rise and Shine, O Lord! (94:1–7))

Psalm 93 provides a picture of the Lord as majestic king, ruling the entire world. Now Psalm 94 calls on this all-powerful God to rise and shine, to get up and do something about the problems that God's people are having with the proud and the wicked. God is also portrayed here as a judge (v. 2). As a judge, God may choose to do some disciplining and teaching of those who are called before the court (v. 10).

In verse 3, "how long" is doubled to emphasize the point. The sense is "How long can the wicked be so successful? It's been long enough Lord! So, Lord, put a stop to it!"

Verses 4–7 bring complaints before the Judge in the form of "they" statements describing the wrongdoing of these evil people. First, they sin with *words* that are boastful and arrogant (v. 4). Second, they sin with *actions*, as they "crush" God's people. That same *crush* verb is used in Isaiah 3:15, when the prophet accuses the people of Jerusalem of "crushing" and "grinding" the poor persons in the city. Psalm 94:6 indicates that these arrogant evildoers go so far as to take the lives of widows, orphans, and strangers. Taken together with prophetic complaints such as those found in Isaiah 1:10–17, 21–26 and 10:1–4, we have a portrayal of the Judge about to throw the book at a group of persons who have been taking advantage of the powerless instead of taking up their cause.

Finally, the psalmist quotes the boasting and arrogant words of those persons who are sure that "the LORD does not see" (v. 7).

God Will Never Give Up! (94:8–15)

Verses 8–11 offer a response to those people who claim that the Lord has no idea about what is going on (v. 7). Such persons are dullards and fools! After all, the Lord made ears and eyes; don't you think the Lord can see and hear? The psalmist suggests that the troubles the people have been experiencing are the Lord's ways of exercising discipline (v. 10). And all our great ideas and plans? Using the thematic word from Ecclesiastes, the writer says our thoughts are all an "empty breath," or nothingness, or "vanity" (v. 11).

In verse 12 is a statement about those who have found happiness. They are those who have been taught "out of your Bible" (a better translation of *torah* than "law" here). Such persons who have absorbed some of the biblical tradition will understand that present troubles are temporary, lasting only until the Lord deals with the wicked (v. 13). They should be assured that the Lord will never give up on his people and will never abandon them. As the all-powerful judge (v. 2), God will eventually see to it that justice is done for God's people.

My Mighty Fortress (94:16–23)

As good teachers sometimes do, the psalmist now tells something of his own story. "Had it not been for the Lord's steady and solid love, I'd have never made it!" the writer says (vv. 16–17). Then, speaking to the Lord in prayer, the psalmist gives thanks for the Lord's love, which has kept him from slipping away (vv. 18–19).

The psalmist continues to experience injustices from governmental leaders (vv. 20–21). But now the writer has a mighty fortress, a stronghold, a rock that he can depend on for safety. And in just a matter of time, the Lord will take care of these enemies!

What Is Being Taught?

Twice in this psalm, reference is made to the Lord's teaching (vv. 10, 12). What is being taught here?

First is teaching about God. God is the Judge (vv. 1–2) who will eventually punish the wicked (v. 23). Though some believe the Lord does not know what is going on (v. 7), God (who made all eyes and ears) hears and sees what is happening to God's people.

Second is teaching about God's people. God's people are at present experiencing suffering (vv. 4–7). This suffering may be God's way of disciplining and teaching (vv. 10, 12). No matter what happens, and no matter when, one thing God's people can count on: God will never abandon them (v. 14)!

Finally, the psalm teaches about God and the individual. I have already experienced God's help in the past, says the writer (vv. 16–19). No matter what troubles may come my way, I know that God is my fortress, a rock-solid support that will never fail (v. 22).

Such faith reaches out toward that which Jesus once described in terms of a person whose house was built on rock (Matt. 7:24–27), or toward that faith expressed in the hymn that says, "On Christ, the solid rock I stand, all other ground is sinking sand."

THE WHOLE WORLD IN HIS HAND
Psalm 95

95:1 O come, let us sing to the LORD;
　　　 let us make a joyful noise to the rock of our salvation!
² Let us come into his presence with thanksgiving;
　　　 let us make a joyful noise to him with songs of praise!
³ For the LORD is a great God,
　　　 and a great King above all gods.
⁴ In his hand are the depths of the earth;
　　　 the heights of the mountains are his also.
⁵ The sea is his, for he made it,
　　　 and the dry land, which his hands have formed.

⁶ O come, let us worship and bow down,
　　　 let us kneel before the LORD, our Maker!
⁷ For he is our God,
　　　 and we are the people of his pasture,
　　　 and the sheep of his hand.

　　　 O that today you would listen to his voice!
⁸　　 Do not harden your hearts, as at Meribah,
　　　 as on the day at Massah in the wilderness,
⁹ when your ancestors tested me,
　　　 and put me to the proof, though they had seen my work.
¹⁰ For forty years I loathed that generation
　　　 and said, "They are a people whose hearts go astray,
　　　 and they do not regard my ways."
¹¹ Therefore in my anger I swore,
　　　 "They shall not enter my rest."

This psalm appears in two quite contrasting musical settings. First, it is familiar to many as part of the church's liturgy, for the morning service of matins:

> O come, let us worship and bow down,
>   let us kneel before the LORD, our Maker!
> For he is our God,
>   and we are the people of his pasture,
>   and the sheep of his hand.
>
> (vv. 6–7)

Second, in paraphrased form, it is familiar in the spiritual "He's Got the Whole World in His Hand": "He's got the whole world in his hand. . . . He's got the little bitty baby in his hand. . . . He's got you and me sister in his hand" (v. 4).

When the psalm is used as part of a liturgy for worship, it is functioning as it has from the beginning. It begins with two sections in the typical pattern of a hymn (see on Psalm 113), with a *call to worship* in the imperative followed by *for* introducing *reasons for worship* (vv. 1–2 + 3–5; 6 + 7a). The psalm concludes with a call to "listen" (vv. 7b–11).

Psalm 95 is fitted carefully into its context. It is linked to Psalm 94 by the "rock" picture in verse 1 (Ps. 94:22; also 92:15). It is also tied to the "kingship of the Lord" psalms with the king imagery (Pss. 93:1; 96:10; 97:1; 98:6; 99:1).

An Invitation to Worship (95:1–5)

The invitation could hardly be stronger, with a quintet of verbs in the imperative mood: "come . . . let us sing . . . let us make a joyful noise. . . . Let us come . . . let us make a joyful noise" (vv. 1–2). This was apparently an invitation to process into the place of worship in the temple.

This introduction indicates a good deal about the sort of worship going on here. It involves singing songs of praise; it is addressed to the Lord, the "rock of our salvation" (see Ps. 89:26); and it will be carried out with joy and enthusiasm.

As noted above, the invitation is followed by some reasons for coming to worship, here introduced by *for* (vv. 3–5). The first reason is because the Lord is great, in fact a *king* above all other gods. (The neighboring "kingship of God" psalms are listed above.) This kingship is illustrated by referring to the work of the Lord's hands. The extremes are named to indicate the whole: the Lord has made the sea and the dry land (Gen. 1:1–10). The depths of the earth and the heights of the mountains are also in the Lord's hands. The Lord, in other words, is a great God because of the Lord's work of *creation*.

"Let Us Bow Down" (95:6–7a)

Verses 1 and 2 are an invitation to join in the procession. The second invitation, in verse 6, is addressed to those already in the temple, inviting them to worship and bow down. They bow before the Lord, the King, because this is the way one approaches a king. When Nathan came in to see David, "he did obeisance to the king, with his face to the ground" (1 Kings 1:23).

The first hymn (vv. 1–5) stresses the work of the King as creator and sustainer of the earth and all creation; this hymn focuses on the Lord as *maker of the people* (v. 6) and as the One who cares for them as a shepherd cares for the sheep of the flock. Psalm 100:3 ties these two notions together:

> It is he that made us, and we are his;
> we are his people, and the sheep of his pasture.

The two opening hymns in Psalm 95 exhibit a good deal of creative imagination. God is rock, king, maker of sea and land, and shepherd. The people are subjects of the King or sheep belonging to the Shepherd.

A Sermon (95:7b–11)

The first hymn invites hearers to join the procession into the temple. The second is a call to bow down and kneel. Now that the congregation has assembled, a short sermon follows.

The sermon begins with an invitation to listen (v. 7b). Then the preacher calls forth some negative examples from the past. After coming out of Egypt, the Israelites traveled through the desert wilderness. The Lord provided food for them in the form of manna and quail (Exodus 16; Numbers 11). When they were short of water, Moses struck a rock, and water came streaming out. But there had been so much complaining and quarreling among the people that Moses called the place Massah and Meribah, which mean "testing" and "quarreling" (Exod. 17:1–7). And now, says this preacher speaking in the name of the Lord, "don't test me again as you tested me at that time!" (vv. 7b–9; Ps. 106:32–33 also recalls this incident).

As reported in Numbers 14:26–28, the forty years in the wilderness was a time of punishment for the people's unfaithfulness. Here, too, it is remembered as a time when the Lord was angry with the people. Because they were not faithful to the Lord, the Lord let them wander in the wilderness, and they did not see the promised land. They did not enter the promised rest (Deut. 12:9).

"But now," says this sermon, "do not be like those people! Listen to the voice of the Lord!"

A Sabbath Rest Remains for God's People

One of the great biblical preachers once looked at this psalm and updated it for use in a new situation (Heb. 3:7–4:13). That preacher focused on the words "O that today you would listen to [God's] voice!" The sermon began by quoting verses 7–11 of Psalm 95. This served as a reminder of how persons can wrongly respond to what God has done for them by rebelling, going astray, testing God.

The message of the sermon is simple: "Don't be like those people in the wilderness! As long as you have a chance, as long as there is a 'today,' hear and believe the good news, and enter into the sort of life that allows you to let your weight down on God, to rest on God, trusting God's promises. Such is the sort of Sabbath rest promised to God's people, who know that whatever may happen, they are the people of his pasture, and the sheep of his hand."

THE SINGING TREES
Psalm 96

96:1 **O sing to the LORD a new song;**
    sing to the LORD, all the earth.
2 **Sing to the LORD, bless his name;**
    tell of his salvation from day to day.
3 **Declare his glory among the nations,**
    his marvelous works among all the peoples.
4 **For great is the LORD, and greatly to be praised;**
    he is to be revered above all gods.
5 **For all the gods of the peoples are idols,**
    but the LORD made the heavens.
6 **Honor and majesty are before him;**
    strength and beauty are in his sanctuary.

7 **Ascribe to the LORD, O families of the peoples,**
    ascribe to the LORD glory and strength.
8 **Ascribe to the LORD the glory due his name;**
    bring an offering, and come into his courts.

⁹ Worship the LORD in holy splendor;
    tremble before him, all the earth.

¹⁰ Say among the nations, "The LORD is king!
    The world is firmly established; it shall never be moved.
    He will judge the peoples with equity."
¹¹ Let the heavens be glad, and let the earth rejoice;
    let the sea roar, and all that fills it;
¹²   let the field exult, and everything in it.
    Then shall all the trees of the forest sing for joy
¹³   before the LORD; for he is coming,
    for he is coming to judge the earth.
    He will judge the world with righteousness,
    and the peoples with his truth.

> Let every heart prepare him room
> and heav'n and nature sing,
> and heav'n and nature sing,
> and heav'n, and heav'n and nature sing!

Such are some of the lines from "Joy to the World," the well-known Christmas carol. According to that carol, there is such joy at the coming of the Lord that both heaven and nature break into singing, and "fields and floods, rocks, hills, and plains repeat the sounding joy."

According to Psalm 96, there is such joy at the Lord's kingship that heaven and earth rejoice, the seas and the fields exult, and the trees of the forest sing for joy (vv. 11–12).

The psalm falls into three sections: a call to *all the earth* to sing praise and tell what God has done (vv. 1–6), a call to *all the earth* to worship (vv. 7–9), and an announcement that the Lord will come to judge *the earth* (vv. 10–13).

The Start of Something Big (96:1–6)

According to its form, this opening section follows the pattern of a typical hymn (see on Psalm 113), with a call to "sing . . . bless . . . tell . . . declare" (vv. 1–3) followed by reasons for these activities, introduced by *for* (vv. 4–6).

The content of this hymn, however, is hardly typical. The first three verses indicate what is to come. First, this is to be a fresh, new contribution to the musical tradition of the synagogue. Second, the author thinks big. Those invited to join in singing are not just those present in the synagogue but "all the earth." Those to be addressed are not just Israel but "the nations" or "all the peoples." Third, the author's notion of God is also big. This is no regional deity but the Lord of "all the earth" who "made the heavens." The making of the heavens is an exceptionally marvelous work; Psalm 8 develops it more fully. The Lord occupies a position above all gods. (The author shares in the views of his time that there were other gods.) These "gods" are really idols who have done nothing, in contrast to the Lord's activities. Fourth, the themes of this singing will be stories about the Lord's saving acts and marvelous works (vv. 2–3; note, for example, the gathering of such stories in Psalm 107).

What did the singing of such a psalm sound like? We do not know. But in view of psalms such as 33 and 150, one may imagine a mighty chorus, accompanied by skilled instrumentalists, playing cymbals and tambourines and stringed instruments, perhaps with some dancers (Ps. 150:4), all led with the sound of a trumpet.

Worship the Lord, All the Earth (96:7–9)

This section follows a pattern known from Psalm 29. Whereas those words were addressed to the heavenly beings, however, these are addressed to human beings. Once again, one sees the large dimensions of this psalm. Called to worship are the "families of the peoples" and "all the earth."

Both verses 6 and 8 assume the existence of the temple and the restoration of the practice of offering sacrifices.

The Lord Is King (96:10–13)

Once again, the viewpoint of this part of the psalm is worldwide. Verse 3 was a call to declare the Lord's glory "among the nations"; here that command is carried out. The Lord, the King, will carry out the task of judging the nations of the world.

Now the psalm moves into the distant future, the end time, when the Lord will judge. The scope of that judging includes all "the peoples" (vv. 10, 13), the earth, the world (v. 13). This last judgment will be good news for Israel. In fact, nature itself will rejoice at this final settling of accounts. The heavens and the earth will be glad, as will the sea and the fields. Even the trees of the forest will sing with joy.

JOY TO THE WORLD
Psalm 97

> 97:1 The Lord is king! Let the earth rejoice;
>   let the many coastlands be glad!
> 2 Clouds and thick darkness are all around him;
>   righteousness and justice are the foundation of his throne.

³ Fire goes before him,
   and consumes his adversaries on every side.
⁴ His lightnings light up the world;
   the earth sees and trembles.
⁵ The mountains melt like wax before the LORD,
   before the Lord of all the earth.

⁶ The heavens proclaim his righteousness;
   and all the peoples behold his glory.
⁷ All worshipers of images are put to shame,
   those who make their boast in worthless idols;
   all gods bow down before him.
⁸ Zion hears and is glad,
   and the towns of Judah rejoice,
   because of your judgments, O God.
⁹ For you, O LORD, are most high over all the earth;
   you are exalted far above all gods.

¹⁰ The LORD loves those who hate evil;
    he guards the lives of his faithful;
    he rescues them from the hand of the wicked.
¹¹ Light dawns for the righteous,
    and joy for the upright in heart.
¹² Rejoice in the LORD, O you righteous,
    and give thanks to his holy name!

This is the second of three consecutive psalms that the lectionary assigns for Christmas Day. What does an Old Testament hymn have to do with the festival celebrating the birth of Jesus the Messiah?

Psalm 96 calls for joyful singing, celebrating the mighty acts of God's salvation: "Then shall all the trees of the forest sing for joy" (96:12). Psalm 97 focuses on the Lord's rule as king, and that is cause for rejoicing: "The LORD is king! Let the earth rejoice; let the many coastlands be glad" (v. 1).

"Joy to the world, the Lord is come" is the way the Christmas carol begins. Those words catch what Psalm 97 is all about.

The psalm divides into three segments, each marked with two words indicating joy: the earth is called to rejoice and be glad (vv. 1–5); Zion is glad and rejoices (vv. 6–9); the righteous experience joy and are called to rejoice (vv. 10–12).

Let the Whole Earth Rejoice (97:1–5)

This psalm portrays the Lord as king (v. 1). What could that mean? Immediately the psalm reveals a certain mystery about this declaration.

This King's throne is surrounded by clouds and thick darkness, with fire and lightning. The earth quakes, and the mountains melt like wax. So it is with the King, the Lord!

But more is said, in the imaginative language of this description of the presence of God. The Lord's throne is founded on two pillars, marking the characteristics of this King's reign: one is marked *righteousness*; the other *justice*.

This is also a down-to-earth psalm. The thematic word in this first section is *earth*, which frames verses 1 through 5 and appears again in verse 4. The earth is called on to rejoice over the Lord's being king (v. 1). At the terrors of the Lord's fire and lightning, the earth looks on and trembles (v. 4). The mighty mountains melt before Yahweh, who is Lord of all the earth (v. 5).

The psalm begins with the declaration that the Lord is king and invites the earth to rejoice (v. 1). The description of the coming of the Lord uses the typical language of *theophany*, or revealing of God (see also Pss. 18:7–15 and 50:1–6). Here is a picture of the Lord ruling the earth, and the foundations of that rule are justice and righteousness.

Let the Towns of Judah Rejoice (97:6–9)

The *whole earth* focus of verses 1–5 continues in verses 6–7. All people can see the splendor of Yahweh, "the LORD," and anyone with some other god is shamed. In fact, when the Lord appears as king, all other heavenly beings (the existence of these beings or gods is assumed) will bow down!

The focus narrows, and the speaker begins to speak *to* God, rather than *about* God (vv. 8–9). The good news is that the Lord is ruling as king (v. 1). Because that is so, Jerusalem (Zion) and the towns of Judah are rejoicing. Their God, the Lord, ranks above all the "gods." And, to come back down to earth, the earth is ruled by the Lord, too (vv. 8–9).

Let Each Individual Rejoice! (97:10–11)

The psalm ends as it began, on a note of rejoicing. The psalmist has just announced, "For you, O LORD, are most high over all the earth; you are exalted far above all gods" (v. 9). The first two parts of the psalm have emphasized the Lord's might as king, as judge, and as the one exalted above the earth and the gods. All of this is cause for celebration and rejoicing, on the part of Jerusalem, the outlying towns, the peoples of the earth, even the population of the heavens!

But where does this leave the individual believer who is worshiping in the temple? Verses 10–11 speak about these persons, promising them the

Lord's love and protection. And there will be joy! Finally, the psalm
invites the "righteous," that is, the congregation of worshipers of the
Lord, to rejoice and give thanks (v. 12).

A Joyful Christmas

With good reason the churches have selected three of these "Lord is
king" psalms (96, 97, 98) as readings for Christmas Day. All three have
something of the sounds of Christmas about them, with heaven and
nature singing (Psalm 96), with the whole earth rejoicing (Psalm 97), and
with the sounding of trumpets and horns (Psalm 98). "I've got the joy,
joy, joy, joy down in my heart" goes the old gospel song. This psalm
(97:11) comes close to saying the same thing.

FIT FOR A KING
Psalm 98

A Psalm.

98:1 **O sing to the LORD a new song,**
     for he has done marvelous things.
   His right hand and his holy arm
     have gotten him victory.
  2 **The LORD has made known his victory;**
     he has revealed his vindication in the sight of the nations.
  3 **He has remembered his steadfast love and faithfulness**
     to the house of Israel.
   All the ends of the earth have seen
     the victory of our God.

  4 **Make a joyful noise to the LORD, all the earth;**
     break forth into joyous song and sing praises.
  5 **Sing praises to the LORD with the lyre,**
     with the lyre and the sound of melody.
  6 **With trumpets and the sound of the horn**
     make a joyful noise before the King, the LORD.

  7 **Let the sea roar, and all that fills it;**
     the world and those who live in it.
  8 **Let the floods clap their hands;**
     let the hills sing together for joy
  9 **at the presence of the LORD, for he is coming**
     to judge the earth.

**He will judge the world with righteousness,
and the peoples with equity.**

Like the "kingship of the Lord" psalms that surround it, Psalm 98 calls for praise to the Lord as king and celebration of the Lord's rule (see Psalms 93, 95, 96, 97, 99). At the center of the psalm is the call to sing praises to "the King, the LORD" (v. 6).

The heading, "A Psalm," designates this as a musical piece suitable for use in worship; the psalm itself suggests instrumental accompaniment (vv. 5–6). The psalm divides into three sections: praise to the Lord because of past victories (vv. 1–3); praise to the Lord, the ruling King (vv. 4–6); praise to the Lord who is coming to judge (vv. 7–9).

Victory Celebration (98:1–3)

The psalm begins by telling *what* it is all about: the gathered people of God are invited to "sing to the LORD a new song." Here is a call to break out of traditional ruts and bring some fresh music into the worship service! Since this call also occurs elsewhere (see Ps. 96:1; also 33:3; 40:3; 144:9; 149:1; Isa. 42:10), the point appears to have been an important one to make. There must have been those who wanted only the "old songs" (the good old hymns that everybody knows) and those who wanted to make use of some contemporary ones. This psalm (and the ones listed above) is on the side of those who want to try something new. According to the Bible, the composition of new songs continues even into the music of the heavenly choruses (Rev. 5:9–10).

The psalm continues by indicating *why* the people are invited to sing some new songs: because the Lord has done some marvelous things (v. 1)! The statement is often made that biblical religion is a "historical religion." That is true in the sense that the Bible indicates how God has worked through historical acts, such as the exodus, the conquest of Canaan, and the like. "Historical," however, does not mean that God worked only in the past. The "marvelous things" that God has done continue into the present! If God does some new things, then there ought to be some new songs of praise celebrating them.

Three times the psalm speaks of a "victory" the Lord has accomplished (vv. 1, 2, 3). The Hebrew noun here is *yeshuah*, which can have the sense "rescue, salvation," as well as "victory." The name Jesus is based on the Greek form of the word and has the sense "salvation" (Matt. 1:21). The reference in Psalm 98 is to an act of rescue or saving done by the Lord (v. 1) that is of such significance that the population of the whole

planet knows about it (v. 3). Does this refer to the return from exile and
the rebuilding of the temple after 539 B.C.?

Praise the Lord! (98:4–6)

This section indicates *who* is to praise the Lord, and tells *how* that praising is to be carried out. The end of verse 3 declares that the whole earth
has witnessed God's victory or rescuing action. Now all those peoples of
the earth are invited to respond by joining in praise to the Lord.

How is that praising to be done? By means of singing, with the accompaniment of stringed instruments (the lyre) as well as wind instruments
(the trumpet and horn).

The section begins and ends by declaring that such praise ought to be
joyful. The scene is a magnificent one: the sounds of music are coming
from the entire earth, a mighty "Hallelujah" chorus, praising the Lord,
the King!

The Coming of the Lord (98:7–9)

The final segment of the psalm indicates *who* ought to join in singing the
new song and also provides some fresh reasons *why* the singing of praises ought to be carried out.

The psalmist thinks big. Called on to praise are not just the congregation of the faithful but all who live in the world (v. 7)! Included in the call
to praise are the seas and the variety of creatures that live in the sea (Pss.
8:8; 104:25). The rivers (NRSV, "floods") are called to "clap their hands" for
excitement and joy, as one claps hands at the crowning of a king (2 Kings
11:12). The hills are portrayed as alive with the sound of music as they sing
joyfully at the Lord's coming. Who should join in this praise? All humans
in the world, but also the sea and all life it contains, the rivers, and the hills.

Finally, *why* should they praise God? The eye is now on the future,
when the Lord will come to hold court and judge all those living on earth.

In sum, Psalm 98 calls for praise because of what God has done in the
past (vv. 1–3); it encourages praise to the Lord in the present (vv. 4–6)
and looks forward to the coming of the Lord, when even nature will join
in the celebrating (vv. 7–9).

Aggiornamento

The Italians have a fine word indicating what Psalm 98 is all about. It was
Pope John XXIII who called the church to the work of *aggiornamento*, a
continual updating of old traditions to meet the needs of a new time.

The church is not always so quick to adapt to realities of new situations. I can recall, for example, years of sitting in a church, joining in prayers printed in the back of a hymnbook, asking the Lord for safe passage for all those traveling "by land or by sea." That was fine, except that in those days the air was filled with those traveling by airplane. This psalm calls for a bringing up to date, an *aggiornamento*, so that the church's praises keep up with the marvelous things happening in the world.

Praise that is fresh and creative, that remembers the past while taking place in the present, that anticipates the coming of the Lord in the future—such is the sort of praise called for in these psalms, praise that is fit for a King.

HOLY, HOLY, HOLY
Psalm 99

99:1 The LORD is king; let the peoples tremble!
　　　He sits enthroned upon the cherubim; let the earth quake!
　² The LORD is great in Zion;
　　　he is exalted over all the peoples.
　³ Let them praise your great and awesome name.
　　　Holy is he!
　⁴ Mighty King, lover of justice,
　　　you have established equity;
　　you have executed justice
　　　and righteousness in Jacob.
　⁵ Extol the LORD our God;
　　　worship at his footstool.
　　　Holy is he!

　⁶ Moses and Aaron were among his priests,
　　　Samuel also was among those who called on his name.
　　　They cried to the LORD, and he answered them.
　⁷ He spoke to them in the pillar of cloud;
　　　they kept his decrees,
　　　and the statutes that he gave them.

　⁸ O LORD our God, you answered them;
　　　you were a forgiving God to them,
　　　but an avenger of their wrongdoings.
　⁹ Extol the LORD our God,
　　　and worship at his holy mountain;
　　　for the LORD our God is holy.

The old hymn is one of the standard songs of praise, used at the beginning of a service of worship:

> Holy, holy, holy, Lord God Almighty!
> Early in the morning our song shall rise to thee.
> Holy, holy, holy, merciful and mighty!
> God in three Persons, blessed Trinity!

The hymn is based on the scene in Revelation 4:8–11, where there are creatures singing day and night, "Holy, holy, holy, the Lord God the Almighty. . . ." The hymn recalls the vision of the prophet Isaiah, where he saw and heard the heavenly creatures singing, "Holy, holy, holy is the LORD of hosts" (Isa. 6:3).

Psalm 99 also offers a triple "holy": "Holy is he!" (vv. 3 and 5) and "Holy is the LORD our God" (v. 9, following the Hebrew word order). In order to understand the psalm, it is important to bring the sense of *holy* into sharp focus.

A Note on the Meaning of *Holy*

The fundamental idea behind the Hebrew word *qadosh*, or "holy," is *apart* or *separate*. A place may be *holy* because it is set apart since the Lord has appeared there ("holy ground," Exod. 3:5); or a place may be *holy* because God is described as living there ("holy temple," Ps. 11:4; Hab. 2:20). Persons connected with holy places are themselves called holy (the priests, Lev. 21:6), and even their clothing is "separate" or "holy" (Lev. 16:4, 32). A day may be called holy, that is, separate (Neh. 8:9, 10, 11). The Sabbath day is to be kept separate, or holy (Exod. 20:8–11; Isa. 58:13–14).

To say that God is holy is to stress the otherness or separateness of God. Isaiah saw the Lord and heard the angels singing, "Holy, holy, holy," the repetition emphasizing the idea of separateness (Isa. 6:3). It was twentieth-century theologian Karl Barth who liked to speak of God as "wholly other."

Yet, according to the Bible, the Lord has not cut off contact with humans but has come to live with them. Hosea caught it just right: "I am God and no mortal, the Holy One in your midst" (Hos. 11:9). The Fourth Gospel speaks the same way: "And the Word became flesh and lived among us" (John 1:14).

This psalm concludes the series of "the LORD is King" psalms (Pss. 93, 95–99). Psalm 96:9 speaks of the Lord's "holy splendor," and 97:12 refers to the Lord's "holy name," but none of these hymns speaks of the Lord as holy with the emphasis given that theme in Psalm 99.

These "holy" statements provide a clue to the structure of the psalm, dividing it into three parts. The expression "Holy is he!" concludes verses 1–3 and 4–5. Verses 6–9 conclude with "For holy is the LORD our God" (Hebrew word order).

The King Who Is a Lover (99:1–5)

Like the other "kingship of the Lord" psalms, this one utilizes the picture of a *king* as a way of understanding who God is. The first two sections highlight two aspects of God's kingship. With verses 1–3, the emphasis is on the Lord's *might*. One's eyes are lifted up to view the heavenly King. The proper reaction of the people at the Lord's ruling is to tremble (v. 1). The cherubim were the winged creatures that were part of the decoration of the Lord's throne in the temple. They represented beings residing in heaven; when the Lord is seated on the heavenly throne, the earth itself quakes! Verse 2 continues the description of the Lord's might. Though ruling in Jerusalem on Mount Zion, where the temple is located, the Lord is greater than all the nations around Jerusalem. These nations are called on to praise the Lord's name, because "Holy is he!"

In verses 4–5, the focus is on the Lord's *mercy*. This "Mighty King" is described as a lover, a lover of justice. Now the picture is of the Lord as a judge, seeing to it that justice, equity, and righteousness are established "in Jacob," that is, in the land of Israel.

What does it mean to establish justice and righteousness? The prophets make the matter quite clear. They speak in terms of action, of doing justice (Micah 6:6–8). "Doing justice" involves taking up the cause of the powerless, that is, the widow, the orphan, and the poor (Isa. 1:10–17, 21–26; 10:1–4).

To summarize: God is great and awesome, seated on a heavenly throne, exalted over all the nations of the earth (vv. 1–3). But God is also merciful and good, caring about the sort of treatment that the powerless receive in the nation's courts. This concern for justice and righteousness is also a reason for praising God, the Holy One.

The God Who Answers (99:6–9)

The final section highlights the Lord's work of *answering* the cries of the Lord's people (vv. 6, 8). The theme of the "otherness" or the holiness of God is sounded in verse 9. But the emphasis in verses 6–8 is on the Lord's nearness, responding to the cries of the people in distress. Moses and Aaron bridged the gap between God and people at the time of the exodus from Egypt (Exodus 4, 5–11). Samuel prayed and the Israelites were delivered from the Philistines (1 Sam. 7:7–11) or the Lord sent thunder and rain (1 Sam. 12:6–18). The "pillar of cloud" led the Israelites during the daytime as they made their way out of Egypt at the time of the exodus. Through that cloud, the Lord spoke to the people (Exod. 33:9; Num. 12:5–9).

With verse 8, the psalm writer again remembers how God has answered prayers and forgiven sins. Both are reasons for praising God and declaring God as holy: deliverances from enemies and the forgiveness of sins.

The psalm concludes with a call to praise God, "for the LORD our God is holy" (v. 9).

DOXOLOGY
Psalm 100

A Psalm of thanksgiving.

100:1 **Make a joyful noise to the LORD, all the earth.**
   2   **Worship the LORD with gladness;**
        come into his presence with singing.

   3 **Know that the LORD is God.**
     It is he that made us, and we are his;
     we are his people, and the sheep of his pasture.

   4 **Enter his gates with thanksgiving,**
     and his courts with praise.
     Give thanks to him, bless his name.

   5 **For the LORD is good;**
     his steadfast love endures forever,
     and his faithfulness to all generations.

"Let's close by standing and singing the Doxology" or "Let's begin by singing the Doxology." Such is the way many a church meeting or meal or celebration begins. The paraphrase of this psalm by Isaac Watts, long known as "Old Hundredth," belongs among the most well known hymns of the English-speaking Christian church:

> Praise God, from whom all blessings flow;
> Praise him, all creatures here below;
> Praise him above, ye heav'nly host;
> Praise Father, Son, and Holy Ghost.

The standard form of the hymn of praise in the book of Psalms is a *call to praise* in the imperative mood, followed by *reasons* for that praise (see on Psalm 113). Psalm 100 is dominated by a series of seven imperative verbs: "Make . . . Worship . . . come . . . Know . . . Enter . . . Give . . . bless." The psalm invites a people gathered before the temple area to praise God (vv. 1–4) and then gives reasons indicating why praise is appropriate (v. 5).

After the string of six hymns celebrating the kingship of the Lord (Psalms 93, 95–99), this seventh psalm concludes the series of hymns with seven invitations to join in activities aimed at praising God. The heading identifies the psalm as one aimed at giving thanks to the Lord (see v. 4).

Who We Are (100:3)

Six of the imperatives found in sequence in this psalm have to do with actions. The central one, however, expresses an intellectual activity, "Know" (v. 3). This central statement indicates who the Lord is and who those are who worship the Lord. "The LORD" translates the Hebrew name Yahweh, which is the personal name for God, as revealed to Moses (Exod. 3:13–15). To say, "Yahweh is God," is thus to say that the God revealed to the Hebrews is the one and only God, the God of the entire universe.

And who are we, who sing and pray this psalm? The answer is given in terms of relationship to God. We have been created by God and we belong to God. To put it another way, we are God's people. Or to express things in pictorial terms, God is the shepherd, and we are the sheep of God's pasture.

In sum, Yahweh, the God of the Hebrews, is the one God who rules the world and universe. And we are those whom God created and who remain God's people. As a shepherd cares for sheep, so our God cares for us.

What We Are to Do (100:1–4)

The remaining six imperative verbs are linked to an invitation to praise God. They provide for us a rather complete description of what praising God means.

Praising the Lord ought to be *joyful* and marked by *gladness*, according to verses 1 and 2. Since the psalm speaks of "noise," we can be sure that there is a certain *enthusiasm* involved in praising. And praise is not confined to the people of Israel but is *universal*; here the whole earth is invited to join in.

Part of the "joyful noise" was *singing*. One wonders: Since peoples were apparently present from the nations of the world, did they sing in Hebrew? Whatever was done, the singing must have been loud (noise!), radiating happiness, and done on the move, as the people "came into the presence" of the Lord.

Verse 4 indicates something of the content of the singing. Apparently, these were songs expressing *thanksgiving* to God; the idea of thanks is expressed twice in verse 4. The people sang as they walked into the temple, not only thanking God but also simply *praising* (this is also the sense of "blessing") the Lord.

We, who are God's people, are invited to praise God with enthusiasm, joy, and thanksgiving.

Why We Should Praise (100:5)

Praising God, the psalms point out, is a reasonable thing to do. As noted above, the structure of the psalms of praise consists of a call to praise and reasons for praising. This psalm concludes in verse 5 with a triple set of reasons for giving praise to the Lord.

The Lord's goodness and steadfast love are often paired as reasons for praising (Pss. 106:1; 107:1; 118:1–4; 136:1, with repetitions of the reasons for praising throughout). "Steadfast love" (Hebrew, *hesed*) is that love that loves no matter what (see the discussion with Psalm 136). Psalm 99:6–8 gives some examples of the Lord's faithful care of the Lord's people; in Psalm 100, the declaration is made that this sort of faithfulness will always be there. The sense of "faithfulness" is reliable support; the same Hebrew root appears as the word for the sturdy pillars (NRSV, "supports") *supporting* the door frame in 2 Kings 18:16.

Worship and Witness

The centerpiece of this psalm, verse 3, tells us something about ourselves. In telling us who we are, that telling always relates us to God: God made us, and we belong to God. We are, in fact, God's people.

The writer of 1 Peter once reminded a Christian congregation who they were, and the description resonates with the description in this psalm: "But you are a chosen race, a royal priesthood, a holy nation, *God's own people*."

Then the writer added some words telling what God's own people are called to do: "proclaim the mighty acts of him who called you out of darkness into his marvelous light" (1 Peter 2:9).

God's people are called to worship and also to witness—or, in the words of Psalm 100 and 1 Peter, to praise and to proclaim.

THE WAY TO WALK
Psalm 101

Of David. A Psalm.

101:1 I will sing of loyalty and of justice;
    to you, O LORD, I will sing.
2 I will study the way that is blameless.
    When shall I attain it?

I will walk with integrity of heart
    within my house;
3 I will not set before my eyes
    anything that is base.

I hate the work of those who fall away;
    it shall not cling to me.
4 Perverseness of heart shall be far from me;
    I will know nothing of evil.

5 One who secretly slanders a neighbor
    I will destroy.
A haughty look and an arrogant heart
    I will not tolerate.

6 I will look with favor on the faithful in the land,
    so that they may live with me;
whoever walks in the way that is blameless
    shall minister to me.

7 No one who practices deceit
    shall remain in my house;
no one who utters lies
    shall continue in my presence.

8 Morning by morning I will destroy
    all the wicked in the land,
cutting off all evildoers
    from the city of the LORD.

A number of psalms are connected with events in the life of the king. These are classified as *royal psalms* and include Psalms 2, 18, 20, 21, 45, 72, 89, 101, 110, 132, and 144. Some of these psalms describe the king in extravagant terms and eventually became the seedbed for messianic hope (see the discussion of Psalm 2).

Psalm 101 is concerned with the behavior of the monarch, offering a
description of that behavior entirely in "I" form. This would then be a
piece the king could recite at such a time as his coronation; it could, of
course, be repeated at other times.

The heading links the psalm with David the king (see on Psalm 3) and
identifies the piece as a psalm, that is, a composition to be sung, possibly
with musical accompaniment. The psalm begins with three resolutions:
"I will sing . . . I will study . . . I will walk" (vv. 1–2). The rest of Psalm
101 provides further description of the singing, the studying, and the
walking (vv. 3–8).

Singing, Studying, and Walking (101:1–2a)

Psalm 100, a hymn of praise, concludes with a declaration about the
Lord's goodness, steadfast love (*hesed*), and faithfulness. Psalm 101 hooks
up with the *hesed* theme, now translating the word as "loyalty."

What would it mean to "sing of loyalty"? The word *hesed* means God's
unconditional love toward humans, the sort of love the New Testament
calls *agape* (1 Corinthians 13) and George Matheson's hymn describes as
the "love that will not let me go" (for *hesed*, see on Psalm 136). The
Psalms sing a great deal about this loyalty or steadfast love; note the "new
song" in Psalm 98:1–3 and especially Psalm 136 with its refrain "for his
steadfast love endures forever." Psalm 136 provides an example of what
it means to "sing of steadfast love" or "loyalty."

The sense of "justice" (Hebrew, *mishpat*) is right relationships among
persons. Psalm 99 praises the Lord for establishing these kinds of relationships in the courts (v. 4). The prophets speak a good deal about
"doing justice," which involves taking up the cause of the widow, the
orphan, and the poor (Isa. 1:10–17, see v. 17; 1:21–26, see vv. 21 and 23;
Amos 5:21–24; Micah 6:6–8). The prophet Isaiah sang an unforgettable
song about justice, or more exactly, the lack of it in the city where he
lived (Isa. 5:1–7, see v. 7).

This is a song for the king to sing. The king begins by announcing that
the song will be about those twin themes that are pillars of biblical religion: steadfast love and justice.

The psalm invites the king to sing but also to *study*. The book of
Psalms began with a picture of a person who was happy, and that happiness resulted from studying the Bible (Ps. 1:1–3). Psalm 101 invites the
king to do some thinking about ethics; in the language of the Psalms,
about how one ought to *walk*. What sort of things would be expected of
a king who sang hymns to the Lord and was thus a believer? The remainder of the psalm provides a picture of how such a believing king ought to
"walk," that is, how the king ought to live.

Video of a King (101:2b–8)

What we have in Psalm 101 is not a *portrait* of a king (like those flattering paintings on the walls of European palaces, inspired more by the fees than the facts) but rather a description of a good king *in action*. We could think of it as videotape showing short scenes from the life of the king.

The first scene shows the king moving about the palace, a man of obvious honesty and good taste (vv. 2b–3). The "heart" is the innermost part of a person. The king has resolved to walk with "integrity of heart"; the same thing is said in the negative with the declaration that "perverseness of heart" will be far from this king, as will all evil (v. 4).

The next scenes, focusing on gossipers and the arrogant, deal with familiar themes known from Proverbs, which would have been a part of the king's education. Proverbs 30:10, for example, has some advice for those living in the royal residence:

> Do not slander a servant to a master,
> or the servant will curse you.

The "haughty look" in Psalm 101:5 is literally "eyes lifted up high," so that one "looks down the nose" at another. Such arrogance is the first in the list of things the Lord hates (Prov. 6:16–19; 21:4; see also Ps. 131:1). This is the external symptom of an inner attitude, an "arrogant heart" (Ps. 101:5).

The camera was on the king's eyes in verse 3. In verse 5 it is on the eyes of the haughty. Verse 6 again focuses on the eyes of the king (literal Hebrew, "my eyes are upon the faithful in the land"). This time the statement is a positive one. The king has noticed certain faithful persons and will reward them with staff positions in the royal residence. The king has been studying the "way that is blameless" (v. 2); those who walk in that way will one day have a job in the palace.

If verse 6 describes those who will be given a position on the royal staff, verse 7 provides the other side of the picture. Persons who lack integrity will be ousted. The Hebrew again focuses on the eyes, "before my eyes" (NRSV, "in my presence"). Finally, verse 8 articulates the ruler's continuing resolve to rid Jerusalem of crime.

Not Just for Kings

This royal psalm adds a few more details to the description of what a king ought to be like. Here is a motion picture of a good ruler going about his work, helping the faithful to prosper, and punishing those who are evil (see Rom. 13:3).

Those familiar with the Old Testament will recognize in this portrayal of a good king the picture of what a ruler ought to be like, as provided in wisdom literature, especially the book of Proverbs. Those who are also familiar with the New Testament will discover here, as in the other royal psalms, features of the One who announced that with his presence, the kingdom of God was at hand (Mark 1:14–15). The old psalm thus becomes part of the good news, intended for all peoples, not just for kings.

GOD KNOWS HOW MUCH I WANT TO STAY
Psalm 102

A prayer of one afflicted, when faint and pleading before the LORD.

102:1 Hear my prayer, O LORD;
　　　let my cry come to you.
　　2 Do not hide your face from me
　　　in the day of my distress.
　　　Incline your ear to me;
　　　answer me speedily in the day when I call.

　　3 For my days pass away like smoke,
　　　and my bones burn like a furnace.
　　4 My heart is stricken and withered like grass;
　　　I am too wasted to eat my bread.
　　5 Because of my loud groaning
　　　my bones cling to my skin.
　　6 I am like an owl of the wilderness,
　　　like a little owl of the waste places.
　　7 I lie awake;
　　　I am like a lonely bird on the housetop.
　　8 All day long my enemies taunt me;
　　　those who deride me use my name for a curse.
　　9 For I eat ashes like bread,
　　　and mingle tears with my drink,
　　10 because of your indignation and anger;
　　　for you have lifted me up and thrown me aside.
　　11 My days are like an evening shadow;
　　　I wither away like grass.

　　12 But you, O LORD, are enthroned forever;
　　　your name endures to all generations.
　　13 You will rise up and have compassion on Zion,
　　　for it is time to favor it;
　　　the appointed time has come.

¹⁴ **For your servants hold its stones dear,**
  and have pity on its dust.
¹⁵ **The nations will fear the name of the LORD,**
  and all the kings of the earth your glory.
¹⁶ **For the LORD will build up Zion;**
  he will appear in his glory.
¹⁷ **He will regard the prayer of the destitute,**
  and will not despise their prayer.

¹⁸ **Let this be recorded for a generation to come,**
  so that a people yet unborn may praise the LORD:
¹⁹ **that he looked down from his holy height,**
  from heaven the LORD looked at the earth,
²⁰ **to hear the groans of the prisoners,**
  to set free those who were doomed to die;
²¹ **so that the name of the LORD may be declared in Zion,**
  and his praise in Jerusalem,
²² **when peoples gather together,**
  and kingdoms, to worship the LORD.

²³ **He has broken my strength in midcourse;**
  he has shortened my days.
²⁴ **"O my God," I say, "do not take me away**
  at the midpoint of my life,
 you whose years endure
  throughout all generations."

²⁵ **Long ago you laid the foundation of the earth,**
  and the heavens are the work of your hands.
²⁶ **They will perish, but you endure;**
  they will all wear out like a garment.
 You change them like clothing, and they pass away;
²⁷ **but you are the same, and your years have no end.**
²⁸ **The children of your servants shall live secure;**
  their offspring shall be established in your presence.

> "Time to come in now!"
> the mellow voice of love in the
> darkening dust of a distant day,
> my barefoot, carefree days
> of firefly lanterns,
> cricket-chirped curfews
> and the serious business of play.
>
> No harshness to remember,
> but firmness born of care,

the loving care of Mother;
she knew how much we liked to play.

"Time to come in now!"
I seem to hear God say
in the deepening dusk of my
sunset day.

God knows how much I want to stay.
(Gerhard Frost, "God Knows,"
in *Seasons of a Lifetime*, p. 153)

These lines catch the sentiments of the psalmist in Psalm 102, conscious that time is running out (vv. 3, 11) and asking God to allow her to live a while longer (v. 24).

Psalm 102 is the only *individual lament* in Book IV (Psalms 90–106) and is made up of the typical elements of that type (see on Psalm 13). Verses 1–2 express a *request* or *call for help*; verses 3–11 are *complaints*; verses 12–22 express *trust* and *praise*; verses 23–24 are again *complaint* and *request*; and verses 25–28 conclude the psalm with *praise*.

The heading indicates that this is a prayer from one who is hurting badly. The fact that there are no hints that the psalm was used as part of a worship service suggests that these lament psalms could be used in the midst of real life, either alone or in a circle of family or friends.

This psalm is exceptionally rich in poetic imagery, speaking of days like smoke or an evening shadow (vv. 3, 11), bones burning like a furnace (v. 3), heart and self withering like grass (vv. 4, 11). The writer feels like an owl in the wilderness or a bird on a housetop (vv. 6–7). Food tastes like ashes, and drink is mixed with tears (v. 9). The earth and the heavens will pass away like a worn-out garment (v. 26).

"I Wither Away like Grass" (102:1–11)

The urgency of the writer's situation is indicated with the opening call for help in verses 1–2, following the Hebrew word order: "LORD, hear my prayer!" It is important that the one praying have the Lord's attention. It is also important that the prayer be answered "speedily," the request being made first in negative and then in positive form (v. 2).

Verses 3–11 present the complaint of the psalm, in "I," "they," and "you" forms. The major emphasis is on the "I" complaint (vv. 3–7, 9, 11), with a "they "complaint in verse 8 and a harsh "you" complaint (directed against the Lord) in verse 10.

These "I" complaints are exceptionally lively, made with an unusual variety of poetic imagery. The first complaint is bracketed with laments over the shortness of "my days" (vv. 3, 11). These days disappear "like smoke," and "my bones burn like a furnace" (v. 3). The days go away as quickly as the evening shadows, and "I wither away like grass" (v. 11). Such a lament over the shortness of life is found in a good number of biblical texts (Job 14:1; Pss. 39:4–6; 49:10–12, 20; 90:5–6; 103:14–16; Eccl. 3:19–22; 6:12).

The "withered grass" image also appears in verse 4, followed by a literal complaint describing the psalmist's lack of appetite and resultant weight loss (vv. 4–5). Life's supportive rhythms are disturbed: the psalmist has trouble eating (v. 4), drinking (v. 9), and sleeping (v. 7). Verses 6 and 7 offer unusual uses of bird imagery to describe the human situation.

The "they" complaint in verse 8 indicates that the psalmist's fellow human beings only make the situation worse. Verse 10 is a bitter complaint directed against "you," that is, against God. "Rather than helping me," says the psalmist, "you have picked me up and thrown me away, like so much garbage!" As has been noted, "my days" of verse 11 then ties up with the same expression that appeared at the beginning of the lament in verse 3. The words are those of a person who senses that death is near: "I wither away like grass."

"All Who Hold Its Stones Dear" (102:12–22)

After this intensely individual section, the psalmist has spliced into Psalm 102 a piece concerned with the future of Jerusalem. After the gloomy attention to the brevity and frailty of human existence, the psalm modulates into a major key, with a sharp "But you, O LORD!" putting the focus on the eternity and the power of the Lord (vv. 12–13).

These words were written after the destruction of Jerusalem in 587 B.C. (vv. 13–14). Biblical scholar Claus Westermann, who experienced the destruction of the city of Berlin in World War II, reflects on verse 14: "all who have experienced their city's destruction understand such phrases as 'hold her stones dear' and 'have pity on her dust'" (*The Living Psalms*, p. 114).

Verses 15–17 portray a day in the future when the nations will stream to worship in a rebuilt Jerusalem (see Isa. 2:1–5), and when the Lord will hear the prayers of persons like the one praying this psalm. The composer of Psalm 102 is so certain that the Lord will deliver those who are suffering and will rebuild Jerusalem that she asks that the story be written down, for the sake of children and even those yet to be born (vv. 18–22; on the theme of concern for the children, see Exod. 12:26; 13:14–15; Deut. 6:20–25; Josh. 4:6–7; Joel 1:2–3).

"Not at the Midpoint of My Life" (102:23–28)

After the lengthy segment in verses 12–22 concerned with the nation and the nations, the writer returns to his own situation. The psalmist is again concerned with "my days" (vv. 3, 11), fearing that the Lord is going to pull him out at halftime rather than letting him finish the whole game (vv. 23–24).

In contrast to the frailty and temporality of the psalmist's own life (v. 23), the psalm again speaks of the might (vv. 25–26) and the enduring character (v. 27) of the Lord. Finally, the psalm ends on a hopeful note about the future of the "people yet unborn" (v. 28; see v. 18).

Happy New Year

The lectionary assigns Psalm 102 to be read on New Year's Eve, no doubt because at the end of another year one is especially aware of the swift passing of the days. The psalm offers a good many reminders that we will not live forever. Life has a midpoint, which ought not be the end point (vv. 23–24). Job spoke of his days going by "swifter than a weaver's shuttle" (Job 7:6); this psalm speaks of the days disappearing like smoke or the evening shadows or the withering grass (vv. 3, 11).

But those pictures are not the whole story. Psalm 102 holds this realistic view of the brevity of human life against the background of the eternity of God (vv. 12, 24, 27). This God has a reputation for answering prayer (v. 2) and even for giving those to whom God is saying, "Time to come in now!" (though they want so much to stay) a new sort of life (John 14:1–7; Rom. 8:38–39; 1 Corinthians 15).

AMAZING GRACE
Psalm 103

Of David.

> 103:1 Bless the LORD, O my soul,
> and all that is within me,
> bless his holy name.
> ² Bless the LORD, O my soul,
> and do not forget all his benefits—
> ³ who forgives all your iniquity,
> who heals all your diseases,

⁴ who redeems your life from the Pit,
    who crowns you with steadfast love and mercy,
⁵ who satisfies you with good as long as you live
    so that your youth is renewed like the eagle's.

⁶ The LORD works vindication
    and justice for all who are oppressed.
⁷ He made known his ways to Moses,
    his acts to the people of Israel.
⁸ The LORD is merciful and gracious,
    slow to anger and abounding in steadfast love.
⁹ He will not always accuse,
    nor will he keep his anger forever.
¹⁰ He does not deal with us according to our sins,
    nor repay us according to our iniquities.
¹¹ For as the heavens are high above the earth,
    so great is his steadfast love toward those who fear him;
¹² as far as the east is from the west,
    so far he removes our transgressions from us.
¹³ As a father has compassion for his children,
    so the LORD has compassion for those who fear him.
¹⁴ For he knows how we were made;
    he remembers that we are dust.

¹⁵ As for mortals, their days are like grass;
    they flourish like a flower of the field;
¹⁶ for the wind passes over it, and it is gone,
    and its place knows it no more.
¹⁷ But the steadfast love of the LORD is from everlasting to
    everlasting on those who fear him,
    and his righteousness to children's children,
¹⁸ to those who keep his covenant
    and remember to do his commandments.

¹⁹ The LORD has established his throne in the heavens,
    and his kingdom rules over all.
²⁰ Bless the LORD, O you his angels,
    you mighty ones who do his bidding,
    obedient to his spoken word.
²¹ Bless the LORD, all his hosts,
    his ministers that do his will.
²² Bless the LORD, all his works,
    in all places of his dominion.
    Bless the LORD, O my soul.

The old hymn remains a favorite:

> Amazing grace, how sweet the sound,
> That saved a wretch like me!
> I once was lost, but now am found;
> Was blind, but now I see.

The Old Testament equivalent for "amazing grace," that is, God's astonishing love, is *hesed*, usually translated as "steadfast love." That notion is at the center of Psalm 103, with the word occurring in verses 4, 8, 11, and 17.

The psalm is carefully constructed, following the basic format of a *hymn* (see on Psalm 113), with *calls to praise* in verses 1–2 and 20–22 supported by *reasons* for praise in verses 6–10, 11–14, 15–18, and 19.

Renewed like an Eagle (103:1–5)

The expression "Bless the LORD, O my soul" that frames Psalms 103 and 104 has the sense of a charge to oneself: "Now praise the Lord!" Instead of saying, "Remember the good things the Lord has done!" (Psalms 104, 105), Psalm 103 says, "*Don't forget* the good things God has done!" The danger of forgetting is especially a theme in Deuteronomy: "take care that you do not forget the LORD, who brought you out of the land of Egypt" (Deut. 6:12; see also 4:9, 23; 32:18).

After the opening call to praise, the reasons for praise are listed. The Lord forgives wrongdoing and heals diseases. The Lord rescues from near death ("the Pit"). The Lord treats the person like royalty, here described as dressed for the day of coronation (Ps. 21:3) with a crown made of steadfast love and mercy. The eagle is a symbol for fresh, youthful strength (see Isa. 40:31). Biblical scholar Claus Westermann writes, "The sequence of six verbs here—forgive, heal, redeem, crown, satisfy, renew—shows how God's actions encompass the whole of human life. Here is no abstract forgiveness of sin, but the whole person is involved, body and soul" (*Ausgewählte Psalmen*, p. 169; my translation).

The Lord's Amazing Grace (103:6–19)

This section of the psalm can be divided into three parts, each containing the Hebrew word *hesed*, which means God's amazing grace.

1. Verses 6–10 speak of the Lord's *inclusive* love, for *all* who are oppressed. "The Lord does mighty acts" is the sense of the first line. Verse 7 refers to the exodus, the central act of deliverance in the Old Testament. Verses 8–10 speak of how the Lord relates to humans in view of their *fallibility*, their tendency to do wrong. The assertion in verse 8 is

like a creed and stands at the center of the entire psalm (see also Exod. 34:6). The Hebrew root for the word translated "merciful" is *reḥem*, "womb." Thus the picture behind "merciful" is the kind of affection a mother has for a child of her own womb; the word could be translated "motherly love."

The accent in "steadfast love" is love that is undeserved; verse 10 provides an example of how that steadfast love works. The Lord does not deal with us according to the readout on a cosmic computer that has kept track of our actions but with the kind of mercy and love that a mother has for her own child.

2. Verses 11–14 offer three comparisons. The first is spatial: the Lord's love is as high as the sky and as wide as the distance from east to west; in other words, it cannot be measured. The second comparison is from family life: the Lord's love is like that of a father for his children. The story of God as "waiting father" in Luke 15 may be viewed as an expansion of this idea (see also Jer. 31:9 and Hos. 11:1–7). The psalm therefore balances the notion of God's "motherly love" with the comparison of God's love to that of a father for his children. Finally, the Lord loves us, says the psalmist, despite our weaknesses. The Lord, after all, made us and knows that we have been constructed out of dust (Gen. 2:7; 3:19; Ps. 104:29).

3. Verses 15–18 provide yet another angle on the Lord's steadfast love, this time in contrast to human *mortality*. This lament about the shortness of human life is a familiar theme in the Psalms (90:5–6; 102:11) as well as in other parts of the Old Testament (Job 14; Isa. 40:6–7). In contrast to humans who flourish for a time and then die, the Lord's love lasts forever.

This sort of love calls forth a response from the Lord's people in the form of remembering the covenant and the commandments.

Praise to the King (103:19–22)

After the pictures of the Lord as loving parent, Psalm 103 concludes with a picture of the Lord as heavenly king, ruling over all that exists. All the beings that exist in heaven are called to praise the Lord (see Pss. 29:1–3; 148:1–4). The psalm comes back down to earth with the call to "all his works" in verse 22 (see 104:13, 24) and ends as it began, with the psalmist telling himself to praise the Lord.

An Amazing Impact

In its present context, Psalm 103 is linked with Psalm 104 because only these two psalms begin and end with "Bless the LORD, O my soul." At the center of Psalm 103 is the Lord's steadfast love. God is portrayed as loving with motherly affection ("mercy," "merciful," in vv. 4, 8) and also fatherly compassion (v. 13). Psalm 103 tells of a God who *delivers* the nation from bondage (v. 7) and the individual from sin (vv. 10–13). In Psalm 104, God is not parent but rather king in heaven (vv. 1–4) and also creator, cloud rider, sustainer of all life. Taken together, these two psalms complement one another. Psalm 103 speaks of *salvation*, the second article of the Apostle's Creed; the concern of Psalm 104 is *creation* (the first article) and *the Spirit* (the third article).

Few psalms have had the impact of Psalm 103. Lectionaries list it as a reading for 8 Epiphany, the Sundays between September 11 and 17 (A), August 21 and 27 (C), May 24 and 28 (B), and St. Michael and All Angels. It is traditionally read at Thanksgiving services. Its musical settings range from the hymn "My Soul Now Praise Your Maker!" by Catherine Winkworth to "Bless the Lord" from the 1972 musical *Godspell*.

"THE WORLD IS SO FULL OF A NUMBER OF THINGS"
Psalm 104

104:1 Bless the LORD, O my soul.
    O LORD my God, you are very great.
    You are clothed with honor and majesty,
2   wrapped in light as with a garment.
    You stretch out the heavens like a tent,
3   you set the beams of your chambers on the waters,
    you make the clouds your chariot,
      you ride on the wings of the wind,
4 you make the winds your messengers,
    fire and flame your ministers.

5 You set the earth on its foundations,
    so that it shall never be shaken.
6 You cover it with the deep as with a garment;
    the waters stood above the mountains.
7 At your rebuke they flee;
    at the sound of your thunder they take to flight.
8 They rose up to the mountains, ran down to the valleys
    to the place that you appointed for them.
9 You set a boundary that they may not pass,
    so that they might not again cover the earth.

10 You make springs gush forth in the valleys;
    they flow between the hills,

[11] giving drink to every wild animal;
     the wild asses quench their thirst.
[12] By the streams the birds of the air have their habitation;
     they sing among the branches.
[13] From your lofty abode you water the mountains;
     the earth is satisfied with the fruit of your work.

[14] You cause the grass to grow for the cattle,
     and plants for people to use,
     to bring forth food from the earth,
[15]   and wine to gladden the human heart,
     oil to make the face shine,
     and bread to strengthen the human heart.
[16] The trees of the LORD are watered abundantly,
     the cedars of Lebanon that he planted.
[17] In them the birds build their nests;
     the stork has its home in the fir trees.
[18] The high mountains are for the wild goats;
     the rocks are a refuge for the coneys.
[19] You have made the moon to mark the seasons;
     the sun knows its time for setting.
[20] You make darkness, and it is night,
     when all the animals of the forest come creeping out.
[21] The young lions roar for their prey,
     seeking their food from God.
[22] When the sun rises, they withdraw
     and lie down in their dens.
[23] People go out to their work
     and to their labor until the evening.

[24] O LORD, how manifold are your works!
     In wisdom you have made them all;
     the earth is full of your creatures.
[25] Yonder is the sea, great and wide,
     creeping things innumerable are there,
     living things both small and great.
[26] There go the ships,
     and Leviathan that you formed to sport in it.

[27] These all look to you
     to give them their food in due season;
[28] when you give to them, they gather it up;
     when you open your hand, they are filled with good things.
[29] When you hide your face, they are dismayed;
     when you take away their breath, they die
     and return to their dust.

30 **When you send forth your spirit, they are created;**
    and you renew the face of the ground.

31 **May the glory of the LORD endure forever;**
    may the LORD rejoice in his works—
32 **who looks on the earth and it trembles,**
    who touches the mountains and they smoke.
33 **I will sing to the LORD as long as I live;**
    I will sing praise to my God while I have being.
34 **May my meditation be pleasing to him,**
    for I rejoice in the LORD.
35 **Let sinners be consumed from the earth,**
    and let the wicked be no more.
    Bless the LORD, O my soul.
    Praise the LORD!

The lines appear on the first page of Robert Louis Stevenson's book *A Child's Garden of Verses:*

> The world is so full of a number of things
> I'm sure we should all be as happy as kings.

These words could be taken as a title for Psalm 104, which delights in the "number of things" with which the world is filled.

A Pair of Psalms

Psalm 104 is the second in a series of four hymns that conclude Book IV of the Psalter. Psalms 103 and 104 have in common beginnings and endings that occur only here in the Bible: "Bless the LORD, O my soul." The contents of the two psalms are quite different, however. Psalm 103 centers on the steadfast love (*hesed*) and compassion of the Lord. As it concludes, Psalm 103 describes the Lord as heavenly *king* (v. 19) and calls on the "works" of the Lord to join in praise (v. 22), thus anticipating the theme of Psalm 104 ("works," 104:24). Psalm 104 picks up the picture of the Lord as *king* in heaven (vv. 1–4) but then moves quickly to describe the Lord's involvement with the earth and its creatures (vv. 5–30).

These two psalms are complementary in what they say about God. According to Psalm 103, God is the parent, compassionate, healing, merciful, and forgiving. Psalm 104 portrays God as creator, cloud rider, sustainer of the trees, the birds, all creatures, including humans. Taken together, these two psalms offer an Old Testament summary of God's work. Thinking in terms of the Apostle's Creed, Psalm 103 speaks of *redemption* (the second article) while Psalm 104 deals with *creation* (the first article) and the *work of the Spirit* (the third article).

The psalm consists of the basic elements of a *hymn* (see on Psalm 113), with *calls to praise* (vv. 1a, 35c) framing *reasons* for praise (vv. 1b–35b). The main body of the psalm may be divided into two parts that begin with "O LORD" (vv. 1b–23, 24–30) and a final section calling for the enduring of the honor of "the LORD" (vv. 31–35b).

How Great Thou Art (104:1–23)

After the brief call to praise, "Bless the LORD, O my soul," the focus of Psalm 104 is on God in the heavens. The Lord is great—constructing the heavens, using the clouds as a chariot, riding on the wind—and yet has a personal relationship with the psalmist, who addresses the Lord as "my God" (vv. 1–4).

With verse 5 the spotlight shifts to the earth and remains there, the word *earth* occurring seven times in the remainder of the psalm (vv. 5, 9, 13, 14, 24, 32, 35). "You spread waters over the earth as easily as one spreads a blanket on a bed," says the psalm in verse 6. "You set a boundary . . . so that they might not again cover the earth" (v. 9).

With verses 10–13, everything is in motion. Water gushes forth from springs and runs down through the valleys. For the first time in the psalm, one encounters animal life. First to appear are "wild animals" and "wild asses," making their way across the plains to the streams to drink. Trees grow on the banks of the streams. The sound of thunder (v. 7) is now balanced with the singing of the birds in the trees (v. 12). The Lord sends rain and "the earth is satisfied with the fruit of your work" (v. 13). The Lord is both creator and sustainer, responsible for the initial gushing of springs and flowing of streams but also for the continued sending of rain.

The 1990 Imax film *Blue Planet*, using satellite photographs of the earth from outer space, notes that 75 percent of the earth's surface is water and shows dramatically that ours is indeed a "blue planet," "covered with the deep as with a blanket" (v. 6, paraphrased).

Only at this somewhat late point in the psalm, at verse 14, do human beings appear on the scene, after the mention of cattle and in the context of references to trees, birds, storks, wild goats, and rock badgers (NRSV, "coneys"). For the cattle, the Lord provides grass. For humans, the Lord provides bread. One does not, however, live by bread alone (Deut 8:3; Matt 4:4)! The Lord also provides wine to add joy to life (Eccl. 9:7; 10:19; Sir. 40:20) and oil, which contributes beauty and fragrance (Esth. 2:12; Ps. 133:2; Eccl. 9:8; Amos 6:6).

But enough said about humans! In this psalm, they are only one species among many. Psalm 104 also indicates that the Lord is involved in forest management, planting the huge Lebanon cedars that provide a home for the birds, including the stork. The high mountains provide habitat for the wild goats and rock badgers.

To this point, the psalm has been describing the living *spaces* for the various species on earth. With verses 19–23 the focus shifts to the planetary rhythms of *time*. In biblical fashion (Gen. 1:5, 8, etc.), the psalm speaks first about the night. The cosmic choreography is impressive: the sun sets, darkness descends, and the animals go out into the forest. God even directs the nocturnal hunting of the young lions (v. 21). When the sun rises, the animals draw back and humans step onto the scene until evening, when the next day begins.

Lord, How Great Are Your Works! (104:24–30)

Another "O LORD" initiates the second major section of the psalm (v. 24). After marveling that "the world is so full of a number of things," as the child's verse puts it, the psalmist considers the sea, which is huge and filled with a variety of forms of life, small and big (see Ps. 69:34). Humans have a place in this scene: they have built ships and pilot them on the seas. What purpose does the mysterious sea monster serve, swimming and leaping through the waves? "You formed him," says the psalmist to the Lord, "just to play!" The Jewish Publication Society translation suggests that the monster is the Lord's pet, "Leviathan that you formed to sport with."

The psalmist reflects on the array of creatures that have paraded by. The Lord made them all (v. 24), and they depend on the Lord for food and for life itself (vv. 27–30). In contrast to the royal imagery of verses 1–4, the Lord is now portrayed as a farmer going out to feed the animals, giving each its assigned portion (see also Ps. 145:15–16). If the divine caretaker does not show his face, these animals are terrified. And when the Lord removes their life-support system, they die. When God sends forth new spirit, or breath, new creatures appear on the scene. God is also involved in causing new plants to grow, renewing the surface of the ground each springtime.

I Will Sing to the Lord (104:31–35)

The psalm ends on a (mostly) joyful note, expressing the hope that the Lord will be happy with what has been created and with this poem

(vv. 31, 34) and reporting the writer's happiness. But Psalm 104 is in touch with reality. Verse 32 is a reminder of the Lord's power and of the potential for natural disaster. With but a glance the Lord can make the earth quake or volcanoes erupt.

In a final reference to the earth, the psalm acknowledges the reality of sin and wickedness (v. 35ab). The psalmist does not choose to dwell on these realities, but this observation indicates that the psalmist's theology is down-to-earth, rejoicing in God's good gifts but also aware of the pain and hurt that people, even God's people, must endure.

Down-To-Earth Theology

To summarize Psalm 104 and consider its relation to our lives today:

1. The psalm is not human centered but all-of-life centered. Psalm 8 describes the responsibility of humans as royalty, installed by the Lord to rule over creation. In Psalm 104, humans are only a part of the great family of creatures the Lord has made.
2. The psalm does not picture an idealized wonderland without sin but is aware of violence in nature (vv. 21, 32) and history (v. 35).
3. Joy, delight, and play are important in this psalm. The purpose of wine is to make people happy (v. 15); the psalmist hopes that the Lord will be happy in his works (v. 31) and declares that he himself is happy in the Lord (v. 34). And the only purpose for the great sea monsters is to frolic in the ocean waters (v. 26)!
4. The psalm does not present a deistic picture of a God who creates and then lets the earth and its creatures go on their own. The Lord is involved in making grass grow and in the production of bread, wine, and oil (vv. 14–15), in the maintaining of the rhythm of the cosmos (v. 20) and in the care and feeding of animals (vv. 21, 27–30). God has a part in annual renewal of the ground (v. 30) and also in earthquakes and volcanoes (v. 32).
5. This mighty God, Creator and Actor in both nature and history, relates to individuals. The writer addresses the Lord as "my God" (vv. 1, 33), brings praise to God (v. 33), and hopes to please God with his poem (v. 34).
6. The lectionaries assign the psalm to the day of Pentecost because of the reference to the Spirit (vv. 24–30).
7. For an outstanding interpretation of the psalm, listen to the choral setting of verse 33, "O Lord God," by Paul Tschesnokoff (for a CD recording, contact Luther College, Decorah, Iowa).

TIME TO REMEMBER
Psalm 105

105:1 O give thanks to the LORD, call on his name,
    make known his deeds among the peoples.
2 Sing to him, sing praises to him;
    tell of all his wonderful works.
3 Glory in his holy name;
    let the hearts of those who seek the LORD rejoice.
4 Seek the LORD and his strength;
    seek his presence continually.
5 Remember the wonderful works he has done,
    his miracles, and the judgments he has uttered,
6 O offspring of his servant Abraham,
    children of Jacob, his chosen ones.

7 He is the LORD our God;
    his judgments are in all the earth.
8 He is mindful of his covenant forever,
    of the word that he commanded, for a thousand generations,
9 the covenant that he made with Abraham,
    his sworn promise to Isaac,
10 which he confirmed to Jacob as a statute,
    to Israel as an everlasting covenant,
11 saying, "To you I will give the land of Canaan
    as your portion for an inheritance."

12 When they were few in number,
    of little account, and strangers in it,
13 wandering from nation to nation,
    from one kingdom to another people,
14 he allowed no one to oppress them;
    he rebuked kings on their account,
15 saying, "Do not touch my anointed ones;
    do my prophets no harm."

16 When he summoned famine against the land,
    and broke every staff of bread,
17 he had sent a man ahead of them,
    Joseph, who was sold as a slave.
18 His feet were hurt with fetters,
    his neck was put in a collar of iron;
19 until what he had said came to pass,
    the word of the LORD kept testing him.
20 The king sent and released him;
    the ruler of the peoples set him free.

²¹ He made him lord of his house,
    and ruler of all his possessions,
²² to instruct his officials at his pleasure,
    and to teach his elders wisdom.

²³ Then Israel came to Egypt;
    Jacob lived as an alien in the land of Ham.
²⁴ And the LORD made his people very fruitful,
    and made them stronger than their foes,
²⁵ whose hearts he then turned to hate his people,
    to deal craftily with his servants.

²⁶ He sent his servant Moses,
    and Aaron whom he had chosen.
²⁷ They performed his signs among them,
    and miracles in the land of Ham.
²⁸ He sent darkness, and made the land dark;
    they rebelled against his words.
²⁹ He turned their waters into blood,
    and caused their fish to die.
³⁰ Their land swarmed with frogs,
    even in the chambers of their kings.
³¹ He spoke, and there came swarms of flies,
    and gnats throughout their country.
³² He gave them hail for rain,
    and lightning that flashed through their land.
³³ He struck their vines and fig trees,
    and shattered the trees of their country.
³⁴ He spoke, and the locusts came,
    and young locusts without number;
³⁵ they devoured all the vegetation in their land,
    and ate up the fruit of their ground.
³⁶ He struck down all the firstborn in their land,
    the first issue of all their strength.

³⁷ Then he brought Israel out with silver and gold,
    and there was no one among their tribes who stumbled.
³⁸ Egypt was glad when they departed,
    for dread of them had fallen upon it.
³⁹ He spread a cloud for a covering,
    and fire to give light by night.
⁴⁰ They asked, and he brought quails,
    and gave them food from heaven in abundance.
⁴¹ He opened the rock, and water gushed out;
    it flowed through the desert like a river.

⁴² **For he remembered his holy promise,**
     and Abraham, his servant.

⁴³ **So he brought his people out with joy,**
     his chosen ones with singing.
⁴⁴ **He gave them the lands of the nations,**
     and they took possession of the wealth of the peoples,
⁴⁵ **that they might keep his statutes**
     and observe his laws.
     Praise the LORD!

Like other institutions of our time, many a congregation or church body has a "Visioning Committee" or a "Task Force for the Future" that is assigned to think about the years ahead. Psalm 105 may suggest something quite different. It could be that, after reflecting on Psalm 105, a congregation might decide to establish a "Remembering Committee" or a "Task Force for the Past." In any case, the focus of this psalm is on the past, or more precisely, on the Lord's "wonderful works" done in the past.

Psalm 105 follows the pattern of a hymn (see Psalm 113), beginning with a *call to praise* (vv. 1–6), continuing with *reasons* for praise (vv. 6–45a), and concluding with another *call to praise* (v. 45b). The psalm opens with a series of ten imperatives, inviting the congregation to worship and climaxing with a call to *remember*: "give thanks . . . call . . . make known . . . Sing . . . sing praises . . . tell . . . Glory . . . Seek . . . seek . . . Remember." As is the case with such psalms as 78, 106, 135, and 136 and with portions of psalms such as 22:4–5, 9–10, 24, the writer believes it important for the gathered congregation not only to plan for the future but also to attend to the "wonderful works" that the Lord has done in the past.

Psalms 105 and 106 are similar in theme, both recalling the "mighty doings of the LORD" (Ps. 106:2). Book IV begins with Psalm 90, which reflects on the passage of time and asks the Lord to give guidance in the use of the gift of time (90:12). Book IV now ends with two psalms also concerned with time, recalling what God has done in times past.

Remember! (105:1–6)

The series of ten imperatives as the psalm begins suggests that it was designed to be used in the context of congregational worship. The Lord's people, the "children of Jacob," are encouraged first of all to give the Lord thanks and then, in the same breath, to "make known his deeds among the peoples." The same pattern is repeated as they are encouraged to sing praises to the Lord and then to tell of "his wonderful works."

Since these works took place in the past, this is a time to remember what they were. What follows in Psalm 105 illustrates what this telling ought to sound like.

The Lord Will Remember (105:7–11)

The Hebrew text called those listening to "remember" (v. 5) and now, using the same verb, assures those persons that the Lord will remember (NRSV, "is mindful of") the covenant agreement between God and the people. The terms of that covenant are then reviewed: the Lord promised Abraham a land, many descendants, blessing, and that Abraham's descendants would be a blessing to others (Gen. 12:1–2). The text here mentions only the promised land; knowledge of the other three elements of the promise is assumed.

Remember How the Lord Protected! (105:12–15)

Now the recital of the "wonderful works" begins, recalling both acts and words of the Lord. At the beginning of the people's history, the Lord protected them from other nations and spoke to leaders of other nations, saying, "Don't harm them!"

Remember Joseph! (105:16–22)

The speaker assumes that the people know these stories and does not retell them but alludes to them. It was the Lord who was working through Joseph (v. 17), who eventually rose to the position of the Egyptian king's trusted assistant and teacher.

Remember the Exodus! (105:23–38)

The story of the plagues and the exodus is told with a good deal of action: every sentence in the Hebrew of this section begins with a verb. Most often the subject of the verb is the Lord, indicating who was controlling all these events. The outline of the story was familiar to those who originally heard it in this version: Israel came to Egypt; the Lord prospered the Israelites; and then the Lord turned the hearts of the Egyptians against Israel (vv. 23–25). When their lives had become miserable, the Lord acted by sending Moses and Aaron, who performed an astounding number of "signs" and "miracles" among the Egyptians. These climaxed in the death of all firstborn creatures, animal and human, and then the people's escape.

Remember the Wilderness! (105:39–43)

It was the Lord, Psalm 105 continues, who provided protection and lead-ing in the wilderness years and who miraculously provided food and water. The psalm begins with a call to the people to "remember" (v. 5). It continues by saying that the Lord has remembered his covenant with the ancestors (vv. 9–10) and now ties up this recital of the Lord's mighty acts by referring back to the promise to Abraham (v. 42).

Great Expectations (105:43–45)

The story of the Lord's mighty acts concludes with a summary of the exodus and a remembering of the conquest of the land. After this telling of what God has done comes an indication of why these stories have been told: so that those who hear them might be faithful covenant partners with the Lord (v. 45)!

Why Remember?

In our own time, remembering the past is hardly as popular as envision-ing the future. Yet Psalm 105 and the others listed above suggest that such remembering is an essential part of the biblical faith. A person with amnesia, who has forgotten the past, will have a difficult time knowing who he or she is and what he or she is to be about.

It is possible for a people, even a congregation, to have amnesia and forget who they are and why they exist. Psalm 105 suggests not just a committee of a few but a commitment of a whole people to keeping alive the story of God's mighty acts in their past through the telling of stories and the singing of songs (v. 2). Such a telling and singing of what God has done could lead to remembering who God's people are and to living in a manner worthy of such a people (v. 45; see 1 Peter 2:9–10).

OLD STORIES FOR A NEW TIME
Psalm 106

> 106:1 **Praise the LORD!**
> **O give thanks to the LORD, for he is good;**
> **for his steadfast love endures forever.**
> ² **Who can utter the mighty doings of the LORD,**
> **or declare all his praise?**
> ³ **Happy are those who observe justice,**
> **who do righteousness at all times.**

⁴ Remember me, O LORD, when you show favor to your people;
　　help me when you deliver them;
⁵ that I may see the prosperity of your chosen ones,
　　that I may rejoice in the gladness of your nation,
　　that I may glory in your heritage.

⁶ Both we and our ancestors have sinned;
　　we have committed iniquity, have done wickedly.
⁷ Our ancestors, when they were in Egypt,
　　did not consider your wonderful works;
　　they did not remember the abundance of your steadfast love,
　　but rebelled against the Most High at the Red Sea.
⁸ Yet he saved them for his name's sake,
　　so that he might make known his mighty power.
⁹ He rebuked the Red Sea, and it became dry;
　　he led them through the deep as through a desert.
¹⁰ So he saved them from the hand of the foe,
　　and delivered them from the hand of the enemy.
¹¹ The waters covered their adversaries;
　　not one of them was left.
¹² Then they believed his words;
　　they sang his praise.

¹³ But they soon forgot his works;
　　they did not wait for his counsel.
¹⁴ But they had a wanton craving in the wilderness,
　　and put God to the test in the desert;
¹⁵ he gave them what they asked,
　　but sent a wasting disease among them.

¹⁶ They were jealous of Moses in the camp,
　　and of Aaron, the holy one of the LORD.
¹⁷ The earth opened and swallowed up Dathan,
　　and covered the faction of Abiram.
¹⁸ Fire also broke out in their company;
　　the flame burned up the wicked.

¹⁹ They made a calf at Horeb
　　and worshiped a cast image.
²⁰ They exchanged the glory of God
　　for the image of an ox that eats grass.
²¹ They forgot God, their Savior,
　　who had done great things in Egypt,
²² wondrous works in the land of Ham,
　　and awesome deeds by the Red Sea.

²³ Therefore he said he would destroy them—
     had not Moses, his chosen one,
   stood in the breach before him,
     to turn away his wrath from destroying them.

²⁴ Then they despised the pleasant land,
     having no faith in his promise.
²⁵ They grumbled in their tents,
     and did not obey the voice of the Lᴏʀᴅ.
²⁶ Therefore he raised his hand and swore to them
     that he would make them fall in the wilderness,
²⁷ and would disperse their descendants among the nations,
     scattering them over the lands.

²⁸ Then they attached themselves to the Baal of Peor,
     and ate sacrifices offered to the dead;
²⁹ they provoked the Lᴏʀᴅ to anger with their deeds,
     and a plague broke out among them.
³⁰ Then Phinehas stood up and interceded,
     and the plague was stopped.
³¹ And that has been reckoned to him as righteousness
     from generation to generation forever.

³² They angered the Lᴏʀᴅ at the waters of Meribah,
     and it went ill with Moses on their account;
³³ for they made his spirit bitter,
     and he spoke words that were rash.

³⁴ They did not destroy the peoples,
     as the Lᴏʀᴅ commanded them,
³⁵ but they mingled with the nations
     and learned to do as they did.
³⁶ They served their idols,
     which became a snare to them.
³⁷ They sacrificed their sons
     and their daughters to the demons;
³⁸ they poured out innocent blood,
     the blood of their sons and daughters,
   whom they sacrificed to the idols of Canaan;
     and the land was polluted with blood.
³⁹ Thus they became unclean by their acts,
     and prostituted themselves in their doings.

⁴⁰ Then the anger of the Lᴏʀᴅ was kindled against his people,
     and he abhorred his heritage;

⁴¹ **he gave them into the hand of the nations,**
so that those who hated them ruled over them.
⁴² **Their enemies oppressed them,**
and they were brought into subjection under their power.
⁴³ **Many times he delivered them,**
but they were rebellious in their purposes,
and were brought low through their iniquity.
⁴⁴ **Nevertheless he regarded their distress**
when he heard their cry.
⁴⁵ **For their sake he remembered his covenant,**
and showed compassion according to the abundance of
his steadfast love.
⁴⁶ **He caused them to be pitied**
by all who held them captive.

⁴⁷ **Save us, O LORD our God,**
and gather us from among the nations,
that we may give thanks to your holy name
and glory in your praise.

⁴⁸ **Blessed be the LORD, the God of Israel,**
from everlasting to everlasting.
And let all the people say, "Amen."
Praise the LORD!

"Tell me a story!" is the child's request. And the love for stories does not stop with childhood. Those who write novels or produce movies or television shows know that human beings are so constructed that they enjoy being caught up in a good story.

Much of the Bible has come to us in the form of stories. Fortunate is the child who has grown up living in the world of these stories and who has thereby learned something about who God is and that God cares about her or him.

Psalm 106 does not so much tell stories as refer to them, as if the reader or hearer already knows them. What the psalm is really about is giving these stories a new audience, retelling these old stories for a new time.

Like Psalms 103 and 104, Psalms 105 and 106 may be considered a pair. Both begin with "O give thanks to the LORD," and both end with "Praise the LORD." Both tell stories from the past history of the people of Israel.

The mood of the two psalms, however, differs. Psalm 105 focuses on the "wonderful works" of God, whereas in Psalm 106 the focus is on the inappropriate ways in which humans have reacted to God's wonderful works.

Since verse 47 assumes that the people have been scattered "among the nations," Psalm 106 may be dated sometime after 587 B.C. , when the Babylonian exile began.

A short introduction calls for praise (vv. 1–5). The main part of the psalm is a collection of stories about the past sins of the people, with a few references to the Lord's acts of saving them (vv. 6–46; see vv. 8–12, 23, 30–31, 43–46). Verse 47 expresses the point of the psalm, and verse 48 is a conclusion to Book IV.

Remember Us, Lord! (106:1–5)

The psalm begins with a *call to praise*, followed by a *reason* for praising ("for his steadfast love endures"; also Pss. 107:1; 118:1; 136:1). The answer to the question in verse 2, "Who can utter the mighty doings of the LORD?" is "No one!" Verse 3 is one of the "happy are" statements that occur in the book of Psalms (see on Ps. 1:1). Verse 4 comes right to the point of the psalm (expanded upon in v. 47), indicating that the people are in difficulties and need to be delivered or saved. The psalmist assumes the Lord will indeed save the people and asks that he, too, might experience that new life of freedom, where the Lord's people will again prosper and where the psalmist can once again rejoice and take pride in being a part of that people.

Stories of Sinning and Some Deliverances (106:6–46)

The clue to understanding the purpose of these stories is found in verse 47. The people are in trouble, scattered among the nations. The psalmist is telling these old stories, readdressing them to a new situation, to help these exiled and discouraged people to ask God to save them.

Verse 6 invites the people to join in a triple confession of sinning, committing iniquity, and doing wickedly. The stories that follow provide concrete illustrations of sinning and also give some examples of what God did to help.

Verses 7–12: They Rebelled, the Lord Delivered

The first old story to be retold is the exodus. After the people experienced deliverance from bondage in Egypt, they developed theological amnesia. They forgot God's love and rebelled against the Lord. When they were faced with the sea ahead of them and the enemies behind them, the Lord delivered them and they burst into song.

Verses 13–23: They Switched Religions, the Lord Delivered

The second story takes place in the wilderness. The people worshiped a golden calf instead of worshiping the Lord (Exodus 32). Their theological amnesia is cited once again (v. 21), but because of the intervention of Moses, they were not destroyed.

Verses 24–31: They Switched Religions, the Lord Forgave

This time, the people decided they didn't want the promised land, disobeyed the Lord, and switched to the worship of Baal. They experienced a plague but were not destroyed, because Phinehas prayed for them and the Lord acted again and stopped the plague.

Verses 32–33: They Rebelled at Meribah, the Lord Provided Water

The people rebelled, Moses and Aaron doubted, but the Lord saved them by providing water (Num. 20:2–13).

Verses 34–46: They Switched Religions, Became Captives, and the Lord Delivered Them

The reference here is to the stories told in the book of Judges. This time the people got caught up in the religion of the Canaanites (vv. 35–39). Time and again they were taken captive, but time and again the Lord also heard their cries for help and delivered them (see Judges 2–16).

Do It Again, Lord! (106:47, 48)

Now comes the point of all these stories. To paraphrase the prayer of the psalmist in verse 47: "We are in trouble, Lord, so we are praying for help. Save us once again" (vv. 10, 23, 30, 43). "Bring us back home to Jerusalem so we can give you thanks and praise."

With verse 48, the editor of the book of Psalms has provided a doxology to conclude Book IV of the collection of psalms (see also 41:13; 72:18–20; 89:52; and Psalm 150; see "Going by the Book" in the Introduction).

Why Tell Those Stories?

Christians and Jews have a long tradition of telling stories from the Bible. They retell these stories because they help to understand about God and about God's relationship to us.

The writer of Psalm 106 tells some old stories but tells them for a new time, to bring a word to a people in exile. They are discouraged, wondering whether God can help and whether God will help. "God did it before, God can do it again!" says this psalm.

Once the teacher of a college course in the Bible stopped in a bank, borrowed a sign, and hung it around his neck before the class arrived. The sign said, "Teller." When the students asked about the sign, the teacher said, "That's what I am. A teller. And if we consider ourselves to be believers continuing in the biblical tradition, that's what we all are."

Indeed we are—tellers of old stories for new times.

5. Book V
(PSALMS 107–150)

CONSIDER THE STEADFAST LOVE OF THE LORD!
Psalm 107

107:1 O give thanks to the LORD, for he is good;
for his steadfast love endures forever.
2 Let the redeemed of the LORD say so,
those he redeemed from trouble
3 and gathered in from the lands,
from the east and from the west,
from the north and from the south.

4 Some wandered in desert wastes,
finding no way to an inhabited town;
5 hungry and thirsty,
their soul fainted within them.
6 Then they cried to the LORD in their trouble,
and he delivered them from their distress;
7 he led them by a straight way,
until they reached an inhabited town.
8 Let them thank the LORD for his steadfast love,
for his wonderful works to humankind.
9 For he satisfies the thirsty,
and the hungry he fills with good things.

10 Some sat in darkness and in gloom,
prisoners in misery and in irons,
11 for they had rebelled against the words of God,
and spurned the counsel of the Most High.
12 Their hearts were bowed down with hard labor;
they fell down, with no one to help.
13 Then they cried to the LORD in their trouble,
and he saved them from their distress;
14 he brought them out of darkness and gloom,
and broke their bonds asunder.

¹⁵ Let them thank the LORD for his steadfast love,
    for his wonderful works to humankind.
¹⁶ For he shatters the doors of bronze,
    and cuts in two the bars of iron.

¹⁷ Some were sick through their sinful ways,
    and because of their iniquities endured affliction;
¹⁸ they loathed any kind of food,
    and they drew near to the gates of death.
¹⁹ Then they cried to the LORD in their trouble,
    and he saved them from their distress;
²⁰ he sent out his word and healed them,
    and delivered them from destruction.
²¹ Let them thank the LORD for his steadfast love,
    for his wonderful works to humankind.
²² And let them offer thanksgiving sacrifices,
    and tell of his deeds with songs of joy.

²³ Some went down to the sea in ships,
    doing business on the mighty waters;
²⁴ they saw the deeds of the LORD,
    his wondrous works in the deep.
²⁵ For he commanded and raised the stormy wind,
    which lifted up the waves of the sea.
²⁶ They mounted up to heaven, they went down to the depths;
    their courage melted away in their calamity;
²⁷ they reeled and staggered like drunkards,
    and were at their wits' end.
²⁸ Then they cried to the LORD in their trouble,
    and he brought them out from their distress;
²⁹ he made the storm be still,
    and the waves of the sea were hushed.
³⁰ Then they were glad because they had quiet,
    and he brought them to their desired haven.
³¹ Let them thank the LORD for his steadfast love,
    for his wonderful works to humankind.
³² Let them extol him in the congregation of the people,
    and praise him in the assembly of the elders.

³³ He turns rivers into a desert,
    springs of water into thirsty ground,
³⁴ a fruitful land into a salty waste,
    because of the wickedness of its inhabitants.
³⁵ He turns a desert into pools of water,
    a parched land into springs of water.

36 **And there he lets the hungry live,**
    and they establish a town to live in;
37 **they sow fields, and plant vineyards,**
    and get a fruitful yield.
38 **By his blessing they multiply greatly,**
    and he does not let their cattle decrease.

39 **When they are diminished and brought low**
    through oppression, trouble, and sorrow,
40 **he pours contempt on princes**
    and makes them wander in trackless wastes;
41 **but he raises up the needy out of distress,**
    and makes their families like flocks.
42 **The upright see it and are glad;**
    and all wickedness stops its mouth.
43 **Let those who are wise give heed to these things,**
    and consider the steadfast love of the LORD.

The opening verse of Psalm 106 declares, "O give thanks to the LORD, for he is good; for his steadfast love endures forever." The remainder of the psalm gives examples of the people's rebellions again God, making the point that, despite these, the Lord continued to love them (Ps. 106:43–46).

Psalm 107 also begins with "O give thanks to the LORD, for he is good; for his steadfast love endures forever." But here the continuation is quite different from that of Psalm 106. In Psalm 107, this opening "O give thanks" is like a text for a sermon; examples of the Lord's steadfast love in action follow.

A clue to the point of the psalm may be found in comparing the beginning and ending. The first verse celebrates the Lord's steadfast love. The main part of the psalm gives examples of what that love has done and calls for thanks and praise (vv. 8, 15, 21–22, 31–32). The last verse invites reflection on these matters: "Let those who are wise give heed to these things, and consider the steadfast love of the LORD."

"The steadfast love of the LORD" is what Psalm 107 is about.

Introducing Book V

Psalm 107 opens the fifth and final "book" of the Psalms. This is the longest of the books (forty-four psalms) and contains the longest of the psalms, Psalm 119. Some links connect Book V's opening psalm with Psalm 106, the last plsam in Book IV: verse 1 of each psalm is identical (but for the "Praise the LORD" at the opening of Psalm 106); Psalm

106:47 offers the prayer "gather us from among the nations," and Psalm 107:3 states that the Lord's people have been "gathered in from the lands."

Book V contains a number of smaller collections: Davidic psalms are gathered at the beginning (Psalms 108–110) and end (Psalms 138–145); the "Egyptian Hallel" in Psalms 113–118 is a grouping of psalms long used as part of the Passover liturgy; the "Songs of Ascent" are collected in Psalms 120–134; and the book concludes with a quintet of psalms that begin and end with "Hallelujah," translated in the NRSV "Praise the LORD" (Psalms 146–150).

After an introductory call to give thanks for the Lord's steadfast love (vv. 1–3), Psalm 107 provides four reports of that steadfast love in action (vv. 4–9, 10–16, 17–22, 23–32), each repeating a refrain celebrating that steadfast love (vv. 8, 15, 21, 31). Verses 33–42 are a celebration of the Lord's blessings. Verse 43 sounds like a word from an editor/teacher, linking up with the "steadfast love" theme at the beginning.

Thank the Lord! (107:1–3)

The opening verse is an invitation to give thanks and provides two reasons for thanksgiving: (1) the Lord is good; (2) the Lord's steadfast love endures (see also Pss. 106:1; 118:1; 136:1). Those who are invited to give thanks are persons who have experienced some sort of deliverance from the Lord. The next section provides some examples.

Steadfast Love in Action (107:4–32)

The first example of the Lord's saving actions (vv. 4–9) has to do with persons who were lost, hungry, and thirsty in the desert. They prayed, and the Lord led them to a town. Let them give thanks to the Lord, who found them and fed them (vv. 8–9)!

Next is a reference to those enduring the harshness of imprisonment (vv. 10–16). The precise nature of the crime and punishment is not clear; apparently these persons were being punished for some sort of religious crime. But God could forgive them, says the psalm, and in fact rescued ("saved") them. Let these, too, give thanks to the Lord, who set them free (vv. 15–16)!

The next group is identified as those who became sick because of their sins (vv. 17–22). These persons were near death. They prayed to the Lord and were healed. Let them thank the Lord, offer sacrifices, and sing stories of what the Lord has done (vv. 21–22)!

The longest description of persons in distress tells of those involved in a storm at sea (vv. 23–32). The situation is grave and dramatically described (vv. 25–27). The dangers of the sea were well known to biblical writers:

> Those who sail the sea tell of its dangers,
>   and we marvel at what we hear.
> In it are strange and marvelous creatures,
>   all kinds of living things, and huge sea monsters.
>   (Sir. 43:24–25)

The sailors described in Psalm 107 had used up all their options and did not know what to do. They prayed, and the Lord calmed the sea and enabled them to reach their destination. Again, it is a time for thanks to God!

Blessings and Deliverance (107:33–43)

The previous section provided examples of the Lord's work of rescuing, or *saving* (vv. 6, 13). In addition to these dramatic acts of God is the quiet, sustaining work of God's *blessing*. God can work through nature to punish people (vv. 33–34), but God can also bring about good conditions for growing and harvesting and allowing cattle to multiply (vv. 35–38).

The psalm concludes with a statement that shows both sides of God's actions, *rescuing* from distress and *blessing* with the building of families (vv. 39–42). A final word to the wise invites reflection on the Lord's steadfast love (v. 43).

Once More, Amazing Grace

What could Psalm 107 mean for our own time? At the center of the psalm is that word *hesed*, which is translated "steadfast love" or which could be translated as "amazing grace." It occurs at the beginning and end (vv. 1, 43) and in each of the four examples (vv. 8, 15, 21, 31). This is the love of God that loves no matter what, like the love of a parent for a child or the love between husband and wife (see also on Psalm 136).

The lectionary connects this psalm with Job's account of the Lord commanding the sea, "Thus far shall you come, and no farther!" (Job 38:1–11) and also with the story of Jesus stilling the storm

(Mark 4:35–41). When Jesus says to the sea, "Peace! Be still!" he is doing just what his Father does!

PSALMS RECYCLED
Psalm 108

A Song. A Psalm of David.

108:1 My heart is steadfast, O God, my heart is steadfast;
    I will sing and make melody.
    Awake, my soul!
 ² Awake, O harp and lyre!
    I will awake the dawn.
 ³ I will give thanks to you, O Lord, among the peoples,
    and I will sing praises to you among the nations.
 ⁴ For your steadfast love is higher than the heavens,
    and your faithfulness reaches to the clouds.

 ⁵ Be exalted, O God, above the heavens,
    and let your glory be over all the earth.
 ⁶ Give victory with your right hand, and answer me,
    so that those whom you love may be rescued.

 ⁷ God has promised in his sanctuary:
    "With exultation I will divide up Shechem,
    and portion out the Vale of Succoth.
 ⁸ Gilead is mine; Manasseh is mine;
    Ephraim is my helmet;
    Judah is my scepter.
 ⁹ Moab is my washbasin;
    on Edom I hurl my shoe;
    over Philistia I shout in triumph."

¹⁰ Who will bring me to the fortified city?
    Who will lead me to Edom?
¹¹ Have you not rejected us, O God?
    You do not go out, O God, with our armies.
¹² O grant us help against the foe,
    for human help is worthless.
¹³ With God we shall do valiantly;
    it is he who will tread down our foes.

How were the Psalms written? Did the authors compose them as new pieces, or did they utilize existing poems and hymns and prayers? Or did they do both?

We do not know the answer to most of these questions about the composition of each psalm and the formation of the book of Psalms. Psalm 108, however, provides a few clues. The first section, verses 1–5, is almost identical with Psalm 57:7–11. The second part of Psalm 108, verses 6–13, is practically identical with Psalm 60:5–12. In this case it appears that the writer fashioned this new psalm by recycling, by splicing together parts from two older ones.

The heading for Psalm 57 associates it with David running from Saul, and that for Psalm 60 with another specific event in David's life. The recycled segments are given a new heading in Psalm 108: "A Song" (Hebrew *shir*, using the same Hebrew root as occurs in "I will sing" in v. 1) and "A Psalm" (Hebrew *mizmor*, the same root as in the word translated "and make melody"). At some point, an editor took the new psalm and made it the first of a three-part Davidic collection at this point in Book V.

I Will Sing and Make Melody (108:1–5)

The psalm begins with a *hymn*, resolving to sing praises (vv. 1–3), indicating why such praises are appropriate (v. 4), and then ending with a wish that God be exalted (v. 5). See the comments on Psalm 57:7–11.

Give Us a Victory, Lord! (108:6–13)

The second part of Psalm 108 picks up verses 5–12 of Psalm 60, a *community lament*. The typical elements of a lament are present here (see on Psalm 13): *request* (108:6, 12), *"you" complaint* (vv. 10–11), *affirmation of trust* (v. 13). In addition, the psalm includes a *word from God*, spoken by a priest or prophet (vv. 7–9). For explanation of this section, see the commentary on Psalm 60:5–12.

The New Psalm (108:1–13)

In its new form, this psalm, composed of parts of two other psalms, functions as a community lament. We have seen the elements of the lament in verses 6–13. Verses 1–5 may then be understood as a *vow to praise*, the one element of the standard lament form missing in verses 6–13.

The second part of the psalm asks for the Lord's help (verses 6, 12). The first part assumes that help will be given and, therefore, that praise and thanksgiving will be in order.

LIKE A SHADOW AT EVENING
Psalm 109

To the leader. Of David. A Psalm.

109:1 Do not be silent, O God of my praise.
　² For wicked and deceitful mouths are opened against me,
　　speaking against me with lying tongues.
　³ They beset me with words of hate,
　　and attack me without cause.
　⁴ In return for my love they accuse me,
　　even while I make prayer for them.
　⁵ So they reward me evil for good,
　　and hatred for my love.

　⁶ They say, "Appoint a wicked man against him;
　　let an accuser stand on his right.
　⁷ When he is tried, let him be found guilty;
　　let his prayer be counted as sin.
　⁸ May his days be few;
　　may another seize his position.
　⁹ May his children be orphans,
　　and his wife a widow.
　¹⁰ May his children wander about and beg;
　　may they be driven out of the ruins they inhabit.
　¹¹ May the creditor seize all that he has;
　　may strangers plunder the fruits of his toil.
　¹² May there be no one to do him a kindness,
　　nor anyone to pity his orphaned children.
　¹³ May his posterity be cut off;
　　may his name be blotted out in the second generation.
　¹⁴ May the iniquity of his father be remembered before the LORD,
　　and do not let the sin of his mother be blotted out.
　¹⁵ Let them be before the LORD continually,
　　and may his memory be cut off from the earth.
　¹⁶ For he did not remember to show kindness,
　　but pursued the poor and needy
　　and the brokenhearted to their death.
　¹⁷ He loved to curse; let curses come on him.
　　He did not like blessing; may it be far from him.
　¹⁸ He clothed himself with cursing as his coat,
　　may it soak into his body like water,
　　like oil into his bones.
　¹⁹ May it be like a garment that he wraps around himself,
　　like a belt that he wears every day."

²⁰ May that be the reward of my accusers from the LORD,
   of those who speak evil against my life.
²¹ But you, O LORD my Lord,
   act on my behalf for your name's sake;
   because your steadfast love is good, deliver me.
²² For I am poor and needy,
   and my heart is pierced within me.
²³ I am gone like a shadow at evening;
   I am shaken off like a locust.
²⁴ My knees are weak through fasting;
   my body has become gaunt.
²⁵ I am an object of scorn to my accusers;
   when they see me, they shake their heads.

²⁶ Help me, O LORD my God!
   Save me according to your steadfast love.
²⁷ Let them know that this is your hand;
   you, O LORD, have done it.
²⁸ Let them curse, but you will bless.
   Let my assailants be put to shame; may your servant be glad.
²⁹ May my accusers be clothed with dishonor;
   may they be wrapped in their own shame as in a mantle.
³⁰ With my mouth I will give great thanks to the LORD;
   I will praise him in the midst of the throng.
³¹ For he stands at the right hand of the needy,
   to save them from those who would condemn them to death.

This is the prayer of a person who is hurting badly. Others have been spreading lies and spewing hate, while the psalmist has been praying for them (109:4–5).

The one praying is experiencing poverty on the outside and heart trouble on the inside (v. 22). Two pictures express the nearness of death: the psalmist's life is like the evening shadows that disappear as the sun goes down; his life is of no more value than that of a locust, shaken off as a crop-destroying pest (v. 23; see Exod. 10:12–19). The one praying is weak, pale, and thin because of fasting (v. 24).

In addition, there are those in the community who continue with their false accusations and their scorn (vv. 20, 25; see also vv. 1–5). Feeling like an enemy of those who once were friends, having prayers and kindness rejected, experiencing personal pain—such is the situation of this psalmist, who is hurting badly.

The note to the music director in the heading identifies this as a *miz-mor*, a piece to be done with musical accompaniment, and a part of the collection of psalms associated with David (see on Psalm 3).

The psalm consists of the elements typical of an *individual lament* (see on Psalm 13): *request* in verses 1, 20–21, and 26–29; *"they" complaint* in verses 2–5; *"I" complaint* in verses 22–25; *vow to praise* in verses 30–31. The absence of complaint against the Lord ("you" complaint) is somewhat unusual.

What is both peculiar and problematic about this psalm is the lengthy section of curses in verses 6–19. The bitter spirit here expressed accounts for the fact that the psalm is seldom used in either preaching or teaching.

The Silence of God (109:1–5)

The initial concern of the psalm is with words. The "they" complaint tells of words of certain persons who are wicked and deceitful, liars, filled with hate, aggressive and evil, and who are making the psalmist's life miserable (vv. 2–5).

What of the words of God? The previous psalm cited words of promise from a God who would help people in need (Ps. 108:7–9). But for this psalmist, there have been no words of promise from God, in fact, no words at all. God has been silent (109:1).

Finally, there are the words of the psalmist. These had been loving words of prayer on behalf of persons out to destroy him, directed to a God who does not respond (vv. 4–5).

The remainder of the psalm must be heard against this background of words of hate, words of love, and the absence of any words from God.

The Sentiments of a Hurting Human (109:6–19)

This has been the difficult and controversial part of the psalm, so much so that theologians and biblical scholars as well as compilers of texts for preaching have suggested eliminating the psalm altogether from use in preaching or teaching. Another suggestion is represented by the translators of the NRSV, who make an addition to the Hebrew text by inserting "They say" before verse 6, suggesting that the ones who spoke these words were the wicked and deceitful persons described in verses 2–5 (see the NRSV footnote at v. 6).

The most natural way to read the section, however, is as the words of the writer of the psalm. But the words should be read in their context: as expressing the sentiments of a human being who has experienced too much the ever-present slandering words of others and the absence of any word from God.

The language of verses 6–15 is not an invention of the psalmist. This is vocabulary typical of the time, used for wishing ill upon enemies. Some examples from other parts of the Bible include several psalmists speaking to God about enemies: "O God, break the teeth in their mouths. . . . Let them vanish like water that runs away. . . . Let them be like the snail that dissolves into slime" (Ps. 58:6–9); "Let their eyes be darkened so that they cannot see . . . let no one live in their tents. . . . Let them be blotted out of the book of the living" (Ps. 69:23–28); "Happy shall they be who take your little ones and dash them against the rock!" (Ps. 137:9). Such was the way people spoke of enemies. For further examples, one can read the list of curses on those who break the commandments in Deuteronomy 28:15–46. Books have been written collecting other curses that will fall on those who break treaties in the world of the Ancient Near East. These difficult verses in Psalm 109 should be read against the background of a culture where such language and wishes were not unfamiliar.

Verses 6–7 express the psalmist's wish that a dishonest lawyer will get the enemy convicted in court. Verses 8–12 wish the death of the enemy and the suffering of the families at home, with no one to care for the children. Verses 13–15 express the desire that this person be totally forgotten! Verse 16 provides some reasons for these violent wishes. Finally, verses 17–19 suggest that these enemies ought to get a taste of their own medicine!

Your Steadfast Love (109:20–31)

Central to the final segment of Psalm 109 is the notion of the Lord's steadfast love. This section begins with a double request, expressing the psalmist's wishes concerning the enemies and then concerning himself (vv. 20–21). Worth noting is the fact that these curses do not function automatically; their carrying out is left to the Lord (v. 20). The point of the entire psalm is expressed in the last words of verse 21: "deliver me!"

Verses 22–25 offer complaints in the "I" or "they" (only 25:b) form. Poor and weak, the psalmist sees his life as nearing its end (vv. 22–24). Others in the community only make things more miserable (v. 25).

Another double wish occurs in verses 26–29. First, the psalmist asks twice for the Lord's help ("Help me. . . . Save me"), basing these requests on the Lord's steadfast love. The second part of the wish is that the enemies be shamed.

As is typical of laments (see Psalm 13), the piece ends with a vow to praise the Lord in the congregation (vv. 30–31).

For the Brokenhearted Only

It is possible that this psalm can be understood only by persons who have been badly hurt by friends. These friends have turned against them just at the time when they need support. Such was the situation of this psalmist (vv. 1–5, 22–25).

Twice the writer refers to heart problems (vv. 16, 22), not the sort that can be solved by a bypass operation but symptoms of the inner pain that results from rejection by friends. It is possible that only such situations of acute disappointment and pain can explain the bitterness of the middle section of Psalm 109.

Jesus advised loving one's enemies and praying for those who persecute (Matt. 5:44). This psalmist had been doing precisely those things but received only hatred and evil in response (vv. 4–5). It must have been too much, and he fired off a string of curses, then left things in God's hands (v. 20). This was not the sort of response that Jesus would one day call for. It was perhaps an all-too-human response, of the sort that we might make, knowing that like the psalmist, we, too, need to be helped and saved (v. 26).

SEATED AT THE RIGHT HAND OF THE FATHER
Psalm 110

Of David. A Psalm.

110:1 **The LORD says to my lord,**
         "Sit at my right hand
         until I make your enemies your footstool."

   2 **The LORD sends out from Zion**
         your mighty scepter.
         Rule in the midst of your foes.
   3 **Your people will offer themselves willingly**
         on the day you lead your forces
         on the holy mountains.
      From the womb of the morning,
         like dew, your youth will come to you.
   4 **The LORD has sworn and will not change his mind,**
         "You are a priest forever according to the order
         of Melchizedek."

   5 **The Lord is at your right hand;**
         he will shatter kings on the day of his wrath.
   6 **He will execute judgment among the nations,**
         filling them with corpses;
      he will shatter heads
         over the wide earth.

⁷ **He will drink from the stream by the path;**
therefore he will lift up his head.

Sunday after Sunday, Christian people all over the world gather for worship and, in a variety of languages, recite these words from the Apostles' Creed:

> On the third day he rose again.
> He ascended into heaven,
>   and is *seated at the right hand of the Father.*

The creed picked up this expression from the New Testament:

> Who is to condemn? It is Christ Jesus, who died, yes, who was raised, who is at the right hand of God, who indeed intercedes for us. (Rom. 8:34)

> God put this power to work in Christ when he raised him from the dead and seated him at his right hand in the heavenly places. (Eph. 1:20)

> But when Christ had offered for all time a single sacrifice for sins, "he sat down at the right hand of God." (Heb. 10:12)

See also Acts 2:32–33; 7:55; Heb. 1:13; 8:1; 1 Peter 3:22.

The writers of the New Testament understood the resurrection of Jesus as the fulfillment of this psalm. In fact, Psalm 110 is the most-quoted Old Testament text in the entire New Testament. What was the sense of this psalm before the time of the Christ?

The heading indicates that the psalm is a part of a Davidic collection (see on Psalm 3) and is a psalm, or *mizmor*, that is, a song that can be sung to musical accompaniment.

The first line provides the clue for understanding the whole. Since "the LORD" is a translation of Yahweh, the Hebrew name for God, the psalm could be translated

> Yahweh says to my king,
>   "Sit at my right hand
> until I make your enemies your footstool."
>   (Ps. 110:1)

The psalm belongs to the group of psalms that play a role in the life of the king, the *royal psalms* (see the comments on Psalm 2). Apparently Psalm 110 was once a part of the ritual used for the installation of a new king (see also Psalms 2, 72, 101).

Psalm 110 falls into two parts, each introduced with a quotation from the Lord: "The LORD says . . ." (vv. 1–3); "The LORD has sworn . . ." (vv. 4–7). Since the Hebrew text is exceptionally difficult, there are uncertainties in the translation and the sense of the psalm.

The Lord Says to the King . . . (110:1–3)

The first of the Lord's words to the king are an invitation and a promise. If this psalm was used as part of a ceremony for installing a new king, as seems likely, the words identified as words of the Lord would have been spoken by a priest or some other person from the temple staff. "Sit at my right hand" is an invitation to take the place of honor and authority, just to the right of the King (see also 1 Kings 2:19; Pss. 45:9; 80:17). Today, when a colleague or assistant is described as "his or her right-hand man or woman," those notions of honor and authority persist.

The promise in verse 1 is concerned with military matters, specifically "enemies" (the same Hebrew word is translated as "foes" in v. 2). Here is the expression of a theme typical to the royal psalms: the Lord will make the king victorious in warfare (see also Pss. 21:8–12; 72:4, 8–11). The New Testament writers understand this promise to be fulfilled ultimately in the resurrection of Jesus (see the texts cited above).

Verse 2 expresses another wish for the king regarding military matters. The sense is "May you one day rule over those who are now your enemies!" The translation of verse 3 is not certain and the meaning is not clear. Apparently, this is another promise to the king that he will have military success.

The Lord Has Sworn to the King . . . (110:4–7)

The first saying referred to the installation of the king as a political and military leader. The second saying assigns religious responsibilities to the king, designated as a "priest forever according to the order of Melchizedek." Melchizedek was king of Jerusalem when it was a Canaanite city, long before the Israelites conquered it. Genesis 14:18–20 indicates that he was both a political and religious leader. When David became king in Jerusalem, he apparently inherited some of these ancient traditions associated with the city, including the functioning of the king in matters of religion (2 Sam. 6:17–18) as well as matters of state.

Verses 5–6 again speak of the anticipated extensive ("over the wide earth") military successes of the king. The meaning of verse 7 is uncertain.

The Seedbed for Messianic Hope

As the years went on, this royal psalm had its contribution to make to the people's hopes for a mighty ruler, a "second David." When taken together, the royal psalms portray an impressive ruler indeed: this king from the line of David will be a military victor, will rule all nations, will rule forever, will establish righteousness and justice, and will bring peace, *shalom*, to a war-torn people (see the discussion with Psalm 2). Psalm 110 again speaks of military victories and then adds to the portrait the detail about Melchizedek and the promise of the king being seated at the right hand of the Lord.

The writer of Hebrews saw the risen Christ in the light of the words about Melchizedek (Hebrews 7). When Jesus was raised from the dead, the New Testament writers understood what was going on as the fulfillment of the promise of Psalm 110:1. When Christians confess their faith, they affirm with the New Testament that the one about whom Psalm 110 was ultimately speaking is Jesus, the Messiah.

THE ABC'S OF THEOLOGY
Psalm 111

111:1 **Praise the LORD!**
> **I will give thanks to the LORD with my whole heart,**
>> **in the company of the upright, in the congregation.**
> 2 **Great are the works of the LORD,**
>> **studied by all who delight in them.**
> 3 **Full of honor and majesty is his work,**
>> **and his righteousness endures forever.**
> 4 **He has gained renown by his wonderful deeds;**
>> **the LORD is gracious and merciful.**
> 5 **He provides food for those who fear him;**
>> **he is ever mindful of his covenant.**
> 6 **He has shown his people the power of his works,**
>> **in giving them the heritage of the nations.**
> 7 **The works of his hands are faithful and just;**
>> **all his precepts are trustworthy.**
> 8 **They are established forever and ever,**
>> **to be performed with faithfulness and uprightness.**
> 9 **He sent redemption to his people;**
>> **he has commanded his covenant forever.**
>> **Holy and awesome is his name.**
> 10 **The fear of the LORD is the beginning of wisdom;**
>> **all those who practice it have a good understanding.**
>> **His praise endures forever.**

On the outer wall at the entrance to the library at Augustana College in Sioux Falls, South Dakota, are the words "The fear of the Lord is the beginning of wisdom." That motto, which occurs in Proverbs 1:7 and also in Psalm 111:10, suggests that the first step in becoming well educated, or in the language of the Bible, the first step in becoming *wise*, is to be rightly related to God. To fail to get right with God at the beginning of a period of intensive study, this saying suggests, could mean the failure of the entire enterprise. Citing this motto from the wisdom teachers, Psalm 111 is concerned with becoming well educated and wise.

A Pair of Acrostics

Psalms 111 and 112 are a pair and should be considered together. In form they are similar, each beginning with "Praise the LORD," each consisting of twenty-two lines divided into ten verses, and each an alphabetical acrostic (see the comments on Psalms 9–10). In the case of these two psalms, each line begins with a successive letter of the Hebrew alphabet, running from *alef* to *tav*, that is, from *a* to *z*.

When it comes to content, the two psalms are complementary. The focus of Psalm 111 is on God, and that of Psalm 112 is on human beings. Taken together, they provide a picture of what the Bible says concerning *theology* and *anthropology*, especially as presented by the teachers of wisdom.

Though not evident in the English translation, it must be remembered that the succession of lines after the initial "Praise the LORD" in these psalms follows the pattern of the Hebrew alphabet. Such a formal restriction places certain constraints on an author, which have resulted here in a lack of longer, connected units. Verses 1–4 present a call to praise ("Praise the LORD") and a vow to praise (v. 1) and then offer some general statements about the Lord's actions, framed by references to "great works" (v. 2) and "wonderful deeds" (v. 4). Verses 5–9 speak in more specific terms, framed by mention of the covenant, and verse 10 is a summary statement, reflecting the viewpoint of Israel's wisdom teachers.

Praise the Majestic and Merciful Lord! (111:1–4)

The call to "praise the LORD" (Hebrew, *hallelujah*) appears often in the succession of psalms running from 111 through 118, so that this might be called a collection of "Hallelujah" psalms. The usual form of the *hymn* is to issue a *call to praise* that is then followed by *reasons for praise* (see Psalm 113). This psalm follows that pattern, with the call in verse 1 and reasons following in verses 2–9.

The psalm refers to the "works of the LORD" (v. 2) and God's "wonderful deeds" (v. 4). Written recollections of these deeds must have been available at the time this psalm was produced, since the psalm speaks of those who "study" the "works of the LORD." These study sessions appear to have been pleasant experiences, no doubt carried out in the presence of others, since the psalm describes them in terms of delight (v. 2).

Two pictures describing the Lord are called forth in verses 3 and 4. The Lord is like a king whose work is honorable and majestic (v. 3). The reference to the Lord's mercy in verse 4 suggests that the Lord is also like a loving mother, since the root meaning of the Hebrew word behind "mercy" (*reḥem*) is "womb." The segment in verses 2–4 is framed by references to the Lord's contact with people, in terms of great works and wonderful deeds.

Praise the Caring and Rescuing Lord! (111:5–9)

Still determined by the pattern of a hymn, the psalm provides further reasons for praise, now recalling some of the Lord's mighty acts. Verse 5 is a remembrance of the miraculous feeding of the people as they wandered through the wilderness (Exodus 16; Numbers 11), and "the heritage of the nations" in verse 6 calls to mind the gift of the promised land. Verses 7 and 8 make some general statements about the Lord's works and teachings. Verse 9 recalls the exodus from Egypt ("redemption") and also the making of the covenant at Mount Sinai, linking up with the same theme in verse 5.

A Word for Those Who Study (111:10)

The psalm concludes with a word about beginning the quest for wisdom. The first step is to have a proper attitude of *reverence* toward the holy and awesome God (see also Job 28:28; Prov. 1:7; 9:10). Once this theological awareness is in place, the psalm commends study (v. 2). The inscription on the front of the college library was quite appropriate!

The *content* of such study, according to verse 2, is to be the "works of the LORD." Verses 5–6 hint at those mighty works with allusions to the miraculous feeding in the wilderness, the covenant, and the conquest of the land of Canaan.

The *manner* of study is described as not a drudgery but a delight (v. 2). Both teachers and students are invited to participate in an educational program that is theological in content (vv. 9–10) and joyful in its execution. The learning atmosphere is the same as that portrayed in Psalm 1:2, which also refers to the *delight* of studying the teachings about the Lord.

The *result* of such enjoyable learning about God will be "good sense" (NRSV, "a good understanding"; but see the translation of the same Hebrew as "good sense" in Prov. 13:15). Since this closing saying speaks of only the "beginning" of the process, such study will result in an ever-deepening wisdom.

Finally, this study is carried out in a *context* where the Lord is praised, as both the beginning and ending of this psalm suggest.

THE ABC'S OF ANTHROPOLOGY
Psalm 112

112:1 **Praise the LORD!**
  Happy are those who fear the LORD,
  who greatly delight in his commandments.
2 **Their descendants will be mighty in the land;**
  the generation of the upright will be blessed.
3 **Wealth and riches are in their houses,**
  and their righteousness endures forever.
4 **They rise in the darkness as a light for the upright;**
  they are gracious, merciful, and righteous.
5 **It is well with those who deal generously and lend,**
  who conduct their affairs with justice.
6 **For the righteous will never be moved;**
  they will be remembered forever.
7 **They are not afraid of evil tidings;**
  their hearts are firm, secure in the LORD.
8 **Their hearts are steady, they will not be afraid;**
  in the end they will look in triumph on their foes.
9 **They have distributed freely, they have given to the poor;**
  their righteousness endures forever;
  their horn is exalted in honor.
10 **The wicked see it and are angry;**
  they gnash their teeth and melt away;
  the desire of the wicked comes to nothing.

Psalms 112 and 111 are a pair and should be considered together. Both begin with "Praise the LORD," and both are acrostics, the first word in each line beginning with the letters of the Hebrew alphabet in sequence (see the comments on Psalm 111; also Psalms 9–10). Certain phrases occur in both psalms, for example, Psalms 111:3b and 112:3b, which are identical in Hebrew. Especially interesting is a comparison of Psalm 111:4b, which says that the Lord is "gracious and merciful," with 112:4b, which says that those who fear the Lord are "gracious, merciful, and righteous."

While there are such obvious similarities, each psalm also has its own point to make. The focus of Psalm 111 is on God, whereas Psalm 112 offers instruction about human beings. The theme of Psalm 111 is sounded in verse 2: "Great are the works of the LORD, studied by all who delight in them." The theme of Psalm 112 is struck by verse 1: "Happy are those who fear the LORD, who greatly delight in his commandments."

The expression "those who fear the LORD" at the start of Psalm 112 links up with "the fear of the LORD" at the end of Psalm 111. Psalm 112 begins with a general picture of the happy state of those who fear the Lord (vv. 1–3) and continues with concrete descriptions of the lives of such persons (vv. 5–10).

Human Happiness (112:1–4)

A number of psalms speak of happiness, each adding its own color to the biblical portrait (Pss. 1:1; 41:1; 65:4; 89:15; 119:1–3; 128:1). According to this saying, true happiness is to be found in having the right attitude of honor toward the Lord and then in carrying out the Lord's commandments, which are concerned with relationships to God and to fellow human beings (Exod. 20:1–11, 12–17). Psalm 111 spoke of the delight of studying the works of the Lord; Psalm 112 speaks of the delight of living in the way of the Lord's commandments. This life of honoring God and following God's commandments is not a drudgery but a delight (112:1)!

Verses 2 and 3 provide illustrations of the biblical notion of *blessing*. There are two fundamental shapes to God's activity in the Bible: *saving* (such as the rescue from Egypt or the deliverance achieved on the cross) and *blessing*. Here is a good illustration of that second activity. Those who are "blessed" will have many descendants who will enjoy wealth and influence in the land, and the effect of their good lives will be enduring.

These "blessed" persons are described as God-like (compare v. 4b with Ps. 111:4b) and as lighting up a dark world (v. 4a; see also Matt. 5:14–16).

Lives That Are Lit Up (112:5–10)

The remainder of Psalm 112 makes clear that the world in which these blessed persons live is a world with problems. Verse 4 refers to the darkness; verse 7 speaks of evil; verse 8 hints at hostility; and the psalm concludes with a reference to the wicked (v. 10).

Against this background of darkness and evil in the world, the lives of these who are blessed (vv. 1–2) are now described. Things will go well for those persons who have been blessed with wealth and who share that wealth and are concerned for the poor. Their good lives will be remembered forever (vv. 5–6)!

Verses 7 and 8 indicate that even though, externally, enemies are making life difficult, these persons who "fear the LORD" have an inner confidence and security. Twice these lines refer to the "heart," the innermost part of a person, describing an inner security and steadiness, rooted in a right relationship to the Lord.

More is said about the sort of lives led by these persons who fear the Lord and who are blessed: once again, they share their wealth with the poor (v. 9; see also v. 5). The picture behind the expression, "their horn is exalted," is that of an animal whose head is lifted high above others and is thus in a superior position (see also Pss. 75:5, 10; 92:10; 132:17; Luke 1:69, NRSV footnote).

The psalm concludes in verse 10 with the promise that the wicked will not be successful.

The ABC's of Biblical Faith

Psalms 111 and 112 are instructional in intent and have the marks of the "wisdom teachers," who produced material such as that found in the book of Proverbs. Psalm 111:10 is thematic for Proverbs (Prov. 1:7), and the acrostic patterns in these two psalms are obvious devices for effective teaching and learning.

Taken together, Psalms 111 and 112 provide a teacher's summary of the essentials of the faith. This instruction is carried out in an atmosphere of worship and fear of the Lord (111:1, 10; 112:1). It is for those already convinced of the validity of faith in the God of the Bible. Such learning is a delightful experience (111:2; see also 112:1).

Psalm 111 focuses on *theology*, that is, what can be known about God. The Lord is loving and merciful, as seen in the events in the people's history, such as the feeding in the wilderness, the covenant, and the conquest of the land of Canaan (111:4–7). The Lord is known through wonderful acts of deliverance ("deeds," "works," "redemption"; 111:4, 6, 9) and also through the quiet activities of blessing ("provides food," 111:5). Humans are to respond to the Lord's actions by praise (vv. 1, 10) and by study that begins with a right attitude toward the Lord (vv. 10, 2).

Psalm 112 has its focus on *anthropology*, that is, what can be said about human beings. Human happiness is to be found in a life honoring the Lord and living according to the commandments (112:1). Such lives will enjoy the Lord's blessings (vv. 2–3). Though living in an evil world (vv. 4, 7–8, 10), God's people will be secure and steady because their hearts are with the Lord (vv. 7–8). Having experienced the Lord's saving and blessing, they will share what God has given them with the poor (vv. 5, 9).

These two alphabetical psalms articulate two themes: the greatness of the works of the Lord (111:2) and the happiness of those who worship the Lord (112:1).

THE PRINCE AND THE PEASANT MAIDEN
Psalm 113

113:1 Praise the LORD!
　　Praise, O servants of the LORD;
　　praise the name of the LORD.

　2 Blessed be the name of the LORD
　　from this time on and forevermore.
　3 From the rising of the sun to its setting
　　the name of the LORD is to be praised.
　4 The LORD is high above all nations,
　　and his glory above the heavens.

　5 Who is like the LORD our God,
　　who is seated on high,
　6 who looks far down
　　on the heavens and the earth?
　7 He raises the poor from the dust,
　　and lifts the needy from the ash heap,
　8 to make them sit with princes,
　　with the princes of his people.
　9 He gives the barren woman a home,
　　making her the joyous mother of children.
　　Praise the LORD!

For Jewish people, the festival of Passover continues to be the central event of the year. The celebration occurs in the home. The table is set with one empty place for Elijah, should the prophet decide to leave his heavenly chariot for a time and visit (2 Kings 2:11). Songs are sung and stories are told, especially the story of the exodus. Each year in this setting, in Jewish homes throughout the world, Psalms 113–118, called the "Egyptian Hallel" (*hallel* means "praise"), are read or sung, recalling the story of the deliverance from Egypt (Psalm 114) and concluding with expressions of hope for deliverance from death (Ps. 118:14–17). Psalm 113 is the introduction to this sequence of psalms for Passover and sets the tone with the picture of God that it presents.

A Model Hymn

Psalm 113 offers a clear example of the structure of the *hymn of praise* in the psalms. It begins (and ends) with a *call to praise* in the imperative mood (vv. 1–3, 9c) and continues by offering *reasons for praise*, speaking first of the Lord's might (vv. 4–6) and continuing with illustrations of the Lord's loving care (vv. 7–9ab). This call-to-praise plus reasons-for-praise pattern is basic to the type of psalm identified as a hymn.

The position of Psalm 113 as introductory to the Psalms 113–118 group offers suggestions for the psalm's interpretation. Psalm 113 speaks of the Lord's might and mercy and provides two examples from the lives of individuals. Psalm 114, with its focus on the exodus, exemplifies the Lord's might and mercy in the lives of a people. The Psalms as a whole tell the stories of both: God delivering an individual and God delivering a people.

Time and Space (113:1–3)

This psalm begins with a triple call to praise:

> Praise the LORD [Hebrew, *hallelu-yah*]!
> Praise [*hallelu*], O servants of the LORD;
> praise [*hallelu*] the name of the LORD.
>
> (v. 1)

The word *blessed* in verse 2 means the same as "praised." The first call asks that the Lord's praise continue throughout all *time* (v. 2). The second calls for praise from "the rising of the sun to its setting," from east to west, throughout all *space*. When these psalms are used in worship, they encourage the "servants of the LORD" not to think too small!

Praise Is a Reasonable Thing! (113:4–9)

Following the typical pattern of the hymn, the call to praise is followed by a number of reasons. Praise is shown to be a reasonable thing for human beings to do.

The first reasons concern the Lord's *might* (vv. 4–6). The psalm uses a spatial image to convey the notion of the greatness of God: God is seated on high and looks down upon heaven and earth. The same notion is expressed in Isaiah 6:1 and 57:15.

The next reasons for praising the Lord focus on the Lord's *loving care*. The psalm provides two concrete examples. The Lord looks down upon the earth, sees a person who is poor and needy, and raises that person to a position of political importance. Was this in answer to the prayers of that poor person? This could be the case, but the text does not say. The important thing is to recognize what the Lord has done and then to join in praising.

The second example speaks of a woman who had been infertile but who has now become a mother. The psalm closes with a picture of this young Jewish woman in her home, happily playing with her children. It was the Lord who gave this couple their children (v. 9), and therefore it is appropriate to praise the Lord.

Claus Westermann has captured the astonishing dimensions of Psalm 113. The psalm reaches, he says, from the majesty of the Lord high above all the heavens to a little room in a house where a mother rejoices with her child. It extends from the festivity of a hymn sung at worship to everyday life in a village where the men sit together in the evening (Westermann, *The Psalms*, p. 88).

God Is Great, God Is Good

Psalm 113 provides a commentary on the family prayer often used before meals: "God is great, God is good, and we thank him for this food." That short prayer expresses the two dimensions of the Bible's description of God.

According to the biblical story, when Elkanah and Hannah finally had a child, whom they named Samuel, Hannah prayed to the Lord with a song of joy. In the course of the prayer she cited words found in this psalm: "He raises up the poor from the dust; he lifts the needy from the ash heap" (1 Sam. 2:8).

According to Luke's Gospel, after Mary heard Elizabeth's words of congratulation on Mary's pregnancy, she spoke words similar to those of Hannah and this psalm: "My soul magnifies the Lord, and my spirit rejoices in God my Savior. . . . He has brought down the powerful from their thrones, and lifted up the lowly" (Luke 1:46–55).

In speaking of the Lord's *might* and *loving care*, the words of Hannah and of Mary and of Psalm 113 capture the two poles in the biblical description of who God is.

It was the Dane Søren Kierkegaard who once told a story about a young prince who was riding through the countryside and noticed a beautiful peasant maiden working in a field. The prince immediately fell in love with her. But because the prince did not want to force her affection, he went back to the castle, laid aside his royal garments, and came to the village where the maiden lived, disguised as a common peasant. He made her acquaintance and won her love, and only then did he reveal his true identity.

So it was with God, said Kierkegaard. God did not force God's affec-
tions on human beings; God did not force people to sing praises but came
to the world disguised as a carpenter's son. This pattern of laying aside
the trappings of royalty and reaching out to win the love of a beloved is
reminiscent of the story of the good news about Jesus; note Paul's telling
of the story in Philippians 2:5–11.

THE DAY THE SEA RAN AWAY
Psalm 114

114:1 **When Israel went out from Egypt,**
　　　　the house of Jacob from a people of strange language,
　　² **Judah became God's sanctuary,**
　　　　Israel his dominion.

　　³ **The sea looked and fled;**
　　　　Jordan turned back.
　　⁴ **The mountains skipped like rams,**
　　　　the hills like lambs.

　　⁵ **Why is it, O sea, that you flee?**
　　　　O Jordan, that you turn back?
　　⁶ **O mountains, that you skip like rams?**
　　　　O hills, like lambs?

　　⁷ **Tremble, O earth, at the presence of the LORD,**
　　　　at the presence of the God of Jacob,
　　⁸ **who turns the rock into a pool of water,**
　　　　the flint into a spring of water.

In Jewish homes throughout the world, the deliverance of the
Israelites from Egypt, the exodus, is celebrated with the springtime festival of Passover. The house is given a thorough spring cleaning, the table
is elegantly set, and the family is gathered, maybe with a few guests. The
candles are lit, and the story of the exodus is told, sung, and enacted.
Then Psalms 113 and 114 are recited. After these psalms, a blessing is
said and the meal begins. After the meal, Psalms 115–118 are sung or
recited. The central event in the Old Testament story is the deliverance
from Egypt, and that event is at the center of Psalm 114.

A Psalm That Tells a Story

This long Jewish tradition provides some clues for understanding the
psalm. Psalm 114 should be read in connection with Psalm 113 and in the

context of Psalms 113–118. While Psalm 113 is a model of the hymn in the Old Testament (see the comments on that psalm), Psalm 114 has a somewhat unique form. It is perhaps best described as a psalm that tells a story.

The first section describes the escape from Egypt in highly imaginative terms (vv. 1–4). After this description come some playful questions, directed to the sea, the river, the mountains and hills (vv. 5–6). The psalm ends with a description of the coming of the Lord (vv. 7–8).

When the Sea Ran Away (114:1–4)

This psalm is about the exodus from Egypt. Its first three words in Hebrew are literally translated "when-they-went-out, Israel, from-Egypt." The Greek version of the psalm begins, "In the *exodus*. . . ." The focus is immediately on the event that is central to the faith of the Old Testament.

The psalm provides an excellent example of the poetic technique of synonymous parallelism (see the Introduction). In the first verses, "Israel" is balanced by "house of Jacob," and "Egypt" is balanced by "people of strange language." Reading through the psalm, one finds the balancing terms *Judah/Israel*, *sanctuary/dominion*, *sea/Jordan*, *fled/turned back*, and so on.

The psalm writer was aware of the linguistic differences between Israelites and Egyptians, referring to the latter's "strange language." Recall that Joseph called for a translator when he met his brothers, pretending he did not understand their Hebrew (Gen. 42:23). In verse 1, "Israel" refers to the whole people. Verse 2 assumes the split between Israel and Judah after the death of Solomon in 922 B.C.

Verse 3 balances the miracle of the parting of the Red Sea, or Sea of Reeds (Exodus 14–15), with the story of the miraculous crossing of the Jordan River (Josh. 3:14–17). The excitement of the events propels the writer into poetry, personifying sea and river, mountains and hills.

The Coming of the Lord (114:5–8)

Verses 3–4 have described the extraordinary movements of the waters and the mountains. The questions are, What did the sea see that caused it to run away? What caused the Jordan River to flow backward, clearing a pathway for the Israelites to cross (Josh. 3:14–17)? What could make the mountains and hills skip about like sheep?

Verses 7–8 provide the answers: it was the presence of the Lord that brought about all these reactions in nature. These verses describe a *theophany*, which means an appearance of God. Psalm 29 also speaks of nature's reactions at the presence of the Lord (Sirion is another name for Mount Hermon):

> He makes Lebanon skip like a calf,
>   and Sirion like a young wild ox.
>   (Ps. 29:6)

Now, in Psalm 114, the earth is addressed as a person and called to "tremble" at the Lord's presence. The psalm ends with recollections of the miraculous provision of water when the Israelites were wandering in the wilderness (see Exod. 17:6; Num. 20:11).

The Exodus Model

It has been pointed out above that Psalms 113 and 114 play a central role in the Jewish festival of Passover, which recalls the events surrounding the exodus as the great act of deliverance in Israel's history.

When the early Christians sought to describe the crucifixion and resurrection of Jesus, one of the sources for imagery and language was the exodus story. That account of deliverance from bondage became one of the models used for describing the deliverance achieved on the cross. Jesus is presented in John's Gospel as the Passover lamb (John 19:14, 36) or the Lamb of God (John 1:29). Paul uses Passover imagery in writing to the church at Corinth, declaring, "Our Passover Lamb is Christ, who has already been sacrificed" (1 Cor. 5:7, CEV).

Jews remember and celebrate the deliverance from Egypt with the Passover meal. Christians celebrate the deliverance from sin and death achieved by God through Christ with the Lord's Supper. Both meals remember and celebrate mighty acts of God.

OURS IS THE EARTH
Psalm 115

> 115:1 Not to us, O LORD, not to us, but to your name give glory,
>   for the sake of your steadfast love and your faithfulness.
>   2 Why should the nations say,
>   "Where is their God?"
>
>   3 Our God is in the heavens;
>   he does whatever he pleases.
>   4 Their idols are silver and gold,
>   the work of human hands.

⁵ They have mouths, but do not speak;
   eyes, but do not see.
⁶ They have ears, but do not hear;
   noses, but do not smell.
⁷ They have hands, but do not feel;
   feet, but do not walk;
   they make no sound in their throats.
⁸ Those who make them are like them;
   so are all who trust in them.

⁹ O Israel, trust in the LORD!
   He is their help and their shield.
¹⁰ O house of Aaron, trust in the LORD!
   He is their help and their shield.
¹¹ You who fear the LORD, trust in the LORD!
   He is their help and their shield.

¹² The LORD has been mindful of us; he will bless us;
   he will bless the house of Israel;
   he will bless the house of Aaron;
¹³ he will bless those who fear the LORD,
   both small and great.

¹⁴ May the LORD give you increase,
   both you and your children.
¹⁵ May you be blessed by the LORD,
   who made heaven and earth.

¹⁶ The heavens are the LORD's heavens,
   but the earth he has given to human beings.
¹⁷ The dead do not praise the LORD,
   nor do any that go down into silence.
¹⁸ But we will bless the LORD
   from this time on and forevermore.
   Praise the LORD!

"In the beginning . . . God created the heavens and the earth." This is the way the Bible begins. Psalm 115 has the same broad focus. "May you be blessed by the LORD," it says, "who made heaven and earth" (v. 15).

For the People's Worship

There are a number of unanswered questions in connection with the production of this psalm. Why do a number of ancient manuscripts join Psalms 114 and 115 into one psalm? What is the relationship between verses 4–8 of this psalm and verses 15–18 of Psalm 135, which are almost identical? The writers of these psalms drew on common materials or borrowed from each other in ways that are no longer clear to us.

The psalm begins with an affirmation that honor belongs to the Lord and a complaint about the nations, in question form (vv. 1–2). Verses 3–8 answer the question in verse 2 concerning the whereabouts of God and continue with a satirical description of the powerlessness of the gods these nations worship. Verses 9–13 are a triple call for trust in the Lord, followed by a triple announcement of blessing. The psalm concludes with a double blessing (vv. 14–15); some observations on heaven, earth, and the dead; and a final call to praise the Lord (vv. 16–18).

The repetitive form of verses 9–11 and 12–13, as well as the changes of speakers, suggests that the psalm was used by the people in public worship, as a liturgy.

Where Is Their God? (115:1–2)

There are hints here that the people of Israel are having problems with the nations surrounding them. These neighbors are raising a theological question. They look at Israel and say, "Where is their God?" The situation must have been such that there were doubts about the Lord's presence with Israel.

In this situation, the psalm begins with a doubled declaration that all honor should be given to the Lord, because of the Lord's covenant love and loyalty toward Israel (*hesed*; see on Psalm 136) and because of the Lord's faithfulness.

But Israel's neighbors are raising questions about the whereabouts of Israel's God.

Our God, Their Gods (115:3–8)

The questions are answered quickly with a statement about where God is and an additional declaration about God's freedom to do whatever God pleases (v. 3). Following this, the psalmist goes on the offensive, speaking to the gathered congregation about the "gods" of the neighbors. They cannot "do what they please"; in fact, they can do nothing at all (vv. 4–7)! The Lord, the God of Israel, is the one who made the heavens and the earth (v. 15). These "gods" can do nothing, have made nothing, and in fact have themselves been "made" (the same verb as in v. 15) by people who then turn around and worship them (v. 8). One is reminded of the satire on idol worship in Isaiah 44:9–20, where the prophet shows the silliness of people who will wear themselves out making a god (44:12) and then call for help to the thing they themselves have put together (44:17). Psalm 115 points up the foolishness of those who make idols and then rely on the things they have made for help (v. 8).

Who Do You Trust? (115:9–15)

After describing those who put their trust in things they themselves have made, the psalm issues a call to the people gathered for worship to put their trust in the Lord (vv. 9–11). Those addressed are first "Israel," the people as a whole; then the "house of Aaron," which refers to the clergy or priests; and finally those who "fear the Lord," which is probably a reference to foreigners who have joined in with the people of Israel to worship the Lord (Isa. 56:6). In this connection, one thinks of the "God-fearers," Gentiles who joined in synagogue worship, mentioned in the New Testament (Acts 10:2, 22; 13:16, 26). To *trust* in the Lord means to rely on the Lord, like a child resting in its mother's arms (Psalm 131; see also the other "psalms of trust," such as 11, 16, 23, 27, 62, 63). The Lord is their "help," who intervenes actively to rescue people in trouble, and also their "shield," which refers to defending the people from attackers.

The same three groups are mentioned as the speaker promises those gathered that the Lord has remembered them and will bless them all (vv. 12–13). A final wish for the congregation asks that the Lord *bless* them (on "blessing," see on Psalm 144). This is not a god who cannot do anything, like the gods described in verses 4–7, but the God who made the heavens and the earth (v. 15).

Ours Is the Earth (115:16–18)

Verses 16–18 speak in terms of three realms. The Lord is in the heavens, humans have been given the earth, and the dead exist in a place where there is only silence. The psalm concludes with a resolution to praise the Lord forever and a call to praise (in Hebrew, "Praise the LORD" is "Hallelujah").

What is striking in considering this psalm at the beginning of a new millennium is the comment that "the earth he has given to human beings" (v. 16). Ecologists and environmentalists as well as poets and prophets are calling our attention to what has been happening to the fragile planet we call home. Our oceans and lakes and rivers have become polluted; our air is no longer clear and clean; our soils have been poisoned by chemicals. Our forests, the lungs of the planet, are being destroyed, and we are losing thousands of species of life.

At this time in the history of life on our planet, words from the Bible that we have not noticed catch our attention. Our "spaceship Earth" is a wonderland filled with God's creatures and maintained through God's care (Psalm 104). Humans have been given dominion over the earth and are called to act as responsible royalty (Psalm 8; see also Gen. 1:26–28), not only tilling the land but also keeping it (see Gen. 2:15 and context).

Verse 16 from Psalm 115 puts it clearly and simply: this blue planet that we call our home has been given to us as a gift, and the giver is the Lord. The heavens are the Lord's, but the earth is ours (v. 16).

THE POWER OF A PRAYER
Psalm 116

116:1 I love the LORD, because he has heard
    my voice and my supplications.
2 Because he inclined his ear to me,
    therefore I will call on him as long as I live.
3 The snares of death encompassed me;
    the pangs of Sheol laid hold on me;
    I suffered distress and anguish.
4 Then I called on the name of the LORD:
    "O LORD, I pray, save my life!"

5 Gracious is the LORD, and righteous;
    our God is merciful.
6 The LORD protects the simple;
    when I was brought low, he saved me.
7 Return, O my soul, to your rest,
    for the LORD has dealt bountifully with you.

8 For you have delivered my soul from death,
    my eyes from tears,
    my feet from stumbling.
9 I walk before the LORD
    in the land of the living.
10 I kept my faith, even when I said,
    "I am greatly afflicted";
11 I said in my consternation,
    "Everyone is a liar."

12 What shall I return to the LORD
    for all his bounty to me?

¹³ I will lift up the cup of salvation
   and call on the name of the Lord,
¹⁴ I will pay my vows to the Lord
   in the presence of all his people.
¹⁵ Precious in the sight of the Lord
   is the death of his faithful ones.
¹⁶ O Lord, I am your servant;
   I am your servant, the child of your serving girl.
   You have loosed my bonds.
¹⁷ I will offer to you a thanksgiving sacrifice
   and call on the name of the Lord.
¹⁸ I will pay my vows to the Lord
   in the presence of all his people,
¹⁹ in the courts of the house of the Lord,
   in your midst, O Jerusalem.
   Praise the Lord!

Psalm 116 is sung or recited each year at Passover time in Jewish homes to this day. It is a part of the collection of psalms running from 113–118, called the "Egyptian Hallel" (Egyptian praise), centering on the story of the exodus from Egypt.

Psalm 113 is a hymn, portraying both the might and the caring concern of the Lord. Psalm 114 focuses on the story of the exodus, when the Lord delivered the people of Israel out of slavery in Egypt into a new life as free people. Psalm 115 is a call to praise and trust this God who not only delivered Israel but continues to help and bless them and all who fear the Lord.

Psalm 114 tells the story of the *nation's* deliverance from bondage in Israel and is followed by brief words of praise (Ps. 115:1, 18). Psalm 116 now tells the story of an *individual's* deliverance from death and is again followed by brief words of praise, in Psalm 117.

The psalm contains the typical elements of a *song of thanksgiving* (see the comments on Psalm 30). It begins with a *short summary* of the deliverance experienced and a *vow to call on the Lord* for a lifetime (vv. 1–2), then tells the *story of the deliverance* (vv. 3–11). The final section provides the script for the fulfillment of the *vow to praise and to give thanks* (vv. 12–19).

A Near-Death Experience (116:1–2, 3–11)

The psalm begins by summarizing what the writer has experienced. The writer is speaking about the Lord, addressing the gathered congregation (vv. 18–19). "The Lord has answered my prayers," the psalmist says, "and

I'll keep calling on the Lord for help for the rest of my life" (vv. 1–2, paraphrase).

The psalm does not describe the specific situation out of which the psalmist was delivered. It does, however, indicate that this situation was very serious, a matter of death or life: "The snares of death encompassed me . . . I suffered distress and anguish" (v. 3). This psalm was the prayer of a person facing death: "O LORD, . . . save my life!" (v. 4).

As the story continues, the psalm makes some theological statements. Here are listed a number of general characteristics of God, who is identified as gracious, righteous, merciful, and protective of ordinary people. Then follows a summary of the writer's own experience: "when I was brought low, he saved me" (vv. 5–6).

Now the psalm switches back and forth, the writer addressing himself (v. 7), then the Lord, this time in a summary statement recalling the serious situation: "You have delivered my soul from death" (v. 8). Again addressing the gathered congregation, the one who has been delivered describes life as a walk with the Lord. Despite personal difficulties and attacks from others, the psalmist continued to believe and trust in the Lord and was finally delivered (vv. 9–11).

Calling on the Name of the Lord (116:12–19)

The last part of the psalm is a fulfilling of the promise to call on the name of the Lord, as announced in verse 2. In the presence of the gathered congregation, the psalmist gives thanks to the God who has rescued him (vv. 12–14). Lifting the "cup of salvation" apparently refers to a liturgical act of thanksgiving. Verse 15 affirms the value of each of the Lord's people. The death of any one of these is costly in the Lord's eyes.

The psalm concludes with the psalmist promising to be the Lord's servant and offering a sacrifice and a prayer in the temple, thereby fulfilling the vow to call on the Lord for a lifetime (v. 2).

The Power of a Prayer

This psalm was written because someone experienced being delivered from death and then being given a fresh start at a new life. This person begins the psalm with a declaration "I love the LORD" and with a vow to call on the Lord for the remainder of a lifetime.

The psalmist also has a story to tell, and tells it to the gathered congregation. The situation had been desperate, filled with distress and anguish. Death seemed to reach into life, snaring and surrounding this person (v. 3). Days were filled with weeping; weakness had made even walking difficult (v. 8).

In this situation the psalmist had prayed a simple and direct prayer: "O LORD, I pray, save my life" (v. 4)! The Lord did save, and finally the psalmist could relax and recover and rest (vv. 6–7) and also walk again, "in the land of the living" (v. 9). With words addressed to himself, the psalmist declares that it was the Lord who gave help through all of this (v. 7).

The telling of the story continues. While going through these trials, the psalmist had complained, "I am greatly afflicted!" and "Everyone is a liar!" But despite all these pains and lies, the psalmist remained loyal to the Lord: "I kept my faith" (vv. 10–11).

A near-death experience, a desperate prayer, a dramatic restoration to life, once again walking around in the land of the living—this was the chain of events that the psalmist experienced!

All of this led to a changed life and a rededication to a life of service and of thanks and praise to the Lord (vv. 16–17). The person who wrote this psalm told this story in the presence of others who had gathered for worship, so that they might learn that prayer does change things. After all, the psalmist had prayed, "LORD, . . . save my life!"—and there he was, standing before them, alive!

PRAISE FROM THIS PLANET
Psalm 117

117:1 **Praise the LORD, all you nations!**
　　　　Extol him, all you peoples!
　2 **For great is his steadfast love toward us,**
　　　　and the faithfulness of the LORD endures forever.
　　　　Praise the LORD!

The story of the Lord's delivering Israel from Egypt in Psalm 114 is followed by a psalm that celebrates God's power over all the nations of the earth (Ps. 115:1–8). In a similar manner, the account of the Lord's delivering an individual from death in Psalm 116 is followed by a psalm calling on all nations of the earth to praise the Lord as their God.

In Psalms 114–115 and 116–117, all parts of the "Egyptian Hallel" (see on Psalm 113), an account of a particular deliverance is followed by an assertion of universal sovereignty. The God who heard the prayer of the people Israel (Exod. 3:7) and of a persecuted individual (Ps. 116:4) is also the God of all the peoples of the planet.

Psalm 117 is built on the pattern of the hymn (see on Psalm 113), with opening and closing *calls to praise* ("Praise the LORD" in vv. 1 and 2c) enclosing *reasons for praise* (v. 2a).

Two things are noteworthy about this psalm. First, with but seventeen words in Hebrew, it is the shortest one (Psalm 134 is runner-up, with twenty-three words). Second, though short in length, it is among the broadest of the psalms in scope. All the nations, all the people of this planet, are invited to praise the Lord, because of the Lord's steadfast love (Hebrew, *hesed* = unmotivated love) and faithfulness.

With this declaration of such a wide-hearted love, the psalm anticipates those words of Jesus in the Fourth Gospel, declaring that God so loved (Greek, *agape* = unmotivated love) the people of this planet that God gave God's only Son to die, so that they might have everlasting life (John 3:16).

When the apostle Paul was making the point that God's love was for all the people of the earth, he listed four passages from the Old Testament to nail down his point. Among those passages was the first verse of Psalm 117, calling for praise from the entire planet: "Praise the Lord, all you Gentiles, and let all the peoples praise him" (Rom. 15:11).

I LIVE TO TELL THE STORIES
Psalm 118

118:1 **O give thanks to the LORD, for he is good;**
     his steadfast love endures forever!

2 **Let Israel say,**
     "His steadfast love endures forever."
3 **Let the house of Aaron say,**
     "His steadfast love endures forever."
4 **Let those who fear the LORD say,**
     "His steadfast love endures forever."

5 **Out of my distress I called on the LORD;**
     the LORD answered me and set me in a broad place.
6 **With the LORD on my side I do not fear.**
     What can mortals do to me?
7 **The LORD is on my side to help me;**
     I shall look in triumph on those who hate me.
8 **It is better to take refuge in the LORD**
     than to put confidence in mortals.
9 **It is better to take refuge in the LORD**
     than to put confidence in princes.

¹⁰ All nations surrounded me;
    in the name of the LORD I cut them off!
¹¹ They surrounded me, surrounded me on every side;
    in the name of the LORD I cut them off!
¹² They surrounded me like bees;
    they blazed like a fire of thorns;
    in the name of the LORD I cut them off!
¹³ I was pushed hard, so that I was falling,
    but the LORD helped me.
¹⁴ The LORD is my strength and my might;
    he has become my salvation.

¹⁵ There are glad songs of victory in the tents of the righteous:
    "The right hand of the LORD does valiantly;
¹⁶   the right hand of the LORD is exalted;
    the right hand of the LORD does valiantly."
¹⁷ I shall not die, but I shall live,
    and recount the deeds of the LORD.
¹⁸ The LORD has punished me severely,
    but he did not give me over to death.

¹⁹ Open to me the gates of righteousness,
    that I may enter through them
    and give thanks to the LORD.

²⁰ This is the gate of the LORD;
    the righteous shall enter through it.

²¹ I thank you that you have answered me
    and have become my salvation.
²² The stone that the builders rejected
    has become the chief cornerstone.
²³ This is the LORD's doing;
    it is marvelous in our eyes.
²⁴ This is the day that the LORD has made;
    let us rejoice and be glad in it.
²⁵ Save us, we beseech you, O LORD!
    O LORD, we beseech you, give us success!

²⁶ Blessed is the one who comes in the name of the LORD.
    We bless you from the house of the LORD.
²⁷ The LORD is God,
    and he has given us light.
    Bind the festal procession with branches,
    up to the horns of the altar.

²⁸ **You are my God, and I will give thanks to you;**
you are my God, I will extol you.

²⁹ **O give thanks to the LORD, for he is good,**
for his steadfast love endures forever.

High above the plains and rolling hills of Bavaria in southern Germany rises the Coburg Castle. Today's visitor walks into the courtyard to find a massive sculpture of Martin Luther holding a Bible. Luther hid out in the Coburg from the end of April to the beginning of October in 1530. He wrote a good many pieces for publication during these months, including extensive commentaries on Psalms 117 and 118. On the wall of the room where he did his writing was painted, in large letters, a quotation from Psalm 118:17, in German. The restored quote can still be seen on that wall. It translates "I shall not die, but I shall live, and recount the deeds of the Lord." This psalm Luther named his favorite, and this text became his personal motto.

A Script for a Liturgy

Psalm 118 is marked by an unusual number of repeated phrases: "His steadfast love endures forever" and "Let X now say" in verses 1–4; "the LORD [is] on my side" in verses 6–7; "better . . . than" in verses 8 and 9; "surrounded" and "in the name of the LORD I cut them off" in verses 10–12; "right hand of the LORD" in verses 15–16. These repetitions, as well as hints of a procession into the temple (vv. 19, 26–27), suggest that the psalm was used as a script for a liturgy, with various groups that were present in the congregation speaking parts.

The psalm is located as the last of the "Egyptian Hallel" psalms (see on Psalm 113) and, in contrast to the theme of death found in Psalm 116, speaks with great confidence about triumph, salvation, and life (vv. 5–7, 14, 17).

The psalm begins with a call to give thanks (vv. 1–4), continues with a story of a deliverance (vv. 5–18) and a script for a processional (vv. 19–28), and concludes in verse 29 with a repetition of verse 1, tying the psalm together.

O Give Thanks! (118:1–4)

The opening of the psalm indicates that it was used in community worship, first calling on all present to "give thanks" and then addressing in turn the entire assembly (Israel), the priests (house of Aaron), and visitors (those who fear the Lord) to join in the praise of the Lord. The formula found in verse 1 also occurs at the beginnings of Psalms 106 and 107, throughout Psalm 136, and often in Chronicles (1 Chron. 16:34; 2 Chron. 5:11–14; 7:1–3; 20:21).

We can imagine this psalm as a lively liturgy, with a leader giving the call to worship in verse 1 and then calling on the various groups listed in verses 2–4 to respond.

Telling What the Lord Has Done (118:5–18)

At the end of this section, the speaker refers to "recounting the deeds of the Lord" (v. 17). The section running from verses 5–18 is a personal testimony given before the congregation, thus providing an example of such a recounting.

The testimony begins in verse 5 with a short summary of what the speaker has experienced. The Hebrew behind "distress" has the sense of being cramped or narrow. The one praying had been squeezed, cramped, pressed, but then the Lord put that person in "a broad place." Luther's comments, written from exile in the Coburg Castle, advise:

> You must learn to call [on God]. Do not sit by yourself or lie on a couch, hanging and shaking your head. Do not destroy yourself with your own thoughts by worrying. . . . Say to yourself, "Come on, you lazy bum; down on your knees, and lift your eyes and hands toward heaven!" (*Selected Psalms III*, 14:60–61)

The psalmist's trust in the Lord is expressed in verses 6–9. Paul's words, "If God is for us, who is against us?" in Romans 8:31 are reminiscent of verse 6. The writer to the Hebrews quotes verse 6 in Hebrews 13:6.

Verses 10–18 tell of the distress and the deliverance that the psalmist experienced. Do verses 10–13 and 15–16 report a military victory? In that case, the speaker would be a king, telling of experiences while leading Israel's armies. But the words could also be an individual's dramatic description of difficulties faced and deliverance experienced.

One thing is clear in this section: it was the Lord who helped the person who had "called on the LORD." That was stated in verse 5 and is restated in verses 13b, 14, 18b, and in the victory songs of verses 15–16.

The central thematic statement of the psalm appears in verse 17. Martin Luther saw in it the story of his own life and the purpose for his living and thus put these words on the wall of his study at Coburg Castle as his personal motto. The psalmist looks back at difficult times as the Lord's punishment and is glad to be alive (v. 18).

Open the Gates! (118:19–29)

Here is a hint that the psalm was used as a script for some sort of liturgical ceremony. One could imagine a procession waiting outside for the gates to the temple area to be opened (vv. 19–20b; see Ps. 24:7–10). With verse 21, the individual who told the story of deliverance (vv. 10–18) gives public thanks to the Lord.

The sense of verse 22 is that a person once rejected by the community has now become a prominent leader. The verse is often cited in the New Testament in reference to Jesus Christ, sometimes with verse 23 (Matt. 21:42; Mark 12:10–11; Luke 20:17; Acts 4:11; 1 Peter 2:4–8).

Verse 24 is often cited on special days or times of festivals. When Jesus arrived in Jerusalem on Palm Sunday, the crowds shouted words from verse 26 (Matt. 21:9; Mark 11:9–10; Luke 13:35; 19:38). Verse 27b refers to an action connected with the procession; the details are not clear. With verse 29, the psalm wraps up by referring back to verse 1.

Living to Tell the Stories

This has been one of the most popular of the psalms in both Judaism and Christianity. In both traditions, it is connected with the central act of deliverance: the exodus for Jews, the resurrection for Christians.

For Jews, Psalm 118 is part of the "Egyptian Hallel" and is therefore sung or read in connection with the story of the exodus from Egypt at Passover time each year. If Psalm 114 provides a description of the deliverance at the Sea of Reeds, Psalm 118 provides a script for celebrating that deliverance and, in fact, for celebrating all the saving acts of God. Verses 5–18 tell the story of one such saving act, and verse 17 promises more, similar stories. Verse 21 speaks again of the Lord's saving, and verse 25 calls for more such actions.

In the New Testament, the psalm provided a clue for understanding the event of the resurrection of Jesus at Easter. Resurrection is not to be separated from crucifixion. Jesus is identified as "the stone that the builders rejected," which has now become "the chief cornerstone" (Matt. 21:42; Mark 12:10; Luke 20:17; Acts 4:11; 1 Peter 2:7; and contexts for all these references). The event of the resurrection is "the Lord's doing . . . marvelous in our eyes" (Ps. 118:23; see Matt. 21:42; Mark 12:11).

Selected portions of Psalm 118 are also part of liturgies for burial (for example, vv. 5, 8–9, 15–17, 19–20). Those words still visible on the wall in Coburg Castle continue to catch both the promise and the task set before believers: "I shall not die, but I shall live, and recount the deeds of the Lord."

A PSALM FOR SOJOURNERS
Psalm 119

119:1 Happy are those whose way is blameless,
who walk in the law of the LORD.
2 Happy are those who keep his decrees,
who seek him with their whole heart,
3 who also do no wrong,
but walk in his ways.
4 You have commanded your precepts
to be kept diligently.
5 O that my ways may be steadfast
in keeping your statutes!
6 Then I shall not be put to shame,
having my eyes fixed on all your commandments.
7 I will praise you with an upright heart,
when I learn your righteous ordinances.
8 I will observe your statutes;
do not utterly forsake me.

9 How can young people keep their way pure?
By guarding it according to your word.
10 With my whole heart I seek you;
do not let me stray from your commandments.
11 I treasure your word in my heart,
so that I may not sin against you.
12 Blessed are you, O LORD;
teach me your statutes.
13 With my lips I declare
all the ordinances of your mouth.
14 I delight in the way of your decrees
as much as in all riches.
15 I will meditate on your precepts,
and fix my eyes on your ways.
16 I will delight in your statutes;
I will not forget your word.

17 Deal bountifully with your servant,
so that I may live and observe your word.
18 Open my eyes, so that I may behold
wondrous things out of your law.
19 I live as an alien in the land;
do not hide your commandments from me.
20 My soul is consumed with longing
for your ordinances at all times.

²¹ You rebuke the insolent, accursed ones,
    who wander from your commandments;
²² take away from me their scorn and contempt,
    for I have kept your decrees.
²³ Even though princes sit plotting against me,
    your servant will meditate on your statutes.
²⁴ Your decrees are my delight,
    they are my counselors.

²⁵ My soul clings to the dust;
    revive me according to your word.
²⁶ When I told of my ways, you answered me;
    teach me your statutes.
²⁷ Make me understand the way of your precepts,
    and I will meditate on your wondrous works.
²⁸ My soul melts away for sorrow;
    strengthen me according to your word.
²⁹ Put false ways far from me;
    and graciously teach me your law.
³⁰ I have chosen the way of faithfulness;
    I set your ordinances before me.
³¹ I cling to your decrees, O LORD;
    let me not be put to shame.
³² I run the way of your commandments,
    for you enlarge my understanding.

³³ Teach me, O LORD, the way of your statutes,
    and I will observe it to the end.
³⁴ Give me understanding, that I may keep your law
    and observe it with my whole heart.
³⁵ Lead me in the path of your commandments,
    for I delight in it.
³⁶ Turn my heart to your decrees,
    and not to selfish gain.
³⁷ Turn my eyes from looking at vanities;
    give me life in your ways.
³⁸ Confirm to your servant your promise,
    which is for those who fear you.
³⁹ Turn away the disgrace that I dread,
    for your ordinances are good.
⁴⁰ See, I have longed for your precepts;
    in your righteousness give me life.

⁴¹ Let your steadfast love come to me, O LORD,
    your salvation according to your promise.

⁴² Then I shall have an answer for those who taunt me,
   for I trust in your word.
⁴³ Do not take the word of truth utterly out of my mouth,
   for my hope is in your ordinances.
⁴⁴ I will keep your law continually,
   forever and ever.
⁴⁵ I shall walk at liberty,
   for I have sought your precepts.
⁴⁶ I will also speak of your decrees before kings,
   and shall not be put to shame;
⁴⁷ I find my delight in your commandments,
   because I love them.
⁴⁸ I revere your commandments, which I love,
   and I will meditate on your statutes.

⁴⁹ Remember your word to your servant,
   in which you have made me hope.
⁵⁰ This is my comfort in my distress,
   that your promise gives me life.
⁵¹ The arrogant utterly deride me,
   but I do not turn away from your law.
⁵² When I think of your ordinances from of old,
   I take comfort, O Lord.
⁵³ Hot indignation seizes me because of the wicked,
   those who forsake your law.
⁵⁴ Your statutes have been my songs
   wherever I make my home.
⁵⁵ I remember your name in the night, O Lord,
   and keep your law.
⁵⁶ This blessing has fallen to me,
   for I have kept your precepts.

⁵⁷ The Lord is my portion;
   I promise to keep your words.
⁵⁸ I implore your favor with all my heart;
   be gracious to me according to your promise.
⁵⁹ When I think of your ways,
   I turn my feet to your decrees;
⁶⁰ I hurry and do not delay
   to keep your commandments.
⁶¹ Though the cords of the wicked ensnare me,
   I do not forget your law.
⁶² At midnight I rise to praise you,
   because of your righteous ordinances.
⁶³ I am a companion of all who fear you,

of those who keep your precepts.
64 The earth, O LORD, is full of your steadfast love;
    teach me your statutes.

65 You have dealt well with your servant,
    O LORD, according to your word.
66 Teach me good judgment and knowledge,
    for I believe in your commandments.
67 Before I was humbled I went astray,
    but now I keep your word.
68 You are good and do good;
    teach me your statutes.
69 The arrogant smear me with lies,
    but with my whole heart I keep your precepts.
70 Their hearts are fat and gross,
    but I delight in your law.
71 It is good for me that I was humbled,
    so that I might learn your statutes.
72 The law of your mouth is better to me
    than thousands of gold and silver pieces.

73 Your hands have made and fashioned me;
    give me understanding that I may learn your commandments.
74 Those who fear you shall see me and rejoice,
    because I have hoped in your word.
75 I know, O LORD, that your judgments are right,
    and that in faithfulness you have humbled me.
76 Let your steadfast love become my comfort
    according to your promise to your servant.
77 Let your mercy come to me, that I may live;
    for your law is my delight.
78 Let the arrogant be put to shame,
    because they have subverted me with guile;
    as for me, I will meditate on your precepts.
79 Let those who fear you turn to me,
    so that they may know your decrees.
80 May my heart be blameless in your statutes,
    so that I may not be put to shame.

81 My soul languishes for your salvation;
    I hope in your word.
82 My eyes fail with watching for your promise;
    I ask, "When will you comfort me?"
83 For I have become like a wineskin in the smoke,
    yet I have not forgotten your statutes.

84 How long must your servant endure?
   When will you judge those who persecute me?
85 The arrogant have dug pitfalls for me;
   they flout your law.
86 All your commandments are enduring;
   I am persecuted without cause; help me!
87 They have almost made an end of me on earth;
   but I have not forsaken your precepts.
88 In your steadfast love spare my life,
   so that I may keep the decrees of your mouth.

89 The LORD exists forever;
   your word is firmly fixed in heaven.
90 Your faithfulness endures to all generations;
   you have established the earth, and it stands fast.
91 By your appointment they stand today,
   for all things are your servants.
92 If your law had not been my delight,
   I would have perished in my misery.
93 I will never forget your precepts,
   for by them you have given me life.
94 I am yours; save me,
   for I have sought your precepts.
95 The wicked lie in wait to destroy me,
   but I consider your decrees.
96 I have seen a limit to all perfection,
   but your commandment is exceedingly broad.

97 Oh, how I love your law!
   It is my meditation all day long.
98 Your commandment makes me wiser than my enemies,
   for it is always with me.
99 I have more understanding than all my teachers,
   for your decrees are my meditation.
100 I understand more than the aged,
   for I keep your precepts.
101 I hold back my feet from every evil way,
   in order to keep your word.
102 I do not turn away from your ordinances,
   for you have taught me.
103 How sweet are your words to my taste,
   sweeter than honey to my mouth!
104 Through your precepts I get understanding;
   therefore I hate every false way.

105 Your word is a lamp to my feet
        and a light to my path.
106 I have sworn an oath and confirmed it,
        to observe your righteous ordinances.
107 I am severely afflicted;
        give me life, O LORD, according to your word.
108 Accept my offerings of praise, O LORD,
        and teach me your ordinances.
109 I hold my life in my hand continually,
        but I do not forget your law.
110 The wicked have laid a snare for me,
        but I do not stray from your precepts.
111 Your decrees are my heritage forever;
        they are the joy of my heart.
112 I incline my heart to perform your statutes
        forever, to the end.

113 I hate the double-minded,
        but I love your law.
114 You are my hiding place and my shield;
        I hope in your word.
115 Go away from me, you evildoers,
        that I may keep the commandments of my God.
116 Uphold me according to your promise, that I may live,
        and let me not be put to shame in my hope.
117 Hold me up, that I may be safe
        and have regard for your statutes continually.
118 You spurn all who go astray from your statutes;
        for their cunning is in vain.
119 All the wicked of the earth you count as dross;
        therefore I love your decrees.
120 My flesh trembles for fear of you,
        and I am afraid of your judgments.

121 I have done what is just and right;
        do not leave me to my oppressors.
122 Guarantee your servant's well-being;
        do not let the godless oppress me.
123 My eyes fail from watching for your salvation,
        and for the fulfillment of your righteous promise.
124 Deal with your servant according to your steadfast love,
        and teach me your statutes.
125 I am your servant; give me understanding,
        so that I may know your decrees.
126 It is time for the LORD to act,

for your law has been broken.
¹²⁷ Truly I love your commandments
    more than gold, more than fine gold.
¹²⁸ Truly I direct my steps by all your precepts;
    I hate every false way.

¹²⁹ Your decrees are wonderful;
    therefore my soul keeps them.
¹³⁰ The unfolding of your words gives light;
    it imparts understanding to the simple.
¹³¹ With open mouth I pant,
    because I long for your commandments.
¹³² Turn to me and be gracious to me,
    as is your custom toward those who love your name.
¹³³ Keep my steps steady according to your promise,
    and never let iniquity have dominion over me.
¹³⁴ Redeem me from human oppression,
    that I may keep your precepts.
¹³⁵ Make your face shine upon your servant,
    and teach me your statutes.
¹³⁶ My eyes shed streams of tears
    because your law is not kept.

¹³⁷ You are righteous, O LORD,
    and your judgments are right.
¹³⁸ You have appointed your decrees in righteousness
    and in all faithfulness.
¹³⁹ My zeal consumes me
    because my foes forget your words.
¹⁴⁰ Your promise is well tried,
    and your servant loves it.
¹⁴¹ I am small and despised,
    yet I do not forget your precepts.
¹⁴² Your righteousness is an everlasting righteousness,
    and your law is the truth.
¹⁴³ Trouble and anguish have come upon me,
    but your commandments are my delight.
¹⁴⁴ Your decrees are righteous forever;
    give me understanding that I may live.

¹⁴⁵ With my whole heart I cry; answer me, O LORD.
    I will keep your statutes.
¹⁴⁶ I cry to you; save me,
    that I may observe your decrees.
¹⁴⁷ I rise before dawn and cry for help;

I put my hope in your words.
¹⁴⁸ My eyes are awake before each watch of the night,
    that I may meditate on your promise.
¹⁴⁹ In your steadfast love hear my voice;
    O LORD, in your justice preserve my life.
¹⁵⁰ Those who persecute me with evil purpose draw near;
    they are far from your law.
¹⁵¹ Yet you are near, O LORD,
    and all your commandments are true.
¹⁵² Long ago I learned from your decrees
    that you have established them forever.

¹⁵³ Look on my misery and rescue me,
    for I do not forget your law.
¹⁵⁴ Plead my cause and redeem me;
    give me life according to your promise.
¹⁵⁵ Salvation is far from the wicked,
    for they do not seek your statutes.
¹⁵⁶ Great is your mercy, O LORD;
    give me life according to your justice.
¹⁵⁷ Many are my persecutors and my adversaries,
    yet I do not swerve from your decrees.
¹⁵⁸ I look at the faithless with disgust,
    because they do not keep your commands.
¹⁵⁹ Consider how I love your precepts;
    preserve my life according to your steadfast love.
¹⁶⁰ The sum of your word is truth;
    and every one of your righteous ordinances endures forever.

¹⁶¹ Princes persecute me without cause,
    but my heart stands in awe of your words.
¹⁶² I rejoice at your word
    like one who finds great spoil.
¹⁶³ I hate and abhor falsehood,
    but I love your law.
¹⁶⁴ Seven times a day I praise you
    for your righteous ordinances.
¹⁶⁵ Great peace have those who love your law;
    nothing can make them stumble.
¹⁶⁶ I hope for your salvation, O LORD,
    and I fulfill your commandments.
¹⁶⁷ My soul keeps your decrees;
    I love them exceedingly.
¹⁶⁸ I keep your precepts and decrees,
    for all my ways are before you.

169 Let my cry come before you, O LORD;
     give me understanding according to your word.
170 Let my supplication come before you;
     deliver me according to your promise.
171 My lips will pour forth praise,
     because you teach me your statutes.
172 My tongue will sing of your promise,
     for all your commandments are right.
173 Let your hand be ready to help me,
     for I have chosen your precepts.
174 I long for your salvation, O LORD,
     and your law is my delight.
175 Let me live that I may praise you,
     and let your ordinances help me.
176 I have gone astray like a lost sheep; seek out your servant,
     for I do not forget your commandments.

Psalm 119 is designed for people who understand life to be a journey through territory that is not their homeland. In other words, this is a psalm for persons who understand themselves as sojourners.

The psalm begins by portraying life as a "way" and the living of life as walking in that way:

> Happy are those whose way is blameless,
>   who walk according to the teaching of the LORD.
>   (v. 1, my translation)

The writer of the psalm declares, "I am a sojourner on earth" (v. 19, RSV). The word *sojourner* means a resident alien, a foreigner who lives in a place other than his or her homeland. Such a person needs the word of the Lord as a light to find the way (v. 105) and needs the Good Shepherd for times when, like a lost sheep, he or she has lost the way (v. 176).

This picture of the believer as a person on the way, passing through a foreign land, is a key for understanding the psalm as a whole.

A Love for Learning

While this is the longest psalm in the Bible, it is not the most difficult to understand. The psalm is built according to a clear acrostic pattern. It is made up of twenty-two eight-verse units, corresponding to the twenty-two letters of the Hebrew alphabet. Each line of each unit begins with a successive letter of the Hebrew alphabet: each of verses 1–8 begins with *alef*, the first letter of the alphabet; each of verses 9–16 begins with *bet*, the second letter; and so on. A number of psalms follow an acrostic pattern (see the listing with the comments on Psalms 9–10), but this is the only one that uses each letter eight times.

Why this unusual pattern? It appears that this is a teacher's device to aid in memorizing the psalm. The content of the psalm indicates that it is indeed to be understood as "teaching" (see v. 1 above).

An important clue for understanding this psalm relates to the word *torah*, which in the Hebrew language can mean teaching, instruction, or law. That word is of central importance to this psalm, occurring twenty-five times. It should be translated as "teaching" or "instruction," not as "law" (see the comments in connection with Psalm 1). The Jewish Publication Society (JPS) translation, for example, translates it in the first two ways. This more appropriate translation gives a different ring to the entire psalm and helps clear up a number of difficult passages. "O, how I love your teaching" (v. 97, JPS) or "I love your teaching" (v. 113, JPS), for example, is more understandable and more appropriate than "I love your law" (NRSV).

Psalm 119 begins with introductory comments, addressed to readers, concerning finding happiness (vv. 1–3; see also Psalm 1). The remainder of the psalm consists of words addressed to God, a *prayer* made up of twenty-two eight-verse sections. Each section uses a number of words for God's written directives for humans: commandments, statutes, ordinances, decrees, words, precepts, promise, and *torah* (translated by the NRSV as "law" but, as indicated above, better understood as "teaching").

1. The Way of Happiness (119:1–8)

A good way to get started with this psalm is to read through Psalm 1, another teaching or *torah* psalm. That psalm also has a link with the Hebrew alphabet: the first word of Psalm 1 begins with *alef*, the first letter of the alphabet, and the last word begins with *tav*, the last letter. The first psalm tells of the happiness of those who live their lives according to the teaching (*torah*) of the Lord (Ps. 1:2). Verse 1 of Psalm 119 introduces the psalm by sounding the same theme.

2. A Word for Young People (119:9–16)

Psalm 119 is concerned about helping persons find the right way through life and begins with advice for young people. At the beginning and the end of this section are statements about the Lord's *word*, which provides direction for "keeping their way pure" or staying on track (v. 9) and which ought to be studied (NRSV, "meditate") and not forgotten (vv. 15–16).

3. A Sojourner's Life (119:17–24)

With verse 19, the writer identifies himself as a *sojourner* (RSV; NRSV, "alien"), that is, as one living in a land temporarily, as on a visit. The sojourner's life picks up direction from the Bible. The sojourner's prayer is "Open my eyes, that I may perceive the wonders of your teaching" (v. 18, JPS).

4. I Did It Your Way (119:25–32)

The central word in this segment is *way*, partly because each line in this section begins with *d* in Hebrew, and *derek* is the Hebrew for "way." *Derek* is the first word in verses 26, 27, 29, 30, 32).

The psalmist is again thinking of life as "on the way" and offers some reflections on that theme. He asks the Lord to teach him the way to go and to help him understand the Lord's directives (v. 27). The psalmist promises to study the wondrous things the Lord has done (v. 27). He also asks that the Lord remove all "false ways" from him and provide for him further instruction (v. 29). Finally, the psalmist announces his choice of the way of faithfulness (v. 30) and announces, "My way, Lord, is your way" (v. 32, paraphrase).

5. Teach Me Your Way, Lord (119:33–40)

The "way" theme continues in verse 33 and also in the prayer of verse 35, "Lead me in the path . . . ," as well as verse 37. Life is pictured as a journey along a way, down a path. Once again there is a request for instruction, indicating the pedagogical concern of this prayer-psalm: "Teach me" (v. 33; see also vv. 12, 26).

6. Love Me, Save Me (119:41–48)

This segment provides a glimpse of the psalmist's situation. Certain persons are taunting him, apparently because of his faith in the Lord (v. 42). Despite these difficulties, the psalmist continues to speak of the delight he finds in the commandments and promises to keep on studying (vv. 47–48).

7. Reflections on Remembering (119:49–56)

This is the *zayin* or *z* section of the psalm. One of the most important words beginning with that letter in the Hebrew text is *zekōr*, "remember."

Three verses here begin with that word and can provide the basis for some reflections on remembering. In a situation of some distress (v. 50), the psalmist takes comfort in remembering the Lord's promises (vv. 49–50). Another source of comfort is the Lord's ordinances, the structures the Lord has established for the ordering of life (v. 52). The writer remembers these structures and again takes comfort. Finally, when day is done, the psalmist remembers the Lord in prayers in the night (v. 55). In times of difficulty, suggests this psalm, remember God's promises, God's ordering of life, God's name in prayer.

8. The Earth Is Full of Your Steadfast Love (119:57–64)

If *remember* is one of the most important biblical Hebrew words beginning with *z* (the previous section), then *hesed*, "steadfast love," is surely one of the most important in this *h* section. That word begins the last sentence of this section, in verse 64 ("Your *hesed*, O LORD, fills the earth"; my translation). (For a psalm that celebrates this *hesed* in each verse, see Psalm 136.)

9. Teaching and Learning (119:65–72)

There are two requests in this section, each of them asking the Lord to "teach me" (vv. 66, 68). The same Hebrew verb occurs in verse 71, this time with the sense "learn." In keeping with the instructional tone of the entire psalm, this section is a prayer request to be taught by the Lord. The psalmist had strayed from the right path (v. 67) and had experienced opposition from certain "arrogant" persons. But through all this he has learned, and in fact takes delight in, the Lord's teaching (v. 70; NRSV, "law"). The key word in this *t* section of the psalm is the Hebrew *tob*, "good" (vv. 65 [NRSV, "well"], 68 (twice), 71, and 72 [NRSV, "better"]).

10. Your Teaching Is My Delight (119:73–80)

The prayer in verse 73 sets the tone for this part of the psalm. This is the *y* section of the Hebrew alphabet, and an important *y*-word in Hebrew is *yad*, which means "hand." The writer acknowledges that the Lord's hands have made him, asks for understanding, and declares that "your teaching [NRSV, "law"] is my delight" (v. 77).

11. Like a Wineskin in the Smoke (119:81–88)

This section hints at the dire situation of the one writing Psalm 119. It begins and ends with descriptions of the writer's difficulties: the writer is yearning to be rescued (v. 81, "salvation") and appeals to the Lord's steadfast love to save his life (v. 88). He is running out of patience (v. 82), experiencing persecution (vv. 84–87), and compares himself to a dried-out, brittle leather container for wine (v. 83).

12. I Am Yours; Save Me (119:89–96)

At the heart of this segment is a cry for help in a desperate situation: "save me!" (v. 94). This is the only imperative verb in this segment of the psalm. This cry to the Lord for help does not come out of the blue, from just anyone. It is coupled with a reminder of who the psalmist is, or better, of *whose* the psalmist is: "I am yours; save me!" (v. 94).

13. O How I Love Your Teaching! (119:97–104)

This is how the JPS translation translates verse 97, following with "It is my study all day long." This love for the Lord's teaching expresses itself in a life marked by study (v. 97), by right living (v. 101), and by enjoyment (v. 103).

14. Your Word Is a Lamp (119:105–112)

The picture running through this psalm is that of life as a journey. This segment assumes that it is a journey through the darkness (see Ps. 23:4). In such a situation, the Lord's word is like a flashlight helping one find the way (see also Prov. 6:23; John 8:12). "Darkness" becomes a metaphor, including personal affliction (v. 107) as well as attacks from certain wicked persons (v. 110).

15. Half-hearted Religion (119:113–120)

In Hebrew, the opening word in this *s* section (translated "double-minded") may indicate a branch that is forked. The reference here is to a person who has double loyalties or, as one Hebrew dictionary puts it, is half-hearted.

Running through the Bible is the notion that one cannot be loyal to two gods but must choose one (Josh. 24:15; 1 Kings 18:21, both in their contexts). In this psalm are two pictures for God: "hiding place" (also Ps 32:7; translated "secret place" in 1 Sam. 19:2) and "shield" (Ps. 119:114).

16. Do Something, Lord! (119:121–128)

The situation that lies behind these words is that of a person who understands himself to be God's servant (vv. 122, 124, 125) but who is now fearing oppressors (v. 121) and certain godless ones (v. 122). This person is running out of patience, waiting for the Lord to act (vv. 123, 126), but in the meantime is seeking to walk on the path the Lord desires (v. 128).

17. Lord, Be Gracious and Make Your Face Shine (119:129–136)

The language here reminds one of the benediction in Numbers 6:24–26, although here the direction of the words is different. In Numbers, the words are directed from the Lord to the people; here the direction is from the one praying to the Lord. The psalmist asks, "Be gracious to me" (v. 132) and "Make your face shine upon your servant" (v. 135).

Verse 130 offers a picture of the process of teaching scripture: such work is described as "the *unfolding* of your words." The Hebrew word is that used for the opening of a door, such as the door of a great temple (2 Chron. 29:3). To teach the Bible is to open doors!

18. "That I May Live" (119:137–144)

This segment speaks much of righteousness, because this is the *ṣ* section of the psalm, and *ṣedeq*, "righteousness," is one of the great words of the faith (here vv. 137, 138, 142, 144). The sense of the word is that everything is in order and in right relationship; *b'ṣedeq* in modern Hebrew has the sense "in order." The psalmist is experiencing bad times (vv. 141, 143) and seeks, finally, to live (v. 144).

19. Lord, Preserve My Life (119:145–152)

Like the previous segment, this one is concerned about the preservation of the writer's life (v. 149). The segment begins with a doubled "I cry" and "I cry to you." The cries are desperate, "with my whole heart" (v. 145), and accompanied with a request to "save me" (v. 146).

20. Give Me Life (119:153–160)

The segment begins with the cry to God, "*Look* on my misery and rescue me," expressed by a Hebrew word beginning with *r*, the thematic letter for this segment. The word also begins verses 158 and 159 (NRSV, "look at" and "consider"). Once again, the concern of the psalm is for life itself.

It asks for rescue from misery (vv. 153, 157) and pleads three times for life (vv. 154, 156, 159).

21. Lord, Grant Us *Shalom* (119:161–168)

At the center of this *s* section is a statement about *shalom*, the Hebrew word for peace and prosperity. Though suffering from undeserved persecution (vv. 161, 163), the psalmist maintains a discipline of daily praise (v. 164) and testifies to the *shalom* that the love of the Lord's teachings has given (v. 165).

22. A Lost Sheep (119:169–176)

The psalm comes to an end with cries for understanding and for rescue (vv. 169–170), with promises of praise (vv. 171–172), and with a request for the Lord's helping hand (v. 173). The psalmist again affirms delight in the Lord's teaching (v. 174) and asks once more for the gift of life (v. 175). Finally, the psalm provides a hint as to the psalmist's self-understanding. The psalmist is not proud and self-satisfied but is rather like a sheep that has lost its way. The final prayer provides another clue to that self-understanding: "I have gone astray like a lost sheep; seek out your servant."

A Sojourner's Life

From the start, Psalm 119 assumes that life is always "on the way" and that those persons are happy whose lives follow the way marked out by the teaching of the Lord (vv. 1–3).

The psalm is concerned with teaching, especially teaching young people (vv. 9–12). It can effectively be read aloud in a group, a section at a time, pausing after each section to ask, "What does this say about God and the ways of our lives?

The psalm prays that our ways be faithful to the Lord's teaching (v. 5) and asks that the Lord instruct us in this way (v. 33) and lead us along the right path (v. 35), so that life may be found (v. 37). The word of scripture is a light to help find the way in the darkness (v. 105), and the Lord watches over all our ways (v. 168). And should one's life leave the right path so that one is like a lost sheep, one can pray to the Lord who searches for the lost (v. 176). Those who have lived lives along this way are ready to sing praises to the Lord (vv. 171, 172, 175), whose hand has been ever ready to help (v. 173).

The next grouping of psalms (Psalms 120–134) continues to develop the theme of life as a way, or a journey, or a sojourn.

A SOJOURNER'S STORY
Psalm 120

A Song of Ascents.

120:1 In my distress I cry to the LORD,
      that he may answer me:
² "Deliver me, O LORD,
      from lying lips,
      from a deceitful tongue."

³ What shall be given to you?
      And what more shall be done to you,
      you deceitful tongue?
⁴ A warrior's sharp arrows,
      with glowing coals of the broom tree!

⁵ Woe is me, that I am an alien in Meshech,
      that I must live among the tents of Kedar.
⁶ Too long have I had my dwelling
      among those who hate peace.
⁷ I am for peace;
      but when I speak,
      they are for war.

Psalm 120 is the first of a series of psalms running from 120 to 134, each of which is identified as "A Song of Ascents," literally, "A Song for the Going Up." This expression appears to refer to "going up" to Jerusalem; the same Hebrew word appears in the reference to the tribes who "go up" to Jerusalem in Psalm 122:4. This group of fifteen psalms seems to have been used for going up to Jerusalem for one of the festivals held there (see Deut. 16:16), and thus these have been called *pilgrimage psalms*. These psalms were likely gathered together as a special collection to be used on such pilgrimages.

The Pilgrimage Psalms (Psalms 120–134)

The fifteen psalms in this grouping have a number of things in common. Each has the heading "A Song of Ascents." With the exception of Psalm 132, they are short. Their concerns are often about family matters (Psalms 127, 128, 133), and they often deal with rural issues and the life of the farmer (Psalm 126). In a lecture series on these psalms, Martin Luther said that they "deal with important teaching and almost all of the articles of our Christian faith, of preaching, forgiveness of sins, the cross, love, marriage, authorities, so that they set forth as it were a summary of all essential teachings" (Muelhaupt, *D. Martin Luthers Psalmen-Auslegung*, volume 3:599 [my translation]). In a recent study of Psalms 120–134, Klaus Seybold concludes that the world of these psalms

> is the world of the simple person and the little people, of the farmer, the handworker, the mother with small children, the father of the family, who works from early until late, who experiences both tears and jubilation, who rejoices at the festivals and thinks about religious matters. These psalms are witnesses from everyday life, witnesses of folk poetry and folk piety. All of this makes them especially precious (*Die Wallfahrtspsalmen*, p. 42 [my translation]).

A Sojourner's Story

The writer of Psalm 120 is identified as "an alien in Meshech," living "among the tents of Kedar" (v. 5). These are names of nomadic tribal groups of uncertain location but far from Jerusalem (see Isa. 21:16–17; Jer. 49:28–33). Was the psalmist living in such a faraway place? Or were these names being used figuratively, indicating that the writer has been living among war-loving foreigners?

The Hebrew word behind "alien" (*gēr*) denotes a person who lives in a place temporarily, with a permanent home somewhere else. Another translation of that word is "sojourner," from the French meaning "for a day." This is a sojourner's psalm, written by a citizen of Jerusalem who is temporarily living away from that city.

The psalm begins with a short summary of an answered prayer (vv. 1–2). The first verse should be translated "In my distress I cried to the Lord, and he answered me," rather than with the NRSV translation. This short summary of a deliverance from trouble is typical at the beginning of a "song of thanksgiving" (for example, Ps. 30:1; 116:1–2).

Verse 2 quotes the prayer of the one living as a sojourner in a foreign land. The nature of the psalmist's difficulties comes into focus: certain persons in this foreign environment were guilty of lying and deceit, sins of the tongue. Verses 6–7 indicate that these persons were making plans for war.

So how should these deceivers and liars be punished? This is the question raised in verse 3. They who are "for war" (v. 7) should themselves experience the hostility of warriors directed against them (v. 4). The "glowing coals of the broom tree" likely refers to the fires used for shaping and sharpening the points of arrows used in warfare.

Verse 5 expresses the writer's lament over living away from the homeland. The psalmist is living far away from home, not happily, and speaks of having lived for a long time "among those who hate peace [*shalom*]" (v. 6). The dilemma of the situation is expressed succinctly in verse 7: "I am for peace [*shalom*]; but when I speak, they are for war."

Such has been the psalmist's situation. But now, the psalmist is back in the temple, giving thanks for having been delivered (v. 1).

The Sojourner's Story and My Story

This is the leadoff psalm in the collection of psalms designed for those "going up" to Jerusalem. By the time the collection was made, it was clear that most persons who would hear these psalms, in fact, most worshipers of the Lord, would not be living in Jerusalem but would be living as Jews in foreign places.

The cry "Woe is me, that I am living as a sojourner" would be the cry of every believer living away from Israel. Such persons could identify with Psalm 120. Believers in Yahweh who had to live in places where other gods were worshiped could also understand the references to the deceit, the lies, the warlike notions of those in the places where they lived.

This psalm holds out some hope for such people living far from home. This is a sojourner's story about answered prayers and about deliverance. As such, it comes as good news for all sojourners, wherever in the world they live as "aliens and exiles." Such persons are "God's own people," whether their time of residence is the time of the psalmist, the first century A.D. (1 Peter 2:9–12), or the twenty-first century.

ON THE ROAD AGAIN
Psalm 121

A Song of Ascents.

121:1 I lift up my eyes to the hills—
  from where will my help come?
 2 My help comes from the LORD,
  who made heaven and earth.

 3 He will not let your foot be moved;
  he who keeps you will not slumber.
 4 He who keeps Israel
  will neither slumber nor sleep.

 5 The LORD is your keeper;
  the LORD is your shade at your right hand.

⁶ The sun shall not strike you by day,
    nor the moon by night.

⁷ The LORD will keep you from all evil;
    he will keep your life.
⁸ The LORD will keep
    your going out and your coming in
    from this time on and forevermore.

While cleaning off a basement bookshelf, I discovered an old King James Version of the Bible, once used as a textbook for a college course. In the margin alongside Psalm 121 is written "the traveler's psalm," a notation from a class lecture. "This is a psalm to read before setting out on a journey," I recall the professor saying.

The psalm itself, however, suggests a broader application. It is still suited for the beginning of a journey, say, from Minneapolis to St. Louis. But it is also suited for the journey of a lifetime, viewing all of life as a sojourn.

In this short farewell liturgy, verses 1–2 are to be spoken by the person or persons about to set out, and verses 3–8 are spoken by those staying behind.

A Way to Say Goodbye (121:1–2)

Psalm 121 begins with the anxious question of one about to set out on a journey (v. 1). There is a moment of anxiety at the outset of any long trip: Will we arrive safely? Will we get there without an accident? In the case of this psalm, the question is asked by one setting out for Jerusalem. Who knew what dangers might lie ahead, along those roads that twist and turn their way through the mountains (Luke 10:25–37)?

After the worried question in verse 1, the traveler answers the question with a confession of trust. The question was, "Where will my help come from?" The answer: "My help comes from the LORD, who made heaven and earth."

Behind the faith that finds expression in verses 1 and 2 are the fundamental convictions that run through these *pilgrimage psalms*: (1) the Lord is *mighty*, maker of heaven and earth; (2) the Lord is *caring* (expressed in the repeated "my help").

A Promise for a Journey (121:3–6)

In the second part of this farewell liturgy, others address the one about to set out. This could have been a relative or friend or a group staying at home.

The traveler's confession in verse 2 had recalled the Lord's might but also the Lord's nearness and care. The remainder of the psalm develops that second theme, using the word *keep* a half dozen times.

Felix Mendelssohn recognized the significance of verse 4 when he made it the thematic statement of his chorus in *Elijah*: "He, watching over Israel, slumbers not nor sleeps." Luther called this a "Psalm of Comfort" and summarized its message by saying it teaches

> that we should remain steadfast in faith and await God's help and protection. Because even though it appears that God is sleeping or snoring . . . this is certainly not so, despite the way we feel and think. God is surely awake and watching over us. . . . Eventually we'll learn that, if we can only hold fast. (Mülhaupt, *D. Martin Luthers Psalmen-Auslegung*, volume 3:599 [my translation])

Verses 5–6 speak of the Lord's "keeping" as *protecting from danger*, and first of all from the danger of too much sun. Sunstroke was a serious problem for those living in the biblical lands. Elisha once treated a young man who had been struck down by the sun (2 Kings 4:18–37). The apocryphal book of Judith reports that Judith's husband "had died during the barley harvest. For as he stood overseeing those who were binding sheaves in the field, he was overcome by the burning heat, and took to his bed and died" (Judith 8:2–3).

My father was a private pilot. I recall a time when I was a boy flying with him in a small Aeronca Champion over the farms surrounding our hometown. In a field below we saw a farmer we knew, sitting on a tractor, plowing a field, in the middle of a hot July day. There was not a cloud in the sky, and these were the days before there were air-conditioned cabs on tractors. My father maneuvered the plane until the shadow was over our friend's tractor. We watched as he looked around; then he heard the plane, took off his straw hat, and waved to us! When I read verse 5, "the LORD is your shade," I think of that farmer and that airplane ride. Isaiah 49:2 uses the same imagery: "in the shadow of his hand he hid me."

Exposure to moonlight was thought to cause mental disturbances; the word *lunatic*, from the Latin *luna*, "moon," still reflects this notion. The sense of these two verses is to assure the traveler of the Lord's protection in the daytime as well as through the night.

A Promise for a Lifetime (121:7–8)

The thematic word *keep* occurs three times in the final segment of the psalm, but now the sphere of the Lord's watching activity is expanded in an astonishing way. Verses 3–6 are concerned about a specific journey; now the psalm asserts that "the Lord will keep you from *all* evil" and "will keep *your life*." The biblical expression "going out and coming in" refers to all of one's activities, the "comings and goings" that make up our day-by-day lives (see Deut. 28:6; 31:2; Josh. 14:11).

The psalm thus concludes by declaring that the Lord will watch over everything the individual does, not only for the duration of a journey but "from this time on and forevermore."

The Roads of Our Lives

This "traveler's psalm" is well suited for a time of farewell. But the movement of the psalm itself suggests a wider application, referring to life itself as a journey, a sojourn. The psalm's use in services for both baptism and burial indicates that this wider application has been recognized by the church.

"Life as a journey" is a familiar theme in the Bible. When the aged Jacob met Pharaoh, he said with a sigh, "The years of my earthly sojourn are one hundred thirty" (Gen. 47:9). Another psalmist prays, "Hear my prayer, O LORD. . . . For I am your passing guest, a sojourner, like all my forebears" (Ps. 39:12; NRSV adapted). The New Testament pictures the lives of Abraham and Sarah as sojourners, ever on the way (Heb. 11:9, RSV).

We may not be so fond of this image of life as a journey, ourselves ever on the way. We may prefer the image of a circle, ourselves in the center, family and friends gathered around. But this circular imagery is the way in which the rich but foolish farmer understood life. He himself was in the middle, ever working to widen the expanse of his possessions and property, but never suspecting that his earthly sojourn was about to end (Luke 12:13–21)!

Our view of life may tend toward the sentiments of the comfortable old song that pictures a small cottage and a cozy room, populated by "just Molly and me, and baby makes three." But the melody running through the biblical stories of God's people, and the one to which this psalm is suited, is a newer, more bracing tune. This psalm is more suited to Willy Nelson's "On the Road Again."

The call of Jesus was never "gather around me" or even "listen to me." Rather, it was and remains "Follow me!" This is a call to take up the life of the sojourner. The New Testament names this a call to a life of discipleship.

PRAY FOR THE PEACE OF JERUSALEM
Psalm 122

A Song of Ascents. Of David.

122:1 I was glad when they said to me,
        "Let us go to the house of the LORD!"
    ² Our feet are standing
        within your gates, O Jerusalem.

    ³ Jerusalem—built as a city
        that is bound firmly together.
    ⁴ To it the tribes go up,
        the tribes of the LORD,
      as was decreed for Israel,
        to give thanks to the name of the LORD.
    ⁵ For there the thrones for judgment were set up,
        the thrones of the house of David.

    ⁶ Pray for the peace of Jerusalem:
        "May they prosper who love you.
    ⁷ Peace be within your walls,
        and security within your towers."
    ⁸ For the sake of my relatives and friends
        I will say, "Peace be within you."
    ⁹ For the sake of the house of the LORD our God,
        I will seek your good.

If there is one Hebrew word that is known the world over, it is the word for peace: *shalom*. If there is one city in Israel that is internationally known, it is Israel's capital: Jerusalem. Psalm 122 is concerned for both: peace and Jerusalem. One memorable sentence ties the two together: "Pray for the peace of Jerusalem" (v. 6). In Hebrew, the words sing: *sha-e-lu sha-lom yi-ru-sha-la-yim.*

Once again, the setting of the psalm in the context of the fifteen pilgrimage psalms (see the comments with Psalm 120) helps to understand it. Psalm 120 spoke of the psalmist as a sojourner, living far from home (120:5). Psalm 121 provided a prayer for one setting out on a pilgrimage. With Psalm 122, the one who so joyously anticipated visiting the city has arrived: "Our feet are standing within your gates, O Jerusalem" (122:2).

Three times Jerusalem is mentioned in Psalm 122, once in each of the major sections: anticipation and arrival in Jerusalem (vv. 1–2); Jerusalem, city for pilgrimages (vv. 3–5); pray for the peace of Jerusalem (vv. 6–9). (See the comments on the "songs of Zion" with Psalm 87.)

Jerusalem: Anticipation and Arrival (122:1–2)

One of the popular festivals still celebrated by Jewish people today is named Simchat Torah, which means "joy in the scriptures." The festival occurs in the fall and is marked by a good deal of singing and even dancing with the Torah scrolls. The first word of Psalm 122 is "I rejoiced" or "I was glad," a verbal form of the same word *simchat*. That word sets the mood of this psalm: joy.

Verse 1 tells of the joy in anticipating the trip to Jerusalem for one of the annual festivals. Deuteronomy 16:16 lists them: unleavened bread, or Passover, in the spring; "weeks," or Pentecost, seven weeks after Passover; and "booths," or Sukkot, in the fall. Entire families attended these events, and one can imagine the good times that were had in worshiping together, singing and exchanging stories, reuniting with families and friends. The twelve-year-old son of Mary and Joseph caused his parents considerable worry when he did not return on time from one of these festivals (Luke 2:41–52)!

On arrival, the psalmist addresses the city as if to say, "Jerusalem, here we are" (v. 2). The same sense of joy at being in the Jerusalem temple is expressed in Psalm 84.

Jerusalem: Place for Pilgrimages (122:3–5)

The fifteen psalms from 120–134 are labeled psalms of *ascent*; the same Hebrew word appears in verse 4 when it speaks of the tribes that "go up" to Jerusalem.

Why these visits to Jerusalem? These were massive festivals organized for the purpose of giving thanks to the Lord, says verse 4. One can imagine singing hymns of praise, meeting old friends, times of visiting, families enjoying these days together. "How very good and pleasant it is," said another psalm writer, "when God's people gather together!" (Psalm 133:1, my translation).

Psalm 122 indicates that there was another reason for these gatherings: this was also the time for the settling of legal disputes and court cases (v. 5). King Solomon had built a special "Hall of Justice" where such activities took place (1 Kings 7:7).

Jerusalem: Pray for Peace! (122:6–9)!

The psalm begins with a cry of joy at being in Jerusalem, and it concludes with a call for prayer. At both the beginning (v. 2, "O Jerusalem") and ending, the city is personified and addressed ("you," "your").

Concern for *shalom* is expressed three times. First, all hearing the psalm are encouraged to pray for the city's peace (v. 6a). Then the psalmist addresses the city itself, wishing prosperity for those who love it and peace and security for those living there (vv. 6b–7). The final wish for peace is accompanied by reasons: friends and relatives live there (v. 8), and the temple is there (v. 9). Because of all this, the psalmist promises the city, "I will seek your good" (v. 9).

The Holy City

Since the fundamental meaning of the word *holy* is "separate, set apart," the adjective is certainly appropriate for describing Jerusalem. Jews sing of "Jerusalem the golden" and in 1996 celebrated the three-thousand-year anniversary of the city's founding. Christians make pilgrimages to Jerusalem, look forward to a "new Jerusalem" (Rev. 3:12; 21:2, 9–14), and celebrate the city in hymns such as "Jerusalem, My Happy Home," "Jerusalem the Golden," and "Jerusalem, Thou City Fair and High."

This psalmist addressed the city as a person. Jesus looked at the city, was deeply moved, and also addressed it as a person, through tears:

If you, even you, had only recognized on this day the things that make for peace! (Luke 19:42)

Jerusalem, Jerusalem, the city that kills the prophets and stones those who are sent to it! How often have I desired to gather your children together as a hen gathers her brood under her wings, and you were not willing! (Matt 23:37)

Jerusalem. It may be that one must make a pilgrimage to the city to begin to understand the memories, the dreams, the power associated with that place. Abraham Heschel wrote,

Jerusalem, the mother of Israel, we enter your walls as children who have always honored you, who have never been estranged from you. Your weight has been weighed in tears shed by our people for nearly two thousand years. Laughter was suppressed when we thought of your being in ruins. . . . "Wherever I go, I go to Jerusalem," said Rabbi Nahman. . . .

For more than three thousand years we have been in love with Jerusalem. She occupied our hearts, filled our prayers, pervaded our dreams. Continually mourning her loss, our grief was not subdued when celebrating festivities, when arranging a dinner table, when painting our homes. No meal was concluded without imploring: "Build Jerusalem, speedily, in your own days. . . ."

She is a city in a state of trance. Here the prophets lived and ceased to live but their exaltation stayed on. Here the trees praise, the streets say grace, and my steps give thanks. The way of Jerusalem is a way of exaltation. She is so much more than what you see. . . . Jerusalem, the charismatic city, is like a Hasidic master, whose sheer presence is a bestowal, whose heart and mind are never disengaged from God. (*Israel: An Echo of Eternity* pp. 16, 26, 29–30)

WE'VE HAD IT, LORD!
Psalm 123

A Song of Ascents.

123:1 **To you I lift up my eyes,**
    O you who are enthroned in the heavens!
  ² **As the eyes of servants**
    look to the hand of their master,
  as the eyes of a maid
    to the hand of her mistress,
  so our eyes look to the LORD our God,
    until he has mercy upon us.

  ³ **Have mercy upon us, O LORD, have mercy upon us,**
    for we have had more than enough of contempt.
  ⁴ **Our soul has had more than its fill**
    of the scorn of those who are at ease,
    of the contempt of the proud.

This collection of *pilgrimage psalms* (120–134) begins with the psalmist living far away from Jerusalem (Ps. 120:5). It continues with words of blessing for the journey to Jerusalem (Psalm 121) and with a report of the arrival in that city (Psalm 122).

Psalm 123 consists mainly of words addressed to God. It is the first prayer in this sequence. Did the editors intend it to be understood as a prayer that is prayed on arrival at the gates of the temple?

This prayer is made up of the typical elements of the *lament* (see on Psalm 13). It displays a unique feature in that it starts out as the lament of an individual (v. 1) and continues as the lament of a group (vv. 2–4). Verse 1 is the *address,* verse 2 an *affirmation of trust,* verse 3a a *request,* and verses 3b–4 a *complaint* in the "we" form ("Our soul . . .").

All Those Eyes (123:1–2)

The psalm begins by playing on the notion of *eyes;* the word occurs in each of the first four lines of the Hebrew text. The writer speaks of "my eyes," then of "the eyes of servants," then of "the eyes of a maid," and finally of "our eyes," that is, the eyes of the whole group that is praying. These words are reminiscent of the prayer used by Jews and Christians at mealtime: "The eyes of all look to you, and you give them their food in due season" (Ps. 145:15; see also Ps. 104:27).

Of interest in this psalm are the pictures that are used for God. God is a king, enthroned in the heavens (v. 1). God is a master, on whom servants are dependent. God is a mistress, on whom a maid depends. These pictures of God are of help in our own understanding of God. Two dimensions may be seen: God is *mighty*, high and lifted up, enthroned in the heavens; God is also *caring* and can be *counted on*, just as servants may count on the care of their master or mistress.

We've Had It, Lord! (123:3–4)

The point of the lament comes to expression in the urgent double request of verse 3. "Have mercy upon us, O LORD!" is the psalmist's prayer. The sense is "Lord, we've had it! Now help us out!" The word *contempt* is doubled for emphasis. The specific nature of the difficulty assumed in verses 3 and 4 is not clear. In any case, the psalmist and the group of believers being represented are experiencing hostility from those neighbors near whom they live.

Pictures of God

These pilgrimage psalms are especially rich in the variety of manners in which God is described. God is the creator of the heavens and the earth, who cares for individuals (121:1–2). God is the watchman, looking after God's people in the daytime and also at night (121:3–8). In Psalm 123, God is portrayed as king, enthroned in the heavens but approachable from earth. God is also pictured as master, to whom servants may bring their requests and on whom they depend. Finally, God is portrayed as mistress, a woman, and God's people as a maid who depends on that mistress.

When the wisdom teachers taught, they made use of a good number of comparisons: "Like a gold ring or an ornament of gold is a wise rebuke to a listening ear" (Prov. 25:12; note also vv. 3, 11, 13, 20, 26, 28 in the same chapter). When Jesus spoke about God and people, he used pictures and stories, called parables, to make his preaching and teaching clear. The variety of ways of portraying God in Psalms 120–134, through pictures, similes, stories, and other devices, can be an encouragement to our own efforts to speak of God creatively and effectively in our time.

IF GOD IS FOR US . . .
Psalm 124

A Song of Ascents. Of David.

124:1 **If it had not been the** LORD **who was on our side**
      —let Israel now say—
   2 **if it had not been the** LORD **who was on our side,**
      when our enemies attacked us,
   3 **then they would have swallowed us up alive,**
      when their anger was kindled against us;
   4 **then the flood would have swept us away,**
      the torrent would have gone over us;
   5 **then over us would have gone**
      the raging waters.

   6 **Blessed be the** LORD,
      who has not given us
      as prey to their teeth.
   7 **We have escaped like a bird**
      from the snare of the fowlers;
   the snare is broken,
      and we have escaped.

   8 **Our help is in the name of the** LORD,
      who made heaven and earth.

"If God is for us," wrote the apostle Paul, "who is against us?" He continued with the statement that "neither death, nor life, nor angels, nor rulers, nor things present, nor things to come, nor powers, nor height, nor depth, nor anything else in all creation, will be able to separate us from the love of God in Christ Jesus our Lord" (Rom. 8:31, 38–39). Something of the same spirit of triumphant confidence in the Lord rings through the opening words of Psalm 124: "If it had not been the LORD who was on our side. . . ."

The Community Gives Thanks

The psalm is related to its neighbors in this collection of *pilgrimage psalms*. With Psalm 123, the community asked for help: "Have mercy upon us, O LORD." Psalm 124 celebrates help that has been received (vv. 1–5) and declares, "Our help is in the name of the LORD." Psalm 125 then provides a picture of those who trust in the Lord's help (125:1–2).

The call in verse 1 for the congregation to participate, "let Israel now say," suggests that the psalm was used in a liturgical setting, with worship leader (v. 1) and responding people (vv. 2–8). Psalm 129 uses a similar "let Israel now say" device (see also Psalm 118:2–4).

The psalm consists of an opening *call to the congregation* (v. 1), a *confession of trust* (vv. 2–5), words of *praise* (vv. 6–7), and a final *affirmation of trust* (v. 8).

If the Lord Had Not Been for Us . . . (124:1–5)

The worship leader invites the congregation to imagine a hypothetical situation. He invites them to say together, "If the LORD had not been for us . . ." (a more literal translation of the Hebrew). One can imagine hearing that phrase a second time, this time with more power: *"If the LORD had not been for us. . . ."*

After the doubled "if" statements comes a brief explanation, putting those statements in a context: "when our enemies attacked us." "What if the Lord had not been on our side?" The potential consequences are listed, in the form of figures of speech: We would have been swallowed alive, like lambs swallowed by wolves! We would have been swept downstream, like those caught in a mighty flood! We would have been drowned by torrential waters (vv. 4–5)!

We've Flown Away! (124:6–8)

These words of blessing are words of praise: "Blessed be the LORD," followed by reasons for praising. Once again, the language is figurative: the Lord did not give us over to these animals who would have chewed us up (v. 6)! The Lord has allowed us to escape, like birds escaping from traps set by bird catchers (v.7; compare Eccl. 9:12).

The psalm comes to a close in verse 8 with the congregation confessing trust in the Lord. This confession is very close to the individual's declaration of trust in Psalm 121:2, an indication of the similar themes and language in these pilgrimage psalms.

If God Is for Us . . .

Informing Psalm 124 are two distinct actions on the part of God, both indicated in verse 8. First, God is the *creator* who made the heavens and the earth. Second, this mighty Creator is also "our help," the *deliverer* who rescued the Lord's people from an enemy attack (vv. 1–5). Psalm 123:3–4 exemplifies the sort of cry for help that came out of such a desperate situation; Psalm 124 praises God because the prayer has been answered and the deliverance has come about. The same twin aspects of the Lord's activity are expressed in Psalm 121:2.

The imagery of "the Lord on our side" that occurs in verses 1–5 is also found in the climactic section that concludes the eighth chapter of Paul's letter to the Christians at Rome. "If God is for us"—let the people now say—"If God is for us, who is against us? . . . Who is to condemn? . . . Who will separate us from the love of Christ? . . . In all these things, we are more than conquerors through him who loved us" (Rom. 8:31–39).

LIKE A CITY SET IN THE HILLS
Psalm 125

A Song of Ascents.

125:1 **Those who trust in the LORD are like Mount Zion,**
    which cannot be moved, but abides forever.
² **As the mountains surround Jerusalem,**
    so the LORD surrounds his people,
    from this time on and forevermore.
³ **For the scepter of wickedness shall not rest**
    on the land allotted to the righteous,
    so that the righteous might not stretch out
    their hands to do wrong.
⁴ **Do good, O LORD, to those who are good,**
    and to those who are upright in their hearts.
⁵ **But those who turn aside to their own crooked ways**
    the LORD will lead away with evildoers.
    Peace be upon Israel!

At the beginning of these pilgrimage psalms were the words of one setting out for Jerusalem: "I lift up my eyes to the hills" (Ps. 121:1). This act of looking toward the mountains was the first step on the way to Jerusalem.

The writer of Psalm 125, once again, has an eye on the mountains. As the psalmist looks at the mighty hills surrounding Jerusalem, a parallel comes to mind. Just as the mountains surround, protect, watch over Jerusalem, so the Lord surrounds, protects, watches over the Lord's people! The Lord as mountain range: a fresh picture for understanding God! And an appropriate one for pilgrims on their way toward the holy city.

A Psalm of Trust

Psalm 125 begins with a pair of *comparisons*, illustrating the protection given those who trust in the Lord (vv. 1–2). It continues with a *promise* of the Lord's protection (v. 3) and concludes with a *prayer* for the people (v. 4) and an announcement about the fate of evildoers (v. 5a). The psalm ends with a word of blessing for Israel (see also Ps. 128:6).

Especially dominant in this psalm is the element of *trust*, sounded in verses 1 and 2.

The Mountains of Jerusalem (125:1–2)

The first two statements offer comparisons with the mountains of Jerusalem. In verse 1, *believers*, "those who trust in the LORD," are compared to Mount Zion, the major mountain in the area of the city. A number of psalms celebrate the city and this mountain and the joys of living there: Psalms 46; 78:67–69; 87. The point of the comparison in verse 1 is that those who trust in the Lord will enjoy secure and long lives.

The imagery shifts with verse 2. Now it is not believers but *God* who is compared to the mountains. The psalm writer has been traveling for days and has seen Jerusalem from afar. The sight of the city nestled in the middle of the protecting mountains strikes the psalmist as a good illustration of God's relationship to God's people: God surrounds them, protects them, cares for them. Once again, the duration of the relationship between God and people is emphasized: "forevermore."

A Promise and a Prayer (125:3–5)

Verse 3 promises that foreign powers will not rule Jerusalem, "the land allotted to the righteous." Such foreign rule would bring with it a temptation for the citizens to pick up wrongful pagan customs.

Verses 4–5ab offer a double prayer, first asking that the Lord do good to those who are upright, then that God punish those who are "crooked," that is, those who do evil.

The psalm begins with a pair of pictures of the lives of those who trust in the Lord: they are as sturdy and solid as Mount Zion, and they are surrounded by the Lord's care just as Jerusalem is surrounded by the Judean mountains. It concludes with a wish for those who place their trust in the Lord: *Shalom*, peace, be upon Israel!

The last and the first words of that wish tie the psalm together. Israel, the people of God, will find peace when they let the weight of their cares down on the sturdy support of the Lord. They will discover *shalom* when they look up and discover they are like a city set in the hills, surrounded by a love even mightier than the mountains.

BETWEEN MEMORY AND HOPE
Psalm 126

A Song of Ascents.

126:1 When the LORD restored the fortunes of Zion,
    we were like those who dream.
2 Then our mouth was filled with laughter,
    and our tongue with shouts of joy;
then it was said among the nations,
    "The LORD has done great things for them."
3 The LORD has done great things for us,
    and we rejoiced.

4 Restore our fortunes, O LORD,
    like the watercourses in the Negeb.
5 May those who sow in tears
    reap with shouts of joy.
6 Those who go out weeping,
    bearing the seed for sowing,
shall come home with shouts of joy,
    carrying their sheaves.

This prayer of the people looks back at a good time in the past (vv. 1–3) and asks the Lord to bring about more good times in the future (vv. 4–6). This psalm of the community remembers when the Lord restored the good fortunes of the people (v. 1) and asks that the Lord restore that time of good fortune again (v. 4). Psalm 126 comes from a people who are living between the times, between a good time remembered and another good time hoped for.

Dreamers and Dry Riverbeds

This is a psalm of special beauty, with its images of dreamers laughing and shouting and of dry riverbeds flowing with water (vv. 1, 4). One can hear the laughter of those who are joyful and also the weeping of those who are sad (vv. 5–6). It is a *community lament* (see the comments on Psalm 44), a prayer of the people Israel from a time of difficulty.

The psalm divides into two sections, the first remembering what the Lord has done for the people in the past (vv. 1–3) and the second asking that the Lord help the people once again in the future (vv. 4–6).

"We Were Like Those Who Dream" (126:1–3)

"When the LORD restored the fortunes of Zion" is a reference to the time when the people of Judah were set free from living as exiles in Babylon (587–539 B.C.). Psalm 137 came out of that time of exile and remembers its sadness:

> By the rivers of Babylon—
> there we sat down and there we wept
> when we remembered Zion. . . .
> How could we sing the LORD's song
> in a foreign land?
>
> (vv. 1, 4)

Psalm 126 recalls the joy of release from captivity, speaking of laughter and joy. It was too good to be true, and the people walked around as if in a dream! (The apostle Peter also thought he was dreaming when he was set free from captivity; see Acts 12:6–11.)

Even the surrounding nations recognized the significance of the release from captivity and gave proper credit, saying, "The LORD has done great things for them" (v. 2). With verse 3, the delivered people happily make that statement their own.

Like Streams of Water in the Desert (126:4–6)

The first half of the psalm looked to the past. But now, with the *request* in verse 4, the focus is on the future. The writer has seen how the dry creeks in the Negeb, the desert to the south of Jerusalem, can become streams of cool, clear water. Here is the picture for this prayer. "Take away our dryness, Lord! Make us like those dry creeks that become rivers of rushing, flowing water!"

Psalm 126 concludes with another picture illustrating the prayer. The psalmist says, "Lord, this is a time of planting. The people of Israel are going about their work with heavy hearts. There is much sadness because of our political situation. Grant that there may soon be a change of fortunes, so that we may experience the sort of joy that comes with a good harvest" (see v. 5).

Verse 6 contrasts the present time of "sowing" with a more hopeful future time, when there will be a harvest accompanied by shouts of joy.

Living between Memory and Hope

Few passages in the Bible indicate more clearly that, in the biblical view, our lives are played out in the space between recalling what God has done for us in the past and hoping that God will grant our prayers for the future. To put it another way, we could find our own location between verses 3 and 4 of this psalm. We recall and hear told what the Lord did for our people in the past (vv. 1–3). Now we pray for the Lord's continued help in the future, hoping for the time when we, too, "shall come home with shouts of joy."

Some things in the past should be forgiven (for example, "our trespasses") and then forgotten. Others, such as the "great things the Lord has done for us," should be remembered, even celebrated. Remembering what God has done can help shape our prayers and hopes concerning what God may yet do.

Even pilgrims look forward to a time of finishing their work, picking up their sheaves, and coming home, accompanied by shouts of joy.

A WORD FOR WORRIERS AND WORKAHOLICS
Psalm 127

A Song of Ascents. Of Solomon.

127:1 Unless the LORD builds the house,
        those who build it labor in vain.
    Unless the LORD guards the city,
        the guard keeps watch in vain.
  2 It is in vain that you rise up early
        and go late to rest,
    eating the bread of anxious toil;
        for he gives sleep to his beloved.

  3 Sons are indeed a heritage from the LORD,
        the fruit of the womb a reward.

⁴ **Like arrows in the hand of a warrior**
   are the sons of one's youth.
⁵ **Happy is the man who has**
   his quiver full of them.
 He shall not be put to shame
   when he speaks with his enemies in the gate.

Our age has added a new word to the English language: *workaholic*. A workaholic is a person obsessed with his or her work. This is a person who neglects family and friends and self because of work and who lives to work, rather than works to live. While the word *workaholic* is an invention of the late twentieth century, the reality is nothing new. Psalm 127 has a word about work, about worry, and about family.

Back to the Basics

This is the eighth in the collection of *pilgrimage psalms*, designed to be used on the way to one of the annual festivals in Jerusalem (see the comments with Psalm 120). The heading associates it with Solomon, probably because he built the "house" in Jerusalem, the temple.

   The psalm is neither praise nor lament and in fact is not even addressed to God (contrast Ps. 126:4). It offers *instruction* on some of the basics of life, such as work and worry, stress and sleep (vv. 1–2), and family (vv. 3–5).

On Work and Worry (127:1–2)

High up on the outer wall of the courthouse in Leipzig, Germany, in full view of those in the center of the city, are the words of the first verse of this psalm:

   Wo der Herr nicht das Haus baut, so arbeiten unsonst,
      die daran bauen.

("Unless the LORD builds the house, those who build it labor in vain.") Whoever designed and built that courthouse thought it appropriate to remind those entering the building that what they did there was of interest to the Lord.

   The three sayings in verses 1–2 are linked by the word translated "in vain." The Hebrew word means "worthless"; in Psalm 60:11 it refers to human help as worthless.

   The expression "build a house" can have the literal sense of erecting a structure, like Solomon's temple or the courthouse in Leipzig. But in the

Bible, it can also mean to build up a family. In the book of Ruth, the townspeople say concerning Ruth, "May the LORD make the woman who is coming into your house like Rachel and Leah, who together *built up the house of Israel*" (Ruth 4:11). The text is saying that the Lord should be a part of the process of marrying and raising a family. "A prudent wife is from the LORD," says Proverbs 19:14, and the story of Isaac and Rebekah in Genesis 24 provides a narrative illustration of the Lord's involvement in the marriage of two persons.

Running alongside this statement about house building in Psalm 127 is a saying about the Lord guarding a city. The Hebrew behind the words translated "guards" and "guard" is *shamar*, the same word used six times in Psalm 121 and translated there as "keep." Psalm 121 declares that the Lord "keeps" the traveler as well as the whole people. This saying suggests that the relationship of the citizens to the Lord is of essential importance for the security of the city.

The third activity that is "in vain" or "worthless" is getting up early, going to bed late, and worrying overmuch about one's work. As the third in this trio of "in vain" sayings, this one is the climax. What exactly is being said here?

The teachers in Israel whose teachings are found collected in Proverbs had a good deal to say about work. Mostly their words could be summarized "Get up early! Work hard! Don't sleep too much!" For example:

> Go to the ant, O sluggard;
>> consider her ways and be wise. . . .
>
> How long will you lie there, O sluggard?
>> When will you arise from your sleep?
>
> A little sleep, a little slumber,
>> a little folding of the hands to rest,
>
> and poverty will come upon you like a vagabond.
>> (Prov. 6:6–11, RSV)

> Love not sleep, lest you come to poverty;
>> open your eyes, and you will have plenty of bread.
>> (Prov. 20:13, RSV)

> As a door turns on its hinges,
>> so does a sluggard on his bed.
>> (26:14, RSV; see also vv. 13–16)

There are plenty of examples from Proverbs and other wisdom literature that advise putting in a good day's work. But here, in Psalm 127, are words advising against pushing too hard, against burning the midnight oil. Work is good, but the combination of work and worry ("anxious toil") is lethal, or, as the psalm puts it, "in vain."

Sleep, by contrast, is one of God's gifts, according to this psalm. Humans get up early and go to bed late, all to earn money to buy food. But sleep, says the psalm, comes as a gift from the Lord. "Sweet is the sleep of a laborer," says another wise teacher (Eccl. 5:12, RSV; see also 8:16).

My friend Gerhard Frost said to me one morning, "I just had one of those nights when I was lying awake, baby-sitting the world." Says Psalm 127, "Relax. Have a good sleep. You can let God take care of the world for one night!" "For he gives sleep to his beloved," says verse 2. In Charles Peguy's poem "Sleep," God says, "Sleep is perhaps the most beautiful thing I have created. And I myself rested on the seventh day." The poem continues, with God still speaking:

> Poor people, they don't know what is good.
> They look after their business very well
>   during the day.
> But they haven't enough confidence in me
>   to let me look after it during the night.
> As if I wasn't capable of looking
>   after it during one night. . . .
> And I say Blessed, blessed is the man
>   who puts off what he has to
>   do until tomorrow.
> Blessed is he who puts off.
>   That is to say, Blessed is he who hopes.
>   And who sleeps.
>   (from *Basic Verities*, 27, 28, 31)

On Family and Happiness (127:3–5)

The psalm begins by speaking of the Lord's involvement in building a house. The second part of Psalm 127 speaks of the Lord's involvement in building a family (for "build" in this second sense, see Ruth 4:11).

The psalm has spoken of the Lord building, guarding, giving sleep, and now the topic is the Lord giving children. Nothing is said here about biology or family planning. Children simply appear as an inheritance (as one might inherit a house or a farm) and as a reward. They are a gift.

The point of verse 4 is that children born to a young couple can protect and care for parents when they are old. Verse 5 adds another page to the "Happy is . . ." book of the Bible (Psalm 1, for example). A "quiver full," a large family, is a source of joy. Should a parent need to appear in court, held in the city gate, children will be there to provide support!

House building and security, working and resting, stress and sleep, the gift of family—these are the commonplace themes of this psalm aimed at worriers and workaholics.

THE JOYS OF WORK AND FAMILY
Psalm 128

A Song of Ascents.

128:1 **Happy is everyone who fears the LORD,**
  who walks in his ways.
 2 **You shall eat the fruit of the labor of your hands;**
  you shall be happy, and it shall go well with you.

 3 **Your wife will be like a fruitful vine**
  within your house;
 your children will be like olive shoots
  around your table.
 4 **Thus shall the man be blessed**
  who fears the LORD.

 5 **The LORD bless you from Zion.**
  May you see the prosperity of Jerusalem
  all the days of your life.
 6 **May you see your children's children.**
  Peace be upon Israel!

Psalms 127 and 128 deal with the same themes: the balancing of work and rest, the happiness of family life, the building of a house and a home, the gift of children.

This is the ninth in the series bearing the label "A Song of Ascents," that collection of psalms designed to be used in connection with pilgrimages to Jerusalem (see on Psalm 120). These psalms seem to follow the course of the pilgrimage. With Psalms 125, 126, 128, and continuing with 129, 132, and 133, we begin to hear mention of Zion, that mountain where the temple is located. As the pilgrimage begins to near its goal, the psalms speak more and more of that place.

The first section of the psalm is framed by statements that speak of the person who "fears the Lord" (vv. 1, 4). Within this frame are sayings addressed to "you," that is, to the person being instructed. The psalm concludes with two further sayings in "you" form, wishing well for those who have come to worship (vv. 5–6).

Happiness in Work and with Family (128:1–4)

Like a number of psalms (1; 41:1; 65:4; 89:15; 119:1–3; 127:5), Psalm 128 is concerned with human happiness. It begins by declaring that the person will be happy who "fears the LORD." This expression does not mean to "be afraid of God" but to be related to the Lord in an attitude of love and respect, like the attitude of a child toward a parent. One hears of the "fear of the LORD" in other psalms and especially in Proverbs, where it is identified as "the beginning of knowledge" (1:7; see also Prov. 1:29; 2:5; 3:7; 8:13). Such an attitude is also a mark of the good wife (Prov. 31:30).

Another mark of the happy person has to do with the living of daily life in accord with the Lord's will, here described as "walking in his ways." The life of the believer is not just talking the talk but also walking the walk. Psalm 119 also begins by linking happiness with the right sort of "walking," that is, with the right carrying out of day-by-day activities (Ps. 119:1–6).

Psalm 128 begins with a general observation about the person who is truly happy. Verses 2–3 fill out the picture of happiness, with words addressed to those hearing the psalm.

Psalm 127 had something to say to "workaholics" (Ps. 127:2). Psalm 128 offers a promise to the person who is rightly related to the Lord (v. 1) and who works: you will enjoy success in your work. Here is no talk of great riches but a promise of being able to make a living and, once again, a promise of happiness and of things going well.

After speaking of *work*, the psalm has a word about *family*. The wife is portrayed as a vine, and children are branches growing out from this vine. Parents know the experience of watching as each child grows, learns to stand, and then is just tall enough to see over the kitchen table. Another one "shoots up," as promised in this psalm (v. 3)!

Verse 4 is stronger in the Hebrew, beginning with the word *hinnēh*, which has the sense "Behold!" or "Look! (see Ps. 133:1). "Look! The one who fears the Lord will be blessed in this way" says this verse in the Hebrew, reaching back to tie up with "who fears the LORD" verse 1. The sense of *blessing* thus includes that which makes for human happiness: success in work and the joy of family.

Prosperity, Posterity, and Peace (128:5–6)

The psalm closes with words of benediction, such as might have been pronounced by a priest to a group of pilgrims in Jerusalem. The Lord's "blessing," as described above, is wished for each person. This is not just a wish for individuals but a hope for a lifetime of prosperity for Jerusalem.

If children are the Lord's gifts (Pss. 127:3–5; 128:1–4), so are grand-children! Psalm 128 expresses the wish that those gathered will live to see that next generation. The conclusion is an expressed hope for *shalom* (peace and well-being), not only for those gathered in the temple or those in Jerusalem but for Israel, the entire people of God.

As these pilgrims see first the mountains about Jerusalem (Ps. 125:2) and then Mount Zion itself (125:1), these psalms begin to speak more about the fortunes of Zion (Ps. 126:1), and also its misfortunes (Ps. 129:5). The pilgrimage psalms speak of the joys in gathering together as comparable to the dew on Mount Zion (Ps. 133:3). They affirm Zion as the place where the Lord lives in a special way (Ps. 132:13–18) and wish these travelers the Lord's blessings as they leave Zion (Pss. 128:5; 134:3).

The Best Things in Life

"The best things in life are free" goes the old saying. The pair of Psalms 127 and 128 identifies some of those "best things" with the blessings of the Lord on the Lord's people. The Lord blesses those people by prospering their labors, enabling them to find joy in work, protecting their city, providing them with peace, giving the gift of children and grand-children, even giving the gift of sleep.

Such are the common things and the common themes these pilgrimage psalms are about.

LIFE REVIEW
Psalm 129

A Song of Ascents.

129:1 **"Often have they attacked me from my youth"**
         —let Israel now say—
    2 **"often have they attacked me from my youth,**
         yet they have not prevailed against me.
    3 **The plowers plowed on my back;**
         they made their furrows long."
    4 **The LORD is righteous;**
         he has cut the cords of the wicked.
    5 **May all who hate Zion**
         be put to shame and turned backward.
    6 **Let them be like the grass on the housetops**
         that withers before it grows up,

⁷ with which reapers do not fill their hands
  or binders of sheaves their arms,
⁸ while those who pass by do not say,
  "The blessing of the LORD be upon you!
  We bless you in the name of the LORD!"

One of the techniques used in counseling troubled persons is called a "life review." The one being counseled is asked to look back and review the course of his or her life, in order to put the difficulties of the present in perspective.

The psalmists use this technique of reviewing a life. Psalm 71 is a prayer from an older person, facing difficulties in the immediate future and asking the Lord, "Do not cast me off in the time of old age" (Ps. 71:9). That psalmist affirms trust in the Lord by looking back and recalling how the Lord has helped in the past "from my youth" (v. 5). And again, "O God, *from my youth* you have taught me" (Ps. 71:17).

That expression "from my youth" occurs only in Psalms 71 and 129. In Psalm 71, it calls for a review of an individual's life. Now, in Psalm 129, the psalm writer is recalling the history of the nation, portrayed as a person (see also Hosea 11). A life review can be helpful for a person and also for a people.

One Nation's Story

This *pilgrimage psalm* was used in connection with periodic journeys to Jerusalem (see on Psalm 120). Once again, Zion, the mountain on which Jerusalem is built, is mentioned (Ps. 129:5; also Pss. 125:1; 126:1; 128:5). The psalm was designed for some sort of worship service, with a worship leader calling out the first lines, "Often have they attacked me from my youth," then inviting the congregation to repeat the line as a response— "let Israel now say" (see also Ps. 124:1–2). The psalm begins with a recalling of the nation's story (vv. 1–4), continues with the expression of a wish that Israel's enemies be shamed (vv. 5–8a), and concludes with a blessing (v. 8bc).

Life Review: A History of Being Helped (129:1–4)

The psalmist recalls that the story of the people Israel has not been all sweetness and roses. "Often have they attacked me," says the psalmist, and then he invites the congregation to join in that statement. Now the people are speaking of Israel's experience: "Often have they attacked me from my youth, yet they have not prevailed against me" (v. 2). "We've suffered lots of adversities and battles," the worshipers are saying, "but somehow we have survived!" One could read through the books of Samuel and Kings to get a sense of the adversities suffered in the early years of the nation's history.

Verse 3 offers a gruesome picture of what Israel has suffered. These enemies have ripped up Israel as plows would rip up a person's back, leaving deep gashes.

Verse 4 comes as a word of praise and thanks: the Lord is righteous and has slashed the ropes with which the wicked had bound up the Lord's people.

Prayer for the People (129:5–8)

These psalms in the collection from 120 to 134 were meant for people on their way to Zion, the place where the Lord was thought to be especially present. One can imagine the excitement as the city began to come into sight.

Verse 5 states the wish that enemies of the city be shamed and turned back. This is the thematic statement; the following verses play on that theme. Verse 6 wishes that the people's enemies be like the little patches of grass that grow on the flat roof of a house; when the hot sun beats down and the hot winds blow, the grass withers, dries up, and blows away. So may these enemies of Zion disappear! There will not be even a handful of growth to be harvested or tied up into bundles (v. 7).

At harvesttime, the workers normally greeted one another with words wishing the Lord's blessing. Boaz, for example, greeted his field workers by saying, "The LORD be with you," and they responded with "The LORD bless you" (Ruth 2:4). But for this "crop," these enemies, there will be no harvest. The Zion haters will dry up and blow away (v. 6).

These wishes expressed in this prayer *against* the enemy are thus prayers *for* Israel, God's people.

A Prayer for Pilgrims

Pilgrims are people who are on a journey to a future that has some uncertainties. Will the journey be a safe one? Will we encounter hostility? Will we be welcomed when we arrive?

Psalm 129 is realistic about the potential dangers of the coming journey but also remembers the Lord's help in the past. It anticipates the greeting that those making the journey will hear upon arrival: "We bless you in the name of the LORD."

OUT OF THE DEPTHS I CRY
Psalm 130

A Song of Ascents.

130:1 **Out of the depths I cry to you, O LORD.**
  2   **Lord, hear my voice!**
       Let your ears be attentive
         to the voice of my supplications!

  3 **If you, O LORD, should mark iniquities,**
       Lord, who could stand?
  4 **But there is forgiveness with you,**
       so that you may be revered.

  5 **I wait for the LORD, my soul waits,**
       and in his word I hope;
  6 **my soul waits for the Lord**
       more than those who watch for the morning,
       more than those who watch for the morning.

  7 **O Israel, hope in the LORD!**
       For with the LORD there is steadfast love,
       and with him is great power to redeem.
  8 **It is he who will redeem Israel**
       from all its iniquities.

It was a cold, rainy January day when we visited the Dachau concentration camp memorial, not far from Munich, Germany. Our guide was a German friend who had been held in the camp as a fourteen-year-old boy because his father, an officer in the German army, had taken part in a plot on Hitler's life and the whole family was being punished. Our friend told us the story: his father had been executed; the family was arrested and sent to Dachau.

A visit to Dachau is an event never to be forgotten. One sees photographs and films depicting life in the camp. In the gray mist we walked across the area where the barracks had been. We came to the buildings housing the ovens of the crematorium.

Jewish, Catholic, and Protestant chapels have been built at the camp. Whoever designed the Protestant house of worship had Psalm 130 in mind. On the wall in black letters are these words:

Aus der Tiefe rufe ich Herr, zu Dir.
Herr, höre meine Stimme!

("Out of the depths I cry to you, O LORD. Lord, hear my voice!"
Ps. 130:1.) What words could one use to commemorate some of the most
horrible atrocities committed on the planet? Those designing the chapel
at Dachau reached for these words from Psalm 130.

The power of this psalm has long been recognized. The ancient
church ranked it as one of the seven "penitential psalms" to be used at
times of confession of sin (see on Psalm 6). It is known as *De Profundis*,
the first words in the Latin translation. Modern pastoral handbooks rec-
ommend the psalm for the most difficult times: stillbirth, death shortly
after birth, burial.

The psalm is made up of elements of the *individual lament* (see on
Psalm 13) shaped to fit the situation. Verses 1–2 are a *request* for a hearing, with verses 3–4 related to that request. Verses 5–6 offer an *affirmation of trust*, and verses 7–8 expand this individual lament to address the
gathered congregation. The *complaint* must be inferred; the psalmist is
"in the depths," and the word of *praise* is absent.

Lord, Hear My Voice! (130:1–4)

The psalm begins with an urgent cry for help: "Out of the depths I cry to
you, O LORD." Behind this request is an implied complaint: "Lord, I'm
about to go under, and you aren't paying any attention!" The person crying for help is pictured as in deep water, drowning. The same imagery
opens Psalm 69:

> Save me, O God,
>   for the waters have come up to my neck.
> I sink in deep mire,
>   where there is no foothold;
> I have come into deep waters,
>   and the flood sweeps over me.

The problem of the one crying out is not just one of physical pain; nor
is it only an emotional problem, a case of depression. It is not only a spiritual problem, that of being weighed down with sin. In fact, the person
crying out does not "have" a problem at all. At issue is survival. In this
psalm, it is a matter of life—or death.

With verse 3, the tone of the psalm begins to change. The person praying looks inward and sees only failure: "If you, O LORD, should
mark iniquities, Lord, who could stand?" Then the psalmist looks at God
and sees some grounds for hope, because "there is forgiveness with
you" (v. 4).

Waiting and Hoping (130:5–8)

The final segment of the psalm is an expression of *trust* in the Lord, as
is typical for psalms of lament. Now the imagery is that of a watchman, weary after staying at the post through the long hours of the
night. "Watchman, what of the night?" is the call to the city's sentinel
(Isa. 21:11, RSV). One can imagine the eager watchman waiting for the
first rays of morning light. The psalmist says that she is longing for the
Lord more than those weary sentinels.

How could the "I cry" of the person about to go under be transformed
into the "I hope" of one who expects to be rescued (v. 5)? The answer lies
in the attitude of trust expressed in verse 7 and, ultimately, in the Lord's
steadfast love: "For with the LORD there is steadfast love, and with him is
great power to redeem." This "steadfast love" is the sort of love that
keeps on loving, no matter what. The same Hebrew word (*hesed*) is used
for the love that young Hosea had for his wife, even after her unfaithfulness (Hosea 1–3). This is the kind of love that never gives up, like that of
the father who never gave up on his rebellious son and kept hoping, waiting, watching for his return (Luke 15). Because of this love that will not
let go, the "I cry" of the one about to go under is finally taken up into the
congregation's affirmation of trust in the Lord, who will come to the rescue (vv. 7–8). The psalm began as an individual's cry for help. It comes
to a close as a call to the gathered community to continue hoping and
trusting in the Lord.

Into Another Key

Certainly, the apostle Paul understood this psalm. He knew what it was
to be in the depths, to be able to say "the waters have come up to my
neck" (Ps. 69:1). Paul wrote, "Three times I was shipwrecked; for a night
and a day I was adrift at sea" (2 Cor. 11:25). Paul also knew something
about God's steadfast love and modulates his own affirmation of trust
into a brighter, gospel key:

> For I am convinced that neither death, nor life, nor angels, nor rulers, nor
> things present, nor things to come, nor powers, nor height, nor depth, nor
> anything else in all creation, will be able to separate us from the love of
> God in Christ Jesus our Lord. (Rom. 8:38–39)

The good news is this, says the apostle: no matter how deep you've
gotten in over your head, no matter how low your life has sunk, no matter how badly you've gotten bogged down in the muck and the mire, you
are never out of the range of God's love.

Our cries from the depths, says Psalm 130, can be stilled and transformed into waiting and hoping in the Lord.

ON LETTING YOUR WEIGHT DOWN
Psalm 131

A Song of Ascents. Of David.

131:1 **O LORD, my heart is not lifted up,**
        my eyes are not raised too high;
     I do not occupy myself with things
        too great and too marvelous for me.
   2 **But I have calmed and quieted my soul,**
        like a weaned child with its mother;
     my soul is like the weaned child that is with me.

   3 **O Israel, hope in the LORD**
        from this time on and forevermore.

One of my teachers told this story: A young pilot once succeeded in
convincing his grandmother to take her first airplane ride with him in his
small private plane. The takeoff went smoothly, and they were soon
cruising over the town where she lived and the farm where she had been
born. Then her grandson noticed that his passenger was tense and pale
and that her knuckles were white as she hung onto the arms of the seat
for dear life. When he landed the plane, the rest of the family waiting on
the ground couldn't wait to get her reaction. "Grandma, how did you like
the ride?" they asked. "Oh it was fine," she said, "but let me tell you a
secret. I never really let all my weight down."

The flight would have been so much more enjoyable had she only
relaxed and let her weight down.

Psalm 131 is an invitation to relax, to let one's weight down, to live a
life of trust in the Lord.

Words of Hope and Trust

This *pilgrimage psalm* (see on Psalm 120) is linked to Psalm 130 by the
common statement "O Israel, hope in the LORD" (130:7; 131:5). Psalm
130 centers on the theme of hope, even in desperate times. At the center
of Psalm 131 is an unforgettable picture of trust. Taken together, these
psalms speak words of hope to persons who quietly entrust their lives to
the care of a loving God.

One of the standard elements in a psalm of lament is the *affirmation of trust* (see on Psalm 13). Psalm 131 is an example of that element developing into an entire psalm. (For a listing of other psalms of trust, see the comments on Psalm 11.)

After an address to the Lord, the psalm makes three negative statements (verse 1). Verse 2 makes a positive statement that is illustrated with a picture, and verse 3 concludes the psalm with a word addressed to the gathered congregation.

If the NRSV translation is correct ("like the weaned child that is with me"), the author of the psalm could be a mother.

Lord, I'm Not Proud (131:1)

In Psalm 101:5, a ruler says, "A haughty look and an arrogant heart I will not tolerate." The author of Psalm 131 uses the same language in declaring to the Lord, "My heart is not lifted up, my eyes are not raised too high." If my eyes are "raised high," the only way I can see others is to look down my nose at them. This sort of body language is an expression of arrogance, an attitude of self-promotion that finally ends up in wanting to take over matters properly belonging to God.

In the next lines the psalmist owns to mystery, admitting that there are certain questions about life she cannot answer. The wisdom teachers spoke the same way, saying, "Three things are too wonderful [the same Hebrew word is translated "marvelous" in Ps. 131:1] for me" (Prov. 30:18–19).

Like a Child with a Mother (131:2)

The picture of the God-person relationship here is clear: God is portrayed as a mother, the psalmist as a child. While feminine pictures for God in the Bible are rare, they are present. In Isaiah 49:15, the Lord speaks to the people, saying,

> Can a woman forget her nursing child . . . ?
> Even these may forget,
>   yet I will not forget you.

God is compared to a woman, nursing a child. For other examples portraying God as a woman, see Numbers 11:11–15; Deuteronomy 32:18; Isaiah 66:13; Luke 15:8–10.

The RSV translation of Psalm 131:2 reads,

> But I have calmed and quieted my soul,
>> like a child quieted at its mother's breast;
>> like a child that is quieted is my soul.

In this psalm, the Lord is like a mother, the psalmist a child depending on that mother.

A Word to the Congregation (131:3)

Psalm 131 concludes with words also found in Psalm 130:7, encouraging the congregation to hope in the Lord. Psalm 130 provided a *reason* for hoping, that is, the Lord's steadfast love and power. Psalm 131 suggests a *duration* for hoping in the Lord, that is, forever. As in Psalm 130, the life of the individual is also considered in the context of the life of the community.

Taken together, these two psalms speak words of hope to those in the depths of despair. They encourage a patient and trusting lifestyle, not preoccupied with status and peer approval. They advise owning up to mystery and wonder in the world and letting down the weight of cares and worries into the arms of a God who loves as a mother loves a child.

KING DAVID, MOUNT ZION
Psalm 132

A Song of Ascents.

132:1 **O LORD, remember in David's favor**
all the hardships he endured;
² **how he swore to the LORD**
and vowed to the Mighty One of Jacob,
³ **"I will not enter my house**
or get into my bed;
⁴ **I will not give sleep to my eyes**
or slumber to my eyelids,
⁵ **until I find a place for the LORD,**
a dwelling place for the Mighty One of Jacob."

⁶ **We heard of it in Ephrathah;**
we found it in the fields of Jaar.
⁷ **"Let us go to his dwelling place;**
let us worship at his footstool."

8 Rise up, O Lᴏʀᴅ, and go to your resting place,
     you and the ark of your might.
9 Let your priests be clothed with righteousness,
     and let your faithful shout for joy.
10 For your servant David's sake
     do not turn away the face of your anointed one.

11 The Lᴏʀᴅ swore to David a sure oath
     from which he will not turn back:
   "One of the sons of your body
     I will set on your throne.
12 If your sons keep my covenant
     and my decrees that I shall teach them,
   their sons also, forevermore,
     shall sit on your throne."

13 For the Lᴏʀᴅ has chosen Zion;
     he has desired it for his habitation:
14 "This is my resting place forever;
     here I will reside, for I have desired it.
15 I will abundantly bless its provisions;
     I will satisfy its poor with bread.
16 Its priests I will clothe with salvation,
     and its faithful will shout for joy.
17 There I will cause a horn to sprout up for David;
     I have prepared a lamp for my anointed one.
18 His enemies I will clothe with disgrace,
     but on him, his crown will gleam."

This is the tenth of eleven *royal psalms* scattered throughout the book of Psalms. Originally composed for use in connection with events in the life of the king, these psalms eventually became the seedbed for messianic hope. (See the discussion and listing of royal psalms in connection with the comments on Psalm 2.)

Place and Person

The heading identifies this as another of the *pilgrimage psalms*, to be used in connection with journeys to Jerusalem (see on Psalm 120). As a royal psalm, Psalm 132 was first used when King David brought the ark of the covenant, the portable shrine for the worshiping of the Lord in the wilderness, to be installed in Jerusalem. (See the comments on the "songs of Zion" with Psalm 87.)

The psalm begins with David's vow to the Lord to find a central *place* for the ark and continues with an account of the bringing of the ark to that place in Jerusalem (vv. 1–10). In the second part, the focus is on a *person*, the Lord vowing to David to keep a descendant of David on the throne, *if* the covenant was kept (vv. 11 and 12). Finally, verses 13–18 again speak of the *place*, Zion, that the Lord has chosen.

The Chosen Place: (132:1–10)

This psalm was written as a prayer on behalf of King David. "Remember," says the writer, "how David wanted to have a place for worship of the Lord." David's desire to find a place for the Lord was remembered in Stephen's sermon in Acts 7:46, which appears to cite this psalm. Second Samuel 5 tells of David's taking Jerusalem from Philistine control and making it the political capital for Israel. The ark was a portable altar, the center of worship in the wilderness. It had been left out in the country at a place called Kiriath-jearim. Then 2 Samuel 6 reports on the celebration and parade as David brought the ark to Jerusalem, making that city also the people's religious capital. So Jerusalem became the "place for the LORD" that David had hoped for.

The Chosen Person (132:11–12)

Speaking through the prophet Nathan, the Lord had promised David that his line would continue and his throne would be established forever (2 Sam. 7:14–16; see also Acts 2:30). That promise is stated here, but with an important condition: "If your sons keep my covenant and my decrees that I shall teach them, their sons also, forevermore, shall sit on your throne" (Ps. 132:12). The royal line of David would continue, *if* David's successors were faithful to the covenant with the Lord.

Chosen Place, Chosen Person (132:13–18)

Zion was the mountain where the temple was located. The Lord promised to bless that place and its people and priests (vv. 15–16). The Lord will cause a king ("horn") to rule there, and that king will be victorious over Israel's enemies (see also Luke 1:69). And in fact, says the Lord, "This is my resting place forever; here I will reside" (v. 14).

Since Jerusalem is identified as the Lord's residence forever, pilgrims made journeys to that city year after year, decade after decade. This psalm about the place (Zion = Jerusalem) and the person (the son of David, the "anointed one," vv. 11, 17) who ruled there fits well into a collection of psalms designed for those making a pilgrimage to the city.

Whatever Happened to the Promises?

When the Babylonians captured and then burned Jerusalem in 587 B.C. , the chosen person was taken into exile and the chosen place was destroyed (2 Kings 25). The collection of writings from Deuteronomy through 2 Kings (with the exception of Ruth, not at this location in the Hebrew Bible) was composed to answer the question "Why did the Lord let this happen?"

The answer was that Jerusalem and the monarchy were destroyed because the people had broken the covenant. King after king failed to measure up to the covenant stipulations. Time and again the people failed to establish justice, as the prophets pointed out.

But the royal psalms survived, and the promises they contained were transposed into a new key. What were originally descriptions of the ruling king were pushed into the future and, taken together, provided a portrait of a great future king, a messiah (anointed one), who would come from the line of David. This great king would rule with righteousness and justice, would bring about peace, and would rule forever, seated at the right hand of God.

Those who name themselves Christians understand the promises of the royal psalms to be fulfilled in the person of Jesus of Nazareth, named Messiah (Matt. 16:13–20 and the testimony of the New Testament).

HOW SWEET IT IS!
Psalm 133

A Song of Ascents.

133:1 **How very good and pleasant it is**
      when kindred live together in unity!
   2 **It is like the precious oil on the head,**
      running down upon the beard,
   on the beard of Aaron,
      running down over the collar of his robes.
   3 **It is like the dew of Hermon,**
      which falls on the mountains of Zion.
   For there the LORD ordained his blessing,
      life forevermore.

A friend returned from a trip to Israel with a new song—a popular Israeli folk song, he said, taken from the Bible. He began to strum his guitar, and he sang the first line of Psalm 133 in Hebrew:

Hee-nay mah tov oo-mah na-eem,
she-vet a-cheem gam ya-chad.

"Behold, how good and how pleasant is the dwelling of brothers together" runs the literal translation; "when kindred live together in unity" is the NRSV translation.

The song became a part of my teaching material, in classrooms, camps, and churches. Then one day I received a postcard from a young woman who had learned the song in my class a decade earlier. "Now I'm a camp counselor here in New York," she wrote, "and I taught my campers that Hebrew song. We were out hiking one day and we sang it. Suddenly another group of campers came running out of the woods and began singing along. They were Jewish kids from New York City! I think God must have enjoyed hearing us Christians and Jews singing that psalm together."

A musical setting for a psalm starts in Israel, moves to the midwestern United States, and emerges decades later when it is sung outdoors by young Jewish and Christian campers who happen to meet in New York. "How very good and pleasant it is" indeed.

Psalm 133 begins with a proverbial saying (v. 1), continues with a pair of similes illustrating the proverb (vv. 2–3a), and concludes with a word about blessing (v. 3b). As the second to last of the pilgrimage psalms (see on Psalm 120), it reflects on the pleasant experience of fellow believers gathering together in Jerusalem for a time.

A Good Time Together (133:1–3)

The saying in verse 1 is a proverb, similar to those found in the book of Proverbs. As such, it contains "the wisdom of many in the wit of one," as has been said. The Hebrew word translated "pleasant" is *nā'îm*, from which the name Naomi is derived (see Ruth 1:20). The literal Hebrew "brothers" is rightly translated for our time by "brothers and sisters" or "kindred" (NRSV) or even "God's people" (TEV).

The poet/teacher wants to emphasize the point about the goodness of being together and therefore supplies two pictures. "Precious oil" was a pleasant-smelling, refreshing liquid used as a body oil (Ps. 23:5; Amos 6:6; Micah 6:15). Since it was also used at the installation of a priest, the priest Aaron is mentioned (see Lev. 8:12). The generous quantity of oil adds to the picture of the community gathering as a sweet, pleasant time together.

The writer's imagination generates another picture in verse 3. Mount Hermon is far to the north of Jerusalem, some fifty miles to the northeast of the Sea of Galilee. It is mentioned here as a place where the dew is heavy. Since this is poetry and not meteorology, one need not worry over whether Hermon's dew actually reaches the mountains around Jerusalem.

The psalm ends with a word about *blessing*, the Lord's giving of good gifts to the Lord's people.

Visiting with Garfinkel

The story is told about a Jewish man who never failed to attend synagogue services on Friday evenings. He often made the point, however, that he didn't really believe in God. And so it happened that one Friday evening when he returned from services, his children asked him, "Dad, if you don't believe in God, why do you go to synagogue every Friday?" He answered, "Garfinkel is my best friend. He goes to synagogue each week to visit with God. I go to visit with Garfinkel." The community gathered each week to be in the presence of God. Another important aspect of that gathering is being in the presence of others!

Psalm 73 tells the story of a person who was near losing faith. Then one time when that person joined the gathered community in worship, he or she could once again perceive the reality of God (see vv. 16–17). The writer of the letter to the Hebrews once advised young Christians to encourage one another in good deeds, "not neglecting to meet together, as is the habit of some, but encouraging one another" (Heb. 10:25).

Placed in a collection of psalms to be used at times of gathering in Jerusalem, Psalm 133 expresses delight in times of being together with other believers. That joy is given expression in the words of a proverb to be spoken or, better yet, to be sung: "How wonderful it is, how pleasant, for God's people to live together in harmony!"

PRAISES IN THE NIGHT
Psalm 134

A Song of Ascents.

134:1 **Come, bless the Lord, all you servants of the Lord,**
      who stand by night in the house of the Lord!
   2 **Lift up your hands to the holy place,**
      and bless the Lord.

   3 **May the Lord, maker of heaven and earth,**
      bless you from Zion.

The collection of fifteen psalms running from 120 to 134 begins with words from those far away from Jerusalem, anticipating the journey to the house of the Lord (Psalms 120–122). The one about to set out acknowledges trust in the Lord, "who made heaven and earth" (Ps. 121:2). The collection now comes to a conclusion with a word of blessing at an evening service. This is a word from the Lord, "maker of heaven and earth" (Ps. 134:3). At both the beginning and ending of these pilgrimage psalms is a reminder of the greatness of the God these people worship.

As the last of these songs for pilgrimage, this one has a concluding function. It begins by inviting all to praise (the sense of "bless" here) the Lord (vv. 1–2) and then wishes the Lord's blessing from Mount Zion on those gathered (v. 3).

Psalm 134 is linked to Psalm 133 by the fact that both begin with the same Hebrew exclamation, *hinnēh*, translated by the exclamation point at the end of the first verse of each psalm. With Psalm 134, the exclamation is an invitation to a group gathered for worship at night. Isaiah 30:29 appears to refer to a similar evening worship service: "You shall have a song as in the night when a holy festival is kept" (see also Ps. 119:62).

Psalm 134 issues an invitation to worshipers: "Lift up your hands to the holy place, and bless the LORD" (v. 2). This was apparently a posture for prayer. "I lift up my hands toward your most holy sanctuary," says Psalm 28:2, providing another example of this stance. As in verse 1, the sense of "bless" here is "praise."

This psalm and the collection of pilgrimage psalms comes to a conclusion with a word wishing God's blessings, that is, a benediction (see also Num. 6:24–26). Here "bless" has the sense of the Lord watching over and caring for each person present (the Hebrew is a singular "you" here). As was the case in Psalm 121, the "maker of heaven and earth" is also concerned about one individual worshiper.

With this benediction, these psalms designed to fit a journey to Jerusalem come to a close. On further reflection, they seem also to fit the journey of a lifetime.

THIS IS YOUR GOD
Psalm 135

135:1 **Praise the LORD!**
Praise the name of the LORD;
give praise, O servants of the LORD,
2 **you that stand in the house of the LORD,**

in the courts of the house of our God.
3 Praise the LORD, for the LORD is good;
  sing to his name, for he is gracious.
4 For the LORD has chosen Jacob for himself,
  Israel as his own possession.

5 For I know that the LORD is great;
  our Lord is above all gods.
6 Whatever the LORD pleases he does,
  in heaven and on earth,
  in the seas and all deeps.
7 He it is who makes the clouds rise at the end of the earth;
  he makes lightnings for the rain
  and brings out the wind from his storehouses.

8 He it was who struck down the firstborn of Egypt,
  both human beings and animals;
9 he sent signs and wonders
  into your midst, O Egypt,
  against Pharaoh and all his servants.
10 He struck down many nations
  and killed mighty kings—
11 Sihon, king of the Amorites,
  and Og, king of Bashan,
  and all the kingdoms of Canaan—
12 and gave their land as a heritage,
  a heritage to his people Israel.

13 Your name, O LORD, endures forever,
  your renown, O LORD, throughout all ages.
14 For the LORD will vindicate his people,
  and have compassion on his servants.

15 The idols of the nations are silver and gold,
  the work of human hands.
16 They have mouths, but they do not speak;
  they have eyes, but they do not see;
17 they have ears, but they do not hear,
  and there is no breath in their mouths.
18 Those who make them
  and all who trust them
  shall become like them.

19 O house of Israel, bless the LORD!
  O house of Aaron, bless the LORD!

20 **O house of Levi, bless the Lord!**
  You that fear the Lord, bless the Lord!
21 **Blessed be the Lord from Zion,**
  he who resides in Jerusalem.
  Praise the Lord!

After the collection of pilgrimage psalms running from Psalm 120 to 134, the book of Psalms now returns to something more traditional: a *hymn of praise*. At some point in its history, Psalm 135 was sung in the temple in Jerusalem (vv. 2, 19–21). The psalm begins and ends with "Hallelujah" ("Praise the Lord"), thus marking it as a hymn. It is made up of the typical elements of the hymn of praise (see Psalm 113 for the pattern): a *call to praise* in the imperative (vv. 1–3) followed by *reasons* for praise introduced by *for* (vv. 4, 5–12). Verse 13 addresses the Lord in "you" form with praise, and verse 14 again provides a reason. Verses 15–18 pick up some traditional words about idols (see also Ps. 115:4–8), and the psalm comes to a close with a quintuple call to praise (bless) the Lord and a final "Hallelujah."

Praise and Sing! (135:1–3)

The psalm begins with several links to the psalms just before it in the canon. Psalm 134 addresses worshipers as "servants of the Lord" who "stand . . . in the house of the Lord" (134:1). Psalm 135 addresses the gathered congregation with nearly the same words (135:1–2). Psalm 134 calls for praise; Psalm 135 also calls for praise and then offers that praise.

This introductory section consists of *calls to praise* in the imperative ("Praise!" in vv. 1–3a) and also some quite general *reasons for praise* ("for the Lord is good . . . for he is gracious," v. 3b).

Why We Should Praise (135:4–14)

After this opening call to praise and sing, the psalm provides some more specific reasons for praising. Praising God is a reasonable thing to do!

Reason number one: *the Lord has chosen Israel as the Lord's own possession*. The Hebrew for "possession" is *segullah*, which means an especially valuable possession. Ecclesiastes speaks of "silver and gold and the treasure [*segullah*] of kings" (Eccl. 2:8). King David describes his possessions by saying, "I have a *treasure* of my own of gold and silver" (1 Chron. 29:3). The term is also used of God's people in Exodus 19:5 and Deuteronomy 7:6, as well as in 1 Peter 2:9, which identifies Christians as "a people for [Christ's] possession" (NRSV footnote).

Reason number two for praising is stated in verse 5: *the Lord is great.*
The next lines expand on that greatness. The Lord has control over all
that exists in the universe, here described as heaven and earth, "the seas
and all deeps" (v. 6). When one sees a mighty cumulonimbus cloud
parked majestically in the blue sky, or when one senses a storm coming
on, with lightning and rain and wind, one ought to remember that "whatever the LORD pleases he does" (v. 6). According to this psalm, the Lord
controls all of these events.

Verse 5 indicates a third reason to praise: *the Lord is above all gods.* This
theme is developed in verses 15–18.

The fourth reason for praising the Lord reaches back into history, to
the time of the exodus from Egypt. The "signs and wonders" of verse 9
refer to the plagues (Exodus 7–12). Verses 10 and 11 refer to the conquest of the promised land, and verse 12 provides a summary: *the Lord
gave the land as an inheritance.*

With verse 13, the psalm addresses words of praise to the Lord per-
sonally in "you" language. Here praise is set in the context of eternity,
and a promise is made that God will continue to have compassion and
help Israel (v. 14).

A Comment about Idols (135:15–18)

One short comment made earlier in the course of the hymn needs further explanation. In verse 5 the psalmist says, "Our Lord is above all
gods." In verses 15–18 this notion is expanded on. Using material known
by other psalmists (see Ps. 115:4–8), the writer pokes fun at the powerlessness of idols and finally concludes that worshipers become like that
which they worship (v. 18)! The contrast between the powerlessness of
these idols and the might of the Lord (vv. 4–12) could not be sharper.
One is reminded of the bitter prophetic satire on idols and those who
make them in Isaiah 44:9–20.

Concluding Praises (135:19–21)

The psalm ends as it began, with calls to praise the Lord. Various groups
are present during the service of worship: the "house of Israel" refers to
the whole congregation; "Aaron" and "Levi" are groups of priests and
assistants. Does "You that fear the LORD" refer to believing non-
Israelites, joining in for worship? (See the "God-fearers" who appear in
Acts 10:2; 13:16; 16:14.)

This Is Your God

Following on the pilgrimage psalms, Psalm 135 is a magnificent hymn that expresses the essentials of what the psalms say about God:

The Lord is good (v. 3). This goodness is evident in the fact that the Lord chose Israel as the Lord's own treasured possession (v. 4), delivered them from Egyptian bondage, and gave them a land (vv. 8–12). And the Lord's loving care for the people will carry into the future (vv. 13–14).

The Lord is great (v. 5a). This greatness is illustrated in three ways: (1) the Lord is greater than any other gods that may inhabit the universe (vv. 5b, 15–18); (2) the Lord has control over nature (vv. 6–7); (3) the Lord controls history. The Lord acted in Israel's past history, rescuing them from Egyptian bondage and giving them a land (vv. 8–12), and will continue to act on Israel's behalf in their future (vv. 13–14).

Praise the Lord (vv. 1–3, 13, 19–21). Because of the Lord's goodness and greatness, all God's people are called to praise. What this psalm says *about* God is framed by *praise addressed to God*. To put it another way: according to this psalm, theology is best done in the context of doxology.

AMAZING GRACE
Psalm 136

136:1 **O give thanks to the LORD, for he is good,**
> **for his steadfast love endures forever.**
² **O give thanks to the God of gods,**
> **for his steadfast love endures forever.**
³ **O give thanks to the Lord of lords,**
> **for his steadfast love endures forever;**

⁴ **who alone does great wonders,**
> **for his steadfast love endures forever;**
⁵ **who by understanding made the heavens,**
> **for his steadfast love endures forever;**
⁶ **who spread out the earth on the waters,**
> **for his steadfast love endures forever;**
⁷ **who made the great lights,**
> **for his steadfast love endures forever;**
⁸ **the sun to rule over the day,**
> **for his steadfast love endures forever;**
⁹ **the moon and stars to rule over the night,**
> **for his steadfast love endures forever;**

¹⁰ who struck Egypt through their firstborn,
  for his steadfast love endures forever;
¹¹ and brought Israel out from among them,
  for his steadfast love endures forever;
¹² with a strong hand and an outstretched arm,
  for his steadfast love endures forever;
¹³ who divided the Red Sea in two,
  for his steadfast love endures forever;
¹⁴ and made Israel pass through the midst of it,
  for his steadfast love endures forever;
¹⁵ but overthrew Pharaoh and his army in the Red Sea,
  for his steadfast love endures forever;
¹⁶ who led his people through the wilderness,
  for his steadfast love endures forever;
¹⁷ who struck down great kings,
  for his steadfast love endures forever;
¹⁸ and killed famous kings,
  for his steadfast love endures forever;
¹⁹ Sihon, king of the Amorites,
  for his steadfast love endures forever;
²⁰ and Og, king of Bashan,
  for his steadfast love endures forever;
²¹ and gave their land as a heritage,
  for his steadfast love endures forever;
²² a heritage to his servant Israel,
  for his steadfast love endures forever.

²³ It is he who remembered us in our low estate,
  for his steadfast love endures forever;
²⁴ and rescued us from our foes,
  for his steadfast love endures forever;
²⁵ who gives food to all flesh,
  for his steadfast love endures forever.
²⁶ O give thanks to the God of heaven,
  for his steadfast love endures forever.

The Jewish Talmud notes that Psalm 136

equates the most awesome Divine miracles, i.e. , He divided the Sea of
Reeds into parts (v. 13) with the apparently mundane and routine task of
providing for daily sustenance, i.e. , He gives bread to all living creatures
(v. 25). This teaches that . . . the provision of daily sustenance is as significant as the splitting of the sea.

In consideration of these things, the Talmud calls Psalm 136 the "Great
Hallel," the great psalm of praise, "because it underscores God's most

enduring achievement—the sustenance of every living thing" (Fever, *Tehillim/Psalms*, p. 1607).

Jewish commentators point out that there are twenty-six verses in this psalm. The number 26 is of significance because when the numerical value of the Lord's Hebrew name Yahweh is counted (YHWH = 10 + 5 + 6 + 5), the total is 26. The bare framework of the psalm testifies to the reality of Yahweh, the Lord!

The psalm links up with Psalm 135, since both are hymns of praise to the God who works in nature and in history.

A call to praise and to give thanks (vv. 1–3) is followed by a recalling of God's work of creation (vv. 4–9) and of the events of the exodus, the guiding through the wilderness, and the conquest of the promised land (vv. 10–22). With the final section, the speaker changes ("us") and the worshiping congregation is tied to these events of past history (vv. 23–25). The last verse links with the first.

The most striking feature of the psalm is the repeated refrain, "for his steadfast love endures forever." That repetition indicates that with this refrain, we are at the heart of the psalm.

The Heartbeat of the Psalm (136:1–3)

Psalm 136 was designed to be read or sung or chanted aloud, with a group repeating each response, in the manner of Psalm 118:1–4 (see also Sirach 51). The best way to sense the meaning of this psalm is to read it aloud in a group. One person should read the first line of each verse with the others joining in on each refrain. After a half dozen repetitions, the refrain sinks in: "for his steadfast love endures forever." If one were to ask a worshiper what had been learned at the morning's service, the answer would be clear: God's steadfast love endures forever!

The statement in verse 1 is found often in the Bible: see Psalms 106:1; 107:1; 118:1–4; as well as 1 Chronicles 16:34; 2 Chronicles 5:11–14; 7:1–3; 20:21; Ezra 3:10–11, and other places.

A good equivalent for *hesed*, the Hebrew word translated here as "steadfast love," is *amazing grace*. The word *hesed* comes up often in Hosea; it means the love and loyalty that ought to exist between a husband and wife (Hos. 2:19). When Hosea's wife was unfaithful and drifted into a life of prostitution, the prophet discovered he still loved her and bought her out of slavery (Hos. 3:1–2). That sort of "love that loves no matter what" is *hesed*. *Hesed* is love with a strong element of loyalty. And that sort of loyal love became the model for understanding the Lord's love for Israel.

The Story of God's Work in Creation (136:4–9)

The word translated "wonders" can refer to things beyond the realm of understanding, such as the way of an eagle or a serpent or a ship or a man and a woman (Prov. 30:18–19). The reference also can be to the Lord's great acts on behalf of the people in history that evoke awe (note the historical psalms 78:4; 105:2; 106:2). The language links up with that of the creation account in Genesis 1:14–19.

The Story of God's Acts in History (136:10–22)

The psalm lists a series of the Lord's wondrous deeds in the realm of history. Here is a recollection of the exodus from Egypt (Ps. 136:10–15) as well as the leading through the wilderness, including the killing of a pair of famous kings (vv. 16–20) and the gift of the promised land (vv. 21–22).

Our Story (136:23–26)

Now, for the first time, the community reciting these stories appears: "It is he who remembered *us*" (v. 23). First, the worshipers recall how the Lord helped at a time when they were in deep trouble (v. 23). Then they remember how often the Lord rescued them from enemies (v. 24). These recollections of the people bring the stories of God's mighty acts up to date and into the lives of the gathered community.

Finally, the community recalls how God provides food for all creatures, human and nonhuman alike (v. 25; see also Pss. 104:14–15, 27–28; 145:15–16; 146:7; 147:9). In this way, Psalm 136 puts the gift of daily food on the same plane as the great acts of creation, exodus, and conquest. All are workings out of the Lord's amazing grace. The prayer "O give thanks to the LORD, for he is good, for his steadfast love endures forever" is as appropriate from an individual over a plate of food as it was from a people who had just escaped from slavery into freedom. In both cases, the prayers are expressions of thankful hearts, amazed that the God of heaven cares about this people, or about this person.

CAN WE TAKE OUR RELIGION ALONG?
Psalm 137

> 137:1 **By the rivers of Babylon—**
>   **there we sat down and there we wept**
>   **when we remembered Zion.**

2 **On the willows there**
   we hung up our harps.
3 **For there our captors**
   asked us for songs,
   and our tormentors asked for mirth, saying,
   "Sing us one of the songs of Zion!"

4 **How could we sing the LORD's song**
   in a foreign land?
5 **If I forget you, O Jerusalem,**
   let my right hand wither!
6 **Let my tongue cling to the roof of my mouth,**
   if I do not remember you,
   if I do not set Jerusalem
   above my highest joy.

7 **Remember, O LORD, against the Edomites**
   the day of Jerusalem's fall,
   how they said, "Tear it down! Tear it down!
   Down to its foundations!"
8 **O daughter Babylon, you devastator!**
   Happy shall they be who pay you back
   what you have done to us!
9 **Happy shall they be who take your little ones**
   and dash them against the rock!

The question raised in Psalm 137 is one that concerns any group of believers as they move through history: How can we sing the Lord's song in a foreign land? Put in other words: How can we be faithful to the religion we have inherited and yet also relevant to the world in which we live?

Can We Take Our Religion Along?

This psalm is unique in the book of Psalms because it indicates the historical situation out of which it comes. The persons speaking in the psalm are in Babylon on the Euphrates River, recalling their lives in Zion, that is, in Jerusalem.

How did they come to be in Babylon? In 587 B.C., Jerusalem was destroyed by the Babylonians, and the majority of Jewish citizens were deported to live in Babylon. This began the period of the Babylonian exile, which lasted until the Persians conquered Babylon in 539 B.C. Along with Isaiah 40–55, Psalm 137 is one of the sources for picking up the mood of these Jews living in the capital city of the Babylonian Empire.

While the exile was a political crisis, with Jerusalem left a heap of rubble, it was also a religious crisis. How could a powerful God have let this happen? And the mood of the people in exile? The prophet picks up what they have been saying: "My way is hidden from the LORD" (Isa. 40:27); "The LORD has forsaken me, my Lord has forgotten me" (Isa. 49:14). It was a religious crisis, indeed.

The exiles wondered if God had forgotten them and abandoned them. This psalm reports another question: Can we continue to sing our old songs and hymns here in Babylon? In other words: Can our religion make the move from Jerusalem to a new world?

Psalm 137 falls into three sections, each driven by the verb *remember*. In the first, a singer *remembers* Zion/Jerusalem (vv. 1–4); then, the writer vows to *remember* Jerusalem (vv. 5–6); finally, the writer asks the Lord to *remember* the crimes of Jerusalem's enemies (vv. 7–9).

We Remember Zion (137:1–3)

The city of Babylon was the capital of the most powerful empire of its day. The achievements of Babylonian science, especially in astronomy, were breathtaking. And in Babylon were the famed "hanging gardens" that King Nebuchadnezzar had constructed for one of his wives.

Psalm 137 comes from a small Jewish community gathering by the Euphrates River. Far from home, with only the memory of the temple, these Jews worshiped. That worship included stories from the people's past history with the Lord (Deuteronomy–2 Kings); preaching from prophetic figures, such as the prophet of Isaiah 40–55 and Ezekiel; and songs, such as Psalm 137.

According to this psalm, their captors asked them to "sing us one of the songs of Zion." Did these Babylonians want to hear songs in praise of Zion and Jerusalem, such as Psalms 46 and 84? Or just any of the religious songs of these Jews? Certainly, they did not want to join in on a friendly hymn sing on the banks of the Euphrates! Their intentions were hostile. They were captors, and they were seeking to make the lives of their Jewish captives miserable. The psalmist says in effect, "We sang, we remembered Zion, and we wept because we couldn't sing anymore."

If I Do Not Remember You . . . (137:4–6)

Verse 4 expresses the central question of this psalm: Is our religion portable, transportable? Can we worship our Lord in a foreign land? a pagan land? a secular land?

With verses 5–6, the writer of the psalm speaks a resounding yes to these questions. To give that yes the strongest possible emphasis, the composer makes some public vows. Never will this singer forget Jerusalem. Should this happen, the musician asks that the ability to write and to speak be taken away! This is a powerful vow, from a writer and speaker! But Jerusalem would always be this person's highest joy (v. 6).

The Talmud says that verse 6, "if I do not set Jerusalem above my highest joy," should be read at a wedding to the bridegroom as he awaits the arrival of the bride, as a reminder that *no* joy, not even that of marriage, could be as great as the joy associated with Jerusalem.

Lord, Remember Our Enemies (137:7–9)

The final "Remember" is directed to the Lord. Verses 7–9 contain some exceptionally harsh words, often cut out when the psalm is printed in a hymnbook. These are very human words, from one who has had enough oppression. The Edomites were bitter enemies because they had refused to help when Jerusalem was being destroyed by the Babylonians (Obadiah 12–13). Verse 9 is a violent wish, inexcusable but not atypical for a violent time (see also 2 Kings 8:12; Isa. 13:16; Hos. 10:14; 13:16; Nah. 3:10).

Recycling, Rewriting, and Remembering

Can this old psalm still be used in the life and worship of the twenty-first-century church? Two extremes ought to be avoided.

Some psalms, such as Psalm 23, are easily *recycled* and seem to fit into almost any situation. But this will not work for Psalm 137. Verses 7–9 could not be read in a congregational setting without some sort of commentary.

Some would advise *rewriting* certain of the Psalms; in the case of Psalm 137, this would mean cutting out the last three verses. Such an approach, however, has the danger of eliminating those parts of the Psalms not suited to twenty-first-century sensitivities.

The best clue for the appropriation of Psalm 137 may be found in that word *remember*. The names Babylon and Edom call for some remembering of historical situations, and such a remembering can help explain (but not excuse) the very human words of verses 7–9, from persons who are hurting badly. That *remembering* ought also to include other words about attitude toward enemies, from both the Old Testament (2 Chron. 28:8–15) and the New (Matt. 5:43–48).

Finally, the advice to remember Jerusalem will be quite welcome to those whose faith has at its center a cross and an empty tomb, both located in that city.

THE LORD AND THE LOWLY
Psalm 138

Of David.

138:1 I give you thanks, O LORD, with my whole heart;
       before the gods I sing your praise;
  2 I bow down toward your holy temple
       and give thanks to your name for your steadfast love and your
       faithfulness;
       for you have exalted your name and your word
       above everything.
  3 On the day I called, you answered me,
       you increased my strength of soul.

  4 All the kings of the earth shall praise you, O LORD,
       for they have heard the words of your mouth.
  5 They shall sing of the ways of the LORD,
       for great is the glory of the LORD.
  6 For though the LORD is high, he regards the lowly;
       but the haughty he perceives from far away.

  7 Though I walk in the midst of trouble,
       you preserve me against the wrath of my enemies;
       you stretch out your hand,
       and your right hand delivers me.
  8 The Lord will fulfill his purpose for me;
       your steadfast love, O LORD, endures forever.
       Do not forsake the work of your hands.

When the Bible speaks about God, it often speaks in extremes. God is "high above all nations" and yet concerned about the poor man and the childless woman (Ps. 113:4, 7–9). The Lord is enthroned in heaven and yet watches all the earth's inhabitants (Ps. 33:13). God speaks in Isaiah 57:15: "I dwell in the high and holy place, and also with those who are contrite and humble in spirit."

This sort of notion comes to expression in verse 6 of Psalm 138: "For though the LORD is high, he regards the lowly; but the haughty he perceives from far away." This is a psalm about the Lord and the lowly.

Psalm 138 is the first in a final collection of eight Davidic psalms in the Psalter (Psalms 138–145; on David, see on Psalm 3). Psalms of thanks and praise (Psalms 138, 145) frame a group of individual laments (Psalms 139–144).

This *song of thanksgiving* begins with an account of answered prayer

(vv. 1–3), continues with a word about the kings of the earth (vv. 4–6), and concludes with an affirmation of trust and a request for help (vv. 7–8).

Wholehearted Thanks (138:1–3)

The psalm gets right to the point: "I thank you" is the first word in the Hebrew text. The perspective of this psalm is broad ("All the kings of the earth . . . ," v. 4), and the psalmist immediately sets this "thank you" in that wide setting, referring to the gods of the nations of the earth (v. 1).

The writer appears to assume the existence of these gods, as do the prophecies in the second part of Isaiah. But these gods are powerless and their idols are, in the view of the prophet, quite ludicrous (see Isa. 41:21–24; 43:11–13; 44:6–8, 9–20).

The one praying in Psalm 138 is in the outer court of the temple in Jerusalem (v. 2). "Give thanks" occurs a second time, establishing the theme of the psalm. The psalmist is thankful for those familiar characteristics of the Lord: steadfast love (*hesed*; see on Psalm 136) and faithfulness.

Songs of thanksgiving such as this one typically refer to a specific action of God for which the writer is thankful. This time the psalmist says simply, "I prayed, you answered" (v. 3).

This Is Our God (138:4–6)

The perspective of Psalm 138 is global. After speaking of the gods of the earth (v. 1), the psalm portrays a scene where all the kings of the earth are singing praise to the Lord ("LORD" is emphasized, occurring four times in this section). As reasons for this praise, verses 4 and 5 speak of the words, the ways, and the glory of the Lord. Of central importance is the statement in verse 6, which frames the matter in extremes. The Lord is on high but watches over those who are lowly (see also Pss. 14:2; 34:15, 17; 102:18–20).

You Are with Me (138:7–8)

"Though I walk in the midst of trouble, you preserve me" is an affirmation of trust that reminds one of Psalm 23:4: "Even though I walk through the darkest valley. . . ." Psalm 138 also includes a promise for deliverance from enemies. After a second reference (v. 8) to the Lord's *steadfast love* (also v. 2), the psalm concludes with a request for the Lord's continuing care: "Do not forsake the work of your hands."

Amazing Grace

This psalm is framed by references to the Lord's *hesed,* or steadfast love, or amazing grace (vv. 2, 8). The psalmist is thankful for that *hesed* (v. 2) and trusts that it will endure (v. 8). At the heart of the psalm is a declaration illustrating that steadfast love. The Lord who is high and exalted cares for the lowly (v. 6).

The New Testament centers on a dramatic illustration of the shape of that divine *hesed,* in the Gospel stories of a Son sent into the world (John 3:16) and of One who was God's equal and then became a servant who suffered, died, and was exalted (Phil. 2:5–11).

"THANK YOU FOR ME"
Psalm 139

To the leader. Of David. A Psalm.

139:1 O LORD, you have searched me and known me.
  2 You know when I sit down and when I rise up;
      you discern my thoughts from far away.
  3 You search out my path and my lying down,
      and are acquainted with all my ways.
  4 Even before a word is on my tongue,
      O LORD, you know it completely.
  5 You hem me in, behind and before,
      and lay your hand upon me.
  6 Such knowledge is too wonderful for me;
      it is so high that I cannot attain it.

  7 Where can I go from your spirit?
      Or where can I flee from your presence?
  8 If I ascend to heaven, you are there;
      if I make my bed in Sheol, you are there.
  9 If I take the wings of the morning
      and settle at the farthest limits of the sea,
  10 even there your hand shall lead me,
      and your right hand shall hold me fast.
  11 If I say, "Surely the darkness shall cover me,
      and the light around me become night,"
  12 even the darkness is not dark to you;
      the night is as bright as the day,
      for darkness is as light to you.

¹³ **For it was you who formed my inward parts;**
   you knit me together in my mother's womb.
¹⁴ **I praise you, for I am fearfully and wonderfully made.**
   Wonderful are your works;
   that I know very well.
¹⁵   **My frame was not hidden from you,**
   when I was being made in secret,
      intricately woven in the depths of the earth.
¹⁶ **Your eyes beheld my unformed substance.**
   In your book were written
      all the days that were formed for me,
      when none of them as yet existed.
¹⁷ **How weighty to me are your thoughts, O God!**
   How vast is the sum of them!
¹⁸ **I try to count them—they are more than the sand;**
   I come to the end—I am still with you.

¹⁹ **O that you would kill the wicked, O God,**
   and that the bloodthirsty would depart from me—
²⁰ **those who speak of you maliciously,**
   and lift themselves up against you for evil!
²¹ **Do I not hate those who hate you, O LORD?**
   And do I not loathe those who rise up against you?
²² **I hate them with perfect hatred;**
   I count them my enemies.
²³ **Search me, O God, and know my heart;**
   test me and know my thoughts.
²⁴ **See if there is any wicked way in me,**
   and lead me in the way everlasting.

It was a child's bedtime prayer that helped me understand this psalm.

In those days I heard those prayers almost every evening. Three sons slept together in a basement bedroom. After a story or two and some conversation about the day, it was time for prayers. The pattern of the first and last sons was always the same: "Thank you for my mom and dad, thank you for my brothers and sister, thank you for my dog, Amen." But the middle son added a personal touch. After the thanks for parents, siblings, and dog came an addition: "Thank you for me." A healthy appreciation for the gift of life, it seemed to me—not just for life in general but for a specific, individual life.

This psalm expresses the same sense of individual appreciation: "You knit *me* together in my mother's womb. I praise you" (vv. 13–14a).

For the heading, see the comments on Psalms 3 and 4. The psalm falls into four sections: "Lord, you know me" (vv. 1–6); "I'm never away from you" (vv. 7–12); "You created me" (vv. 13–18); "Deal with the wicked, Lord" (vv. 19–24).

The psalm appears to have come from a person who has been falsely accused by certain "wicked" persons (vv. 19–22). The psalmist asks the Lord, "Search me . . . know my heart" (v. 23). Now the Lord's investigation has been completed (v. 1), and the mood of the psalm is one of thankful praise (vv. 2–18).

You Know Me, Lord (139:1–6)

The focus of this section is on the Lord's *knowing* (vv. 1, 2, 4, 6). This is not a theological assertion about omniscience but rather a statement of faith that the Lord knows everything about the particular individual who is praying.

This knowing includes knowing one's actions (vv. 2–3) as well as one's words, even before they are spoken (v. 4). After reflecting on such knowing, the psalmist reacts with amazement and praise: "Wonderful!" (v. 6).

I'm Never Away from You (139:7–12)

Again, this is not a theoretical statement about the omnipresence of God but rather an assertion about a specific person. The prophet Jonah learned from experience that it was impossible to escape the Lord's presence (Jonah 1:3). The psalmist here asserts the same thing.

Verse 8 speaks of the vertical extremes: one cannot escape the Lord by running to heaven, nor down to Sheol, the region of the dead. As Job said, "Sheol is naked before God" (Job 26:6).

Verses 9–10 express the impossibility of escaping from God in terms of the four points of the compass. One must think of facing east; then the "wings of the morning" is to the east, where the sun rises, and the "limits of the sea" is to the west. "Your right hand" would be the south, and "your hand"–that is, the left hand—the north (Dahood, *Psalms III*, pp. 285–91).

The Lord also sees in the darkness. According to Sirach, "the eyes of the Lord are ten thousand times brighter than the sun; they look upon every aspect of human behavior and see into hidden corners" (Sirach 23:19; also Heb. 4:13).

God the Knitter (139:13–18)

The Psalms have a great variety of pictures of God, including God as king, shepherd, father, mother. In verse 13 of Psalm 139, God is portrayed as a knitter! The notion also occurs in Job 10:11: "You clothed me with skin and flesh, and knit me together with bones and sinews."

The image invites reflection. I watched a Norwegian American mother-in-law knit a series of six Norwegian sweaters for our family. The process appears unbelievably complex, controlling the threads, getting the colors right, developing the patterns. If it is complicated to knit a Norwegian sweater, how much more complicated must it be (one feels certain) to knit a Norwegian! Or an African, a Russian, or a Korean! On reflection, the psalmist can only say, "I praise you, for I am fearfully and wonderfully made" (v. 14).

Verse 16 expresses the notion of a book where the psalmist's days have already been recorded. The same idea occurs in the notion of God's "record" in Psalm 56:8 and the "book of the living" in Psalm 69:28. Is this a basis for a doctrine of "predestination"? Patrick Miller has commented on the matter of predestination:

> It has always been a theological claim that works better as a personal conviction about one's own destiny's being set in the purpose of God than it does as an effort to work out logically the mystery of God's purpose for others. (*Interpreting the Psalms*, p. 147)

The conviction that "I am still *with* you" expresses a powerful biblical theme; see comments on Psalm 23:4.

Deal with the Wicked, Lord! (139:19–24)

The very harsh words about the wicked in verses 19–22 may be explained, but not excused, by the situation that called them forth. It appears that the psalmist and the Lord together have been falsely accused. The psalmist expresses hatred against these accusers, viewed as enemies of the psalmist and of God (vv. 21–22). In this difficult personal situation, the writer declares himself innocent of these charges and asks for God's guidance (vv. 23–24).

These are hard words for the Christian reader, who has been taught to "love your enemies and pray for those who persecute you" (Matt. 5:44). But they are also very human words, giving expression to the feelings of the psalmist. Vengeance, it will be noted, is left in God's hands (v. 19).

On Being Zusya

In some ways, Psalm 139 can be classified as a "creation psalm." The psalm does not speak of God creating the heavens and the earth, calling into existence a planet here or a galaxy there. It speaks rather of God creating an individual, or more accurately, it says to God, *"You* created *me. You* knit *me* together in my mother's womb" (v. 13). This creating activity is presented as a reason for praise (v. 14).

People, in other words, are not mass-produced but custom-made. The story is told about young Rabbi Zusya, who was quite discouraged about his failures and weaknesses. Said an older rabbi to him, "When you get to heaven, God is not going to say to you, 'Why weren't you Moses?' No, God will say, 'Why weren't you Zusya?' So why don't you stop trying to be Moses, and start being the Zusya God created you to be?"

This unusual psalm speaks about the God who is everywhere present (vv. 7–12) and yet who knows me, leads me, and holds me (v. 10) and has even knit me together in the womb (v. 13). Perhaps the most comforting word is that no matter what, the one whom God has knit together can always say, "God, I am still with you" (v. 18).

DELIVER ME FROM EVIL!
Psalm 140

To the leader. A Psalm of David.

140:1 **Deliver me, O LORD, from evildoers;**
      protect me from those who are violent,
  2 **who plan evil things in their minds**
      and stir up wars continually.
  3 **They make their tongue sharp as a snake's,**
      and under their lips is the venom of vipers.   *Selah*

  4 **Guard me, O LORD, from the hands of the wicked;**
      protect me from the violent
      who have planned my downfall.
  5 **The arrogant have hidden a trap for me,**
      and with cords they have spread a net,
      along the road they have set snares for me.   *Selah*

  6 **I say to the LORD, "You are my God;**
      give ear, O LORD, to the voice of my supplications."
  7 **O LORD, my LORD, my strong deliverer,**
      you have covered my head in the day of battle.
  8 **Do not grant, O LORD, the desires of the wicked;**
      do not further their evil plot.   *Selah*

⁹ Those who surround me lift up their heads;
   let the mischief of their lips overwhelm them!
¹⁰ Let burning coals fall on them!
    Let them be flung into pits, no more to rise!
¹¹ Do not let the slanderer be established in the land;
    let evil speedily hunt down the violent!

¹² I know that the LORD maintains the cause of the needy,
     and executes justice for the poor.
¹³ Surely the righteous shall give thanks to your name;
     the upright shall live in your presence.

The request in the Lord's Prayer "Deliver us from evil" comes out of a long tradition of requests for rescue (Pss. 6:4; 119:153), or reports of such deliverance, in the Psalms (Pss. 18:19; 34:7; 91:14; 116:8). Psalm 140 is one example of a prayer from an individual who is hurting badly and who prays, "Deliver me from evil."

For the heading, see the comments on Psalm 4. This third psalm in the Psalter's final Davidic collection is the second in a sextet of *laments* (Psalms 139–144). The usual elements of the lament are present (see on Psalm 13), with *Selah* marking points of division (vv. 3, 5, 8; see on Psalm 3). This psalm consists of *requests* with *"they" complaints* (vv. 1–3, 4–5), an *affirmation of trust* coupled with a *request* (vv. 6–8), *"they" complaints* and *requests* again (vv. 9–11), an *affirmation of trust* (v. 12), and a *vow to praise* (v. 13). The fact that nine of the thirteen verses in the psalm contain requests says something of the urgent nature of this prayer for help. The doubled "protect me from the violent" (the Hebrew is identical in vv. 1, 4) also testifies to the urgent situation.

Deliver Me, Protect Me (140:1–5)

The sense of the verb *deliver* is to pull something or someone out of a situation as one might pull stones out of the wall of a house (Lev. 14:40, 43). The prayer is that the Lord will pull the one praying out of the situation with evildoers. What are these persons doing? Pictured as poisonous snakes, their evil deeds have to do with their tongues, that is, with slanderous or lying speech.

Verse 1 asked for the Lord to intervene and deliver; verse 4 requests a defensive sort of action of protecting and guarding. Once again, picture language is used to describe what the enemies are doing. Like a hunter setting traps, they have set traps for the psalmist. (Psalm 141:9–10 uses similar hunting metaphors.)

My Strong Deliverer (140:6–11)

Verses 6–7 offer affirmations of trust in the form of confessions of faith: "You are my God . . . my Lord, my strong deliverer, you have covered my head"—that is, you have been my safety helmet! The request in verse 8 is a negative one, that the Lord not prosper the enemies. The psalmist's wishes that the Lord deal with the enemies continue in verses 9–11. Verse 9 again indicates that their evildoing has to do with what they are saying (also v. 3), and verse 11 identifies their violence as slander (see also vv. 1, 4). Does the reference to "burning coals" refer to some sort of volcanic eruption, such as that which consumed Sodom and Gomorrah (Gen. 19:24; also Ps. 11:6)? In any case, the coals and the pits are used as metaphors for evil. Far from praying *for* these enemies, the psalmist wishes them the worst!

Deliverer of the Poor and Needy (140:12–13)

The psalm ends with the writer affirming trust in the Lord as the defender and deliverer of the poor and needy, in whose ranks the psalmist is to be found. In relationship to the goods of their society, these persons are poor and needy; in relationship to the Lord, they are the righteous and upright.

The Psalms, the Powerless, and the Prophets

The theme of the Lord's care for the powerless is sounded in these words about the poor and needy. The theme continues to be heard in psalms such as 145:14–21; 146:7–9; 147:3, 6 ("the brokenhearted," "the down-trodden"). In fact, it runs through the Bible, from legal materials (Exod. 22:21–24; Lev. 19:9–10; 25:35–38; Deut. 24:14–22), through Proverbs (14:21; 22:22–23; 23:10–11; 29:14), the Prophets (Isa. 1:16–17, 23; Amos 4:1; 5:12; 8:4–6), and into the New Testament (James 1:27–2:7), all of which should be read in their broader context. The tradition of concern for social justice is an ancient and central one for biblical faith.

While Psalm 140 is not one of the more well known psalms, it was quoted by the apostle Paul, who cited from verse 3 in his listing of statements about human evil in Romans 3:13.

EVENING PRAYER
Psalm 141

A Psalm of David.

141:1 I call upon you, O LORD; come quickly to me;
        give ear to my voice when I call to you.

² **Let my prayer be counted as incense before you,**
       and the lifting up of my hands as an evening sacrifice.

³ **Set a guard over my mouth, O LORD;**
       keep watch over the door of my lips.
⁴ **Do not turn my heart to any evil,**
       to busy myself with wicked deeds
   in company with those who work iniquity;
       do not let me eat of their delicacies.

⁵ **Let the righteous strike me;**
       let the faithful correct me.
   Never let the oil of the wicked anoint my head,
       for my prayer is continually against their wicked deeds.
⁶ **When they are given over to those who shall condemn them,**
       then they shall learn that my words were pleasant.
⁷ **Like a rock that one breaks apart and shatters on the land,**
       so shall their bones be strewn at the mouth of Sheol.

⁸ **But my eyes are turned toward you, O GOD, my Lord;**
       in you I seek refuge; do not leave me defenseless.
⁹ **Keep me from the trap that they have laid for me,**
       and from the snares of evildoers.
¹⁰ **Let the wicked fall into their own nets,**
       while I alone escape.

A portion of this psalm is well known in those communities where
worship includes a traditional evening service of vespers. In the canticle
Domine clamavi, the leader sings,

> Let my prayer be counted as incense before you;
>   and the lifting up of my hands as an evening sacrifice.
>
> (v. 2)

The gathered congregation responds,

> I call upon you, O LORD; come quickly to me;
>   give ear to my voice when I call to you.
>
> (v. 1)

The canticle continues with other verses from the psalm (see Canticle
5, *Lutheran Book of Worship*).

The imagery is striking: prayers rise to God in heaven just as the
sweet-smelling smoke of incense rises. The picture is of persons with
their hands stretched up, praying.

This is the fourth in the concluding collection of psalms associated with David (Psalms 138–145; see comments on Psalm 4). It is a prayer for help from one troubled by certain wicked persons.

My Prayer as Incense (141:1–2)

The one praying needs the Lord's immediate attention (v. 1). The prayer is part of an evening service where sacrifices are offered. The book of Ezra refers to such a service: "At the evening sacrifice I got up from my fasting, with my garments and my mantle torn, and fell on my knees, spread out my hands to the LORD my God, and said . . ." (Ezra 9:5–6; see also Dan. 9:20–21 and Judith 9:1).

As the smoke from the sacrifice rises in the evening sky, the psalmist imagines those clouds carrying her prayers along to God in heaven. The author of Revelation reports on a vision: "And the smoke of the incense, with the prayers of the saints, rose before God" (Rev. 8:4).

Guard My Mouth (141:3–7)

After the quiet and calming imagery of smoke rising gently in the evening sky, Psalm 141 comes back down to earth with a very practical prayer. The psalmist is concerned about words, specifically about inappropriate words. The concern is expressed in two pictures, asking the Lord to be a guard watching what proceeds from the writer's mouth and a watchman keeping an eye on what proceeds from her lips. But any evil expressing itself in words would originate in the depths of the heart and would be encouraged by associating with the wrong crowd. Thus the sense of the prayer is "Lord, help me to watch my words, and to keep the right sort of company" (vv. 3–4).

The prayer continues in verse 5, expressing the psalmist's wish that the Lord help her to take positive criticism from the faithful and to refuse company with the wicked. "Eventually," believes the psalmist, "these wicked persons will learn that what I said was good and right. And they will be smashed and scattered, like a rock is smashed and the pieces are scattered about" (vv. 6–7).

My Eyes Are on You, Lord (141:8–10)

Psalm 123 speaks about eyes that are lifted up:

> To you I lift up my eyes,
>   O you who are enthroned in the heavens!

> As the eyes of servants
>   look to the hand of their master,
> as the eyes of a maid
>   to the hand of her mistress,
> so our eyes look to the LORD our God,
>   until he has mercy upon us."
>
> (vv. 1–2)

In verse 8 of Psalm 141, the writer affirms trust in the Lord with this language of eyes toward God. The request is clear: Do not leave me defenseless, God!

Verses 9 and 10 express a double request: "Keep me safe from my enemies; punish them and let me escape!"

His Eye Is on the Sparrow

This psalm seems unusually preoccupied with the psalmist's own person, speaking of the voice, the hands, the mouth, the lips, the heart, the head, and the eyes. The person praying is in big trouble—involving the psalmist totally!

In such a situation, the one praying lifts up voice, hands, and eyes to the Lord. Like the faithful servant or maid, the psalmist has an eye on the Master and is confident of being helped (Psalm 123). Jesus reversed the direction of watching and spoke of the eyes of God: "If God the Father has an eye on the sparrow," he said, "don't you think God keeps an eye on you?" (see Matt. 10:29–31).

NOBODY CARES ABOUT ME!
Psalm 142

A Maskil of David. When he was in the cave. A Prayer.

142:1 With my voice I cry to the LORD;
    with my voice I make supplication to the LORD.
² I pour out my complaint before him;
    I tell my trouble before him.
³ When my spirit is faint,
    you know my way.

In the path where I walk
    they have hidden a trap for me.
⁴ Look on my right hand and see—

> there is no one who takes notice of me;
>> no refuge remains to me;
>> no one cares for me.
>
> ⁵ I cry to you, O LORD;
>> I say, "You are my refuge,
>> my portion in the land of the living."
> ⁶ Give heed to my cry,
>> for I am brought very low.
>
> Save me from my persecutors,
>> for they are too strong for me.
> ⁷ Bring me out of prison,
>> so that I may give thanks to your name.
> The righteous will surround me,
>> for you will deal bountifully with me.

At the center of Psalm 142 is the cry of a person who is lonely and hurting: "there is no one who takes notice . . . no one cares for me" (v. 4). The heading suggests a situation where the psalm would have been appropriate, identifying it as a prayer of David "when he was in the cave"; both 1 Samuel 22 and 24 tell of David running from Saul and hiding in a cave. The point is that this prayer for help fits a desperate situation. (For "Maskil," see the comments on Psalm 32.)

The psalm consists of the typical elements of the *individual lament* (see on Psalm 13): *introduction* (vv. 1–2), *affirmation of trust* (vv. 3a, 5, 7b), *"they" complaint* (vv. 3b-4); *requests* (vv. 6–7a, to "Bring me out of prison"), and *vow to praise* (v. 7a, "so that I may give thanks to your name").

You Know My Way (142:1–3a)

Right from the start this sounds like the prayer of a desperate person. This is not silent prayer but a cry for help that is emphatically vocal (v. 1). The psalmist's complaint comes gushing out and includes a recital of the troubles being experienced (v. 2).

What were those troubles? The psalm only hints at the situation of the one praying. That person is "in prison" (v. 7), which could be a figure of speech for a loss of freedom or, as seems more likely, a real incarceration. In any case, the one praying can hardly go on (v. 3a), suffers entrapments from certain persecutors (vv. 3b, 6b), and has no one who helps or even cares (v. 4). The psalmist sums it up: "I am brought very low" (v. 6).

Speaking to the Lord, the writer of Psalm 23 expresses no fear of evil because "you are with me" (Ps. 23:4). This psalmist also expresses confidence in the Lord, saying, "You know my way" (Ps. 142:3).

Save Me, Lord (142:3b–7)

The complaints multiply. Those who are making the psalmist's life miserable are trying to trap him, just as one would set a trap for an animal (v. 3b).

The usual place for a helper is at the right side: "Because [the Lord] is *at my right hand*, I shall not be moved," says Psalm 16:8. The Apostles' Creed speaks of the risen Christ as "seated *at the right hand* of the Father" (see also Ps. 110:5). But there is no helper at the right hand of this psalmist. The psalmist says, "There is no place to hide, and there is no person who cares for me or even who notices me" (v. 4).

Verse 5 addresses the Lord directly with an affirmation of trust. Here are two pictures. The Lord is a *refuge*. The word is used for a place of safety; here it is the Lord who is the person with whom safety is to be found. "My *portion*" refers to the dividing up of the promised land after the conquest. The Israelite tribes were each given a share of the land, except for the tribe of Levi; from them would come the priests, the clergy, responsible for the worship life of the people and to be supported by offerings given at the shrine. The matter is explained in Deuteronomy 10:8–9:

> The LORD set apart the tribe of Levi to carry the ark of the covenant of the LORD, to stand before the LORD to minister to him. . . . Therefore Levi has no allotment [portion] or inheritance with his kindred; the LORD is his inheritance.

(See also Num. 18:20; Josh. 13:14). The tradition that the Lord is the "portion" for the Levites is here "turned into a confession that the LORD is the basis of existence" (Mays, *Psalms*, p. 432; see also Ps. 73:26).

With verse 6 comes the first desperate request, asking the Lord to pay attention! The request is supplied with a reason in the form of an "I" complaint: "for I am brought very low."

The point of the psalm comes to expression in the cry for help in verse 6b. The vow to praise the Lord in verse 7 is an element typical for these psalms of lament (see on Psalm 13). The psalm comes to a close on a note of calm confidence in the Lord's goodness; Psalm 13 also concludes with a reference to the Lord's bountiful dealings.

Mood Indigo

The lines from the Duke Ellington blues classic "Mood Indigo" seem to catch the feelings of the writer of Psalm 142:

> 'Cause there's nobody who cares about me,
> I'm just a soul who's bluer than blue can be.

> When I get that mood indigo,
> I could lay me down and die.

"I've Got a Right to Sing the Blues" is the title of another classic blues tune. These modern-day laments put into words the conviction that there are times in life when one's spirit is faint (v. 3), when one is brought very low (v. 6), and when one is certain that "there's nobody who cares about me" (v. 4).

Articulating these feelings of sadness and loneliness can certainly be healthful and helpful. The hymn "What a Friend We Have In Jesus" suggests going even further:

> Have we trials and temptations?
> Is there trouble anywhere?
> We should never be discouraged—
> Take it to the Lord in prayer.

> Do your friends despise, forsake you?
> Take it to the Lord in prayer.
> In his arms he'll take and shield you;
> You will find a solace there.

"Take it to the Lord in prayer," the hymn recommends. Psalm 142 would agree.

TEACH ME THE WAY I SHOULD GO
Psalm 143

A Psalm of David.

143:1 **Hear my prayer, O LORD;**
give ear to my supplications in your faithfulness;
answer me in your righteousness.
2 **Do not enter into judgment with your servant,**
for no one living is righteous before you.

3 **For the enemy has pursued me,**
crushing my life to the ground,
making me sit in darkness like those long dead.
4 **Therefore my spirit faints within me;**
my heart within me is appalled.

5 **I remember the days of old,**

I think about all your deeds,
I meditate on the works of your hands.
6 I stretch out my hands to you;
my soul thirsts for you like a parched land.   *Selah*

7 Answer me quickly, O LORD;
my spirit fails.
Do not hide your face from me,
or I shall be like those who go down to the Pit.
8 Let me hear of your steadfast love in the morning,
for in you I put my trust.
Teach me the way I should go,
for to you I lift up my soul.

9 Save me, O LORD, from my enemies;
I have fled to you for refuge.
10 Teach me to do your will,
for you are my God.
Let your good spirit lead me
on a level path.

11 For your name's sake, O LORD, preserve my life.
In your righteousness bring me out of trouble.
12 In your steadfast love cut off my enemies,
and destroy all my adversaries,
for I am your servant.

Psalm 143 is the last in the series of seven psalms that the early church named the *penitential psalms*, that is, psalms that were used to direct the practice of repentance (Psalms 6, 32, 38, 51, 102, 130, 143). The expression of repentance comes to focus in verse 2 with the statement "for no one living is righteous before you." Paul appears to be paraphrasing these words in his assertion in Romans 3:20, "For 'no human being will be justified in his sight' by deeds prescribed by the law," and in Galatians 2:16, "No one will be justified by the works of the law." In contrast to assertions of innocence, such as may be heard in Psalms 7:8 and 26:1–6, 11, this psalm asserts the common guilt of all human beings (143:2b).

The heading links Psalm 143 with David (see the comments on Psalm 3). The psalm is made up of typical elements of the *individual lament* (see on Psalm 13), with a *request* (vv. 1–2), *complaint* in "they" (v. 3) and "I" forms (v. 4), an *affirmation of trust* recalling the Lord's saving acts in the past and expecting such help in the present (vv. 5–6), and finally a series of *requests* supported by statements of *trust* in verses 7–12. The "Teach me" request is emphasized by the doubling in verses 8 and 10.

The psalm can be considered in two major segments: verses 1–6, marked by *Selah* at the end (see on Psalm 3), and verses 7–12, the series of *requests*.

Hear Me, Help Me (143:1–6)

"Hear my prayer, O LORD" is the cry of one who considers himself a servant (v. 12), asking the Master for help. The one praying dares ask for help because of the Lord's *faithfulness*. The same Hebrew root is used for the pillars supporting the doors of the temple (2 Kings 18:16); the idea is that of steady support (v. 1).

In some cases a psalmist will encourage the Lord to give him or her a judicial examination because the psalmist is certain of innocence (Pss. 7:8; 26:1–2). This psalm is not like that. The one praying asks *not* to be examined on the grounds that *no one living* is innocent before God (v. 2). This assertion of universal sinfulness is picked up by Paul in his letters to the Romans (3:20) and to the Galatians (2:16).

The psalm refers to "the enemy" or "enemies" in verses 3, 9, and 12. The identity of these persons is not entirely clear. Have they caused the psalmist to sit in prison (v. 3; see Ps. 142:7), or is this a figure of speech? In any case, they have been making life miserable, and the psalmist asks to be saved from them (v. 9) and even asks the Lord to destroy them (v. 12). Verse 4 expresses the low point of the writer's situation. The psalmist then looks back, recalling the mighty acts that the Lord did in the past (v. 5). The effect is to set the difficulties of the present time in some sort of broader perspective (see also Ps. 22:4–5, 9–10). The Lord has helped before; perhaps he will help again! Finally, all that the one in trouble can do is to stretch out hands to the Lord for help, in a typical posture of one crying out for aid (v. 6; see also Jer. 4:31; Lam. 1:17). *Selah* marks a pause.

Save Me, Teach Me (143:7–12)

The second section of Psalm 143 is made up of a string of requests directed to the Lord, sometimes with reasons to support the requests. "Answer me" repeats the cry in verse 1, now with more urgency. The Lord must respond quickly, lest the psalmist die and go to the "Pit," the place of the dead. Verse 8 expresses trust that the Lord will help by morning and then asks for instruction in "the way I should go," that is, in how life ought to be lived.

The most immediate need is expressed in the "Save me" of verse 9. The problem of the enemies must be dealt with! Verse 10 looks to life after having been delivered from enemies and is once again a request for instruction on living according to God's will. Life is pictured as walking, and God is asked to lead the walker onto the right paths.

The psalm concludes in verses 11–12 with a series of urgent cries for help: "preserve my life . . . bring me out of trouble . . . cut off my enemies . . . destroy all my adversaries." Why should the Lord help this particular person praying? For the second time the psalmist reminds the Lord who it is that is praying: "I am your servant" (also v. 2).

Forgive Me, Save Me, Teach Me

Psalm 143 makes contact with our own lives at three points. First, it remains *a prayer for a time of repentance, or sorrow over sins.* Verse 2b, read in the context of the passages from Romans and Galatians listed above, makes clear the biblical teaching that *all* humans have failed to do God's will! The psalm is rightly counted among those called penitential.

Second, like all laments, this is *an urgent prayer in a time of trouble* and thus can serve to guide our own prayers in such times. The psalmist reminds God of his or her difficult situation (vv. 3–4) and then asks to be delivered from these difficulties (vv. 6–7, 9, 11, 12). The prayer *against* the enemies in verse 12, however, will have to be changed to a prayer *for* enemies, in the light of the words of Jesus in Matthew 5:43–48.

Finally, this is *a prayer asking for instruction* (vv. 8, 10). The source of this instruction is to be God ("for you are my God," v. 10), and the content is quite down-to-earth ("the way I should go . . . on a level path," vv. 8, 10). Where could one find further presentations of this sort of teaching? To begin with, Psalms 1, 19, and 119, among others, speak of offering *torah*, "instruction." To continue, one can read through the Psalms and ask, "What does this tell me about God, about humans, and about the earth and its creatures?"

SET ME FREE, BLESS US ALL
Psalm 144

Of David.

144:1 **Blessed be the LORD, my rock,**
      who trains my hands for war, and my fingers for battle;
  2 **my rock and my fortress,**
      my stronghold and my deliverer,

my shield, in whom I take refuge,
 who subdues the peoples under me.

3 O LORD, what are human beings that you regard them,
 or mortals that you think of them?
4 They are like a breath;
 their days are like a passing shadow.

5 Bow your heavens, O LORD, and come down;
 touch the mountains so that they smoke.
6 Make the lightning flash and scatter them;
 send out your arrows and rout them.
7 Stretch out your hand from on high;
 set me free and rescue me from the mighty waters,
 from the hand of aliens,
8 whose mouths speak lies,
 and whose right hands are false.

9 I will sing a new song to you, O God;
 upon a ten-stringed harp I will play to you,
10 the one who gives victory to kings,
 who rescues his servant David.
11 Rescue me from the cruel sword,
 and deliver me from the hand of aliens,
 whose mouths speak lies,
 and whose right hands are false.

12 May our sons in their youth
 be like plants full grown,
 our daughters like corner pillars,
 cut for the building of a palace.
13 May our barns be filled,
 with produce of every kind;
 may our sheep increase by thousands,
 by tens of thousands in our fields,
14 and may our cattle be heavy with young.
 May there be no breach in the walls, no exile,
 and no cry of distress in our streets.

15 Happy are the people to whom such blessings fall;
 happy are the people whose God is the LORD.

Everyone is interested in what is new, whether it be a new automobile, a new play, a new book, or a new song. One aspect of humans being created "in the image of God" is the ability to produce new things, as God did in those first days of creation.

"I will sing a new song to you, O God," says the psalmist in verse 9. The one who composed Psalm 144 was a writer who worked with words, a musician who worked with melodies, and a performer who played them on a "twelve-stringed harp," the ancient equivalent of a twelve-string guitar (v. 9).

This artist was also a believer, whose musical talents resulted in this song about the Lord, here described as "my rock."

Psalms Recycled

As has always been the case with composers, from Bach to Elton John and beyond, a "new song" is not necessarily entirely new. Psalm 144 is a good example of how words (and probably melodies) from older psalms were recycled for use in later days. This writer is using materials from Psalm 18 (compare the first verses of each) and Psalm 33 (compare 144:15b and 33:12; there are many other examples of picking up materials from each of these psalms).

While the psalm identifies itself as the prayer of a king (see vv. 2, 10–11) and could therefore be classified as a *royal psalm* (see the discussion with Psalm 2), it appears that in its present form, materials from older royal psalms (vv. 1–11) have been recycled for use in a later time, most likely in the postexilic period when the relationship to hostile foreigners was a problem (see Neh. 9:2; Isa. 56:3; and others).

Set Me Free (144:1–11)

The heading "Of David" (see on Psalm 3) marks this as the seventh of eight psalms in this final Davidic collection, running from Psalms 138 to 145.

The first part of the psalm consists of elements familiar from the *psalms of lament* (see on Psalm 13). Verses 1–2 offer words of *praise and trust*. Here are a series of metaphors for God: "my rock . . . my fortress . . . my stronghold . . . my deliverer . . . my shield." The same images appear in Psalm 18:1–2; for comments on these images, see the commentary on that psalm.

Verses 3 and 4 offer a *lament* in the form of reflections on human mortality. In asking, "What are human beings?" the psalmist picks up a theme paralleled in Psalm 8:4. Whereas Psalm 8 reflected on the insignificance of humans in the context of the vast *space* of the universe, Psalm 144 reflects on human insignificance in the context of *time*, similar to a good many laments about the brevity of life (Job 14:1; Pss. 39:4–6; 49:12, 20; 90:5–6; 146:3–4; Eccl. 3:19–21; Sirach 18:7–14).

The central concern of this recycled psalm is expressed in the *request for help* in verses 5–8. The one praying asks the Lord to come down and help, describing the appearing of the Lord (theophany) in terms of a storm, with language reminiscent of other biblical theophanies (Judg. 5:4–5; Pss. 18:7–17; 29:3–9). The request comes to sharp focus in verse 7. The psalmist is being harassed by "aliens," hostile neighbors, and asks the Lord to "set me free and rescue me" (see also "Rescue me" of v. 11).

In a manner typical of the psalms of lament, the writer offers a *vow to praise* in verses 9–10. After promising to compose and perform a new song (v. 9), the writer reminds God of past acts of deliverance and victory for David and other kings (v. 10).

Verse 11 was originally a *request for help* on the part of the king praying this psalm (see also v. 7). Here it becomes the prayer of the people experiencing persecution from their own enemies.

Bless Us (144:12–15)

The two fundamental shapes of God's activity as described in the Bible are *deliverance* (in the Old Testament, the exodus; in the New Testament, the crucifixion and resurrection) and *blessing* (the giving of everyday gifts, such as health, good weather, good crops). These two are evident in Psalm 144. Verses 1–11 ask for the Lord's deliverance ("set me free and rescue me," vv. 7, 11), and this final section is a request for the blessings of growth in the family (v. 12), abundant crops and cattle (vv. 13–14a), and *shalom*, or peace, in society (v. 14b).

The psalm concludes with a declaration of the happiness of God's people who have experienced such deliverance and blessings (v. 15; see the other "happy are" statements in the Psalms, such as 1:1; 2:12; 41:1; 65:4; 89:15; 119:1–3; 127:5; and 128:1; and the comments on Ps. 2:12).

Rescuing and Blessing

Psalm 144 provides a good example for observing these two basic forms of God's activity as described in the Bible. When people are in trouble, whether experiencing political bondage (the situation of Israel in Egypt; see the book of Exodus) or the bondage of sin, death, and the devil (the situation of all humans; see Romans 3), God responds to cries for help by *rescuing* them (the exodus; the crucifixion and resurrection). Psalm 144:1–11 is a cry for the Lord to *rescue*.

But God's actions are not limited to these remarkable instances, nor to single dramatic events of saving or healing in the life of an individual. Verses 12–15 speak of the quiet, ongoing, ordinary actions of God,

including giving growth to children, providing sun and rain and good
weather for the growing of crops, seeing to the birth and growth of
sheep and cattle, and providing security and *shalom* in the community.
These everyday gifts are the work of God, who also sends *blessing*
(v. 15).

THE ABC'S OF PRAISE
Psalm 145

Praise. Of David.

145:1 **I will extol you, my God and King,**
>   **and bless your name forever and ever.**
> 2 **Every day I will bless you,**
>   **and praise your name forever and ever.**
> 3 **Great is the LORD, and greatly to be praised;**
>   **his greatness is unsearchable.**

> 4 **One generation shall laud your works to another,**
>   **and shall declare your mighty acts.**
> 5 **On the glorious splendor of your majesty,**
>   **and on your wondrous works, I will meditate.**
> 6 **The might of your awesome deeds shall be proclaimed,**
>   **and I will declare your greatness.**
> 7 **They shall celebrate the fame of your abundant goodness,**
>   **and shall sing aloud of your righteousness.**

> 8 **The LORD is gracious and merciful,**
>   **slow to anger and abounding in steadfast love.**
> 9 **The LORD is good to all,**
>   **and his compassion is over all that he has made.**

> 10 **All your works shall give thanks to you, O LORD,**
>   **and all your faithful shall bless you.**
> 11 **They shall speak of the glory of your kingdom,**
>   **and tell of your power,**
> 12 **to make known to all people your mighty deeds,**
>   **and the glorious splendor of your kingdom.**
> 13 **Your kingdom is an everlasting kingdom,**
>   **and your dominion endures throughout all generations.**

> **The LORD is faithful in all his words,**
>   **and gracious in all his deeds.**

14 **The LORD upholds all who are falling,**
   and raises up all who are bowed down.
15 **The eyes of all look to you,**
   and you give them their food in due season.
16 **You open your hand,**
   satisfying the desire of every living thing.
17 **The LORD is just in all his ways,**
   and kind in all his doings.
18 **The LORD is near to all who call on him,**
   to all who call on him in truth.
19 **He fulfills the desire of all who fear him;**
   he also hears their cry, and saves them.
20 **The LORD watches over all who love him,**
   but all the wicked he will destroy.

21 **My mouth will speak the praise of the LORD,**
   and all flesh will bless his holy name forever and ever.

Words from Psalm 145 continue to be used as a prayer before mealtime. In the *Small Catechism*, Martin Luther suggested that when it is mealtime, "the children and the members of the household are to come devoutly to the table, fold their hands, and recite: 'The eyes of all look to you, and you give them their food in due season. You open your hand, satisfying the desire of every living thing'" Psalm 145:15–16 (p. 55).

The use of this psalm at mealtime was not new with Luther. It is also a traditional Jewish table blessing.

Praise!

The heading "Praise" occurs only here in the Psalter. The psalm is linked with David, since it is the final Davidic psalm in the collection of Psalms 138–145 and the final Davidic psalm in the entire book of Psalms. With its concluding words "My mouth will speak the praise of the LORD" it points ahead, providing an introduction to the quintet of psalms that closes the entire book.

This is an acrostic psalm, each line beginning with a successive letter of the Hebrew alphabet (see on Psalms 9–10). Concluding the final Davidic collection and coming near the end of the Psalter, Psalm 145 has an especially comprehensive focus. The word *all*, for example, occurs seventeen times in the Hebrew text (sixteen times in the NRSV)!

The psalm is framed by *vows to praise* (vv. 1–2, 21). Within this frame, the psalm suggests *reasons* for praise: the Lord is great (vv. 4–6) and the Lord is good (vv. 7–10). The Lord's kingdom is everlasting (vv. 11–13), and the Lord sustains all living things (vv. 14–16). Finally, the Lord is near to those calling on him (vv. 17–20).

God Is Great (145:1–6, 21)

The writer of Psalm 145 thinks big. In the first line, the *alef* line (the first letter of the Hebrew alphabet), the psalmist addresses God as king and vows to praise God forever and ever. The "king" picture for God comes up again with the words about "your kingdom" in verses 11–13.

Biblical hymns are typically made up of a call to praise followed by reasons for praise (see on Psalm 113). In this case a vow to praise frames the psalm (vv. 1–2, 21). The main part of the psalm then furnishes reasons for praising. The first of these reasons is God's *greatness*, stated at the beginning (v. 3) and end (v. 6) of this segment. The writer is thinking of the "mighty acts" (v. 4) that God has done; one thinks immediately of the deliverance from Egypt, the leading through the wilderness, the conquest of the promised land. Stories about these mighty acts, or wondrous works, or awesome deeds, had been told in the past and continued to be told at the time of the psalmist. These great deeds are worthy of reflection and meditation (v. 5), and stories about them will be told from generation to generation.

God Is Good (145:7–10)

If the Lord's greatness is reason for singing praise, God's *goodness* also calls forth praise. There is plenty of that goodness (v. 7), and the Lord gives it to *all* people, and in fact, to all that the Lord has made (v. 9). This is the first occurrence of the word *all*, which will sound through the remainder of the psalm.

Verses 8 and 9 reach back to the ancient confession in Exodus 34:6, heard also in Psalm 103:8 (see the comments on that text). If the Lord has been good to all that the Lord has made (v. 9), then it is reasonable that all, both humans ("your faithful") and the remainder of creation, should give thanks (v. 10).

God Is a King Who Cares (145:11–20)

Psalm 145 began with the picture of God as king (v. 1), and now that royal picture is expanded on. As is said in verses 5–6, the Lord has done mighty deeds (v. 12) worthy of being reported to all peoples. The King will rule forever (v. 1), and therefore the kingdom will endure forever.

"God is great, God is good" runs the children's mealtime prayer. Beginning with verse 13b, the psalm tells of God's goodness, again providing reasons for praising God. The abstract language about faithfulness and graciousness is balanced by concrete references to holding up those who are falling and picking up all who are bent over with life's burdens (see also Ps. 146:8).

Verses 15 and 16 have long been used as part of a prayer before mealtime. Luther suggested using these words from Psalm 145, followed by the Lord's Prayer and then the words "Lord God heavenly Father, bless us and these your gifts, which we receive from your bountiful goodness through Jesus Christ our Lord. Amen" (*Small Catechism*).

The psalm winds down by speaking of the *nearness* of the Lord (vv. 18–20). Again, the universal note is sounded: the Lord will be near to *all* who pray to the Lord, to *all* who fear the Lord. The Lord will hear their prayer and deliver them from dire situations. The Lord also "watches over all who love him"; the Hebrew word for "watch" is a form of *shamar*, the key word in Psalm 121, there translated "keep."

The ABC's of the Faith

This is a hymn of praise, but it can also serve as a review of what the Psalms say about God.

God is *great*, says Psalm 145, a king ruling an everlasting kingdom and a doer of mighty acts (vv. 1, 12–13, and 5, 6, 12).

God is also *good to all* (v. 9). This goodness takes the form of caring for the hurting (v. 14) and providing nourishment for all creatures that God has created (v. 16). It also means hearing the prayers of those in trouble (v. 19) and keeping watch over God's people (v. 20). In the repeated accent on *all* (vv. 8–20) is the same wide-heartedness as in John 3:16, "so that *everyone* who believes in him may not perish."

I PLEDGE ALLEGIANCE
Psalm 146

146:1 **Praise the LORD!**
Praise the LORD, O my soul!
2 **I will praise the LORD as long as I live;**
I will sing praises to my God all my life long.

3 **Do not put your trust in princes,**
in mortals, in whom there is no help.

⁴ When their breath departs, they return to the earth;
    on that very day their plans perish.

⁵ Happy are those whose help is the God of Jacob,
    whose hope is in the LORD their God,
⁶ who made heaven and earth,
    the sea, and all that is in them;
  who keeps faith forever;
⁷   who executes justice for the oppressed;
    who gives food to the hungry.

  The LORD sets the prisoners free;
⁸   the LORD opens the eyes of the blind.
  The LORD lifts up those who are bowed down;
    the LORD loves the righteous.
⁹ The LORD watches over the strangers;
    he upholds the orphan and the widow,
    but the way of the wicked he brings to ruin.
¹⁰ The LORD will reign forever,
    your God, O Zion, for all generations.
  Praise the LORD!

One of the first things learned in elementary school when I was growing up was the "Pledge of Allegiance." Each day began in the same way. We students walked into the room and took our seats. Then the teacher entered. We stood up, placed our right hands over our hearts, looked at the red, white, and blue flag before us, and solemnly promised, "I pledge allegiance to the flag."

There was a patriotic spirit in the church, too. In the front of our church stood two flags: the United States flag and the "Christian flag," indicating that these were to be the twin loyalties of a Christian American. And on the coins and bills minted and printed in our country the words are still there: "In God We Trust."

Psalm 146 is about allegiance, about trust. Its concern is "To whom do we owe our allegiance? Whom do we trust?"

The Closing Quintet (Psalms 146–150)

Psalms 138–145 make up the final collection of psalms associated with David. That collection ends with the psalmist's promise "My mouth will speak the praise of the LORD" (Ps. 145:21). Psalms 146–150 then articulate the praise promised at the end of Psalm 145.

Psalms 146–150 form a unit, each beginning and ending with the call to "Praise the LORD!" (in Hebrew, "Hallelujah!"). This makes for ten "Hallelujahs"; Psalm 150 itself contains another ten.

These five psalms have a number of common themes. They speak of the work of God as creator and sustainer of life (146:6; 147:4, 8–9, 14–18; 148:5–6). They also speak frequently of the Lord's work as deliverer of people in distress (147:2–3, 12–14, 19–20; 148:14; 149) and of the Lord's concern for the powerless (146:7b-9; 147:2–3, 6, 9).

The circle of those invited to praise expands in these psalms. This closing quintet begins with an individual calling him- or herself to praise ("O my soul," 146:1) and resolving to do so (146:2). It continues with a call to the people of Jerusalem (147:12) or Israel (149:2) to praise and concludes with an invitation to "everything that breathes" to join in the praises of the Lord (150:6).

The structure of Psalm 146 reflects the pattern of the *hymn* (see Psalm 113). It begins with a *call to praise* (vv. 1–2) and supplies a number of *reasons* for praising (vv. 5–9). Verses 3 and 4 expand on the typical pattern with an offer of *instruction*. Verse 10 consists of a confession of faith and a final call to "Praise the LORD!

Who Can I Trust? (146:1–4)

While statements like the American "Pledge of Allegiance" are reminders of the loyalty persons owe to nations, verses 3–4 in Psalm 146 caution against giving one's *ultimate* allegiance to any human institution. Political leaders, after all, are human, with the faults that are common to all humans. The books of Kings and Chronicles remain reminders of the fallibility of those persons who held office in ancient Israel and Judah. As an example, one need only read through the stories about David in 2 Samuel 11 and the following chapters.

This psalm also is a reminder that political leaders won't be around forever. They are "mortal," says the NRSV translation; the Hebrew says they are '*ādām* (mortals) and will return to the '*adāmāh* (earth; vv. 3–4). The Hebrew play on words could be reproduced by saying they are *humans* and will return to the *humus*. One day their breath, or "wind," as the word could be translated, will quit blowing (see also Ps. 104:29), and their plans and platforms and promises will disappear with them.

Verses 1 and 2 suggest another sort of allegiance that will never disappoint. Here is a trust in God that can be expressed in praise for a lifetime! The same resolve is expressed in Psalm 104:33.

Who Is Truly Happy? (146:5–9)

The book of Psalms begins with a description of those who are truly happy (Psalm 1), and the same "happiness" theme sounds as the Psalter draws to a conclusion. The reasons for happiness are stated clearly: those persons are truly happy who acknowledge that their helper and the one in whom they hope is the Lord, the God of their people (146:5).

After the theme is stated in verse 5, the following sentences provide illustrations of the theme. First, the Lord is *creator* of the heavens, the earth, and the seas. (The same three-part division lies behind Psalm 104: heavens, vv. 1–9; earth, vv. 10–24; seas, vv. 25–26). The Lord is also the *caregiver* who delivers the oppressed and imprisoned and provides food for the hungry.

The Lord's special concern is for the powerless—the widow, the orphan, the oppressed, and the stranger (146:7, 9). With the reference contrasting the righteous (v. 8) and the wicked (v. 9), one again detects an echo of Psalm 1 (v. 6).

True happiness, according to Psalm 146, involves placing one's hope in the God of Jacob and relying on that God for help.

Who Can I Trust? (146:10)

The psalm begins with some instruction, advising any who heard not to place their trust "in princes," that is, in any human rulers or institutions. The psalm continues with a picture of the happiness of those who hope in the Lord. The psalm concludes with the assertion that the one in whom those worshiping can place their trust and their hope is the Lord, who "will reign forever."

This is language of kingship, familiar from the middle of the book of Psalms (Psalms 93, 95–99) and from the dramatic announcement that sets off the story told in the New Testament: "the kingdom of God is at hand" (Mark 1:14, NRSV footnote). In fact, the promises of God's deliverance in verses 7b–9 of Psalm 146 look very much like a preview of that story.

CONSIDER THE RAVENS
Psalm 147

147:1 **Praise the Lord!**
How good it is to sing praises to our God;
for he is gracious, and a song of praise is fitting.

2 The Lᴏʀᴅ builds up Jerusalem;
  he gathers the outcasts of Israel.
3 He heals the brokenhearted,
  and binds up their wounds.
4 He determines the number of the stars;
  he gives to all of them their names.
5 Great is our Lord, and abundant in power;
  his understanding is beyond measure.
6 The Lᴏʀᴅ lifts up the downtrodden;
  he casts the wicked to the ground.

7 Sing to the Lᴏʀᴅ with thanksgiving;
  make melody to our God on the lyre.
8 He covers the heavens with clouds,
  prepares rain for the earth,
  makes grass grow on the hills.
9 He gives to the animals their food,
  and to the young ravens when they cry.
10 His delight is not in the strength of the horse,
  nor his pleasure in the speed of a runner;
11 but the Lᴏʀᴅ takes pleasure in those who fear him,
  in those who hope in his steadfast love.

12 Praise the Lᴏʀᴅ, O Jerusalem!
  Praise your God, O Zion!
13 For he strengthens the bars of your gates;
  he blesses your children within you.
14 He grants peace within your borders;
  he fills you with the finest of wheat.
15 He sends out his command to the earth;
  his word runs swiftly.
16 He gives snow like wool;
  he scatters frost like ashes.
17 He hurls down hail like crumbs—
  who can stand before his cold?
18 He sends out his word, and melts them;
  he makes his wind blow, and the waters flow.
19 He declares his word to Jacob,
  his statutes and ordinances to Israel.
20 He has not dealt thus with any other nation;
  they do not know his ordinances.
  Praise the Lᴏʀᴅ!

At the center of this psalm, one hears the cries of a nest full of young ravens. Amid the sounds of musical productions in the temple (vv. 1, 7) and of wind, rain, and hail in the countryside (vv. 8, 17–18) are those raven cries. Quite remarkably, this psalm asserts that the God who controls the wind and the rain also cares about these tiny creatures: God "gives to the animals their food, and to the young ravens when they cry" (v. 9). This psalm invites us to do what Jesus once advised: to consider the ravens (Luke 12:24).

Psalm 147 is the second in the quintet of psalms that close the Psalter (see the comments on Psalm 146). It divides into three parts, each part made up of the elements of a *hymn* (see on Psalm 113), with a *call to praise* followed by *reasons* for praising. Each part also contains some *observations* about God.

Praise the Lord! (147:1–6)

Each of these concluding five psalms begins with the call "Praise the Lord!" which translates the Hebrew "Hallelujah!" After that initial *call to praise*, verse 1 offers an observation in praise of praise. Verses 2–6 follow with *reasons* for praising God. The Lord works in history, now engineering the rebuilding of Jerusalem and acting to bring the exiles home and to heal broken bodies as well as broken hearts. The imagery is that of a new exodus, where those who have been living outside the homeland are finally coming home, where they will find *shalom*—that is, peace, prosperity, and good crops (v. 14).

There is no doubt about who is responsible for this new beginning. It is the Lord who builds, gathers, heals, and binds up (vv. 2–3).

Verse 4 presents the Lord's work in nature as a second reason for praise. The Lord creates a certain number of stars, names them, and thus controls them (Gen. 2:18–20). Verse 5 offers an observation about God's greatness and the impossibility of understanding God.

Sing to the Lord! (147:7–11)

Here a pair of imperatives to praise ("Sing . . . make melody") are provided with reasons (vv. 8–9), and the section again closes with an observation about God and people (vv. 10–11). The reasons for praise have to do with the Lord and nature. In speaking of rain, the psalm mentions the meteorological preparation for rain as well as the results of the rain, the growth of grass (v. 8; note also the choice wheat in v. 14).

Next, the focus is on the animals, referring first to the larger land animals. The old gospel song declares that God's "eye is on the sparrow" (see Matt. 10:29); the psalmist speaks of the Lord's ear, which is tuned to the cry of the young raven (v. 9). The Lord's care for young ravens is also mentioned in Job 38:41: "Who provides for the raven its prey, when its young ones cry to God, and wander about for lack of food?"

Why should ravens be singled out?

The medieval Jewish exegete David Kimchi suggested that raven mothers abandoned their young ones because the tiny birds were white at birth and the parents imagined they were not their own offspring! And so, wrote Kimchi, "the Holy One, blessed be he, provides for them mosquitoes which they devour" (in Risse, *"Gut ist es,"* p. 255). The notion about the irresponsibility of raven parents persists; in the German language, a mother who abandons young children is called a *Rabenmutter* (raven mother).

Jesus, too, was impressed by the Lord's care for ravens: "Consider the ravens: they neither sow nor reap, they have neither storehouse nor barn, and yet God feeds them" (Luke 12:24).

After this attention to the earth and its creatures, Psalm 147 offers an observation concerning God's relationship to people. Not much impressed by the strength of the sturdiest draft horse or the speed of an Olympic runner, the Lord takes pleasure in those who place their confidence in the Lord's reliable love (*hesed*; vv. 10–11).

Praise the Lord, Jerusalem! (147:12–20)

The final section of Psalm 147 is again made up of a call to praise, identifying who should praise (v. 12), followed by reasons for praising (vv. 13–19) and a final observation about the Lord and Israel in the context of all nations (v. 20).

The psalm begins with a focus on the saving work of the Lord (vv. 2–3). Now it speaks of the Lord's work of blessing, which shows itself in the Lord providing a situation of security in Jerusalem so that young children can grow up in safety and peace (vv. 13–14a). God's blessing also includes providing conditions so that crops will grow and provide food (v. 14b).

The theme of verses 15–19 is God's word (vv. 15, 18, 19). While that word can bring about events in history (Isa. 9:8; 55:10–11; Jer. 23:18–20), the emphasis here is on the word of God and nature. That word causes snow and hail, frost and cold, warmth and thawing. These weather phenomena affect all people (Matt. 5:45). The psalm concludes with observations about the special privileges of Israel, the people who have received God's word in the form of scripture (vv. 19–20).

Quoth the Raven

At the center of this psalm is the voice of that young raven, crying to the Lord for food. Should it happen that some tired scholar, in the manner of Edgar Allen Poe, at some "midnight dreary," pondering "weak and weary, over many a quaint and curious volume of forgotten lore" should ask whether the steadfast love of this God could ever fail, that scholar might be surprised to hear a mysterious, rasping, haunting voice declaring but one gospel word: "Nevermore!"

"IT'S CLAPPING!"
Psalm 148

148:1 Praise the LORD!
  Praise the LORD from the heavens;
    praise him in the heights!
² Praise him, all his angels;
    praise him, all his host!

³ Praise him, sun and moon;
    praise him, all you shining stars!
⁴ Praise him, you highest heavens,
    and you waters above the heavens!

⁵ Let them praise the name of the LORD,
    for he commanded and they were created.
⁶ He established them forever and ever;
    he fixed their bounds, which cannot be passed.

⁷ Praise the LORD from the earth,
    you sea monsters and all deeps,
⁸ fire and hail, snow and frost,
    stormy wind fulfilling his command!

⁹ Mountains and all hills,
    fruit trees and all cedars!
¹⁰ Wild animals and all cattle,
    creeping things and flying birds!

¹¹ Kings of the earth and all peoples,
    princes and all rulers of the earth!
¹² Young men and women alike,
    old and young together!

¹³ Let them praise the name of the LORD,
    for his name alone is exalted;
    his glory is above earth and heaven.

14 **He has raised up a horn for his people,**
  praise for all his faithful,
  for the people of Israel who are close to him.
Praise the LORD!

Gerhard Frost once reflected on this psalm:

> We sat together,
> this tall man and a tiny child,
> before the fireplace.
> Enthralled with this, her first,
> and looking up at me,
> she said, "It's clapping!"
>
> I would have said, "It's crackling,"
> and so would you—
> victims of the dulling years—
> but who is right?
> Who has really heard?
> Can fire praise by crackling?
>
> No, she's the one
> who has found the word.
> Indeed, it's clapping,
> "Praise the Lord!"
> (*Blessed is the Ordinary*, p. 84)

"All God's children got a place in the choir," goes an old song. The boundaries of Psalm 148 push even further to include places not only for all God's children but for all *creation*. The choir of those praising here includes children and senior citizens but also creeping things and cattle, fire (see Frost's poem, above) as well as hail and snow, and sun, moon, and stars!

The psalm begins by speaking of praise of the Lord from the heavens (vv. 1–6), continues with praise from the earth (vv. 7–12), and concludes with a call for all to join in (vv. 13–14).

Praise from the Heavens (148:1–6)

The opening segment provides an insight into the Old Testament view of the universe. Humans live on the earth, along with the variety of creatures God has created (vv. 7–12). Above the earth are the heavens, where the angels reside (vv. 1–2).

The "heavens" can also be called the "firmament" or "dome" (Ps. 19:1; Gen. 1:6–8). Above that solid dome are waters (Ps. 148:4). When it rains, windows in the dome slide open to allow water to come down. At the time of the great flood, "all the fountains of the great deep burst forth, and the windows of the heavens were opened" (Gen. 7:11).

Verses 5–6 pick up on the creation story in Genesis 1. God gave the command and all was *created* (the Hebrew word *bārā'*, as used in Genesis 1): the sun and moon, the stars and planets, the waters above the heavens.

Praise from the Earth (148:7–12)

"In the beginning . . . God created the heavens and the earth," the Bible begins. With this segment of Psalm 148, it is time to hear praises from the earth. First to be mentioned are those aspects of the created world that evoke fear: sea monsters, fire, hail and storm, all are called to praise the Lord (vv. 7–8). The words of the psalm break open the traditional compartments of our thinking. Not only kings and people but also humpback whales, hurricanes, and blizzard winds are called to join in praise (vv. 7–8)!

The listing continues: again, the call to praise is inclusive, addressed to mountains and trees, wild and domestic animals, creeping things and flying birds (vv. 9–10). How do these creatures praise the Lord? It appears that praise need not be limited to words. According to Psalm 150, one can praise God with dance, with trumpets, stringed instruments, and percussion! If human dance can express praise, why not the dance of the loons on a Minnesota lake? If the sound of a trumpet can express praise, why not the sound of a trumpeter swan?

Verses 11 and 12 call on all human beings to praise by naming the extremes of the groups: from the political leaders in the world's centers of power to the boys and girls playing in the streets of a village. All can praise the Lord, and this psalm calls them to do so.

Let the Praises Begin! (148:13–14)

The concluding words tie together the twin themes of the psalm, declaring that the Lord's honor is higher than the earth and the heavens. To "raise up a horn" means to restore strength and honor (Pss. 75:4–5; 112:9). Claus Westermann once observed, "It is praise which binds humans with all other creatures." According to this psalm, praise is the business of all that exists. Psalm 150 will carry this theme even further.

LET THE FAITHFUL DANCE!
Psalm 149

149:1 **Praise the LORD!**
Sing to the LORD a new song,
his praise in the assembly of the faithful.
2 **Let Israel be glad in its Maker;**
let the children of Zion rejoice in their King.
3 **Let them praise his name with dancing,**
making melody to him with tambourine and lyre.
4 **For the LORD takes pleasure in his people;**
he adorns the humble with victory.
5 **Let the faithful exult in glory;**
let them sing for joy on their couches.
6 **Let the high praises of God be in their throats**
and two-edged swords in their hands,
7 **to execute vengeance on the nations**
and punishment on the peoples,
8 **to bind their kings with fetters**
and their nobles with chains of iron,
9 **to execute on them the judgment decreed.**
This is glory for all his faithful ones.
Praise the LORD!

At the center of Psalm 149 is the people of God, identified at the beginning (v. 1), the middle (v. 5), and the end (v. 9) as "the faithful" or "faithful ones." The Hebrew word in all three contexts is *hasidim*, which is sometimes translated as "saints" (NIV). In using this term for God's people, the psalm is picking up a theme from the end of Psalm 148. There "his faithful" is further defined with the balancing expression "the people of Israel who are close to him" (148:14).

In Psalm 149, these faithful persons are the ones who assemble for worship (v. 1); they are invited to rejoice in their worship (v. 5), and they are promised that one day they shall live in splendor or glory (v. 9).

The psalm is made up of two parts that are built around the central call to the faithful in verse 5. Verses 1–4 consist of a call to praise (vv. 1–3), as well as a reason for praising (verse 4). Verses 6–9 again offer a third-person call to praise (v. 6), and the section closes with a declaration that the faithful ones are experiencing honor, or glory (v. 9).

These "faithful ones," these "saints," are at the center of this psalm, quite literally. Verse 5 reads, "Let the faithful exult in glory; let them sing for joy on their couches." This is the central verse of the psalm, with four verses on either side. Even more interesting, the expression "faithful in glory" is precisely at the center of the Hebrew original of the psalm: there are twenty-six words leading up to it and twenty-six words that follow (see also the discussion on Psalm 23).

Let the People Dance and Sing! (149:1–5)

Once again, the call goes out for some new choir music (v. 1; see also Pss. 33:3; 40:3; the openings of Psalms 96 and 98; and the hymn in Isa. 42:10). While it is possible for a congregation in bad times to sing songs of lament, or even not to sing at all (Psalm 137), the call here is clearly for songs of rejoicing, in good times. Such rejoicing takes expression not only in songs of praise, even new songs of praise, but also in nonword form. The people are called to dance, to beat the tambourine, and to play the harp (NRSV, "lyre"), all to the honor of the Lord (vv. 4–5).

Let the People Praise! (149:6–9)

After the somewhat odd call to rejoice and sing while lying on couches (v. 5), the people are called to an action that involves having praises in their mouths and swords in their hands (v. 6). Is this some sort of call to war, to go into battle singing war songs and brandishing weapons and finally to capture the leaders of the enemy? This is the impression one gets when reading verses 6–9. The "call to battle" was well known in ancient Israel (see Micah, Isaiah, Jeremiah, etc.). Or is this the script for some sort of ritual celebration, recalling an actual victory or in anticipation of a future one? Since it is so near the end of the Psalter, Psalm 149 could be pointing ahead to an anticipated victory over all enemy nations in the distant future.

What about the King?

The psalm begins with a picture of the people of Israel celebrating with their King on Mount Zion. This language of Zion and of kingship in Psalm 149, the second-to-last psalm, is reminiscent of similar language in Psalm 2, the second psalm. In that liturgy used for the coronation of a new king, the Lord promises, "I have set my king on Zion, my holy hill" (Ps. 2:6).

In Psalm 149:2, Israel is called to be glad as they look back to what their Maker has done. This verse, read in the light of Psalm 2, which precedes it, and the Gospels that follow, could well be looking toward the coming of the One who was greeted on a Sunday in Jerusalem as king (John 12:13, in the context of 12:12–19).

FROM KING DAVID TO DUKE ELLINGTON
Psalm 150

150:1 Praise the LORD!
      Praise God in his sanctuary;
         praise him in his mighty firmament!
    2 Praise him for his mighty deeds;
         praise him according to his surpassing greatness!

    3 Praise him with trumpet sound;
         praise him with lute and harp!
    4 Praise him with tambourine and dance;
         praise him with strings and pipe!
    5 Praise him with clanging cymbals;
         praise him with loud clashing cymbals!
    6 Let everything that breathes praise the LORD!
      Praise the LORD!

The most remarkable exposition of this psalm in my memory took place neither from a lectern in a theological school nor from a pulpit in a church. Rather, it was in a college cafeteria, at one o'clock in the morning, after the annual spring formal dance. The band was packing up. Most of the students had left. A half dozen faculty members were standing around the piano, chatting with the leader of the band. His name was Duke Ellington.

The conversation turned to religion and Ellington's recent sacred compositions. "Would you tell us about your recording of Psalm 150?" someone asked. "Oh, yeah," said the bandleader, and he called to a singer walking by, "Toney Watkins, come over here!" He came, and they gave us their rendition of Psalm 150, Ellington on the piano and Toney Watkins singing the words: "Praise the Lord with the sound of the trumpet!" Ellington looked up from the keyboard and smiled: "And that, my friends, is where Cat Anderson takes off on a marvelous trumpet ride."

Psalm 1 introduces the book of Psalms as a collection suitable for meditation and identifies the Psalter as a prayer book. Psalm 150 suggests that the psalms be accompanied by instrumental music and dancing. The book of Psalms is not only a prayer book but also a hymnbook, or to use the Hebrew title, a book of "praises."

Praise—that is what this psalm is about, and that is what the whole book of Psalms is about. The German theologian Ludwig Koehler once wrote, "The deeper one descends through the centuries into the breadth and depth of the Old Testament writings, the louder the praise and laud of God can be heard" (quoted in Westermann, *Praise and Lament*, p. 7).

Those words could be said for the book of Psalms: the deeper one descends into the collection, the louder one hears the praises of God.

This psalm provides a primer for praising. It deals with the basic questions: the why, the how, and the who of praising God.

Those Mighty Acts (150:1–2)

The first word of the psalm is *Hallelujah*, which is the call "Praise Yahweh" (NRSV, "Praise the LORD"), the God of Israel. The sort of praise commended here is not just an appreciative "Oh, what a beautiful morning!" but rather a focused "Thank you, Lord, for this beautiful morning!"

The psalm begins by locating the One who is to be praised in the heavenly holy place, the "firmament" high above the earth, where God dwells (see Gen. 1:6–8). Built on the typical pattern of a *hymn* (see on Psalm 113), the *call to praise* is followed by *reasons* for praising. *Why* praise God? The Lord has done "mighty deeds" and is great. (Psalm 106 provides a recital of those mighty deeds; Pss. 71:16 and 145:4, 12 refer to them.)

Strike Up the Band! (150:3–5)

How should God be praised? This is the special concern of this final psalm. "Praise God with musical instruments," Psalm 150 says. The exact shapes and sounds of these instruments continue to be debated among specialists. What is clear is that all classes of instruments are to be taken up in praise, including wind, strings, and percussion.

What is also quite clear is that this praise is not timid. It is to be done with enthusiasm. Here is a call not only for cymbals but for "loud clashing cymbals!"

Duke Ellington's recording *A Second Sacred Service* includes his setting of Psalm 150, "Praise God and Dance," featuring singer Alice Babs and trumpet player Cat Anderson. The album jacket reports on the reaction to the concert given in the ancient church of Santa Maria del Mar in Barcelona, Spain. With the finale, Psalm 150, the congregation took the words quite literally and burst into the aisles, dancing!

Who Is Invited to Praise? (150:6)

The final lines of this final psalm issue an invitation. And *who* is invited to this party? The answer is clear and could not be more inclusive. The invitation to praise goes out not only to Israel, not only to Israel and the church, not only to those participating in the world's great religions, not only even to humans but to "everything that breathes."

Psalm 104 indicates that those beings that God gives breath (v. 29) range from the tiniest creatures in the sea to birds and storks and wild asses and even sea monsters romping in the world's oceans. If one could hear all the sounds of praise emanating from this blue planet, one would be able to detect not only the elegies of Ellington or the cantatas of Bach but also the gentle whir of a hummingbird's wing or the sturdy *cantus firmus* and counterpoint of the humpback whale.

Bibliography

FOR FURTHER READING

Commentaries

Dahood, Mitchell. *Psalms III.* (101–150). Garden City: Doubleday and Company, Inc., 1970.

Fever, Avrohom Chaim. *Tehillim/Psalms,* in ArtScroll Tanach Series. Brooklyn: Mesorah Publications, 1977, 1985.

Hossfeld, F.-L. , and E. Zenger. *Die Psalmen I: Psalm 1–50. Die Neue Echter Bibel.* Würzburg: Echter Verlag, 1993.

Kraus, Hans-Joachim. *Psalms 1–59* and *Psalms 60–150.* Translated by H. C. Oswald. Minneapolis: Augsburg Publishing House, 1988, 1989.

Mays, James L. *Psalms.* Interpretation: A Bible Commentary for Teaching and Preaching. Louisville, Ky.: Westminster John Knox Press, 1994.

McCann, J. Clinton, Jr. *The Book of Psalms.* Vol. 4 of *The New Interpreter's Bible.* Nashville: Abingdon Press, 1996.

Poteat, Edwin McNeill. "Exposition of Psalms 42–89." In *The Book of Psalms,* Vol. 4 of *The Interpreter's Bible.* Nashville: Abingdon Press, 1955.

Seybold, Klaus. *Die Psalmen. Handbuch zum Alten Testament I/15.* Tübingen: J. C. B. Mohr (Paul Siebeck), 1996.

Other Works Cited

Berlin, Adele. *Introduction to Hebrew Poetry.* Vol. 4 of *The New Interpreter's Bible.* Nashville: Abingdon Press, 1996.

Frost, Gerhard E. *Blessed Is the Ordinary: Reflections.* Minneapolis: Winston Press, 1980.

———. *Seasons of a Lifetime: A Treasury of Meditations.* Minneapolis: Augsburg Publishing House, 1989.

Frost, Robert. *The Poetry of Robert Frost,* edited by Edward Connery Lathem. New York: Henry Holt & Co. , 1969.

Heschel, Abraham. *Israel: An Echo of Eternity.* New York: Farrar, Straus & Giroux, 1967.

———. *The Prophets.* New York: Harper & Row, 1962.

Holladay, William L. *The Psalms through Three Thousand Years: Prayerbook of a Cloud of Witnesses.* Minneapolis: Fortress Press, 1993.

Indexes for Worship Planning. Minneapolis: Augsburg Fortress, 1996.

Limburg, James. "Psalms, Book of." In *The Anchor Bible Dictionary,* vol. 5, edited by David Noel Freedman. New York: Doubleday, 1992.

Luther, Martin. *Selected Psalms III.* Vol. 14 of *Luther's Works,* edited by Jaroslav Pelikan. St. Louis: Concordia Publishing House, 1958.

———. *Small Catechism.* Translation and introduction by Timothy J. Wengert. Minneapolis: Fortress Press, 1994.

Lutheran Book of Worship. Minneapolis: Augsburg Publishing House, 1978.

Lutheran Book of Worship: Minister's Edition. Minneapolis: Augsburg Publishing House, 1978.

Mays, James L. *The Lord Reigns: A Theological Handbook to the Psalms.* Louisville, Ky.: Westminster John Knox Press, 1994.

Miller, Patrick D. *Interpreting the Psalms.* Philadelphia: Fortress Press, 1986.

———. *They Cried to the Lord: The Form and Theology of Biblical Prayer.* Minneapolis: Fortress Press, 1994.

Mülhaupt, E., ed., *D. Martin Luthers Psalmen-Auslegung.* Vol. 2. Göttingen, 1962; Vol. 3. Göttingen: Band, 1965.

Peguy, Charles. *Basic Verities.* Translated by Anne and Julia Green. New York: Random House, Inc. , 1943.

Risse, Siegfried. *"Gut ist es, unserem Gott zu singen": Untersuchungen zu Psalm 147.* Münster: Oros Verlag, 1995.

Seybold, Klaus. *Die Wallfahrtspsalmen.* Neukirchen-Vluyn: Neukirchener Verlag, 1978.

Stein, Joseph, Jerry Bock, and Sheldon Harnick. *Fiddler on the Roof.* New York: Pocket Books, 1966.

Westermann, Claus. *Ausgewählte Psalmen.* Göttingen: Vandenhoeck & Ruprecht, 1984.

———. *Der Psalter.* 2d ed. Stuttgart: Calwer Verlag, 1969.

———. *The Living Psalms.* Translated by J. R. Porter. Grand Rapids: Wm. B. Eerdmans Publishing Co. , 1989.

———. *Praise and Lament in the Psalms.* Translated by Keith R. Crim and Richard N. Soulen. Atlanta: John Knox Press, 1981.

————. *The Psalms: Structure, Content and Message.* Translated by Ralph D. Gehrke. Minneapolis: Augsburg Publishing House, 1980.

Wiesel, Elie. *One Generation After.* New York: Avon Books, 1965.

Wright, G. Ernest. *God Who Acts.* London: SCM Press, 1952.